ORGANIZATIONAL PSYCHOLOGY

ORGANIZATIONAL PSYCHOLOGY

Critical concepts in psychology

Edited by Jo Silvester

**Volume III
Enhancing Performance in Organizations**

LONDON AND NEW YORK

First published 2008
by Routledge
2 Park Square, Milton Park, Abingdon, Oxon, OX14 4RN, UK

Simultaneously published in the USA and Canada
by Routledge
270 Madison Avenue, New York, NY 10016

*Routledge is an imprint of the Taylor & Francis Group,
an informa business*

Editorial material and selection © 2008 Jo Silvester;
individual owners retain copyright in their own material

Typeset in Times New Roman by Keyword Group Ltd.
Printed and bound in Great Britain by
TJI Digital, Padstow, Cornwall

All rights reserved. No part of this book may be reprinted or reproduced or utilised in any form or by any electronic, mechanical, or other means, now known or hereafter invented, including photocopying and recording, or in any information storage or retrieval system, without permission in writing from the publishers.

British Library Cataloguing in Publication Data
A catalogue record for this book is available
from the British Library

Library of Congress Cataloging in Publication Data
A catalog record for this book has been requested

ISBN 10: 0-415-40008-2 (Set)
ISBN 10: 0-415-40011-2 (Volume III)

ISBN 13: 978-0-415-40008-4 (Set)
ISBN 13: 978-0-415-40011-4 (Volume III)

Publisher's Note

References within each chapter are as they appear in the original complete work

CONTENTS

Acknowledgements — vii

Introduction — 1

PART 5
Individual and group performance — 5

36 Does the transactional–transformational leadership paradigm transcend organizational and national boundaries? — 7
BERNARD M. BASS

37 The romance of leadership as a follower-centric theory: a social constructionist approach — 27
JAMES R. MEINDL

38 The bases of social power — 40
JOHN R.P. FRENCH, JR. AND BERTRAM RAVEN

39 Teams in organizations: recent research on performance and effectiveness — 56
RICHARD A. GUZZO AND MARCUS W. DICKSON

40 Sparkling fountains or stagnant ponds: an integrative model of creativity and innovation implementation in work groups — 89
MICHAEL A. WEST

41 Frontiers in group dynamics: concept, method and reality in social science; social equilibria and social change — 119
KURT LEWIN

CONTENTS

42 **Cognition and corporate governance: understanding boards of directors as strategic decision-making groups** 161
DANIEL P. FORBES AND FRANCES J. MILLIKEN

43 **Social identity and self-categorization processes in organizational contexts** 187
MICHAEL A. HOGG AND DEBORAH J. TERRY

PART 6
Organizational performance 219

44 **Principles of sociotechnical design revisited** 221
ALBERT CHERNS

45 **Motivation through the design of work: test of a theory** 230
J. RICHARD HACKMAN AND GREG R. OLDHAM

46 **Work control and employee well-being: a decade review** 260
DEBORAH J. TERRY AND NERINA L. JIMMIESON

47 **Organizational change and development** 311
KARL E. WEICK AND ROBERT E. QUINN

48 **Overcoming resistance to change** 338
LESTER COCH AND JOHN R.P. FRENCH, JR.

49 **Counterproductive behaviours at work** 360
ADRIAN FURNHAM AND JOHN TAYLOR

50 **What *is* the difference between organizational culture and organizational climate? A native's point of view on a decade of paradigm wars** 411
DANIEL R. DENISON

ACKNOWLEDGEMENTS

The publishers would like to thank the following for permission to reprint their material:

The American Psychological Association for permission to reprint Bernard M. Bass, 'Does the transactional–transformational leadership paradigm transcend organizational and national boundaries?', *American Psychologist*, 52(2), 1997, pp. 130–139. Copyright © 1997 by the American Psychological Association.

Reprinted from *Leadership Quarterly*, 6, James R. Meindl, 'The romance of leadership as a follower-centric theory: a social constructionist approach', pp. 329–341, copyright © 1995, with permission from Elsevier.

The Institute for Social Research of the University of Michigan for permission to reprint John R. P. French, Jr. and Bertram H. Raven, 'The bases of social power', in D. Cartwright (ed.), *Studies in Social Power*, 1959, pp. 150–167. Copyright 1959 by the University of Michigan.

The Annual Review of Psychology for permission to reprint Richard A. Guzzo and Marcus W. Dickson, 'Teams in organizations: recent research on performance and effectiveness', *Annual Review of Psychology*, volume 47, pp. 307–338, copyright © 1996 by Annual Reviews. www.annualreviews.org.

Blackwell Publishing for permission to reprint Michael A. West, 'Sparkling fountains or stagnant ponds: an integrative model of creativity and innovation implementation in work groups', *Applied Psychology: An International Review*, 51(3), 2002, pp. 355–387.

Sage Publications Ltd. for permission to reprint Kurt Lewin, 'Frontiers in group dynamics', *Human Relations*, 1, 1947, pp. 5–41. Copyright © The Tavistock Institute, London, UK, 1947.

The Academy of Management (NY) in the format of Other Book via Copyright Clearance Center for permission to reprint Daniel P. Forbes and Frances J. Milliken, 'Cognition and corporate governance: understanding boards of directors as strategic decision-making groups', *Academy of Management Review*, 24(3), 1999, pp. 489–505. Copyright © 1999 by Academy of Management (NY).

ACKNOWLEDGEMENTS

The Academy of Management (NY) in the format of Other Book via Copyright Clearance Center for permission to reprint Michael A. Hogg and Deborah J. Terry, 'Social identity and self-categorization processes in organizational contexts', *Academy of Management Review*, 25(1), 2000, pp. 121–140. Copyright © 2000 by Academy of Management (NY).

Sage Publications Ltd. for permission to reprint Albert B. Cherns, 'Principles of sociotechnical design revisited', *Human Relations*, 40(3), 1987, pp. 153–161. Copyright © The Tavistock Institute, London, UK, 1987.

Reprinted from *Organizational Behavior and Human Performance*, 16, J. Richard Hackman and Greg R. Oldham, 'Motivation through the design of work: test of a theory', pp. 250–279, copyright © 1976, with permission from Elsevier.

John Wiley & Sons Ltd. for permission to reprint Deborah J. Terry and Nerina L. Jimmieson, 'Work control and employee well-being: a decade review', in C. L. Cooper and I. T. Robertson (eds), *International Review of Industrial and Organizational Psychology*, Vol. 14, 1999, pp. 95–148, copyright © 1999 John Wiley & Sons Ltd.

The Annual Review of Psychology for permission to reprint Karl E. Weick and Robert E. Quinn, 'Organizational change and development', *Annual Review of Psychology*, volume 50, pp. 361–386, copyright © 1999 by Annual Reviews. www.annualreviews.org.

Sage Publications Ltd. for permission to reprint Lester Coch and John R. P. French, Jr., 'Overcoming resistance to change', *Human Relations*, 1(4), 1948, pp. 512–532. Copyright © The Tavistock Institute, London, UK, 1948.

Palgrave Macmillan for permission to reprint Adrian Furnham and John Taylor, 'Counterproductive behaviours at work', in *The Dark Side of Behaviour at Work: Understanding and Avoiding Employees Leaving, Thieving and Deceiving*, 2004, pp. 83–129.

The Academy of Management (NY) in the format of Other Book via Copyright Clearance Center for permission to reprint Daniel R. Denison, 'What *is* the difference between organizational culture and organizational climate? A native's point of view on a decade of paradigm wars', *Academy of Management Review*, 21(3), 1996, pp. 619–654. Copyright © 1996 by Academy of Management (NY).

Disclaimer

The publishers have made every effort to contact authors/copyright holders of works reprinted in *Organizational Psychology: Critical Concepts in Psychology*. This has not been possible in every case, however, and we would welcome correspondence from those individuals/companies whom we have been unable to trace.

INTRODUCTION

According to Parker and Wall (1998) these are exciting times for job and work design. The introduction of new organizational forms has provided increased opportunities to create more fulfilling and effective work environments, and organizational psychologists have been central to these efforts. John Patrick identifies three ways in which individual work performance can be enhanced. The first of these is to ensure that people with the right knowledge, skills and abilities are selected into an organization. The second is to provide training and development opportunities; making sure that appropriate knowledge and skills continue to grow. The third involves designing the work environment and jobs to enable employees to work optimally and is the focus of this third volume in the Critical Concepts series.

Although some of the papers included in Volume III look at individual-level factors, the majority describe research concerned with how performance can be enhanced by individuals working together. The readings explore the rich history of organizational psychology in the evolution of theory and practice to support the healthy and productive workplace. This is an area where organizational psychologists can be proud of innovations in theory and practice that have had a major positive impact on how people work. Not surprisingly, this volume includes several early texts on the social bases of power, group dynamics and organizational change that have become classics in the field. These papers are a pertinent reminder of the important contributions made by social scientists to the early development of organizational psychology as an academic discipline. They remind us, however, that we still face similar challenges in our efforts to understand and model dynamic processes of change at work.

The first section in this volume begins with two papers that explore different aspects of leadership. There is little escaping the fact that leadership has proven to be a tremendously popular concept in organizational psychology and management more generally. The search for individual characteristics that predict successful leaders has been a strong research theme, and researchers have concentrated on understanding how individual and environmental factors interact to produce leaders. The first paper in this volume by Bass (1997) discusses the universality of the

INTRODUCTION

transactional–transformational leadership paradigm. He suggests, that no matter what country one happens to be in, it would seem that employees' ideals about what good leadership should be involves transformational-type behaviour. In the next paper, Meindl (1995) questions this romantic notion of leadership and develops a 'follower-centric' theory based on a social constructivism. The third paper, by French and Raven (1959) is a classic description of the different bases of social power that individuals use within organizations to achieve their objectives. It is included as a reminder of the importance of power and politics in organizational psychology research.

Groups and team working are two forms of work design that have been universally popular and the next papers focus on this area. In their review of the team-working literature, Guzzo and Dickson (1996) present evidence to support the use of teams as a strategy for enhancing organizational functioning. In his paper, West (2002) describes the important role played by groups in creativity at work. He argues that diversity of knowledge among team members is important as a predictor of innovation.

It seems that work design, more than any other subject in organizational psychology, is replete with classic texts that still have relevance today. In some cases they tackle research topics that have become the preserve of other academic disciplines such as organizational sociology. Others describe methods that have slipped out of favour in mainstream organizational psychology. Lewin's (1947) classic paper on group dynamics compares methods and concepts traditionally used in social science with those of the empirical sciences. It is a paper that continues to have relevance to present-day debates and controversies about methodologies and epistemologies. Sixty years on, Lewin's work reminds us of the rich opportunities and considerable challenges inherent in researching social change.

The last two papers in the first section consider how individuals conceptualize themselves and behave in relation to their work groups. In their paper, Forbes and Milliken (1999) explore the demographics of boards of directors, and factors that lead individual members to influence strategic decisions. Hogg and Terry (2000) examine how social identity and self-categorization processes might be used to explain organizational behaviour during events such as mergers and acquisitions.

Most of the papers in the second section of this volume look at how work can be designed to increase performance. They consider why, despite the continually changing workplace, planned changes are often so difficult to implement. In his paper, Cherns (1987) reviews research evidence for principles of sociotechnical design. Hackman and Oldham's (1976) paper is another classic in the field of organizational design, which considers how work might be designed to motivate employees. Their model identifies the conditions needed (e.g. employees' psychological states, attributes and job characteristics) for individuals to become internally motivated at work. In a more recent paper, Terry and Jimmieson (1999) review the literature concerned with employee control and well-being. They assess whether jobs that impose limitations are more likely to generate unfavourable work outcomes and suggest that future researchers should focus on the mechanisms underpinning the effects of work control.

The next two papers are concerned with organizational change and development. In their review paper, Weick and Quinn (1999) examine the speed of change in organizations, differences between episodic and continuous change, and conceptualizations of inertia. In another classic paper, Coch and French (1948) argue that whilst change is a necessary part of organizational functioning, employees' resistance to change can lead to higher rates of turnover, increased grievances and aggression. Coch and French look at why employees resist change and what can be done to overcome this resistance. Continuing with the theme of resistance, Furnham and Taylor (2004) consider how work-group norms and management practices can contribute to counterproductive work behaviour including thieving, deception, bullying and absenteeism. Finally, Denison's (1996) paper asks 'What *is* the difference between organizational culture and organizational climate' and takes a 'native's point of view on a decade of paradigm wars'. He examines the similarities and differences between the quantitative culture research and organizational climate literature and suggests that climate and culture should be viewed as different interpretations rather than phenomena.

Reference

Parker, S. & Wall, T. (1998). *Job and Work Design: Organizing Work to Promote Well-Being and Effectiveness*. London: Sage Publications.

Part 5

INDIVIDUAL AND GROUP PERFORMANCE

36

DOES THE TRANSACTIONAL–TRANSFORMATIONAL LEADERSHIP PARADIGM TRANSCEND ORGANIZATIONAL AND NATIONAL BOUNDARIES?

Bernard M. Bass

Source: *American Psychologist* 52(2) (1997): 130–139.

Abstract

There is universality in the transactional–transformational leadership paradigm. That is, the same conception of phenomena and relationships can be observed in a wide range of organizations and cultures. Exceptions can be understood as a consequence of unusual attributes of the organizations or cultures. Three corollaries are discussed. Supportive evidence has been gathered in studies conducted in organizations in business, education, the military, the government, and the independent sector. Likewise, supportive evidence has been accumulated from all but 1 continent to document the applicability of the paradigm.

Evidence supporting the transactional–transformational leadership paradigm has been gathered from all continents except Antarctica—even offshore in the North Sea. The transactional–transformational paradigm views leadership as either a matter of contingent reinforcement of followers by a transactional leader or the moving of followers beyond their self-interests for the good of the group, organization, or society by a transformational leader. The paradigm is sufficiently broad to provide a basis for measurement and understanding that is as universal as the concept of leadership itself. Here, universal does not imply constancy of means, variances, and correlations across all situations but rather explanatory constructs good for all situations. Numerous investigations (field studies, case histories, management games, interviews, and laboratory studies) point to the robustness of the effects of transformational and charismatic leadership (Dorfman, 1996).

Although I focus here on the transactional–transformational conceptualization derived from Burns (1978) and elaborated by Bass (1985), it is one among a number of neocharismatic conceptualizations built around similar leader behaviors and perceptions with slight variations in emphases (House, 1995). Referred to as the "New Leadership" (Bryman, 1992), these conceptualizations include the 1976 theory of charisma (House, 1977), the attributional theory of charisma (Conger & Kanungo, 1987), the leadership challenge (Kouzes & Posner, 1987), and visionary leadership (Sashkin, 1988). This new leadership does not replace the conceptions of leadership as exchanges of reinforcements by the leader that are contingent on followers' performance. Rather, the new leadership adds the role of the transformational leader in enlarging and elevating followers' motivation, understanding, maturity, and sense of self-worth. Graen and Uhl-Bien (1991) found that although leader–member exchange may begin with a simple transactional relationship, for effectiveness, it needs to become transformational.

Numerous reasons bolster the universality argument. First, leadership, as such, is a universal phenomenon. No society has been found where it is completely absent (Murdock, 1967). Still, the leadership that occurs is affected by the organizations and cultures in which it appears. To export participative management from the United States to more authoritarian countries involves preaching Jeffersonian democracy to managers who believe in the Divine Right of Kings (Haire, Ghiselli, & Porter, 1966). Nonetheless, the globalization of industry and the media has made the task easier to spread systematic approaches to leadership.

Second, laypeople repeatedly ask, "Are leaders born or made?" and usually argue about how much they are made. However, recent findings about heritability (Rose, 1995) may suggest otherwise. In a study of 100 sets of monozygotic and dizygotic twins, T. Vernon (personal communication, March 31, 1995) reported that monozygotic twins were much more alike than dizygotic twins in their self-perceived transformational leadership behaviors as measured by the Multifactor Leadership Questionnaire (MLQ Form 5X; Bass & Avolio, 1995). As much as 40% of the variance could be attributed to heritability. Transactional managing by exception and laissez-faire leadership were similarly affected by heritability. Only transactional contingent reward failed to register a significant effect of inheritance. To the degree that heritability is culture free, it means that a universal constraint is placed on how much contingencies of training, culture, and organization vitiate possible transformational leadership effects.

Third, knowledge work will dominate the 21st century. It requires more envisioning, enabling, and empowering leadership, all of which are central to transformational leadership as defined by Kouzes and Posner (1987). The leadership must go beyond the transactional reward–punishment exchange relationship.

Fourth, the socially oriented transformational leader engages in moral uplifting of followers. Moral absolutes may be involved. It is absolutely true that crying "fire!" in a crowded theater is absolutely wrong. It is absolutely good to help the many without harming any.

Fifth, the transactional–transformational leadership paradigm can be extended to describe teams and group effects as well as how whole organizations differ (Avolio & Bass, 1994). People jockey for positions in a transactional group, whereas they share common goals in a transformational group. Rules and regulations dominate the transactional organization; adaptability is a characteristic of the transformational organization. The team MLQ has been developed to assess teams, as teams, in terms of the components of transformational and transactional team mores (Avolio & Bass, 1995). Correspondingly, raters have been able to complete reliable and valid descriptions of their organizations using the Organizational Description Questionnaire (Bass & Avolio, 1993a). The paradigm can even be extended to the international behavior of nations. Kissinger (1994) repeatedly described the international diplomacy of nations as justified by either self-interest (transactional) or moral principles (transformational). Britain was transactional in maintaining its "splendid isolation" and the European balance of powers by taking sides with whichever side was weaker. It was transformational when it outlawed and fought the slave trade as a matter of moral principle.

Sixth, pop culture and its fads sweep across the world. Worldwide webs of communication, trade, and travel and the international transfer of technology contribute to the convergence of requirements and role models for leadership. Most business and industrial managers everywhere are more pragmatic and less idealistic than most leaders of social movements (England, 1976). Organizations are continually seeking benchmarks to see what they can do to become closer in practice to the best of their counterparts. They learn, change, and become more alike. So do cultures. It may not be politically correct to say so, but less developed cultures change as a consequence of the diffusion of ideas and practices from more developed cultures.

Seventh, the United States provides important sources of communalities in the postindustrialized world. English has become the world's language of business, and much of American management practices and management education have been adopted universally. The United States dominates the worldwide entertainment industry. The master of business administration program has gone global. Recently, the British Ministry adopted American-style "publish or perish" rules for supporting higher education.

Five universals

Lonner (1980) listed four kinds of universals or regularities in leader–follower relations that transcend cultures and organizations: simple, variform, functional, and systematic. I add a fifth—variform functional. A *simple universal* about leadership is demonstrated by General Norman Schwarzkoff's (1994) statement that anytime a group of human beings come together, there is always a leader. Furthermore, he did not see any difference in the characteristics required for successful leadership of Macedonia by Alexander the Great and successful leadership at IBM by

Lou Gerstner. A *variform universal* is a simple regularity influenced to some extent by cultures or organizations. Ordinarily, business organizations almost everywhere are headed by a single executive officer or managing director, but in Germany, a technical and a commercial director may share authority and responsibilities. A *functional universal* is a relation that is universal between variables. Such a functional universal is the correlation between laissez-faire leadership and perceived ineffectiveness. Everywhere, the assigned leader who frequently avoids responsibilities and shirks duties is perceived as ineffective and dissatisfying by followers. A more dynamic rubric is a *variform functional universal*. Almost everywhere, a positive, sizable correlation is found between attributed charisma and satisfaction with it. But a slightly negative correlation emerged in one large sample of government economists rating their supervisors (Avolio, Bass, & Jung, 1996). A *systematic behavioral universal* is a theory about relationships that explain if–then outcomes across cultures and organizations. The full-range model of transformational and transactional leadership provides the measurable relationships for such a theory. The model and the theory underlying it are systematically universal, although they include variform and variform functional universals. When exceptions to the generalizations occur, they usually are circumstances explained by the peculiarities of the culture or organization.

In sum, universal means a universally applicable conceptualization. At the individual level of measurement, each individual leader has a profile of transactional and transformational scores that can be reliably and validly discriminated from the norms for his or her group, organization, or culture: The means will vary in understandable ways, as will the variances, as one moves from one context to another. Considerable functional uniformities in correlations with outcomes will be observed, with understandable exceptions (Bass, Burger, Doktor, & Barrett, 1979).

Variation occurs because the same concepts may contain specific thought processes, beliefs, implicit understandings, or behaviors in one culture but not another. Misumi's (1985) performance–maintenance distinctions transfer for electronics plant supervisors across Britain, the United States, Japan, and Hong Kong, but the specific behaviors reflecting the two styles differ markedly (Smith, Misumi, Tayeb, Peterson, & Bond, 1989). The linkages among concepts may strengthen or weaken as one moves from one culture to another. For example, Indonesian inspirational leaders need to persuade their followers about the leaders' own competence, a behavior that would appear unseemly in Japan. Contingent rewarding is more implicit in Japan than in the United States (Yokochi, 1989). Nevertheless, the concepts of inspiration and contingent reward appear to be as universal as the concept of leadership itself. In the same way, the contribution to the extra effort of followers of a leader's inspiration and a leader's promises of reward will vary to some degree. Nevertheless, inspirational leadership is more strongly correlated with extra effort of followers in most organizations and cultures than is contingent reward leadership (viz., Druskat, 1994; Salter, 1989).

Dorfman and Ronen (1991) accounted for people's favoring of differences over similarities of leadership across cultures. The differences intrigue people; the sameness bores them. Differences give people more to say. Significant differences are a matter of having large enough samples. It is effect sizes that need to be large for people to dwell on the differences. Some suggest that because much of the theories and methods of the transactional–transformational leadership paradigm originated in the culturally individualistic United States, the paradigm is likely to have little relevance in countries with collectivistic cultures. The opposite appears to be more likely. Transformational leadership emerges more readily in the collectivistic societies of East Asia (Jung, Bass, & Sosik, 1995). Currently, House (1995) is heading a 60-nation study in which measures of charismatic leadership have been developed indigenously in the same three industries in each of the nations. So far, preliminarily, he has concluded that the similarities of findings outweigh the differences.

At first, it appeared implicitly to me that transformational leadership was limited to leaders in the upper echelons of organizations. So, when I collected the first interview and survey data in 1980, they were data from and about senior executives and U.S. Army colonels describing their leaders (Bass, 1985). But by 1985, it had been discovered that transformational leadership was much more universal in that it could be displayed by middle managers, Army noncommissioned officers and lieutenants, first-level supervisors, and team leaders with no formal rank in their organizations. By 1992, it was clear from empirical evidence that transformational leadership could be exhibited by samples ranging from housewives active in the community (Avolio & Bass, 1994) and students (Avolio, Waldman, & Einstein, 1988) to Japanese CEOs (Bass & Yokochi, 1991), world-class leaders of movements, and presidents of the United States (Bass, Avolio, & Goodheim, 1987). Also, as people began to work toward transformational teams, it became clear that members of a team could learn how to make a team more transformational (Avolio & Bass, 1995).

A variety of contingency theories of leadership have been advanced, with varying research support. Little empirical evidence supports Hersey–Blanchard's (Hersey & Blanchard, 1969) model of situational leadership contingent on the followers' maturity. After more than 400 publications, controversy remains about Fiedler's (1983) saw-toothed theory that task-oriented leaders are most effective when they are faced with situations that are highly favorable or highly unfavorable to them and relations-oriented leaders do best when they are faced with situations that are in-between in favorableness. Equally researched is House's (1971) path–goal theory, which states that the effective leader clarifies the transactional exchange and the path the subordinate needs to follow for goal attainment. Contingencies include the motivation of the subordinate and the structure of the situation. But supporting evidence is mixed. Although contingencies do have some validity, overall, better leaders integrate a task-oriented and a relations-oriented approach (Blake & Mouton, 1964) as well as demonstrate their ability to clarify the path to the goals (Bass, 1960, 1990).

Since 1980, general findings have been assembled that the best of leaders are both transactional and transformational. Again, for many situations, the circumstances may not make that much difference. In fact, the leadership behavior may affect the contingent condition more than the reverse. Thus, the transactional leader works within the constraints of the organization; the transformational leader changes the organization (Bass, 1985). Transformational leadership and transactional leadership may be affected by contingencies, but most contingencies may be relatively small in effect.

Conceptualization

Leaders and followers enter into an exchange beginning with a process of negotiation to establish what is being exchanged and whether it is satisfactory (Hollander, 1986). This transactional leadership depends on the leader's power to reinforce subordinates for their successful completion of the bargain. Reinforcement can be materialistic or symbolic, immediate or delayed, partial or whole, implicit or explicit, and in terms of rewards or resources. Nevertheless, Levinson (1980) suggested that if you limit yourself to transactional leadership of a follower with rewards of carrots for compliance, or punishments with a stick for failure to comply with agreed-on work to be done by the follower, the follower will continue to feel like a jackass. Among other things, the follower's sense of self-worth must be addressed to engage and commit the follower (Shamir, 1991). And that is one of the strongest motivators that transformational leadership adds to the transactional exchange.

Authentic transformational leaders motivate followers to work for transcendental goals that go beyond immediate self-interests. What is right and good to do becomes important. Transformational leaders move followers to transcend their own self-interests for the good of the group, organization, or country. Transformational leaders motivate followers and other constituencies to do more than they originally expected to do as they strive for higher order outcomes (Burns, 1978). Self-interested pseudotransformational leaders may impress their followers in the same way, but their own purposes are clearly different and are likely to be exploitative rather than uplifting.

Until 1980, experimental and survey leadership research was limited mainly to the effects of leadership on lower order changes with leaders and followers at lower levels of organizations or in temporary groups—a reason that made more appealing explanations in terms of simple cost-benefit exchanges. The new paradigm of transformational and transactional leadership paralleled completion of more leadership research at the higher levels of organizations and intrinsic motivation. The old paradigms of task-oriented or relations-oriented leadership, directive or participative leadership, and autocratic or democratic leadership and related exchange theories of leadership ignored effects on leader–follower relations of the sharing of vision, symbolism, imaging, and sacrifice.

Empirical support for universality

Development of the multifactor leadership questionnaire

In 1980, 70 South African senior executives were asked if they could identify someone in their lives who had raised their consciousness; elevated their motivation on Maslow's (1954) hierarchy of needs; or moved them to go beyond their self-interests for the good of their group, organization, or society. (These effects were Burns's [1978] definition of the transforming leader.) All were able to do so. After identifying such an individual, the executives reported that the leader motivated them to extend themselves, to develop themselves, and to become more innovative. The executives were motivated to emulate their transformational leader. They became committed to the organization as a consequence of belief in the leader. They exerted extra effort for their leader (Bass, 1985).

The original MLQ (Bass, 1985) began with the executives' statements and those from the literature on charisma and contingent reinforcement. The 141 statements were sorted by 11 trained judges into transformational and transactional leadership. Then, they were administered as MLQ Form 1 to senior U.S. Army officers to rate how much each statement described their superior officers on magnitude estimation scales of frequency ranging from 0 (the behavior is observed *not at all*) to 4 (the behavior is observed *frequently, if not always*). Numerous factor analyses of the frequencies of the behaviors rated by subordinates in this and subsequent studies of business executives, agency administrators, and U.S. Army colonels were completed (for summaries, see Bass, 1985; Bass & Avolio, 1993b). The factor studies suggested that the transformational statements could be assigned to four interrelated components: Idealized Influence (or Charisma), Inspirational Motivation, Intellectual Stimulation, and Individualized Consideration. The transformational components are intercorrelated. Nevertheless, they are assessed separately because they are conceptually distinct and important for diagnostic purposes. Analogously, anxiety and depression correlate highly but need to be treated differently. The transformational components are as follows:

> *Idealized Influence (Charisma)*—leaders display conviction; emphasize trust; take stands on difficult issues; present their most important values; and emphasize the importance of purpose, commitment, and the ethical consequences of decisions. Such leaders are admired as role models generating pride, loyalty, confidence, and alignment around a shared purpose. A subjective component of attributed charisma may spin off from idealized influence, a behavioral component, for a fifth transformational component. (Components better describe the conceptually but not empirically distinct constructs. The same leaders tend to be high or low in each, but the behaviors involved are different and require different remediations.)

Inspirational Motivation—leaders articulate an appealing vision of the future, challenge followers with high standards, talk optimistically with enthusiasm, and provide encouragement and meaning for what needs to be done.

Intellectual Stimulation—leaders question old assumptions, traditions, and beliefs; stimulate in others new perspectives and ways of doing things; and encourage the expression of ideas and reasons.

Individualized Consideration—leaders deal with others as individuals; consider their individual needs, abilities, and aspirations; listen attentively; further their development; advise; teach; and coach.

Transactional leadership, using a carrot or a stick, contains three components usually characterized as instrumental in followers' goal attainment.

Contingent Reward—leaders engage in a constructive path–goal transaction of reward for performance. They clarify expectations, exchange promises and resources for support of the leaders, arrange mutually satisfactory agreements, negotiate for resources, exchange assistance for effort, and provide commendations for successful follower performance.

Active Management by Exception—leaders monitor followers' performance and take corrective action if deviations from standards occur. They enforce rules to avoid mistakes.

Passive Management by Exception—leaders fail to intervene until problems become serious. They wait to take action until mistakes are brought to their attention.

Laissez-Faire Leadership, a nonleadership component, also emerges—leaders avoid accepting their responsibilities, are absent when needed, fail to follow up requests for assistance, and resist expressing their views on important issues. Before the MLQ Form 5 was revised, an unpublished factor analysis of 4 of the 10 items such as "avoids interfering with the way I do my job" could be seen as empowering subordinates rather than as laissez-faire leadership (Bass, 1996).

According to a higher order factor analysis, the factors can be ordered from highest to lowest in activity as follows: Transformational Leadership, Contingent Reward, Active Management by Exception, Passive Management by Exception, and Laissez-Faire Leadership (Bass, 1985). Correspondingly, confirmed subsequently in an array of empirical studies, as noted in the first corollary that is presented, the components can also be ordered on a second dimension—effectiveness.

Transformational Leadership tends to be most effective, followed in order of effectiveness by Contingent Reward, Active Management by Exception, Passive Management by Exception, and Laissez-Faire Leadership (Avolio & Bass, 1990).

In the numerous factor analyses that have been reported, consistent with the original research (Bass, 1985; Bycio, Hackett, & Allen, 1995), Charismatic and Inspirational Leadership form a single factor. Sometimes a transformational factor appears. The boundaries between Contingent Reward and Individualized Consideration also may blur. Although both involve helping fulfill the needs of followers, Individualized Consideration focuses more attention on personal growth and recognition, whereas Contingent Reward attends more to promising or providing material rewards and resources.

A survey of empirical analyses and three meta-analyses (Gaspar, 1992; Lowe, Kroeck, & Sivasubramaniam, 1996; Patterson, Fuller, Kester, & Stringer, 1995) suggested that, generally, the MLQ components of Transformational Leadership correlate highly (.50 to .80) with each other but less so with Contingent Reward (.30 to .50). They correlate near zero with Management by Exception and moderately to highly negative with Laissez-Faire Leadership.

Howell and Avolio (1993) used partial least squares regression analysis with data collected on MLQ Form 10 from a sample of 250 executives rated by their direct reports, which supported the discriminant and convergent validity of a complex transactional–transformational factor structure. These results have been replicated with a total of 3,786 cases from 14 samples using MLQ-5X (Avolio, Bass, & Jung, 1996).

Many factor analyses have been completed for data from the United States and abroad. Koh (1990) found a similar factor structure for Singaporean school principals. Included were Charisma–Inspiration, Intellectual Stimulation, Individualized Consideration, Contingent Reward, Active and Passive Management by Exception, and Laissez-Faire Leadership. Garcia (1995) produced similar results with U.S. salespeople, and Druskat (1994) did so with Roman Catholic clergy. Nonetheless, particularly when abbreviated scales were used, as at the U.S. Air Force Academy (Curphy, 1990) and in a Dutch study (Den Hartog, Van Muijen, & Koopman, 1994), fewer factors could emerge as factor solutions. Minimally, a composite transformational factor and active and passive transactional factors were likely to appear in these diverse studies. Nonetheless, LISREL analyses involving 3,786 cases indicated that a more complex model of seven factors including Charisma–Inspiration, Intellectual Stimulation, Individualized Consideration, Contingent Reward, Active and Passive Management by Exception, and Laissez-Faire Leadership best fit the data in contrast to factor solutions with fewer factors (Avolio et al., 1996).

The universality of three propositions

Three corollaries for the theory underlying the model were presented by Bass and Avolio (1993b). With each corollary, some of the supporting empirical work is noted, which was completed in different countries and types of organizations to suggest that variform, functional, and systematic universals are involved.

The first corollary is that there is a hierarchy of correlations among the various leadership styles and outcomes in effectiveness, effort, and satisfaction. Transformational leaders are more effective than those leaders practicing contingent reward; contingent reward is somewhat more effective than active management by exception, which in turn is more effective than passive management by exception. Laissez-faire leadership is least effective. The patterns are similar for extra effort and for satisfaction with the leadership. The hierarchy remains, but is less steep, when objective, independent outcome criteria of effectiveness are used.

The corollary, first verified in the United States (Waldman, Bass, & Einstein, 1986), is applicable to results from India, Spain, Singapore, Japan, China, Austria, and a number of other countries. In Bombay, Dennyson Pereira (1986) found general support for the correlational hierarchy for managers in a large manufacturing organization, as did Roberto Pascual in Bilbao, Spain; Jaime Filella in Barcelona, Spain; Roger Gill in Singapore; Nokko Yokochi in Japan (Yokochi, 1989); Steyrer and Mende (1994) in Austria in diverse sectors of business and industrial management; and Davis, Guan, Luo, and Maahs (1996) in a Chinese state enterprise.

To illustrate, 120 Austrian branch bank managers and their subordinates who described them completed the MLQ in German. Significant correlations were found between the extent to which the managers were perceived as transformational rather than transactional and the extent to which their banks increased subsequently in customer market share and several other criteria of customer business.

The same kind of results were reported for Federal Express managers in the United States (Hater & Bass, 1988) and for financial executives in Canada (Howell & Avolio, 1993). A similar hierarchy of correlations emerged for New Zealand professionals and administrators (Bass, 1985), U.S. nursing administrators (Arnold, 1990), and U.S. religious ministers (Onnen, 1987). Similar hierarchical results have been reported in the profit and nonprofit sectors for middle managers in the United States, Canada, Belgium, Japan, and elsewhere (Bass & Avolio, 1993b) and for the military in the United States, Canada, and Germany (Boyd, 1988).

Between 1989 and 1993, in Italy, Avolio and I systematically collected immediate subordinates' MLQ ratings of Fiat's senior managers (Bass & Avolio, 1990, 1991, 1994). For almost 200 of the senior executives described by their 1,032 immediate subordinates, the hierarchy of correlations held up. The same was true for 30 senior managers of Swedish multinationals described by their subordinates and for 500 participants in training in the Binghamton, New York, area coming from 10 different types of organizations such as business, education, health care, government, law enforcement, and social services.

Lowe et al. (1996) completed a meta-analysis involving from 1,295 to 5,475 cases. The hierarchy of correlations emerged for results based on subordinates' ratings as well as for those based on organizational outcomes—independent performance appraisals, career advancement, performance of the units led, and so forth. Results were the same for both published and unpublished reports.

I do not wish to imply that one has here a functional universal that is invariant. On the contrary, it is a variform functional universal when samples can be compared where everything but nationality is controlled (Boyd, 1988). Although the overall order of effects generally remained, variations appeared in the size of the differential correlations. Boyd compared 700 North Atlantic Treaty Organization (NATO) field grade officers. Although transformational leadership did remain more highly correlated with effective outcomes than did transactional leadership, with these military data, contingent reward was less effective and management by exception was more effective than usually obtained with civilian samples. The pattern for Canadian officers was particularly divergent from U.S. and German results in that Canadian transactional leadership correlated close to zero with effectiveness. Although passive and active management by exception were not separated in Boyd's scoring of the data, active management by exception undoubtedly would have been more highly correlated with effectiveness and passive management by exception would have been less so, judging from a meta-analysis by Gaspar (1992) that compared military and civilian MLQ results.

Gaspar's (1992) meta-analysis of MLQ findings involved 957 military respondents with 577 to 2,141 civilian counterparts describing their superiors. Overall, the hierarchy of correlations with objective outcomes and perceived effectiveness was elevated in the military respondents as compared with civilians. For the military respondents, the mean correlation of the MLQ transformational factor scores with objective performance ranged from .46 to .57. The comparable results for the civilians ranged from .26 to .29. For the military personnel, objective performance correlated .46 with contingent reward; the comparable result was .20 for the civilians. Objective performance correlated .26 with active management by exception for the military respondents and −.27 for the civilians. The correlation was .32 with passive management by exception for the military respondents and −.07 for the civilians. When perceived effectiveness was the criterion outcome, the correlations were elevated (partly because of the bias of same-source variance). Military transformational leadership components correlated from .51 to .75 with perceived effectiveness. For the civilians, the correlations were from .47 to .57. The military–civilian differences in mean size of correlations with outcomes and the reverse direction with management by exception pointed to a variform, not a simple, universal in the leadership – outcome correlations.

The second corollary is that there is a one-way augmentation effect. When stepwise regression is used, measures of transformational leadership add to measures of transactional leadership in predicting outcomes, but not vice versa. Definitive analyses supporting the augmentation effect were completed with a representative sample of U.S. Navy officers using retrospective outcomes (Yammarino & Bass, 1990) and Canadian managers using outcomes collected a year after the measurements of leadership (Howell & Avolio, 1993). Comparable results were obtained in India (Pereira, 1986) and the Dominican Republic (Davis, 1994). In Singapore, Koh (1990) found the augmentation effect generalized for 90 secondary school principals when the criteria predicted by transformational leadership added to transactional leadership were commitment and satisfaction. However, it failed to do so when the criteria involved turnover or academic performance. The augmentation effect appears to be a variform functional universal.

The third corollary is that in whatever the country, when people think about leadership, their prototypes and ideals are transformational. Supportive evidence comes from a variety of sources: (a) Bass and Avolio (1989) showed that Lord's prototype leader was correlated with transformational, not transactional, leadership in an American sample. (b) In training efforts in various types of organizations and participants from the United States, Canada, South Africa, Spain, Austria, Sweden, Italy, Israel, and elsewhere, an exercise has been conducted routinely in the Full Range of Leadership Development Program with several thousand participants (Avolio & Bass, 1990). Participants are asked to describe an ideal leader who has been of consequence to them in their own lives. The traits and behaviors that are mentioned to describe the leader are almost invariably transformational, not transactional. (c) Using the MLQ items as a preference survey, Chinese police and Taiwanese company employees chose transformational rather than transactional leadership (Singer & Singer, 1990). (d) When U.S. undergraduates were asked to list up to 25 traits of leadership, the MLQ-like transformational factors emerged. Their implicit traits of leadership included charismatic, dedicated, intelligent, and sensitive (Offerman, Kennedy, & Wirtz, 1994).

Although the three corollaries appear to be universal, this does not mean the levels of perceived leadership in self and others will be invariant among the different nationalities. For instance, among Boyd's (1988) NATO officers, contingent reward was less effective for Canadian officers than for German or American officers. Self-ratings in Japan were not as inflated as they are in the United States or Europe (Yokochi, 1989). The size of the means, variances, and correlations will vary to some degree, yet the overall patterns of results generally remain the same everywhere. For instance, in Sri Lanka, the leader stereotype is a Ceylonese John Wayne, a hard task master, or a benevolent dictator. Nevertheless, when Weathersby (1993) asked 44 Sri Lankan managers to reflect individually and collectively about their experiences, over time they ended up espousing transformational approaches.

The three corollaries were found to hold when the MLQ was presented in translation in various European and Asian languages. One unpublished Chinese version of MLQ Form 5 suitably backtranslated was used in an unpublished study of managerial motivation in the People's Republic of China by Wang Ming Xhou. Another independently translated, unpublished version of Form 5 by Singer and Singer (1990) and an unpublished Chinese version of Form 5X by Li Baiqing were modified and used by Davis et al. (1996) in a Chinese state enterprise. Translations have been made of the MLQ in Spanish (Molero Alonso, 1994; replicated in Venezuela, Mexico, the Dominican Republic [Davis, 1994], and Puerto Rico),

French (duplicated in Quebec, Canada, and France), Italian (Aparo, 1993), German (Steyrer & Mende, 1994), and Dutch (Den Hartog et al., 1994), as well as other languages more distant from English, such as Hebrew, Arabic (Al-Anazi, 1993), and Japanese (Yokochi, 1989). Nonetheless, although the concepts and components of transformational and transactional leadership transfer, the specific behaviors involved may be different, particularly as one crosses into the non-Western world.

Cultural contingencies

Variform universals and variform functional universals still leave room for contingency analyses to assess how much situational context affects the general means, variances, and correlations. Dorfman (1994) cautioned about applying U.S.-developed leadership models to other cultures and agreed with Adler (1984) that the devil is in the details. Thus, the impact of charismatic leadership on employee satisfaction was greater on the American employees for whom correlations of .50 and .70 were found, as compared with correlations of .29 and .57 for the Mexican employees (Dorfman & Howell, 1988). (Some of the darker history of charismatic Mexican political leaders may have lowered the Mexican results.) U.S. employees also generated higher correlations between contingent reward and the measures of satisfaction with work and with supervision (.48 and .73, respectively) in contrast to the Mexican employees (.19 and .58, respectively).

In Indonesia, inspirational leaders boast about their own competence to create pride and respect in themselves. In so doing, such transformational leaders aim to reduce subordinates' feelings of fear and shame. But, it would be unseemly for leaders to be so boastful in Japan.

There are cultural contingencies in manifesting individualized consideration. According to interviews by Yokochi (1989) with 17 Japanese CEOs of some of the largest Japanese firms and MLQ questionnaire surveys of 135 Japanese managers at levels below them, effective Japanese executives tended to be much more transformational than transactional. The three corollaries held up. Nonetheless, although the concepts and components of transformational and transactional leadership transfer, the specific behaviors involved may be different, particularly as one crosses into the non-Western world. In Yokochi's study, the transformational factor of Individualized Consideration emerged from a different set of items in Japan because such consideration is expected from one's supervisor as a matter of course, although it remains unspoken. The mutual obligation between the leaders and the followers in collectivistic cultures facilitates the transformational leaders' individualized consideration. Leaders in collectivistic cultures likewise already have a moral responsibility to take care of their subordinates, to help them prepare a career development plan, to attend their funeral ceremonies and birthday parties, and to counsel followers about personal problems. In turn, subordinates have a moral obligation to reciprocate with unquestioning loyalty and obedience. Indeed, transformational leadership may be far more pervasive in collectivistic societies than in the individualistic societies of the West (Jung, Bass, & Sosik, 1995).

Transformational leadership may be autocratic and directive or democratic and participative. Leaders can be intellectually stimulating to their followers when they authoritatively direct the followers' attention to a hidden assumption in their thinking. Leaders could also be intellectually stimulating when they ask whether their group would be ready to look together for hidden assumptions. In the individualistic societies of North America, more participative leadership would be expected of its transformational leaders. In the collectivistic societies of Asia, more directiveness would be expected of its transformational leaders. How participative or directive the transformational leaders will be—how much they will depend on authority—would also depend on the issue involved. One would expect to see more authoritative transformational leadership when policy decisions rather than workplace decisions are being made.

Contingent reward may be the least universal component in concepts, behaviors, and effects. As noted earlier, there was no heritability effect in the display of contingent reward (T. Vernon, personal communication, March 31, 1995). Also, it seems to be particularly contingent on the way superior–subordinate relations are organized in different countries and on the idiosyncrasies of national history. Japan, India, Britain, and Egypt provide illustrations of the divergences. In the West, performing better than other members of one's team is ordinarily commendable. Contingent reward may be expected as a matter of equity. In Japan, it may be a cause for disharmony and loss of face. Pay differentials are small and along with promotions are not by one's immediate superior but by the amorphous company, consistent with its standards, values, history, and traditions. In India, implicit is the preference of many subordinates for a dependent personal relationship rather than a contractual one with their leader (Sinha, 1984). Earley (1988) noted that English workers do not value praise, criticism, and general conversation with their superiors as much as do workers in the United States and Ghana. English workers, therefore, are likely to be less responsive to contingent rewards. In particular, those in heavy industry distrust feedback from their supervisors. Perhaps contingent reward needs to be sought in the English workers' interactions with their shop stewards. Egypt is dominated by large public organizations. These are highly structured and centralized bureaucracies with little room for supervisors to practice contingent rewarding (Badran & Hinings, 1981).

Organizational contingencies

Mechanistic organizations were expected to reveal more individual transactional leaders and organic organizations more individual transformational leaders (Bass, 1985). However, Singer and Singer (1990) failed to find such differences when results for members of police organizations were compared with those in business firms in New Zealand and Taiwan. But, the three corollaries tend to hold up across organizations, with a few exceptions. Organizational outliers have appeared on occasion when multiple samples of data have been collected in different units or organizations. Thus, in all but 1 of the 14 samples mentioned earlier, analyzed by Avolio et al. (1996), the usual expected strong correlation emerged between the leader's inspirational motivation and satisfaction with the leader. Thirteen samples generated correlations greater than .60. In 1 sample, an unexpected correlation of −.21 appeared! There is a possible explanation. The outlier sample consisted of professional economists working in a federal agency. Either their supervisors were irrelevant in that setting or the respondents subscribed to Williamson's (1975) theory that organizations are internal competitive marketplaces.

Kennedy (1994) found an outlier within the sample of offshore oil platform supervisors when he obtained onshore bosses' ratings of the offshore supervisors, platform by platform. Generally, the expected positive correlations were obtained between boss-rated performance of the supervisors on a platform and the supervisors' transformational leadership according to their subordinates, but the correlation was −.57 for the boss-rated performance and the transformational supervisors' behavior according to subordinates on one of the platforms. The result may have been due to a distant, tough, no-nonsense onshore boss rating the supervisors on the basis of his view of appropriate management. In the same way, Kennedy found that the mean for management by exception for offshore North Sea oil platform supervisors was much higher than for civilian norms in general. Kennedy's finding is understandable if one appreciates how, as in the military, a premium is placed on safety and effective reaction to emergencies.

Universality or specificity?

Many situational contingencies may be posed as variform functional universals that raise or lower the means, variances, and correlations with outcomes. But the issue remains as to whether the portion of the accountable variance due to a contingent situation remains small, although interesting, or becomes so large as to call into question the argument endorsing the universality of transactional–transformational behaviors and their effects.

The cultural as well as organizational influences on leadership and interpersonal behavior are well-documented (Bass, 1990). Differences in cultural beliefs, values, and norms moderate leader–follower relations. Nonetheless, certain generalizations appear warranted. Transformational leadership tends to be more effective and satisfying than contingent rewarding, contingent rewarding is more effective and satisfying than managing by exception, and managing by exception is more effective and satisfying than laissez-faire leadership. Transformational leadership tends to add to the effects of transactional leadership, not substitute for the latter. The ideals and implicit theories of leadership tend to be transformational rather than transactional. Borrowing from Podsakoff, MacKenzie, Moorman, and Fetter (1990) and Shamir, House, and Arthur (1993), to refute the transactional–transformational distinction will require finding conditions, cultures, and organizations in which trust between the leader and the led is unimportant and the led have no concern for self-esteem, intrinsic motivation, consistency in self-concept, actions taken for the leader, or meaningfulness in their work and lives. Such contexts are likely to prove to be the exception rather than the rule.

Author's note

This article was delivered as the Distinguished Scientific Contributions Award Address at the Society for Industrial and Organizational Psychology, Orlando, FL, May 1995.

I am indebted to P. W. Dorfman for the liberal view of the meaning of *universality*. The full-range model and much of the relevant research emerged from collaboration with B. J. Avolio, F. J. Yammarino, and many others at the Center for Leadership Studies. I also thank W. F. Ulmer for comments on an earlier version of this article.

References

Adler, N. J. (1984). Understanding ways of understanding: Cross-cultural management methodology reviewed. *Advances in International Comparative Management, 1,* 31–67.

Al-Anazi, F. B. (1993). *The relationship between new leadership styles and organization: An empirical investigation of transformational and transactional leadership.* Unpublished doctoral dissertation, University of Liverpool, Liverpool, England.

Aparo, A. (1993). Multidimensional management. *Isvor Notizie, VII*(17), 6–8.

Arnold, J. W. (1990). *A comparison of home care nursing supervisors' self-described leadership styles and staff nurses' descriptions of the supervisors' leadership styles.* Unpublished master's thesis. University of Akron.

Avolio, B. J., & Bass, B. M. (1990). *The Full Range of Leadership Development: Basic/advanced manuals.* Binghamton, NY: Bass/Avolio and Associates.

Avolio, B. J., & Bass, B. M. (1994). *Evaluate the impact of the Full Range of Leadership Training: Final report to the Kellogg Foundation.* Binghamton: State University of New York at Binghamton, Center for Leadership Studies.

Avolio, B. J., & Bass, B. M. (1995). *Team leadership, team development and effectiveness: Final report to the Eisenhower Fund.* Binghamton: State University of New York at Binghamton, Center for Leadership Studies.

Avolio, B. J., Bass, B. M., & Jung, D. I. (1996). *Replicated confirmatory factor analyses of the Multifactor Leadership Questionnaire* (Form 5X; Rev.; CLS Tech. Rep. No. 96–1). Binghamton: State University of New York at Binghamton, Center for Leadership Studies.

Avolio, B. J., Waldman, D. A., & Einstein, W. O. (1988). Transformational leadership in a management game simulation. *Group and Organization Studies, 13,* 59–80.

Badran, M., & Hinings, B. (1981). Strategies of administrative control and contextual constraints in a less-developed country: The case of Egyptian public enterprise. *Group and Organization Studies, 2,* 3–21.

Bass, B. M. (1960). *Leadership, psychology and organizational behavior.* New York: Harper.

Bass, B. M. (1985). *Leadership and performance beyond expectations.* New York: Free Press.

Bass, B. M. (1990). *Bass and Stogdill's handbook of leadership: Theory, research and management applications* (3rd ed.). New York: Free Press.

Bass, B. M. (1996). *A new paradigm of leadership: An inquiry into transformational leadership.* Washington, DC: U.S. Army Research Institute for the Behavioral and Social Sciences.

Bass, B. M., & Avolio, B. J. (1989). Potential biases in leadership measures: How prototypes, leniency, and general satisfaction relate to ratings and rankings of transformational and transactional leadership constructs. *Educational and Psychological Measurement, 49,* 509–527.

Bass, B. M., & Avolio, B. J. (1990). Training and development of transformational leadership: Looking to 1992 and beyond. *European Journal of Industrial Training, 14,* 21–27.

Bass, B. M., & Avolio, B. J. (1991). *The diffusion of transformational leadership in organizational settings.* Turin, Italy: ISVOR-Fiat.

Bass, B. M., & Avolio, B. J. (1993a). Transformational leadership and organizational structure. *International Journal of Public Administration Quarterly, 17,* 112–121.

Bass, B. M., & Avolio, B. J. (1993b). Transformational leadership: A response to critiques. In M. M. Chemers & R. Ayman (Eds.), *Leadership theory and research: Perspectives and directions* (pp. 49–80). New York: Academic Press.

Bass, B. M., & Avolio, B. J. (1994). *Improving organizational effectiveness through transformational leadership.* Thousand Oaks, CA: Sage.

Bass, B. M., & Avolio, B. J. (1995). *The Multifactor Leadership Questionnaire.* Palo Alto, CA: Mind Garden.

Bass, B. M., Avolio, B. J., & Goodheim, L. (1987). Biography and the assessment of transformational leadership at the world-class level. *Journal of Management, 13,* 7–19.

Bass, B. M., Burger, P. C., Doktor, R., & Barrett, G. (1979). *Assessment of managers: An international comparison.* New York: Free Press.

Bass, B., & Yokochi, N. (1991, Winter/Spring). Charisma among senior executives and the special case of Japanese CEO's. *Consulting Psychology Bulletin, 1,* 31–38.

Blake, R. R., & Mouton, J. S. (1964). *The managerial grid.* Houston, TX: Gulf.

Boyd, J. T., Jr. (1988). *Leadership extraordinary: A cross national military perspective on transactional versus transformational leadership.* Unpublished doctoral dissertation. Nova University.

Bryman, A. (1992). *Charisma and leadership in organizations.* London: Sage.

Burns, J. M. (1978). *Leadership.* New York: Harper & Row.

Bycio, P., Hackett, R. D., & Allen, J. S. (1995). Further assessments of Bass's (1985) conceptualization of transactional and transformational leadership. *Journal of Applied Psychology, 80,* 468–478.

Conger, J. A., & Kanungo, R. N. (1987). Toward a behavioral theory of charismatic leadership in organizational settings. *Academy of Management Review, 12,* 637–647.

Curphy, G. I. (1990). *An empirical study of Bass's (1985) theory of transformational and transactional leadership.* Unpublished doctoral dissertation, University of Minnesota, Twin Cities Campus.

Davis, D. D. (1994, July). *A test of Bass's model of transformational leadership in the Dominican Republic.* Paper presented at the meeting of the International Congress of Applied Psychology, Madrid, Spain.

Davis, D. D., Guan, P. L., Loo, J. J., & Maahs, C. J. (1996). *Need for continuous improvement, organizational citizenship, transformational leadership and service climate in a Chinese enterprise.* Unpublished manuscript.

Den Hartog, D. N., Van Muijen, J., & Koopman, P. (1994, July). *Transactional vs. transformational leadership.* Paper presented at the meeting of the International Congress of Applied Psychology, Madrid, Spain.

Dorfman, P. W. (1994, April). *Cross-cultural research: Issues and assumptions.* Paper presented at the meeting of the Society for Industrial and Organizational Psychology, Nashville, TN.

Dorfman, P. W. (1996). International and cross-cultural leadership. In J. Punnitt & O. Shanker (Eds.), *Handbook for international management research* (pp. 267–349). Cambridge, MA: Blackwell.

Dorfman, P. W., & Howell, J. P. (1988). Dimensions of national culture and effective leadership patterns. *Advances in International Comparative Management, 3,* 127–150.

Dorfman, P. W., & Ronen, S. (1991, August). *The universality of leadership theories: Challenges and paradoxes.* Paper presented at the meeting of the Academy of Management, Miami Beach, FL.

Druskat, V. U. (1994). Gender and leadership style: Transformational and transactional leadership in the Roman Catholic Church. *Leadership Quarterly, 5,* 99–119.

Earley, P. C. (1988, April). *Contributions of intercultural research to the understanding of performance feedback.* Paper presented at the meeting of the Society for Industrial and Organizational Psychology, Dallas, TX.

England, G. W. (1976). *The manager and his values: An international perspective.* Cambridge, MA: Balinger.

Fiedler, F. E. (1983). The contingency model—A reply to Ashour. *Organizational Behavior and Human Performance, 9,* 356–368.

Garcia, J. L. (1995). *Transformational leadership processes and salesperson performance effectiveness.* Unpublished doctoral dissertation, Fielding Institute, Santa Barbara, CA.

Gaspar, S. (1992). *Transformational leadership: An integrative review of the literature.* Unpublished doctoral dissertation, Western Michigan University.

Graen, G., & Uhl-Bien, M. (1991). The transformation of professionals into self-managing and partially self-designing contributors: Toward a theory of leadership making. *Journal of Management Systems, X,* 25–39.

Haire, M., Ghiselli, E., & Porter, L. (1966). *Managerial thinking: An international study.* New York; Wiley.

Hater, J. J., & Bass, B. M. (1988). Supervisors 'evaluations and subordinates' perceptions of transformational and transactional leadership. *Journal of Applied Psychology, (73),* 695–702.

Hersey, P., & Blanchard, K. H. (1969). *Management of organizational behavior.* Englewood Cliffs, NJ: Prentice Hall.

Hollander, E. P. (1986). On the central role of leadership processes. *International Review of Applied Psychology, 35,* 39–52.

House, R. J. (1971). A path–goal theory of leader effectiveness. *Administrative Science Quarterly, 16,* 321–338.

House, R. J. (1977). A 1976 theory of charismatic leadership. In J. G. Hunt & L. L. Larson (Eds.), *Leadership: The cutting edge* (pp. 199–272). Carbondale: Southern Illinois University Press.

House, R. J. (1995). Leadership in the twenty-first century: A speculative inquiry. In A. Howard (Ed.), *The changing nature of work* (pp. 411–450). San Francisco: Jossey-Bass.

Howell, J. M., & Avolio, B. J. (1993). Transformational leadership, transactional leadership, locus of control, and support for innovation: Key predictors of consolidated business-unit performance. *Journal of Applied Psychology, 78,* 891–902.

Jung, D. I., Bass, B. M., & Sosik, J. (1995). Collectivism and transformational leadership. *Journal of Management Inquiry, 2,* 3–18.

Kennedy, D. A. (1994, July). *Effective workplace leadership skills of an offshore first-line supervisor.* Paper presented at the meeting of the International Congress of Applied Psychology, Madrid, Spain.

Kissinger, H. (1994). *Diplomacy.* New York: Random House.

Koh, W. (1990). *An empirical validation of the theory of transformational leadership in secondary schools in Singapore.* Unpublished doctoral dissertation. University of Oregon, Concordia.

Kouzes, J. M., & Posner, B. Z. (1987). *The leadership challenge: How to get extraordinary things done in organizations.* San Francisco: Jossey-Bass.

Levinson, H. (1980). Power, leadership, and the management of stress. *Professional Psychology, 11,* 497–508.

Lonner, W. J. (1980). The search for psychological universals. In H. C. Triandis & W. W. Lambert (Eds.), *Handbook of cross-cultural psychology* (pp. 143–204). Boston: Allyn & Bacon.

Lowe, K. B., Kroeck, K. G., & Sivasubramaniam, N. (1996). Effectiveness correlates of transformational and transactional leadership: A meta-analytic review. *Leadership Quarterly, 7,* 385–391.

Maslow, A. H. (1954). *Motivation and personality.* New York: Harper.

Misumi, J. (1985). *The behavioral science of leadership: An interdisciplinary research program.* Ann Arbor: University of Michigan Press.

Molero Alonso, F. (1994). *Carisma y liderazgo carismático: Una aproximacion empirica desde las perspectivas de Bass y Friedman* [Charisma and leadership: An empirical bringing together of the perspectives of Bass and Friedman]. Unpublished doctoral dissertation, Universidad National de Educacion a Distancia, Madrid, Spain.

Murdock, G. (1967). *Ethnographic atlas.* Pittsburgh. PA: University of Pittsburgh Press.

Offerman, L. R., Kennedy, J. K., & Wirtz, P. W. (1994). Implicit theories: Content, structure and generalizability. *Leadership Quarterly, 5,* 43–58.

Onnen, M. K. (1987). *The relationship of clergy and leadership characteristics to growing or declining churches.* Unpublished doctoral dissertation, University of Louisville.

Patterson, C., Fuller, J. B., Kester, K., & Stringer, D. Y. (1995, May). *A meta-analytic examination of leadership style and selected follower compliance outcomes.* Paper presented at the meeting of the Society for Industrial and Organizational Psychology, Orlando, FL.

Pereira, D. (1986, July). *Transactional and transformational leadership scores of executives in a large Indian engineering firm.* Paper presented at the meeting of the International Congress of Applied Psychology, Jerusalem.

Podsakoff, P. M., MacKenzie, S. B., Moorman, R. H., & Fetter, R. (1990). Transformational leader behaviors and their effects on followers' trust in leader, satisfaction, and organizational citizenship behaviors. *Leadership Quarterly, 1,* 107–142.

Rose, R. (1995). Genes and human behavior. *Annual Review of Psychology, 46,* 625–654.
Salter, D. J. (1989). *Leadership styles in the United States Marine Corps transport helicopter squadrons.* Unpublished master's thesis. Naval Postgraduate School, Monterey, CA.
Sashkin, M. (1988). The visionary leader. In J. A. Conger & R. N. Kanungo (Eds.), *Charismatic leadership: The elusive factor in organizational effectiveness* (pp. 122–160). San Francisco: Jossey-Bass.
Schwarzkopf, N. A. (1994, July 21). *Hitler and Stalin: Legacy of hate* [Interview by C. Kuralt]. New York: CBS Television.
Shamir, B. (1991). Meaning, self and motivation in organizations. *Organization Studies, 12,* 405–424.
Shamir, B., House, R. J., & Arthur, M. B. (1993). The motivational effects of charismatic leadership: A self-concept based theory. *Organization Science, 4,* 577–594.
Singer, M. S., & Singer, A. E. (1990). Situational constraints on transformational versus transactional leadership behavior, subordinates' leadership preference, and satisfaction. *Journal of Social Psychology, 130,* 385–396.
Sinha, J. (1984). A model of effective leadership styles in India. *International Studies of Management and Organization, 14,* 86–98.
Smith, P. B., Misumi. J. J., Tayeb, M., Peterson, M., & Bond, M. (1989). On the generality of leadership style measures across cultures. *Journal of Occupational Psychology, 62,* 97–109.
Steyrer, J., & Mende, M. (1994, July). *Transformational leadership: The local market success of Austrian branch bank managers and training applications.* Paper presented at the meeting of the International Congress of Applied Psychology, Madrid, Spain.
Waldman, D., Bass, B. M., & Einstein, W. O. (1986). *Effort, performance and transformational leadership in industrial and military settings* (Working Paper 84–78). Binghamton: State University of New York.
Weathersby, R. (1993). Sri Lankan managers' leadership conceptualizations as a function of ego development. In J. Demick & P. M. Miller (Eds.), *Development in the workplace* (pp. 67–89). Hillsdale, NJ: Erlbaum.
Williamson, O. E. (1975). *Markets and hierarchies.* New York: Free Press.
Yammarino, F. J., & Bass, B. M. (1990). Long-term forecasting of transformational leadership and its effects among naval officers: Some preliminary findings. In K. E. Clark & M. B. Clark (Eds.), *Measure of leadership* (pp. 151–169). West Orange, NJ: Leadership Library of America.
Yokochi, N. (1989). *Leadership styles of Japanese business executives and managers: Transformational and transactional.* Unpublished doctoral dissertation, United States International University, San Diego, CA.

37

THE ROMANCE OF LEADERSHIP AS A FOLLOWER-CENTRIC THEORY

A social constructionist approach

James R. Meindl

Source: *Leadership quarterly* 6(3) (1995): 329–341.

Abstract

This article uses the romance of leadership notion to develop a follower-centric perspective on leadership. A social constructionist view is highlighted. I clarify some of the assumptions of this approach, contrasting them with those of a more leader-centered perspective. In an effort to increase the testability of this approach, I outline a general model, paving the way for generating individual- and group-level hypotheses, and discuss implications for practice and for future leadership research.

Introduction

Hollander (1978) once wrote that leadership is the union of leaders, followers, and situations. Over the years, leadership studies have tended to emphasize the thoughts, actions, and personas of leaders over those of followers. In addition, leadership situations have tended to be defined from the perspectives of leaders and not of followers. This article attempts to provide a more follower-centric perspective. I use the "romance of leadership" notion and its emphasis on social construction to provide a complement to leader-centric perspectives. In doing so, I clarify and further elaborate the approach developed in two earlier papers (Meindl, 1990, 1993), articulating hypotheses at the group and individual levels of analysis. Other approaches are possible (e.g., Lord & Maher, 1991). For those readers interested in using the romance of leadership notion as an entre for their own studies of leadership, this and the previous two papers together will provide useful background.

The romance of leadership notion (Meindl, Ehrlich, & Dukerich, 1985) refers to the prominence of leaders and leadership in the way organizational actors and observers address organizational issues and problems, revealing a potential "bias" or "false assumption-making" regarding the relative importance of leadership factors to the functioning of groups and organizations. Some researchers see in this a rationale or justification for abandoning the study of leadership, portraying it in anti-leadership terms (Yukl, 1989; Bass, 1990). This is a mistaken view. The romance of leadership notion embraces the phenomenological significance of leadership to people's organizational experiences. As such, it can be used as a point of departure for theorizing about leadership in a way that operates from a set of assumptions which distinguishes it from other leader-centric approaches. Thus, rather than being anti-leadership, the romance of leadership, and the perspective it provides, is more accurately portrayed as an alternative to theories and perspectives that place great weight on "leaders" and on the substantive significance of their actions and activities. The romance of leadership notion emphasizes followers and their contexts for defining leadership itself and for understanding its significance. It loosens traditional assumptions about the significance of leaders to leadership phenomena.

Toward social construction

The romance of leadership emphasizes leadership as a social construction. Attention is focused on the development of theory and hypotheses regarding the features, outcomes, and implications of the social construction process, as it occurs among followers and as it is affected by the contexts in which they are embedded. It seeks to understand the existence of general and more situation-specific concepts of "leaders" and how they are conceptualized and otherwise constructed by actors and observers. Although there are currently many available perspectives that highlight the thoughts and phenomenology of the leader, the romance of leadership is about the thoughts of followers: how leaders are constructed and represented in their thought systems. The romance of leadership perspective focuses on the linkage between leaders and followers as constructed in the minds of followers. Rather than assuming leaders and followers are linked in a substantially causal way, it assumes that the relationship between leaders and followers is primarily a constructed one, heavily influenced by interfollower factors and relationships. The behavioral linkages between the leader and follower are seen as a derivative of the constructions made by followers. The behavior of followers is assumed to be much less under the control and influence of the leader, and more under the control and influence of forces that govern the social construction process itself.

Away from leader personality and behavior

One aspect of a leader-centric perspective is a focus on the persona of the leader. The romance of leadership perspective moves a researcher away from the personality of the leader as a significant, substantive, and causal force on the thoughts and actions of followers. It instead places more weight on the images of leaders that followers construct for one another. It assumes that followers react to, and are more influenced by, their constructions of the leader's personality than they are by the "true" personality of the leader. It is the personalities of leaders as imagined or constructed by followers that become the object of study, not "actual" or "clinical" personalities per se.

Similarly, this approach does not explain or deal with the behavior of the leader and the direct impact of that behavior on followers. In other words, direct effects of the actions and activities of the leader, independent of and unmoderated or unmediated by social construction processes, are not addressed. Thus, leadership is assumed to be revealed not in the actions or exertions of the leader but as part of the way actors experience organizational processes. In essence, leadership is very much in the eyes of the beholder: followers, not the leader—and not researchers—define it. From this perspective, the idea that leadership cannot and does not occur without followers is taken literally to be true.

The subjectivity of leader effectiveness

No behaviors on the part of the leader are assumed to represent "more" or "better" leadership than any others, independent of the constructions of followers. It is assumed instead that any given behavioral exertion of "leadership" by the leader can be associated with a wider range of constructions, and imbued with a wider range of meanings, than is otherwise assumed. In this perspective, the predefined, behavioral measures/definitions/concepts of leadership normally used by researchers are taken to represent indirect, rough "clues" to the constructions of leaders and leadership made by followers. As such, the "variance" in leadership ratings made by followers is assumed to reveal a variance of constructions and not assumed to reveal variations in the behavioral effectiveness of the leader. A leader-centric research agenda seeks to understand what behaviors by the leader cause certain reactions among followers (leader behaviors causing followership) and what behaviors are more or less effective in doing so (given, say, certain types of followers and situations). By contrast, the follower-centric agenda of romance of leadership seeks to understand the variance of constructions as influenced by social processes that occur among followers and by salient contextual/situational factors, and their implications for behavior.

The construction of charismatic leadership

Leader-centric approaches to charismatic leadership tend to emphasize the close and special interpersonal linkages that exist between leaders and their followers, highlighting the behavioral processes between them that cause these relationships. In the present approach, these charismatic relationships are assumed to exist in the minds of followers and are treated as a byproduct of interfollower processes and activities. So, instead of understanding a particular social relationship that develops between a leader and a follower mainly in terms of the interaction dynamics that occur within it, this approach seeks to examine that same relationship as a function of the network of relationships in which the followers are embedded. The role that peers play in constructing for followers the nature of their linkages to the leader is emphasized, as is the nature of the contexts and settings in which charisma constructions are more or less likely to develop.

Emergent leadership and hierarchical relationships

Prominent in this approach is the idea that leadership is an emergent phenomenon. Leadership is considered to have emerged when followers construct their experiences in terms of leadership concepts—that is, when they interpret their relationship as having a leadership-followership dimension. Given this emergent definition of leadership, it becomes crucial to understand when and under what conditions such construals are likely to occur among group members—when and what sort of leadership criteria are used to make sense of self in relation to other group members, tasks, and outcomes. Thus, in research designed to pursue this idea, less importance is placed on discovering who emerges as the leader and what he or she had to do to get there—a leader-centric agenda—and more emphasis is placed on discovering when and under what conditions alternative forms of leadership emerge, as the way that followers make sense of and evaluate their organizational experiences.

In this vein, it is not assumed that the construction of leadership is an integral part of formal, hierarchical relationships. Thus, to speak of a "leader," reference is being made only to those figures who are defined as leaders by followers in a relationship that has been constructed by them as entailing issues of leadership and of followership on their part. In this sense, the formality of hierarchical "power" differentials that exist between a superior and a subordinate is conceptually independent from that of leadership emergence. This, then, is not a theory of the formal positions of leadership but a theory about whether or not leadership emerges as an "overlay" to whatever other formal or informal dimensions individuals use to think about their relationships to other group members and to the tasks at hand.

Leadership ratings as self-reports

Reports made by followers regarding their leaders are treated as information regarding the constructions of followers, not as information about the qualities and activities of the leader as with more leader-centric approaches. For example, the commonly employed distinctions between transactional and transformational leadership ratings are used here as rough approximations of two alternative leadership constructions that can occur and that can be employed by followers in various situations and contexts. Furthermore, the correlation between various constructions (leadership ratings made by followers) and their judgments of the effectiveness and personal satisfaction with the leader are taken as evidence of the use of alternative leadership criteria, not as an objective measure of the impact of the leader's behavior on dependent followership variables or criteria.

Although the use of correlated perceptions in making inferences regarding leadership has often been problematic, the romance of leadership approach treats correlated perceptions (and variations of those correlations, variations in concepts, and ratings of self as correlated or not with ratings of the leader) as data relevant to understanding the process and the contents of construction. Such correlations and their variations reveal the thought systems and ideologies regarding leadership that are employed by followers. The assumption is that these systems and ideologies are important causes of "followership."

Applications and practice

Those who are interested in practical applications may begin to see the implications of this perspective around the issues of control and followership. Whereas the leader-centric perspective favors the rather direct control of followers—by engaging in so-called leadership behaviors—the present approach would emphasize more indirect and less tightly controlled effects on followers. Manipulations of contexts and constructions, rather than of leader behaviors, would, in a sense, constitute the "practice" of leadership. Rather than searching for the right personality, one would search for the opportunity to create the right impression. Reputations would be more significant than actions. Rather than being concerned about engaging in the right practices, one would be concerned about creating the right "spin." Rather than schooling leaders in the proper exertions of leadership, training and development programs would represent opportunities to inculcate potential followers with the "right way" to construct leadership. The creation and sustenance of interpretive dominance regarding leadership would have the highest priority.

A general framework for research

The perspective outlined above can be used as a general framework from which a number of researchable models, with testable hypotheses, might be developed. One of these is described below. It simplies and unifies work being done and planned on the romance of leadership notion and the follower-centric view that it provides. The individual aspects of the model focus on the situational and individual difference variables that influence the construction of leadership within individual actors. The group-level aspects of the model focus on the intermember processes that take place within a group or larger collective, emphasizing social processes. The model is focused on construction, referring to: (1) the emergence, in the thought systems of actors and observers, of leadership as a way to understand and address organizational issues; and (2) alternative constructions concerning the definition, criteria, or "theory-in-use" through which leaders are evaluated. Variations in the constructions of leadership are the immediate, dependent variables of interest.

```
┌─────────────────────────────────────────────┐
│  ┌──────────────────┐   ┌──────────────────┐│
│  │ Individual Level │   │   Group Level    ││
│  │    Processes     │   │    Processes     ││
│  └──────────────────┘   └──────────────────┘│
└─────────────────────┬───────────────────────┘
                      │
                      ▼
          ┌─────────────────────┐
          │ Social Construction │
          │         of          │
          │     Leadership      │
          └──────────┬──────────┘
                     │
                     ▼
┌────────────────────────────────────────────┐
│  ┌──────────────┐       ┌──────────────┐   │
│  │ Commitment to│◄─────►│ Self-Defined │   │
│  │  the Leader  │       │ Followership │   │
│  └──────────────┘       └──────────────┘   │
└────────────────────┬───────────────────────┘
                     │
                     ▼
            ┌─────────────────┐
            │   Followership  │
            │     Action      │
            └─────────────────┘
```

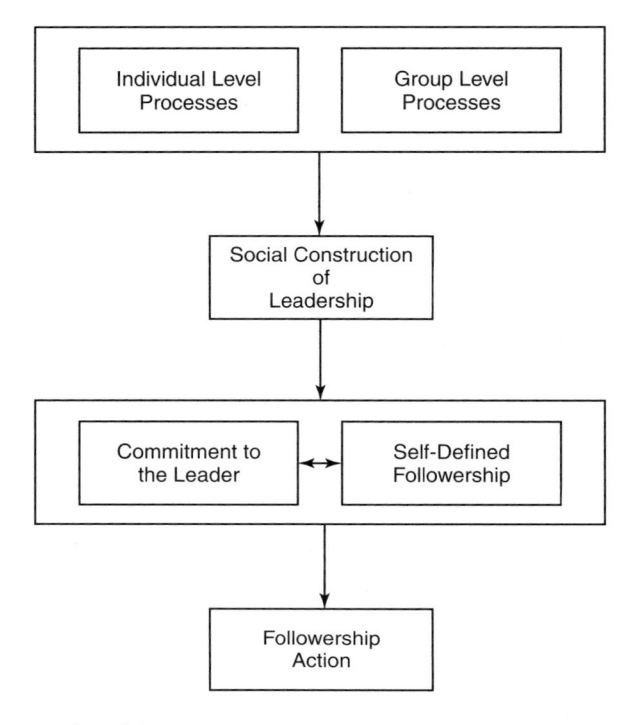

Figure 1 A general model.

A simple overarching model is depicted in Figure 1. It highlights two interrelated outcomes: followers' orientation to the leader and to the self. These are treated as the immediate, psychological precursors to overt acts of followership. These attitudes involve a self-perception by followers that they are, indeed, followers, who are committed to the causes, missions, goals, and aspirations that the leader presumably embodies, exemplifies, and symbolizes. The self-definition of followers and their commitments to the personification of causes, as embodied in the figure of the leader, are the outputs of leadership concepts and ideologies, judgments, and evaluations that have been formulated as part of the social construction process. Through this process, followers understand themselves and each other and their relationships to organizational tasks. These social constructions, in turn, are generated by processes at the level of individuals and of groups, combining with each other to produce leadership as it occurs from the perspectives of followers.

Modeling individual-level processes

Within this general framework, one can attempt to identify: (1) the sets of input variables that are linked to alternative constructions of leadership in the minds of individual actors, (2) the underlying mechanisms through which those variables operate and exert their influence, and (3) the immediate outcomes of those alternative constructions. Input variables that are connected to alternative constructions can be divided, as is commonly done, into those that are associated with individual followers and those that emanate from the social-organizational contexts in which followers are embedded. On the output side, evidence of alternative constructions can be seen in various attributions of leadership made by followers and in their use of alternative criteria through which evaluations of leadership are made. Mechanisms that link input variations to outcomes are attitudinal in nature, working through cognitive and affective channels.

One avenue of research is to explore the covariations between input factors, such as individual difference variables, and evidence of alternative constructions, such as attributions of leadership. Meindl and Ehrlich (1988) constructed a "romance of leadership scale" (RLS). This was conceptualized as a generalized propensity to see leadership as more or less important to the general functioning of organizations. Initial work on that scale, reported in Meindl (1990), found, on the input side, evidence linking various individual difference variables—such as locus of control and age—with scores on that scale. On the output side, another study found that RLS scores were linked to the tendency to "see" more or less charisma in highly public leaders, such as the president of the United States and CEOs of well-known corporations.

In parallel to the work done on the individual differences, it is possible to examine situational factors on the input side. The underlying assumption is that certain contextual features, quite independently of the personal attributes of followers, alter the nature of the emergent leadership constructions. These include factors such as performance cues (that is, information about how well or how poorly the group or organization is accomplishing its tasks) and perceptions of crisis. A study by Pillai and Meindl (1991a) found evidence of the increased use of charismatic criteria for emergent leadership among members in task groups that were exposed to a crisis versus members who were in groups operating under less threatening circumstances. With respect to performance cues, Pillai and Meindl (1991b) manipulated the information raters received regarding the performance patterns of a company. Exposing different raters to the same description of a leader but varying the patterns of firm performance, evidence was found indicating that certain patterns (such as a turnaround) are more likely to cause an attribution of charisma than other patterns. Evidence obtained in these studies suggests that the presence or absence of crisis influences leadership ratings depending upon the broad domain of leadership being evaluated. As a general rule, those attributes typically associated with "tranformational" leadership—such as charisma—are more affected by contextual cues—such as crisis perceptions—than those typically linked with "transactional" forms of leadership.

An interesting direction for exploring the individual-level model would be to focus on the precise cognitive/affective mechanisms that alter the use of various leadership constructions. The arousal levels of followers seem a likely candidate in this regard. The notion here is that various individual and situational factors combine to produce a level of psycho-physiological arousal in followers, which in turn influence the kinds of leadership constructions that emerge. Meindl, Mayo, and Pastor (1994) advanced the hypothesis that higher arousal levels would lead to the development and/or use of more tranformational, "charismatic" constructions than lower levels of arousal. As a corollary, one could expect that perceptions and use of tranformational attributes and criteria for evaluating leadership would covary with differing arousal levels to a greater degree than transactional ratings.

This arousal-level factor can be modeled as either a situational or individual difference variable. In other words, one can refer to the origins of arousal as "state-based" (that is, induced externally, perhaps by certain situational events) or as "trait-based" (that is, emanating from the personality of the follower). Experimental studies designed to explore a state-based arousal mechanism could independently manipulate some aspect of arousal and examine its effects on leadership perceptions, holding constant some presentation of leadership stimuli to followers. Mood manipulations might be useful (e.g., Lewter & Lord, 1992), but one must be careful about what aspect of arousal is being manipulated. There is reason to believe that mood states vary along two underlying dimensions of activation level and positivity/negativity (Larsen & Diener, 1992; Russell, 1980; Watson & Tellegen, 1985). Studies designed to examine state-based arousal effects on leadership perceptions might examine each of these underlying components, separately and in combination.

A general, trait-based arousal mechanism can be found in the concept of "affect intensity" (Larsen & Diener, 1987). This is an individual difference variable that refers to the tendency of some people to generally over- or underreact, affectively or emotionally, to potentially arousing events in their environment. This trait-based mechanism, though, acts in combination with situational contexts. Under nonarousing conditions, high- and low-reactivity people cannot be differentiated. This mechanism only comes into play under arousing conditions. In terms of its impact on leadership constructions, high- and low-affect-intensity followers would, under the right conditions, be expected to exhibit differing arousal levels and, hence, make more and less respective use of charismatic attributes in their constructions. Indeed, affect intensity might function as a moderator in models that link the perception of crisis to perceptions of leadership.

Modeling group-level processes

In addition to the individual-level processes that give rise to constructions of leadership, there are a host of allied social processes—within groups of followers—that might influence individual member's constructions. These group-level processes function to fix the level of inputs in the individual-level model but also cause the constructions of individual members to become a collaborative, negotiated, intersubjectively shared system of leadership concepts that link and unify followers within the group. These processes are those traditionally labeled as "social influence," arising out of the interactions that take place among fellow group members.

In general, such processes work in the direction of generating, among fully embedded members, isopraxisms out of the otherwise independent, potentially diverse, and idiosyncratic constructions.

Studies that seek to find evidence of social construction can take a number of different tacts (see Chen & Meindl, 1991, for one example), but analyses that focus on the network of interactions within groups and organizations can perhaps provide the most direct information regarding the microprocesess involved. To that end, Meindl (1990, 1993) proposed a social contagion model of charismatic leadership in which longitudinal and cross-sectional studies linking interaction-network characteristics to the diffusion of leadership concepts, attributions, and evaluations within groups are implied.

Interaction networks are important to this perspective because they are the channels of communication and influence through which the social construction of leadership takes place. Taking a cross-sectional perspective, where the reseacher is working at the group level of analysis, evidence of a contagion process would be revealed in the residual pattern and distribution of leadership constructions within a group of followers. Although the contents of those contructions, and how they vary across groups, will be interesting to document, a focus on variation in content (examining the mean differences of leadership construction between organizations or groups of followers) is less useful for examining the contagion notion than is a focus on the relative variance of those constructions within different groups of followers, when these groups vary significantly from one another in terms of important network characteristics. For example, given a social contagion hypothesis, certain network parameters should be correlated with the dispersion of leadership constructions within a group. That is because the evidence of a social contagion process is revealed in the residue of more or less homogeneous leadership constructions that conform to network parameters. One might well expect, for example, that the relative density of network ties would predict the relative dispersion of leadership constructions: In groups of followers characterized by high-density networks, the residual constructions of leadership, across group members, ought be more homogenous than in groups characterized by lower-density networks, everything else being equal (such as time and size). The same might be expected for other group-level variables, such as cohesion. Preliminary evidence suggests that such a cross-sectional methodology is fruitful (Pastor, Meindl, & Mayo, 1994).

Although concepts such as social contagion and interaction networks describe group phenomena, this does not mean that only between-groups analyses are appropriate. Indeed, valuable evidence pertaining to a social contagion-interaction network model of leadership can be obtained by conducting analyses of individuals within groups. One research strategy would be to examine if the positions of individual followers within a group's network predict what their views of leadership will be. For example, one might hypothesize that "deviant" views of leadership (that is, views that are at variance with the central tendency of the group) would be greatest or most likely to occur in followers who are at the sociometric fringes of the group. Thus, network-position parameters, such as the centrality of the follower within the group, ought to be inversely correlated with the deviation from the group's mean leadership contruction: those followers who occupy central positions within the group will have greater weight in determining, and hence have views that are more indicative of, the mean than less central followers.

With respect to the discussion above, one might speculate that the "shape" of the social network within which the followers in a group communicate and influence one another would be correlated with the shape of the distribution of leadership constructions among them. The shape of the network is described by well-known network parameters; the shape of the distribution of constructions can be described by its mathematical moments. The first moment—the mean of a distribution—is less meaningful than higher moments such as variance (second moment), skew (third moment), and kurtosis (fourth moment), for describing the distribution of leadership constructions as they would be predicted by the social contagion notion.

Whereas cross-sectional studies can observe evidence of the expected residue of a contagion process having taken place, longitudinal studies can observe evidence of this process more directly. As described in Meindl (1990), a social contagion view of leadership highlights the spreading of leadership concepts within a group of followers over time. Here, observations of temporal order are a paramount concern for the researcher: in whose mind and when do various constructions of leadership take hold? Again, given that social contagion and other forms of social influence are likely to occur through interaction networks, one would expect that some emerging social construction of leadership would flow through sociometric channels, being picked up and perhaps modified, in a sequential fashion, by individual followers who reside in those channels. Clearly, longitudinal perspectives of this sort offer some of the most exciting opportunities to examine the social construction of leadership, as it occurs in groups and organizations, but they have yet to be done.

Quite apart from social contagion notions, other group-level processes can also be examined. For example, the notion of group composition has had a long tradition in the analysis of small groups and has been reincarnated in the management literature under the general rubrics of group demography and organizational diversity. The variables and processes highlighted by those concepts offer yet another set of opportunities for exploring leadership as social construction at the group level. It is possible to formulate some initial, simple models upon which future work might be elaborated. A general model is depicted in Figure 2. Here, group composition is seen as influencing the interaction dynamics that occur among individual followers. Hereogeneous groups increase the range of perspectives, attitudes, and opinions regarding task-related matters and alter the socioemotional climate of the group via situated identities and stereotypes made operative as a result of any salient social categories. The interaction dynamics that result are, in turn, hypothesized to determine the construction of leadership through their effects on various cognitive and affective attitudinal mechanisms.

```
        ┌─────────────┐
        │    Group    │
        │ Composition │
        └──────┬──────┘
               │
               ▼
        ┌─────────────┐
        │ Interaction │
        │  Dynamics   │
        └──────┬──────┘
               │
               ▼
   ┌─────────────────────────────┐
   │ ┌──────────┐   ┌──────────┐ │
   │ │Cognitive │◄─►│ Affective│ │
   │ │Mechanism │   │Mechanism │ │
   │ └──────────┘   └──────────┘ │
   └──────────────┬──────────────┘
                  │
                  ▼
          ┌──────────────┐
          │ Construction │
          │      of      │
          │  Leadership  │
          └──────────────┘
```

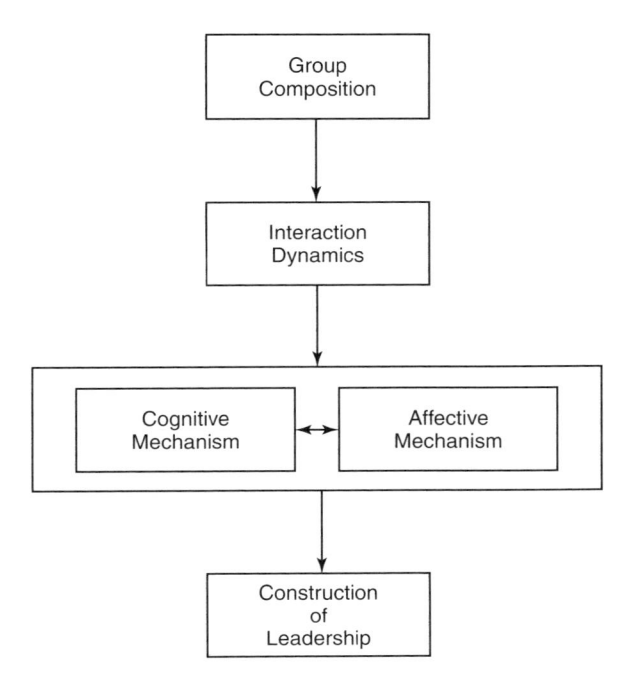

Figure 2 A group-level model.

Specific hypotheses along these lines can be developed and tested. As one example, group composition might be operationalized as an index of demographic diversity (in terms of gender, race, ethnicity, etc.). Interaction dynamics may be assumed to be more conflict ridden in heterogeneous groups than in homogeneous ones and, as a result, perceptions regarding the need for greater integration and group cohesion would be heightened, along with an increase in the general level of stress and arousal that individuals experience and that pervade group atmosphere. The results of a recent study by Mayo, Meindl, and Pastor (1994) indicate that such reactions are likely to produce an increased use of charismatic criteria as a way to evaluate leadership. That is, the correlation between perceptions of charisma and evaluative judgments about leadership effectiveness would be greater across heterogeneous groups and weaker across more homogeneous groups of followers.

Conclusion

This article set forth some statements regarding the "romance of leadership" as a way to define and understand leadership. I realize that my efforts may strike some readers as radical and others, perhaps, as plain silly. Both reactions are likely to stem from my deliberate eschewal of leaders—their personas and behaviors—from consideration. Those who chafe at the decidedly one-sided emphasis on followers may yearn for a more "balanced" approach, such as might come from an interactionist (leader × follower, person × situation) perspective (e.g., Mowday & Sutton, 1993). Such an approach suggests an integration of theoretical work done on both the leader- and follower-centric sides. Even if that were ultimately desirable, however, attempted integrations at this point are extremely premature, given the long development of leader-centric approaches and the newness of follower-centric ones. There is simply not yet enough follower-centric work with which to integrate effectively. Any integration will be heavily biased in the direction of leader-centric traditions, concepts, and research agendas. Better to let alternative traditions develop on their own, unencumbered by each other's assumptions and biases.

Those who have aspirations for an "objective" theory of leadership will find great difficulty with the inherently subjectivistic, social constructionist view being advanced here. Years ago, Calder (1977), among others, reminded us that leadership as a concept was not invented by social scientists but borrowed by them from the cultural, linguistic vernacular of commonly employed concepts social actors use to make sense of the world around them and to communicate it to others. The point is that much of the trouble with conventional leadership research is attributable to the conceptual difficulties encountered when theorists and research scientists attempt to impose outside, objective, third-party definitions of what is inherently subjective. Much sweat and tears have gone into redoubled efforts to remediate leadership studies by disentangling, decoupling, or separating leadership from its origins: objectifying it—cleaning it up, so to speak—so that researchers can better work with it as a scientific construct, independent of its lay meanings. But another response is possible, one which embraces rather than resists leadership's origins in lay psychology. Given its cultural ontology, it seems at least permissible—perhaps even desirable—to return leadership study to a focus on what actors and observers construct as a normal part of their social experiences. The fact that leadership and the figure of the leader are prominent in these constructions is something that itself is worthy of study.

A subjectivist definition and a social construction view of leadership does not imply that it cannot be studied through normal scientific processes of inquiry. As I have tried to show, it is possible to use the romance of leadership notion, with its constructionistic, followership-centric bent, to formulate testable hypotheses. Although I have focused on individuals and groups in this article, there are likely many exciting possibilities for research at all levels of analysis, the only real limitation being the creativity and interest of the researcher.

References

Bass, B.M. (1990). *Bass & Stogdill's handbook of leadership.* 3rd edition. New York: Free Press.

Calder, B.J. (1977). An attribution theory of leadership. In B.M. Staw & G.R. Salancik (Eds.), *New directions in organizational behavior* (pp. 179–204). Chicago: St. Clair.

Chen, C.C., & Meindl, J.R. (1991). The construction of leadership images in the popular press: The case of Donald Burr and People Express. *Administrative Science Quarterly, 36,* 521–551.

Hollander, E.P. (1978). *Leadership dynamics.* New York: Free Press.

Larsen, R.J., & Diener, E. (1987). Affect intensity as an individual difference characteristic: A review. *Journal of Research in Personality, 21,* 1–37.

Larsen, R.J., & Diener, E. (1992). Promises and problems with the circumplex model of emotion. *Review of Personality and Social Psychology,* 13, 25–59.

Lewter, J., & Lord, R.G. (1992). Affect and the multifactor leadership questionnaire: A replication and extension. Paper presented at the Academy of Management Meeting, Las Vegas, NV, August.

Lord, R.G., & Maher, K.J. (1991). *Leadership and information processing: Linking perceptions and organizational performance.* New York: Routledge, Chapman & Hall.

Mayo, M., Meindl, J.R., & Pastor, J.C. (1994). Diversity and leadership: The effects of relational demography on the emergence of charismatic leadership. Unpublished manuscript, School of Management, State University of New York at Buffalo.

Meindl, J.R. (1990). On leadership: An alternative to the conventional wisdom. In B.M. Staw & L.L. Cummings (Eds.), *Research in organizational behavior* (Vol. 12, pp. 159–203). Greenwich, CT: JAI Press.

Meindl, J.R. (1993). Reinventing leadership: A radical, social psychological approach. In J.K. Murnighan (Ed.), *Social psychology in organizations* (pp. 89–118). Englewood Cliffs, NJ: Prentice-Hall.

Meindl, J.R., & Ehrlich, S.B. (1988). Developing a romance of leadership scale. Silver Anniversary Proceedings, Eastern Academy of Management Meetings, Washington, DC, May.

Meindl, J.R., Ehrlich, S.B., & Dukerich, J.M. (1985). The romance of leadership. *Administrative Science Quarterly, 30,* 78–102.

Meindl, J.R., Mayo, M.C., & Pastor, J.C. (1994). The effects of arousal on attributions of charisma. Unpublished manuscript, School of Management, State University of New York at Buffalo.

Mowday, R.T., & Sutton, R.I. (1993). Organizational behavior: Linking individuals and groups to contexts. *Annual Review of Psychology, 44,* 195–229.

Pastor, J.C., Meindl, J.R., & Mayo, M. (1994). Teacher as leader: A network analysis of charisma perceptions in the classroom. Unpublished manuscript, School of Management, State University of New York at Buffalo.

Pillai, R., & Meindl, J.R. (1991a). The impact of a performance crisis on attributions of charismatic leadership: A preliminary study. Best Paper Proceedings of the 1991 Eastern Academy of Management Meetings, Hartford, CT, May.

Pillai, R., & Meindl, J.R. (1991b). The effects of a crisis on the emergence of charismatic leadership: A laboratory study. Best Paper Proceedings of the 1991 Academy of Management Meetings, Miami, FL, August.

Russell, J.A. (1980). A circumplex model of affect. *Journal of Personality and Social Psychology, 39,* 1161–1178.

Watson, D., & Tellegen, A. (1985). Toward a consensual structure of mood. *Psychological Bulletin, 98,* 219–235.

Yukl, G.A. (1989). *Leadership in organizations.* 2nd edition. Englewood Cliffs, NJ: Prentice Hall.

38

THE BASES OF SOCIAL POWER

John R. P. French, Jr. and Bertram Raven

Source: D. Cartwright (ed.), *Studies in Social Power,* Ann Arbor, MI: Institute for Social Research, 1959, pp. 150–167.

The processes of power are pervasive, complex, and often disguised in our society. Accordingly one finds in political science, in sociology, and in social psychology a variety of distinctions among different types of social power or among qualitatively different processes of social influence (1, 6, 14, 20, 23, 29, 30, 38, 41). Our main purpose is to identify the major types of power and to define them systematically so that we may compare them according to the changes which they produce and the other effects which accompany the use of power. The phenomena of power and influence involve a dyadic relation between two agents which may be viewed from two points of view: (a) What determines the behavior of the agent who exerts power? (b) What determines the reactions of the recipient of this behavior? We take this second point of view and formulate our theory in terms of the life space of P, the person upon whom the power is exerted. In this way we hope to define basic concepts of power which will be adequate to explain many of the phenomena of social influence, including some which have been described in other less genotypic terms.

Recent empirical work, especially on small groups, has demonstrated the necessity of distinguishing different types of power in order to account for the different effects found in studies of social influence. Yet there is no doubt that more empirical knowledge will be needed to make final decisions concerning the necessary differentiations, but this knowledge will be obtained only by research based on some preliminary theoretical distinctions. We present such preliminary concepts and some of the hypotheses they suggest.

Power, influence, and change

Psychological change

Since we shall define power in terms of influence, and influence in terms of psychological change, we begin with a discussion of change. We want to define change at a level of generality which includes changes in behavior, opinions, attitudes, goals, needs, values and all other aspects of the person's psychological field. We shall use the word "system" to refer to any such part of the life space.[1] Following Lewin (26, p. 305) the state of a system at time 1 will be denoted $s_1(a)$.

Psychological change is defined as any alteration of the state of some system a over time. The amount of change is measured by the size of the difference between the states of the system a at time 1 and at time 2: $\text{ch}(a) = s_2(a) - s_1(a)$.

Change in any psychological system may be conceptualized in terms of psychological forces. But it is important to note that the change must be coordinated to the resultant force of all the forces operating at the moment. Change in an opinion, for example, may be determined jointly by a driving force induced by another person, a restraining force corresponding to anchorage in a group opinion, and an own force stemming from the person's needs.

Social influence

Our theory of social influence and power is limited to influence on the person, P, produced by a social agent, O, where O can be either another person, a role, a norm, a group or a part of a group. We do not consider social influence exerted on a group.

The influence of O on system a in the life space of P is defined as the resultant force on system a which has its source in an act of O. This resultant force induced by O consists of two components: a force to change the system in the direction induced by O and an opposing resistance set up by the same act of O.

By this definition the influence of O does not include P's own forces nor the forces induced by other social agents. Accordingly the "influence" of O must be clearly distinguished from O's "control" of P (Chapter 11). O may be able to induce strong forces on P to carry out an activity (i.e., O exerts strong influence on P); but if the opposing forces induced by another person or by P's own needs are stronger, then P will locomote in an opposite direction (i.e., O does not have control over P). Thus psychological change in P can be taken as an operational definition of the social influence of O on P only when the effects of other forces have been eliminated.

It is assumed that any system is interdependent with other parts of the life space so that a change in one may produce changes in others. However, this theory focuses on the primary changes in a system which are produced directly by social influence; it is less concerned with secondary changes which are indirectly effected in the other systems or with primary changes produced by nonsocial influences.

Commonly social influence takes place through an intentional act on the part of O. However, we do not want to limit our definition of "act" to such conscious behavior. Indeed, influence might result from the passive presence of O, with no evidence of speech or overt movement. A policeman's standing on a corner may be considered an act of an agent for the speeding motorist. Such acts of the inducing agent will vary in strength, for O may not always utilize all of his power. The policeman, for example, may merely stand and watch or act more strongly by blowing his whistle at the motorist.

The influence exerted by an act need not be in the direction intended by O. The direction of the resultant force on P will depend on the relative magnitude of the induced force set up by the act of O and the resisting force in the opposite direction which is generated by that same act. In cases where O intends to influence P in a given direction, a resultant force in the same direction may be termed positive influence whereas a resultant force in the opposite direction may be termed negative influence.

If O produces the intended change, he has exerted positive control; but if he produces a change in the opposite direction, as for example in the negativism of young children or in the phenomena of negative reference groups, he has exerted negative control.

Social power

The *strength of power* of O/P in some system a is defined as the maximum potential ability of O to influence P in a.

By this definition influence is kinetic power, just as power is potential influence. It is assumed that O is capable of various acts which, because of some more or less enduring relation to P, are able to exert influence on P.[2] O's power is measured by his maximum possible influence, though he may often choose to exert less than his full power.

An equivalent definition of power may be stated in terms of the resultant of two forces set up by the act of O: one in the direction of O's influence attempt and another resisting force in the opposite direction. Power is the maximum resultant of these two forces:

$$\text{Power of O/P}(a) = (f_{a,x} - f_{\overline{a,x}})^{\max}$$

where the source of both forces is an act of O.

Thus the power of O with respect to system a of P is equal to the maximum resultant force of two forces set up by any possible act of O: (a) the force which O can set up on the system a to change in the direction x, (b) the resisting force[3] in the opposite direction. Whenever the first component force is greater than the second, positive power exists; but if the second component force is greater than the first, then O has negative power over P.

It is necessary to define power with respect to a specified system because the power of O/P may vary greatly from one system to another. O may have great power to control the behavior of P but little power to control his opinions. Of course a high power of O/P does not imply a low power of P/O; the two variables are conceptually independent (Chapter 11).

For certain purposes it is convenient to define the range of power as the set of all systems within which O has power of strength greater than zero. A husband may have a broad range of power over his wife, but a narrow range of power over his employer. We shall use the term "magnitude of power" to denote the summation of O's power over P in all systems of his range.

The dependence of s(a) on O

Several investigators have been concerned with differences between superficial conformity and "deeper" changes produced by social influence (1, 5, 6, 11, 12, 20, 21, 22, 23, 26, 36, 37). The kinds of systems which are changed and the stability of these changes have been handled by distinctions such as "public vs. private attitudes," "overt vs. covert behavior," "compliance vs. internalization," and "own vs. induced forces." Though stated as dichotomies, all of these distinctions suggest an underlying dimension of the degree of dependence of the state of a system on O.

We assume that any change in the state of a system is produced by a change in some factor upon which it is functionally dependent. The state of an opinion, for example, may change because of a change either in some internal factor such as a need or in some external factor such as the arguments of O. Likewise the maintenance of the same state of a system is produced by the stability or lack of change in the internal and external factors. In general, then, psychological change and stability can be conceptualized in terms of dynamic dependence. Our interest is focused on the special case of dependence on an external agent, O (31).

In many cases the initial state of the system has the character of a quasi-stationary equilibrium with a central force field around $s_1(a)$ (26, p. 106). In such cases we may derive a tendency toward retrogression to the original state as soon as the force induced by O is removed.[4] Let us suppose that O exerts influence producing a new state of the system, $s_2(a)$. Is $s_2(a)$ now dependent on the continued presence of O? In principle we could answer this question by removing any traces of O from the life space of P and by observing the consequent state of the system at time 3. If $s_3(a)$ retrogresses completely back to $s_1(a)$, then we may conclude that maintenance of $s_2(a)$ was completely dependent on O; but if $s_3(a)$ equals $s_2(a)$, this lack of change shows that $s_2(a)$ has become completely independent of O. In general the degree of dependence of $s_2(a)$ on O, following O's influence, may be defined as equal to the amount of retrogression following the removal of O from the life space of P:

Degree of dependence of $s_2(a)$ on $O = s_2(a) - s_3(a)$.

A given degree of dependence at time 2 may later change, for example, through the gradual weakening of O's influence. At this later time, the degree of dependence of $s_4(a)$ on O, would still be equal to the amount of retrogression toward the initial state of equilibrium $s_1(a)$. Operational measures of the degree of dependence on O will, of course, have to be taken under conditions where all other factors are held constant.

Consider the example of three separated employees who have been working at the same steady level of production despite normal, small fluctuations in the work environment. The supervisor orders each to increase his production, and the level of each goes up from 100 to 115 pieces per day. After a week of producing at the new rate of 115 pieces per day, the supervisor is removed for a week. The production of employee A immediately returns to 100 but B and C return to only 110 pieces per day. Other things being equal, we can infer that A's new rate was completely dependent on his supervisor whereas the new rate of B and C was dependent on the supervisor only to the extent of 5 pieces. Let us further assume that when the supervisor returned, the production of B and of C returned to 115 without further orders from the supervisor. Now another month goes by during which B and C maintain a steady 115 pieces per day. However, there is a difference between them: B's level of production still depends on O to the extent of 5 pieces whereas C has come to rely on his own sense of obligation to obey the order of his legitimate supervisor rather than on the supervisor's external pressure for the maintenance of his 115 pieces per day. Accordingly, the next time the supervisor departs, B's production again drops to 110 but C's remains at 115 pieces per day. In cases like employee B, the degree of dependence is contingent on the perceived probability that O will observe the state of the system and note P's conformity (5, 6, 11, 12, 23). The level of observability will in turn depend on both the nature of the system (e.g., the difference between a covert opinion and overt behavior) and on the environmental barriers to observation (e.g., O is too far away from P). In other cases, for example that of employee C, the new behavior pattern is highly dependent on his supervisor, but the degree of dependence of the new state will be related not to the level of observability but rather to factors inside P, in this case a sense of duty to perform an act legitimately prescribed by O. The internalization of social norms is a related process of decreasing degree of dependence of behavior on an external O and increasing dependence on an internal value; it is usually assumed that internalization is accompanied by a decrease in the effects of level of observability (37).

The concepts "dependence of a system on O" and "observability as a basis for dependence" will be useful in understanding the stability of conformity. In the next section we shall discuss various types of power and the types of conformity which they are likely to produce.

The bases of power

By the basis of power we mean the relationship between O and P which is the source of that power. It is rare that we can say with certainty that a given empirical case of power is limited to one source. Normally, the relation between O and P will be characterized by several qualitatively different variables which are bases of power (30, Chapter 11). Although there are undoubtedly many possible bases of power which may be distinguished, we shall here define five which seem especially common and important. These five bases of O's power are: (1) reward power, based on P's perception that O has the ability to mediate rewards for him; (2) coercive power, based on P's perception that O has the ability to mediate punishments for him; (3) legitimate power, based on the perception by P that O has a legitimate right to prescribe behavior for him; (4) referent power, based on P's identification with O; (5) expert power, based on the perception that O has some special knowledge or expertness.

Our first concern is to define the bases which give rise to a given type of power. Next, we describe each type of power according to its strength, range, and the degree of dependence of the new state of the system which is most likely to occur with each type of power. We shall also examine the other effects which the exercise of a given type of power may have upon P and his relationship to O. Finally, we shall point out the interrelationships between different types of power, and the effects of use of one type of power by O upon other bases of power which he might have over P. Thus we shall both define a set of concepts and propose a series of hypotheses. Most of these hypotheses have not been systematically tested, although there is a good deal of evidence in favor of several. No attempt will be made to summarize that evidence here.

Reward power

Reward power is defined as power whose basis is the ability to reward. The strength of the reward power of O/P increases with the magnitude of the rewards which P perceives that O can mediate for him. Reward power depends on O's ability to administer positive valences and to remove or decrease negative valences. The strength of reward power also depends upon the probability that O can mediate the reward, as perceived by P. A common example of reward power is the addition of a piece-work rate in the factory as an incentive to increase production.

The new state of the system induced by a promise of reward (for example the factory worker's increased level of production) will be highly dependent on O. Since O mediates the reward, he controls the probability that P will receive it. Thus P's new rate of production will be dependent on his subjective probability that O will reward him for conformity minus his subjective probability that O will reward him even if he returns to his old level. Both probabilities will be greatly affected by the level of observability of P's behavior. Incidentally, a piece rate often seems to have more effect on production than a merit rating system because it yields a higher probability of reward for conformity and a much lower probability of reward for nonconformity.

The utilization of actual rewards (instead of promises) by O will tend over time to increase the attraction of P toward O and therefore the referent power of O over P. As we shall note later, such referent power will permit O to induce changes which are relatively independent. Neither rewards nor promises will arouse resistance in P, provided P considers it legitimate for O to offer rewards.

The range of reward power is specific to those regions within which O can reward P for conforming. The use of rewards to change systems within the range of reward power tends to increase reward power by increasing the probability attached to future promises. However, unsuccessful attempts to exert reward power outside the range of power would tend to decrease the power; for example if O offers to reward P for performing an impossible act, this will reduce for P the probability of receiving future rewards promised by O.

Coercive power

Coercive power is similar to reward power in that it also involves O's ability to manipulate the attainment of valences. Coercive power of O/P stems from the expectation on the part of P that he will be punished by O if he fails to conform to the influence attempt. Thus negative valences will exist in given regions of P's life space, corresponding to the threatened punishment by O. The strength of coercive power depends on the magnitude of the negative valence of the threatened punishment multiplied by the perceived probability that P can avoid the punishment by conformity, i.e., the probability of punishment for nonconformity minus the probability of punishment for conformity (11). Just as an offer of a piece-rate bonus in a factory can serve as a basis for reward power, so the ability to fire a worker if he falls below a given level of production will result in coercive power.

Coercive power leads to dependent change also; and the degree of dependence varies with the level of observability of P's conformity. An excellent illustration of coercive power leading to dependent change is provided by a clothes presser in a factory observed by Coch and French (3). As her efficiency rating climbed above average for the group the other workers began to "scapegoat" her. That the resulting plateau in her production was not independent of the group was evident once she was removed from the presence of the other workers. Her production immediately climbed to new heights.[5]

At times, there is some difficulty in distinguishing between reward power and coercive power. Is the withholding of a reward really equivalent to a punishment? Is the withdrawal of punishment equivalent to a reward? The answer must be a psychological one—it depends upon the situation as it exists for P. But ordinarily we would answer these questions in the affirmative; for P, receiving a reward is a positive valence as is the relief of suffering. There is some evidence that conformity to group norms in order to gain acceptance (reward power) should be distinguished from conformity as a means of forestalling rejection (coercive power) (5).

The distinction between these two types of power is important because the dynamics are different. The concept of "sanctions" sometimes lumps the two together despite their opposite effects. While reward power may eventually result in an independent system, the effects of coercive power will continue to be dependent. Reward power will tend to increase the attraction of P toward O; coercive power will decrease this attraction (11, 12). The valence of the region of behavior will become more negative, acquiring some negative valence from the threatened punishment. The negative valence of punishment would also spread to other regions of the life space. Lewin (25) has pointed out this distinction between the effects of rewards and punishment. In the case of threatened punishment, there will be a resultant force on P to leave the field entirely. Thus, to achieve conformity, O must not only place a strong negative valence in certain regions through threat of punishment, but O must also introduce restraining forces, or other strong valences, so as to prevent P from withdrawing completely from O's range of coercive power. Otherwise the probability of receiving the punishment, if P does not conform, will be too low to be effective.

Legitimate power

Legitimate power is probably the most complex of those treated here, embodying notions from the structural sociologist, the group-norm and role oriented social psychologist, and the clinical psychologist.

There has been considerable investigation and speculation about socially prescribed behavior, particularly that which is specific to a given role or position. Linton (29) distinguishes group norms according to whether they are universals for everyone in the culture, alternatives (the individual having a choice as to whether or not to accept them), or specialties (specific to given positions). Whether we speak of internalized norms, role prescriptions and expectations (34), or internalized pressures (15), the fact remains that each individual sees certain regions toward which he should locomote, some regions toward which he should not locomote, and some regions toward which he may locomote if they are generally attractive for him. This applies to specific behaviors in which he may, should, or should not engage; it applies to certain attitudes or beliefs which he may, should, or should not hold. The feeling of "oughtness" may be an internalization from his parents, from his teachers, from his religion, or may have been logically developed from some idiosyncratic system of ethics. He will speak of such behaviors with expressions like "should," "ought to," or "has a right to." In many cases, the original source of the requirement is not recalled.

Though we have oversimplified such evaluations of behavior with a positive-neutral-negative trichotomy, the evaluation of behaviors by the person is really more one of degree. This dimension of evaluation, we shall call "legitimacy." Conceptually, we may think of legitimacy as a valence in a region which is induced by some internalized norm or value. This value has the same conceptual property as power, namely an ability to induce force fields (26, p. 40–41). It may or may not be correct that values (or the superego) are internalized parents, but at least they can set up force fields which have a phenomenal "oughtness" similar to a parent's prescription. Like a value, a need can also induce valences (i.e., force fields) in P's psychological environment, but these valences have more the phenomenal character of noxious or attractive properties of the object or activity. When a need induces a valence in P, for example, when a need makes an object attractive to P, this attraction applies to P but not to other persons. When a value induces a valence, on the other hand, it not only sets up forces on P to engage in the activity, but P may feel that all others ought to behave in the same way. Among other things, this evaluation applies to the legitimate right of some other individual or group to prescribe behavior or beliefs for a person even though the other cannot apply sanctions.

Legitimate power of O/P is here defined as that power which stems from internalized values in P which dictate that O has a legitimate right to influence P and that P has an obligation to accept this influence. We note that legitimate power is very similar to the notion of legitimacy of authority which has long been explored by sociologists, particularly by Weber (42), and more recently by Goldhammer and Shils (14). However, legitimate power is not always a role relation: P may accept an induction from O simply because he had previously promised to help O and he values his word too much to break the promise. In all cases, the notion of legitimacy involves some sort of code or standard, accepted by the individual, by virtue of which the external agent can assert his power. We shall attempt to describe a few of these values here.

Bases for legitimate power

Cultural values constitute one common basis for the legitimate power of one individual over another. O has characteristics which are specified by the culture as giving him the right to prescribe behavior for P, who may not have these characteristics. These bases, which Weber (42) has called the authority of the "eternal yesterday," include such things as age, intelligence, caste, and physical characteristics. In some cultures, the aged are granted the right to prescribe behavior for others in practically all behavior areas. In most cultures, there are certain areas of behavior in which a person of one sex is granted the right to prescribe behavior for the other sex.

Acceptance of the social structure is another basis for legitimate power. If P accepts as right the social structure of his group, organization, or society, especially the social structure involving a hierarchy of authority, P will accept the legitimate authority of O who occupies a superior office in the hierarchy. Thus legitimate power in a formal organization is largely a relationship between offices rather than between persons. And the acceptance of an office as *right* is a basis for legitimate power—a judge has a right to levy fines, a foreman should assign work, a priest is justified in prescribing religious beliefs, and it is the management's prerogative to make certain decisions (10). However, legitimate power also involves the perceived right of the person to hold the office.

Designation by a legitimizing agent is a third basis for legitimate power. An influencer O may be seen as legitimate in prescribing behavior for P because he has been granted such power by a legitimizing agent whom P accepts.

Thus a department head may accept the authority of his vice-president in a certain area because that authority has been specifically delegated by the president. An election is perhaps the most common example of a group's serving to legitimize the authority of one individual or office for other individuals in the group. The success of such legitimizing depends upon the acceptance of the legitimizing agent and procedure. In this case it depends ultimately on certain democratic values concerning election procedures. The election process is one of legitimizing a person's right to an office which already has a legitimate range of power associated with it.

Range of legitimate power of O/P

The areas in which legitimate power may be exercised are generally specified along with the designation of that power. A job description, for example, usually specifies supervisory activities and also designates the person to whom the job-holder is responsible for the duties described. Some bases for legitimate authority carry with them a very broad range. Culturally derived bases for legitimate power are often especially broad. It is not uncommon to find cultures in which a member of a given caste can legitimately prescribe behavior for all members of lower castes in practically all regions. More common, however, are instances of legitimate power where the range is specifically and narrowly prescribed. A sergeant in the army is given a specific set of regions within which he can legitimately prescribe behavior for his men.

The attempted use of legitimate power which is outside of the range of legitimate power will decrease the legitimate power of the authority figure. Such use of power which is not legitimate will also decrease the attractiveness of O (11, 12, 36).

Legitimate power and influence

The new state of the system which results from legitimate power usually has high dependence on O though it may become independent. Here, however, the degree of dependence is not related to the level of observability. Since legitimate power is based on P's values, the source of the forces induced by O include both these internal values and O. O's induction serves to activate the values and to relate them to the system which is influenced, but thereafter the new state of the system may become directly dependent on the values with no mediation by O. Accordingly this new state will be relatively stable and consistent across varying environmental situations since P's values are more stable than his psychological environment.

We have used the term legitimate not only as a basis for the power of an agent, but also to describe the general behaviors of a person. Thus, the individual P may also consider the legitimacy of the attempts to use other types of power by O. In certain cases, P will consider that O has a legitimate right to threaten punishment for nonconformity; in other cases, such use of coercion would not be seen as legitimate. P might change in response to coercive power of O, but it will make a considerable difference in his attitude and conformity if O is not seen as having a legitimate right to use such coercion. In such cases, the attraction of P for O will be particularly diminished, and the influence attempt will arouse more resistance (11). Similarly the utilization of reward power may vary in legitimacy; the word "bribe," for example, denotes an illegitimate reward.

Referent power

The referent power of O/P has its basis in the identification of P with O. By identification, we mean a feeling of oneness of P with O, or a desire for such an identity. If O is a person toward whom P is highly attracted, P will have a desire to become closely associated with O. If O is an attractive group, P will have a feeling of membership or a desire to join. If P is already closely associated with O he will want to maintain this relationship (39, 41). P's identification with O can be established or maintained if P behaves, believes, and perceives as O does. Accordingly O has the ability to influence P, even though P may be unaware of this referent power. A verbalization of such power by P might be, "I am like O, and therefore I shall behave or believe as O does," or "I want to be like O, and I will be more like O if I behave or believe as O does." The stronger the identification of P with O the greater the referent power of O/P.

Similar types of power have already been investigated under a number of different formulations. Festinger (7) points out that in an ambiguous situation, the individual seeks some sort of "social reality" and may adopt the cognitive structure of the individual or group with which he identifies. In such a case, the lack of clear structure may be threatening to the individual and the agreement of his beliefs with those of a reference group will both satisfy his need for structure and give him added security through increased identification with his group (16, 19).

We must try to distinguish between referent power and other types of power which might be operative at the same time. If a member is attracted to a group and he conforms to its norms only because he fears ridicule or expulsion from the group for nonconformity, we would call this coercive power. On the other hand if he conforms in order to obtain praise for conformity, it is a case of reward power. The basic criterion for distinguishing referent power from both coercive and reward power is the mediation of the punishment and the reward by O: to the extent that O mediates the sanctions (i.e., has means control over P) we are dealing with coercive and reward power; but to the extent that P avoids discomfort or gains satisfaction by conformity based on identification, regardless of O's responses, we are dealing with referent power. Conformity with majority opinion is sometimes based on a respect for the collective wisdom of the group, in which case it is expert power. It is important to distinguish these phenomena, all grouped together elsewhere as "pressures toward uniformity," since the type of change which occurs will be different for different bases of power.

The concepts of "reference group" (40) and "prestige suggestion" may be treated as instances of referent power. In this case, O, the prestigeful person or group, is valued by P; because P desires to be associated or identified with O, he will assume attitudes or beliefs held by O. Similarly a negative reference group which O dislikes and evaluates negatively may exert negative influence on P as a result of negative referent power.

It has been demonstrated that the power which we designate as referent power is especially great when P is attracted to O (2, 7, 8, 9, 13, 23, 30). In our terms, this would mean that the greater the attraction, the greater the identification, and consequently the greater the referent power. In some cases, attraction or prestige may have a specific basis, and the range of referent power will be limited accordingly: a group of campers may have great referent power over a member regarding campcraft, but considerably less effect on other regions (30). However, we hypothesize that the greater the attraction of P toward O, the broader the range of referent power of O/P.

The new state of a system produced by referent power may be dependent on or independent of O; but the degree of dependence is not affected by the level of observability to O (6, 23). In fact, P is often not consciously aware of the referent power which O exerts over him. There is probably a tendency for some of these dependent changes to become independent of O quite rapidly.

Expert power

The strength of the expert power of O/P varies with the extent of the knowledge or perception which P attributes to O within a given area. Probably P evaluates O's expertness in relation to his own knowledge as well as against an absolute standard. In any case expert power results in primary social influence on P's cognitive structure and probably not on other types of systems. Of course changes in the cognitive structure can change the direction of forces and hence of locomotion, but such a change of behavior is secondary social influence. Expert power has been demonstrated experimentally (8, 33). Accepting an attorney's advice in legal matters is a common example of expert influence; but there are many instances based on much less knowledge, such as the acceptance by a stranger of directions given by a native villager.

Expert power, where O need not be a member of P's group, is called "informational power" by Deutsch and Gerard (4). This type of expert power must be distinguished from influence based on the content of communication as described by Hovland et al. (17, 18, 23, 24). The influence of the content of a communication upon an opinion is presumably a secondary influence produced after the *primary* influence (i.e., the acceptance of the information). Since power is here defined in terms of the primary changes, the influence of the content on a related opinion is not a case of expert power as we have defined it, but the initial acceptance of the validity of the content does seem to be based on expert power or referent power. In other cases, however, so-called facts may be accepted as self-evident because they fit into P's cognitive structure; if this impersonal acceptance of the truth of the fact is independent of the more or less enduring relationship between O and P, then P's acceptance of the fact is not an actualization of expert power. Thus we distinguish between expert power based on the credibility of O and informational influence which is based on characteristics of the stimulus such as the logic of the argument or the "self-evident facts."

Wherever expert influence occurs it seems to be necessary both for P to think that O knows and for P to trust that O is telling the truth (rather than trying to deceive him).

Expert power will produce a new cognitive structure which is initially relatively dependent on O, but informational influence will produce a more independent structure. The former is likely to become more independent with the passage of time. In both cases the degree of dependence on O is not affected by the level of observability.

The "sleeper effect" (18, 24) is an interesting case of a change in the degree of dependence of an opinion on O. An unreliable O (who probably had negative referent power but some positive expert power) presented "facts" which were accepted by the subjects and which would normally produce secondary influence on their opinions and beliefs. However, the negative referent power aroused resistance and resulted in negative social influence on their beliefs (i.e., set up a force in the direction opposite to the influence attempt), so that there was little change in the subjects' opinions. With the passage of time, however, the subjects tended to forget the identity of the negative communicator faster than they forgot the contents of his communication, so there was a weakening of the negative referent influence and a consequent delayed positive change in the subjects' beliefs in the direction of the influence attempt ("sleeper effect"). Later, when the identity of the negative communicator was experimentally reinstated, these resisting forces were reinstated, and there was another negative change in belief in a direction opposite to the influence attempt (24).

The range of expert power, we assume, is more delimited than that of referent power. Not only is it restricted to cognitive systems but the expert is seen as having superior knowledge or ability in very specific areas, and his power will be limited to these areas, though some "halo effect" might occur. Recently, some of our renowned physical scientists have found quite painfully that their expert power in physical sciences does not extend to regions involving international politics. Indeed, there is some evidence that the attempted exertion of expert power outside of the range of expert power will reduce that expert power. An undermining of confidence seems to take place.

Summary

We have distinguished five types of power: referent power, expert power, reward power, coercive power, and legitimate power. These distinctions led to the following hypotheses.

1. For all five types, the stronger the basis of power the greater the power.
2. For any type of power the size of the range may vary greatly, but in general referent power will have the broadest range.
3. Any attempt to utilize power outside the range of power will tend to reduce the power.
4. A new state of a system produced by reward power or coercive power will be highly dependent on O, and the more observable P's conformity the more dependent the state. For the other three types of power, the new state is usually dependent, at least in the beginning, but in any case the level of observability has no effect on the degree of dependence.
5. Coercion results in decreased attraction of P toward O and high resistance; reward power results in increased attraction and low resistance.
6. The more legitimate the coercion the less it will produce resistance and decreased attraction.

Notes

1. The word "system" is here used to refer to a whole or to a part of the whole.
2. The concept of power has the conceptual property of *potentiality*; but it seems useful to restrict this potential influence to more or less enduring power relations between O and P by excluding from the definition of power those cases where the potential influence is so momentary or so changing that it cannot be predicted from the existing relationship. Power is a useful concept for describing social structure only if it has a certain stability over time; it is useless if every momentary social stimulus is viewed as actualizing social power.
3. We define resistance to an attempted induction as a force in the opposite direction which is set up by the same act of O. It must be distinguished from opposition which is defined as existing opposing forces which do not have their source in the same act of O. For example, a boy might resist his mother's order to eat spinach because of the manner of the induction attempt, and at the same time he might oppose it because he didn't like spinach.
4. Miller (33) assumes that all living systems have this character. However, it may be that some systems in the life space do not have this elasticity.
5. Though the primary influence of coercive power is dependent, it often produces secondary changes which are independent. Brainwashing, for example, utilizes coercive power to produce many primary changes in the life space of the prisoner, but these dependent changes can lead to identification with the aggressor and hence to secondary changes in ideology which are independent.

References

1. Asch, S. E. *Social psychology*. New York: Prentice-Hall, 1952.
2. Back, K. W. Influence through social communication. *J. abnorm. soc. Psychol.*, 1951, **46**, 9–23.
3. Coch, L., & French, J. R. P., Jr. Overcoming resistance to change. *Hum. Relat.*, 1948, **1**, 512–532.
4. Deutsch, M., & Gerard, H. B. A study of normative and informational influences upon individual judgment. *J. abnorm. soc. Psychol.*, 1955, **51**, 629–636.

5. Dittes, J. E., & Kelley, H. H. Effects of different conditions of acceptance upon conformity to group norms. *J. abnorm. soc. Psychol.*, 1956, **53**, 100–107.
6. Festinger, L. An analysis of compliant behavior. In Sherif, M., & Wilson, M. O., (Eds.). *Group relations at the crossroads*. New York: Harper, 1953, 232–56.
7. Festinger, L. Informal social communication. *Psychol. Rev.*, 1950, **57**, 271–82.
8. Festinger, L., Gerard, H. B., Hymovitch, B., Kelley, H. H., & Raven, B. H. The influence process in the presence of extreme deviates. *Hum. Relat.*, 1952, **5**, 327–346.
9. Festinger, L., Schachter, S., & Back, K. The operation of group standards. In Cartwright, D., & Zander, A. *Group dynamics: research and theory*. Evanston: Row, Peterson, 1953, 204–23.
10. French, J. R. P., Jr., Israel, Joachim & Ås, Dagfinn "Arbeidernes medvirkning i industribedriften. En eksperimentell undersøkelse." Institute for Social Research, Oslo, Norway, 1957.
11. French, J. R. P., Jr., Levinger, G., & Morrison, H. W. The legitimacy of coercive power. In preparation.
12. French, J. R. P., Jr., & Raven, B. H. An experiment in legitimate and coercive power. In preparation.
13. Gerard, H. B. The anchorage of opinions in face-to-face groups. *Hum. Relat.*, 1954, **7**, 313–325.
14. Goldhammer, H., & Shils, E. A. Types of power and status. *Amer. J. Social.*, 1939, **45**, 171–178.
15. Herbst, P. G. Analysis and measurement of a situation. *Hum. Relat.*, 1953, **2**, 113–140.
16. Hochbaum, G. M. Self-confidence and reactions to group pressures. *Amer. soc. Rev.*, 1954, **19**, 678–687.
17. Hovland, C. I., Lumsdaine, A. A., & Sheffield, F. D. *Experiments on mass communication*. Princeton: Princeton Univer. Press, 1949.
18. Hovland, C. I., & Weiss, W. The influence of source credibility on communication effectiveness. *Publ. Opin. Quart.*, 1951, **15**, 635–650.
19. Jackson, J. M., & Saltzstein, H. D. The effect of person-group relationships on conformity processes. *J. abnorm. soc. Psychol.*, 1958, **57**, 17–24.
20. Jahoda, M. Psychological issues in civil liberties. *Amer. Psychologist*, 1956, **11**, 234–240.
21. Katz, D., & Schank, R. L. *Social psychology*. New York: Wiley, 1938.
22. Kelley, H. H., & Volkart, E. H. The resistance to change of group-anchored attitudes. *Amer. soc. Rev.*, 1952, **17**, 453–465.
23. Kelman, H. Three processes of acceptance of social influence: compliance, identification and internalization. Paper read at the meetings of the American Psychological Association, August 1956.
24. Kelman, H., & Hovland, C. I. "Reinstatement" of the communicator in delayed measurement of opinion change. *J. abnorm. soc. Psychol.*, 1953, **48**, 327–335.
25. Lewin, K. *Dynamic theory of personality*. New York: McGraw-Hill, 1935, 114–170.
26. Lewin, K. *Field theory in social science*. New York: Harper, 1951.
27. Lewin, K., Lippitt, R., & White, R. K. Patterns of aggressive behavior in experimentally created social climates. *J. soc. Psychol.*, 1939, **10**, 271–301.
28. Lasswell, H. D., & Kaplan, A. *Power and society: A framework for political inquiry*. New Haven: Yale Univer. Press, 1950.
29. Linton, R. *The cultural background of personality*. New York: Appleton-Century-Crofts, 1945.

30. Lippitt, R., Polansky, N., Redl, F., & Rosen, S. The dynamics of power. *Hum. Relat.*, 1952, **5**, 37–64.
31. March, J. G. An introduction to the theory and measurement of influence. *Amer. polit. Sci. Rev.*, 1955, **49**, 431–451.
32. Miller, J. G. Toward a general theory for the behavioral sciences. *Amer. Psychologist*, 1955, **10**, 513–531.
33. Moore, H. T. The comparative influence of majority and expert opinion. *Amer. J. Psychol.*, 1921, **32**, 16–20.
34. Newcomb, T. M. *Social psychology.* New York: Dryden, 1950.
35. Raven, B. H. The effect of group pressures on opinion, perception, and communication. Unpublished doctoral dissertation, University of Michigan, 1953.
36. Raven, B. H., & French, J. R. P., Jr. Group support, legitimate power, and social influence. *J. Person.*, 1958, **26**, 400–409.
37. Rommetveit, R. *Social norms and roles.* Minneapolis: Univer. Minnesota Press, 1953.
38. Russell, B. *Power: A new social analysis.* New York: Norton, 1938.
39. Stotland, E., Zander, A., Burnstein, E., Wolfe, D., & Natsoulas, T. Studies on the effects of identification. University of Michigan, Institute for Social Research. Forthcoming.
40. Swanson, G. E., Newcomb, T. M., & Hartley, E. L. *Readings in social psychology.* New York: Henry Holt, 1952.
41. Torrance, E. P., & Mason, R. Instructor effort to influence: an experimental evaluation of six approaches. Paper presented at USAF-NRC Symposium on Personnel, Training, and Human Engineering. Washington, D. C., 1956.
42. Weber, M. *The theory of social and economic organization.* Oxford: Oxford Univer. Press, 1947.

39
TEAMS IN ORGANIZATIONS
Recent research on performance and effectiveness

Richard A. Guzzo and Marcus W. Dickson

Source: *Annual Review of Psychology* 47 (1996): 307–338.

Abstract

This review examines recent research on groups and teams, giving special emphasis to research investigating factors that influence the effectiveness of teams at work in organizations. Several performance-relevant factors are considered, including group composition, cohesiveness, and motivation, although certain topics (e.g. composition) have been more actively researched than others in recent years and so are addressed in greater depth. Also actively researched are certain types of teams, including flight crews, computer-supported groups, and various forms of autonomous work groups. Evidence on basic processes in and the performance effectiveness of such groups is reviewed. Also reviewed are findings from studies of organizational redesign involving the implementation of teams. Findings from these studies provide some of the strongest support for the value of teams to organizational effectiveness. The review concludes by briefly considering selected open questions and emerging directions in group research.

Introduction

Scope and objectives

For more than a decade now, psychology has enjoyed a rekindled interest in groups and teams. Chapters in previous *Annual Review of Psychology* volumes have considered group research (e.g. Levine & Moreland 1990) and organizational behavior (e.g. Wilpert 1995), but this chapter is unique because of its special focus on team performance in organizational contexts, especially in work organizations.

The literature reviewed considers, among other emphases, research conducted in organizational settings with groups or teams that must meet the demands of producing goods or delivering services. Although we review some research conducted in other than organizational settings, we emphasize studies in which the dependent variables were clearly indicative of performance effectiveness rather than studies on intragroup or interpersonal processes in groups (e.g. studies of conformity, opinion change, conflict). We also include studies of interventions made to test the efficacy of techniques intended to improve team effectiveness. Such interventions may be targeted at individual team members (e.g. enhancing member skills that are important to team performance), at teams as performing units (e.g. team development interventions), or at the organizations in which teams work. Thus, research on larger-scale organizational change efforts of which the implementation or enhancement of teams are one part of an overall change strategy is included. Lastly, we emphasize research in the 1990s, though we do refer to earlier works.

Definitional struggles

Work group/team

What is a work group? A variety of definitions have been offered (Guzzo & Shea 1992), but one we adopt owes its origins to the work of Alderfer (1977) and Hackman (1987). A "work group" is made up of individuals who see themselves and who are seen by others as a social entity, who are interdependent because of the tasks they perform as members of a group, who are embedded in one or more larger social systems (e.g. community, organization), and who perform tasks that affect others (such as customers or coworkers).

"Team" has largely replaced "group" in the argot of organizational psychology. Is this a mere matter of wording or are there substantive differences between groups and teams? For many, "team" connotes more than "group." Katzenbach & Smith (1993), for example, assert that groups become teams when they develop a sense of shared commitment and strive for synergy among members. The definition of work groups presented above, we believe, accommodates the uses of the many labels for teams and groups, including empowered teams, autonomous work groups, semi-autonomous work groups, self-managing teams, self-determining teams, self-designing teams, crews, cross-functional teams, quality circles, project teams, task forces, emergency response teams, and committees—a list that represents, but does not exhaust, available labels. Consequently, we use the labels "team" and "group" interchangeably in this review, recognizing that there may be degrees of difference, rather than fundamental divergences, in the meanings implied by these terms. We use the terms interchangeably as a convenience. The word "group" predominates in the research literature—intergroup relations, group incentives, group dynamics—and though it uses "group" as its root word, we believe the literature has great relevance for understanding virtually all forms of teams in organizations, too.

Effectiveness

There is no singular, uniform measure of performance effectiveness for groups. We prefer to define it broadly, as have Hackman (1987) and Sundstrom et al (1990). Accordingly, effectiveness in groups is indicated by (*a*) group-produced outputs (quantity or quality, speed, customer satisfaction, and so on), (*b*) the consequences a group has for its members, or (*c*) the enhancement of a team's capability to perform effectively in the future. Research that assesses one or more of these three aspects of effectiveness is of primary interest in this review.

Framework for the review

We begin with recent research on several long-standing issues relevant to work-group effectiveness, including team cohesiveness, team composition and performance, leadership, motivation, and group goals. They are generic issues in the sense that they pertain to almost all teams doing almost all kinds of work. Although not the only performance-relevant research topics, they are the ones most actively investigated in recent years.

We then consider research on the performance of different kinds of groups, including cockpit crews and electronically mediated groups, as well as groups created to solve problems (quality circles, task forces) and autonomous work groups. The next section explicitly addresses teams and the organizational systems in which they are embedded and focuses on the interconnections between team and organization.

The final section offers selected conclusions and flags open questions and new directions for future research. The section concludes with a brief discussion of points of leverage for effecting change in teams.

New looks at long-standing issues in group performance

Cohesiveness

Reviews of cohesiveness research have appeared in recent years (e.g. Evans & Dion 1991, Guzzo & Shea 1992). The former review found a substantial positive association between cohesion and performance while the latter offered a more qualified conclusion. Smith et al (1994) report a positive correlation between a cohesiveness-like measure of top management teams in small high-technology firms and firm financial performance. Zaccaro et al (1995) reported that highly task-cohesive military teams under high temporal urgency performed as well on a decision task as did either high task-cohesive or low task-cohesive teams under low temporal urgency, suggesting that task cohesion can improve team decision making under time pressure. The topic of cohesiveness is still very much an unsettled concern in the literature. It is certainly related to issues of familiarity, which are discussed at other points in the chapter.

Group composition

Group composition refers to the nature and attributes of group members, and it is one of the most frequently studied group design variables. Most of the empirical research on composition and work-group performance in recent years has investigated variables associated with team effectiveness without intervening or experimenting to affect those variables. The typical model of study has been to assess the performance of existing groups or teams in organizations over time and to relate that performance to measured aspects of group composition.

Other studies investigated group composition as one of several possible design variables for groups. Group design refers to issues of staffing (who is in the group, what the group size should be), specifying the group's task and members' roles, and creating organizational support systems (e.g. training opportunities) for groups. Studies conducted with teams in organizational settings are of particular interest here.

One study that related team effectiveness to composition and other potential design variables was reported by Campion et al (1993). They studied 80 work groups in a financial services firm and found broad evidence of relationships between effectiveness and 19 design variables clustered into five categories: team job design (e.g. amount of self-management in the team), interdependence among team members, composition (especially the heterogeneity of members), intragroup processes, and contextual factors (e.g. managerial support). Campion et al found team size to be positively related to effectiveness and found heterogeneity of members' background and expertise to be unrelated or negatively related to effectiveness, depending on the specific criterion measure.

Another study examining some of the same issues was reported by Magjuka & Baldwin (1991). Here the focus was on factors that contribute to the successful implementation of team-based employee-involvement programs and the longer-term effective performance of teams in such programs. Through teams employees have voice in organizational affairs, gain access to information and address problems previously reserved for management, and take on new and varied responsibilities. On the basis of results from their national survey, Magjuka & Baldwin identified factors thought to contribute to the effectiveness with which employee involvement teams are designed and implemented. They then obtained additional data and examined relationships between these factors and effectiveness for 72 teams in two manufacturing firms. They found that larger team size, greater within-team heterogeneity (in terms of the kinds of jobs team members held), and greater access to information were positively associated with team effectiveness. The implications of these findings for designing and implementing employee involvement teams are straightforward. Other factors such as hours spent in meetings and members' wages did not relate to effectiveness.

Heterogeneity and performance

The extent to which team effectiveness is affected by the heterogeneity among members is a complicated matter. Magjuka & Baldwin (1991) and Campion et al (1993), as noted above, offer seemingly contradictory findings. Jackson et al (1995), in their paper on diversity in organizations, reviewed and summarized empirical evidence from a number of related disciplines about the link between diversity (that is, within-group heterogeneity) and team effectiveness. Their reading of the literature is that heterogeneity is positively related to the creativity and the decision-making effectiveness of teams. Note that heterogeneity is broadly defined here and refers to the mix of personalities, gender, attitudes, and background or experience factors. For example, Bantel & Jackson (1989) found that organizational innovations in the banking industry were positively associated with heterogeneity of functional expertise among members of the top management teams of firms in that industry. Watson et al (1993) reported that, overtime (15 weeks), initial performance differences between newly formed culturally homogeneous and culturally diverse groups disappeared and eventually "crossed-over," such that culturally heterogeneous groups that initially performed poorly relative to homogeneous groups later performed better than homogeneous groups on selected aspects of task performance (namely, generating alternative solutions and applying a range of perspectives in analyzing business cases). Overall, the Campion et al (1993) finding of a nil or negative association between the heterogeneity of group members' backgrounds and team effectiveness appears to be more the exception than the rule (Jackson et al 1991), though evidence supporting the value of member heterogeneity for team performance is clearest in the domains of creative and intellective tasks. The processes (cognitive, social) through which heterogeneous group compositions have their effect on team performance are far from fully specified, though Jackson et al (1995) explore possible mediating processes.

Heterogeneity of members also appears to have other, performance-related consequences. Jackson et al (1991) reported that heterogeneity among members of top management teams in bank holding companies was positively related to turnover in those teams. Wiersema & Bird (1993) found similar, if stronger, results in a sample of Japanese firms. Turnover is usually thought of as dysfunctional for team effectiveness, though it is possible that the consequences of losing and replacing members could work to the advantage of teams in some circumstances.

Familiarity and performance

Another aspect of group composition that has recently been studied for its relationship to team performance is that of familiarity among members. Goodman & Leyden (1991) examined, over the course of 15 months, the productivity (in tons per shift) of coal-mining crews who differed in the extent to which members were familiar with each other, their jobs, and their mining environment. Results indicated that lower levels of familiarity were associated with lower levels of productivity. Watson et al (1991) studied groups who spent more than 30 hours in decision-making tasks and found that group decision-making effectiveness (relative to individual decision-making effectiveness) rose over time, a finding they attribute at least in part to the effects of increased familiarity among members. Dubnicki & Limburg (1991) found that older health-care teams tend to be more effective in certain ways, though newer teams express more vitality. Thus, some evidence indicates that teams composed of individuals who are familiar with one another carry out their work with greater effectiveness than teams composed of strangers. However, one should bear in mind that some older evidence indicates that there may be a point, perhaps two or three years after a group is formed, at which group longevity and member familiarity become detriments to group performance (Katz 1982). In the later section on cockpit crews we provide further discussion of team member familiarity.

Leadership and group performance

The effects on group performance of leaders' expectations of group performance were studied in a field experiment by Eden (1990a). The purpose of the intervention was to raise, through information provided by an '"expert," group leaders' expectations of their group's performance in a training setting. The groups were platoons in the Israeli Defense Forces in training that lasted 11 weeks. Platoons training under leaders who held high expectations performed better on physical and cognitive tests at the end of training than did comparison platoons. This research extends prior work on the effects of expectations on performance (Eden 1990b) and indicates that such expectancy effects occur in the absence of any lowered expectations for comparison groups.

Jacobs & Singell (1993) offer a different perspective on how individual leaders can affect team performance. They examined the effects of managers (after controlling for other variables) on the won-lost record of professional baseball teams over two decades and found it was possible to identify superior managers. Superior managers were effective through at least two possible processes: by exercising excellent tactical skills or by improving the individual performances of team members.

George & Bettenhausen (1990) studied groups of sales associates reporting to a store manager and found that the favorability of leaders' moods was inversely related to employee turnover. Another study in business organizations examined the position-based power dominance of firms' chief executive officers (CEOs) and their top-management team size as predictors of firm performance (Haleblian & Finkelstein 1993). The study found that firms' performance was worse in turbulent environments when the CEO was dominant and better when top-management team size was greater.

Motivation and group performance

In recent years motivation in groups has received more theoretical rather than empirical attention. Much of this attention is devoted to understanding motivation at a collective (group, team) level rather than to strictly confining the motivation construct to an individual level of analysis. For example, Shamir (1990) analyzed three different forms of collectivistic work motivation: calculation (rewards or sanctions are anticipated to follow from group performance), identification (one's self-concept is influenced by membership in a group), and internalization (acceptance of group beliefs and norms as a basis for motivated behavior). Each orientation is considered viable in different circumstances. Guzzo et al (1993) introduced the concept of group potency and defined it as the group's collective belief that it can be effective. They differentiated the construct from other related constructs (e.g. collective efficacy) and reviewed evidence that the strength of this motivational belief significantly predicted group effectiveness in customer service and other domains. Guzzo et al (1993) maintained an interest in motivation at the group level of analysis, not at the individual level of analysis.

Individual motivation within groups also has received attention, especially as individual motivation is related to group-level factors. Earley (1994) provided empirical evidence on the role of individualism-collectivism (a culture-based individual difference) in shaping the impact of motivational (self-efficacy) training for individuals. Group-focused training was found to have a stronger impact on collectivist individuals, and self-focused training was found to have a greater impact on individualists. For Earley, a central research question was how individual motivation is affected by the match of motivational training to the individual values of trainees. Sheppard (1993) offered an interpretation of individual task-performance motivation in groups that drew heavily on expectancy theory (e.g. Vroom 1964), reinterpreting within the expectancy theory framework evidence on individual motivational deficits in the form of social loafing and free-riding in groups.

Group goals

Related to issues of group motivation are issues of group goals and goal-setting. Goals for group performance can take many forms: quantity, speed, accuracy, service to others, and so on (see Brawley et al 1992 for an exploration of the types of goals set by sports teams). And the evidence is clear that, compared with the absence of goals (or the presence of ill-defined goals), specific, difficult goals for groups raise group performance on those dimensions reflecting the content of the goal (Weldon & Weingart 1993). That is, goals for quantity tend to raise quantity, goals for speed tend to raise speed, and so on.

There are occasional reports of failures of group goals to induce performance effects (see Fandt et al 1990 for an example). Despite the exceptions, there does appear to be a strong evidentiary basis for the performance effects of goals. In light of this, research has been redirected toward understanding the processes through which goals have their effects. Weingart (1992), for example, examined in a laboratory experiment member effort and planning, two possible mediators of goal effects, and found evidence indicating that member effort mediated the impact of goal difficulty on performance. The quality of the planning process also affected group performance in the expected direction but was not observed to be a result of goal levels. Weldon et al (1991) and Weingart & Weldon (1991) also provide evidence that group goals raise member effort, but only in the former study did that effort translate into increased group performance. Other possible mediators of the effects of group goals include the degree of cooperation and communication they stimulate in groups (Weldon & Weingart 1993; see also Lee 1989, Locke & Latham 1990).

Goals for group performance often coexist with goals for individual performance. When group and individual goals conflict, dysfunctions can result. However, it is not necessarily the case that even when group and individual goals are compatible the presence of both results in levels of performance higher than when either goal type exists alone. Specifically, Mitchell & Silver (1990) found that the presence of both individual and group goals resulted in performance no greater than that attained in the presence of group goals alone. Self-efficacy has also been explored in this context, with Lee (1989) showing that team goal-setting mediated the relationship between team-member self-efficacy and winning percentage among several female field hockey teams.

Other issues

Other issues of long-standing interest because of their relationship to group performance effectiveness include feedback and communication in groups. For example, in a study of a collegiate volleyball team, de Armas Paredes & Riera-Milian (1987) found won-lost records to be related to the quality of intrateam communication. The performance effects of feedback were investigated in a study of railway work crews by Pearson (1991), who found small but statistically significant increases in productivity over time as a consequence of receiving performance feedback. The effect of task-performance feedback also was investigated by McLeod et al (1992). However, they found no significant change in task performance effectiveness attributable to such goal-referenced feedback. They also investigated the effects of feedback that concerned interpersonal processes in groups and did detect a change in the dominance behavior of individuals attributable to it.

Kinds of groups

The preceding section reviewed recent research on long-standing issues of relevance to group performance. Issues such as composition, motivation, and leadership are of near-universal importance to groups. They are relevant to many types of teams in many kinds of settings. In this section we consider recent research on particular types of groups.

Many classifications of groups into types have been offered. Hackman's (1990) book, for example, organizes its reports of groups into categories such as service (e.g. delivery) and performing (e.g. symphonic) teams. In this section we, too, specify different kinds of groups on the basis of the work they do. We do not offer the following categories as a typology that we expect to have value outside of the confines of this review. Instead, the categorizations defined below are a matter of convenience for organizing recent research literature.

Flight crews: teams in the cockpit

"The crew concept" in airlines has had many names over the years. The phrase "Cockpit Resource Management" initially took hold. More recently, this focus has come to be known as "Crew Resource Management" (CRM) owing, in part, to the recognition of the importance of including persons not actually in the cockpit (e.g. controllers, flight attendants, etc) as part of the team (Lauber 1993).

CRM has been defined as "using all available resources—information, equipment, and people—to achieve safe and efficient flight operations" (Lauber 1984). The practical importance of such a program is shown in the fact that over 70% of all severe aircraft accidents between 1959 and 1989 were at least partially attributable to flight crew behavior.

In general, CRM training includes "not only optimizing the person-machine interface and the acquisition of timely, appropriate information, but also interpersonal activities including leadership, effective team formation and maintenance, problem solving and decision making, and maintaining situation awareness. ... It represents anew focus on crew-level (as opposed to individual-level) aspects of training and operations" (Helmreich & Foushee 1993, p. 4). Helmreich & Wilhelm (1991) noted that CRM training is generally well received by trainees and leads to positive changes in crew members' attitudes about both crew coordination and personal capabilities (or self-efficacy). However, they also acknowledge that in a small percentage of trainees there is a "boomerang effect" in which attitudes become less positive.

Related to CRM training is Line-Oriented Flight Training (LOFT), which is a broad category encompassing flight simulations conducted for several purposes (e.g. to qualify as a pilot, for training). Butler (1993) asserted that LOFT is most important as a training methodology to reinforce CRM concepts and training. This type of LOFT is called CRM LOFT, and it is ongoing, systematic flight simulation of realistic problem situations that require the type of decision-making skills and crew communication that are taught in CRM training. Wiener et al (1993) provide an excellent review of literature on CRM training and LOFT.

CRM and crew communication

Communication is one of the major areas covered in CRM training (Orlady & Foushee 1987). In the context of CRM training, communication includes such things as "polite assertiveness and participation, active listening, and feedback" (Orlady & Foushee 1987, p. 199). Though effective communication is almost universally recognized as crucial to effective flight crew performance, and CRM training is generally seen as improving communication skills of flight crew members, there is little experimental or quasi-experimental research on the effectiveness of CRM's communication training for improving outcomes. Instead, the majority of the research examines the effects of CRM training on process variables.

Effective crew coordination is in large part a function of effective crew communication, and so we note research by Stout et al (1994), though not quite a CRM-based study. Their preliminary investigations used a low-fidelity flight simulator, and they examined the interactions among two-person teams of undergraduate volunteers. They found that, when team members must act interdependently to perform effectively, increased levels of such team process and communication behaviors as providing information before it is needed, planning, asking for input, and stepping in to help others were all related to increased effectiveness. Urban et al (1995) had similar results in another non-CRM laboratory study in which they examined the impact of workload and team structure on effectiveness.

CRM and decision making

Diehl (1991) suggested that 50% of all accident-related errors are errors of decision. Thus, the question of whether CRM can enhance the quality of decision making in the cockpit is an important one.

Flight crews are in some ways like many other types of groups that make decisions. Power dynamics are present, and traditional group decision-making pitfalls (e.g. groupthink, risky shift) must be avoided. Flight crews are similar to other groups in that they determine what the situation is, assess available options, and choose among them.

In other ways, though, decision making in the cockpit is unlike other group-decision situations. One significant difference is that crew decision making is hierarchically managed decision making: Each member of the crew contributes his or her knowledge and opinions, and the captain is the final decision-maker. Finally, there is a great variety of expertise available in a flight crew, making flight crews perhaps more heterogeneous than many other types of decision-making groups (Orasanu 1993).

Contextual variables

There are several contextual variables that play a role in airline crew performance and process. One of the most significant is the limited duration of flight crews' existence as a unit. In the commercial airline industry, a given flight crew will probably only work together for at most four days, and sometimes will be together for only part of one day. Indeed, commercial airline flight crews perhaps most closely resemble project teams or task forces in that they are composed of persons with expertise in a specific area (e.g. navigator, captain) and work together for a limited period of time, after which members are reassigned to other flight crews.

Because of this, CRM training and LOFT are conducted in the context of a team (all of the members of a CRM or LOFT flight crew are trainees). Further, the training is not done with the intention of strengthening *that particular* team, but rather with the goal of making the individuals more effective in whatever team/flight crew they find themselves.

Crews learn to develop relationships quickly (Bowers et al 1993a, Foushee et al 1986). This process can be facilitated by the standard preflight briefing. In this meeting, the captain lays out his or her expectations for the crew and states the goals of the flight (Ginnett 1993).

Finally, and most significantly, Foushee et al (1986) found that newly formed crews communicate less effectively and are more likely to have accidents than are crews that have been intact for at least a short time. This is the primary reason that Hackman (1993) recommended that the system of scheduling flight crews be modified, though he recognized that there would be strong resistance to this idea by flight crew personnel. Note that this mirrors the studies cited earlier suggesting that teams composed of individuals who are familiar with each other will in general be more effective than teams composed of people who do not know each other at all, as is often the case in newly formed cockpit crews. Indeed, the United States Army embraced this view when they mandated "battle-rostering" of crews (assigning aviation crews who work together for extended periods of time). However, recent research by Leedom & Simon (1995) suggested that battle-rostering for the long-term may lead to overconfidence—and errors—among aviators.

Leedom & Simon (1995) also noted that the underlying purpose of battle-rostering and other tactics to increase team member familiarity is to increase predictability of behavior in the team setting. They explored the effectiveness of standardized behavior-based training to improve team coordination and functioning and found that this approach led to higher levels of performance than did battle-rostering and that it did so without the potential overconfidence effects found with battle-rostering. Thus, the issue of crew structure and familiarity remains open.

A second contextual issue is the increasing level of automation in the cockpit. With new aircraft designs and the emergence of the "glass cockpit," crews face new issues of communication, interaction, and decision making. One reason for the emergence of new automation is the attempt by aircraft manufacturers to reduce human decision making as much as possible—because people too often make bad decisions (Billings 1991). Bowers et al (1993b) found in a simulator test that the addition of automation decreased the perceived workload, but this decrease in workload did not necessarily result in increased performance. In fact, in difficult situations the nonautomated crews made better decisions than the automated crews.

Further, Costley et al (1989) found that there were lower communication rates in more automated aircraft, though there was no decrease in operational actions.

Military flight crews

Although there are of course many similarities between military flight crews and commercial flight crews, there are also some significant differences between the two. Military flight crews may be significantly larger, for example, and they are likely to remain together as a unit for much longer periods of time than are commercial flight crews, owing to battle-rostering (described in the preceding section). Further, issues of rank of personnel may play a greater role in the military flight crews, and this may be at odds with the assertiveness taught in most CRM-type training. Finally, military flights in peacetime are almost always training flights of some kind, whereas commercial flights are for the purpose of transportation of cargo and passengers rather than for training (Prince & Salas 1993).

Despite those differences, CRM and LOFT-type training programs have been developed by several branches of the military (often called Air Crew Training, or ACT) (Prince & Salas 1993). These ACT programs have generally similar results to CRM training and LOFT, and the research findings from one area generally mirror those of the other. For example, the finding that there is a high correlation between CRM-type behaviors and objective and subjective measures of the effectiveness of aircrews (Povenmire et al 1989) could easily have come from either the commercial or the military air crew research programs.

Further, Prince & Salas (1993) note several similarities between military and commercial research into the origins of flight difficulties. These included problems with the exchange of information in the cockpit, the distribution and level of priority of tasks, and relationships within the crew.

It is important to note that CRM- and LOFT-type training has not yet fully taken root in the military's flying culture, and that the programs that have been developed vary from one service branch to another and from one command to another. This lack of consistency across commands and services may make full-scale adoption and acceptance of such programs more difficult to achieve in the military than in the commercial airlines.

Overall effectiveness of CRM training and loft

As noted above, there is a great deal of research on the effectiveness of CRM training and LOFT, and this body of work is explored in much greater detail in Wiener et al (1993) than can be covered here.

In summary, however, compared with no training of crews in CRM, training in CRM results in more crews being rated by crew evaluators as above average and fewer being rated as below average (Helmreich et al 1990). Further, skills learned in CRM training and LOFT are often cited by pilots as playing a key role in their handling of crisis situations (e.g. National Transportation Safety Board 1990a,b).

Computer-assisted groups

The continuing spread of computerization has been accompanied by an expansion of research on groups that use computers in their work. This research has in large part focused on comparing computer-mediated group meetings with non-computer-mediated meetings and, where work is done by groups, on idea generation and choice making.

An interpretation and annotated bibliography of studies, especially experiments, on computer-assisted groups, is provided by Hollingshead & McGrath (1995). They identified fifty research reports over two decades yielding about 150 findings relevant to task performance in computer-mediated groups. Almost all studies were done in laboratories with ad hoc groups. Overall, Hollingshead & McGrath found that computer-mediated groups tended to be characterized by less interaction and exchange than face-to-face groups and tend to take longer in their work. Whether computer-mediated or face-to-face groups are superior in task performance (on dimensions other than speed) appears to depend on the task. Specifically, computer-mediated groups appear superior at generating ideas but face-to-face groups appear superior on problem-solving tasks and tasks requiring the resolution of conflicts (of preferences, for example). They also suggest that a large part of the effect of computer technology in groups may be due to structuring of the task imposed by the use of computer technology rather than other aspects of the electronic medium.

It is interesting to note that increased structuring of the task—whether by computers or by nontechnological means—seems to enhance group processes. Consider, for example, the "stepladder technique," in which a core group of perhaps two members make a tentative decision, and with each successive "step" a new member is added and a presentation is made of the group's current ideas, followed by a renewed discussion of the possibilities. Rogelberg et al (1992) found that groups using this highly structured process produced higher quality solutions (to a survival problem) than did groups using conventional discussion methods. Further, Hartell (1991) demonstrated that teams of undergraduates trained in and utilizing a system of Problem Identification/Verification dealt with trouble-shooting tasks more effectively than teams who were not trained.

Creativity and brainstorming

Examples of research on brainstorming can be found in the work of Gallupe, Valacich, and colleagues. Dennis & Valacich (1993) reported that electronically interacting groups (i.e. communicating via computers) produced more ideas during a brainstorming task than did nominal groups (i.e. those whose members did not interact). Gallupe et al (1991, 1992, 1994) compared face-to-face brainstorming with electronic brainstorming groups and found the latter to be superior or the equal of interacting groups. These studies suggest that the electronic brainstorming medium reduces the extent to which the production of new ideas is blocked by such things as listening to others or waiting for a turn to speak.

Sainfort et al (1990) compared experimental groups using a computer-aided decision system, a videotape training system in conflict resolution, or no support system. They found that the computer-aided groups generated more potential solutions to the problem and perceived themselves as making greater progress than either of the other groups. Also, both technology groups (computer and videotape) were significantly more effective in solving the problem than the control group. All of this research corresponds to the conclusions of Hollingshead & McGrath (1995).

Decision making

McLeod's (1992) meta-analysis of 13 studies examined the relationship between various electronic group decision support systems and group process outcomes. It was shown that the use of electronic group support systems in group decision making leads to increases in decision quality, level of focus on task, equality of participation, and the length of time required to reach a decision. However, use of a group decision support system led to decreases in overall consensus and in satisfaction with the process and the decision.

George et al (1992) examined whether the inclusion of a facilitator among groups making decisions using an electronic meeting system would have an effect on the group process or quality of decisions made. They found that there were no differences in either group process or outcomes (i.e. decision quality) between groups that determined their own group process and those for whom the group process was determined by a facilitator. Similarly, Archer (1990) found that if the phases of a decision process in a complex business situation were organized and rational, there was no difference in decision quality between computer-mediated and face-to-face decision making.

Contextual issues

Contextual factors other than the computer programs themselves also play a role in computer-assisted groups. Valacich et al (1994) found significantly different results between groups using the same computer-mediated communication system when all members of the group were in one room as opposed to when the members were dispersed. In this case, the dispersed group generated more unique solutions and solutions of higher quality than did the proximate group.

Communication patterns

Several authors have reached similar conclusions about communication patterns in groups who communicate solely or primarily by computer. For example, Kiesler & Sproul (1992) found that communication in such groups is characterized by greater direct advocacy, greater equality of participation (even when members are of different status levels), more extreme or risky decisions, and more hostile or extreme communications (e.g. "flaming") than in face-to-face groups. Dubrovsky et al (1991) also found that social-status inequalities were less salient in groups who communicated and made decisions by electronic mail than in face-to-face groups. However, they also found that differences in influence based on differences in expertise were less pronounced in e-mail groups. They refer to these phenomena as "the equalization effect."

In some computer-mediated decision systems, communication among members is anonymous. Jessup et al (1990) reported three experiments in which they showed that when there was anonymity in the group decision-making process, members were more critical of ideas proposed, more probing in their questioning, and more likely to generate questions and ideas.

Group processes

Sambamurthy et al (1993) found that experimental groups using a computerized group decision support system to make budget allocation decisions had better organized decision processes than did groups using a paper-and-pencil version of the decision support system and than a control group to which no decision support system was provided. However, the computerized system also appeared to reduce the thoroughness of the discussion and led to a less intensely critical decision process. Likewise, Poole et al (1993) found that use of a group-decision support system improved the organization of subjects' decision-making process but may have led to less thorough and critical discussion. Keys et al (1988) used undergraduates in a study of the effects of use of a decision-support system in a business strategy game, and found that students in the computer condition did more and better planning than those in a control condition. Aiken &Riggs (1993) examined the applicability of a group decision-support system, in which communication among group members was almost entirely electronic, to the question of group creativity. They found that groups using the group decision-support system were more productive and more satisfied with the process because of such things as increased participation, synergy, and enhanced structure.

Shortfalls of computer-mediated group work

Computer-mediated group work is not always superior to face-to-face interaction, however. Straus & McGrath (1994) found that the productivity (in terms of quantity but not quality) of face-to-face groups on discussion tasks exceeded that of electronically mediated groups and that this productivity difference was greatest on those tasks requiring higher levels of coordination among group members. Lea & Spears (1991) confirmed previous research that groups communicating by way of computers produce more polarized decisions than do face-to-face groups. Adrianson & Hjelmquist (1991) found less conformity and opinion change in groups using computer-mediated communication than in those using face-to-face communication and found that personality characteristics of group members were only weakly related to these communication patterns.

Other technologies

Computers are, of course, not the only technological innovation used for group communication and decision making. More simplistic technology such as teleconferencing has also been introduced. Interestingly, the negative interpersonal interactions found in computer-based communications (e.g. "flaming," increased time to decision) appear to be absent in teleconferencing, which is much more similar to face-to-face communications. Groups making decisions via teleconferencing tend to take less time than do face-to-face groups, and members tend to perceive the leader as taking on fewer leadership roles (Rawlins 1989).

Summary

Technological systems that more closely mimic face-to-face interaction (e.g. videophones and videoconferencing) are becoming more widely available, and these advances will spur new research into their use as group decision-making tools. Simultaneously, use of systems in which there is no real-time communication is also becoming more and more common (e.g. group-ware, list-servers). These communication systems provide ample opportunities for research. We believe that technology-based group communication and decision-making systems will continue to thrive and that researchers will have to struggle to keep up with the pace of programmer advances and practitioner usage.

Defined problem-solving groups

Some groups are created for the specific purpose of generating solutions to problems. Quality circles and task forces are two such kinds of groups.

Quality circles

Quality circles were developed as a means to generate ideas that, if implemented, would raise the product quality by reducing defects, error rates, and so on. Quality circles were a precursor in the United States to the more recent "total quality movement" in which many mechanisms of quality (and, more generally, productivity) improvement are implemented to foster continuous improvements in the quality of products and of services. Quality circles typically are 6–12 employees who perform related jobs and who meet to discuss problems—and opportunities—to raise the quality or productivity of their part of an organization. They generate solutions that may or may not be implemented by the organization. The introduction of quality circles usually is accompanied by training in group process (e.g. in structured techniques for diagnosing problems and brainstorming) as well as training in aspects of quality management, such as in working with statistical indicators of quality.

Although quality circles have been a popular form of groups in organizations, evidence suggests that quality circles have relatively little enduring impact on organizational effectiveness (Lawler et al 1992) and research on them has diminished. Steel et al (1990) studied quality circles over a 14-month period in a United States federal mint and found no evidence that they affected important organizational outcomes. Quality circles may sometimes be successful at generating so-called big hits early on (i.e. quality improvements that have substantial economic value to a firm) but the evidence does not indicate that quality circles can maintain such contributions over time.

Task forces

Task forces are another kind of group created to solve problems. They are temporary, created with a relatively well-bounded mandate to be fulfilled. Task forces have a more limited time horizon than do quality circles; once the task is accomplished, the task force can disband. May & Schwoerer (1994) reported on the creation of task forces to develop and implement ways of reducing the incidence of cumulative trauma disorders (or CTDs) that result from repetitious, forceful movements in a meat-packing plant. (Carpal tunnel syndrome is one such disorder.) Teams were made up of 7–9 volunteers representing several functions (e.g. medical, management) and were trained in substantive issues related to CTDs. The teams appeared successful in decreasing the incidence and severity of CTDs, though the number of production days lost to injuries was unaffected. The authors of the report also presented their views on the appropriate structure, training, and support of task forces similar to those studied.

Autonomous work groups

We use the label "autonomous work groups" as a synonym for "self-managing teams" and for "empowered teams." These are teams of employees who typically perform highly related or interdependent jobs, who are identified and identifiable as a social unit in an organization, and who are given significant authority and responsibility for many aspects of their work, such as planning, scheduling, assigning tasks to members, and making decisions with economic consequences (usually up to a specific limited value) (e.g. see Dobbelaere & Goeppinger 1993).

The concept of autonomous work groups has been in the literature for half a century. However, there was little momentum for their adoption in US work-places until the past decade or so as firms reduced levels of management, thus giving over to lower-level employees responsibilities in the past held by management, and as firms sought new ways of increasing employee involvement and productivity. Autonomous work groups are inherent in many recent attempts to radically transform organizational work systems, a topic discussed in the next section on teams and organizational change. This section deals with research specifically targeted at autonomous work groups.

Cohen & Ledford (1994) studied a large sample of self-managing teams at different levels and in varying functions in a service organization. These self-managing teams had been in existence for two years on average. They were systematically matched against comparable traditionally managed teams. Further, teams were screened from the sample when they did not unambiguously fulfill the definition of self-management. Criteria of team effectiveness included ratings on different dimensions of performance (e.g. quality, productivity, safety) obtained from different sources (team members and higher levels of management) as well as indicators of effectiveness from company records, such as customer complaints and monetary losses due to absenteeism. Ratings indicated that self-managing teams were more effective than their comparison groups. However, no significant differences were observed on measures of effectiveness based on company records. Work-related attitudes (e.g. satisfaction) were more favorable among members of self-managing teams.

Cordery et al (1991) reported a study of autonomous work groups at a greenfield site. A greenfield site is a new physical location of work. In this study of mineral processing plants in Australia, work groups at the new plant site were compared with groups in existing sites. An important differentiating feature of the new site was that an organizational structure unlike those at any existing sites was implemented. That organizational structure "centered on the operation of autonomous work groups in the processing area" (Cordery et al 1991, p. 465). Greenfield teams in this site had decision-making responsibility for such things as allocating work, attending to administrative matters, and setting priorities, as well as having influence on hiring decisions. Their members also acquired multiple skills and worked under a pay-for-skills reward system. Traditional (nonautonomous) groups, against which autonomous work groups were compared, also existed in parts of the new plant and in the established site. The primary intervention was thus a change in the nature of group work, in the competencies of members (through multiskilling), and in groups' supporting organizational context (reward system, authority system, information availability). This intervention secondarily influenced individual inputs through its creation of multiskilled group members.

The Cordery et al (1991) data indicated that autonomous work groups were associated with more favorable employee attitudes than were traditional work groups, though this difference abated over time (measurements were made at 8 and 20 months after the greenfield start-up). However, both turnover and absenteeism were higher among members of autonomous work groups in comparison with traditional groups.

The Cordery et al (1991) study was much like an earlier study by Wall et al (1986) that contrasted autonomous work groups in greenfield and established sites engaged in food production. The earlier study also found higher turnover among employees in the greenfield site. However, the findings of these two studies contradict the report by Weisman et al (1993), who found that higher retention (i.e. lower turnover) among nurses was associated with self-management practices. A previous review of research by Beekun (1989) concluded that the use of autonomous work teams is associated with decreases in absenteeism and turnover. Other results that differed from Cordery et al (1991) were reported by Wall et al (1986), who found less evidence of positive attitudinal consequences of autonomous work groups than did the latter study. Barker's (1993) case study report noted that members of self-managing teams had lower levels of absenteeism and tardiness because the members of the teams enforced attendance and on-time norms much more strictly than managers had enforced those policies prior to the implementation of teams.

Overall there is substantial variance in research findings regarding the consequences of autonomous work groups on such measures as productivity, turnover, and attitudes. This variance may indicate that the effects of autonomous work groups are highly situationally dependent. That is, the effects of autonomous work-group practices may depend on factors such as the nature of the work force (e.g. its dominant values) and the nature of the organization (e.g. information and reward systems). Smith & Comer (1994) did address the proposition that the success enjoyed by self-organizing teams (self-organizing teams are similar to autonomous work groups) may depend on the situation. Through a laboratory experiment, Smith & Comer demonstrated that self-managing groups can be expected to be more successful in turbulent environments. This study is unique in its attempt to provide direct answers to complex questions about the "fit" of autonomous (and related forms of) work groups. Considerably more research will be required, given the number of possible factors that could moderate the impact of autonomous work groups in organizations.

Teams and change in organizational systems

Groups are almost always embedded in larger social systems (e.g. communities, schools, business organizations). These social systems that surround teams define a major part of the context in which team performance occurs. As Levine & Moreland (1990) have pointed out, too much past research on group performance effectiveness has been devoid of attention to the linkages between group performance and aspects of the social systems in which groups are located. For theorists such as McGrath (1991), a fundamental assumption about the nature of groups is that they are partially nested within, and loosely-coupled to, a surrounding social system. "Partially nested" refers to the fact that individuals often are members of more than one group and that groups may be parts of more than one social system. "Loosely coupled" refers to the fact that there are few clear, mechanistic-like connections either between groups and surrounding systems or within groups, a point similar to Guzzo & Shea's (1992) metaphor of groups being systems more like clouds than clocks. Another of McGrath's (1991) fundamental assertions about the nature of groups is that in such systems they perform multiple tasks concurrently.

There are several consequences of taking seriously the concept of the embeddedness of teams in organizations. One is that team performance effectiveness and the factors that bring it about are tied to the nature and effectiveness of the entire organization. Changes in team effectiveness can thus have consequences for change in the larger system, such as when improved performance by a team or set of teams is thought to yield greater profits for a business. Perhaps we usually think of team-organization linkages in just this way: that team performance contributes to organizational performance.

The regularity and strength of such linkages between the performance of components (individuals, teams, departments) and overall organizational effectiveness is explored in Harris (1994). That work mostly addresses the apparent paradox that investments in computer technology may bring about improvements in performance at the component level but do not necessarily translate into larger system improvements. It also raises widely applicable issues about measurement, the nature of social systems, and cross-level influences. In light of these considerations, it could be quite wrong to make the easy assumption that improvements in team performance yield gains for the whole organization.

Team-organization linkages also imply that changes in the larger social system can bring about changes in the teams situated in it. That is, one need not directly intervene into teams to change their performance: Interventions into the surrounding organizational system may bring about improved (or, if the intervention is a poor one, reduced) team performance.

The teams-in-organizational-context perspective is complex. It obscures cause-and-effect relations so perceptible from experimental studies of groups stripped of context. It implies that the effects of interventions made at one level (individual, group, organization) may reside at another level. And it implies that multiple simultaneous influences on and of teams may be taking place in these social systems. Complicated though it is, it is imperative to examine research evidence on teams and change in organizational systems.

Research evidence on teams and organizational change tends to be of a unique character. Understandably there are fewer controlled, experiment-like methods and far more case studies and surveys. This is an embodiment of a classical trade-off of rigor for relevance in research. However, there are by now quite large numbers of less-rigorous but highly relevant research reports. It is likely that weaknesses of research design in some are at least partly compensated by strengths in the research designs of other reports.

An indication of just how many such reports exist is given by Macy & Izumi (1993). They presented the results of a meta-analysis of 131 field studies (yielding 506 effect-size estimates) of organizational change that appeared over a 30-year period. Interestingly, they encountered 1800 studies, only 131 of which provided sufficient quantitative data for their meta-analysis. (Of these 131 studies, 88.5% were published in refereed journals.) We focus first on their findings with regard to broad organizational change and then address those findings most specific to teams in organizations.

In regard to overall organizational change, Macy & Izumi (1993) found that indicators of financial performance show the greatest improvements when multiple changes are simultaneously made in aspects of organizational structure, human resource management practices, and technology. Macy & Izumi report a +0.37 correlation between the number of changes made ("action levers" in their terminology) and indicators of financial performance. Other criteria of change (e.g. employee attitudes) showed no such relationship. But of the many action levers that can be pulled in large-scale organizational change efforts, which specific ones have the greatest impact?

With effect-size measures of financial performance as dependent variables, the action levers with the greatest impact included the creation of autonomous work groups and team development interventions. Group-oriented interventions also showed evidence of improving behavioral measures of performance such as turnover and absenteeism. Other interventions showing appreciable relationships to financial indicators of organizational performance included job redesign, increased employee involvement, changes (mostly flattening) of organizational hierarchies, and changes in workflow. (Macy & Izumi 1993 suggest viewing these findings with caution owing to the sometimes small number of cases on which they are based.) Employee attitudes showed little systematic improvement with these interventions.

In summary, according to Macy & Izumi (1993): Multifaceted, system-wide organizational interventions show the most reliable positive impact on organizational effectiveness, team-oriented interventions are one of a few subsets of interventions that have the most notable effects, and team-oriented interventions affect both financial and behavioral measures of performance.

A nonquantitative, comprehensive review of research evidence on teams, organizational systems, and effectiveness was provided by Applebaum & Blatt (1994). Applebaum & Blatt described alternative organizational systems in which teams are of greater or lesser significance as well as attempts to transform organizations to more team-based social systems. Historically, according to these authors, teams are significant elements in Swedish sociotechnical and Japanese lean-production models of work organization. In contrast, teams have not been emphasized in German or traditional American human resource models of organization.

With existing models of work organization such as these as a backdrop, Applebaum & Blatt (1994) examined experiments in workplace innovation in American organizations. Applebaum & Blatt draw on two lines of evidence about the use of innovative work practices and their impact. One line of evidence consists of 12 large surveys reported between 1982 and 1993. The other consists of 185 case studies.

With regard to teams, Applebaum & Blatt (1994) related that in recent years many US organizations have been experimenting with team-based work arrangements. More specifically, it was estimated in 1990 that 47% of large US companies made use of self-directed, autonomous work teams and that there was a strong growth trend in the use of such teams from 1987 to 1990 (Lawler et al 1992).

Quality circles were the most frequently implemented type of team, estimated to be present in 66% of the largest companies in the United States (Lawler et al 1992). Another estimate of the popularity of teams in organizations was provided by Gordon (1992). Gordon reported that 80% of organizations with 100 or more employees used teams in some way and that 50% of employees in these organizations are members of at least one team at work.

There are, however, many variations in team-based organizational practices. In some organizations the introduction or renewed emphasis on teams represents only a small marginal change to standard operating procedures while in others the adoption of teams is a part of a large-scale attempt at radical organizational transformation. Further, in some but not all organizations the implementation of team-based work arrangements may be accompanied by changes in hiring, compensation, decision making, technology, and other processes. As Applebaum & Blatt (1994) aptly noted, in practice "teams" is one of several "commonly abused terms" (p. 72). Given this variation, the path to unambiguous conclusions about the connections between teams and organizational effectiveness is often quite hard to find. The following conclusions are offered cognizant of the caveats and qualifications required by the state of the research evidence.

Applebaum & Blatt (1994), largely on the basis of their review of case studies, concluded that there is clear evidence that team-based work arrangements bring about improved organizational performance, especially in measures of efficiency (e.g. reduced cycle times in production) and quality (e.g. fewer defects in products). Some research reports run counter to this conclusion (e.g. Robertson et al 1992). However, Applebaum & Blatt's (1994) conclusions are supported by the work of Levine & D'Andrea Tyson (1990), who examined the effects of employee participation on productivity. Levine & D'Andrea Tyson identified three forms of participation: consultative, representative, and substantive, the latter form constituting the greatest degree of participation. Consultative participation, for example, may come through the creation of quality circles, representative participation through labor-management committees, and substantive participation through autonomous work groups. Cotton (1993) also largely concurred, identifying autonomous work groups and self-determining teams as structures that provide far more participation than quality circles or various forms of representative participation. Levine & D'Andrea Tyson (1990) reviewed empirical evidence from diverse sources (e.g. organizational psychology, economics, industrial relations) and concluded that "participation *usually* leads to small, short-run improvements in performance and *sometimes* leads to significant, long-lasting improvements in performance" (p. 203, emphasis in original) and that "there is usually a positive, often small effect of participation on productivity, sometimes a zero or statistically insignificant effect, and almost never a negative effect" (pp. 203–4). Substantive participation, according to Levine & D'Andrea Tyson, is the form most likely to result in significant, long-lasting increases in productivity, and work teams are the primary means by which substantive participation is attained. Cotton (1993), too, found self-directed work teams to be "an effective way to improve employee productivity and attitudes" (p. 199) and found little evidence that consultative or representative participation has the same consequences.

A national survey of 727 US work establishments conducted in 1991 also is a source of evidence on the impact of team-based organizational arrangements (see Spaeth & O'Rourke 1994 for a description of the survey procedures). An establishment is a location of employment. Small business enterprises are more likely to have a single establishment whereas large enterprises have many. The relationship between performance and the team-based work practices was analyzed by Kalleberg & Moody (1994). They found that organizations adopting sets of practices that included teams as an important element of organization design tended to excel on several performance dimensions (e.g. employee relations, product quality) though not on the dimension of customer service. Note that in this survey performance was assessed by ratings (rather than, say, by measures of output) made by an establishment's representative, the same representative who provided other information about their establishment. Thus, in this survey, the potential exists that some part of the observed relationships are attributable to a response-response bias.

In summary, ample evidence indicates that team-based forms of organizing often bring about higher levels of organizational effectiveness in comparison with traditional, bureaucratic forms. This evidence, however, is confounded because more than one change (e.g. more than just the creation of teams) typically is implemented in studies of organizational change, and measures of effectiveness reflect more than just those contributions uniquely attributable to teams. The question "What makes teams effective?" is directly addressed by research on group composition, leadership, goal setting, and the like. In contrast, researchers on teams and organizational change ask "To what extent do teams as elements in larger social systems contribute to system effectiveness?" For many group researchers and theorists this is a rather nontraditional question. And it is a vexing question for all, although there is consistent, and sometimes quite powerful evidence that teams contribute to organizational effectiveness.

Discussion

This review has sampled a wide-ranging collection of research studies on team effectiveness, focusing on work teams in organizational systems. Studies emphasized in the review are those centrally concerned with some aspect of effectiveness as a dependent variable and with changes and interventions made to influence the effectiveness with which teams perform. Rather than restating the findings in summary form, this final section considers selected issues raised by the research review. We first highlight three open issues (out of many) in team effectiveness research. Then, newer waves in team research are identified and briefly considered, including those most directly related to issues discussed in this review. Finally, we discuss "points of leverage" for intervening to affect team performance. Thoughts on future research and theorizing are offered throughout.

Open questions

What is diversity? How does it affect team performance? These two open questions about team composition and effectiveness provide fertile soil for further research and theorizing.

Diversity

Diversity refers to dissimilarity among members in terms of gender, ethnicity, race, personality, culture, and functional experience, among other things. There is evidence that team effectiveness is well-served by diverse members when teams perform cognitive, creativity-demanding tasks. This is not to say that diverse membership might not pay off in enhanced effectiveness in other task domains: rather, too little is now known to draw firm conclusions. Also, it is not known whether all forms of diversity contribute in similar portions or in similar ways to team performance on intellective tasks. In fact, there is a real need to develop theory and data on the ways in which dissimilarity among members contributes to task performance. Just as research on goal and team performance has begun to emphasize the mediating processes connecting goals and team effectiveness, research on diversity in teams should increasingly emphasize the processes that mediate its effects.

Familiarity

When does familiarity help and hurt team effectiveness? Research on familiarity among coal-mining crews, cockpit crews, and other work groups shows a benefit to familiarity. That is, the greater the familiarity among members of a group, the greater their performance. However, other research indicates that too-familiar cockpit crews may, in fact, be more inclined to make errors. Perhaps the value of familiarity is time-dependent. That is, high familiarity among members (or high interpositional knowledge, as discussed by Cannon-Bowers et al 1995) may have the greatest utility early in a team's existence, perhaps by fostering the rapid appearance of coordination and integration of team members' efforts. High familiarity may have value at other times, too, such as in times of stress or high demand. However, familiarity may eventually become a liability as the lack of membership change (and thus the lack of any unfamiliar members being introduced into a team) contributes to stultification and entropy in teams. The venerable work by Katz (1982) suggested that communication within and between teams declines as teams age, thus communication may be an important mediator of the effects of familiarity.

Team boundaries

Where are team boundaries? The boundaries of teams are imaginary lines of demarcation separating member from outsider. Boundaries are essential to the definition of teams (Sundstrom et al 1990) and to the psychology of being a member of the in-group vs the out-group. In many instances team boundaries are reinforced by such things as uniforms and the use of space or turf. However, the boundaries of teams may at other times be quite difficult to discern. "Virtual teams"—teams whose members are connected through a network of computers—are examples of teams whose boundaries of inclusion and exclusion may be quite difficult to establish, especially if individuals may selectively join an electronic conversation for some but not all of the team's existence. But problems of establishing team boundaries are not limited to electronic groups. Vandermark (1991) and Lichtenberg et al (1990) suggested that there are benefits to including as team members persons who might traditionally have been considered on the periphery. Vandermark (1991) raised the issue with regard to the inclusion of cabin crews in the cockpit resource management training of flight crews; Lichtenberg et al (1990) raised the issue with regard to psychiatric aides and their role in teams of health-care professionals. Further, viewing teams as entities embedded in larger systems populated by individuals who are members of more than one team also can complicate the identification of team boundaries. We believe that future research is needed to clarify issues of inclusion and exclusion by virtue of team boundaries (for further discussion, see Guzzo 1996), how boundaries relate to effectiveness, and how the nature of boundaries might shape the effects of interventions intended to raise team performance.

New waves, new directions

We briefly consider three areas of research in which there have been recent surges of interest: electronically mediated teams, interventions for enhancing team effectiveness, and teams in the context of social systems.

Electronically mediated teams

Although the first studies of electronically mediated teams were done nearly two decades ago, the pace of research on such teams has accelerated in recent years. No doubt this is attributable to many factors, not the least of which is the decreasing expense of the technology needed for such research. And new technologies (e.g. videoconferencing, communication, and support software for groups) continually create opportunities to conduct new research. There is no doubt that electronically mediated teams will become an increasingly common feature of the organizational landscape. We therefore suggest that research on electronically mediated groups break free from the tradition of comparing those groups to face-to-face groups. Instead, future research should accept such groups on their own terms. It should focus instead on contrasting technologies and on team effectiveness under different ways of utilizing available technologies. From a practical point of view we need more research on how to maximize team effectiveness with new technologies. From a theoretical point of view we need better insights and explanations of the drivers of the dynamics of team performance and effectiveness under such technologies.

Interventions

New ways of intervening to improve team effectiveness are in the works. Many of these are tied to a foundation of research on teamwork and effectiveness in military teams. Salas et al (1995) pointed out that, although there have been few direct tests of team-training interventions in recent research on military teams, knowledge has progressed to a point where such training interventions are now possible, grounded in workable conceptualizations of competencies and task requirements in teams. New ways of intervening are also on the horizon due to new methodologies of team research and new theoretical models of team performance (e.g. see Guzzo & Salas 1995).

Teams in context

A third notable area of expanding research interest is teams in context. The oft-cited recognition that, historically, the bulk of psychological research has examined teams in the absence of consideration of their contexts is giving way to more frequent studies of teams in naturalistic settings, such as organizations. We expect this shift to be accompanied by new theoretical emphases and insights, especially as they relate to the influence of aspects of the teams' environments. In organizations, such environmental factors could include intraorganizational factors such as reward practices and information systems, as well as extraorganizational factors such as the customer demands and business environments.

Points of leverage

Three primary points of leverage exist for intervening to enhance team effectiveness. One is the design of the group. Design includes such things as specification of membership, of member roles and methods of their coordination, and of goals. Several studies we have reviewed concern design as a point of leverage for raising team effectiveness. Diversity of membership and size of group, for example, have been found to be related to team effectiveness, although the relationships are not completely consistent across all studies or all group tasks. The effect of goals on group performance has been more uniformly found to be positive, although even here we found one study that was an exception to the pattern of evidence. What we are calling "design" is very much like what traditional models of group performance refer to as "inputs" in the input-process-output description of group performance.

The "process" element in the traditional input-process-output model includes both social processes in groups (e.g. cohesiveness) and task processes (e.g. rules of task performance). Group process is thus a second leverage point at which interventions can be made to improve team effectiveness. Some evidence in the literature reviewed found, for example, that group cohesiveness can contribute to performance, and other studies found that structured task processes—such as the stepladder technique for group problem solving—can contribute positively to performance.

The traditional input-process-output model would be too confining if its interpretation were restricted to the idea that inputs (i.e. member characteristics, goals) fully determine group process. Inputs influence group process but may not strongly constrain it. One factor that can strongly constrain group process is the technology with which a group works, such as computers. Our review of computer-assisted groups indeed shows their process to be different (e.g. more equal but less overall member participation) from non-computer-assisted groups and that these differences may or may not result in enhanced effectiveness, depending on factors such as the task.

A third point of leverage for enhancing team effectiveness is the context. That is, team performance can be raised by changing the conditions in which teams perform. Several lines of evidence we have reviewed point to the power of the context as a driver of team effectiveness. Organizational leaders, for example, are a part of the context in which work groups perform, and leaders have been shown to influence team effectiveness. Cockpit resource management and its variations appear to have positive effects on flight crews because such interventions change the organizational context (values, culture) in which crews are formed and carry out their work. Further, large-scale organizational change efforts that change the social system of which teams are a part have been shown to enhance effectiveness. The point of leverage with the most consistent research support for affecting team performance is the context. In fact, it is probably most justifiable to conclude that the greatest changes in team effectiveness are most likely to be realized when changes in teams' organizational context are supported by the appropriate team design and process.

Literature cited

Adrianson L, Hjelmquist E. 1991. Group processes in face-to-face and computer mediated communication, *Behav. Inf. Tech.* 10(4):281–96

Aiken MW, Riggs M. 1993. Using a group decision support system for creativity. *J. Great. Behav.* 27(1):28–35

Alderfer CP. 1977. Group and intergroup relations. In *Improving the Quality of Work Life*, ed. JR Hackman, JL Suttle, pp. 227–96. Pallisades, CA: Goodyear

Applebaum E, Blatt R. 1994. *The New American Workplace*. Ithaca, NY: ILR

Archer NP. 1990. A comparison of computer conferences with face-to-face meetings for small group business decisions, *Behav. Inf. Tech.* 9(4):307–17

Bantel KA, Jackson SE. 1989. Top management and innovations in banking: Does composition of the top teams make a difference? *Strateg. Manage. J.* 10:107–24 (Special issue)

Barker JR. 1993. Tightening the iron cage: concertive control in self-managing teams. *Adm. Sci. Q.* 38:408–37
Beekun RI. 1989. Assessing the effectiveness of socio-technical interventions: antidote or fad? *Hum. Relat.* 47:877–97
Billings CE. 1991. Human-centered aircraft automation: a concept and guidelines. *Tech. Memo. 103885*. Moffett Field. CA: NASA-Ames Res. Cent.
Bowers CA. Braun CC, Holmes BE, Morgan BB Jr. 1993a. The development of aircrew coordination behaviors. In *Proc. Seventh Int. Symp. Aviat. Psychol.* pp. 573–77. Columbus, OH
Bowers CA, Deaton J, Oser RL, Prince C, Kolb M. 1993b. The impact of automation on crew communication and performance. In *Proc. Seventh Int. Symp. Aviation Psychol.* pp. 573–77. Columbus, OH
Brawley LR, Carron AV, Widmeyer WN. 1992. The nature of group goals in sports teams: a phenomenological analysis. *Sport Psychol.* 6:323–33
Butler RE. 1993. LOFT: Full-mission simulation as Crew Resource Management Training. See Wiener et al 1993. pp. 231–59
Campion MA, Medsker GJ, Higgs AC. 1993. Relations between work group characteristics and effectiveness: implications for designing effective work groups. *Pers. Psychol.* 46:823–50
Cannon-Bowers JA, Tannenbaum SI, Salas E, Volpe CE. 1995. Defining competencies and establishing team training requirements. See Guzzo & Salas 1995, pp. 333–80
Cohen SG, Ledford GE Jr. 1994. The effectiveness of self-managing teams: a field experiment *Hum. Relat.* 47:13–43
Cordery JL, Mueller WS, Smith LM. 1991. Attitudinal and behavioral effects of autonomous group working: a longitudinal field study. *Acad. Manage. J.* 34: 464–76
Costley J, Johnson D, Lawson D. 1989. A comparison of cockpit communication B737–B757. In *Proc. Fifth Int. Symp. Aviat. Psychol.* pp. 413–18. Columbus. OH
Cotton JL. 1993. *Employee Involvement*. Newbury Park, CA: Sage
de Armas Paredes M, Riera-Milian MA. 1987. Analisis de la communicacion en un equipo deportivo y su influencia en los resultados de este. [Analysis of communication in a sports team and its influence on performance.] *Bol. Psicol Cuba* 10:37–48 (Abstr.)
Dennis AR, Valacich JS. 1993. Computer brainstorms: more heads are better than one. *J. Appl. Psychol.* 78:531–37
Diehl A. 1991. The effectiveness of training programs for preventing aircrew "error." In *Proc. Sixth Int. Symp. Aviat. Psychol.* pp. 640–55. Columbus: Ohio State Univ.
Dobbelaere AG, Goeppinger KH. 1993. The right way and the wrong way to set up a self-directed work team. *Hum. Resour. Prof.* 5:31–35
Dubnicki C, Limburg WJ. 1991. How do healthcare teams measure up? *Healthc. Forum.* 34(5):10–11
Dubrovsky VJ, Kiesler S, Sethna BN. 1991. The equalization phenomenon: status effects in computer-mediated and face-to-face decision-making groups. *Hum.-Comput. Interact.* 6(2): 119–46
Earley PC. 1994. Self or group? Cultural effects of training on self-efficacy and performance. *Adm. Sci. Q.* 39:89–117
Eden D. 1990a. Pygmalion without interpersonal contrast effects: whole groups gain from raising manager expectations. *J. Appl. Psychol.* 75:394–98

Eden D. 1990b. *Pygmalion in Management: Productivity as a Self-Fulfilling Prophecy.* Lexington, MA: Lexington Books

Evans CR, Dion KL. 1991. Group cohesion and performance: a meta-analysis. *Small Group Res.* 22:175–86

Fandt PM, Richardson WD, Conner HM. 1990. The impact of goal-setting on team simulation experience. *Simul. Gaming.* 21(4): 411–22

Foushee HC, Lauber JK, Baetge MM, Acomb DB. 1986. Crew performance as a function of exposure to high-density, short-haul duty cycles. *NASA Tech. Memo. 88322.* Moffett Field, CA: NASA-Ames Res. Cent.

Gallupe RB, Bastianutti L, Cooper WH. 1991. Brainstorming electronically. *J. Appl. Psychol.* 76:137–42

Gallupe RB, Cooper WH, Grise' M-L, Bastianutti LM. 1994. Blocking electronic brainstorms. *J. Appl. Psychol.* 79: 77–86

Gallupe RB, Dennis AR, Cooper WH, Valacich JS, Bastianutti L, Nunamaker J. 1992. Electronic brainstorming and group size. *Acad. Manage. J.* 35:350–69

George JF, Dennis AR, Nunamaker JF. 1992. An experimental investigation of facilitation in an EMS decision room. *Group Decis. Negot.* 1(1):57–70

George JM, Bettenhausen K. 1990. Understanding prosocial behavior, sales performance, and turnover: a group-level analysis in a service context. *J. Appl. Psychol.* 75: 698–709

Ginnett RC. 1993. Crews as groups: their formation and their leadership. See Wiener et al 1993, pp. 71–98

Goodman PS, Leyden DP. 1991. Familiarity and group productivity. *J. Appl. Psychol.* 76:578–86

Gordon J. 1992. Work teams—How far have they come? *Training.* 29:59–65

Guzzo RA, Salas E, eds. 1995. *Team Effectiveness and Decision Making in Organizations.* San Francisco: Jossey-Bass

Guzzo RA, Shea GP. 1992. Group performance and intergroup relations in organizations. In *Handbook of Industrial and Organizational Psychology*, ed. MD Dunnette. LM Hough, 3:269–313. Palo Alto, CA: Consult. Psychol. Press. 2nd ed.

Guzzo RA, Yost PR, Campbell RJ, Shea GP. 1993. Potency in groups: articulating a construct. *Br. J. Soc. Psychol.* 32(1):87–106

Guzzo RA, 1996. Fundamental considerations about workgroups. In *Handbook of Work Group Psychology*, ed. M West. Chichester: Wiley. In press

Hackman JR. 1987. The design of work teams. In *Handbook of Organizational Behavior*, ed. JW Lorsch, pp. 315–42. Englewood Cliffs, NJ: Prentice-Hall

Hackman JR, ed. 1990. *Groups That Work and Those That Don't.* San Francisco: Jossey-Bass

Hackman JR. 1993. Teams, leaders, and organizations: new directions for crew-oriented flight training. See Wiener et al 1993, pp. 47–70

Haleblian J, Finkelstein S. 1993. Top management team size, CEO dominance, and firm performance: the moderating roles of environmental turbulence and discretion. *Acad. Manag. J.* 36:844–63

Harris DH, ed. 1994. *Organizational Linkages: Understanding the Productivity Paradox.* Washington, DC: Natl. Acad. Press

Hartel CEJ. 1991. *Improving team-assisted diagnostic decision making: some training propositions and an empirical test.* PhD thesis. Colo. State Univ., Fort Collins

Helmreich RL, Foushee HC. 1993. Why crew resource management? Empirical and theoretical bases of human factors training in aviation. See Wiener et al 1993, pp. 3–45

Helmreich RL, Wilhelm JA. 1991. Outcomes of crew resource management training. *Int. J. Aviat. Psychol.* 14:287–300

Helmreich RL, Wilhelm JA, Gregorich SE, Chidester TR. 1990. Preliminary results from the evaluation of cockpit resource management training: performance ratings of flightcrews. *Aviat. Space Environ. Med.* 576–79

Hollingshead AB, McGrath JE. 1995. Computer-assisted groups: a critical review of the empirical research. See Guzzo & Salas 1995, pp. 46–78

Jackson SE, Brett JF, Sessa VI, Cooper DM, Julin JA, Peyronnin K. 1991. Some differences make a difference: individual dissimilarity and group heterogeneity as correlates of recruitment, promotion, and turnover. *J. Appl. Psychol.* 76: 675–89

Jackson SE, May KE, Whitney K. 1995. Understanding the dynamics of diversity in decision-making teams. See Guzzo & Salas 1995, pp. 204–61

Jacobs D, Singell L. 1993. Leadership and organizational performance: isolating links between managers and collective success. *Soc. Sci. Res.* 22:165–89

Jessup LM, Connolly T, Tansik DA. 1990. Toward a theory of automated group work: the deindividuating effects of anonymity. *Small Group Res.* 21(3):333–48

Kalleberg AL, Moody JW. 1994. Human resource management and organizational performance. *Am. Behav. Sci.* 37:948–62

Katz RL. 1982. The effects of group longevity on project communication and performance. *Adm. Sci. Q.* 27:81–104

Katzenbach JR, Smith DK. 1993. The discipline of teams. *Harv. Bus. Rev.* 71: 111–20

Keys B, Burns O, Case T, Wells RA. 1988. Decision support package in a business game: performance and attitudinal affects. *Simul Games.* 19(4):440–52

Kiesier S, Sproul L. 1992. Group decision making and communication technology. *Organizational Behav. Hum. Decis. Process.* 52(1):96–123

Lauber JK. 1984. Resource management in the cockpit. *Air Line Pilot.* 53:20–23

Lauber JK. 1993. Foreword. See Wiener et al 1993, pp. xv–xviii

Lawler EE, Mohrman SA, Ledford G. 1992. *Employee Involvement and TQM: Practice and Results in Fortune 5000 Companies.* San Francisco: Jossey-Bass

Lea M, Spears R. 1991. Computer-mediated communication, de-individuation and group decision-making. *Int. J. Man-Mach. Stud.* 34(2):283–301

Lee C. 1989. The relationship between goal-setting, self-efficacy, and female field hockey team performance. *Int. J. Sport Psychol.* 20(2):147–61

Leedom DK, Simon R. 1995. Improving team coordination: a case for behavior-based training. *Mil. Psychol.* 7(2): 109–22

Levine DI, D'Andrea Tyson L. 1990. Participation, productivity, and the firm's environment. In *Paying For Productivity*, ed. AS Blinder, pp. 183–237. Washington, DC: Brookings Inst.

Levine JM, Moreland RL. 1990. Progress in small group research. *Annu. Rev. Psychol.* 41:585–634

Lichtenberg PA, Strzepek DM, Zeiss AM. 1990. Bringing psychiatric aides into the treatment team: an application of the Veterans Administration's ITTG model. *Gerontol. Geriatri. Educ.* 10(4):63–73

Locke EA, Latham GP. 1990. *A Theory of Goal-Setting and Task Performance.* Englewood Cliffs, NJ: Prentice Hall

Macy BA, Izumi H. 1993. Organizational change, design, and work innovation: a meta-analysis of 131 North American field studies—1961–1991. In *Research in*

Organizational Change and Development, ed. W Passmore. R Woodman, 7:235–313. Greenwich, CT: JAI

Magjuka RJ, Baldwin TT. 1991. Team-based employee involvement programs: effects of design and administration. *Person. Psychol.* 44:793–812

May DR, Schwoerer CE. 1994, Employee health by design: using employee involvement teams in ergonomic job redesign. *Person. Psychol.* 47:861–76

McGrath JE. 1991. Time, interaction, and performance: a theory of groups. *Small Group Res.* 22:147–74

McLeod PL. 1992. An assessment of the experimental literature on electronic support of group work: results of a meta-analysis. *Hum.-Comput. Interact.* 7(3):257–80

McLeod PL, Liker JK, Lobel SA. 1992. Process feedback in task groups: an application of goal setting. *J. Appl. Behav. Sci.* 28: 15–41

Mitchell TR, Silver WS. 1990. Individual and group goals when workers are interdependent: effects on task strategies and performance. *J. Appl. Psychol.* 75:185–93

National Transportation Safety Board. 1990a. *Aircraft Accident Rep.: United Airlines Flight 811, Boeing 747-122, N4713U*. Honolulu, HI, Feb. 24, 1989. (*NTSB/AAR/90/01*). Washington, DC: Natl. Transp. Saf. Board

National Transportation Safety Board. 1990b. *Aircraft Accident Rep: United Airlines Flight 232, McDonnell-Douglas DC-10-10*. Sioux Gateway Airport, Sioux City, 1A, July 19, 1989. (*NTSB/AAR/90/06*). Washington, DC: Natl. Transp. Saf. Board

Orasanu JM. 1993. Decision-making in the cockpit. See Wiener et al 1993, pp. 137–72

Orlady HW, Foushee HC, eds. 1987. *Proc. of the NASA/MAC Workshop on Cockpit Resource Manage.* (*NASA Conf. Publ. 2455*). Moffett Field, CA: NASA-Ames Res. Cent.

Pearson CAL. 1991. An assessment of extrinsic feedback on participation, role perceptions, motivation, and job satisfaction in a self-managed system for monitoring group achievement. *Hum. Relat.* 44:517–37

Poole MS, Holmes M, Watson R, DeSanctis G. 1993. Group decision support systems and group communication: a comparison of decision-making in computer-supported and non-supported groups. *Commun. Res.* 20(2): 176–213

Povenmire HK, Rockway M, Bunecke JL, Patton MW. 1989. Cockpit resource management skills enhance combat mission performance in B-52 simulator. In *Proc. Fifth Int. Symp. Aviat. Psychol.* pp. 310–25. Columbus, OH

Prince C, Salas E, 1993. Training and research for teamwork in the military aircrew. See Wiener et al 1993, pp. 337–66

Rawlins C. 1989. The impact of teleconferencing on the leadership of small decision-making groups. *J. Organ. Behav. Manage.* 10(2):37–52

Robertson D, Rinehart J, Huxley C, and the CAW Research Group on CAMI. 1992. Team concept and Kaizen: Japanese production management in a unionized Canadian auto plant. *Stud. Polit. Econ.* 39: 77–107

Rogelberg SG, Barnes-Farrell JL, Lowe CA. 1992. The stepladder technique: an alternative group structure facilitating effective group decision making. *J. Appl. Psychol.* 77: 730–37

Sainfort FC, Gustafson DH, Bosworth K, Hawkins RP. 1990. Decision support system effectiveness: conceptual framework and empirical evaluation. *Organ, Behav. Hum. Decis. Process.* 45(2):232–52

Salas E, Bowers CA, Cannon-Bowers JA. 1995. Military team research: 10 years of progress. *Mil. Psychol.* 7:55–75

Sambamurthy V. Poole MS, Kelly J. 1993. The effects of variations in GDSS capabilities of decision-making processes in groups. *Small Group Res.* 24(4):523–46

Shamir B. 1990. Calculations, values, and identities: the sources of collectivistic work motivation. *Hum. Relat.* 43:313–32

Sheppard JA. 1993. Productivity loss in performance groups: a motivational analysis. *Psychol. Bull.* 113:67–81

Smith C, Comer D. 1994. Self-organization in small groups: a study of group effectiveness within non-equilibrium conditions. *Hum. Relat.* 47:553–81

Smith KA, Smith KG, Olian JD, Sims HP, O'Bannon DP, Scully J. 1994. Top management team demography and process: the role of social integration and communication. *Adm. Sci. Q.* 39:412–38

Spaeth JL, O'Rourke DP. 1994. Designing and implementing the national organizations study. *Am. Behav. Sci.* 37:872–90

Steel RP, Jennings KR, Lindsey JT. 1990. Quality circle problem solving and common cents: evaluation study findings from a United States federal mint. *J. Appl. Behav. Sci.* 26:365–81

Stout RJ, Salas E, Carson R. 1994. Individual task proficiency and team process: What's important for team functioning? *Mil. Psychol.* 6(3):177–92

Straus SG, McGrath JE. 1994. Does the medium matter? The interaction of task type and technology on group performance and members reactions. *J. Appl. Psychol.* 79: 87–97

Sundstrom E, De Meuse KP, Futrell D. 1990. Work teams: applications and effectiveness. *Am. Psychol.* 45:120–33

Urban JM, Bowers CA, Monday SD, Morgan BB Jr. 1995. Workload, team structure, and communication in team performance. *Mil. Psychol.* 7(2):123–39

Valacich JS, George JF, Nunamaker JF, Vogel DR. 1994. Physical proximity effects on computer-mediated group idea generation. *Small Group Res.* 25(1):83–104

Vandermark MJ. 1991. Should flight attendants be included in CRM training? A discussion of a major air carrier's approach to total crew training. *Int. J. Aviat. Psychol.* 1(1): 87–94

Vroom VH. 1964. *Work and Motivation.* New York: Wiley

Wall TD, Kemp NJ, Jackson PR, Clegg CW. 1986. Outcomes of autonomous work groups: a field experiment. *Acad. Manage. J.* 29:280–304

Watson WE, Kumar K, Michaelsen LK. 1993. Cultural diversity's impact on interaction process and performance: comparing homogeneous and diverse task groups. *Acad. Manage. J.* 36:590–602

Watson WE, Michaelsen LK, Sharp W. 1991. Member competence, group interaction, and group decision making: a longitudinal *study. J. Appl. Psychol.* 76:803–9

Weingart LR. 1992. Impact of group goals, task component complexity, effort, and planning on group performance. *J. Appl. Psychol.* 77:682–93

Weingart LR, Weldon E. 1991. Processes that mediate the relationship between a group goal and group member performance. *Hum. Perform.* 4:33–54

Weisman CS, Gordon DL, Cassard SD, Bergner M. 1993. The effects of unit self-management on hospital nurses' work process, work satisfaction, and retention. *Med. Care.* 31(5):381–93

Weldon E, Jehn KM, Pradhan P. 1991. Processes that mediate the relationship between a group goal and improved group performance. *J. Pers. Soc. Psychol.* 61:555–69

Weldon E, Weingart LR. 1993. Group goals and group performance. *Br. J. Soc. Psychol.* 32:307–34

Wiener EL, Kanki BG, Helmreich RL, eds. 1993. *Cockpit Resource Management*. San Francisco: Academic

Wiersema MF, Bird A. 1993. Organizational demography in Japanese firms: group heterogeneity, individual dissimilarity, and top management team turnover. *Acad. Manage. J.* 36:996–1025

Wilpert B. 1995. Organizational behavior. *Annu. Rev. Psychol.* 46:59–90

Zaccaro SJ, Gualtieri J, Minionis D. 1995. Task cohesion as a facilitator of team decision making under temporal urgency. *Mil. Psychol.* 7(2):77–93

40

SPARKLING FOUNTAINS OR STAGNANT PONDS

An integrative model of creativity and innovation implementation in work groups

Michael A. West

Source: *Applied Psychology: An International Review* 51(3) (2002): 355–387.

Abstract

In this article I synthesise research and theory that advance our understanding of creativity and innovation implementation in groups at work. It is suggested that creativity occurs primarily at the early stages of innovation processes with innovation implementation later. The influences of task characteristics, group knowledge diversity and skill, external demands, integrating group processes and intragroup safety are explored. Creativity, it is proposed, is hindered whereas perceived threat, uncertainty or other high levels of demands aid the implementation of innovation. Diversity of knowledge and skills is a powerful predictor of innovation, but integrating group processes and competencies are needed to enable the fruits of this diversity to be harvested. The implications for theory and practice are also explored.

Introduction

Three themes dominate the writings of researchers investigating creativity and innovation among work teams. The first is the importance of the group task and the demands and opportunities it creates for creativity and innovation. The second is the theme of diversity in knowledge and skills among team members, which researchers suggest is related to both team creativity and innovation. And the third is the theme of team integration—when team members work in integrated ways to capitalise on their diverse knowledge and skills, researchers believe that both creativity and innovation implementation result.

In this paper I argue that what is neglected in the literature and in research designs is a focus on an important fourth element—the extent of external demands, threat or uncertainty and consequent effects upon creativity and innovation implementation in teams. I propose that creativity and innovation implementation represent two stages in the innovation process and that external demands have quite opposite effects on each of these stages. I argue that external demands on the team *inhibit* creativity or idea generation but *encourage* the implementation of creative ideas—or innovation implementation. This proposition has important implications not only for theory in the area, but also for practice. If we ignore the role of external demands, then our theories are likely to be of limited value in predicting team innovation and creativity, and our interventions in teams to promote these outcomes are likely to founder. Ultimately, applying the principles expounded here will enable teams to avoid the fate of stagnation and aspire realistically towards being sparkling fountains of ideas and innovative change.

Whether the context is producing TV programmes, training for war, managing health and illness in hospitals, developing new products in manufacturing organisations, or providing financial services, the use of work groups as a form of work organisation is both ubiquitous and increasing (Guzzo, 1996). Researchers in applied psychology have responded by puzzling over the factors that influence the effectiveness of work groups or teams, from the shopfloor through to top management teams (see for reviews West, 1996; Cohen & Bailey, 1997; West, Borrill, & Unsworth, 1998). Much less energy has been devoted to answering the question "what factors influence the extent to which teams generate and implement ideas for new and improved products, services, and ways of doing things at work?"

Why has so little attention been devoted to understanding the factors that influence group or team innovation? One reason is the confusion in the literature between the two concepts—team innovation and team creativity. Distinguishing between them more clearly can dissipate this confusion. Creativity can be seen as the first stage in the innovation process. Creativity is the development of ideas while innovation implementation is the application of ideas (e.g. for new and improved products, services, or ways of working) in practice (West, 1997). Aphoristically, creativity is thinking about new things, innovation implementation is about doing new things (West & Rickards, 1999). Innovation can then be defined as encompassing both stages—the development of ideas—creativity; followed by their application—the introduction of new and improved products, services, and ways of doing things at work.f Innovation, I shall argue, is therefore a two-component, but essentially non-linear process, encompassing both creativity and innovation implementation. At the outset of the process, creativity dominates, to be superseded later by innovation implementation processes. First I will define creativity and innovation before considering in more detail the notion that there are two relatively distinct components to the innovation process.

Creativity and innovation implementation

Creativity encompasses the processes leading to the generation of new and valued ideas. In informal use, innovation concerns those behavioural and social processes whereby individuals, groups, or organisations seek to achieve desired changes, or avoid the penalties of inaction. Innovation is therefore the introduction of new and improved ways of doing things at work. A fuller, more explicit definition of innovation is "the intentional introduction and application within a job, work team or organization of ideas, processes, products or procedures which are new to that job, work team or organization and which are designed to benefit the job, the work team or the organization" (West & Farr, 1990). Innovation is restricted to *intentional* attempts to bring about benefits from new changes; these might include economic benefits, personal growth, increased satisfaction, improved group cohesiveness, better organisational communication, as well as productivity and economic gains. Various processes and products may be regarded as innovations. They include technological changes such as new products, but may also include new production processes, the introduction of advanced manufacturing technology, or the introduction of new computer support services within an organisation. Administrative changes are also regarded as innovations. New human resource management (HRM) strategies, organisational policies on health and safety, or the introduction of teamwork are all examples of administrative innovations within organisations. Innovation implies novelty, but not necessarily absolute novelty. If teamwork is introduced into a government department, it is considered to be an innovation if it is new in that government department, irrespective of whether it has been introduced into other government departments. Innovations may vary from those that are relatively minor, to those that are of great significance. Some innovations can be introduced in the space of an hour, while others may take several years. Some innovations are unplanned and emerge by accident. One frequently cited example of an emergent innovation is the Post-It notes developed in 3M by an employee who wanted some system of marking the pages of his hymnal when he sang in his church choir. In contrast, some innovations are planned and managed, requiring enormous amounts of an organisation's attention and energy to ensure their effective implementation.

It is generally assumed by researchers that innovation is not a linear process (see for example, Drazin & Schoonhoven, 1996; Van de Ven, 1986; Van de Ven, Schroeder, Scudder, & Polley, 1986; Van de Ven, Polley, Garud, & Venkatraman, 1999) and I have proposed elsewhere (West, 1990) that it may be conceived of as cyclical with periods of innovation initiation, implementation, adaptation, and stabilisation. Creativity is likely to be most evident in the early stages of innovation processes or cycles, when those in teams are required to develop or offer ideas in response to a perceived need for innovation. Creative thinking is also likely when they initiate proposals for change and consider their initial implementation. Such considerations will alert team members to possible impracticalities associated with their ideas and with potential negative reactions from stakeholders.

The employee who discovered the practical value of Post-It notes in 3M was constrained not by technology (the adhesive properties required for the product were already available), but by the resistance and incredulity of others in the organisation. His creative strategy was to provide Post-It notes to the secretaries of senior managers, and they in turn began to demand more of the product, so persuading the Marketing and Production departments of the value of the idea. Thus, creativity is primarily required at early stages of the innovation process. As the innovation is adapted to organisational circumstances and stabilised, there is less need for creativity. Of course, it can be argued that creativity is important throughout the innovation process, but in general, the requirements for creative ideas will be greater at the earlier stages of the innovation process than the later.

This distinction might have limited theoretical import if the factors influencing both creativity and innovation implementation were identical. However, though task characteristics, integrated group functioning, and diversity of knowledge and skills are (I shall argue) requirements for both, the effects of external demands and threat upon creativity and innovation implementation are, I propose, quite opposite (see Fig. 1).

In this paper I argue that four groups of factors together principally determine the level of group innovation:

- Task characteristics
- Group knowledge diversity and skills
- External demands
- Integrating group processes

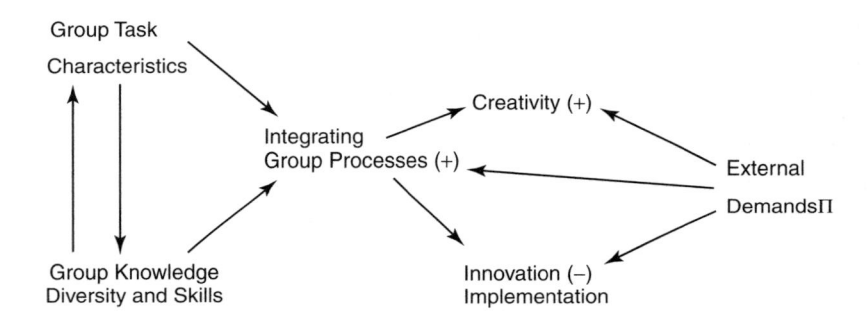

Figure 1 A model of team innovation.

Fig. 1 depicts the principal relationships among these elements and for the rest of this article I explore the propositions illustrated in the figure by reference to the relevant literature.

Group task characteristics

The task a group performs is a fundamental influence on the work group, defining its structural, process, and functional requirements—who is in the group, what their roles are, how they should work together, and the nature and processes of the tasks they individually and collectively perform. Indeed, in one sense a team is defined by the task it is required to perform. For example, Mohrman, Cohen, and Mohrman (1995) define a team as: "a group of individuals who work together to produce products or deliver services for which they are mutually accountable". They go on to propose that "Team members share goals and are mutually held accountable for meeting them, they are interdependent in their accomplishment, and they affect the results through their interactions with one another. Because the team is held collectively accountable, the work of integrating with one another is included among the responsibilities of each member" (pp. 39–40). The task will therefore influence the level of creativity and innovation in the team.

Dimensions for classifying task characteristics include task difficulty; solution multiplicity; intrinsic interest; cooperative requirements (Shaw, 1976); tasks which are unitary versus divisible, conjunctive, disjunctive, and additive (Steiner, 1972); conflict versus cooperation elements; and conceptual versus behavioural components (McGrath, 1984). These classification systems have been developed by social psychologists but have not been fruitful for researchers exploring group performance and innovation in organisational settings, probably because such goals as producing TV programmes, battleground training, health care, product development, and providing financial services cannot be neatly categorised into discrete tasks and sub-tasks (Tschan & von Cranach, 1996). Primary health care teams which maintain and promote the health of people in local communities, have multiple stakeholders and a wide variety of tasks (Slater & West, 1999). Their team tasks are both simple and difficult; unitary and divisible; involve conflict and cooperation; and demand both behavioural and conceptual responses.

Socio-technical systems theory (STST) provides a powerful framework for examining the effects of task design upon work group innovation. Socio-technical systems theorists (Trist & Bamforth, 1951; Emery, 1959; Cooper & Foster, 1971) argue that autonomous work groups provide a structure through which the demands of the social and technical subsystems of an organisation can be jointly optimised. Thus STST proposes that the technical subsystems of any work unit must be balanced and optimised concurrently with the social subsystem—technological and spatial working conditions must be designed to meet the human demands of the social system. The two subsystems are connected by team members' occupational roles and by necessary cooperative and interdependent relationships referred to in Mohrman et al.'s (1995) definition of teams given above. The key to effective performance is then whether the work group can control variance of task performance at source (Cordery, 1996). Such variance control implies innovation, since the work group will introduce new and improved methods of working or technologies in order to achieve control of variance in task performance appropriately.

The joint optimisation of the two subsystems is more likely when autonomous work groups have the following characteristics:

- The team is a relatively independent organisational unit that is responsible for whole tasks.
- The tasks of members are related in content so that awareness of a common task is evoked and maintained and members are required to work interdependently.
- There is a "unity of product and organisation", i.e. the group has a complete task to perform and group members can "identify with their own product" (Ulich & Weber, 1996).

Such conditions, according to theorists, will produce "task orientation", which is a state of interest and engagement produced by task characteristics (Emery, 1959). This is very similar to the concept of intrinsic motivation that Amabile argues is so fundamental to creativity and innovation at work (Amabile, 1983; Amabile & Conti, 1999). According to STST therefore, the task is the central focus of a psychological view of activity (Hacker, 1994). It is the character of the intersection between the group and the organisation that makes the task the most psychologically relevant part of the working conditions (Volpert, 1987). Blumberg (1988) makes the same point and proposes that the task is "the point of articulation between the social and technical systems, linking the job in the technical system with its correlated role behaviour in the social system" (p. 6). To the extent that the three characteristics of autonomous work groups described above are present therefore, the more likely the group is to develop ideas for, and implement new and improved products, processes, or procedures.

The *task* characteristics that evoke "task orientation" or intrinsic motivation according to STST, and thereby innovation, are:

- completeness (i.e. whole tasks)
- varied demands
- opportunities for social interaction
- autonomy
- opportunities for learning
- development possibilities for the task.[1]

Wholeness refers to the independent setting of goals which are embodied in super-ordinate organisational goals; autonomous planning functions include the choice of means for doing the work, including interactions for goal attainment; and feedback on performance refers to the ability of the group to monitor and control variance in performance at source. Gulowsen (1972) suggests the degree of autonomy of the work group can be assessed in relation to group influence over:

- The formulation of goals—what and how much it is expected to produce
- Where to work and number of hours (when to work overtime and when to leave)
- Choice about further activities beyond the given task
- Selection of production methods
- Internal distribution of task responsibilities within the group
- Membership of the group (who and how many people will work in the group)
- Leadership—whether there will be and who will be the leader
- How to carry out individual tasks

Recognising that task requirements and the relationship between the technical and social subsystems have a major influence on levels of group innovation is an important prerequisite for considering the more dynamic influences of other psychological, social psychological, and environmental factors upon group innovation.

In summary, the extent of group autonomy and the task requirements of completeness, varied demands, opportunities for social interaction, opportunities for learning, and development opportunities will predict group creativity and innovation implementation.

Group knowledge diversity and skills

Diversity of knowledge and skills, it is proposed, will contribute to team innovation, dependent upon the sophistication of group processes. Groups composed of people with differing professional backgrounds, knowledge, skills and abilities, will be more innovative than those whose members are similar, because they bring usefully differing perspectives on issues to the group (Paulus, 2000). Their divergence of views will create multiple perspectives and potentially constructive conflict. Diversity contributes to the magnitude of the team's total pool of task-related skills, information, and perspectives. The size of the pool represents the potential for more comprehensive or creative decision making via informational conflict (Milliken & Martins, 1996; Simons, Pelled, & Smith, 1999). If this informational conflict is processed in the interests of effective decision making and task performance rather than on the basis of motivation to win or prevail, or because of conflicts of interest, this in turn will generate improved performance and more innovative actions will be the result (De Dreu, 1997; Hoffman & Maier, 1961; Pearce & Ravlin, 1987; Porac & Howard, 1990; Tjosvold, 1985, 1991, 1998; Paulus, 2000). There is evidence that groups that contain people with diverse but overlapping knowledge domains and skills are particularly creative (Dunbar, 1995, 1997). Dunbar found that successful research teams were heterogeneous, were more likely to make use of analogies to solve problems, and were led by a scientist who was more willing to take risks. Moreover, task characteristics will dictate the requirements for diversity in group members' knowledge and skills. More complete, varied, and developmental tasks will create requirements for a wider range of group member knowledge and skills.[2] And it is this major influencing factor that we explore next.

In considering this question, researchers tend to differentiate between attributes that are directly related to work roles (such as organisational position or specialised technical knowledge), and those that are more enduringly characteristic of the person (such as age, gender, ethnicity, social status, and personality) (Maznevski, 1994). Existing research evidence suggests that diversity of professional background is associated with higher levels of innovation. For example, in a study of 100 primary health care teams, Borrill et al. (2000) found that the greater the number of professional groups represented in the team, the higher the levels of innovation, and the higher the levels of radicalness, magnitude, and novelty of innovation in all domains of the team's activities.

Jackson (1992) suggests that the effects of diversity on team performance are complex; task-related and relations-oriented diversity have different effects which depend also on the team task. She concludes that in relation to tasks requiring creativity and quality of decision making: "the available evidence supports the conclusion that team task-related diversity is associated with better quality team decision-making" (Jackson, 1996, p. 67), citing evidence provided by Filley, House, and Kerr (1976), Hoffman (1979), McGrath (1984), and Shaw (1981). Of course, diversity of background may also be a hindrance, if group processes do not facilitate integration of team members' perspectives.

A significant study of innovation in teams was the UNESCO-sponsored international effort to determine the factors influencing the scientific performance of 1,222 research teams (Andrews, 1979; see also Payne, 1990). Diversity was assessed in six areas: projects; interdisciplinary orientations; specialities; funding resources; R & D activities; and professional functions. Overall, diversity accounted for 10 per cent of the variance in scientific recognition, R & D effectiveness, and number of publications, suggesting that both flexibility of thought and organisation, fostered by diversity, do influence team innovation. This research also indicated that the extent of communication both within and between research teams had strong relationships with scientific recognition of their teams, R & D effectiveness, number of publications, and the applied value of their work.

Zenger and Lawrence (1989) have suggested another interpretation of the effects of diversity on innovation—that functional diversity might influence work group performance as a result of the higher level of external communication that group members initiate, precisely because of their functional diversity. In related research, Ancona and Caldwell (1992) studied 45 new-product teams in five high-technology companies and found that when a work group recruited a new member from a certain functional area in an organisation, communication with that area went up dramatically. Such new links might favour innovation through the incorporation of diverse ideas and models gleaned from these different functional areas.

Consistent with this, Ancona and Caldwell (1992) discovered that the greater the group's functional diversity, the more team members communicated outside the work group's boundaries and the higher their levels of innovation.

In some circumstances, knowledge diversity predicts group innovation but we do not know what types of diversity stimulate innovation and under what circumstances. I suggest that *requisite knowledge diversity* (the amount of knowledge diversity necessary for task performance and to create variety in, and flexibility of, cognitive responses and to encourage constructive controversy) will lead to innovation. Requisite diversity will increase the more complex is the group's task. However, when diversity begins to threaten the group's safety and integration, then creativity and innovation implementation, respectively, will suffer. For example, where diversity reduces group members' clarity about and commitment to group objectives, then innovation attempts will be resisted (these ideas are elaborated below). The challenge is to create sufficient diversity within the team without threatening their shared view of their task and their ability to communicate and work effectively together.

If diversity is maximised at the expense of shared understanding about the group task, it will threaten the ability of the group to innovate effectively. The clarity of the task will therefore influence the requisite level of knowledge diversity in the team. Innovation itself requires agreement about the goals of any change and how these advance the overall objectives of the team. There must be sufficient overlap of group members' mental models for them to coordinate and communicate effectively. Thus the common task (shared goals) will create shared understanding, but within this, greater knowledge diversity will lead to more creativity and innovation.[3]

What is proposed here is an inverted-U relationship between knowledge diversity and integrating group processes. Where diversity is very low, the group pressures will be towards conformity rather than integration. Where diversity is very high, there is unlikely to be adequate shared mental representation of the group and its task to enable integration, communication, and coordination of efforts for innovation. Thus the research team composed of a statistician, Marxist sociologist, quantitative organisational psychologist, social constructionist, and political scientist may be so diverse that they are unable to develop a coherent and innovative programme of research to discover under what circumstances nursing teams on hospital wards implement innovation.

The model in Fig. 1 also indicates that diversity will itself affect group processes. This is not to suggest that the less diverse a group is, the better integrated and safer it will be for its members. On the contrary, it is likely that members only learn integrating skills and discover safety through the effective management of diversity. Where the group is homogeneous then there will be strong pressures for conformity. Where the group is heterogeneous there will be pressures to manage (via group processes) the centrifugal forces of diversity that could lead to the disintegration of the group and could also threaten individual members (others' differing perspectives threatening one's own beliefs for example). We only discover a solid sense of safety through the management of apparently threatening environments. The child who explores her environment is more confident than the child who never strays from her mother (Bowlby, 1988; Ainsworth, Blehar, Waters, & Wall, 1978; Hazan & Shaver, 1987).

In summary therefore: Knowledge and skill diversity in groups foster innovation.

External demands

The external context of the group's work, be it organisational climate, support systems, market environment, or environmental uncertainty, is likely to have a highly significant influence both on its creativity and innovation implementation. People, groups, and organisations will innovate partly in response to external threat. But such threats or demands will inhibit creativity. A wealth of evidence suggests that, in general, creative cognitions occur when individuals are free from pressure, feel safe, and experience relatively positive affect (Claxton, 1997, 1998). For example, using the Luchins Water jars problems (Rokeach, 1950), it is possible to demonstrate how time pressures inhibit creative problem solving. Moreover, psychological threats to face or identity are associated with rigid thinking (Cowen, 1952). Time pressure can also increase rigidity of thinking on work-related tasks such as selection decisions (Kruglansky & Freund, 1983). Wright (1954) asked people to respond to Rorschach inkblots tests; half were hospital patients awaiting an operation and half were "controls". The former gave more stereotyped responses, and were less fluent and creative in completing similes (e.g. "as interesting as ..."), indicating the effects of stress or threat upon their capacity to generate creative responses.

In contrast, among individual health workers we have found in a number of studies that high work demands are significant predictors of individual innovation (Bunce & West, 1995, 1996; West, 1989). Indeed, studies of work role transitions show that changing role objectives, strategies, or relationships is a common response to the demands of new work environments (West, 1987a, 1987b). In a recent study of over 10,000 health care workers, work overload emerged as a significant predictor of innovation (Hardy & West, 2000). Of course, excessive work demands can have detrimental effects also on stress levels, absenteeism, and turnover. But the point here is that individuals innovate in response to high levels of demand—and groups comprise individuals. Borrill et al. (2000) recently explored innovation in 100 UK primary health care teams. Innovations reported by the teams were rated blind by external raters who were experts in the domain of primary health care. The external demands of the health care environment were assessed using a UK government index of health and illness for each local area (the Jarman Index). Perceived levels of participation by team members were also measured using the Team Climate Inventory (Anderson & West, 1998). Where levels of participation in the team were high, team innovation was also high, but only in environments characterised by high levels of ill health, with strong external demands on the health care professionals. Our research in manufacturing organisations (West, Patterson, Pillinger, & Nickell, 1998) and in hospitals (West & Anderson, 1992) suggests that external demands have a significant impact also upon organisational innovation (and therefore will likely have an impact upon group innovation). In a longitudinal study of 81 manufacturing organisations, the lower their market share in relation to their primary products, the higher was the level of companies' product and technological innovation. It seems that the threat of being a small player in a competitive situation spurs innovation. Moreover, the extent of environmental uncertainty reported by senior managers in these organisations (in relation to suppliers, customers, market demands, and government legislation) was a significant predictor of the degree of innovation in organisational systems, i.e. in work organisation and people management practices. Taken together, these findings suggest that if the environment of teams and organisations is threatening and uncertain, the more likely it is that they will innovate in order to reduce the uncertainty or threat.

Earlier, it was suggested that creative processes (idea generation) occur in the earlier stages of the innovation process, while innovation implementation processes occur predominantly at later stages. What is suggested therefore is that external demands will *inhibit* creativity which occurs in the earlier stages of the innovation process, but they will *facilitate* innovation (via innovation implementation) at later stages. Creativity requires an undemanding environment, while implementation requires precisely the opposite.

Why is there this consistency of findings about the influence of external demands across levels of analysis? Innovation implementation involves changing the status quo, which implies resistance, conflict, and a requirement for sustained effort. A team that attempts to implement innovation is likely to encounter resistance and conflict among others in the organisation, and therefore sustained effort is required to overcome these disincentives to innovate. But effort itself is aversive—like most species, we strive to achieve our goals while expending the minimum effort necessary. So the effort required to innovate has to be motivated, at least partly, by external demands.[4] But what form do external demands take and how does this component of the model described in Fig. 1 relate to other factors influencing innovation (task characteristics, team member knowledge and skill diversity, and integrating processes)? External demands are likely to take the form of *uncertainty* (experienced as potentially threatening)—compare this with Burns and Stalker's (1961) finding that a strong relationship existed between environmental uncertainty and organic structures in organisations, which themselves facilitate innovation. The price of crude oil is a constant uncertainty in petroleum refining and retailing organisations, and this prompts continuous innovation in retail operations to win customer loyalty. Another form of external demand is *time constraints* imposed by the organisation or environment. Where customers demand ever shorter lead times (the time from placing an order to its delivery), manufacturers or suppliers of services must innovate in their work processes in order to satisfy their customers' demands. *Competition* is clearly a form of demand which economists have long identified as a force for innovation. The *severity or challenge* of the environment is also an important influence (as the work of Borrill et al., 2000 described above clearly suggests). This aspect of demand is distinct from the task characteristics described by STST. For example, two health care teams may perform exactly the same diagnostic, treatment, and preventive health care functions, but the team operating in a deprived inner city environment faces far greater demands than that in a well-to-do suburban area.

What is intuitively apparent is that the relationship between external demands and innovation implementation cannot be linear. Extreme demands or sustained high levels are likely to produce paralysis or learned helplessness. When individuals are confronted by sustained demands that they cannot meet, they are likely to respond with apathy or learned helplessness (Maier & Seligman, 1976). So either very low or very high levels of demands will be associated with relatively low levels of innovation implementation—an inverted-U relationship.

What of the relationship between external demands and task characteristics? So far, it has been proposed that the task characteristics suggested by STST (a whole task, tasks of members are content inter-related, unity of team with its product or service, varied demands, opportunities for social interaction, autonomy, opportunities for learning, task development opportunities) will foster intrinsic motivation, and thereby, innovation attempts. It has also been suggested that external demands will encourage innovation implementation. This leads to the following propositions:

- Where the level of group task characteristics that encourage intrinsic motivation and external demands is high, then innovation implementation will be at a high level.
- Where the level of group task characteristics that encourage intrinsic motivation is high and external demands are low, then innovation implementation will be moderate.
- Where the level of group task characteristics that encourage intrinsic motivation is low and external demands are high, then innovation implementation will be moderate.
- Where the level of group task characteristics that encourage intrinsic motivation and external demands is low, then innovation implementation will be low.

These propositions suggest that either high levels of task characteristics encouraging intrinsic motivation *or* high levels of external demands are necessary for innovation implementation. Below I discuss in detail the relationship between external demands and integrating group processes. I suggest that high levels of external demands (or threats) increase group cohesion—and the corollary, high levels of internal group cohesion enable the group to cope more effectively with threat and uncertainty (Mullen & Copper, 1994).[5]

In summary, this section has presented arguments for the following proposition: External demands, threat, and uncertainty motivate groups to innovate at work.

Thus far we have considered what are structural and given features of workgroups or teams: the task, member knowledge diversity, and external demands. The influence of these factors will be affected by how group members interact together to jointly optimise the technical and social subsystems of the group (in STST terms), or how they work together to achieve their group goals (which are likely to include innovation)—in short integrating group processes. Without effective integrating group processes, groups will be simply stagnant ponds from which no creative ideas or innovative changes emerge. It is to a consideration of the dynamic, mediating effects of integrating group processes that we finally turn.

Group processes

Fig. 2 shows the key group processes that enable the team to translate the effects of task characteristics and the effects of diversity of knowledge into the generation and implementation of ideas for new and improved products, processes, services, or ways of working. Knowledge diversity and external demands will both influence group processes such as developing and redeveloping shared objectives, participation, management of conflict, the influence of minorities in the group, support for ideas to introduce new ways of doing things, and reflexivity. We consider each of these processes below.

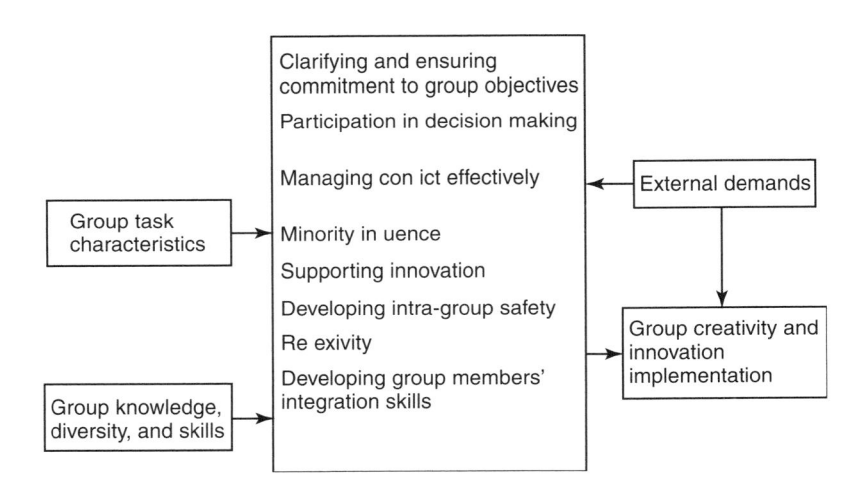

Figure 2 Integrating group processes in a model of team innovation.

Clarifying and ensuring commitment to shared objectives

Ensuring clarity of and commitment to shared team objectives is a sine qua non for integrating knowledge diversity to meet task requirements for teamwork. In the context of group innovation, ensuring clarity of team objectives is likely to facilitate innovation by enabling focused development of new ideas, which can be filtered with greater precision than if team objectives are unclear. Theoretically, clear objectives will only facilitate innovation if team members are committed to the goals of the team since strong goal-commitment will be necessary to maintain group member persistence for innovation implementation in the face of resistance from organisational members.

Pinto and Prescott (1987), in a study of 418 project teams, found that a clearly stated mission was the only factor which predicted success at all stages of the innovation process (conception, planning, execution, and termination). Research evidence from studies of the top management teams of hospitals (West & Anderson, 1996) and of primary health care teams (Borrill et al., 2000) provides clear support for the proposition that clarity of and commitment to team goals is associated with high levels of team innovation. Where group members do not share a commitment to a set of objectives (or a vision of the goals of their work) the forces of disintegration created by disagreements, diversity, and the emotional demands of the innovation process are likely to inhibit innovation.

Participation in decision making

Research on participation in decision making has a long history in both social and industrial/organisational psychology, and suggests that participation fosters integration and commitment (Bowers & Seashore, 1966; Coch & French, 1948; Lawler & Hackman, 1969; Locke, 1991; Locke & Latham, 1990; Heller, Pusić, Strauss, & Wilpert, 1998). But we should be wary of assuming a link with creativity at the early stages of the innovation process. Research on brainstorming consistently shows that nominal groups (individuals working alone, whose efforts are then aggregated) outperform groups where individuals brainstorm together (Diehl & Stroebe, 1987) because when others are talking in groups it is not possible to share one's ideas. Moreover, individuals in groups may be apprehensive about sharing their ideas for fear of evaluation (social inhibition) and individuals may "free ride", or make less effort when their efforts appear dispensable because of others' high performance (Kerr & Bruun, 1983). Individuals working in groups tend also to converge in the rate and type of ideas generated (Larey & Paulus, 1999) and the lowest performers in the group may have the most impact as a result of downward comparison processes (Camacho & Paulus, 1995). These conclusions are based largely on experimental studies in laboratory rather than field-based settings. One organisational study (Sutton & Hargadon, 1996) suggested a number of benefits including positive feelings among participants and customers (who also took part in the groups), development of organizational memory, and skill development.

Participation in teams can, under appropriate conditions, lead to high levels of creativity. Group members can be motivated to perform at higher levels of creativity by social comparison processes (providing group members and teams with a comparison standard) and providing feedback on individual performance (Paulus, Dzindolet, Poletes, & Camacho, 1993; Paulus, Larey, Putman, Leggett, & Roland, 1996).

Sharing ideas with others in a team (via sustained participation) can increase the chances of producing quite novel ideas, but this requires also that group members attend to one another's ideas (Paulus, 2000). And recent research evidence suggests that enhanced creativity can occur as a result of group participation not just during but also after group meetings (Paulus & Yang, in press). But it is clear that many of the benefits of group participation for the generation of creative ideas are manifested only if the group has appropriate teamworking skills (a point elaborated below).

There are obvious reasons for supposing that participation will be linked to team innovation. To the extent that information and influence over decision making are shared within teams, and there is a high level of interaction among team members, the cross-fertilisation of perspectives which can spawn creativity and innovation (Cowan, 1986; Mumford & Gustafson, 1988; Pearce & Ravlin, 1987; Porac & Howard, 1990) is more likely to occur. More generally, high participation in decision making means less resistance to change and therefore greater likelihood of innovations being implemented. When people participate in decision making through having influence, interacting with those involved in the change process, and sharing information, they tend to invest in the outcomes of those decisions and to offer ideas for new and improved ways of working (Kanter, 1983; King, Anderson, & West, 1992). Studies of teams in oil companies, health care, TV programme production organisation, and in top management, support this proposition (Burningham & West, 1995; Borrill et al., 2000; Carter & West, 1998; Poulton & West, 1999; West, Patterson & Dawson, 1999).

Managing conflict effectively

Many scholars believe that the management of competing perspectives is fundamental to the generation of creativity and innovation (Mumford & Gustafson, 1988; Nemeth & Owens, 1996; Tjosvold, 1998). Such processes are characteristic of task-related or information conflict (as opposed to conflicts of interest, emotional, or interpersonal conflict—see De Dreu & De Vries, 1997) and arise primarily from a common concern with quality of task performance in relation to shared objectives. Information conflict is evidenced by appraisal of, and constructive challenges to, the group's processes and performance. In essence, team members are more committed to performing their work effectively and excellently than they are either to bland consensus or to personal victory in conflict with other team members over task performance strategies or decision options.

Dean Tjosvold and colleagues (Tjosvold, 1982, 1998; Tjosvold & Field, 1983; Tjosvold & Johnson, 1977; Tjosvold, Wedley, & Field, 1986) have presented cogent arguments and strong supportive evidence that such constructive (task-related) controversy in a cooperative group context improves the quality of decision making and creativity. Constructive controversy is characterised by full exploration of opposing opinions and frank analyses of task-related issues. It occurs when decision makers believe they are in a cooperative group context, where mutually beneficial goals are emphasised, rather than in a competitive context; where decision makers feel their personal competence is confirmed rather than questioned; and where they perceive processes of mutual influence rather than attempted dominance.

For example, the most effective self-managing teams in a manufacturing plant that Alper and Tjosvold (1993) studied, were those which had compatible goals and promoted constructive controversy. The 544 employees who made up the 59 teams completed a questionnaire that probed for information about cooperation, competition, and conflict within the team. Teams were responsible for activities such as work scheduling, housekeeping, safety, purchasing, accident investigation, and quality. Members of teams that promoted interdependent conflict management (people cooperated to work through their differences), compared to teams with win/lose conflict (where team members tended to engage in a power struggle when they had different views and interests), felt confident that they could deal with differences. Their managers rated such teams as more productive and innovative. Apparently, because of this success, members of these teams were committed to working as a team.

In a study which focused more directly on innovation (though not in teams) faculty members and employees of a large educational institution reported that when they discussed their opposing views openly, fully, and forthrightly, they developed innovative solutions to problems. But when they discussed issues competitively, or from only one point of view, and were unable to integrate the differing views of colleagues, they were frustrated and developed poor quality and low novelty solutions (Tjosvold & McNeely, 1988).

An important perspective on conflict and creativity is offered by minority influence theory. A number of researchers have shown that minority consistency of arguments over time is likely to lead to change in majority views in groups (Maass & Clark, 1984). The experimental evidence suggests that while majorities bring about attitude change through public compliance prior to attitude change (i.e. the individual first publicly conforms to the majority view prior to internalising that view), minority influence works in the opposite direction. People exposed to a confident and consistent minority change their private views prior to expressing public agreement. Minority influence researchers have labelled this process as "conversion". Research on minority influence suggests that conversion is most likely to occur where the minority is consistent and confident in the presentation of arguments. Moreover, it is a behavioural style of persistence that is most likely to lead to attitude change and innovation (Nemeth & Owens, 1996).

De Dreu and De Vries (1997) suggest that an homogeneous workforce in which minority dissent is suppressed will reduce creativity, innovation, individuality, and independence (De Dreu & De Vries, 1993; see also Nemeth & Staw, 1989). Disagreement about ideas within a group can be beneficial and some researchers even argue that team task or information-related conflict is valuable, whether or not it occurs in a collaborative context, since it can improve decision making and strategic planning (Cosier & Rose, 1977; Mitroff, Barabba, & Kilmann, 1977; Schweiger, Sandberg, & Rechner, 1989). This is because task-related conflict may lead team members to re-evaluate the status quo and adapt their objectives, strategies, or processes more appropriately to their situation (Coser, 1970; Nemeth & Staw, 1989; Thomas, 1979; Roloff, 1987). From the perspective of systems theory, De Dreu invokes the concept of *requisite variety* to suggest that disagreement and variety are necessary for systems to adapt to their environment and perform well (Ashby, 1956).

In a study of newly formed postal work teams in the Netherlands, De Dreu and West found that minority dissent did indeed predict team innovation (as rated by the teams' supervisors), but only in teams with high levels of participation (De Dreu & West, 2000). It seems that the social processes in the team necessary for minority dissent to influence the innovation process, are characterised by high levels of team member interaction, influence over decision making and information sharing. This finding has significant implications too for our understanding of minority dissent in groups operating in organisational contexts.

Overall, therefore, task-related (as distinct from emotional or interpersonal) conflict within a psychosocially safe environment, and minority dissent in a participative environment will lead to innovation by encouraging debate (requisite diversity) and consideration of alternative interpretations of information available, leading to integrated and creative solutions.

Supporting innovation

Innovation is more likely to occur in groups where there is support for innovation, and where innovative attempts are rewarded rather than punished (Amabile, 1983; Kanter, 1983). Support for innovation is the expectation, approval, and practical support of attempts to introduce new and improved ways of doing things in the work environment (West, 1990). Within groups, new ideas may be routinely rejected or ignored, or attract verbal and practical support. Such group processes powerfully shape individual and group behaviour (for reviews see e.g. Hackman, 1992) and will encourage or discourage team members to introduce innovations. In a longitudinal study of 27 hospital top management teams, support for innovation emerged as a powerful group process predictor of team innovation (measured by independent evaluations of implemented innovations) (West & Anderson, 1996). Further studies in TV production teams (Carter & West, 1998), primary health care teams and community mental health teams (Borrill et al., 2000) have strongly supported this finding (see also Agrell & Gustafson, 1996).

Developing intragroup safety

Intragroup safety refers to the sense of psychological or psychosocial safety group members feel in the presence of their fellow group members and especially during whole group interactions. It includes the related concepts of group affective tone, safety climate, and conflict acceptance, which are described below. Groups that consistently develop intragroup safety, it is proposed, by encouraging positive group affect, constructive management of conflict, and creating a climate within which it is safe to learn, will be both more creative and more innovative.

George (1996) uses the term group *affective tone*, to refer to "consistent or homogenous affective reactions within a group". If, for example, members of a group tend to be excited, energetic and enthusiastic, then the group itself can be described as being excited, energetic and enthusiastic. If members of a group tend to be distressed, mistrustful and nervous, then the group also can be described in these terms" (p. 78). George believes that a group's affective tone will determine how innovative (and effective) the group will be. Relevant to this belief is evidence that when individuals feel positive they tend to connect and integrate divergent stimulus materials—they are more creative (Isen & Daubman, 1984; Isen, Daubman, & Nowicki, 1987; Isen, Johnson, Mertz, & Robinson, 1985; Cummings, 1998); see inter-relatedness among diverse stimuli; and use broader, inclusive categories (Isen & Daubman, 1984; Isen, Daubman, & Nowicki, 1987). How does this affect group or team behaviour? George suggests that if all or most individuals in a work group tend to feel positive at work (the group has a "high positive affective tone"), then their cognitive flexibility will be amplified as a result of social influence and other group processes. As a result of these individual and group level processes, the group will develop shared (and flexible) mental models. In effect, groups with a high positive affective tone will be creative.

Prince (1975) argues, on the basis of applied work in organisations focused on increasing creativity, that speculation (a critical creative process) makes people in work settings feel vulnerable because we tend to experience our workplaces as unsafe (a finding also reported by Nicholson & West, 1986 in a study of the experience of work among UK managers). Questioning the person who comes up with an idea too closely, joking about the proposal (even in a light way), or simply ignoring the proposal can lead to the person feeling defensive, which tends to "reduce not only his speculation but that of others in the group". Prince goes on: "The victim of the win-lose or competitive posture is always speculation, and therefore idea production and problem solving. When one speculates he becomes vulnerable. It is easy to make him look like a loser" (Prince, 1975, p. 260).

Jehn (1995) found that norms reflecting the acceptance of conflict within a group, promoting an open and constructive atmosphere for group discussion, enhanced the positive effect of task-based conflict on individual and team performance for 79 work groups and 75 manager groups. Members of high performing groups were not afraid to express their ideas and opinions. Such a finding further reinforces the notion that safety may be an important factor in idea generation or creativity.

Indeed, Tjosvold (1998) makes a strong case, based on his considerable research, that the management of conflict in a cooperative context will lead to a greater sense of integration and safety among the parties. Safety is the *consequence* of the management of diversity in views rather than the cause. If we operate in situations where there is no diversity or there is no conflict, we never have the opportunity to discover safety in our psychosocial environment. In one study in the service sector (West & Wallace, 1991) cohesiveness in primary health care teams predicted levels of team innovation.

Similarly, there is evidence that teams differ in the extent to which they create a climate of safety within which it is possible to engage in group learning. Edmondson (1996) demonstrated differences between teams in a study of hospital patient care, finding significant differences across work groups in their management of medication errors. In some groups, members openly acknowledged and discussed their medication errors (giving too much or too little of a drug, or administering the wrong drug) and discussed ways to avoid their occurrence. In others, members kept information about errors to themselves. Learning about the causes of these errors as a team and devising innovations to prevent future errors were only possible in groups of the former type. Edmondson gives an example of how, in one learning-oriented team, discussion of a recent error led to an innovation in equipment. A pump used to deliver intravenous medications was identified as a source of consistent errors and so was replaced by a different type of pump. She also gives the example of how failure to discuss errors and generate innovations led to costly failure in the Hubble telescope development project. In particular, Edmondson (1996, 1999) argues that learning and innovation will only take place where group members trust other members' intentions. This manifests itself in a group level belief that well-intentioned action will not lead to punishment or rejection by the team, which Edmondson calls "team safety": "The term is meant to suggest a realistic, learning oriented attitude about effort, error and change—not to imply a careless sense of permissiveness, nor an unrelentingly positive affect. Safety is not the same as comfort; in contrast, it is predicted to facilitate risk" (1999, p. 14). Edmondson proposes that perceptions of team safety will lead team members to engage in learning and risk-taking behaviour—that is, to innovation. Her research in 53 teams of a large manufacturer of office furniture revealed that safety was the one consistent predictor of team learning, whether self or observer-rated (Edmondson, 1999).

The proposition that developing group psychosocial safety will increase the level of creativity in work groups is clearly testable. It is not unique to work settings. If we consider the psychosocial environment of the child in a family group or classroom, similar propositions can and have been tested. The strength, for example, of attachment in dyadic and group relationships in childhood influences the predisposition to explore and create (Tidwell, Reis, & Shaver, 1996). The conclusion is that whereas external demands inhibit creativity and encourage innovation implementation, intra-group safety facilitates the expression of creative ideas *and* the implementation of innovation.

Reflexivity

I have argued elsewhere (West, 1996, 2000) that team reflexivity will also predict group innovation (as well as effectiveness). Team reflexivity is "the extent to which team members collectively reflect upon the team's objectives, strategies and processes as well as their wider organizations and environments, and adapt them accordingly" (West, 1996, p. 559), There are three central elements to the concept of reflexivity—*reflection*, *planning*, and *action or adaptation*. Reflection consists of attention, awareness, monitoring, and evaluation of the object of reflection. Planning is one of the potential consequences of the indeterminacy of reflection, since during this indeterminacy, courses of action can be contemplated, intentions formed, plans developed (in more or less detail), and the potential for carrying them out is built up. High reflexivity exists when team planning is characterised by greater detail, inclusiveness of potential problems, hierarchical ordering of plans, and long as well as short range planning. The more detailed the implementation plans, the greater the likelihood that they will manifest in innovation (Frese & Zapf, 1994; Gollwitzer, 1996). Indeed the work of Gollwitzer and colleagues suggests that innovation will be implemented almost only when the team has articulated implementation intentions. This is because planning creates a conceptual readiness for, and guides team members' attention towards, relevant opportunities for action and means to implement the innovation. Action refers to goal-directed behaviours relevant to achieving the desired changes in team objective, strategies, processes, organisations, or environments identified by the team. In a variety of studies links between reflexivity and team innovation and effectiveness have been demonstrated (Carter & West, 1998; West, Patterson, & Dawson, 1999; Borrill et al., 2000).

Integration skills

Another potent influence on team innovation is the extent to which team members have the relevant knowledge, skills, and abilities to work effectively in teams— or integration skills. Stevens and Campion (1994) believe that team members require appropriate team knowledge, skills, and abilities (KSAs), which, for more effective communication of the ideas in this article, I will call team integration skills. These are distinct from the technical KSAs that are relevant to task performance (such as medical knowledge for a doctor). These team integration skills are individual, not team, attributes but their deployment directly affects group processes. They include conflict resolution integration skills, such as the skill to recognise and encourage desirable, but discourage undesirable conflict, and the skill to employ integrative (win-win) negotiation strategies. This would include the ability to distinguish between and differentially encourage or discourage respectively task-related conflict and interpersonal conflict (cf. Jehn, 1995). Collaborative problem solving integration skills include the ability to identify situations requiring participative group problem solving; the skill to utilise decentralised communication networks to enhance communication; and the skill to communicate openly and supportively (to send messages which are behaviour-oriented, congruent, and validating). Teamwork integration skills also include goal setting and performance management, such as the skill to monitor, evaluate, and provide feedback on both overall team performance and individual team member performance; and the skill to coordinate and synchronise activities, information, and tasks between members. This work is useful for assessing whether the individuals who make up a team possess the necessary skills, abilities, and knowledge to manage the complexities and challenges of working in a team effectively, and therefore, whether in aggregate, team member skills offer a high level of team competencies in teamworking. The more integration skills the team possesses, the more likely it is that the team will work in integrated ways, not just in terms of team performance, but also in relation to innovation proposals and their successful implementation.

Integrating group processes therefore enable team members to respond to the requirements of the task and innovate by utilising with maximum effort their diverse knowledge and skills, and responding to external demands by developing (in a safe, unthreatening group environment) creative ideas, and implementing them as innovations. The greater the diversity of the team, the higher the levels of external demands, and the more demanding the task, the more will team members be required to develop integrating group processes for successful innovation. Group processes, if sufficiently integrating, will facilitate group creativity and innovation implementation.

This proposition can be tested directly in research but all the propositions presented in this paper have important theoretical and practical implications, and it is to these that we now turn.

Theoretical and practical implications

I have described a model of group creativity and innovation implementation that treats these phenomena as if they were simply dependent variables in a precise experiment in, say, the physical sciences. However, innovation implies reciprocal relationships between variables. For example, innovation may affect the group's level of external demands. The production team on the shopfloor may decide to establish direct relationships with customers in order to speed information flow and reduce task uncertainty. As the primary health care team clarifies its commitment to encourage patients/clients to take responsibility for their own health care, they may change their own membership (taking on a counsellor and health promotion adviser rather than another doctor). The team may also reduce clients' demands for their services as a consequence. Moreover, an innovative group will change managers' perceptions of the team and team members may consequently find they have increasing influence in their organisations. This in turn will affect their subsequent innovation and group processes. Creativity and innovation implementation are also reciprocally interdependent. Of course innovation implementation is dependent upon the quality of the ideas initially developed.[6] Similarly, creativity will be demanded during the innovation implementation process since unanticipated problems are likely to demand yet more creative ideas to aid in their solution.

Innovation is dynamic, so we must aspire to construct dynamic models representing how groups both shape and are shaped by their environments and their innovations. Yet, we are still at an early stage of understanding group creativity and innovation, requiring that we establish basic principles before confronting such complex challenges. We will need models in the future which reciprocally link the organisation and wider environment of the group to characteristics of the group and its task, and to group creativity and innovation implementation. Such dynamic models will enable us to confront more confidently this research area.

Practical implications

In organisational settings where the intent is to encourage teams to be innovative, there are clear practical recommendations that can be derived from the propositions outlined above. First the team's task must be a whole task, that is perceived by the team as significant to the organisation or the wider society; that makes varied demands on team members and requires them to use their knowledge and skills interdependently; that provides opportunities for social contact between them; and provides opportunities for learning, skill development, and task development. The group should be relatively autonomous in the conduct of its work.

Second, the group should be given time during the early stages of the innovation process, in an unpressured environment, to generate creative ideas for new and improved products or ways of working. This may mean taking time away from the usual workplace and working in (ideally) a pleasant and relaxing environment. The services of a skilled facilitator, knowledgeable about research evidence on group creative processes (as opposed to popular belief and consultancy mythology), can help groups to maximise their creative output. An intra-group psychosocial environment experienced by group members as unthreatening will best facilitate such processes.

Third, at later stages of the innovation process, if group members feel pressured, threatened, or uncertain, they are more likely to implement innovations, as long as the threats and uncertainty are created by extra- not intra-group agents—(this is sometimes called the "burning platform" effect) and the level of demand is not crippling. Today, competition, threat, pressure, and uncertainty are characteristic of most public and commercial sector environments, particularly as globalisation increases apace—there is rarely reason to increase the level of demand. But there is much more reason to improve the level of safety and the integration skills of team members.

Fourth, and above all therefore, group members must individually and collectively develop the skills to work well as a team, encouraging integrating group processes to ensure that they innovate effectively. This means continually clarifying and ensuring group member commitment to shared objectives; encouraging information sharing, regular group member interaction, and shared influence over decision making; and encouraging high levels of emphasis on quality, and practical support (time, money, and cooperation) for innovation. It means encouraging group members to regularly reflect upon and adapt their objectives, strategies, and processes—effectively consciously and continually improving their functioning as a group.

Conclusion

For creativity and innovation implementation to emerge from group functioning—for groups to be sparkling fountains of ideas and changes—the context must be demanding but there must be strong group integration processes and a high level of intra-group safety. This requires that members have the integration abilities to work effectively in teams; and that they develop a safe psychosocial climate and appropriate group processes (clarifying objectives, encouraging participation, constructive controversy, reflexivity, and support for innovation). Such conditions are likely to produce high levels of group innovation, but crucially too, the well-being which is a consequence of effective human interaction in challenging and supportive environments.

Acknowledgments

I am grateful to the many colleagues with whom I have had conversations that have influenced my thinking about groups, creativity, and innovation implementation. For commenting on an early draft of this article I thank particularly Nigel Nicholson and Carsten De Dreu, and for their constructive and insightful criticisms, I thank the editor and three anonymous reviewers of this journal.

Notes

1 I would add another characteristic—task significance (Hackman & Oldham, 1975). This refers to the importance of the task in contributing to organisational goals or to the wider society. A lifeboat team in a rural coastal area with busy shipping lanes and a health and safety team in a high-risk industry are likely to be highly intrinsically motivated by the significance of their tasks.
2 This relationship is likely to be, to some extent, reciprocal. Available skills within the team will limit the task that can be performed. If the breast cancer care team has no oncologist then some discussions about diagnosis and treatment will have to be held by people outside the team.
3 Below, I explore how diversity influences integrating group processes.
4 Below it is suggested that where task characteristics are such that the team members are highly intrinsically motivated then the requirement for external demands to motivate innovation implementation will be weak.
5 At the extreme of course, high levels of threat may reduce group cohesion and safety when group members feel the capacities of the group are inadequate to manage the threats or demands.

6 Sternberg and Lubart (1996) refer to synthetic and practical contextual qualities of creativity, which include the extent to which ideas escape the bounds of conventional thinking and the persuasiveness of the ideas to those affected by their implementation.

References

Agrell, A., & Gustafson, R. (1996). Innovation and creativity in work groups. In M.A. West (Ed.), *The handbook of work group psychology* (pp. 317–344). Chichester: John Wiley.

Ainsworth, M.D., Blehar, M.C., Waters, E., & Wall, S. (1978). *Patterns of attachment: A psychological study of the strange situation.* Hillsdale, NJ: Erlbaum.

Alper, S., & Tjosvold, D. (1993). Cooperation theory and self-managing teams on the manufacturing floor. Paper presented at the International Association for Conflict Management, Eugene, OR.

Amabile, T.M. (1983). The social psychology of creativity: A componential conceptualization. *Journal of Personality and Social Psychology*, 45, 357–376.

Amabile, T.M., & Conti, R. (1999). Changes in the work environment for creativity during downsizing. *Academy of Management Journal*, 42, 630–640.

Ancona, D.F., & Caldwell, D.F. (1992). Bridging the boundary: External activity and performance in organisational teams. *Administrative Science Quarterly*, 37, 634–665.

Anderson, J.R. (1991). *The adaptive character of thought.* Hillsdale, NJ: Erlbaum.

Anderson, N., & West, M.A. (1998). Measuring climate for work group innovation: Development and validation of the team climate inventory. *Journal of Organizational Behaviour*, 19, 235–258.

Andrews, F.M. (Ed.) (1979). *Scientific productivity.* Cambridge: Cambridge University Press.

Ashby, W.R. (1956). *An introduction to cybernetics.* London: Methuen.

Blumberg, M. (1988). Towards a new theory of job design. In W. Karwowski, H.R. Parsaei, & M.R. Wilhelm (Eds.), *Ergonomics of hybrid automated systems*, volume 1 (pp. 53–59). Amsterdam: Elsevier.

Borrill, C.S., Carletta, J., Carter, A.J., Dawson, J., Garrod, S., Rees, A., Richards, A., Shapiro, D., & West, M.A. (2000). *The effectiveness of health care teams in the National Health Service.* Birmingham: Aston Centre for Health Service Organization Research.

Bowers, D.G., & Seashore, S.E. (1966). Predicting organizational effectiveness with a four-factor theory of leadership. *Administrative Science Quarterly*, 11, 238–263.

Bowlby, J. (1988). *A secure base: Parent–child attachment and healthy human development.* New York: Basic Books.

Bunce, D., & West, M.A. (1995). Changing work environments: Innovative coping responses to occupational stress. *Work and Stress*, 8, 319–331.

Bunce, D., & West, M.A. (1996). Stress management and innovation interventions at work. *Human Relations*, 49, 209–232.

Burningham, C., & West, M.A. (1995). Individual, climate and group interaction processes as predictors of work team innovation. *Small Group Research*, 26, 106–117.

Burns, T., & Stalker, G.M. (1961). *The management of innovation.* London: Tavistock.

Camacho, L.M., & Paulus, P.B. (1995). The role of social anxiousness in group brainstorming. *Journal of Personality and Social Psychology*, 68, 1071–1080.

Carter, S.M., & West, M.A. (1998). Reflexivity, effectiveness and mental health in BBC-TV production teams. *Small Group Research*, 29, 583–601.

Claxton, G.L. (1997). *Hare brain, tortoise mind*: *Why intelligence increases when you think less*. London: Fourth Estate.
Claxton, G.L. (1998). Knowing without knowing why: Investigating human intuition. *The Psychologist*, *11*, 217–220.
Coch, L., & French, J.R. (1948). Overcoming resistance to change. *Human Relations*, *1*, 512–532.
Cohen, S.G., & Bailey, D.E. (1997). What makes teams work: Group effectiveness research from the shop floor to the executive suite. *Journal of Management*, *23*(3), 239–290.
Cooper, R., & Foster, M. (1971). Sociotechnical systems. *American Psychologist*, *26*, 467–474.
Cordery, J.L. (1996). Autonomous work groups and quality circles. In M.A. West (Ed.), *Handbook of work group psychology* (pp. 225–246). Chichester: John Wiley.
Coser, L.A. (1970). *Continuities in the study of social conflict*. New York: Free Press.
Cosier, R., & Rose, G. (1977). Cognitive conflict and goal conflict effects on task performance. *Organizational Behaviour and Human Performance*, *19*, 378–391.
Cowan, D.A. (1986). Developing a process model of problem recognition. *Academy of Management Review*, *11*, 763–776.
Cowen, E.L. (1952). The influence of varying degrees of psychological stress on problem-solving rigidity. *Journal of Abnormal and Social Psychology*, 47, 420–424.
Cummings, A. (1998). Contextual characteristics and employee creativity: Affect at work. Paper presented at the 13th Annual Conference, Society for Industrial Organizational Psychology. Dallas, USA, April.
De Dreu, C.K.W. (1997). Productive conflict: The importance of conflict management and conflict issue. In C.K.W. De Dreu & E. Van De Vliert (Eds.), *Using conflict in organizations* (pp. 9–22). London: Sage.
De Dreu, C.K.W., & De Vries, N.K. (1993). Numerical support, information processing, and attitude change. *European Journal of Social Psychology*, *23*, 647–662.
De Dreu, C.K.W., & De Vries, N.K. (1997). Minority dissent in organizations. In C.K.W. De Dreu & E. Van De Vliert (Eds.), *Using conflict in organizations* (pp. 72–86). London: Sage.
De Dreu, C.K.W., & West, M.A. (2001). Minority dissent and team innovation: The importance of participation in decision-making. *Journal of Applied Psychology*, *68*(6), 1191–1201.
Diehl, M., & Stroebe, W. (1987). Productivity loss in brainstorming groups: Towards the solution of a riddle. *Journal of Personality and Social Psychology*, *53*, 497–509.
Drazin, R., & Schoonhoven, C.B. (1996). Community, population, and organization effects on innovation: A multilevel perspective. *Academy of Management Journal*, *39*, 1065–1083.
Dunbar, K. (1995). How scientists really reason: Scientific reasoning in real-world laboratories. In R.J. Sternberg & J.E. Davidson (Eds.), *The nature of insight* (pp. 365–395). Cambridge, MA: MIT Press.
Dunbar, K. (1997). How scientists think: On-line creativity and conceptual change in science. In T.B. Ward, S.M. Smith, & J. Vaid (Eds.), *Creative thought*: *An investigation of conceptual structures and processes* (pp. 461–493). Washington, DC: American Psychological Association.
Edmondson, A.C. (1996). Learning from mistakes is easier said than done: Group and organizational influences on the detection and correction of human error. *Journal of Applied Behavioral Science*, *32*(1), 5–28.

Edmondson, A.C. (1999). Psychological safety and learning behavior in work teams. *Administrative Science Quarterly*, *44*, 350–383.
Emery, F.E. (1959). Characteristics of sociotechnical systems. London: Tavistock Insititute of Human Relations, Document No. 527.
Filley, A.C., House, R.J., & Kerr, S. (1976). *Managerial process and organizational behaviour*. Glenview, IL: Scott Foresman.
Frese, M., & Zapf, D. (1994). Action as the core of work psychology: A German approach. In H.C. Triandis, M.D. Dunnette, & L.M. Hough (Eds.), *Handbook of industrial and organizational psychology*, Volume 4 (2nd edn.) (pp. 271–340). Palo Alto, CA: Consulting Psychologists Press.
George, J.M. (1996). Group affective tone. In M.A. West (Ed.), *Handbook of work group psychology* (pp. 77–94). Chichester: John Wiley.
Gollwitzer, P.M. (1996). The volitional benefits of planning. In P.M. Gollwitzer & J.A. Bargh (Eds.), *The psychology of action: Linking cognition and motivation to behaviour* (pp. 287–312). New York: Guilford Press.
Gulowsen, J.A. (1972). A measure of work group autonomy. In L.E. Davis & J.C. Taylor (Eds.), *Design of jobs* (pp. 374–390). Harmondsworth: Penguin.
Guzzo, R.A. (1996). Fundamental considerations about work groups. In M.A. West (Ed.), *Handbook of work group psychology* (pp. 3–24). Chichester: John Wiley.
Hacker, W. (1994). Action regulation theory and occupational psychology: Review of German empirical research since 1987. *The German Journal of Psychology*, *18*, 91–120.
Hackman, J.R. (1992). Group influences on individuals in organisations. In M.D. Dunnette & L.M. Hough (Eds.), *Handbook of industrial and organizational psychology* (Vol. 3). Palo Alto, CA: Consulting Psychologists Press.
Hackman, J.R., & Oldham, G. (1975). Development of the job diagnostic survey. *Journal of Applied Psychology*, *60*, 159–170.
Hardy, G.E., & West, M.A. (2000). Interpersonal attachment and innovation at work. Unpublished manuscript, Department of Psychology, University of Sheffield.
Hazan, C., & Shaver, P. (1987). Romantic love conceptualised as an attachment process. *Journal of Personality and Social Psychology*, *52*, 511–534.
Heller, F., Pusić, E., Strauss, G., & Wilpert, B. (1998). *Organizational participation: Myth and reality*. Oxford: Oxford University Press.
Hoffman, L.R. (1979). Applying experimental research on group problem solving to organizations. *Journal of Abnormal Social Psychology*, *58*, 27–32.
Hoffman, L.R., & Maier, N.R.F. (1961). Sex differences, sex composition, and group problem-solving. *Journal of Abnormal and Social Psychology*, *63*, 453–456.
Isen, A.M., & Daubman, K.A. (1984). The influence of affect on categorization. *Journal of Personality and Social Psychology*, *47*, 1206–1217.
Isen, A.M., Daubman, K.A., & Nowicki, G.P. (1987). Positive affect facilitates creative problem solving. *Journal of Personality and Social Psychology*, *52*, 1122–1131.
Isen, A.M., Johnson, M.M.S., Mertz, E., & Robinson, G.F. (1985). The influence of positive affect on the unusualness of word association. *Journal of Personality and Social Psychology*, *48*, 1413–1426.
Jackson, S.E. (1992). Consequences of group composition for the interpersonal dynamics of strategic issue processing. *Advances in Strategic Management*, *8*, 345–382.
Jackson, S.E. (1996). The consequences of diversity in multidisciplinary work teams. In M.A. West (Ed.), *Handbook of work group psychology* (pp. 53–75). Chichester: John Wiley.

Jehn, K.A. (1995). A multimethod examination of the benefits and detriments of intragroup conflict. *Administrative Science Quarterly, 40*, 256–282.

Kanter, R.M. (1983). *The change masters: Corporate entrepreneurs at work.* New York: Simon & Schuster.

Kerr, N.L., & Bruun, S.E. (1983). Dispensability of member effort and group motivation losses: Free rider effects. *Journal of Personality and Social Psychology, 44*, 78–94.

King, N., Anderson, N., & West, M.A. (1992). Organizational innovation: A case study of perceptions and processes. *Work and Stress, 5*, 331–339.

Kruglansky, A.W., & Freund, T. (1983). The freezing and unfreezing of lay influences: Effects on impressional primacy, ethnic stereotyping and numerical anchoring. *Journal of Experimental Social Psychology, 19*, 448–468.

Larey, T.S., & Paulus, P.B. (1999). Group preference and convergent tendencies in groups: A content analysis of group brainstorming performance. *Creativity Research Journal, 12*, 175–184.

Lawler, E.E. 3rd, & Hackman, J.R. (1969). Impact of employee participation in the development of pay incentive plans: A field experiment. *Journal of Applied Psychology, 53*, 467–471.

Locke, E. (1991). The motivation sequence, the motivation hub, and the motivation core. *Organizational Behavior and Human Decision Making Processes, 50*, 288–299.

Locke, E., & Latham, G. (1990). *A theory of goal setting and task motivation.* Englewood Cliffs, NJ: Prentice-Hall.

Maass, A., & Clark, R.D. (1984). Hidden impacts of minorities: Fifty years of minority influence research. *Psychological Bulletin, 95*(3), 428–450.

McGrath, J.E. (1984). *Groups, interaction and performance.* Englewood Cliffs, NJ: Prentice-Hall.

Maier, S.F., & Seligman, M. (1976). Learned helplessness: Theory and evidence. *Journal of Experimental Psychology: General, 105*, 3–46.

Maznevski, M.L. (1994). Understanding our differences: Performance in decision-making groups with diverse members. *Human Relations, 47*(5), 531–552.

Milliken, F., & Martins, L. (1996). Searching for common threads: Understanding the multiple effects of diversity in organizational groups. *Academy of Management Review, 21*, 402–433.

Mitroff, J., Barabba, N., & Kilmann, R. (1977). The application of behaviour and philosophical technologies to strategic planning: A case study of a large federal agency. *Management Studies, 24*, 44–58.

Mohrman, S.A., Cohen, S.G., & Mohrman, A.M. (1995). *Designing team-based organizations: New forms for knowledge work.* San Francisco: Jossey-Bass.

Mullen, B., & Copper, C. (1994). The relation between group cohesiveness and performance: An integration. *Psychological Bulletin, 115*, 210–227.

Mumford, M.D., & Gustafson, S.B. (1988). Creativity syndrome: Integration, application and innovation. *Psychological Bulletin, 103*, 27–43.

Nemeth, C., & Owens, P. (1996). Making work groups more effective: The value of minority dissent. In M.A. West (Ed.), *Handbook of work group psychology* (pp. 125–142). Chichester: John Wiley.

Nemeth, C., & Staw, B.M. (1989). The trade offs of social control and innovation within groups and organizations. In L. Berkowitz (Ed.), *Advances in experimental social psychology*, Vol. 22 (pp. 175–210). New York: Academic Press.

Nicholson, N., & West, M.A. (1986). *Managerial job change: Men and women in transition.* Cambridge: Cambridge University Press.

Paulus, P.B. (2000). Groups, teams and creativity: The creative potential of idea-generating groups. *Applied Psychology: An International Review, 49,* 237–262.

Paulus, P.B., Dzindolet, M.T., Poletes, G., & Camacho, L.M. (1993). Perception of performance in group brainstorming: The illusion of group productivity. *Personality and Social Psychology Bulletin, 19,* 78–89.

Paulus, P.B., Larey, T.S., Putman, V.L., Leggett, K.L., & Roland, E.J. (1996). Social influence process in computer brainstorming. *Basic and Applied Social Psychology, 18,* 3–14.

Paulus, P.B., & Yang, H. (in press). Idea generation in groups: A basis for creativity in organizations. *Organizational Behavior and Human Decision Processes.*

Payne, R.L. (1990). The effectiveness of research teams: A review. In M.A. West & J.L. Farr (Eds.), *Innovation and creativity at work: Psychological and organizational strategies* (pp. 101–122). Chichester: John Wiley.

Pearce, J. A., & Ravlin, E.C. (1987). The design and activation of self-regulating work groups. *Human Relations, 40,* 751–782.

Pinto, J.K., & Prescott, J.E. (1987). Changes in critical success factor importance over the life of a project. *Academy of Management Proceedings,* 328–332.

Porac, J.F., & Howard, H. (1990). Taxonomic mental models in competitor definition. *Academy of Management Review, 2,* 224–240.

Poulton, B.C., & West, M.A. (1999). The determinants of effectiveness in primary health care teams. *Journal of Interprofessional Care, 13,* 7–18.

Prince, G. (1975). Creativity, self and power. In I.A. Taylor & J.W. Geizels (Eds.), *Perspectives in creativity* (pp. 249–277). Chicago: Aldine.

Rokeach, M. (1950). The effect of perception of time upon the rigidity and concreteness of thinking. *Journal of Experimental Psychology, 40,* 206–216.

Roloff, M.E. (1987). Communication and conflict. In C.R. Berger & S.H. Chaffee (Eds.), *Handbook of communication science* (pp. 484–534). Newbury Park, CA: Sage.

Schweiger, D., Sandberg, W., & Rechner, P. (1989). Experimental effects of dialectical inquiry, devil's advocacy, and other consensus approaches to strategic decision making. *Academy of Management Journal, 32,* 745–772.

Shaw, M.E. (1976). *Group dynamics: The psychology of small group behaviour.* New York: McGraw-Hill.

Shaw, M.E. (1981). *Group dynamics: The psychology of small group behaviour* (2nd edn.). New York: McGraw-Hill.

Simons, T., Pelled, L.H., & Smith, K.A. (1999). Making use of difference: Diversity, debate, and decision comprehensiveness in top management teams. *Academy of Management Journal, 42,* 662–673.

Slater, J.A., & West, M.A. (1999). Primary health care teams. In J.J. Phillips, S.D. Jones, & M.M. Beyerlein (Eds.), *Developing high performance work teams* (pp. 199–213). Alexandria, VA: American Society for Training and Development.

Steiner, I.D. (1972). *Group process and productivity.* New York: Academic Press.

Sternberg, R.J., & Lubart, T.I. (1996). Investing in creativity. *American Psychologist, 51,* 677–688.

Stevens, M.J., & Campion, M.A. (1994). Staffing teams: Development and validation of the Teamwork-KSA test. Paper presented at the 9th annual meeting of the Society of Industrial and Organizational Psychology, Nashville, TN.

Sutton, R.I., & Hargadon, A. (1996). Brainstorming groups in context: Effectiveness in a product design firm. *Administrative Science Quarterly, 41*, 685–718.
Thomas, K.W. (1979). Organizational conflict. In S. Kerr (Ed.), *Organizational behavior* (pp. 151–184). Columbus, OH: Grid Publishing.
Tidwell, M.O., Reis, H.T., & Shaver, P.R. (1996). Attachment, attractiveness, and social interaction: A diary study. *Journal of Personality and Social Psychology, 71*, 729–745.
Tjosvold, D. (1982). Effects of approach to controversy on superiors' incorporation of subordinates' information in decision making. *Journal of Applied Psychology, 67*, 189–193.
Tjosvold, D. (1985). Implications of controversy research for management. *Journal of Management, 11*, 21–37.
Tjosvold, D. (1991). *Team organization: An enduring competitive advantage*. Chichester: John Wiley.
Tjosvold, D. (1998). Co-operative and competitive goal approaches to conflict: Accomplishments and challenges. *Applied Psychology: An International Review, 47*, 285–342.
Tjosvold, D., & Field, R.H.G. (1983). Effects of social context on consensus and majority vote decision making. *Academy of Management Journal, 26*, 500–506.
Tjosvold, D., & Johnson, D.W. (1977). The effects of controversy on cognitive perspective-taking. *Journal of Education Psychology, 69*, 679–685.
Tjosvold, D., & McNeely, L.T. (1988). Innovation through communication in an educational bureaucracy. *Communication Research, 15*, 568–581.
Tjosvold, D., Wedley, W.C., & Field, R.H.G. (1986). Constructive controversy, the Vroom-Yetton Model, and managerial decision-making. *Journal of Occupational Behaviour, 7*, 125–138.
Trist, E.L., & Bamforth, K.W. (1951). Some social and psychological consequences of the longwall method of coal getting. *Human Relations, 4*, 3–38.
Tschan, F., & von Cranach, M. (1996). Group task structure, processes and outcome. In M.A. West (Ed.), *Handbook of work group psychology* (pp. 95–121). Chichester: John Wiley.
Ulich, E., & Weber, W.G. (1996). Dimensions, criteria and evaluation of work group autonomy. In M.A. West (Ed.), *The handbook of work group psychology* (pp. 247–282). Chichester: John Wiley.
Van de Ven, A.H. (1986). Central problems in the management of innovation. *Management Sciences, 32*, 590–607.
Van de Ven, A.H., Polley, D., Garud, R., & Venkatraman, S. (1999). *The innovation journey*. New York: Oxford University Press.
Van de Ven, A.H., Schroeder, R., Scudder, G., & Polley, D. (1986). Managing innovation and change processes: Findings from the Minnesota Innovation Research Program. *Agribusiness Management Journal, 2*, 501–523.
Volpert, W. (1987). Psychische regulation von arbeitstätigkeiten. In U. Kleinbeck & J. Rutenfranz (Eds.), *Arbeitspsychologie, enzyklopädie der psychologie, themenbereich D. Series III, Volume 1* (pp. 1–42). Göttingen: Hogrefe.
West, M.A. (1987a). A measure of role innovation at work. *British Journal of Social Psychology, 26*, 83–85.
West, M.A. (1987b). Role innovation in the world of work. *British Journal of Social Psychology, 26*, 305–315.
West, M.A. (1989). Innovation among health care professionals. *Social Behaviour, 4*, 173–184.

West, M.A. (1990). The social psychology of innovation in groups. In M.A. West & J.L. Farr (Eds.), *Innovation and creativity at work: Psychological and organizational strategies* (pp. 309–333). Chichester: John Wiley.

West, M.A. (Ed.) (1996). *The handbook of work group psychology*. Chichester: John Wiley.

West, M.A. (1997). *Developing creativity in organizations*. Leicester: British Psychological Society.

West, M.A. (2000). Reflexivity, revolution and innovation in work teams. In M. Beyerlein (Ed.), *Product development teams: Advances in interdisciplinary studies of work teams* (pp. 1–30). California: JAI Press.

West, M.A., & Anderson, N. (1992). Innovation, cultural values and the management of change in British hospitals. *Work and Stress, 6*, 293–310.

West, M.A., & Anderson, N. (1996). Innovation in top management teams. *Journal of Applied Psychology, 81*(6), 680–693.

West, M.A., Borrill, C.S., & Unsworth, K.L. (1998). Team effectiveness in organizations. In C.L. Cooper & I.T. Robertson (Eds.), *International review of industrial and organizational psychology*. Vol. 13 (pp, 1–48). Chichester: John Wiley.

West, M.A., & Farr, J.L. (1990). Innovation at work. In M.A. West & J.L. Farr (Eds.), *Innovation and creativity at work: Psychological and organizational strategies* (pp. 3–13). Chichester: John Wiley.

West, M.A., Patterson, M.G., & Dawson, J.F. (1999). A path to profit? Teamwork at the top. *Centrepiece, 4*, 6–11.

West, M.A., Patterson, M., Pillinger, T., & Nickell, S. (1998). *Innovation and change in manufacturing*. Institute of Work Psychology, University of Sheffield, Sheffield S10 2TN.

West, M.A., & Rickards, T. (1999). Innovation. In M.A. Runco & S.R. Pritzker (Eds.), *Encyclopedia of creativity*, Volume 2 (pp. 45–55). London: Academic Press.

West, M.A., & Wallace, M. (1991). Innovation in health care teams. *European Journal of Social Psychology, 21*, 303–315.

Wright, M. (1954). A study of anxiety in a general hospital setting. *Canadian Journal of Psychology, 8*, 195–203.

Zenger, T.R., & Lawrence, B.S. (1989). Organizational demography: The differential effects of age and tenure distributions on technical communication. *Academy of Management Journal, 32*, 353–376.

41

FRONTIERS IN GROUP DYNAMICS

Concept, method and reality in social science; social equilibria and social change

Kurt Lewin

Source: *Human Relations* 1 (1947): 5–41.

One of the byproducts of World War II of which society is hardly aware is the new stage of development which the social sciences have reached. This development indeed may prove to be as revolutionary at the atom bomb. Applying cultural anthropology to modern rather than "primitive" cultures, experimentation with groups inside and outside the laboratory, the measurement of socio-psychological aspects of large social bodies, the combination of economic, cultural, and psychological fact-finding, all of these developments started before the war. But, by providing unprecedented facilities and by demanding realistic and workable solutions to scientific problems, the war has accelerated greatly the change of social sciences to a new development level.

The scientific aspects of this development center around three objectives:

(1) Integrating social sciences.
(2) Moving from the description of social bodies to dynamic problems of changing group life.
(3) Developing new instruments and techniques of social research.

Theoretical progress has hardly kept pace with the development of techniques. It is, however, as true for the social as for the physical and biological sciences that without adequate conceptual development, science cannot proceed beyond a certain stage. It is an important step forward that the hostility to theorizing which dominated a number of social sciences ten years ago has all but vanished. It has been replaced by a relatively wide-spread recognition of the necessity for developing better concepts and higher levels of theory. The theoretical development will have to proceed rather rapidly if social science is to reach that level of practical usefulness which society needs for winning the race against the destructive capacities set free by man's use of the natural sciences.

I should like to survey certain concepts and theories which have emerged mainly from experimental research. They concern:

(a) Quasi-stationary social equilibria and social changes.
(b) Locomotion through social channels.
(c) Social feedback processes and social management.

The last two of these will be dealt with in a later article. A cursory introductory discussion of certain aspects of the present state of affairs in social science is included here for those readers who are interested in the general background of these concepts and in the problems from which they have sprung.

Concept, method, and reality in social science

Developmental stages of sciences

For planning and executing research a clear insight into the present stage of scientific development is needed. Research means taking the next step from the known into the jungle of the unknown. To choose scientifically significant objectives and procedures it does not suffice to be acquainted with the factual knowledge available at a given stage. It is also necessary to free oneself from the scientific prejudices typical of a given developmental stage.

To gain sufficient distance from scientific details and to gain proper perspective for determining next steps the scientist may avail himself of the findings of "comparative theory of science." This discipline deals with the developmental stages of sciences, with their differences and equalities, and can sometimes provide useful yardsticks or way-posts to the empirical scientist.

The types of obstacles which have to be overcome when proceeding to a next scientific step are frequently quite different from what one may expect. Looking backwards it is often hard to understand how anyone could have been influenced by those arguments which have delayed scientific progress for considerable time.

Ernst Cassirer, who has analyzed the developmental stages of the natural sciences, and who had a great gift of viewing logical problems as they appear to the person doing research, points out that scientific progress has frequently the form of a change in what is considered to be "real" or "existing" (7).

The problem of existence in an empirical science

Arguments about "existence" may seem metaphysical in nature and may therefore not be expected to be brought up in empirical sciences. Actually, opinions about existence or nonexistence are quite common in the empirical sciences and have greatly influenced scientific development in a positive and a negative way. Labeling something as "non-existing" is equivalent to declaring it "out of bounds" for the scientist. Attributing "existence" to an item automatically makes it a duty of the scientist to consider this item as an object of research; it includes the necessity of considering its properties as "facts" which cannot be neglected in the total system of theories; finally, it implies that the terms with which one refers to the item are accepted as scientific "concepts" (rather than as "mere words").

Beliefs regarding "existence" in social science have changed in regard to the degree to which "full reality" is attributed to psychological and social phenomena, and in regard to the reality of their "deeper," dynamic properties.

In the beginning of this century, for instance, the experimental psychology of "will and emotion" had to fight for recognition against a prevalent attitude which placed volition, emotion, and sentiments in the "poetic realm" of beautiful words, a realm to which nothing corresponds which could be regarded as "existing" in the sense of the scientist. Although every psychologist had to deal with these facts realistically in his private life, they were banned from the realm of "facts" in the scientific sense. Emotions were declared to be something too "fluid" and "intangible" to be pinned down by scientific analysis or by experimental procedures. Such a methodological argument does not deny existence to the phenomenon but it has the same effect of keeping the topic outside the realm of empirical science.

Like social taboos, a scientific taboo is kept up not so much by a rational argument as by a common attitude among scientists: any member of the scientific guild who does not strictly adhere to the taboo is looked upon as queer; he is suspected of not adhering to the scientific standards of critical thinking.

The reality of social phenomena

Before the invention of the atom bomb the average physical scientist was hardly ready to concede to social phenomena the same degree of "reality" as to a physical object. Hiroshima and Nagasaki seem to have made many physical scientists ready to consider social facts as being perhaps of equal reality. This change of mind was hardly based on philosophical considerations. The bomb has driven home with dramatic intensity the degree to which social happenings are both the result of, and the conditions for the occurrence of, physical events. Gradually, the period is coming to an end when the natural scientist thinks of the social scientist as someone interested in dreams and words, rather than as an investigator of facts, which are not less real than physical facts, and which can be studied no less objectively.

The social scientists themselves, of course, have had a stronger belief in the "reality" of the entities they were studying. Still, this belief was frequently limited to the specific narrow section with which they happened to be familiar. The economist, for instance, finds it a bit difficult to concede to psychological, to anthropological, or to legal data that degree of reality which he gives to prices and other economic data. Some psychologists still view with suspicion the reality of those cultural facts with which the anthropologist is concerned. They tend to regard only individuals as real and they are not inclined to consider a "group atmosphere" as something which is as real and measurable as, let us say, a physical field of gravity. Concepts like that of "leadership" retained a halo of mysticism even after it had been demonstrated that it is quite possible to measure, and not only to "judge," leadership performance.

The denial of existence of a group, or of certain aspects of group life, is based on arguments which grant existence only to units of certain size, or which concern methodologic-technical problems, or conceptual problems.

Reality and dynamic wholes

Cassirer (7) discusses how, periodically throughout the history of physics, vivid discussions have occurred about the reality of the atom, the electron, or whatever else was considered at that time to be the smallest part of physical material. In the social sciences it has usually been not the part but the whole, whose existence has been doubted.

Logically, there is no reason to distinguish between the reality of a molecule, an atom, or an ion, or more generally between the reality of a whole or its parts. There is no more magic behind the fact that groups have properties of their own, which are different from the properties of their subgroups or their individual members, than behind the fact that molecules have properties, which are different from the properties of the atoms or ions of which they are composed.

In the social as in the physical field the structural properties of a dynamic whole are different from the structural properties of subparts. Both sets of properties have to be investigated. When one, and when the other, is important, depends upon the question to be answered. But there is no difference of reality between them.

If this basic statement is accepted, the problem of existence of a group loses its metaphysical flavor. Instead we face a series of empirical problems. They are equivalent to the chemical question whether a given aggregate is a mixture of different types of atoms, or whether these atoms have formed molecules of a certain type. The answer to such a question has to be given in chemistry, as in the social sciences, on the basis of an empirical probing into certain testable properties of the case in hand.

For instance, it may be wrong to state that the blond women living in a town "exist as a group," in the sense of being a dynamic whole which is characterized by a close interdependence of their members. They are merely a number of individuals who are "classified under one concept" according to the similarity of one of their properties. If, however, the blond members of a workshop are made an "artificial minority" and are discriminated against by their colleagues they may well become a group with specific structural properties.

Structural properties are characterized by *relations* between parts rather than by the parts or elements themselves. Cassirer emphasizes that throughout the history of mathematics and physics problems of constancy of relations rather than of constancy of elements have gained importance and have gradually changed the picture of what is essential. The social sciences seem to show a very similar development.

Reality and methods. Recording and experimentation

If recognition of the existence of an entity depends upon this entity's showing properties or constancies of its own, the judgment about what is real or unreal should be affected by changes in the possibility of demonstrating social properties.

The social sciences have considerably improved techniques for reliably recording the structure of small or large groups and of registering the various aspects of group life. Sociometric techniques, group observation, interview techniques, and others are enabling us more and more to gather reliable data on the structural properties of groups, on the relations between groups or subgroups, and on the relation between a group and the life of its individual members.

The taboo against believing in the existence of a social entity is probably most effectively broken by handling this entity experimentally. As long as the scientist merely describes a leadership form he is open to the criticism that the categories used reflect merely his "subjective views" and do not correspond to the "real" properties of the phenomena under consideration. If the scientist experiments with leadership and varies its form, he relies on an "operational definition" which links the concept of a leadership form to concrete procedures of creating such a leadership form or to the procedures for testing its existence. The "reality" of that to which the concept refers is established by "doing something with" rather than "looking at," and this reality is independent of certain "subjective" elements of classification. The progress of physics from Archimedes to Einstein shows consecutive steps by which this "practical" aspect of the experimental procedure has modified and sometimes revolutionized the scientific concepts regarding the physical world by changing the beliefs of the scientists about what is and is not real (7).

To vary a social phenomenon experimentally the experimenter has to take hold of all essential factors even if he is not yet able to analyze them satisfactorily. A major omission or misjudgment on this point makes the experiment fail. In social research the experimenter has to take into consideration such factors as the personality of individual members, the group structure, ideology and cultural values, and economic factors. Group experimentation is a form of social management. To be successful it, like social management, has to take into account all of the various factors that happen to be important for the case in hand. Experimentation with groups will therefore lead to a natural integration of the social sciences, and it will force the social scientist to recognize as reality the totality of factors which determine group life.

Social reality and concepts

It seems that the social scientist has a better chance of accomplishing such a realistic integration than the social practitioner. For thousands of years kings, priests, politicians, educators, producers, fathers and mothers—in fact, all individuals, have been trying day by day to influence smaller or larger groups. One might assume that this would have led to accumulated wisdom of a well integrated nature. Unfortunately nothing is farther from the truth. We know that our average diplomat thinks in very one-sided terms, perhaps those of law, or economics, or military strategy. We know that the average manufacturer holds highly distorted views about what makes a work-team "tick." We know that no one can answer today even such relatively simple questions as what determines the productivity of a committee meeting.

Several factors have come together to prevent practical experience from leading to clear insight (17). Certainly, the man of affairs is convinced of the reality of group life, but he is usually opposed to a conceptual analysis. He prefers to think in terms of "intuition" and "intangibles." The able practitioner frequently insists that it is impossible to formulate simple, clear rules about how to reach a social objective. He insists that different actions have to be taken according to the various situations, that plans have to be highly flexible and sensitive to the changing scene.

If one tries to transform these sentiments into scientific language, they amount to the following statements: (a) Social events depend on the social field as a whole, rather than on a few selected items. This is the basic insight behind the field theoretical method which has been successful in physics, which has steadily grown in psychology and, in my opinion, is bound to be equally fundamental for the study of social fields, simply because it expresses certain basis general characteristics of interdependence. (b) The denial of "simple rules" is partly identical with the following important principle of scientific analysis. Science tries to link certain observable (phenotypical) data with other observable data. It is crucial for all problems of interdependence, however, that—for reasons which we do not need to discuss here—it is, as a rule, impracticable to link one set of phenotypical data *directly* to other phenotypical data. Instead it is necessary to insert "intervening variables" (29). To use a more common language: the practitioner as well as the scientist views the observable data as mere "symptoms." They are "surface "indications of some "deeper-lying" facts. He has learned to "read" the symptoms, like a physicist reads his instruments. The equations which express physical laws refer to such deeper-lying dynamic entities as pressure, energy, or temperature rather than to the directly observable symptoms such as the movements of the pointer of an instrument (7).

The dynamics of social events provides no exception to this general characteristic of dynamics. If it were possible to link a directly observable group behavior, B, with another behavior, B^1,—$B = F(B^1)$ where F means a simple function— then simple rules of procedure for the social practitioner would be possible. When the practitioner denies that such rules can be more than poor approximations he seems to imply that the function, F, is complicated. I am inclined to interpret his statement actually to mean that in group life, too, "appearance" should be distinguished from the "underlying facts," that similarity of appearance may go together with dissimilarity of the essential properties, and *vice-versa,* and that laws can be formulated only in regard to these underlying dynamic entities: $k = F(n, m)$ where k, n, m refer not to behavioral symptoms but to intervening variables (13).

For the social scientist this means that he should give up thinking about such items as group structure, group tension, or social forces as nothing more than a popular metaphor or analogy which should be eliminated from science as much as possible. While there is no need for social science to copy the specific concepts of the sciences, the social scientist should be clear that he, too, needs intervening variables, and that these dynamic facts rather than the symptoms and appearances, are the important points of reference alike for him and for the social practitioner.

"Subjective" and "objective" elements in the social field. The three step procedure

One last point concerning conceptualization and general methodology may be mentioned. To predict the course of a marriage, for instance, a psychologist might proceed in the following way. He might start by analyzing the life space of the husband H. This analysis would involve the relevant physical and social facts in the husband's surroundings, including the expectations and character of his wife W, all represented in the way the husband, H, perceives them. Let us assume that this analysis is sufficiently complete to permit the derivation of the resultant forces on the husband (Fig. 1a). This would be equivalent to a prediction of what the husband actually will do as his next step. The data about the life space of the husband might be sufficiently elaborate to determine the resultant force on the wife W, as he sees her (Fig. 1a). This resultant force, however, would not indicate what the wife will actually do but merely what the husband expects his wife to do.

To derive the next conduct of the wife, her life space would have to be analyzed (Fig. 1b). Usually the wife will see the situation, including herself (W), and her husband, (H), somewhat differently than her husband. Let us assume she sees her husband located in an area corresponding to his own perception of himself; that she perceives her own position, however, as being in region e rather than d; and that the cognitive structure of the intermediate regions b and c are for her too, somewhat different from what they are for her husband. Corresponding to this difference between the life spaces of the husband and wife, the resultant force on the wife (W) may point to the region f rather than to c. This means that the wife will actually move forward f rather than toward c as her husband expected.

The considerations thus far give the basis for predicting the next moves of husband and wife to the region b and f respectively (Fig. 2): analyzing the

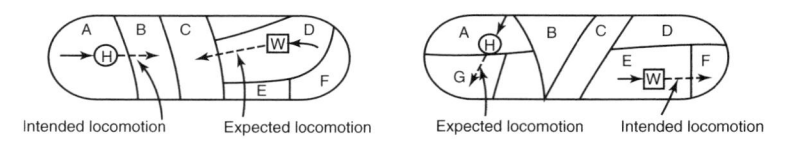

Figure 1 (a) Life space of husband at time 1, (b) Life space of wife at time 1.

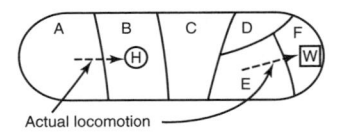

Figure 2 Social field at time 2.

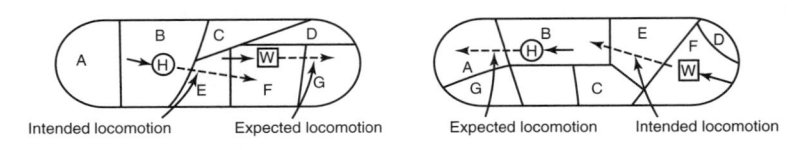

Figure 3 (a) Life space of husband at time 2, (b) Life space of wife at time 2.

two psychological ("subjective") fields gives the basis for predicting the actual ("objective") next step of behavior.

But how do we proceed from here if we are to answer the social problem of the fate of the marriage? Neither husband nor wife had expected their partner to behave as he or she actually did. Obviously, the next step will depend largely on how each will react to this surprise, how each will interpret the conduct of the other, or, more generally speaking, how each will "perceive" the new situation.

The husband who has expected his wife to move from d to c and now sees her moving in the opposite direction, to f, may interpret this to mean that his wife has "changed her mind." In this case he may expect her next move to proceed in the same direction, namely toward g (Fig. 3a). Furthermore, the behavior of his wife is likely to change for him the "meaning" of c, that is, the cognitive structure of the situation. The wife who sees her husband move to b rather than g may perceive this to be an excursion to an activity which would be completed in a certain time after which he would return to a (Fig. 3b). She therefore decides to join her husband in b (Fig. 3b), whereas her husband, having a different perception of the situation (Fig. 3a), intends to move on to f, which he perceives as being closer to his wife.

Obviously, husband and wife will soon be in trouble if they do not "talk things over," that is, if they do not communicate to each other the structure of their life spaces with the object of equalizing them.

This analysis of the history of a marriage has proceeded in a series of three steps: first, a separate analysis of the psychological situation of the husband and that of the wife, at time 1 with the purpose of deriving the next behavior of each. Second, representing the resultant sociological ("objective") situation at time 2. Third, deriving with the help of the laws of perception the resultant psychological situation for husband and wife at time 2. This would give the basis for the next sequence of three steps, starting with the analysis of the psychological situation of the persons involved predict their actual next step.

Such a procedure looks involved, particularly if we consider groups composed of many members. Is it possible to eliminate the "objective," or the "subjective," aspect of this analysis? Actually, social science faces here two types of questions; one concerning the size of units, the other concerning the role of perception in group life. It would be prohibitive if the analysis of group life always had to include analysis of the life space of each individual member.

Analysis of group life, can proceed rather far on the basis of relatively larger units. In the end, of course, the theory of small and large units has to be viewed in social science as well as in physical science, as one theoretical system. But this stage can be reached only after an attack on both the larger and the smaller units.

Unfortunately, treating groups as units does not eliminate the dilemma between "subjective" and "objective" aspects of social fields. It seems to be impossible to predict group behavior without taking into account group goals, group standards, group values, and the way a group "sees" its own situation and that of other groups. Group conflicts would have quite different solutions if the various groups concerned did not perceive differently the situation existing at a given time. To predict or to understand the steps leading to war between two nations A and B it seems to be essential to refer to the group life space of A and to the different group life space of B. This means that the analysis of group interaction has again to follow a three-step procedure, moving from the separate analysis of the life space of each group to the group conduct in the total social field and from there back again to the effect on the group life space.

This procedure of analysis which swings from an analysis of "perception" to that of "action," from the "subjective" to the "objective," and back again is not an arbitrary demand of scientific methodology, nor is it limited to the interaction between groups or between individuals. The procedure mirrors one of the basic properties of group life. Any kind of group action or individual action, even including that of the insane, is regulated by circular causal processes of the following type: individual perception or "fact-finding"—for instance, an act of accounting—is linked with individual action or group action in such a way that the content of the perception or fact-finding depends upon the way in which the situation is changed by action. The result of the fact-finding in turn influences or steers action.

Certain schools in psychology, sociology, and economics have had the tendency to eliminate the problems of perception. The analysis of all social sciences, however, will have to take into account both sections of this circular process. The following discussion of the mathematical representation of social problems should not be misunderstood as trying to minimize the importance of cognitive processes in group life. It is rather based on the conviction that topological and vector psychology has demonstrated the possibility of including them in such a treatment.

Quasi-stationary equilibria in group life and the problem of social change

Periods of social change may differ quite markedly from periods of relative social stability. Still, the conditions of these two states of affairs should be analyzed together for two reasons: (a) Change and constancy are relative concepts; group life is never without change, merely differences in the amount and type of change exist; (b) Any formula which states the conditions for change implies the conditions for no-change as limit, and the conditions of constancy can be analyzed only against a background of "potential" change.

Constancy and resistance to change

It is important to distinguish two questions which are generally not sufficiently separated; the one concerns actual change or lack of change, the other concerns resistance to change. A given group may show little change during a period of, let us say, two weeks. The group may be composed of friends on an island in the middle of their vacation, or a work-team in a factory. Let us assume that the conditions under which this group lives happen to stay constant during this period: no individual leaves or joins the group, no major friction occurs, the facilities for activities or work remain the same, etc. Under these circumstances the constancy of group life, for instance, the unchanged level of production does not require any other "explanation" than the reference to the principle: the same conditions lead to the same effect. This principle is identical with the general idea of lawfulness of group life.

The case would be different if the production level of the work-team were maintained in spite of the fact that a member of the work-team took sick or that inferior or superior material was provided. If, in spite of such changes in the group life setting, production is kept at the same level, then can one speak of "resistance" to change of the rate of production. The mere constancy of group conduct does not prove stability in the sense of resistance to change, nor does much change prove little resistance. Only by relating the actual degree of constancy to the strength of forces toward or away from the present state of affairs can one speak of degrees of resistance or "stability" of group life in a given respect.

The practical task of social management, as well as the scientific task of understanding the dynamics of group life, require insight into the desire for and resistance to, specific change. To solve or even to formulate these questions adequately we need a system of analysis which permits the representation of social forces in a group setting. The following considerations are directed more toward the improvement of these analytical tools than toward the analysis of a particular case.

Social fields and phase spaces

A basic tool for the analysis of group life is the representation of the group and its setting as a "social field." This means that the social happening is viewed as occurring in, and being the result of, a totality of coexisting social entities, such as groups, subgroups, members, barriers, channels of communication, etc. One of the fundamental characteristics of this field is the relative position of the entities, which are parts of the field. This relative position represents the structure of the group and its ecological setting. It expresses also the basic possibilities of locomotion within the field.

What happens within such a field depends upon the distribution of forces throughout the field. A prediction presupposes the ability to determine for the various points of the field the strength and directions of the resultant forces.

According to general field theory the solution of a problem of group life has always to be finally based on an analytical procedure of this type. Only by considering the groups in question in their actual setting, can we be sure that none of the essential possible conduct has been overlooked.

Certain aspects of social problems, however, can be answered through a different analytical device called *"phase space."* The phase space is a system of coordinates, each corresponding to different amounts of intensities of one "property." The phase space does not intend to represent the layout of a field composed of groups, individuals and their ecological setting, but concentrates on one or a few factors. It represents by way of graphs or equations, the quantitative relation between these few properties, variables or aspects of the field, or of an event in it.

For the discussion of the conditions of change we make use of such a phase space, realizing that one has finally to refer back to the actual social field.

Social states as quasi-stationary processes

It is possible to represent the change in discrimination against Negroes in towns A and B by means of a curve in a diagram where the ordinate represents degrees of discrimination and the abscissa time (Fig. 4). In this way the level of discrimination in the two towns can be represented (A is more discriminatory than B), the direction and rapidity of change (gradual decrease in A between the time 2 and 3, sudden increase in B at time 3), the amount of fluctuation (in the period 4—6, A shows relatively much, B relatively little fluctuation).

By "degree of discrimination" we are obviously not referring to the quality of a static object but to the quality of a process, namely the interaction between two populations. Discrimination refers to a number of refusals and permissions, orderings and yieldings, which indicate open and closed possibilities for various individuals in their daily living.

Similarly when speaking of the production level of a work-team one refers to the "flow" of products. In both cases we are dealing with a process which, like a river, continuously changes its elements even if its velocity and direction remain the same. In other words, we refer to the characteristic of quasi-stationary processes. The importance of quasi-stationary equilibria for the psychological problems of individual life has been emphasized by Köehler (10).

In regard to quasi-stationary processes one has to distinguish two questions: (1) Why does the process under the present circumstances proceed on this particular level (for instance, why does the water in this river move with this particular velocity)? and (2) What are the conditions for changing the present circumstances?

ENHANCING PERFORMANCE IN ORGANIZATIONS

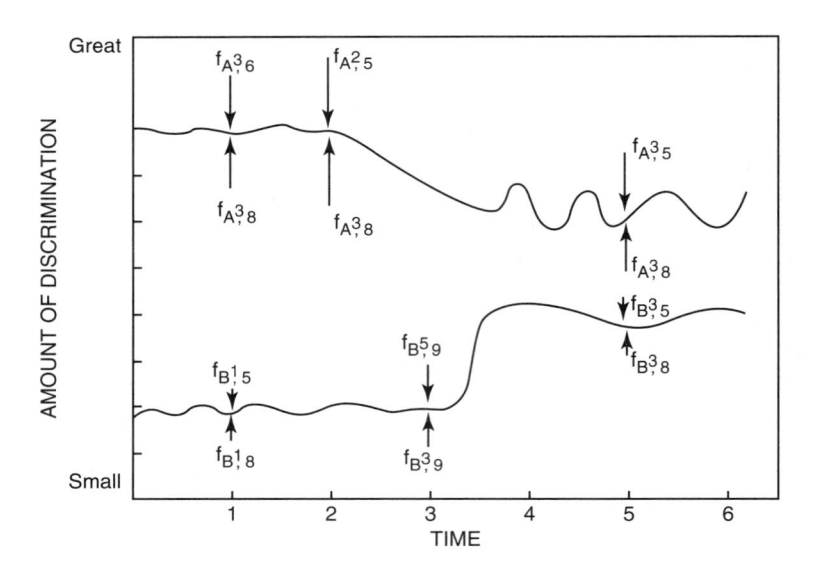

Figure 4 Level of equilibrium and strength of opposing forces.

A general analytic treatment of quasi-stationary social equilibria

Concerning the relation between the character of the process and the present conditions certain analytic statements of a rather general nature can be made.

Frequently, analytic conceptual tools (intervening variables) must be developed to a relatively elaborate stage before they are ready to be linked to observable facts. In the beginning it seems to be easier to make empirical use of secondary derivations; only gradually is one able to design experiments to test the fundamentals more directly. The concept of "force," for instance, is more fundamental than the concept "resultant of forces." It is, however, easier in psychology and sociology to coordinate an observable fact to a resultant of forces than to the components: certain aspects of behavior can be directly related to the resultant force (14), whereas we are able at present to determine psychological component forces only under special conditions (6). We have thought it advisable, therefore, to develop in some detail the conceptual analysis before discussing examples and specific testable theories.

The level of a quasi-stationary process as a quasi-stationary equilibrium

In the case of discrimination, for instance, certain social forces drive toward more discrimination. The interest of certain sections of the white population to keep certain jobs for themselves is such a force; other forces correspond to ideals of the white and colored population about what is "proper" or "not proper" work, etc. Other forces act against greater discrimination: the colored population may show signs of rebellion against higher degrees of discrimination, the white may consider "too much" discrimination unfair, etc. If we indicate the forces toward greater discrimination in the community A by $f_{A,g}$ and the forces toward less discrimination by $f_{A,s}$ we may state that $f_{A,g}$ and $f_{A,s}$ are equal in strength and opposite in direction.[1]

$$f_{A,g} + f_{A,s} = 0 \tag{1}$$

This equation does not determine the absolute strength of the forces. The strength of the opposing forces at the time 1 in town A may be smaller or greater than in town B $|f_{A,g}| > |f_{B,g}|$ (Fig. 4). The strength of the opposing forces may increase without a change of the level. For instance, before the level of discrimination decreased in A the opposing forces may have increased:

$$|f_{A,s}|^2 = |f_{A,g}|^2 > |f_{A,s}|^1 = |f_{A,g}|^1.$$

This would imply that *group tension* has increased. A similar increase of the opposing forces may have occurred in town B at the time 3 prior to the increase in discrimination:

$$|f_{B,s}|^3 = |f_{B,g}|^3 > |f_{B,s}|^1 = |f_{B,g}|^1.$$

Social changes may or may not be preceded by an increase in the opposing forces. Under some conditions, however, social changes can be achieved much easier if the tension is previously decreased. This is important for social management and for the theory of the after effect of changes.

After the discrimination in the town A has decreased the tension may gradually decrease so that

$$|f_{A,s}|^5 < |f_{A,s}|^3.$$

In some cases, however, tension may increase: the decrease of discrimination may lead to a still stronger pressure of the suppressed toward further advances and to an increased counter-pressure. After a change to a higher level of discrimination the opposing forces may decrease again or may remain permanently stronger.

On the whole, then, we can say that a quasi-stationary social state corresponds to equally strong opposing forces but that no general statement concerning their absolute strength is possible.

Force fields

Quasi-stationary processes are not perfectly constant but show fluctuations around an average level L. If we assume the fluctuation to be due to the variation in the strength of an additional force and the amount n of the change of the level L to be a function of the strength of this force, we can state that a force field in the area of fluctuation around L exists which has the following characteristics: the opposing forces on all levels between L and (L + n) and between L and (L − n) are unequal with the stronger force pointing toward the level L.

$$|f_{(L+n),L}| > |f_{(L+n),-L}|; \qquad (2)$$
$$|f_{(L-n),L}| > |f_{(L-n),-L}|$$

The meaning of this statement becomes clearer if we consider the resultant force $f^*_{L,x}$ where $f^*_{L,x} = f_{L,s} + f_{L,g}$. In case of a quasi-stationary process the resultant force on the level L equals zero (Fig. 5).

$$f^*_{L,x} = 0 \qquad (3)$$

The direction of the resultant forces at the "neighboring levels" (L ± n) is *toward* level L, their strength increasing with the distance from L. In other words, the resultant forces in the neighborhood of L have the character of a "positive central force field" (14).[2]

$$f^*_{(L\pm n), L=F(n)} \qquad (4)$$

The character of the function F determines how far, *ceteris paribus*, the social process fluctuates in a specific case.

Changes of the level of quasi-stationary processes will occur if and only if the numerical value of L changes for which the opposing forces are equal. If the resultant force field loses the structure of a central field, the social process loses its quasi-stationary character.

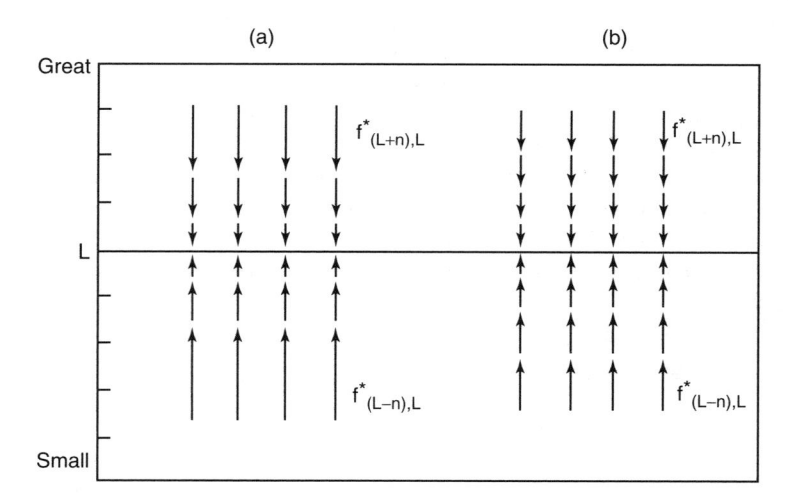

Figure 5 Gradients of resultant forces (f*): (a) Relatively steep gradient, (b) Relatively flat gradient.

Force field within and beyond the neighborhood range

It is important to realize that a quasistationary process presupposes a central structure of the force field only within a certain neighborhood area of L. The statement (4) does not need to hold for n above or below a certain value. In other words, within a certain range stronger forces are necessary to change the level to a larger extent and a weakening of these forces will lead to a return of the process toward the previous level. If, however, the change has once gone beyond this range n to a level (L ± m), the process might show the tendency to move on and not to return to the previous level. This seems to be typical for revolutions after they have once overcome the initial resistance. In regard to the force field, this means that beyond the "neighborhood range" of L the resultant forces are directed away rather than toward L (Fig. 6).

It is obvious that for most problems of management the width of the range in which the process has the character of a stationary equilibrium is of prime importance. This is equally fundamental for the prevention of major managerial catastrophes and for bringing about a desired permanent change.

The effect of various gradients

Before referring to empirical examples let us mention certain additional analytic conclusions. Statement (4) characterizes the structure of the neighboring force field but its gradient is not yet characterized. It might be more or less steep (Fig. 5a and b). The gradient can be different above and below L.

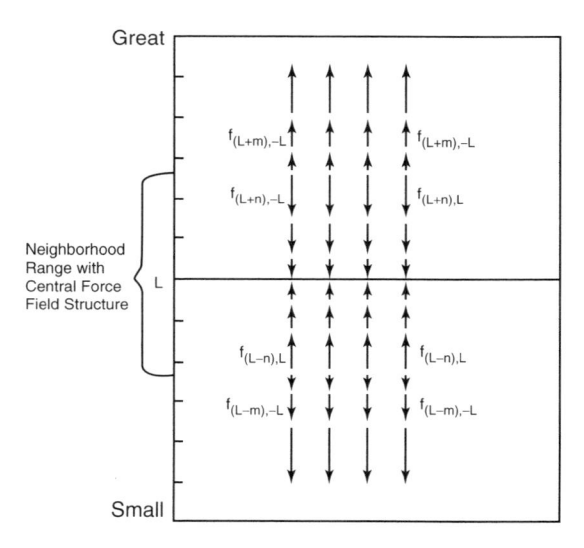

Figure 6 Limits of neighborhood range, showing opposite gradients outside neighborhood range.

(5) Given the same amount of change of the strength of the resultant force ($f^*_{L,x}$), the amount of change of the level of social process will be the smaller, the steeper the gradient.

This holds for permanent changes of L as well as for periodical fluctuations. We have thus far referred to the conduct of the group as a whole. If we consider individual differences within a group we may state:

(6) *Ceteris peribus,* individual differences of conduct in a group will be smaller the steeper the gradient of the resultant force field in the neighborhood of the group level.

Situations of different degrees of permissiveness can be viewed as examples of different steepnesses of the gradient affecting the individuals within a group. The greater range of activities permitted by the democratic leader in the experiment of Lippitt and White (22) was paralleled by greater differences of conduct among the individuals in regard to such items as suggestions to leader, out-of-club-field conversation, and attention demands to companions.

It would be important to relate quantitatively the ease of change of the group level as a whole to the individual differences within the group, although we do not expect to find this relation to be simple.

Examples of quasi-stationary equilibrium in different areas of group life

The following examples are not intended to prove the correctness of a theory for the given case. They are intended mainly to illustrate principles and to prepare the way for the quantitative measurement of social forces. In regard to the specific case they represent hypotheses which have to be tested experimentally.

In the absence of sufficient data on group experiments to illustrate the various analytical principles which should be discussed we have taken the liberty of using somewhat indiscriminately data concerning groups, populations that do not happen to be groups, and individuals.

Level of aggressiveness in democratic and autocratic atmospheres

Lippitt (21) and Lippitt and White (23) have compared the amount of intermember aggression of the same groups of boys in democratic and autocratic atmospheres. Since the personalities and types of activities were kept constant, the change can be attributed to the different social climate or form of leadership. They found that the group average of intermember aggressiveness in autocracy is either very high or very low; in democracy it is on a more medium level (Fig. 7).

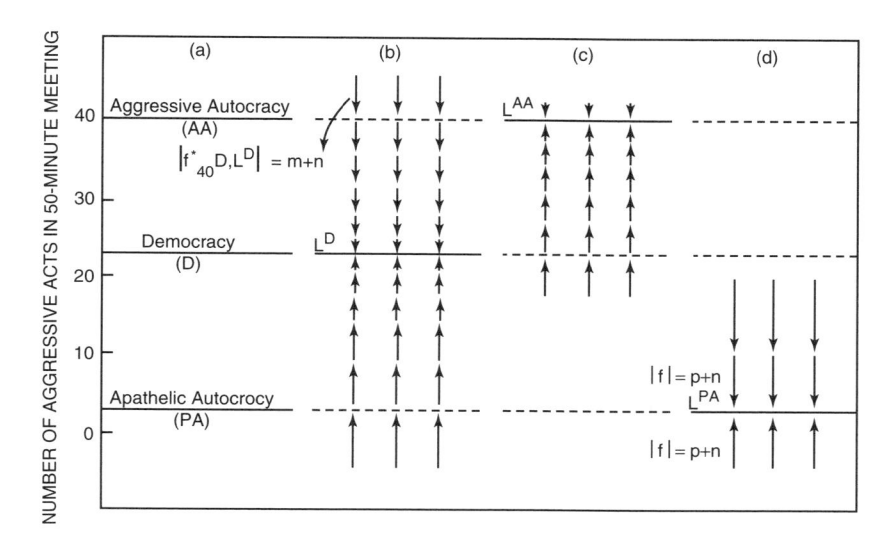

Figure 7 Force fields at the aggressiveness levels for aggressive autocracy, democracy, and apathetic autocracy: (a) Relative Positions of Levels, (b) Levels of democracy, (c) Levels of aggressive autocracy, (d) Levels of apathetic autocracy.

Let us assume that each of these levels of aggressiveness is a quasi-stationary equilibrium, and ask which forces tend to raise and which to lower the level. One factor is the type of activity: a wild game gives more chance for clashes than quiet work; a certain amount of fighting might be fun for boys. Forces against intergroup aggression might be: friendship between members; the presence of an adult leader; the dignified character of the setting.

The actual conduct indicates that in the democratic atmosphere these conflicting forces lead to an equilibrium ($f^*_{L^D,x} = 0$) for $L^D = 23$. This implies a resultant force field of the chracter indicated in Fig. 7b.

If we use the force field in the democratic atmosphere as our base for comparison, the higher level of aggressiveness in aggressive autocratic (AAGr) ($L^{AA} = 40$) could be explained by an increase in the strength of forces toward more aggression or by a diminishing of the forces toward less aggression. Actually both forces seem to have been altered in autocracy: the style of leadership and the irritation due to the restriction of the space of free movement increases the force toward aggressiveness

$$(|f_{AAGr,g}| > |f_{DGr,g}|);$$

Lippitt found that the we-feeling which tends to decrease intermember aggression is diminished in autocracy

$$(|f_{AAGr,s}| < |f_{DGr,s}|).$$

This would suffice to explain why the level of aggression increases in autocracy ($L^D < L^{AA}$). If there were no other changes involved, we could even derive a statement concerning the gradient of the force field in the democratic situation: if the increase of the force $f_{Gr,g}$ equals m and the decrease of the force $f_{Gr,g}$ equals n, the strength of the resultant force at level 40 would be $|f^*_{40^D, L^D}| = m + n$.

How then can aggressiveness in apathetic autocracy (PA) be low ($L^{PA} = 3$)? Lippitt and White (23) found the we-feeling to be low in both types of autocracy; it is unlikely that the irritating effect of the frustrating autocratic leadership should not exist. We are inclined rather to assume that the autocratic leadership form implies an additional force ($f_{Gr,c}$) which corresponds to the higher degree of authoritarian control and which in these situations has the direction against open aggression.

As a rule we can assume that this force is rather strong and is considerably greater than m + n ($f_{PAGr,c} = p > (m+n)$). This autocratic control would keep open aggression very low in spite of the greater force toward aggressions. Only if this control were, out of one reason or other, sufficiently weakened so that $|f_{Gr,c}| < (m+n)$ would the increased tendency toward aggression come into the open.

From this theory one could conclude: Although the resultant force on the level L^{PA} of apathetic autocracy is of course again zero ($f^*_{L^{PA},x} = O$) the opposing components which make up the resultant forces are greater than in the case of democracy. The strength of this additional component is—compared with that in the democratic situation—*ceteris paribus* equal to the pressure of the autocratic control plus the force due to the difference in we-feeling ($|f| = p + n$). In other words we would expect a *high degree of inner tension existing in apathetic autocracy in spite of its appearance of quietness and order*. This additional tension would correspond to opposing forces of the strength $|f| = p + n$ (Fig. 7d).

Since an autocratic atmosphere is less permissive than the democratic atmosphere one may wonder how a high level of in-group aggression can occur in autocracy. The answer lies in the fact that the restrictive character of autocracy has two contradictory effects: (a) it leads to frustration of the group members and therefore to an increase of $f_{P,g}$ in the direction of more aggression. (b) The control aspect of restriction is equivalent to a restraining force $rf_{\overline{P,g}}$ against in-group aggression. This inner contradiction is inherent in every autocratic situation and is the basis of the higher tension level (Fig. 7d.).

From the point of view of management autocratic leadership is confronted with the task of establishing a restraining force field ($rf_{\overline{P,g}}$) of such strength and gradient that the intensity of open in-group aggression does not rise above a certain level. As a first step toward this end, usually, the autocrat tries to strengthen his operational means of control. Strengthening the police or other means of power corresponds to an increase in the "capacity" to control. If this is actually used for stronger suppression, a higher degree of conflict results. This means that a spiral has been set in motion which leads to increasingly more tension, stronger forces toward aggression and suppression.

There are two ways by which autocratic leaders try to avoid this spiral: (1) Restrictive control creates less frustration or at least less open aggression if the individual accepts "blind obedience to the leader" as a value. Germany and Japan are examples of cultures where this attitude is relatively strong. Hitler systematically tried to decrease $f_{P,g}$ through an "education for discipline" in this sense. (2) The second method of reducing $f_{P,g}$ is based on the fact that the tension resulting from a conflict is dynamically equivalent to a "need." Need satisfaction, in this case open aggression, decreases $f_{P,g}$ at least for a certain time. To permit open aggression, but to channel it in a way which is not dangerous for the autocrat is an old technique of social management for autocratic leaders. Another conclusion from the general theory would be that, if the autocratic control in a case of apathetic autocracy were abandoned, a high degree of open aggression should occur as the result of removal of $f_{Gr,c}$. Replacing the autocratic atmosphere with a democratic or laissez-faire atmosphere is equivalent to such a removal. Indeed Lippitt and White (20) observed marked "boiling over" in the first meeting of transition from apathetic autocracy to laissez-faire or, democracy (Fig. 8). It is in line with the theory that this boiling over went to a higher level in the case of transition to laissez-faire than to democracy since the general degree of control or self-control which counteracts intermember aggression is stronger in democracy than in laissez-faire.

This representation by way of a phase space takes into account only certain aspects of the actual processes in the social field. For instance, if authoritarian control weakens to the point of permitting open intermember aggression, this

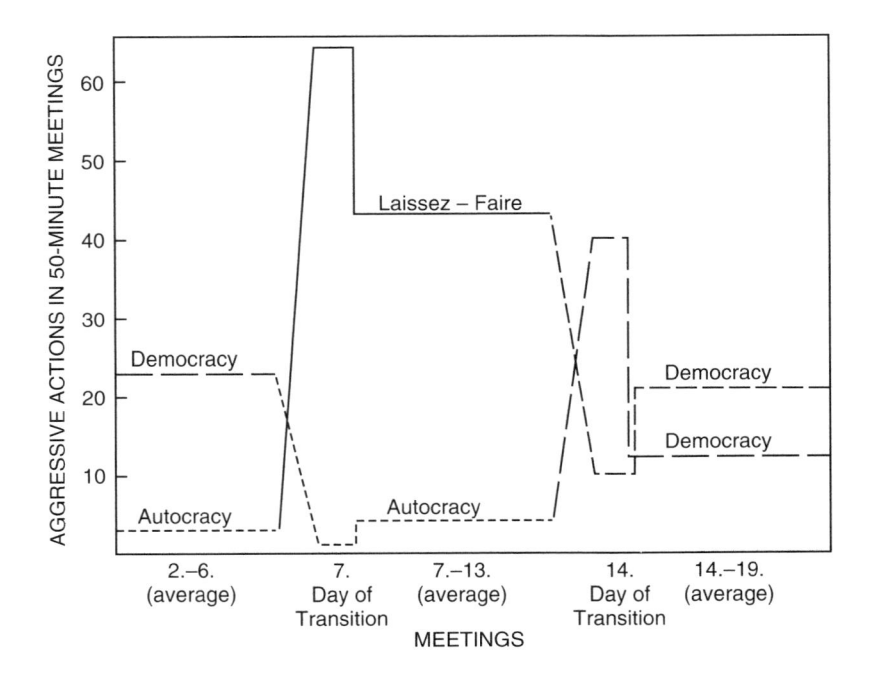

Figure 8 Aggression in two groups of boys.

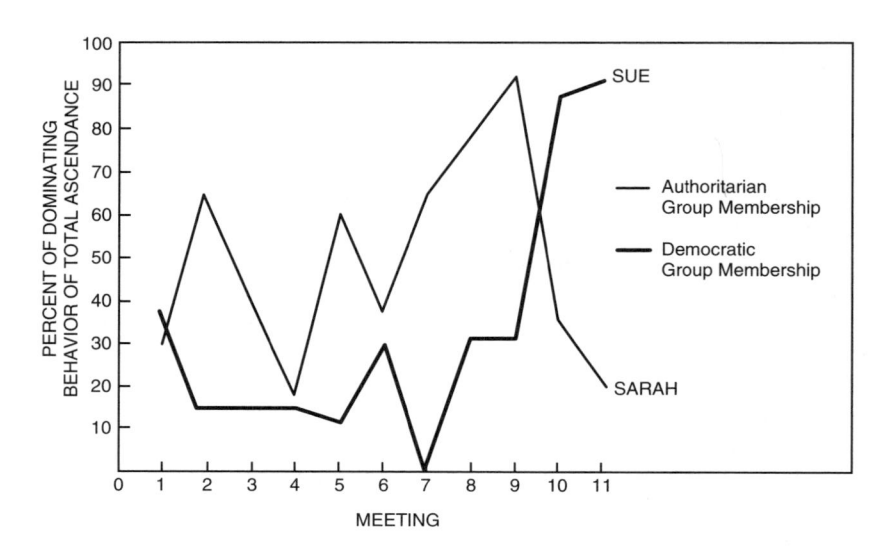

Figure 9 Effect of transfer to a different group.

aggression is likely to weaken still further the level of control (unless the leader is "reacting" to the situation by a heightening of control). These circular causal processes have to be taken into account for prediction.

An atmosphere affecting individual levels of conduct

Figure 9 represents the amount of dominating behavior of a member of an aggressive autocratic group and a member of a democratic group. After an equality at the first meeting, the conduct of the individuals changed in line with the social atmosphere. The two members were changed from one group to the other after the ninth meeting. The fact that after transfer each member rapidly displayed the level of conduct shown by the other member before change, indicates that the strength and the gradient of the resultant force field corresponding to the two atmospheres was approximately the same for both individuals.

Scapegoating and the interdependence of levels of conduct

Data regarding the amount of dominance given and received by individual members of an aggressive autocratic group (Fig. 10 a and b) can serve as an illustration for several general points concerning quasi-stationary processes.

Levels of received hostility as equilibria

It is appropriate to consider such a *passive* property as "being attacked" as a quasi-stationary equilibrium. The amount of aggression received depends partly on the

FRONTIERS IN GROUP DYNAMICS

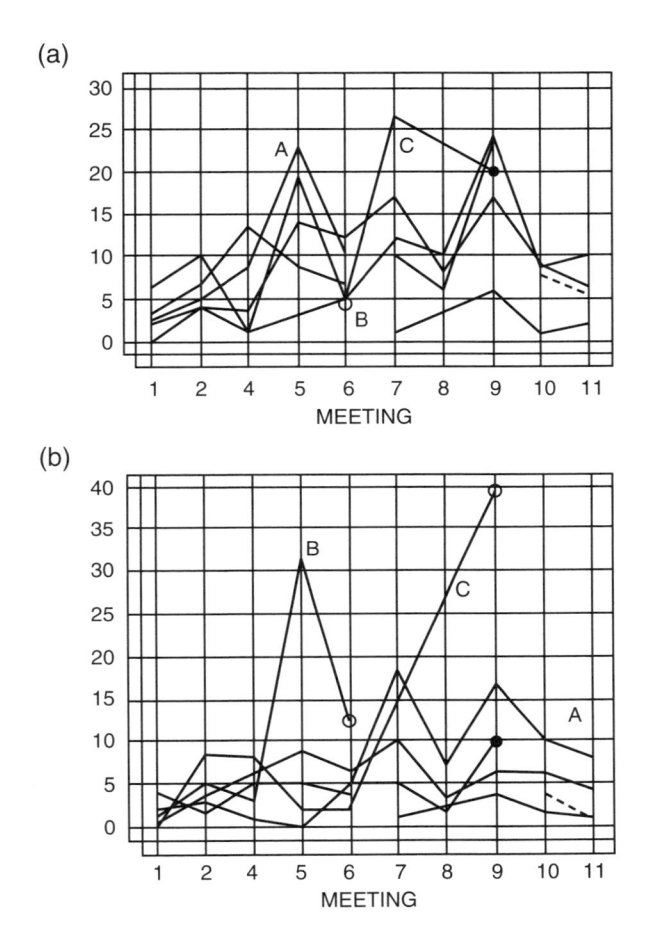

(a)

(b)

Figure 10 (a) Domination dealt out, (b) Domination received.

degree to which the individual provokes or invites aggression and the way he fights or does not fight back. Other factors are the aggressiveness of the other members, the social atmosphere, etc. On the whole then, the constellation is the same as in the forces in other cases of equilibrium: the forces always depend on the characteristics of the group or the individual in question and on his relation to the surroundings

Quitting and the range of the central force field

Scapegoat B (Fig. 10b) quits membership in the club on the sixth day, scapegoat C on the ninth day. These happenings are examples of the general fact that a sufficiently large change of the level of equilibrium leads to a basic change in the character of the total situation: too much received dominance makes the member leave.

One may be tempted to represent the tendency of the individual to leave the club after too much received hostility by means of a central force field with a definite range (see Fig. 6) beyond which the resultant forces are directed away from the level of equilibrium. Such a representation could not indicate, however, that the individual leaves the club since the coordinates of the phase space refer only to time and to the amount of received dominance. To represent this fact one has either to refer to the force constellation in the actual social field or to introduce the degree of "eagerness to belong to the club" as a third dimension of the phase space.

Interaction and circular causal processes

The scapegoats A and B who received much dominating behavior (Fig. 10b) themselves showed much dominating behavior (Fig. 10a). This indicates a close relation between being attacked and attacking. This relation has the character of a circular causal process: the attack of A against B increases B's readiness to attack; the resultant attacks of B raise A's readiness, etc. This would lead to a continuous heightening of the level of equilibrium for A, for B, and for the group as a whole. This holds, however, only within certain limits: if the attack of A is successful B might give in (3). This is another example of the fact that the change of a social process which results from the change of the force field determining the level of equilibrium may in itself effect the total situation in the direction of a further change of the force field. This example can, of course, be regarded as a case of non-equilibrium which corresponds to a constellation of forces away from the present level.

Production in a factory

The output of a factory as a whole or of a work-team frequently shows a relatively constant level of output through an extended period of time. It can be viewed as a quasi-stationary equilibrium. An analysis of the relevant forces is of prime importance for understanding and planning changes.

One of the forces keeping production down is the strain of hard or fast work. There is an upper ceiling for human activity. For many types of work the force away from the strain $f_{P,-st}$ increases faster the closer one comes to the upper limit. The force field has probably a gradient similar to an exponential curve (Fig. 11a).

The common belief views the desire to make more money (f_P, m) as the most important force toward higher production levels. To counter the gradient of the forces $f_{P,-st}$, away from fast work, various incentive systems are used which offer higher rates of pay above a certain standard (Fig. 11b).

Several reasons make it unlikely that the force toward greater output is actually proportional to the unit pay rate in the way indicated in Figure 11b. An increase in earning a certain amount means quite different things to different people.

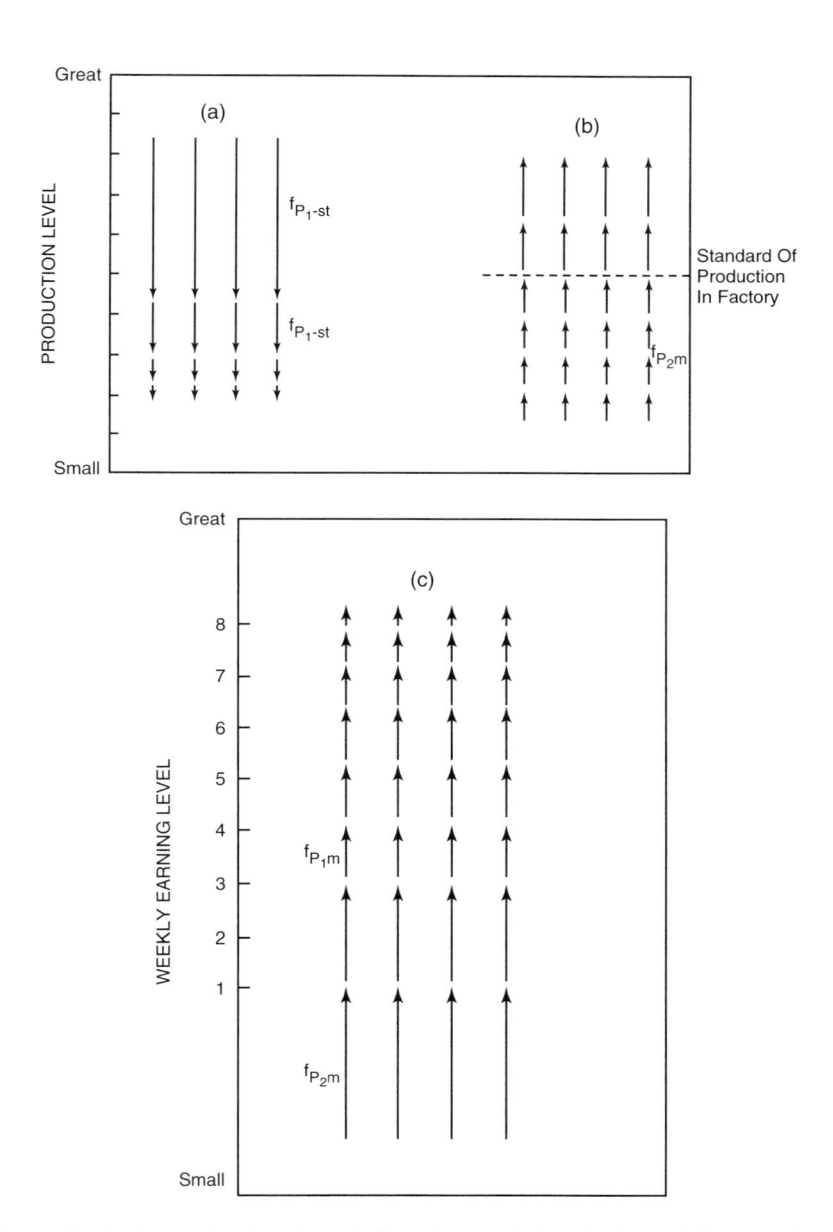

Figure 11 Gradients of certain forces influencing level of production: (a) Forces to lower production attributable to strain-avoidance, (b) Forces to increase production if proportional to money incentive, (c) Gradient of forces toward earning more money.

Some factories which moved from a northern state to the South ten years ago found it impossible for years to reach a level of production which was at all comparable to that of northern workers. One of the reasons was the fact that for the rural southern girls the weekly pay was so much above previous living standards that they did not care to make more money even for a relatively small additional effort.

The relation between the total amount of earnings and the strength and gradient of the force field differs with the sub-culture of the group. One fairly common pattern corresponds to Fig. 11c. A sufficiently low level will lead to a very strong force $f_{P,m}$ toward more income; a sufficiently high level, to a small force toward still higher earnings. In some social groups the units on the scale correspond to ten dollars, in others to a hundred or a thousand dollars. The strength of a force $f_{P,m}$ corresponding to an incentive will depend therefore upon the general "living standards" of the group.

In team work one of the strongest forces is the desire to remain not too far above or below the rest of the group. This holds particularly between "parallel workers" or "friends" in an assembly line (27). An important force against increase of speed may be the fear that a temporary increase of speed would bring about pressure from the supervisor or foreman permanently to keep up the higher speed.

Figure 12 presents data from experiments carried out by Bavelas. The output of the sewing factory as a whole, of the experimental population, and of a control population has a typical quasi-stationary character. After the introduction of pacing cards or group decision the experimental groups show a marked increase to a new level of equilibrium. We will not discuss here the details of the methods used.

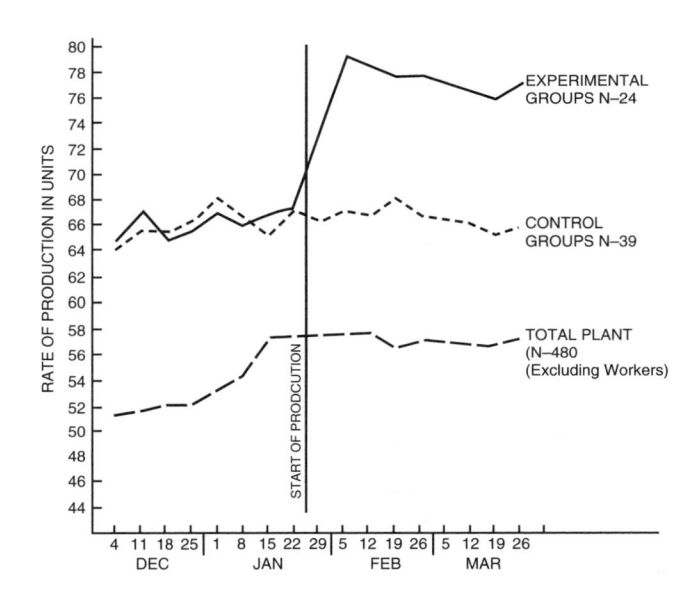

Figure 12 Effect of group decision and pacing cards in a sewing factory.

They seem to be based at least in part on procedures which reduce the forces which tend to keep production down rather than on procedures which add new forces toward higher levels.

Two basic methods of changing levels of conduct

It is of great practical importance for any type of social management that production levels are quasi-stationary equilibria which can be changed either by adding forces in the desired direction or by diminishing opposing forces.

(7) If a change from the level L^1 (Fig. 13a) to L^2 is brought about by increasing the forces toward L^2 (Fig. 13b) the secondary effects should be different from the case where the same change of level is brought about by diminishing the opposing forces (Fig. 13c). In the first case, the process on the new level L^2 would be accompanied by a state of relatively high tension, in the second case by a state of relatively low tension.

Since increase of tension above a certain degree goes parallel with greater fatigue, higher aggressiveness, higher emotionality, and lower constructiveness it is clear that as a rule the second method will be preferable to the high pressure method. (For details about the relation between productivity and tension see Barker, Dembo and Lewin (2).)

Figure 14 offers a striking example of the production of a "nervous" worker which is in line with these considerations. Her average level was above the average of the group; she showed, however, extreme variations in speed and

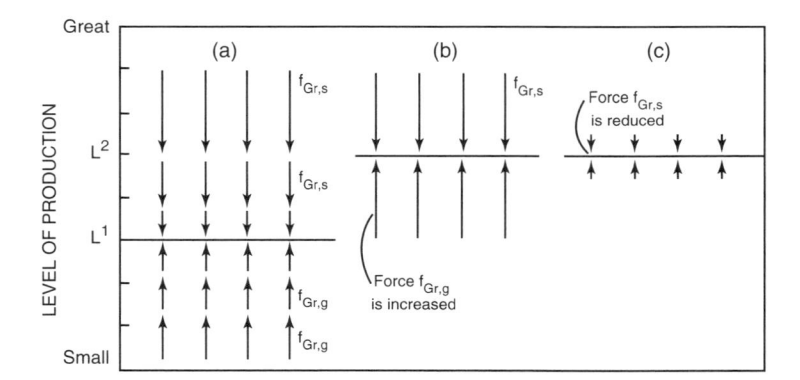

Figure 13 Quasi-stationary equilibria before and after changing levels of production, showing two possible states of tension at the new level: (a) Before changing level of production, (b) After changing production level through strengthening forces toward higher production, (c) After changing production level through reducing forces toward lower production.

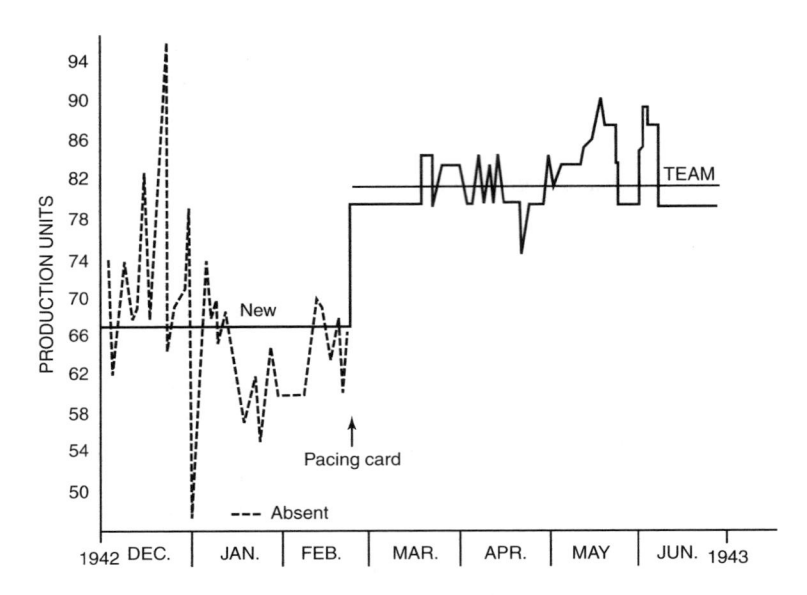

Figure 14 Effect of pacing cards on stability of production.

frequent absenteeism. The use of pacing cards led to an increase in production to an exceptionally high level. At the same time, the fluctuation diminished markedly.

Since restlessness is a common symptom of tension we may assume the greater constancy and the lack of absenteeism to be an expression of the fact that the change of the level of production was accomplished through a change in the force field corresponding to the pattern 13c rather than 13b.

Capacity, learning curves and equilibria

Ability, difficulty and change of difficulty

One factor which affects the level of many social events is "ability." Ability is a popular term which refers to a multitude of very different facts such as the ability to speak French and the ability to take a beating. Nevertheless, in regard to changes the term ability seems to imply a reference to restraining rather than driving forces. Driving forces—corresponding, for instance, to ambition, goals needs or fears—are "forces toward" ($f_{P,s}$) something or "forces away from" something ($f_{P,s}$). They tend to bring about locomotion or changes (14). A "restraining force" is not in itself equivalent to a tendency to change; it merely opposes driving forces, ($rf_{\overline{P,s}}$ means a restraining force opposite to a force $f_{P,s}$; $rf_{\overline{P,-s}}$ is a restraining force opposing $f_{P,-s}$).

A change in ability is equivalent to a change in the "difficulty of a task." Indeed, for the representation as forces in a phase space, both are identical. Always we

FRONTIERS IN GROUP DYNAMICS

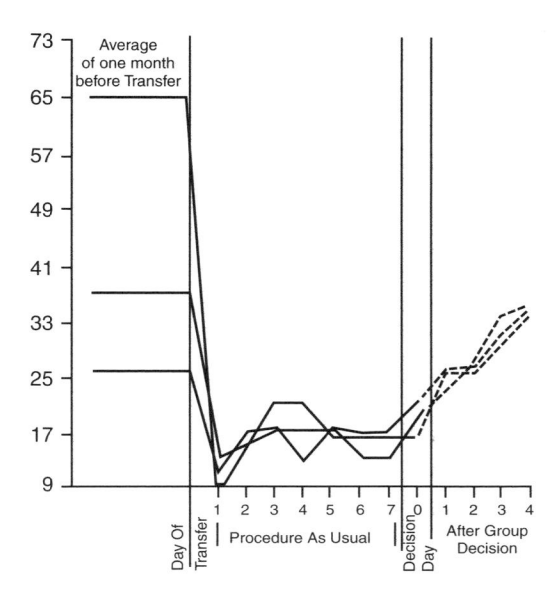

Figure 15 Effect of group decision on slow workers after transfer (double needle machine).

deal with a relation between an individual or group and a task. The term ability or the term difficulty is used according to whether one views the subject or the activity as the variable in this relation.

Figure 15 shows the drop in work output after a worker is transferred—on the same sewing machine—to a different sewing job (5). Although for the two jobs the learning curve of newcomers and the production level of old hands are equal on the average indicating equal difficulty of the two jobs, transferred workers were found to do less well on the new job. For a transferred worker obviously, the new task is more difficult than the previous one.

Let us assume that the resultant force field (of the driving and restraining forces) before transfer corresponds to the central field represented in Fig. 16a. Introducing the new task is equivalent to introducing a stronger restraining force or indeed to adding a field of restraining forces against higher output.

If the transfer to the new job were to leave the force field otherwise unchanged we could make the following conclusion (Fig. 16a and b): the strength of the added restraining force on the second (lower) level L^2 at the time b($\mathrm{rf}_{\overline{L^2,g}})^b$ equal the strength of the resultant driving force existing on the level L^2 at the time a before the change ($|\mathrm{rf}_{\overline{L^2,g}}|^b = |f^*_{L^2,g}|^a$). This would mean that the lowering of the output would be accompanied by an increase in tension.

This is but another example for the theorem: that a change brought about by adding forces in its direction leads to an increase in tension. (In the previous case we had applied this theorem to a change upwards, this time to a change downwards).

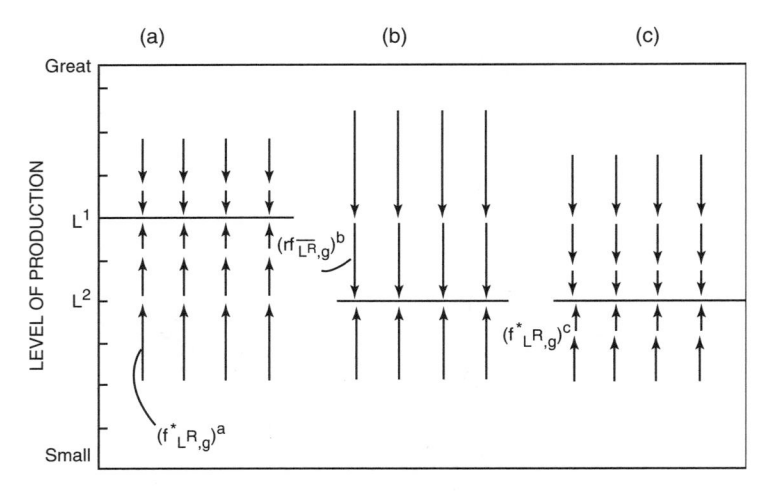

Figure 16 (a) Force field before transfer to new job, (b) Force field after transfer if only restraining forces are added, (c) Force field after transfer if driving force $f_{L^2,g}$ is diminished.

This conclusion, however, is not in line with observations. Actually, the tension after transfer seemed lower, indicating that the change to the lower production level was accompanied by a decrease in the strength of the driving forces toward higher production (Fig. 16c):

$$|f^*_{L^2,g}|^c < |f^*_{L^2,g}|^a$$

There are indications that the transfer in these cases is indeed accompanied by a marked lowering of work moral in the sense of drive to higher production. If this interpretation is correct, learning after transfer should be slow, and indeed it is astonishingly slow (Fig. 15). Although these workers are familiar with the machines, their speed improves so slowly that it is more profitable for the factory to hire new workers than to change the job of experienced workers.

Probably, several factors combine to decrease the force $f_{L^2,g}$ after transfer: a worker in good standing who is proud of his achievement is thrown back into a state of low working status. This is likely to affect his moral and eagerness. The goal of working at a level "above standard" has been a realistic possibility before transfer; now it is "too" high, it is out of reach. The studies on level of aspiration (18) have shown that under these circumstances a person tends to "give up." This would explain the decrease in $f_{L^2,g}$. After group decision the learning curve rises, probably because the setting up of new goals brings about a resultant force toward higher levels without which learning may not take place (15).

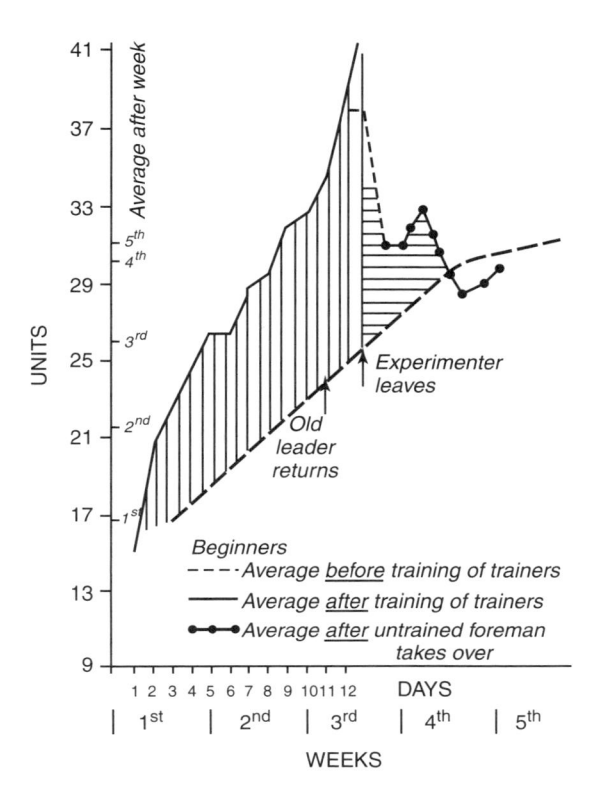

Figure 17 Training of beginners (all stitching machines).

Learning curves as base line for equilibria considerations

There are circumstances under which equilibria must be related to a base line defined in other than absolute values. Bavelas gave special training to a person in charge of training beginners in a factory (5). This led to a considerable steepening of the learning curves of the beginners (Fig. 17). After a few weeks when the specially trained trainer was withdrawn and replaced by the previously employed trainer, the learning curve promptly returned to the level it would have had without the training of the trainer. This and other cases make it probable that under certain circumstances a learning curve can be treated as the base line, that is, a line of "equal level" for determining of force fields.

The inclusion of the learning curve as a possible base could be interpreted as an expression of a general principle:

(8) Social forces should be analyzed on the basis of the relation between social processes and the ability (capacity) of the group (or individual) concerned.

If one accepts this general principle, the treatment of "absolute" standards of processes (height of production, of friendliness, etc.), as the frame of reference for analyzing the forces which determine quasi-stationary equilibria is permissible only if the capacities of the groups concerned do not change during that period.

The combination of "subjective" and "objective" methods

To determine the nature of the forces which are the main variables in a given case a great variety of procedures can be used. An analysis of both the cognitive ("subjective") and behavioral ("objective") aspects of group life requires a combination of methods which lays open the subjective aspects and permits conclusions concerning conduct which can be checked. An example may illustrate the principle involved.

The Division of Program Surveys of the United States Department of Agriculture during the war carried out for the Treasury Department periodic studies of motivation for buying and redeeming war bonds. Interviews indicated the nature of some of the forces toward and away from redemption for individuals in various sections of the population.

The force toward redemption most frequently encountered was found to be financial pressure resulting from an actual emergency like sickness. Forces against redemption were the need for security which is provided by a financial reserve, patriotism, or gaining a higher interest return if bonds are kept longer.

To relate the "subjective" data about the nature of the forces to the curves representing equilibria, such "objective" data as the "capacity" of a population to redeem war bonds, has to be taken into account. Since this capacity depends upon the total amount of war bonds outstanding, it is appropriate according to theorem (8) to base considerations of forces on curves which represent levels of redemption as percentages of this total.

Pearl Harbor, the official entrance of the United States in the war, was accompanied by a marked decline in the level of redemption. From interviews with the population it appears that this is due to an increase of a force against redemption (rather than a decrease of the forces for redemption), namely, a heightened patriotism. From this explanation one would expect that at the end of the war an opposite change would occur. Indeed, Fig. 18 shows an increase of the level of redemption at that time; it can be understood in part as the result of the diminished patriotic motive.

On the whole redemption during the periods from April, 1943, to September, 1944, from October, 1944, to July, 1945, and from August, 1945, to April, 1946, seem to represent three levels of a quasi-stationary process, each period showing typical periodic fluctuations. The change from the first to the second level coincides with the establishing of an easier redemption policy by the

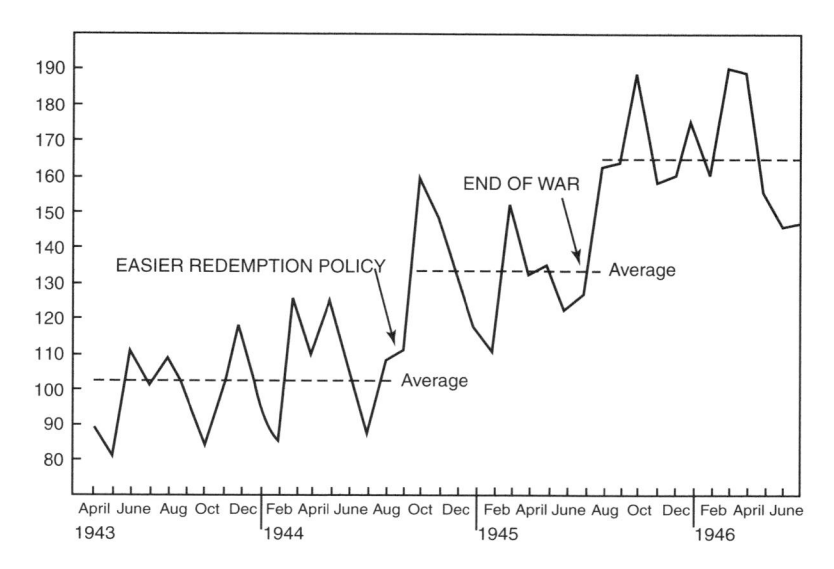

Figure 18 E – bond redemptions as percent of total outstanding.

Treasury Department corresponding to a decrease of the restraining forces against redemption.

The creation of permanent changes

Change of force fields

In discussing the means of bringing about a desired state of affairs one should not think in terms of the "goal to be reached" but rather in terms of a change "from the present level to the desired one." The discussion thus far implies that a planned change consists of transplanting the force field corresponding to an equilibrium at the beginning level L^1 by a force field having its equilibrium at the desired level L^2. It should be emphasized that the total force field has to be changed at least in the area between L^1 and L^2.

The techniques of changing a force field cannot be fully deduced from the representation in the phase space. To change the level of velocity of a river its bed has to be narrowed down or widened, rectified, cleared from rocks, etc. To decide how best to bring about such an actual change, it does not suffice to consider one property. The total circumstances have to be examined. For changing a social equilibrium, too, one has to consider the total social field: the groups and subgroups involved, their relations, their value systems, etc. The constellation of the social field as a whole has to be studied and so reorganized that social events flow differently. The analysis by way of phase space indicates more what type of effect has to be accomplished than how this can be achieved.

Quasi-stationary processes and social "habits"

Influencing a population to make a change such as substituting the consumption of dark bread for white bread means trying to break a well-established "custom" or "social habit." Social habits usually are conceived of as obstacles to change. What does a social habit mean in terms of force fields and what does "breaking of a habit" mean?

If one regards a social stationary process as determined by a quasi-stationary equilibrium one will expect any added force to change the level. We know that the resultant force on a present level L is zero ($f^*_{L,x} = 0$). Adding the force $|f_{L,n}| > 0$ should move the level in the direction of n to a different level $(L + \Delta)$. The amount of change Δ is determined by the equation

$$|f^*(L+\Delta), L| = |f_{L,n}| \tag{5}$$

The idea of "social habit" seems to imply that in spite of the application of a force $f_{L,n}$ the level of the social process will change less than Δ because of some type of "inner resistance" to change. To overcome this inner resistance an additional force seems to be required, a force sufficient to "break the habit," to "unfreeze" the custom.

One could try to deny the existence of such "inner resistance to change" out of social habit.[3] Perhaps social habits merely refer to cases of such steep gradient that adding the force $f_{L,n}$ does not lead to a perceivable change. Such an interpretation hardly suffices. At best, it transforms the problem of habit into the question, why does the resultant force field show such a steep gradient in the immediate neighborhood of L.

The social habit theory answers that the historic constancy creates an "additional force field" which tends to keep up the present level in addition to whatever other forces are keeping the social process at that level. Two statements are implied in such a theory; one asserting the existence of the "additional force field," the other regarding its historical origin. We are here interested mainly in the nature of the additional force field.

Social life proceeding on a certain level leads frequently to the establishment of organizational institutions. They become equivalent to "vested interests" in a certain social level. A second possible source of social habits is related to the value system, the ethos of a group. We shall discuss this in more detail.

Individual conduct and group standards

In discussing force fields we have viewed as "point of application" of the force either an individual or a group as a whole. Let us now consider the relation between the individual and the level of social processes.

An individual P may differ in his personal level of conduct (L^P) from the level which represents group standards (L^{Gr}) by a certain amount n ($|L^{Gr} - L^P| = n$). Such a difference is permitted or encouraged in different cultures to different degrees. If the individual should try to diverge "too much" from group standards he will find himself in increasing difficulties. He will be ridiculed, treated severely and finally ousted from the group. Most individuals, therefore, stay pretty close to the standard of the groups they belong to or wish to belong to.

In other words: the group level is not merely a level of equilibrium resulting from whatever forces $f_{L,g}$ and $f_{L,s}$ the circumstances provide. Frequently this level itself acquires value. It becomes a positive valence corresponding to a central force field with the force $f_{P,L}$ keeping the individual in line with the standards of the group.

Group levels with and without social value and the resistance to change

Although the value character of a group level is rather common, it does not hold for all types of processes. For instance, few individuals know that the level of redemption of war bonds between April, 1943, and August, 1944, was about one per cent. The values which entered into the decisions to redeem did not include the value of keeping the rate of redemption neither above nor below that level. In this respect, the situation is quite different, for instance, from the situation of an individual who tries to keep up with a working team.

Whatever the reason that a certain level acquires or does not acquire value, the difference is important for the problem of change.

Let us assume that for two groups Gr and Gr[1] the resultant force field corresponds to Fig. 19b if we do not take into account the social value of L. In the case of Gr[1], but not in the case of Gr, the level L should have social value for the members; it should correspond to the force field represented in Fig. 19a. Let us assume that a force f were applied on the individual to change his conduct towards g. In Gr[1] the amount of change will be determined by the gradient of the counter-force $f_{(L+n),g}$, in Gr by the combined counter-forces $f_{(L+n),g} + f_{P,L}$ (Fig. 19c). This means:

(10) The greater the social value of a group standard the greater is the resistance of the individual group member to move away from this level.

Many cases of "social habit" seem to refer to group standards with social value and resistance to change can frequently be explained through theorem (10). If this theory is correct certain derivations can be made in regard to the breaking of social habits.

Individual procedures and group procedures of changing social conduct

If the resistance to change depends partly on the value of the group standard for the individual, the resistance to change should be diminished if one uses a procedure which diminishes the strength of the value of the group standard or which changes the level that is perceived by the individual as having social value.

ENHANCING PERFORMANCE IN ORGANIZATIONS

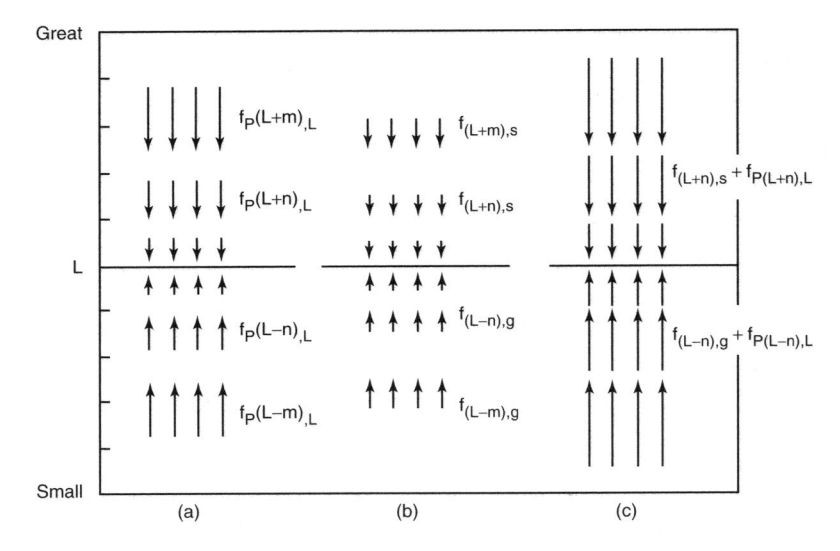

Figure 19 Force fields if the group standard does and does not have social value: (a) Forces on the individual corresponding to the valence of the group standard, (b) Forces on the group standard toward a lower or higher level, (c) Forces field resulting from summation of a. and b.

This second point is one of the reasons for the effectiveness of "group carried" changes (26) which approach the individuals in face-to-face groups. Perhaps one might expect single individuals to be more plyable than groups of like-minded individuals. However, experience in leadership training, in changing of food habits, work production, criminality, alcoholism, prejudices, all seem to indicate that it is usually easier to change individuals formed into a group than to change any one of them separately (19). As long as group values are unchanged the individual will resist changes more strongly the farther he is to depart from group standards. If the group standard itself is changed, the resistance which is due to the relation between individual and group standard is eliminated.

Changing as three steps: unfreezing, moving, and freezing of group standards

A change toward a higher level of group performance is frequently short lived; after a "shot in the arm," group life soon returns to the previous level. This indicates that it does not suffice to define the objective of a planned change in group performance as the reaching of a different level. Permanency of the new level, or permanency for a desired period, should be included in the objective. A successful change includes therefore three aspects: unfreezing (if necessary) the present level L^1, moving to the new level L^2, and freezing group life on the new level. Since any level is determined by a force field, permanency implies that the new force field is made relatively secure against change.

The "unfreezing" of the present level may involve quite different problems in different cases. Allport (1) has described the "catharsis" which seems to be necessary before prejudices can be removed. To break open the shell of complacency and self-righteousness it is sometimes necessary to bring about deliberately an emotional stir-up.

The same holds for the problem of freezing the new level. Sometimes it is possible to establish an organizational set up which is equivalent to a stable circular causal process.

Group decision as a change procedure

The following example of a process of group decision concerns housewives living in a Midwestern town some of whom were exposed to a good lecture about the value of greater consumption of fresh milk and some of whom were involved in a discussion leading step by step to the decision to increase milk consumption (9.25). No high-pressure salesmanship was applied, in fact pressure was carefully avoided. The amount of time used was equal in the two groups. The change in milk consumption was checked after two and four weeks. Figure 20 indicates the superiority of group decision. Similar results were found in regard to evaporated milk.

The effect of individual treatment was compared with the effect of group decision among farm women who had come to the maternity ward of the State Hospital of Iowa. Before their release they received individual instruction concerning the proper formula for feeding babies and the advisability of giving them orange juice and cod liver oil. This procedure was compared with a procedure of discussion

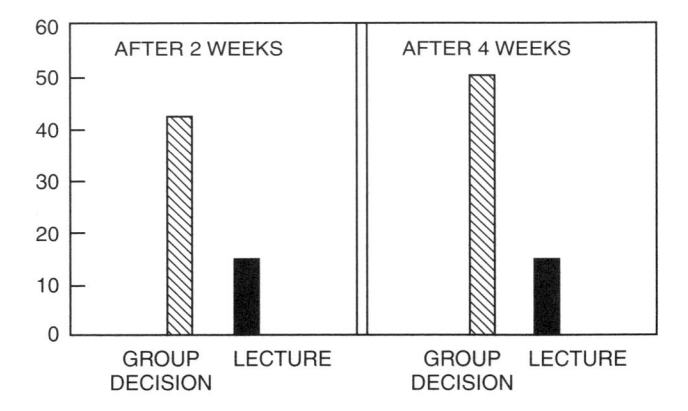

Figure 20 Percentage of mothers reporting an increase in the consumption of fresh milk.

ENHANCING PERFORMANCE IN ORGANIZATIONS

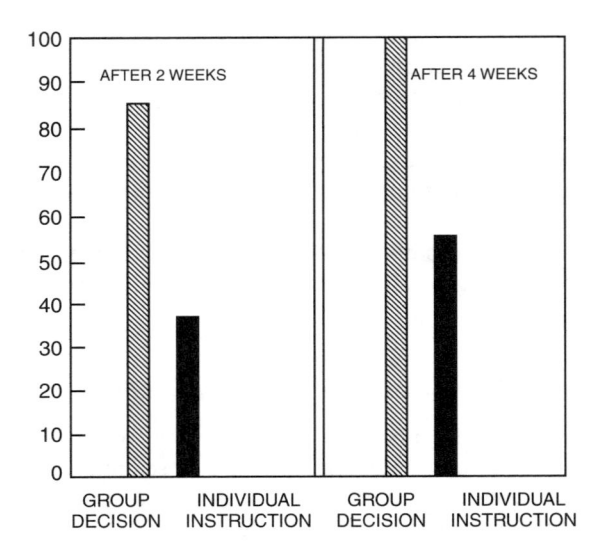

Figure 21 Percentage of mothers following completely group decision or individual instruction in giving orange juice.

and decision carried out with six mothers as a group. In the first case the nutritionist devoted about twenty-five minutes to a single mother, in the second the same amount of time to a group of six mothers.

Figure 21 shows the superiority of the group decision procedure. At four weeks every one of the mothers in the decision group was giving to the baby the advised amount of cod liver oil. Surprisingly, after both procedures there is an improvement between the second and fourth weeks. Figure 22 presents an example of the effect of three group decisions of a team in a factory reported by Bavelas (24) which illustrates an unusually good case of permanency of change measured over nine months.

The experiments reported here cover but a few of the necessary variations. Although in some cases the procedure is relatively easily executed, in others it requires skill and presupposes certain general conditions. Managers rushing into a factory to raise production by group decisions are likely to encounter failure. In social management as in medicine there are no patent medicines and each case demands careful diagnosis. The experiments with group decision are nevertheless sufficiently advanced to clarify some of the general problems of social change.

We have seen that a planned social change may be thought of as composed of unfreezing, change of level, and freezing on the new level. In all three respects group decision has the general advantage of the group procedure.

If one uses individual procedures, the force field which corresponds to the dependence of the individual on a valued standard acts as a resistance to change.

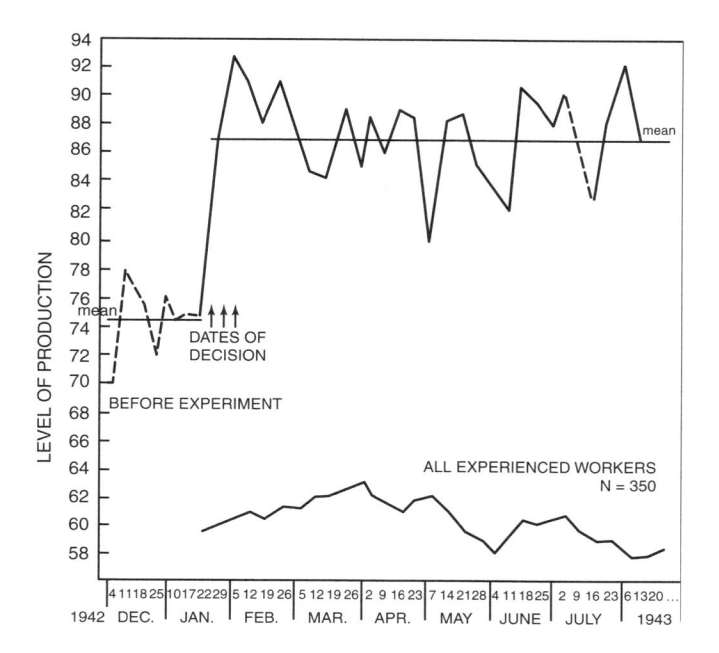

Figure 22 Effect of group decision on sewing machine operators.

If, however, one succeeds in changing group standards, this same force field will tend to facilitate changing the individual and will tend to stabilize the individual conduct on the new group level.

Sometimes the value system of this face-to-face group conflicts with the values of the larger cultural setting and it is necessary to separate the group from the larger setting. For instance, during retraining of recreational leaders from autocratic to democratic patterns Bavelas (4) was careful to safeguard them from interference by the administration of the recreational center. The effectiveness of camps or workshops in changing ideology or conduct depends in part on the possibility of creating such "cultural islands" during change. The stronger the accepted subculture of the workshop and the more isolated it is the more will it minimize that type of resistance to change which is based on the relation between the individual and the standards of the larger group.

One reason why group decision facilitates change is illustrated by Willerman (16). Figure 23 shows the degree of eagerness to have the group change from the consumption of white bread to whole wheat. When the change was simply requested the degree of eagerness varied greatly with the degree of personal preference for whole wheat. In case of group decision the eagerness seems to be relatively independent of personal preference; the individual seems to act mainly as "group member."

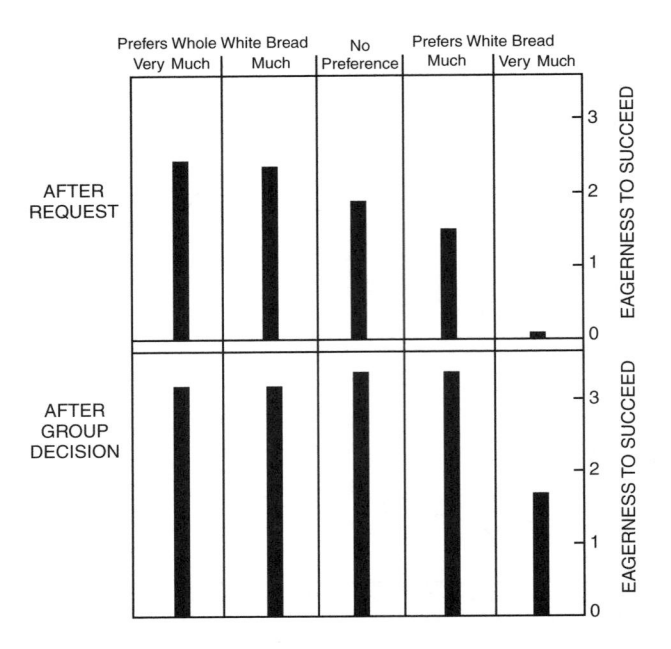

Figure 23 Changing food habits. Relation between own food preferences and eagerness to succeed.

A second factor favoring group decision has to do with the relation between motivation and action. A lecture and particularly a discussion may be quite effective in setting up *motivations* in the desired direction. Motivation alone, however, does not suffice to lead to change. That presupposes a link between motivation and action. This link is provided by the decision but it usually is not provided by lectures or even by discussions. This seems to be, at least in part, the explanation for the otherwise paradoxical fact that a process like decision which takes only a few minutes is able to affect conduct for many months to come. The decision links motivation to action and, at the same time, seems to have a "freezing" effect which is partly due to the individual's tendency to "stick to his decision" and partly to the "commitment to a group." The importance of the second factor would be different for a students' cooperative where the individuals remain together, for housewives from the same block who see each other once in a while and for farm mothers who are not in contact with each other. The experiments show, however, that even decisions concerning individual achievement can be effective which are made in a group setting of persons who do not see each other again.

It would be incorrect to attribute the permanence of the new level entirely to the freezing effect of the decision. In many cases other factors are probably more important. After the housewife has decided to use more milk she might place a standing order with the milkman which could automatically keep milk consumption high. These questions lead to problems of reconstructurization of the social field, particularly to problems of channeling social processes.

Many aspects of social life can be viewed as quasi-stationary processes. They can be regarded as states of a quasi-stationary equilibrium in the precise meaning of a constellation of forces the structure of which can be well defined. These forces have to be identified and will have to be measured quantitatively. A sufficient conceptual analysis is a prerequisite to this step.

The scientific treatment of social forces presupposes analytic devices which are adequate to the nature of social processes and which are technically fitted to serve as a bridge to a mathematical treatment. The basic means to this end is the representation of social situations as "social fields." Some aspects of social processes can be treated by way of systems of coordinates called "phase space."

The use of a phase space for treating a social equilibrium makes it necessary to clarify certain technical questions of analysis, such as the relation between the strength of the opposing forces at a given level of the process, the structure of the force field inside and outside of the neighboring range, the formal conditions of fluctuation and of individual differences, the relation between forces and capacities, and the relation between forces and tension.

This technical analysis makes it possible to formulate in a more exact way problems of planned social changes and of resistance to change. It permits general statements concerning some aspects of the problem of selecting specific objectives in bringing about change, concerning different methods of bringing about the same amount of change, and concerning differences in the secondary effects of these methods. A theory emerges that one of the causes of resistance to change lies in the relation between the individual and the value of group standards. This theory permits conclusions concerning the resistance of certain types of social equilibria to change, the unfreezing, moving, and freezing of a level, and the effectiveness of group procedures for changing attitudes or conduct.

The analytic tools used are equally applicable to cultural, economic, sociological and psychological aspects of group life. They fit a great variety of processes such as production levels of a factory, a work-team and an individual worker; changes of abilities of an individual and of capacities of a country; group standards with and without cultural value; activities of one group and the interaction between groups, between individuals, and between individuals and groups. The analysis concedes equal reality to all aspects of group life and to social units of all sizes. The application depends upon the structural properties of the process and of the total situation in which it takes place.

Our consideration of quasi-stationary equilibrium has been based on analytic concepts which, within the realm of social sciences, have emerged first in psychology. The concepts of a psychological force, of tension, of conflicts as equilibria of forces, of force fields and of inducing fields, have slowly widened their range of application from the realm of individual psychology into the realm of processes and events which had been the domain of sociology and cultural anthropology. From what I have been able to learn recently about the treatment of equilibria by mathematical economics, I am convinced that this treatment, although having a different origin and being based perhaps on a different philosophy, is also fully compatible with our considerations.

The ease of quantitatively measuring economic data on the one hand, and the disturbing qualitative richness of psychological and cultural events on the other has tended to keep the methods of investigating these areas separated. Perhaps, this situation has driven some mathematical economists into an attempt to develop an economics without people and without culture, much in the way that some mathematically inclined psychologists have tried to develop a theory of learning without organisms (12). It is possible, however, to leave the philosophical interpretation in abeyance and to regard the equations of mathematical economics as a treatment of certain aspects of events which are methodologically similar to our treatment of certain aspects of social processes by way of phase spaces; in both cases one has to realize that for prediction it is necessary to refer finally to the total social field with all its essential properties. If one is conscious of the limitation of the separate analytic treatment of certain aspects of the social field, this treatment is a useful and indeed necessary step.

Certainly, mathematical economics has developed powerful analytic tools for treating some basic aspects of group life. If our considerations are correct they mean that it is possible to join hands with mathematical economics and I see no reason why, for instance, the methods of treating economic equilibria (8, 11, 28) or the treatment of the grouping in competitive constellations (30) cannot be applied to other areas of social life.

The analytic tools of mathematical economics should be of great help for carrying through the task of measuring social forces, a task which thus far has been accomplished only in a limited area of individual psychology (6). This task implies three steps; a sufficient development of analytical concepts and theories concerning social forces, their quantification in principle through equations, and measuring concrete cases. It seems that the first step in the treatment of group life has sufficiently progressed to permit a collaboration of the various branches of the social sciences for the second and third task.

For economics the fusion implies the possibility of taking into account the cultural and psychological properties of the population involved and, therefore, of improving greatly the ability of analyzing concrete cases and making correct predictions. Economics will have to be ready to complicate its analytic procedures at certain points, particularly it will have to recognize the cognitive problems mentioned in Section B in the discussion of the three step procedure.

The fusion of the social sciences will make accessible to economics the vast advantages which the experimental procedure offers for testing theories and for developing new insight. The combination of experimental and mathematical procedures has been the main vehicle for the integration of the study of light, of electricity, and of the other branches of physical science. The same combination seems to be destined to make the integration of the social sciences a reality.

Notes

1. The notation of forces follows on the whole the notation I have used for psychological problems (14). $f_{P,g}$ means a force acting on the person P in the direction toward g. $f_{P,-g}$ indicates a force on P in the direction away from g. $rf_{\overline{P,g}}$ is a restraining force against P's moving toward g. $f^*_{P,g}$ means a resultant force which has the direction toward g. The strength of the force $f_{P,g}$ is indicated by $|f_{P,g}|$.

   If not the individual P but a group Gr is viewed as the point of application of the force, a force toward g is indicated as $f_{Gr,g}$ away from g as $f_{Gr,-g}$. To refer to forces acting on different groups A or group B, or on the same group in different positions A and B, we will use the notation $f_{Gr,A,g}$ and $f_{Gr,Bg}$, or the shorter notation $f_{A,g}$ and $f_{B,g}$. The reader should keep in mind, however, that if we say that a force $f_{A,g}$ exists at a position (or a level) A we mean that a force is acting on a group in the position A or that it would act on the group if the group were in that position. The concept of force field refers to such potential positions.

   A force toward g existing at a given time, n, at a place, A, may be notated as $(f_{A,g})$.

2. A positive central force field is defined as a constellation of forces directed toward one region. In a phase space where one dimension is time, one may use this term for a constellation where all forces are directed toward one level.

3. The concept "habit" has played havoc with the progress of psychology for decades. Today it can be regarded as a popular term referring to a conglomeration of various processes. It is to be exchanged for several more adequate concepts (15).

References

1. Allport, G. W. Catharsis and the reduction of prejudice. In Problems of re-education. *J. Soc. Issues,* August, 1945, 3–10.
2. Barker, R., Dembo, T., and Lewin, K. Frustration and regression: an experiment with young children. *Studies in topological and vector psychology II.* Univ. of Iowa Press, 1941.
3. Bateson, G. *Naven.* Cambridge Univ. Press, 1936.
4. Bavelas, A. Morale and the training of leaders. In *Civilian morale* (G. Watson, Ed.). Houghton Mifflin, 1942.
5. Bavelas, A. Unpublished manuscript.
6. Cartwright, D., and Festinger, L. A quantitative theory of decision. *Psychol. Rev.,* 1943, 50, 595–621.
7. Cassirer, E. *Substance and function.* (Tr. by W. C. and M. C. Swabey). Chicago and London: Open Court, 1923.
8. Hicks, J. R. *Value and capital.* Oxford: Clarendon Press, 1939.
9. Klisurich, D. Concepts and sanctions related to milk. Unpublished Master's Thesis deposited in the Library of the State Univ. of Iowa, 1944.
10. Köhler, W. *The place of value in a world of fact.* New York: Liveright, 1938.
11. Lange, O. *Price flexibility and employment.* Univ. of Chicago Press, 1945.
12. Leeper, R. W. *Lewin's topological and vector psychology.* Eugene, Oregon: Univ. of Oregon Press, 1943.
13. Lewin, K. *A dynamic theory of personality.* (Tr. by D. Adams and K. Zener). New York: McGraw-Hill, 1935.
14. Lewin, K. The conceptual representation and the measurement of psychological forces. *Contributions to psychological theory,* Vol. I, No. 4. Duke Univ. Press, 1938.

15. Lewin, K. Field theory of learning. In *The psychology of learning* (H. B. Nelson, Ed.). Forty-first yearbook of the Nat. Society for the Study of Education, Part II. Bloomington, Ill: Public School Publishing Co., 1942.
16. Lewin, K. Forces behind food habits and methods of change. *Bulletin of the National Research Council,* 1943, *108,* 35–65.
17. Lewin, K. Action research and minority problems, *J. Soc. Issues,* 1946, *2.*
18. Lewin, K., Dembo, T., Festinger, L., and Sears, P. Level of aspiration. In *Personality and the behavior disorders,* Vol. I. (J. M. Hunt, Ed.). New York: Ronald Press, 1944.
19. Lewin, K., and Grabbe, P. (Ed.). Problems of re-education. *J. Soc. Issues,* August, 1945.
20. Lewin, K., Lippitt, R., and White, R. Patterns of aggressive behavior in experimentally created "social climates." *J. Soc. Psychol.,* 1939, *10,* 271–299.
21. Lippitt, R. An Experimental study of authoritarian and democratic group atmospheres. *Studies in topological and vector psychology I,* Univ. of Iowa Press, 1940.
22. Lippitt, R., and White, R. Unpublished manuscript reported by White at 1938 meetings of the American Psychological Association.
23. Lippitt, R., and White, R. The "social climate" of children's groups. In *Child behavior and development.* (R. Barker, J. Kounin, and B. Wright, Ed.). New York: McGraw-Hill, 1943.
24. Maier, N. *Psychology in industry.* Houghton Mifflin, 1946.
25. Radke, M., and Klisurich, D. Experiments in changing food habits. Unpublished manuscript.
26. Redl, F. Clinical group work with children. In *Group work and the social scene today.* New York: Association Press, 1943.
27. Roethlisberger, F. J., and Dickson, W. J. *Management and the worker.* Cambridge: Harvard Univ. Press, 1939.
28. Samuelson, P. A. The stability of equilibrium: linear and non-linear systems. *Econometrica,* 1942, *10,* 1–25.
29. Tolman, E. C. The determiners of behavior at a choice point. *Psychol. Rev.,* 1938, *45,* 1–41.
30. Von Neumann, J., and Morgenstern, O. *Theory of games and economic behavior,* Princeton Univ. Press, 1944.

42

COGNITION AND CORPORATE GOVERNANCE

Understanding boards of directors as strategic decision-making groups

Daniel P. Forbes and Frances J. Milliken

Source: *Academy of Management Review* 24(8) (1999): 489–505.

Abstract

Recent research developments underscore the need for research on the processes that link board demography with firm performance. In this article we develop a model of board processes by integrating the literature on boards of directors with the literature on group dynamics and workgroup effectiveness. The resulting model illuminates the complexity of board dynamics and paves the way for future empirical research that expands and refines our understanding of what makes boards effective.

Recent reviews of management research on boards of directors (Johnson, Daily, & Ellstrand, 1996; Pettigrew, 1992) have indicated that, although much has been learned, the time is ripe for reflection and for the exploration of new directions in board research. In particular, Pettigrew has observed that in many studies of boards, "Great inferential leaps are made from input variables such as board composition to output variables such as board performance with no direct evidence on the processes and mechanisms which presumably link the inputs to the outputs" (1992: 171). Pettigrew goes on to argue that future research on boards should focus on the actual behavior of boards, thereby supplementing our knowledge of what boards look like with evidence of what boards do.

The importance of studying board behavior directly is underscored by evidence that practitioners—in some cases, boards themselves—are also beginning to pay more attention to what boards do (Lublin, 1997; Schine, 1997). Whereas in previous decades boards of directors could be characterized as essentially formal and passive institutions that seldom came under public scrutiny (Mace, 1971), boards today are increasingly finding their actions closely monitored by institutional investors (Heard, 1987; Judge & Reinhardt, 1997) as well as by the media (Byrne, 1997; Orwall & Lublin, 1997).

Further evidence of interest in board behavior can be seen in the increased level of legal scrutiny to which boards are subjected and in the growing competitiveness of the market for corporate control (Kesner & Johnson, 1990; Monks & Minow, 1995). Moreover, *Business Week* reported recently that the board of Campbell Soup conducted an internal assessment, in which it determined

> that it wasn't devoting enough time to long-range strategic planning; that some colleagues didn't speak up enough in meetings; that the quality of some committee reports needed upgrading; and that the company had to spend more time broadening and diversifying the skills of directors.
> (Byrne, 1996: 98).

It would have been almost unthinkable to encounter such a rigorous self-analysis from one of the characteristically unresponsive boards documented by Mace (1971) almost 30 years ago. In summary, it appears that as boards assume a more central oversight role in the governance of organizations, researchers and practitioners alike are seeking to better understand the processes and behaviors involved in effective board performance.

In addition, recent research developments have reinforced Pettigrew's (1992) point that it is necessary to go beyond the demography-outcome approach in order to understand fully the performance implications of board characteristics. Reviews of the boards literature indicate that the predictive power of parsimonious models has failed to materialize, even in the most well-researched areas (Johnson et al., 1996). Furthermore, research on demography in other contexts has called into question the assumptions that underlie the search for direct demography-performance links (Lawrence, 1997; Melone, 1994). At the same time, other recent studies have demonstrated the superior explanatory power of studies that incorporate the study of process constructs (Amason & Sapienza, 1997; Ancona & Caldwell, 1992; Smith, Smith, Olian, Sims, O'Bannon, & Scully, 1994).

Here, we propose a model of strategic decision-making effectiveness in U.S.-based boards that bridges some of the gaps that currently characterize much theorizing about boards. We begin by considering the factors that characterize boards as decision-making groups and by discussing some criteria that distinguish effective boards from ineffective ones. Then, drawing on the literature on small-group decision making, we define and develop three critical board processes and two board-level outcomes that we believe serve as mediators of the relationships between commonly studied aspects of board demography and firm performance.

Our analysis focuses on the board's control and service tasks, which, to be performed effectively, require that board members cooperate to exchange information, evaluate the merits of competing alternatives, and reach well-reasoned decisions. We acknowledge that, in practice, it is often difficult for boards to do these things and that on many boards the quantity and quality of substantive interaction are, in fact, minimal. However, the very existence of the board as an institution is rooted in the wise belief that the effective oversight of an organization exceeds the capabilities of any individual and that collective knowledge and deliberation are better suited to this task. The processes we discuss are those that enable boards to achieve their full potential as strategic decision-making groups.

In the course of our discussion, we suggest ways of operationalizing the constructs we identify in an effort to guide future empirical research based on our model. We also explain how the processes we identify are likely to be affected by various aspects of board demography, such as job-related diversity and size. Finally, we discuss ways in which the dynamics of boards as groups may differ among boards of different types of organizations.

Theoretical background

Most scholars agree that predictions about the performance implications of demographic variables are presumed to operate through some set of intervening processes. However, there has been debate over whether the direct study of those intervening processes is necessary. Pfeffer (1983), for example, argues that the study of such processes is not necessary, because executives' beliefs and behaviors can be inferred successfully from demographic characteristics. This argument is essentially one of parsimony: as long as research can explain *what* the group- or organization-level impact of demography is, it is not necessary to determine (or one can speculate about) *why* demography operates in the observed way. This is an appealing argument, and it has provided the inspiration for a great many studies of the demography of top management teams (TMTs) and boards of directors. However, recent research findings suggest at least three reasons why the argument for parsimony over precision in the study of board demography is no longer convincing.

First, recent literature reviews have concluded that board research has failed to establish any clear consensus as to which demographic characteristics lead to which outcomes, even in the most well-researched areas (Daily & Schwenk, 1996; Johnson et al., 1996, Zahra & Pearce, 1989). This conclusion suggests that the influence of board demography on firm performance may not be simple and direct, as many past studies presume, but, rather, complex and indirect. To account for this possibility, researchers must begin to explore more precise ways of studying board demography that account for the role of intervening processes.

Second, the assumptions that underlie the search for direct demography-performance links have been shown to be unreliable. Lawrence (1997), for example, conducted an intensive review of past demographic research, precisely for the purpose of evaluating the assumption that it is unnecessary to test the inferences involved in demography-outcome relationships. She found that, in a majority of cases, the explanations offered for demography-outcome relationships are not supported by studies in which researchers have actually examined the intermediary process phenomena. Recent findings by Walsh (1988) and Melone (1994) also dispute the notion that executive beliefs and behaviors can be inferred reliably from demographic variables alone.

Third, scholars have shown that the study of process constructs has the potential to expand and refine our understanding of group dynamics. For example, Smith and colleagues' study of TMTs (1994) showed that firm performance was impacted (1) directly by demographic variables, (2) indirectly by demographic variables operating through process variables, and (3) directly and independently by additional process variables. The identification of independently predictive processes represents an important complement to knowledge about the direct or indirect effects of board demography. Other studies have shown how a single group characteristic can have multiple implications for group performance. For example, Amason and Sapienza's (1997) study of TMTs shows that group size is positively related to both cognitive conflict and affective conflict—two processes generally understood to have opposite effects on the quality of groups' strategic decisions. Studies that account for such complexities enable researchers to draw more informed conclusions by clarifying the multiple factors that managers must consider in making decisions regarding group design.

These findings demonstrate the value of studying group processes. They indicate that researchers need to incorporate the study of process variables so that they can expand their understanding of the factors that contribute to group performance and address questions concerning the influence of group demography with adequate care. While these lessons are applicable to many areas of group demography, they are particularly applicable to boards.

In the following sections we show how the study of board processes can help to disentangle the predictions offered by multiple theoretical perspectives with regard to board demography. For example, it is plausible that a high proportion of outsiders will enhance some aspects of board functioning, such as board effort norms, as agency theory would suggest, but will have a negative impact on other aspects of board functioning that are beyond the scope of agency theory's rational framework, such as the level of cohesiveness on the board. Attention to process variables permits researchers to develop and test models that reflect these complexities of board dynamics. Researchers will be able to use the knowledge generated by process studies to clarify the tradeoffs associated with various aspects of board design and to resolve long-standing inconsistencies in board research.

Toward a model of board processes

Extensive literature exists on the effectiveness of workgroups in organizations (for reviews, see Bettenhausen, 1991; Cohen & Bailey, 1997; Gist, Locke, & Taylor, 1987). In developing our model of boards as groups, we define workgroups as "intact social systems that perform one or more tasks within an organizational context" (Bettenhausen, 1991: 346), and we believe that all boards qualify as groups in this respect. In addition, we look to the general "heuristic model of group effectiveness" identified by Cohen and Bailey (1997: 244), which is based on earlier models by Hackman and Morris (1975) and Gladstein (1984).

In particular, we value the input-process-output approach this framework uses, as well as its distinction between "task-performance" outcomes and those outcomes concerned with the ability of the group to continue functioning. However, following Goodman, Ravlin, and Schminke (1987), we believe that the specific processes that mediate between board demography and firm performance are likely to depend on factors that are specific to boards as groups and on the specific criteria of effectiveness under consideration. In the sections that follow, we discuss the factors that distinguish boards from other types of workgroups and propose specific criteria that could be used to evaluate the decision-making effectiveness of boards.

Distinctive features of boards as groups

Scholars most commonly describe the board of directors as the formal link between the shareholders of a firm and the managers entrusted with the day-to-day functioning of the organization (Mintzberg, 1983; Monks & Minow, 1995). Consistent with this description, Fama and Jensen have described the board as the "apex of the firm's decision control system" (1983: 311). Like a TMT—another elite workgroup with a major role in the firm's decision control system—boards face complex, multifaceted tasks that involve strategic-issue processing (Jackson, 1992). However, an important difference exists between boards and TMTs in that boards are responsible only for monitoring and influencing strategy—not for implementing strategic decisions or for day-to-day administration (Fama & Jensen, 1983).

Our analysis focuses on the specific board tasks that are most relevant to an understanding of boards as groups: control and service. The board's control task refers to its legal duty to monitor management on behalf of the firm's shareholders and to carry out this duty with sufficient loyalty and care (Monks & Minow, 1995). The board's service task refers to its potential to provide advice and counsel to the CEO and other top managers and to participate actively in the formulation of strategy.

Several additional distinctive features of boards deserve note. First, contemporary boards often include many "outsiders," who have their primary affiliation with another organization. These outsiders serve on only a part-time basis and have limited direct exposure to the firm's affairs. Second, boards average 13 members (Monks & Minow, 1995)—a size considerably greater than that of other workgroups studied in the management literature. The top management teams studied by Eisenhardt and Bourgeois (1988), for example, ranged in size from 5 to 9 members, whereas the workgroups studied by Gersick (1988) and Jehn (1995) averaged 5.6 members and 5.9 members, respectively. Finally, unlike many workgroups, boards function only episodically. Full board meetings are held, on average, only in coordinating the contributions of many members is likely to make it difficult for them to use their knowledge and skills effectively. Large boards also may have difficulty building the interpersonal relationships that further cohesiveness, or maintaining high board effort norms, owing to the potential for "social loafing" that exists in large groups (Latané et al., 1979).

Board tenure

Boards that have served together for a long time are likely to have acquired a high level of firm-specific knowledge and skills. In addition, their members' familiarity with one another is likely to lead to higher levels of cohesiveness and, possibly, to the better use of their knowledge and skills. However, long-tenured boards are also likely to experience lower levels of cognitive conflict, because in working together they are likely to have developed a shared understanding of the issues facing the firm and the appropriate repertoire of responses available to it. In contrast, board members who have only served together a short time will draw more strongly on the understandings they bring with them from their nondirector experiences; therefore, they are likely to have more diverse perspectives on these matters.

In summary, each of the aspects of board demography discussed above is likely to have multiple and contrasting effects on the processes that contribute to effective board performance. Table 1 summarizes our expectations regarding the effects of board demography on board processes.

Board dynamics across different types of boards

In our effort to develop a model of boards as groups that is widely applicable and readily testable, we have been guided by a rather generic conception

Table 1 The effects of board demography on board processes

Board process	Job-related diversity outsiders	Proportion of outsiders	Board size	Board tenure
Effort norms	No hypothesized relationship	Positive	Negative	No hypothesized relationship
Cognitive conflict	Positive	Positive	Positive	Negative
Presence of functional area knowledge & skills	Positive	No hypothesized relationship	Positive	No hypothesized relationship
Presence of firm-specific knowledge & skills	No hypothesized relationship	Negative	No hypothesized relationship	Positive
Use of knowledge & skills	Negative	No hypothesized relationship	Negative	Positive
Cohesiveness	Negative	Negative	Negative	Positive

7 times per year (Monks & Minow, 1995). Committee meetings provide some additional opportunities for intraboard interaction, but, in general, directors still spend less than 2 weeks per year working on the boards they serve (Monks & Minow, 1995).

In summary, boards of directors can be characterized as large, elite, and episodic decision-making groups that face complex tasks pertaining to strategic-issue processing. Because boards are not involved in implementation, the "output" that boards produce is entirely cognitive in nature. In addition, because boards are large, episodic, and interdependent, they are particularly vulnerable to "process losses" (Steiner, 1972)—the interaction difficulties that prevent groups from achieving their full potential. Taken together, these factors suggest that the effectiveness of boards is likely to depend heavily on social-psychological processes, particularly those pertaining to group participation and interaction, the exchange of information, and critical discussion (Butler, 1981; Jackson, 1992; Milliken & Vollrath, 1991).

Criteria of board effectiveness

The model we develop is concerned with two criteria of board effectiveness: (1) board task performance, defined as the board's ability to perform its control and service tasks effectively, and (2) the board's ability to continue working together, as evidenced by the cohesiveness of the board. These are the classic "task" and "maintenance" criteria identified in many past models of group effectiveness (Cohen & Bailey, 1997; Gladstein, 1984). Both are board-level constructs that are distinct from firm performance, but both also contribute to firm performance. Board task performance influences firm performance directly, whereas board cohesiveness does so indirectly by influencing present and future levels of board task performance.

In our model board task performance represents the degree to which boards succeed in fulfilling their control and service tasks. Specific board activities that are critical to the fulfillment of the control task include decisions regarding the hiring, compensation, and replacement of the firm's most senior managers, as well as the approval of major initiatives proposed by management. Specific activities that correspond to the fulfillment of the service task include providing expert and detailed insight during major events, such as an acquisition or restructuring, as well as more informal and ongoing activities, such as generating and analyzing strategic alternatives during board meetings.

Because of the strictly confidential and highly interpretive nature of board activity, it is likely to be extremely difficult for researchers to measure the task performance of boards in ways that are both reliable and comprehensive. Certain publicly announced board actions, such as the adoption of golden parachutes (Singh & Harianto, 1989) or CEO replacement (Boeker, 1992), may be used as proxies for performance on the control dimension. Board performance on the service dimension may be assessed by asking the CEO, a nonmember manager, or an outside consultant to rate the value of the advice and analysis the board contributes to strategic decisions. Alternatively, researchers may regard board task performance as a latent construct.

Board cohesiveness refers to the degree to which board members are attracted to each other and are motivated to stay on the board (Summers, Coffelt, & Horton, 1988). Because boards meet only episodically and are composed of persons for whom directorship is a part-time responsibility, the relationship of directors to the board can be characterized as one of "partial inclusion" (Weick, 1979). Cohesiveness captures the affective dimension of members' inclusion on the board and reflects the ability of the board to continue working together.

In studies of workgroups, researchers have found that when group members are more attracted to one another, they realize higher levels of member satisfaction (Katz & Kahn, 1978; Summers et al., 1988) and higher levels of commitment to the group (Zaccaro & Dobbins, 1989); they are also less likely to engage in excessive turnover (Angle & Perry, 1981; Jaros, 1995; O'Reilly, Caldwell, & Barnett, 1989; Piper, Marache, Lacroix, Richardsen, & Jones, 1983). On boards with very low levels of cohesiveness, members may choose not to stand for reelection, or, in extreme cases, they may resign from the board. Although a certain amount of turnover is normal and even healthy, high levels of turnover are likely to reduce the presence of firm-specific knowledge on the board.

In addition, owing to the tendency of groups to preserve the collective structures they create (Weick, 1979), cohesiveness may influence future board processes as well. For example, in light of past research linking organizational commitment to members' extrarole, prosocial behaviors and a willingness to expend effort on behalf of the organization (O'Reilly & Chatman, 1986), there is reason to expect that high levels of cohesiveness may enhance the future effort norms of the board. Moreover, high levels of cohesiveness may strengthen the future impact of effort norms, because more-cohesive groups are better able to influence their members' behavior (Janis, 1983; Shaw, 1981).

Cohesiveness also can exert a more immediate influence on the task performance of boards—a point we return to later. Cohesiveness can be operationalized using the scales from O'Reilly et al. (1989) that correspond to the affective components of social integration.

Board processes and their impact on board effectiveness

We have argued that board task performance and board cohesiveness are two key criteria by which to assess the effectiveness of boards as decision-making groups and that board task performance is likely to be influenced by social-psychological factors. In this section we discuss three board processes that we propose will significantly influence a board's task performance and cohesiveness: effort norms, cognitive conflict, and the board's use of its knowledge and skills. We also consider the relationship between cohesiveness and board task performance.

Effort norms: ensuring preparation, participation, and analysis

Effort norms are a group-level construct that refers to the group's shared beliefs regarding the level of effort each individual is expected to put toward a task (Wageman, 1995), Effort—an individual-level construct—is a product of motivation and refers to the intensity of individuals' task-performance behavior (Kanfer, 1992) or to the proportion of members' "total cognitive resources [that are] directed toward the target task" (Kanfer, 1992: 79). Norms often exert a strong influence on member behavior (Feldman, 1984; Steiner, 1972), particularly in groups that, like boards, are interdependent (Wageman, 1995). Thus, strong effort norms can be expected to enhance the effort of individual group members (Steiner, 1972; Wageman, 1995), which, in turn, can contribute to the performance of workgroups (Latané, Williams, & Harkins, 1979; Steiner, 1972; Weldon & Gargano, 1985).

Most directors face many competing demands for their time and must keep carefully budgeted schedules (Lorsch, 1989; Mace, 1986). Although most board members face these constraints, the time that directors devote to their tasks can differ considerably across boards, and these differences can significantly determine the degree to which boards are able to represent shareholders' interests successfully and to make contributions to strategy. Mace argues that most boards fall far short of realizing their potential contributions and that this is due, in part, to their failure to even "do the homework" necessary for understanding the company's problems (1986: 107). Similarly, Lorsch argues that directors who devote sufficient time to their duties and seek out the information they need are better able to prevent and manage crises and to govern effectively in times of stability (1989: 191–192).

Although time is an important manifestation of effort, even boards that spend similar amounts of time can exhibit different levels of effort. Past qualitative studies have shown that boards undertake their duties with widely varying degrees of attentiveness, analysis, and participation. Some boards simply "go through the motions" of attending meetings and registering votes, without being mentally engaged with the issues facing the board (Herman, 1981; Mace, 1986). However, there are counterexamples of boards that conduct diligent research on the firms they serve (Lorsch, 1989: 104–105), that participate actively in board discussions (Lorsch, 1989: 118), and that use pocket calculators during meetings (Monks & Minow, 1995: 217). Boards that have standards and expectations promoting such high-effort behaviors among members are more likely to perform their control and service tasks effectively.

Drawing on Wageman's (1995) example, researchers could operationalize effort norms by asking board members to rate the board's support for behaviors with statements such as the following: "carefully scrutinizing the information provided by the firm prior to meetings," "researching issues relevant to the company," "taking notes during meetings," or "participating actively during meetings."

Cognitive conflict: leveraging differences of perspective

Cognitive conflict refers to task-oriented differences in judgment among group members. Jehn defines cognitive conflict as "disagreements about the content of the tasks being performed, including differences in viewpoints, ideas and opinions" (1995: 258). Cognitive conflict differs from effort norms in that effort norms refer to group expectations regarding the intensity of individual behavior, whereas cognitive conflict is concerned with the presence of issue-related disagreement among members. Cognitive conflict is likely to arise in groups that, like boards, are interdependent and face complex decision-making tasks. Because the issues facing boards are complex and ambiguous, board members are liable to characterize issues differently and to hold different opinions about what the appropriate responses to these issues are (Dutton & Jackson, 1987). However, boards are likely to differ considerably in the degree to which they experience cognitive conflict (Byrne, 1997; Monks & Minow, 1995).

Cognitive conflict involves the use of "critical and investigative interaction processes" (Amason, 1996: 104) that can enhance the board's performance of its control role. The presence of disagreement and critical investigation on the board may require CEOs to explain, justify, and possibly modify their positions on important strategic issues and to entertain alternative perspectives and courses of action. Moreover, the existence of cognitive conflict on the board can serve to remind management of the power and role of the board and of the importance of considering shareholder interests in the formulation of strategy even beyond the boardroom.

In addition, cognitive conflict results in the consideration of more alternatives and the more careful evaluation of alternatives—processes that contribute to the quality of strategic decision making in uncertain environments (Eisenhardt, Kahwajy, & Bourgeois, 1997; Jackson, 1992; Milliken & Vollrath, 1991). Watson and Michaelsen (1988) have found that groups performing an intellective task perform better when their interaction behaviors feature the inclusion of multiple viewpoints and the exchange of both positive and negative comments. Likewise, Wanous and Youtz (1986) have found that solution diversity has a positive influence on the quality of group decisions; Schweiger, Sandberg, and Ragan (1986) have found that conflict-inducing techniques contribute to the effectiveness of strategic decision-making groups.

In spite of these beneficial effects of cognitive conflict, cognitive conflict also can arouse negative emotions (Nemeth & Staw, 1989) that diminish interpersonal attraction among members. Findings by Jehn (1995) and Schweiger and colleagues (1986) demonstrate that members of groups with high levels of cognitive conflict experience lower levels of satisfaction with the group and express less desire to remain with the group. Mace (1986) has found evidence that these dynamics can apply to boards as well. Because of the pressures of their competing responsibilities, he observed, many directors respond to high levels of cognitive conflict on the board by reducing, rather than increasing, their commitment to the board (Mace, 1986: 33–36).

One recent example of a reliable operationalization of cognitive conflict is Jehn's (1995) four-item scale for task conflict. Using this scale, researchers could ask respondents to gauge, using Likert-type items, the frequency of conflicts about ideas and the extent of differences of opinion on the board.

The presence and use of knowledge and skills

Boards require a high degree of specialized knowledge and skill to function effectively. Jackson notes that although "an implicit assumption often made in the management literature is that expertise will be used, assuming it is present, psychological research clearly indicates that the availability of expertise in a group does not guarantee the use of that expertise" (1992: 359). Thus, our model accounts for the presence and use of knowledge and skills with two separate constructs: (1) an "input" variable that represents the knowledge and skills present on the board and (2) a "process" variable that represents the way in which those resources are used by the board.

Presence of knowledge and skills

One can characterize the knowledge and skills most relevant to boards on two main dimensions: (1) functional area knowledge and skills and (2) firm-specific knowledge and skills. Functional area knowledge and skills span the traditional domains of business, including accounting, finance, and marketing, as well as those domains that pertain to the firm's relationship with its environment, such as law. Boards—as elite, strategic-issue-processing groups—must have members who possess knowledge and skills in these areas or have access to external networks that can aid in information gathering and problem solving (Ancona & Caldwell, 1988).

Firm-specific knowledge and skills refer to detailed information about the firm and an intimate understanding of its operations and internal management issues. Boards often need this kind of "tacit" knowledge (Nonaka, 1994) in order to deal effectively with strategic issues. In order to make informed decisions regarding diversification or acquisition opportunities, for example, the board may need to have a detailed understanding of how new and existing businesses would complement one another (Farjoun, 1994; Sirower, 1997).

Researchers may assess the knowledge and skills present on the board by asking board members to assess, using a Likert-type scale, the degree to which both types of expertise are present on the board. The scale used to assess the presence of functional area knowledge and skills might include items intended to gauge the presence of knowledge in domains that are common to virtually all businesses, such as finance, accounting, marketing, and law. These items could then be summed to obtain a composite score. Alternatively, because some functional areas are liable to vary in importance across industries, researchers may want to ask respondents to rate the importance of various functional areas to their businesses and use an additive measure that weights more important areas more strongly.

In assessing firm-specific knowledge and skills, researchers could draw on measures similar to those developed by McGrath, MacMillan, and Venkataraman (1995) to measure "comprehension" within executive teams. Specifically, researchers could ask respondents to assess the degree to which the board understands cause-effect relationships involving the needs of customers, sources of risk to the firm, and impediments to output qualify.

Use of knowledge and skills

The use of knowledge and skills refers to the board's ability to tap the knowledge and skills available to it and then apply them to its tasks. The construct, first identified by Hackman and Morris (1975), represents the minimization of "process losses" and the occurrence of "cross-training" and "collective learning" among members (Hackman, 1987: 327). This construct is related to the behavioral dimension of social integration, which refers to a group's ability to cooperate (Cohen & Bailey, 1997). It is also related to Weick and Roberts' concept of heedful interrelating, which they define as a "complex, attentive system [of interaction] tied together by trust," in which individual actions are subordinated and responsive to the demands of "joint action" (1993: 378). The use of knowledge and skills is distinct from cognitive conflict in that the use of knowledge and skills refers to the process by which members' contributions are coordinated, whereas cognitive conflict refers to the content of members' contributions.

If boards are to perform their control task effectively, they must integrate their knowledge of the firm's internal affairs with their expertise in the areas of law and strategy. In addition, if boards are to perform their service task effectively, they must be able to combine their knowledge of various functional areas and apply that knowledge properly to firm-specific issues. In both cases board members must elicit and respect each others' expertise, build upon each others' contributions, and seek to combine their insights in creative, synergistic ways.

Empirical studies of related constructs suggest the importance of the use of knowledge and skills in determining group effectiveness. Wageman (1995), for example, has found that cooperation norms contribute to group performance, particularly in interdependent groups. Similarly, Weick and Roberts (1993) show how heedful interrelating is a prerequisite to the effective performance of flight deck crews. Studies also show that the performance of TMTs is enhanced by group processes similar to the use of knowledge and skills, such as the "smoothness" of group process (Eisenhardt, 1989) and executive team "deftness" (McGrath et al., 1995).

A board's ability to use its knowledge and skills could be operationalized by asking board members to assess the validity of statements like the following, using Likert-type items: "people on this board are aware of each others' areas of expertise," "when an issue is discussed, the most knowledgeable people generally have the most influence," and "task delegation on this board represents a good match between knowledge and responsibilities." In addition, although the construct of executive team deftness is broader than the use of knowledge and skills construct, the scale developed by McGrath and colleagues (1995) to measure deftness contains several items pertaining to the exchange of information within groups that could be adapted for use in this context—for example, "important information often gets withheld on this board" (reverse coded) and "information flows quickly among board members."

Cohesiveness

We have discussed the effects of effort norms, cognitive conflict, and the use of knowledge and skills on board task performance. We now address the potential for board cohesiveness to exert an immediate influence on board task performance.

Because boards are charged with complex, interactive tasks, the degree of interpersonal attraction among members is likely to influence the effectiveness with which those tasks are performed (Williams & O'Reilly, 1998). The relationship between board cohesiveness and board task performance is likely to be curvilinear. Both the control and service components of the board's task require extensive communication and deliberation, and board members must have a certain minimum level of interpersonal attraction in order to engage in these things. In addition, board members must trust each others' judgment and expertise, and such trust will be difficult to sustain on boards with very low levels of interpersonal attraction. Furthermore, cohesiveness has been found to enhance decision making in some ways, such as by promoting earlier and more extensive discussion of alternative scenarios (Hogg, 1996).

However, very high levels of cohesiveness are likely to prove detrimental to the quality of the board's decision making. Highly cohesive boards may be distracted by the proliferation of personal exchanges. In addition, cohesiveness is the most prominent and frequently noted antecedent of "groupthink" (Mullen, Anthony, Salas, & Driskell, 1994)—a dysfunctional mode of group decision making characterized by a reduction in independent critical thinking and a relentless striving for unanimity among members (Janis, 1983). Janis hypothesizes that "for most groups, optimal functioning in decision making tasks may prove to be at a moderate level of cohesiveness" (1983: 248).

Although, as we have noted, cohesiveness is a key determinant of groupthink, it is not sufficient to produce groupthink (Janis, 1983; Mullen et al., 1994). In order to lead to groupthink, cohesiveness also must be accompanied by an absence of cognitive conflict among members. According to Janis (1983), groupthink occurs when members of highly cohesive groups engage in self-censorship and act as "mindguards," pressuring deviant thinkers to conform to majority opinions. But such behaviors do not invariably accompany cohesiveness. It is entirely possible for groups to have high levels of both interpersonal attraction and task-oriented disagreement (Jackson, 1992). In fact, the most effective boards, like the best management teams (Eisenhardt et al., 1997), can be characterized in precisely this way (Byrne, 1996), Cognitive conflict can help to prevent the emergence of groupthink in cohesive groups by fostering an environment characterized by a task-oriented focus and a tolerance of multiple viewpoints and opinions (Bernthal & Insko, 1993; Janis, 1983).

Concluding observations regarding the effects of board processes

The following propositions summarize our predictions regarding the influence of board processes on board effectiveness.

Proposition 1: Board effort norms, cognitive conflict, and the use of knowledge and skills will be positively related to board task performance.

Proposition 2: Cognitive conflict will be negatively related to board cohesiveness.

Proposition 3a: Board cohesiveness will be related in a curvilinear manner to board task performance.

Proposition 3b: The relationship between cohesiveness and board task performance will be moderated by cognitive conflict—that is, cohesiveness will be less likely to detract from board task performance when the board has a high level of cognitive conflict.

In addition to the effects captured in these propositions, we note that the processes discussed above have the potential to influence one another. For example, to the extent that high-effort norms result in more intense participation among members, they may stimulate cognitive conflict and lead to an increased use of members' knowledge and skills. Similarly, cognitive conflict may surface task-relevant information, and, conversely, the elicitation of members' knowledge may give rise to further conflict. However, the exact nature and strength of these relationships are likely to vary. For example, when a board's meetings are dominated by prolonged debates between two individuals, cognitive conflict may actually inhibit the use of members' knowledge and skills. Similarly, the collective experience of cognitive conflict may enhance board effort norms when disagreements are moderate in scale, but conflict may also diminish effort norms if disputes seem unresolvable.

Figure 1 presents a graphical depiction of the relationships proposed in this section.

ENHANCING PERFORMANCE IN ORGANIZATIONS

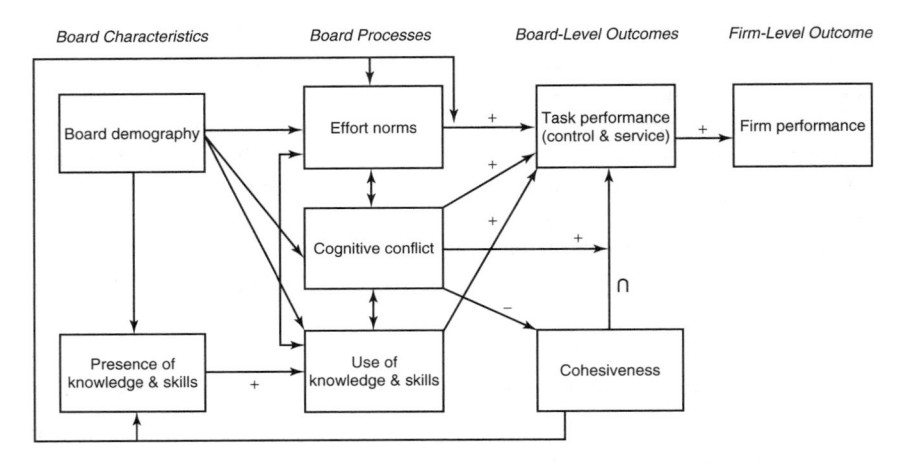

Figure 1 A model of board processes and their impacts on board effectiveness.

The effects of board demography

In this section we illuminate the complexity of board dynamics by showing how a single aspect of board demography can have multiple and contrasting effects on different mediating constructs. This point contradicts the prevailing view, which holds that either (1) there exist unequivocal relationships between board demography and firm performance or (2) demography does not exert a significant influence on board performance (Johnson et al., 1996: 433). We maintain that demography is very likely to be a significant predictor of board behavior but that its effects are too fine grained to be revealed by tests of the demography-performance relationship.

We begin by making a detailed case for the effects of a specific aspect of board demography—job-related diversity—and then offering some speculations regarding the effects of other demographic variables.

Job-related diversity

Forms of diversity that are job related in the context of board work include functional background, industry background, and educational background. Boards exhibit a considerable degree of diversity on these dimensions. Contemporary boards include CEOs who represent a variety of industries and functional backgrounds, as well as significant numbers of lawyers, investment bankers, academics, and nonprofit executives who represent diverse educational and industry backgrounds. Diversity of this sort clearly enhances the presence of functional area knowledge and skills on the board, although diversity is likely to have other influences on board functioning as well.

In their recent review of the literature on the effects of diversity in organizational groups, Milliken and Martins (1996) note that diversity is a "double-edged" sword for groups: although it increases the aggregate level of resources at the group's disposal, it is also associated with higher levels of conflict, interaction difficulties, and lower levels of integration. These double-edged consequences are likely to be particularly pronounced in board settings. Because boards comprise part-timers who interact only periodically, board members have few opportunities to diminish or smooth over the differences that separate them. Thus, consistent with the findings of recent studies on the effects of diversity in organizational groups, diversity can be expected to increase the level of cognitive conflict present on the board and to decrease the board's level of cohesiveness and its use of knowledge and skills.

To the extent that board members have different educational, functional, and industry backgrounds, they are more likely to experience differences in the ways that they perceive, process, and respond to issues they confront on the board (Milliken & Martins, 1996; Williams & O'Reilly, 1998), and these differences are likely to precipitate higher levels of cognitive conflict. Empirical support for this argument can be found in studies of the influence of functional background on executive perception (Dearborn & Simon, 1958; Waller, Huber, & Glick, 1995), as well as in more recent studies of conflict in groups (Eisenhardt & Bourgeois, 1988; Jehn, Northcraft, & Neale, 1997; Pelled, 1993). Moreover, groups with diverse backgrounds are more likely to have access to information and perspectives drawn from outside the group (Ancona & Caldwell, 1992), and attempts to pool and integrate these "exotic" contributions may lead to higher levels of cognitive conflict.

Diverse boards are also more likely to experience communication and coordination difficulties that inhibit the effective use of knowledge and skills, because their members may be unaware of each others' expertise or unable to appreciate its applicability to issues facing the board. In addition, diverse board members may have difficulty understanding one another because of differences in jargon or terminology. These difficulties may prove frustrating to board members, making them less inclined to offer information or opinions that highlight their diversity and more inclined to discuss information that is already shared by the group (Stasser, 1992). A laboratory study by Wittenbaum and Stasser (1996) shows that group members are less likely to share unique information when it is distributed among group members.

Finally, boards whose members have diverse backgrounds are also likely to be less cohesive. Williams and O'Reilly (1998) conclude that demographic diversity is associated with lower levels of interpersonal attraction within groups. The most common explanation for this effect is that demographic differences are associated with differences in attitudes (O'Reilly et al., 1989) and language (Wiersema & Bantel, 1992), which, in turn, lead to less mutually satisfying interactions among members and, ultimately, psychological ties among members that are fewer in number and weaker in strength than they are in more homogeneous groups (Shaw, 1981). Because boards are large groups that meet only episodically, they are unlikely to have time to fully resolve the attitudinal and linguistic differences that divide them, and board cohesiveness will suffer as a result.

Proposition 4: The degree of job-related diversity on the board will be positively related to the presence of functional area knowledge and skills and cognitive conflict on the board but negatively related to the board's cohesiveness and its use of its knowledge and skills.

We have confined our attention to job-related diversity because, unfortunately, the amount of visible diversity on American corporate boards remains very low (Dalton & Daily, 1998). In general, however, the effects of visible diversity are likely to be similar to those that we have outlined for job diversity (Milliken & Martins, 1996). It should be noted that visible diversity is significantly more common on nonprofit boards—a point we return to later.

Other aspects of board demography

As with diversity, other aspects of board demography are likely to have similarly complex effects on board processes. We briefly discuss three of these effects below.

Proportion of outsiders

Outsiders may enhance the effort norms of the board in that they are inclined to conceive of the board's task as a task separate from and complementary to that of management, whereas insiders may view their governance responsibilities as simply an extension of their managerial duties (Mace, 1986). In addition, the presence of outsiders may stimulate a desire on the part of insiders to show that they have their "house in order," leading to higher expectations of effort among them. The presence of outsiders is also likely to enhance the levels of cognitive conflict on the board, because outsiders share significantly fewer experiences with management and are liable to think more freely with regard to the firm's goals and the range of alternatives available to it.

At the same time, however, the presence of outsiders is likely to reduce the presence of firm-specific knowledge on the board, for outsiders lack the intimate understanding of the firm's affairs that insiders possess. Finally, the percentage of outsiders on a board is likely to have a direct negative effect on board cohesiveness. Whereas insiders are well acquainted and must work together regularly, outsiders have their primary affiliations dispersed across many different organizations and are likely to interact only periodically with insiders or with each other.

Board size

Board size is not truly a demographic attribute, but it is an important and much-studied board characteristic that is likely to have important effects on board functioning. Larger boards are likely to have more knowledge and skills at their disposal, and the abundance of perspectives they assemble are likely to enhance cognitive conflict. However, at the same time, the difficulty inherent of the corporate board. This conception is drawn from quantitative and qualitative descriptions of the boards of large, for-profit corporations, such as those in the Fortune 500. We acknowledge, however, that these organizations represent only part of the wide world of organizations and that the functioning of boards as groups may be different in organizations of different types. We address some of these differences below.

Boards of nonprofit organizations

The tasks of nonprofit boards differ in important respects from those of for-profit boards. First, the control function of nonprofit boards must be revised to account for the distinctive legal status of nonprofits, and the service function must be expanded to account for the fact that nonprofit boards typically exert more influence over operating functions than do for-profit boards (Oster, 1996). Second, because of the multifaceted nature of performance in the nonprofit sector (Stone & Brush, 1996), the relationship between board performance and organizational performance may be quite complex. For example, the board's performance of its service function may have a strong influence on certain operational measures of organizational performance, such as the quality of services, but little or no influence on financial measures, such as funding levels, which instead depend heavily on the board's performance of its external functions. In addition, it may actually be part of the control function of nonprofit boards to not only monitor organizational performance but to define and measure it in appropriate ways. In dealing with complexities of this sort, researchers should consider how issues of board effectiveness have been addressed in the nonprofit literature (e.g., Jackson & Holland, 1998).

Demographic differences between nonprofit boards and for-profit boards are also significant. Nonprofit boards include considerably more women and minorities (National Center for Nonprofit Boards, 1996), are larger (averaging 17 members, and often including 30 or more), and consist almost entirely of outsiders (Oster, 1995). Thus, to begin with, nonprofit board processes are likely to be affected by visible diversity, as well as job-related diversity.

Although the impact of these types of diversity is likely to be similar initially (Milliken & Martins, 1996), the salience of visible diversity may decline over time, as Pelled (1996) suggests. In addition, the sense of commitment to organizational objectives that is shared by nonprofit board members may be associated with high levels of cohesiveness. Golden-Biddle and Rao (1997) note that many nonprofit board members face a sharp conflict between the personal aspects of their association and the trusteeship duties their board service carries.

Boards of small firms

The governance of small firms, defined as those with revenues of $25 million or less (d'Amboise & Muldowney, 1988), is distinct from that of larger firms. First, because these firms tend to be undiversified, less structurally complex, and less formalized than their Fortune 500 counterparts, the range and depth of service activities available to the boards of small firms are likely to be greater (Castaldi & Wortman, 1984; Judge & Zeithaml, 1992). Second, because firm size and age are generally thought to be negatively related to the inertial forces that constrain organizational action, there may be a stronger link between the board's service contributions and firm performance (Hambrick & Finkelstein, 1987). Third, because the managers of small firms may be entrepreneurs with relatively little general management experience, the board's own knowledge and skills may be a particularly critical ingredient of its own service effectiveness (Gorman & Sahlman, 1989).

Demographically, the boards of small firms are small, averaging 6 members for Inc. 100 companies (Daily & Dalton, 1993), and even fewer for less-developed firms (Rosenstein, 1988). More important, because the ownership of small firms usually is much more concentrated than that of larger firms, shareholders often are represented directly on the boards of small firms. For example, firms backed by venture capitalists routinely have some or even a majority of their board seats held by their investors (Fried, Bruton, & Hisrich, 1998)—a condition certain to enhance the board's effort norms and to diminish the likelihood of groupthink. However, in owner-managed firms the board may simply have no control function in the conventional sense, because shareholder rights and managerial responsibilities will reside in the same persons.

Boards of high-technology firms

It is possible for industry-based differences among boards of directors to impact their functioning as groups. Perhaps the best illustration of such differences is provided by the boards of high-tech firms. If these boards are to assess the competence of management and provide advice on such issues as a firm's competitive environment, their members must have knowledge and skills that exceed the ordinary requirements of board service (Kotz, 1998). In particular, high-tech boards must have firm-specific knowledge that encompasses the technological intricacies of their firms' products and their production and development (McKenna, 1995). In addition, they may need additional functional area skills that are specific to high-tech environments, such as intellectual property law.

Because of these requirements, the presence and use of the board's knowledge and skills are likely to figure more prominently in these boards than in most others. These requirements may have indirect effects on board functioning as well, because many high-tech boards attempt to address these needs by adjusting the demographics of their boards. For example, high-tech firms tend to enhance the firm-specific knowledge of their boards by including a higher percentage of insiders and by favoring younger directors with current technological knowledge over older directors with prestigious appointments (Kotz, 1998). Finally, because many high-tech firms occupy industry environments characterized by high levels of growth and product differentiability, the boards of such firms may enjoy higher levels of discretion, thereby exerting a stronger influence on firm performance (Hambrick & Abrahamson, 1995).

Limitations and boundary conditions of the model

The model we have presented is characterized by several limitations and boundary conditions that deserve note. First, our discussion is rooted in the upper echelons (Hambrick & Mason, 1984) and strategic choice (Child, 1972) perspectives of organizations. Consistent with these orientations, we have emphasized those aspects of boards that pertain to their ability to influence firm performance by influencing strategic decisions. In this respect our approach differs from other perspectives, such as the institutional (Pfeffer, 1982) or resource dependence perspectives (Pfeffer & Salancik, 1978), which, historically, have emphasized the symbolic and external functions of boards, respectively.

Second, although our model is predicated on the argument that boards can exert a significant influence on organizational performance through the fulfillment of the control and service functions, we acknowledge that, in practice, boards often do not fulfill this potential. We further acknowledge that this potential is not invariant across boards. As we have noted, factors relating to sector, size, and industry may confer on boards a greater or lesser ability to exert this influence. Other factors may influence this ability as well.

Third, the model we have developed is intended to apply primarily to the boards of U.S.-based firms. Boards in other countries often operate in legal, historical, and financial contexts that are very different from those of the United States (Roe, 1993), and for this reason applications of our model to the study of boards in other countries should be undertaken with special care.

Finally, although we are optimistic about the prospects for understanding boards as groups, we caution researchers that not all group processes apply to boards. For example, existing theories of group socialization typically have focused on members' decisions to join or leave groups on the basis of their personal satisfaction with the group experience (Moreland & Levine, 1989). Given that members of boards join as much for organizational as for personal reasons, and serve for specified terms, such theories do not readily explain the dynamics of board membership.

Conclusion

Understanding the nature of effective board functioning is among the most important areas of management research on the horizon. William T. Allen, former Chancellor of the Delaware Chancery Court, noted in a recent speech that "the role of outside director [is] a private office imbued with public responsibility" (Allen, 1992). The same can be said for the role of inside directors. When directors are seen as stewards of organizational resources that impact, for better or for worse, the whole of society, the importance of understanding and improving the way they discharge their responsibilities becomes readily apparent. We believe that management researchers can inform the work of boards in ways that go beyond arguing for the manipulation of composition ratios. By treating boards as decision-making groups and by drawing on existing knowledge of group dynamics in this article, we encourage researchers to focus directly on what boards need to do in order to discharge their responsibilities more effectively.

Future research based on the process-oriented model we have developed here will enable researchers to better explain inconsistencies in past research on boards, to disentangle the contributions that multiple theoretical perspectives have to offer in explaining board dynamics, and to clarify the tradeoffs inherent in board design. Such research will complement and inform the growing interest in opening up the "black box" of organizational demography that has been manifested in recent research on various kinds of organizational groups (Hambrick, 1994; Lawrence, 1997; Pelled, 1996). We have sought to facilitate future empirical research by incorporating established, measurable constructs into our model, as well as by developing and proposing measurement guidelines for several new or adapted constructs.

From a practical standpoint, knowledge of the roles of board processes can help to clarify the complexity of board design to practitioners concerned with the composition of boards and may induce boards to consider adopting process-related interventions to enhance board effectiveness. In these ways research on board processes can help to bring a measure of sophistication and balance to an area of corporate governance that is all too often fraught with contention and ideology.

Acknowledgments

This research was suppoted by a grant from the Tenneco Fund Program at the Stern School of Business, New York University. We are grateful to Theresa Lant, Peter Grinyer, Bill Guth, Dale Zand, Elizabeth Wolfe Morrison, and Susan Jackson for their assistance.

References

Allen, W. 1992. Redefining the role of outside directors in an age of global competition. Speech transcript in R. Monks & N. Minow (Eds.), *Corporate governance*: 487–495. Cambridge, MA: Blackwell Business.

Amason, A. 1996. Distinguishing the effects of functional and dysfunctional conflict on strategic decision making: Resolving a paradox for top management teams. *Academy of Management Journal*, 39: 123–148.

Amason, A., & Sapienza, H. 1997. The effects of top management team size and interaction norms on cognitive and affective conflict. *Journal of Management*, 23: 495–516.

Ancona, D., & Caldwell, D. 1988. Beyond task and maintenance: Defining external functions in groups. *Group & Organization Studies*, 13: 468–494.

Ancona, D., & Caldwell, D. 1992. Demography and design: Predictors of new product team performance. *Organization Science*, 3: 321–341.

Angle, H., & Perry, J. 1981. An empirical assessment of organizational commitment and organizational effectiveness. *Administrative Science Quarterly*, 26: 1–13.

Bernthal, P., & Insko, C. 1993. Cohesiveness without groupthink: The interactive effects of social and task cohesion. *Group & Organization Management*, 18: 66–87.

Bettenhausen, K. 1991. Five years of group research: What we have learned and what needs to he addressed. *Journal of Management*, 17: 345–381.

Boeker, W. 1992. Power and managerial dismissal: Scapegoating at the top. *Administrative Science Quarterly*, 37: 400–421.

Butler, R. 1981. Innovations in organizations: Appropriateness of perspectives from small group studies for strategy formulation. *Human Relations*, 34: 763–788.

Byrne, J. 1996. The best and worst boards: Our new report card on corporate governance. *Business Week*, November 25: 82–106.

Byrne, J. 1997. The best and worst boards: Our report card on corporate governance. *Business Week*, December 8: 90–104.

Castaldi, R., & Wortman, M. 1984. Boards of directors in small corporations: An untapped resource. *American Journal of Small Business*, 9(2): 1–10.

Child, J. 1972. Organization structure, environment and performance: The role of strategic choice. *Sociology*, 6: 2–21.

Cohen, S., & Bailey, D. 1997. What makes teams work: Group effectiveness research from the shop floor to the executive suite. *Journal of Management*, 23: 239–290.

Daily, C., & Dalton, D. 1993. Board of directors leadership and structure: Control and performance implications. *Entrepreneurship Theory & Practice*, 17(3): 65–81.

Daily, C., & Schwenk, C. 1996. Chief executive officers, top management teams and boards of directors: Congruent or countervailing forces? *Journal of Management*, 22: 185–208.

Dalton, D., & Daily, C. 1998. The other ceiling. *Across the Board*, 35: 19.

d'Amboise, G., & Muldowney, M. 1988. Management theory for small business: Attempts and requirements. *Academy of Management Review*, 13: 226–240.

Dearborn, D., & Simon, H. 1958. Selective perception: A note on the departmental identifications of executives. *Sociometry*, 21: 140–144.

Dutton, J., & Jackson, S. 1987. Categorizing strategic issues: Links to organizational action. *Academy of Management Review*, 12: 76–90.

Eisenhardt, K. 1989. Making fast strategic decisions in high-velocity environments. *Academy of Management Journal*, 32: 543–576.

Eisenhardt, K., & Bourgeois, L. 1988. Politics of strategic decision making in high-velocity environments: Toward a midrange theory. *Academy of Management Journal*, 31: 737–770.

Eisenhardt, K., Kahwajy, J., & Bourgeois, L. 1997. How management teams can have a good fight. *Harvard Business Review*, 75(July–August): 77–85.

Fama, E., & Jensen, M. 1983. Separation of ownership and control. *Journal of Law & Economics*, 26: 301–325.

Farjoun, M. 1994. Beyond industry boundaries: Human expertise, diversification and resource-related industry groups. *Organization Science*, 5: 185–199.

Feldman, D. 1984. The development and enforcement of group norms. *Academy of Management Review*, 9:47–53.

Fried, V., Bruton, G., & Hisrich, R. 1998. Strategy and the board of directors in venture capital-backed firms. *Journal of Business Venturing*, 13: 493–503.

Gersick, C. 1988. Time and transition in work teams: Toward a new model of group development. *Academy of Management Journal*, 31: 9–41.

Gist, M., Locke, E., & Taylor, M. 1987. Organizational behavior: Group structure, process, and effectiveness. *Journal of Management*, 13: 237–257.

Gladstein, D. 1984. A model of task group effectiveness. *Administrative Science Quarterly*, 29: 499–517.

Golden-Biddle, K., & Rao, H. 1997. Breaches in the boardroom: Organizational identity and conflicts of commitment in a nonprofit organization. *Organization Science*, 8: 593–611.

Goodman, P., Ravlin, E., & Schminke, M. 1987. Understanding groups in organizations. In L. L. Cummings & B. M. Staw (Eds.), *Research in organizational behavior*, vol. 9: 121–173. Greenwich, CT: IAI Press.

Gorman, M., & Sahlman, W. 1989. What do venture capitalists do? *Journal of Business Venturing*, 4: 231–248.

Hackman, J. 1987. The design of work teams. In J. Lorsch (Ed.), *Handbook of organizational behavior*, 314–342. Englewood Cliffs, NJ: Prentice-Hall.

Hackman, J., & Morris, C. 1975. Group tasks, group interaction process, and group performance effectiveness. A review and proposed integration. In L. Berkowitz (Ed.), *Advances in experimental social psychology*, vol. 8: 45–99. New York: Academic Press.

Hambrick, D. 1994. Top management groups: A conceptual integration and reconsideration of the "team" label. In L. L. Cummings and B. M. Staw (Eds.), *Research in organizational behavior*, vol. 16: 171–213. Greenwich, CT: JAI Press.

Hambrick, D., & Abrahamson, E. 1995. Assessing managerial discretion across industries: A multi-method approach. *Academy of Management Journal*, 38: 1427–1441.

Hambrick, D., & Finkelstein, S. 1987. Managerial discretion: A bridge between polar views of organizational outcomes. In L. L. Cummings and B. M. Staw (Eds.), *Research in organizational behavior*, vol. 9: 369–406. Greenwich, CT: JAI Press.

Hambrick, D., & Mason, P. 1984. Upper echelons: The organization as a reflection of its top managers. *Academy of Management Review*, 9: 193–206.

Heard, J. 1987. Pension funds and contests for corporate control. *California Management Review*, 29(2): 89–100.

Herman, E. 1981. *Corporate control, corporate power*. New York: Cambridge University Press.

Hogg, M. 1996. Social identify, self-categorization and the small group. In E. Witte & J. Davis (Eds.), *Understanding group behavior*, vol. 2: 227–253. Mahwah, NJ: Lawrence Erlbaum Associates.

Jackson, D., & Holland, T. 1998. Measuring the effectiveness of nonprofit boards. *Nonprofit and Voluntary Sector Quarterly*, 27: 159–182.

Jackson, S. 1992. Consequences of group composition for the interpersonal dynamics of strategic issue processing. In J. Dutton, A. Huff, & P. Shrivastava (Eds.), *Advances in strategic management*, vol. 8: 345–382, Greenwich, CT: JAI Press.

Janis, I. 1983. *Groupthink: Psychological studies of policy decisions and fiascoes* (2nd ed.). Boston: Houghton Mifflin.

Jaros, S. 1995. An assessment of Meyer and Allen's three-component model of organizational commitment and turnover intentions. *Proceedings of the Academy of Management*, 317–321.

Jehn, K. 1995. A multimethod examination of the benefits and detriments of intragroup conflict. *Administrative Science Quarterly*, 40: 256–282.

Jehn, K., Northcraft, G., & Neale, M. 1997. *Opening Pandora's box: A field study of diversity, conflict and performance in work groups*. Working paper, Wharton School, University of Pennsylvania, Philadelphia.

Johnson, J., Daily, C., & Ellstrand, A. 1996. Boards of directors: A review and research agenda. *Journal of Management*, 22: 409–438.

Judge, P., & Reinbardt, A. 1997. Seething shareholders. *Business Week*, June 9: 38.

Judge, W., & Zeithaml, C. 1992. Institutional and strategic choice perspectives on board involvement in the strategic decision process. *Academy of Management Journal*, 35: 766–794.

Kanfer, R. 1992. Motivation theory and industrial and organizational psychology. In M. D. Dunnette & L. M. Hough (Eds), *Handbook of industrial and organizational psychology*, vol. 3: 75–170. Palo Alto, CA: Consulting Psychologists Press.

Katz, D., & Kahn, R. 1978. *The social psychology of organizations*. New York: Wiley.

Kesner, I., & Johnson, R. 1990. An investigation of the relationship between board composition and stockholder suits. *Strategic Management Journal*, 11: 327–336.

Kotz, R. 1998. Technology company boards: A new model. *Directors and Boards*, 22(3): 26–28.

Latané, B., Williams, K., & Harkins, S. 1979. Many hands make light the work: The causes and consequences of social loafing. *Journal of Personality and Social Psychology*, 37: 822–832.

Lawrence, B. 1997. The black box of organizational demography, *Organization Science*, 8: 1–22.

Lorsch, J. 1989. *Pawns or potentates: The reality of America's corporate boards*. Boston: Harvard Business School Press.

Lublin, J. 1997. Top executives' departures put heat on boards. *Wall Street Journal*, July 18: B1, B5.

Mace, M. 1971. *Directors: Myth and reality*. Boston: Harvard Business School Press.

Mace, M. 1986. *Directors: Myth and reality* (2nd ed.). Boston: Harvard Business School Press.

McGrath, R., MacMillan, I., & Venkataraman, S. 1995. Defining and developing competence: A strategic process paradigm. *Strategic Management Journal*, 16: 251–275.

McKenna, R. 1995. Boards of a different breed. *Directors and Boards*, 20(1): 20–22.

Melone, N. 1994. Reasoning in the executive suite: The influence of role/experience-based expertise on decision processes of corporate executives. *Organization Science*, 5: 438–455.

Milliken, F., & Martins, L. 1996. Searching for common threads: Understanding the multiple effects of diversity in organizational groups. *Academy of Management Review*, 21: 402–433.

Milliken, F., & Vollrath, D. 1991. Strategic decision-making tasks and group effectiveness: Insights from theory and research on small group performance. *Human Relations*, 44: 1–25.

Mintzberg, H. 1983. *Power in and around organizations*. Englewood Cliffs, NJ: Prentice-Hall.

Monks. R., & Minow, N. (Eds.). 1995. *Corporate governance*. Cambridge, MA: Blackwell Business.

Moreland, R., & Levine, J. 1989. Newcomers and oldtimers in small groups. In P. Paulus (Ed.), *Psychology of group influence* (2nd ed.): 143–186. Hillsdale, NJ: Lawrence Erlbaum Associates.

Mullen, B., Anthony, T., Salas, E., & Driskell, J. 1994. Group cohesiveness and quality of decision making: An integration of tests of the groupthink hypothesis. *Small Group Research*, 25: 189–204.

National Center for Nonprofit Boards. 1996. *A snapshot of America's nonprofit boards*. Washington, DC: National Center for Nonprofit Boards.

Nemeth, C., & Staw, B. 1989. The tradeoffs of social control and innovation in groups and organizations. *Advances in Experimental Social Psychology*, 22: 175–210.

Nonaka, I. 1994. A dynamic theory of organizational knowledge creation. *Organization Science*, 5: 14–37.

O'Reilly, C., Caldwell, D., & Barnett, W. 1989. Work group demography, social integration and turnover. *Administrative Science Quarterly*, 34: 21–37.

O'Reilly, C., & Chatman, J. 1986. Organizational commitment and psychological attachment: The effects of compliance, identification and internalization on prosocial behavior. *Journal of Applied Psychology*, 71: 492–499.

Orwall, B., & Lublin, J. 1997. The plutocracy: If a company prospers, should its directors behave by the book? *Wall Street Journal*, February 24: A1, A8.

Oster, S. 1995. *Strategic management for nonprofit organizations*. New York: Oxford University Press.

Pelled, L. 1993. *Team diversity and conflict: A multivariate analysis*. Working paper, Marshall School of Business, University of Southern California, Los Angeles.

Pelled, L. 1996. Demographic diversity, conflict, and work group outcomes: An intervening process theory. *Organization Science*, 7: 615–631.

Pettigrew, A. 1992. On studying managerial elites. *Strategic Management Journal*, 13: 163–182.

Pfeffer, J. 1982. *Organizations and organization theory*. Boston: Pitman Publishing.

Pfeffer, J. 1983. Organizational demography. In L. L. Cummings & B. M. Staw (Eds.), *Research in organizational behavior*, vol. 5: 299–357. Greenwich, CT: JAI Press.

Pfeffer, J., & Salancik, G. 1978. *The external control of organizations: A resource dependence perspective*. New York Harper & Row.

Piper, W., Marache, M., Lacroix, R., Richardsen, A., & Jones, B. 1983. Average tenure of academic department heads: The effects of paradigm, size and departmental demography. *Administrative Science Quarterly*, 25: 387–406.

Roe, M. 1993. Some differences in corporate structure in Germany, Japan and the United States. *Yale Law Journal*, 102: 2–83.

Rosenstein, J. 1988. The board and strategy: Venture capital and high technology. *Journal of Business Venturing*, 3: 159–170.

Schine, E. 1997. At Disney, Grumpy isn't just a dwarf. *Business Week*, February 24: 38.

Schweiger, D., Sandberg, W., & Ragan, J. 1986. Group approaches for improving strategic decision making: A comparative analysis of dialectical inquiry, devil's advocacy and consensus. *Academy of Management Journal*, 23: 51–71.

Shaw, M. 1931. *Group dynamics: The psychology of small group behavior* (3rd ed.). New York: McGraw-Hill.

Singh, H., & Harianto, F. 1989. Top management tenure, corporate ownership structure and the magnitude of golden parachutes. *Strategic Management Journal*, 10: 143–159.

Sirower, M. 1997. *The synergy trap: How companies lose the acquisition game.* New York: Free Press.
Smith, K., Smith, K., Olian, J., Sims, H., O'Bannon, D., & Scully, J. 1994. Top management team demography and process: The role of social integration and communication. *Administrative Science Quarterly*, 39: 412–438.
Stasser, G. 1992. Pooling of unshared information during group discussion. In S. Worchel, W. Wood, & J. Simpson (Eds.), *Group process & productivity:* 48–67. Newbury Park, CA: Sage.
Steiner, I. 1972. *Group process and productivity.* New York: Academic Press.
Stone, M., & Brush, C. 1996. Planning in ambiguous contexts: The dilemma of meeting needs for commitment and demands for legitimacy. *Strategic Management Journal*, 17: 633–652.
Summers, L., Coffelt, T., & Horton, R. 1988. Work group cohesion. *Psychological Reports*, 63: 627–636.
Wageman, R. 1995. Interdependence and group effectiveness. *Administrative Science Quarterly*, 40: 145–180.
Waller, M., Huber, G., & Glick, W. 1995. Functional background as a determinant of executives' selective perception. *Academy of Management Journal*, 38: 943–974.
Walsh, J. 1988. Selectivity and selective perception: An investigation of managers' belief structures and information processing. *Academy of Management Journal*, 31: 873–896.
Wanous, J., & Youtz, M. 1986. Solution diversity and the quality of group decisions. *Academy of Management Journal*, 29: 149–159.
Watson, W., & Michaelsen, L. 1988. Group interaction behaviors that affect group performance on an intellective task. *Group & Organization Studies:* 13: 495–516.
Weick, K. 1979. *The social psychology of organizing* (2nd ed.). Reading, MA: Addison-Wesley.
Weick, K., & Roberts, K. 1993. Collective mind in organizations: Heedful interrelating on flight decks. *Administrative Science Quarterly*, 38: 357–381.
Weldon, E., & Gargano, G. 1985. Cognitive effort in additive task groups: The effects of shared responsibility on the quality of multiattribute judgments. *Organizational Behavior and Human Decision Processes*, 36: 348–361.
Wiersema, M., & Bantel, K. 1992. Top management team demography and corporate strategic change. *Academy of Management Journal*, 35: 91–121.
Williams, K, & O'Reilly, C. 1998. Demography and diversity in organizations: A review of 40 years of research. *Research in Organizational Behavior*, 20: 77–140.
Wittenbaum, G., & Stasser, G. 1996. Management of information in small groups. In J. Nye & M. Brower (Eds.), *What's social about social cognition?*: 3–28. Thousand Oaks, CA: Sage.
Zaccaro, S., & Dobbins, G. 1989. Contrasting group and organizational commitment: Evidence for differences among multilevel attachments. *Journal of Organizational Behavior*, 10: 267–273.
Zahra, S., & Pearce, J. 1989. Boards of directors and corporate financial performance: A review and integrative model. *Journal of Management*, 15: 291–334.

43

SOCIAL IDENTITY AND SELF-CATEGORIZATION PROCESSES IN ORGANIZATIONAL CONTEXTS

Michael A. Hogg and Deborah J. Terry

Source: *Academy of Management Review* 25(1) (2000): 121–140.

Abstract

Although aspects of social identity theory are familiar to organizational psychologists, its elaboration, through self-categorization theory, of how social categorization and prototype-based depersonalization actually produce social identity effects is less well known. We describe these processes, relate self-categorization theory to social identity theory, describe new theoretical developments in detail, and show how these developments can address a range of organizational phenomena. We discuss cohesion and deviance, leadership, subgroup and sociodemographic structure, and mergers and acquisitions.

Organizations are internally structured groups that are located in complex networks of intergroup relations characterized by power, status, and prestige differentials. To varying degrees, people derive part of their identity and sense of self from the organizations or workgroups to which they belong. Indeed, for many people their professional and/or organizational identity may be more pervasive and important than ascribed identities based on gender, age, ethnicity, race, or nationality. It is perhaps not surprising that social psychologists who study groups often peek over the interdisciplinary fence at what their colleagues in organizational psychology are up to. Some, disillusioned with social cognition as the dominant paradigm in mainstream social psychology, vault the fence, thus fueling recent and not so recent laments within social psychology that the study of groupss may be alive and well, but not in social psychology (e.g., Levine & Moreland, 1990; Steiner, 1974).

Over the past 10 or 15 years, however, there has been a marked revival of interest among social psychologists in the study of groups and group processes (e.g., Abrams & Hogg, 1998; Hogg & Abrams, 1999; Hogg & Moreland, 1995; Moreland, Hogg, & Hains, 1994), even spawning two new journals: *Group Dynamics* in 1996 and *Group Processes and Intergroup Relations* in 1998. The *new* interest in groups is different. There is less emphasis on interactive small groups, group structure, and interpersonal relations within groups, and there is more emphasis on the self concept: how the self is defined by group membership and how social cognitive processes associated with group membership-based self-definition produce characteristically "groupy" behavior. This revival of interest in group processes and identity has been influenced significantly by the development within social psychology of social identity theory and self-categorization theory. A search of *PsychLit* in mid 1997 for the key terms *social identity* and *self-categorization* resulted in a list of almost 550 publications since 1991.

In this article we introduce social identity theory as a platform from which to describe in detail how social categorization and prototype-based depersonalization actually produce social identity phenomena. We explain how these processes, which are the conceptual core of self-categorization theory, relate to the original and more familiar intergroup and self-enhancement motivational perspective of social identity theory. We show how recent conceptual advances based largely, although not exclusively, on self-categorization theory have great but as yet largely unexplored potential for our understanding of social behaviors in organizational contexts. We have tried to energize this potential by describing various speculations, hypotheses, and propositions that can act as a framework for empirical research.

Some of the key theoretical innovations we promote are based on the ideas that (1) social identity processes are motivated by subjective uncertainty reduction, (2) prototype-based depersonalization lies at the heart of social identity processes, and (3) groups are internally structured in terms of perceived or actual group prototypicality of members. After introducing social identity theory and describing self-categorization mechanisms, we discuss cohesion and deviance, leadership, group structure, subgroups, sociodemographic groups, and mergers and acquisitions. We have chosen these group phenomena because they particularly benefit from the self-categorization-based extension of social identity theory. They capture the interplay of intergroup and intragroup relations and the conceptual importance of prototypicality, depersonalization, and uncertainty. They are also particularly organizationally relevant phenomena, where social identity theory can make a contribution.

Before we begin, we underscore two caveats. First, consistent with social identity theory's group level of analysis and cognitive definition of the social group (e.g., Turner, 1982; Turner, Hogg, Oakes, Reicher, & Wetherell, 1987), we consider organizations to be groups, units or divisions within organizations to be groups, professions or sociodemographic categories that are distributed across organizations to be groups, and so forth—all with different social identities and group prototypes. Thus, intergroup relations can exist between organizations, between units or divisions within an organization, between professions that are within but transcend organizations, and so forth. Salience mechanisms, described below, determine which group and, therefore, intergroup relationship is psychologically salient as a basis for self-conceptualization in a given context.

Second, social identity theory is not entirely new to organizational psychologists. Although already adopted to some extent by organizational researchers, Ashforth and Mael (1989) first systematically introduced the theory to organizational psychology (also see Ashforth & Humphrey, 1993, and Nkomo & Cox, 1996) and subsequently published some related empirical work (e.g., Mael & Ashforth, 1992, 1995). Others have also applied it to organizational settings (e.g., Dutton, Dukerich, & Harquail, 1994; Pratt, in press; Riordan & Shore, 1997; Tsui, Egan, & O'Reilly, 1992).

This work, however, often touches only the surface of social identity theory. It focuses on some aspects but does not systematically incorporate significant theoretical developments made since 1987 that focus on self-categorization, group prototypicality, contextual salience, and depersonalization processes (see Pratt, in press). These developments have enabled social identity theorists to extend the theory's conceptual and empirical focus on intergroup phenomena to incorporate a focus on what happens within groups; it has become what could be called an *extended social identity theory*. For example, in recent work on social psychology, researchers have explored social influence and norms (e.g., Turner, 1991); solidarity and cohesion (e.g., Hogg, 1992); attitudes, behavior, and norms (e.g., Terry & Hogg, 1999); small groups (e.g., Hogg, 1996a); group motivation (Hogg, in press a,b; Hogg & Abrams, 1993a; Hogg & Mullin, 1999); and group structure and leadership (e.g., Hogg, 1996b, 1999).[1]

Social identity and self-categorization

Tajfel first introduced the concept of social identity—"the individual's knowledge that he belongs to certain social groups together with some emotional and value significance to him of this group membership" (1972: 292)—to move from his earlier consideration of social, largely intergroup, perception (i.e., stereotyping and prejudice) to consideration of how self is conceptualized in intergroup contexts: how a system of social categorizations "creates and defines an individual's *own* place in society" (Tajfel, 1972: 293). Social identity rests on intergroup social comparisons that seek to confirm or to establish ingroup-favoring evaluative distinctiveness between ingroup and outgroup, motivated by an underlying need for self-esteem (Turner, 1975).

Tajfel (1974a,b) quickly developed the theory to specify how beliefs about the nature of relations between groups (status, stability, permeability, legitimacy) influence the way that individuals or groups pursue positive social identity. Tajfel and Turner (1979) retained this emphasis in their classic statement of social identity theory. The emphasis on social identity as part of the self-concept was explored more fully by Turner (1982). In a comprehensive coverage of relevant research, Hogg and Abrams (1988) then integrated and grounded intergroup, self-conceptual, and motivational emphases. At about the same time, Turner and his colleagues (Turner, 1985; Turner et al., 1987) extended social identity theory through the development of self-categorization theory, which specified in detail how social categorization produces prototype-based depersonalization of self and others and, thus, generates social identity phenomena.

Social identity theory and/or self-categorization theory has been described by social identity theorists in detail elsewhere (e.g., Hogg, 1992, 1993, 1996b; Hogg & Abrams, 1988; Hogg, Terry, & White, 1995; Tajfel & Turner, 1986; for historical accounts see Hogg, in press c; Hogg & Abrams, 1999; Turner, 1996). Because the original form of social identity theory is familiar to organizational psychologists, we do not redescribe it here. Instead, we focus on self-categorization theory, which is less familiar to and less accessible for organizational psychologists in terms of its processes, its relationship to social identity theory, and its potential for explicating organizational processes (Pratt, in press).

Self-categorization theory clearly evolves from Tajfel's and Turner's earlier ideas on social identity. We view it as a development of social identity theory or, more accurately, as that component of an extended social identity theory of the relationship between self-concept and group behavior that details the social cognitive processes that generate social identity effects (e.g., Abrams & Hogg, in press; Hogg, 1996a, in press c; Hogg & Abrams, 1988, 1999, in press; Hogg & McGarty, 1990; Hogg, Terry, & White, 1995). We see no incompatibility between self-categorization theory and the original form of social identity theory but view self-categorization theory, rather, as an important and powerful new conceptual component of an extended social identity theory. The self-categorization component of social identity theory has been very influential in recent developments within social psychology (e.g., Abrams & Hogg, 1999; Oakes et al., 1994; Spears et al., 1997) but has hitherto attracted little attention in organizational psychology (Pratt, in press).

Self-categorization theory

Self-categorization theory specifies the operation of the social categorization process as the cognitive basis of group behavior. Social categorization of self and others into ingroup and outgroup accentuates the perceived similarity of the target to the relevant ingroup or outgroup prototype (cognitive representation of features that describe and prescribe attributes of the group). Targets are no longer represented as unique individuals but, rather, as embodiments of the relevant prototype—a process of *depersonalization*. Social categorization of self—self-categorization—cognitively assimilates self to the ingroup prototype and, thus, depersonalizes self-conception. This transformation of self is the process underlying group phenomena, because it brings self-perception and behavior in line with the contextually relevant ingroup prototype. It produces, for instance, normative behavior, stereotyping, ethnocentrism, positive ingroup attitudes and cohesion, cooperation and altruism, emotional contagion and empathy, collective behavior, shared norms, and mutual influence. Depersonalization refers simply to a change in self-conceptualization and the basis of perception of others; it does not have the negative connotations of such terms as *deindividuation* or *dehumanization* (cf. Reicher, Spears, & Postmes, 1995).

Representation of groups as prototypes

The notion of prototypes, which is not part of the earlier intergroup focus of social identity theory, is absolutely central to self-categorization theory. People cognitively represent the defining and stereotypical attributes of groups in the form of prototypes. Prototypes are typically not checklists of attributes but, rather, fuzzy sets that capture the context-dependent features of group membership, often in the form of representations of exemplary members (actual group members who best embody the group) or ideal types (an abstraction of group features). Prototypes embody all attributes that characterize groups and distinguish them from other groups, including beliefs, attitudes, feelings, and behaviors. A critical feature of prototypes is that they maximize similarities within and differences between groups, thus defining groups as distinct entities. Prototypes form according to the principle of metacontrast: maximization of the ratio of intergroup differences to intragroup differences. Because members of the same group are exposed to similar social information, their prototypes usually will be similar and, thus, shared.

Prototypes are stored in memory but are constructed, maintained, and modified by features of the immediate or more enduring social interactive context (e.g., Fiske & Taylor, 1991). They are highly context dependent and are particularly influenced by what outgroup is contextually salient. Enduring changes in prototypes and, therefore, self-conception can arise if the relevant comparison outgroup changes over time—for instance, if Catholics gradually define themselves in contradistinction to Muslims rather than to Protestants, or if a car manufacturer compares itself to a computer software manufacturer rather than to another car manufacturer. Such changes are also transitory in that they are tied to whatever outgroup is salient in the immediate social context. For instance, a psychology department may experience a contextual change in self-definition if it compares itself with a management school rather than with a history department. Thus, social identity is dynamic. It is responsive, in type and content, to intergroup dimensions of immediate comparative contexts.

Proposition 1: Changes in the inter-organizational comparative context affect the content of organizational prototypes.

As we will see, the content of prototypes strongly influences the group phenomena discussed later in the article.

Self-enhancement and uncertainty reduction motivations

According to social identity theory, social identity and intergroup behavior are guided by the pursuit of evaluatively positive social identity, through positive intergroup distinctiveness, which, in turn, is motivated by the need for positive self-esteem—the self-esteem hypothesis (e.g., Abrams & Hogg, 1988; see also Hogg & Abrams, 1990, 1993b; Hogg & Mullin, 1999; Long & Spears, 1997; Rubin & Hewstone, 1998). Self-categorization theory's focus on the categorization process hints at an additional (perhaps more fundamental), epistemic, motivation for social identity, which has only recently been described—the uncertainty reduction hypothesis (Hogg, in press a,b; Hogg & Abrams, 1993b; Hogg & Mullin, 1999). In addition to being motivated by self-enhancement, social identity processes are also motivated by a need to reduce subjective uncertainty about one's perceptions, attitudes, feelings, and behaviors and, ultimately, one's self-concept and place within the social world. Uncertainty reduction, particularly about subjectively important matters that are generally self-conceptually relevant, is a core human motivation. Certainty renders existence meaningful and confers confidence in how to behave and what to expect from the physical and social environment within which one finds oneself. Self-categorization reduces uncertainty by transforming self-conception and assimilating self to a prototype that describes and prescribes perceptions, attitudes, feelings, and behaviors.

Because prototypes are relatively consensual, they also furnish moral support and consensual validation for one's self-concept and attendant cognitions and behaviors. It is the prototype that actually reduces uncertainty. Hence, uncertainty is better reduced by prototypes that are simple, clear, highly focused, and consensual, and that, thus, describe groups that have pronounced entitativity (Campbell, 1958; also see Brewer & Harasty, 1996; Hamilton & Sherman, 1996; Hamilton, Sherman, & Lickel, 1998; Sherman, Hamilton, & Lewis, 1999), are very cohesive (Hogg, 1992, 1993), and provide a powerful social identity. Such groups and prototypes will be attractive to individuals who are contextually or more enduringly highly uncertain, or during times of or in situations characterized by great uncertainty.

> *Proposition 2*: Subjective uncertainty may produce a prototypically homogenous and cohesive organization or work unit with which members identify strongly.

Uncertainty reduction and self-enhancement are probably independent motivations for social identity processes, and in some circumstances it may be more urgent to reduce uncertainty than to pursue self-enhancement (e.g., when group entitativity is threatened), whereas in others it may be the opposite (e.g., when group prestige is threatened). However, uncertainty reduction may be more fundamentally adaptive because it constructs a self-concept that defines who we are and prescribes what we should perceive, think, feel, and do.

The uncertainty reduction hypothesis has clear relevance for organizational contexts. Indeed, the hypothesis is not inconsistent with Lester's (1987) uncertainty reduction theory that plays an important role in Saks and Ashforth's (1997) multilevel process model of organizational socialization. Although in both cases uncertainty motivates group socialization behaviors, the uncertainty reduction hypothesis specifies self-categorization as the social cognitive process that resolves uncertainty through prototype-based self-depersonalization.

Salience of social identity

The responsiveness of social identity to immediate social contexts is a central feature of social identity theory—and self-categorization theory within it. The cognitive system, governed by uncertainty reduction and self-enhancement motives, matches social categories to properties of the social context and brings into active use (i.e., makes salient) that category rendering the social context and one's place within it subjectively most meaningful. Specifically, there is an interaction between category accessibility and category fit so that people draw on accessible categories and investigate how well they fit the social field. The category that best fits the field becomes salient in that context (e.g., Oakes et al., 1994; Oakes & Turner, 1990).

Categories can be accessible because they are valued, important, and frequently employed aspects of the self-concept (i.e., chronic accessibility) and/or because they are perceptually salient (i.e., situational accessibility). Categories fit the social field because they account for situationally relevant similarities and differences among people (i.e., structural fit) and/or because category specifications account for context-specific behaviors (i.e., normative fit). Once fully activated (as opposed to merely "tried on") on the basis of optimal fit, category specifications organize themselves as contextually relevant prototypes and are used as a basis for the perceptual accentuation of intragroup similarities and intergroup differences, thereby maximizing separateness and clarity. Self-categorization in terms of the activated ingroup category then depersonalizes behavior in terms of the ingroup prototype.

Salience is not, however, a mechanical product of accessibility and fit (Hogg, 1996b; Hogg & Mullin, 1999). Social interaction involves the motivated manipulation of symbols (e.g., through speech, appearance, and behavior) by people who are strategically competing with one another to influence the frame of reference within which accessibility and fit interact. People are not content to have their identity determined by the social cognitive context. On the contrary, they say and do things to try to change the parameters so that a subjectively more meaningful and self-favoring identity becomes salient. For instance, a mixed-sex conversation about the communication of feelings is likely to make sex salient, because the chronically accessible category "sex" is situationally accessible and has good structural and normative fit. Male interactants who find the self-evaluative implications of gender stereotypes about feelings unfavorable might change the topic of conversation to politics so that sex becomes situationally less accessible and now has poor structural and normative fit. In this way a different, and self-evaluatively more favorable, identity may become salient.

This dynamic perspective on identity and self-conceptual salience has clear implications for organizational contexts. Manipulation of the intergroup social comparative context can be a powerful way to change organizational identity (self-conception as a member of a particular organization) and, thus, attitudes, motives, goals, and practices. Organizations or divisions within organizations that have poor work practices or organizational attitudes can be helped to reconstruct themselves, through surreptitious or overt changes in the salience of relevant intergroup comparative contexts (different levels of categorization or different outgroups at the same level of categorization). Such changes affect contextual self-categorization and, therefore, people's internalized attitudes and behaviors (e.g., Terry & Hogg, 1996).

One way in which organizations may deliberately manipulate the intergroup social comparative context is by "benchmarking." An organization selects specific other organizations as a legitimate comparison set, which threatens the group's prestige. This motivates upward redefinition of organizational identity and work practices, to make the group evaluatively more competitive.

Self-categorization theory's focus on prototypes allows some important conceptual developments in social identity theory, which have direct implications for organizational contexts. When group membership is salient, cognition is attuned to and guided by prototypicality. Thus, within groups people are able to distinguish among themselves and others in terms of how well they match the prototype. An intragroup prototypicality gradient exists—some people are or are perceived to be more prototypical than others (Hogg, 1996a,b, 1999). This idea allows social identity theorists to now explicate social identity-based intragroup processes, such as cohesion and social attraction, deviance and overachievement, and leadership and intragroup structural differentiation.

Cohesion and deviance

A development of social identity theory made possible by focusing on how social categorization produces prototype-based depersonalization is the social attraction hypothesis, which approaches group solidarity and cohesion as a reflection of depersonalized, prototype-based interindividual attitudes (Hogg, 1987, 1992, 1993). A distinction is drawn between interindividual evaluations, attitudes, and feelings that are based on and generated by being members of the same group or members of different groups (depersonalized *social attraction*) and those that are based on and generated by the idiosyncrasies and complementarities of close and enduring interpersonal relationships (*personal attraction*).

When a group is salient, ingroup members are liked more if they embody the ingroup prototype. Where the prototype is consensual, certain people are consensually liked, and where all members are highly prototypical, there is a tight network of social attraction. Of course, outgroup members generally are liked less than ingroup members. When a group is not salient, liking is based on personal relationships and idiosyncratic preferences. The prediction is that patterns of liking in an aggregate, and the bases of that liking, can change dramatically when an aggregate becomes a salient group (e.g., when uncertainty or entitativity are high, or when the group is under threat or is engaged in inter-group competition over a valued scarce resource). Social and personal attraction are not isomorphic (see Mullen & Copper, 1994). These predictions have been supported repeatedly by a program of research with laboratory, quasi naturalistic, sports, and organizational groups (Hogg, Cooper-Shaw, & Holzworth, 1993; Hogg & Hains, 1996; Hogg & Hardie, 1991, 1992, 1997; Hogg, Hardie, & Reynolds, 1995; see overviews by Hogg, 1992, 1993).

One practical implication of the idea of depersonalized social attraction in an organizational setting is that organizational or workgroup solidarity and, thus, adherence to group norms are unlikely to be strengthened by activities that strengthen only personal relationships or friendships. Indeed, such activities may compromise solidarity and norm adherence by fragmenting the group into friendship pairs or cliques that show interpersonal dislike for other pairs or cliques. To increase social attraction and solidarity within an organization, managers might, among other things, create uncertainty (this motivates identification), focus on interorganizational competition (this makes the group salient), and emphasize desirable attributes of the organization (this provides positive distinctiveness).

Proposition 3: Social attraction may foster organizational cohesion, and thereby identification and adherence to organizational norms; conversely, interpersonal attraction may fragment the organization and disrupt identification and adherence to norms.

Cohesion and solidarity, and the feelings people have for one another within a group, hinge on the perceived group prototypicality of others. We now discuss two organizationally relevant implications of this idea: (1) the dynamic interplay of group and demographic prototypes that affects cohesion within an organization (relational demography) and (2) the perception and treatment of nonprototypical group members (negative outliers and high flyers).

Relational demography

The social attraction analysis of cohesion has relevance for recent organizational research on relational demography (e.g., Mowday & Sutton, 1993; Riordan & Shore, 1997; Wesolowski & Moss-holder, 1997). Relational demography theorists propose that people in organizations or work units compare their own demographic characteristics (e.g., race, gender, ethnicity) with those of individual other members or the group as a whole, and that perceived similarity enhances work-related attitudes and behavior. The organization or unit provides the context within which similarity comparisons are made. Social identity theory and the social attraction hypothesis provide a much more textured analysis, based on the relative salience of the demographic or organizational group and on the correspondence between demographic and organizational norms/prototypes (see the discussion of group structure below).

Demographic homogeneity may strengthen organizational ingroup prototypes, social attraction, and identification and, thus, adherence to norms, particularly if group norms are not inconsistent with demographic category norms. If the organizational group's norms clash with those of the wider demographic category, then demographic homogeneity may make the wider category and its norms salient and, thus, weaken adherence to the organization's norms. Demographic diversity may weaken the impact of demographic group membership, make the organizational group itself more salient, and, thus, strengthen adherence to organizational norms, particularly if societal relations between demographic groups are harmonious. If, however, relations between demographic groups are conflictual and are emotionally charged, diversity will highlight intergroup relations outside the organization or unit, thus making demographic membership salient and strengthening adherence to demographic—not organizational—norms. This analysis revolves around the contextual salience of demographic or organizational identity—not just the degree of perceived demographic similarity.

Proposition 4: Intraorganizational demographic similarity/diversity will impact organizational behavior via organizational or demographic identity salience; organizational salience and behavior are enhanced by demographic similarity, if organizational and demographic norms are consistent, and by demographic diversity, if there is societal harmony among demographic categories.

Negative outliers and high flyers

A further implication of the social attraction hypothesis is that prototypically marginal ingroup members will be liked less than prototypically central members and that this process will be accentuated under high salience so that marginal members may be entirely rejected as "deviants." A program of laboratory research by Marques and his associates provides good evidence for this process (Marques, 1990; Marques & Paez, 1994; Marques & Yzerbyt, 1988; Marques, Yzerbyt, & Leyens, 1988). By being aprotypical, particularly in a direction that leans toward a salient outgroup, a marginal ingrouper jeopardizes the distinctiveness and prototypical clarity and integrity of the ingroup. This may introduce the threat of uncertainty. Thus, fellow ingroupers, especially those for whom uncertainty is particularly threatening, will strongly reject the deviant in order to consolidate a clear prototype to which they can strongly assimilate themselves through self-categorization.

So-called black sheep studies focus on "negative" deviants: ingroup members who are inclined toward the outgroup prototype. But what about "positive" deviants? These are group members who are aprototypical, but in evaluatively favorable ways—for example, overachievers or high flyers. On the one hand, overachievers should be socially unattractive because they are aprototypical, but, on the other, they should be socially attractive because the group can bask in their reflected glory (cf. Burger, 1985; Cialdini et al., 1976; Cialdini & de Nicholas, 1989; Sigelman, 1986; Snyder, Lassegard, & Ford, 1986; Wann, Hamlet, Wilson, & Hodges, 1995). There is some evidence that people are evaluatively particularly harsh on over-achievers who suffer a setback or experience a fall (e.g., Feather, 1994), but this research does not differentiate between overachievers who are members of a salient ingroup and those who are not.

To investigate this, researchers are conducting a series of laboratory experiments (Fielding & Hogg, 1998). From social identity theory we predict that the immediate and intergroup social context of overachievement determines the evaluation of positive ingroup deviants. There are two dimensions to the model:

1. A functional dimension. Where solidarity and consensual prototypicality are important to the group, perhaps owing to uncertainty concerns, positive deviants are dysfunctional for the group; they will be evaluatively downgraded, much like negative deviants. Where solidarity is less critical and prototypicality less consensual but self-enhancement is important, positive deviants are functional for the group; they will be upgraded as they contribute to a favorable redefinition of ingroup identity.
2. A social attribution dimension. Where positively deviant behavior can be "owned" by the group, the deviant will be favorably evaluated; this would be likely if the deviant modestly attributed the behavior to the support of the group rather than to personal ability and if the deviant had little personal history of overachievement (i.e., was a "new" deviant). Where positively deviant behavior cannot readily be "owned" by the group, the deviant will be unfavorably evaluated; this would be likely if the deviant took full personal credit for the behavior without acknowledging the group's support (i.e., "boasted") and if the deviant had a long personal history of overachievement (i.e., was an enduring deviant).

Proposition 5: Organizations will reject negative organizational deviants. Positive deviants will be accepted where organizational prestige is important but will be rejected where organizational solidarity and distinctiveness are important.

Leadership

In contrast to deviants, prototypical group members are reliably and consensually favorably evaluated when group membership is salient. This idea has recently been extended in order to develop a social identity model of leadership processes in groups (Hogg, 1996b, 1999; also, see Fielding & Hogg, 1997; Hains,

Hogg, & Duck, 1997; Hogg, 1996a; Hogg, Hains, & Mason, 1998). From this perspective, leadership—the focus is largely on emergent leaders—is a structural feature of ingroups (i.e., leaders and followers), which is produced by the processes of self-categorization and prototype-based depersonalization. As group membership becomes more salient, being a prototypical group member may be at least as important for leadership as having characteristics that are widely believed to be associated with a particular type of leader (i.e., being stereotypical of a nominal leader category; see leader categorization theory: Lord, Foti, & De Vader, 1984; Nye & Forsyth, 1991; Nye & Simonetta, 1996; Rush & Russell, 1988). There are three aspects of the process:

(1) Self-categorization constructs a gradient of actual or perceived prototypicality within the group so that some people are more prototypical than others, and they act as a focus for attitudinal and behavioral depersonalization. The person who occupies the contextually most prototypical position embodies the behaviors that others conform to and, thus, *appears* to have exercised influence over other group members. If the social context remains stable, the prototype remains stable, and the same individual appears to have enduring influence. However, the process is automatic. The "leader" merely embodies the aspirations, attitudes, and behaviors of the group but does not actively exercise leadership.

(2) Social attraction ensures that more prototypical members are liked more than less prototypical members; if the prototype is consensual, more prototypical members are consensually liked. There are a number of important implications of this. First, being socially attractive furnishes the leader with the capacity to actively gain compliance with his or her requests—people tend to agree and comply with people they like. Second, this empowers the leader and publicly confirms his or her ability to exercise influence. Third, the prototypical leader is likely to identify strongly with the group and, thus, exercise influence in empathic and collectively beneficial ways, which strengthens his or her perceived prototypicality and consensual social attractiveness. Fourth, consensual attractiveness confirms differential popularity and public endorsement of the leader, imbues the leader with prestige and status, and instantiates an intragroup status differential between leader(s) and followers.

(3) The final process is an attribution one, in which members make the fundamental attribution error (Ross, 1977) or show correspondence bias (Gilbert & Jones, 1986; see also Gilbert & Malone, 1995, and Trope & Liberman, 1993). Members overattribute or misattribute the leader's behavior to personality rather than to his or her prototypical position in the group. Because the behavior being attributed, particularly over an enduring period, includes the appearance or actuality of being influential over others' attitudes and behaviors, being consensually socially attractive, and gaining compliance and

agreement from others, this constructs a charismatic leadership personality for the leader.

A number of factors accentuate this process. First, because prototypicality is the yardstick of group life, it attracts attention and renders highly prototypical members figural against the background of the group, thus enhancing the fundamental attribution error (Taylor & Fiske, 1978). Second, the emerging status-based structural differentiation between leader(s) and followers further enhances the distinctiveness of the leader(s) against the background of the rest of the group. Third, to redress their own perceived lack of power and control, followers seek individualizing information about the leader, because they believe that such information is most predictive of how the leader will behave in many situations (Fiske, 1993; Fiske & Dépret, 1996). Fourth, cultural theories of causes of leadership behavior (e.g., the "great person" theory of leadership) may accentuate the fundamental error (e.g., Morris & Peng, 1994). And fifth, the correspondence bias may be strengthened because followers perceive the leader's behavior to be relatively extreme and distinctive and because they then fail to properly consider situational causes of the behavior (e.g., Gilbert & Malone, 1995; Trope & Liberman, 1993).

Together, these three processes transform prototypical group members into leaders who are able to be proactive and innovative in exercising influence. This also equips leaders to maintain their tenure. They can simply exercise power (more of this below), but they can also manipulate circumstances to enhance their perceived prototypicality: they can exercise self-serving ideological control over the content of the prototype, they can pillory ingroup deviants who threaten the self-serving prototype, they can demonize outgroups that clearly highlight the self-serving ingroup prototype, and they can elevate uncertainty to ensure that members are motivated to identify strongly with a group that is defined as the leader wishes (uncertainty can be managed as a resource by people in power; e.g., Marris, 1996).

The most basic prediction from this model is that as group salience increases, perceived leadership effectiveness becomes more determined by group prototypicality and less determined by possession of general leadership qualities. This prediction has been confirmed in a series of three laboratory studies of emergent leadership (Hains et al., 1997; Hogg et al., 1998, Experiments 1 and 2) and replicated in a field study of outward-bound groups (Fielding & Hogg, 1997). The social attraction and attribution aspects of the model remain to be investigated, as do the many implications described in this section.

We now suggest three organizationally relevant leadership consequences of excessively high group cohesiveness. Such groups may (1) produce leaders who are prototypical but do not possess task-appropriate leadership skills (cf. groupthink); (2) consolidate organizational prototypes that reflect dominant rather than minority cultural attributes and, thus, exclude minorities from top leadership positions; and (3) produce an environment that is conducive to the exercise, and perhaps abuse, of power by leaders.

Prototypical leadership and groupthink

This research may help cast light on groupthink: suboptimal decision-making procedures in highly cohesive groups, leading to poor decisions with potentially damaging consequences (e.g., Janis, 1982). There is now some evidence that the critical component of "cohesiveness" associated with groupthink is social attraction, rather than interpersonal attraction (Hogg & Hains, 1998; see also Turner, Pratkanis, Probasco, & Leve, 1992). If we assume that group prototypes do not necessarily embody optimal procedures for group decision making, then group prototypical leaders are quite likely to be less effective leaders of decision-making groups than are leadership-stereotypical leaders (i.e., leaders who, in this case, possess qualities that most people believe are appropriate for group decision making). This suggests that groupthink may arise because overly cohesive groups "choose" highly prototypical and, thus, perhaps, task-inappropriate members as leaders.

Proposition 6: Strong organizational identification may hinder endorsement of effective leaders, because leadership is based on group prototypicality, and group prototypes may not embody effective leadership properties.

Minorities as organizational leaders

Another implication of this analysis of leadership relates to evidence that minorities (e.g., women and people of color) can find it difficult to attain top leadership positions in organizations (e.g., Eagly, Karau, & Makhijani, 1995). If organizational prototypes (e.g., of speech, dress, attitudes, and interaction styles) are societally cast so that minorities do not match them well, minorities are unlikely to be endorsed as leaders under conditions where organizational pro-totypicality is more important than leadership stereotypicality—that is, when organizational identification and cohesion are very high. This might arise under conditions of uncertainty when, for example, organizations are under threat from competitors or when there is an economic crisis—situations where leaders, rather than managers, may be badly needed.

Proposition 7: Minorities may find it difficult to attain top leadership positions in organizations because they do not fit culturally prescribed organizational prototypes.

Leadership and the exercise of power

An important feature of the model is that the processes of social attraction and prototypical attribution decouple the leader from the group; they create a status-based structural differentiation of leaders(s) and followers, which is endorsed by both leader(s) and followers. This has implications for the role of power in leadership

(Hogg, 1998, 1999; Hogg & Reid, in press). Traditionally, social identity theorists have said little about power, preferring to talk of influence.

Where leaders are merely prototypical, they have influence over followers by virtue of being prototypical; followers automatically comply through self-categorization. It is unnecessary to exercise power to gain influence, and there are strong mutual bonds of liking and empathy between prototypically united leaders and followers that would inhibit the exercise of power in ways that might harm members of the group.

However, once charisma and status-based structural differentiation gather pace, the leader becomes increasingly psychologically and materially separated from the group. This severs the empathic and social attraction bonds that previously guarded against abuse of power. A consensually endorsed, status-based intergroup relationship between leader(s) (probably in the form of a power elite) and followers has effectively come into existence; thus, typical intergroup behaviors are made possible. The leader can discriminate against followers, favor self and the leadership elite, and express negative social attitudes against and develop negative stereotypes of followers (e.g., Goodwin & Fiske, 1996; Goodwin, Gubin, Fiske, & Yzerbyt, in press). Under these conditions leaders are likely to exercise power (in Yukl & Falbe's, 1991, sense of personal power or in Raven's, 1965, sense of reward power, coercive power, or legitimate power) and are able to abuse power—for example, when they feel their position is under threat.

This rigidly hierarchical leadership scenario is most likely to emerge when conditions encourage groups to be cohesive and homogenous, with extremitized and clearly delimited prototypes that are tightly consensual. In an organizational context, extreme societal or organizational uncertainty might produce these conditions (Hogg, 1999; see also Pratto, Sidanius, Stallworth, & Malle, 1994, and Tyler, 1990).

> *Proposition 8*: Subjective uncertainty may produce a prototypically and demographically homogenous organization or work unit that has a hierarchical leadership structure with a powerful leader and that has rigid, entrenched, and "extremist" attitudes and practices.

The progression from benign influence to the possibly destructive wielding of power may not be inevitable. Conditions that inhibit the attribution of charisma and the process of structural differentiation, and that reground leadership in prototypicality, may curb the exercise of power. For example, if a group becomes less cohesive, more diverse, and less consensual about its prototype, followers are less likely to agree on and endorse the same person as the leader. The incumbent leader's power base is fragmented, and numerous new "contenders" emerge. This limits the leader's ability to abuse power and renders the exercise of power less effective. Paradoxically, a rapid increase in cohesiveness, caused, for example, by imminent external threat to the group, may, through a different process, have a similar outcome. Cohesion may make the group so consensual that leader and group become temporarily re-fused. The empathic bond is re-established so that the leader does not need to exercise power to gain influence, and any abuse of power would be akin to abuse of self.

Proposition 9: Emergent leaders may tend to abuse their power unless the organization is highly diverse or highly cohesive.

Group structure

Leadership is only one way in which groups can be internally structured. Groups, such as organizations, are also structured, in various ways, into functional or demographic subgroups. In this section we discuss the relevance of social identity theory to the analysis of relations among subgroups within organizations—in particular, sociodemographic subgroups based on gender, race, ethnicity, and so forth and organizational subgroups within a superordinate organization formed by a merger or acquisition.

Subgroup structure

Almost all groups are vertically organized to contain subgroups, while they themselves are nested within larger groups. Sometimes subgroups are wholly nested within a superordinate group (e.g., a sales department within an organization), and sometimes subgroups are crosscut by the superordinate group (e.g., pilots within an airline). Social identity theorists and those with more general social categorization perspectives make predictions about the nature of relations between subgroups as a function of the nature of the subgroups' relationship to the superordinate group. Much of these scholars' work is framed by the "contact hypothesis," to investigate the conditions under which contact between members of different groups might improve enduring relations between the groups (e.g., Brown, 1996; Gaertner, Dovidio, Anastasio, Bachman, & Rust, 1993; Gaertner, Dovidio, & Bachman, 1996; Gaertner, Rust, Dovidio, Bachman, & Anastasio, 1995; Hewstone, 1994, 1996; Pettigrew, 1998).

Subgroups often resist attempts by a superordinate group to dissolve subgroup boundaries and merge them into one large group. This can be quite marked where the superordinate group is very large, amorphous, and impersonal. Thus, assimilationist strategies within nations, or large organizations, can produce fierce subgroup loyalty and intersubgroup competition. Subgroup members derive social identity from their groups and, thus, view externally imposed assimilation as an identity threat. The threat may be stronger in large superordinate groups because of optimal distinctiveness considerations (Brewer, 1991, 1993). People strive for a balance between conflicting motives for inclusion/sameness (satisfied by group membership) and for distinctiveness/uniqueness (satisfied by individuality). So, in very large organizations, people feel overincluded and strive for distinctiveness, often by identifying with distinctive subunits or departments.

Some research suggests that an effective strategy for managing intersubgroup relations within a larger group is to make subgroup and superordinate group identity simultaneously salient. For example, Hornsey and Hogg (1999, in press a,b) conducted a series of experiments in which they found intersubgroup relations to be more harmonious when the subgroups were salient within the context of a salient superordinate group than when the superordinate group alone or the subgroups alone were salient. This may re-create, in the laboratory, the policy of multiculturalism, adopted by some countries to manage ethnic diversity at a national level (cf. Prentice & Miller, 1999).

The implication for organizations is clear. To secure harmonious and cooperative relations among departments or divisions within a large organization, it may be best to balance loyalty to and identification with the subunit with loyalty to and identification with the superordinate organization, and not overemphasize either one to the detriment of the other. From a social identity perspective, managers might achieve this balance by having a distinct departmental or divisional structure, involving, for example, departmental activities and friendly interdepartmental rivalry, carefully balanced against a clear interorganization orientation and organization-wide activities that emphasize positive distinctiveness and positive organizational identity.

Proposition 10: Harmonious relations among subgroups within an organization are often best achieved by simultaneous recognition of subgroup and organizational identity.

Sociodemographic structure

Intragroup dynamics and structure also are influenced by the sociodemographic structure of society. Most groups, including organizational groups, have a membership that is diverse in terms of race, ethnicity, gender, (dis)ability, and so forth (e.g., Chung, 1997; Cox, 1991; Ibarra, 1995; Kandola, 1995). Organizations are a crucible in which wider intergroup relations, often evaluatively polarized and emotionally charged, are played out; conflict, disadvantage, marginalization, and minority victimization can arise (e.g., Williams & Sommer, 1997; cf. the expectation states theory notion of diffuse status characteristics [de Gilder & Wilke, 1994] and our earlier discussion of relational demography).

As a theory of intergroup relations, social identity theory has direct relevance for the study of sociodemographic diversity within organizations (Brewer, 1996; Brewer, von Hippel, & Gooden, 1999; see also Alderfer & Thomas, 1988; Brewer & Miller, 1996; Kramer, 1991; Oakes et al., 1994). Intraorganizational minority status rests on the dominant composition of the organization—for example, gender may be a minority status in some organizations but not others. Because of the salience of their minority status in the organizational context, members of such groups are likely to be classified and perceived in terms of this status, thus occasioning stereotypical expectations and treatment from members of the dominant group. The likelihood of stereotyped responses increases if the demographic minority categorization (e.g., gender or ethnicity) converges with a role or employment classification within the organization—for instance, if there are relatively few female employees and they are all employed in secretarial or clerical positions. In such circumstances, categorization in terms of the employment classification is facilitated, because it covaries with a salient demographic categorization.

According to Brewer (1996; Brewer et al., 1999; see also Brewer & Miller, 1996), differentiations within categories are more likely to be made when minority status does not correlate with employment classification. If minority group status is not diagnostic of employment categorization, employees will find it necessary, in order to function within the organization, to acknowledge differences within both the minority group and the employment classification. One way in which convergence between minority group status and employment classification can be avoided, and hence stereotyped responses to the minority group can be reduced, is to crosscut organizational roles and social group membership. In a crosscutting structure, minority group memberships and employment classifications are independent of each other; knowing a person's group membership is undiagnostic of employment role or classification. Marcus-Newhall, Miller, Holtz, and Brewer (1993) found that when category membership and role assignment were not convergent (i.e., they were crosscut), category members were less likely to favor their own category on post-test ratings, and they were less likely to differentiate among the categories than in a convergent role structure.

From a social identity perspective, a crosscutting structure is one way to manage diversity effectively in organizations. Another strategy is to create a pluralistic or multicultural normative environment within the organization (Cox, 1991; Kandola, 1995). As discussed above, this involves minority members' balancing subgroup (i.e., demographic minority) and superordinate group (i.e., demographic majority or organization) identification, and majority members' exhibiting normative acceptance and support for cultural diversity within the organization.

To summarize, a crosscutting structure will assist the development of a pluralistic organizational environment, as will reduced marginalization of minority group members, through co-operative intergroup contact (Hewstone & Brown, 1986; see also Deschamps & Brown, 1983) and through intergroup contact that changes members' cognitive representation of the intergroup structure from the perception of separate groups to one that acknowledges plural identities or a common ingroup identity (e.g., Gaertner et al., 1996).

Proposition 11: Conflict arising from sociodemographic diversity within an organization can be moderated by crosscutting demography with role assignments or by encouraging a strategy of cultural pluralism.

Finally, drawing on the uncertainty reduction hypothesis, we would expect organizational uncertainty to generally work against diversity. Organizations facing uncertainty would strive for homogeneity and consensual prototypicality that might marginalize sociodemographic minorities within the organization. The effect would be amplified under conditions of wider societal uncertainty that encourages ethnic, racial, religious, and national identification, and concomitant xenophobia and intolerance.

Mergers and acquisitions

A special case of group structure is the merging of two organizations or the acquisition of one organization by another. Mergers and acquisitions pose special problems of intragroup relations for organizations (e.g., Hakansson & Sharma, 1996; Hogan & Overmyer-Day, 1994). When two organizations merge or, more commonly, one acquires the other, the postmerger entity embraces premerger intergroup relations between the merger "partners." These relations are often competitive and sometimes bitter and antagonistic. Indeed, negative responses and feelings toward the employees of the other organization may jeopardize the success of the merger.

Case studies of mergers confirm this. There are many examples of mergers failing because of "us" versus "them" dynamics that prevail if employees do not relinquish their old identities (e.g., Blake & Mouton, 1985; Buono & Bowditch, 1989). In a laboratory study Haunschild, Moreland, and Murrell (1994) found similar results. People who had worked on a task together in a dyad showed stronger interdyad biases when different dyads were subsequently required to merge than did people who had not previously worked together in their own dyad and, hence, were only nominal groups.

Social identity theorists make clear predictions about the success of a merger. The behaviors that group members adopt to pursue self-enhancement through positive social identity are influenced by *subjective belief structures*: beliefs about the nature of relations between the ingroup and relevant outgroups (Tajfel & Turner, 1979; see also Ellemers, 1993; Ellemers, Doojse, van Knippenberg, & Wilke, 1992; Ellemers, van Knippenberg, de Vries, & Wilke, 1988; Tajfel, 1975; Taylor & McKirnan, 1984; van Knippenberg & Ellemers, 1993). These beliefs concern (1) the stability and legitimacy of intergroup status relations (i.e., whether one's group deserves its status, and the likelihood of a change in status) and (2) the possibility of social mobility (psychologically passing from one group to another) or social change (changing the ingroup's evaluation). Social change can involve direct conflict but also socially creative behavior, such as ingroup bias on dimensions that are not related directly to the basis for the status differentiation (e.g., Lalonde, 1992; Terry & Callan, 1998).

At the interorganizational level, an organization that believes its lower-status position is legitimate and stable and believes that it is possible for members to pass psychologically into the more prestigious organization (i.e., acquire a social identity as a member of the prestigious organization) will be unlikely to show organizational solidarity or engage in interorganizational competition. Instead, members will attempt, as individuals, to disidentify and gain psychological entry to the other organization. This will increase their support for the merger and their commitment to and identification with the new, merged organization.

In contrast, an organization that believes its lower-status position is illegitimate and unstable, that passing is not viable, and that a different interorganizational status relation is achievable will show marked solidarity, engage in direct interorganizational competition, and actively attempt to undermine the success of the merger. Although members of low-status organizations are likely to respond favorably to conditions of high permeability (see Zuckerman, 1979), an opposite effect is likely for employees of the higher-status premerger organization (see Vaughan, 1978). Permeable boundaries pose a threat to the status they enjoy as members of a higher-status premerger organization, so they are likely to respond negatively to permeable intergroup boundaries.

> *Proposition 12*: Lower-status merger partners will respond favorably to a merger, if they believe their status is legitimate and that the boundary between the premerger partners is permeable, and unfavorably, if they believe their status is illegitimate and boundaries are impermeable. Higher-status merger partners will respond unfavorably to permeable boundaries.

In a recent study of employees involved in a merger between two airlines, Terry, Carey, and Callan (in press) found some support for these predictions. Perception of permeable intergroup boundaries in the new organization was associated positively with identification with the new organization and both job-related (organizational commitment and job satisfaction) and person-related (emotional well-being and self-esteem) outcomes among employees of the low-status premerger organization, but negatively with the person-related outcomes among employees of the high-status premerger organization. Analyses showed that these effects were significant after controlling for the type of individual-level constructs that have been considered in previous merger research (e.g., perceived positiveness of the change process and the use of both problem- and emotion-focused coping responses)—a pattern of results that reflects the importance of considering group-level variables in merger research.

Gaertner and colleagues (Anastasio, Bachman, Gaertner, & Dovidio, 1997; Gaertner et al., 1996) also found support for a social categorization approach, in the context of a bank merger. Perception of successful contact between the premerger organizations (e.g., contact between equal-status partners, positive interdependence between the groups, and many opportunities for interaction) reduced intergroup bias, through employees' cognitive representations of the merged group and through low intergroup anxiety. For intergroup evaluative bias on both work-related and sociability dimensions, the belief that the merged organization felt like one group (see van Knippenberg, 1997) was related negatively to intergroup anxiety (and, through reduced anxiety, to low intergroup bias), whereas the perception that the organization felt like two subgroups was related positively to work-related bias. Thus, in contrast to the optimization of subgroup relations in an organizational context (and the management of sociodemographic diversity; see above), a dual identity model does not appear to be useful in the context of a merger, presumably because heightened salience of premerger group identities may threaten the success of this type of organizational change.

One lacuna in social identity research on mergers is the temporal dimension (which is absent from most social psychological research on social identity processes). Mergers take time and move through stages, during which different social identity processes may operate. It would be valuable to track social identity and self-categorization processes in mergers over time, perhaps within the framework of Levine and Moreland's (1994; Moreland & Levine, 1997, in press) diachronic group socialization model.

Another lacuna is uncertainty. Mergers and takeovers often produce enormous uncertainty, which can instantiate precisely the conditions that work against a successful merger. To reduce self-conceptual uncertainty, merger partners resist change and may polarize and consolidate interorganizational attitudes around narrowly prescriptive norms and fierce premerger organizational identification.

Summary, conclusions, and prospects

The aim of this article has been to describe recent theoretical developments within social identity theory that focus, via self-categorization theory, on how social categorization produces prototype-based depersonalization, which is responsible for social identity phenomena. These developments extend social identity theory. They advance our understanding of social identity processes in intergroup contexts and the way in which people may internalize group norms and align their behavior with these norms. They also have produced a new conceptualization of motivation associated with social identity, a better understanding of salience processes, and a new focus on intragroup processes that is now producing social identity models of, for example, cohesion, deviance, group structure, and leadership.

We introduce these new developments to an organizational readership that is familiar with some aspects of social identity theory, but less familiar with more recent self-categorization theory-based developments, in order to show how these developments are relevant to understanding a range of social behaviors in organizational contexts. One of our main aims has been to derive, from these developments, a variety of more or less specific, but testable, speculations and propositions, in order to help frame future research directions in the study of social identity processes and social behavior in organizational contexts.

The challenge for the future is to integrate new social identity mechanisms centrally into theories of organizational behavior. To date, such mechanisms have played a relatively small role in the literature on organizational behavior. Thus, the important role that identifications with the workgroup, organization, and profession, as well as those that emanate from people's sociodemographic background, may play in organizational behavior has yet to be articulated fully.

We suggest that identity-related constructs and processes have the potential to inform our understanding of organizational behavior. Combined with multilevel approaches to organizational research, the use of both individual-level and group-level constructs in models of organizational phenomena could mark the beginning of a new phase of research in organizational behavior. By acknowledging the importance of work-related identities to people's sense of self, a social identity perspective adds to our understanding of organizational attitudes and behavior by drawing on the important link between such identities and the person's sense of self. Such a perspective should improve explanation and understanding of intergroup relations, both within and between organizations.

To maximize the usefulness of the social identity perspective in the organizational arena, there must be significant interchange between social and organizational psychologists. When one is deriving predictions from a social identity perspective on organizational behavior, one finds the results from laboratory-based social psychological research invaluable, as are the insights that have been gained from field research in the organizational context. It is this type of interchange that will further our understanding of how identity-related constructs and processes impact organizational phenomena, and it should lead, in turn, to extensions of and refinements to social identity theory itself. We are confident that the extent of theoretical interchange between organizational and social psychologists studying social identity mechanisms can increase (e.g., Hogg & Terry, in press), and we are extremely optimistic about the potential that this interchange has for the development of both disciplines.

Note

1 For general developments, see books by Abrams and Hogg (1990, 1999); Hogg and Abrams (1988); Hogg and Terry (in press); Oakes, Haslam, and Turner (1994); Robinson (1996); Spears, Oakes, Ellemers, and Haslam (1997); Terry and Hogg (1999); Turner et al. (1987); and Worchl, Morales, Páez, and Deschamps (1998).

References

Abrams, D., & Hogg, M. A. 1988. Comments on the motivational status of self-esteem in social identity and intergroup discrimination. *European Journal of Social Psychology*, 18: 317–334.

Abrams, D., & Hogg, M. A. (Eds.). 1990. *Social identity theory: Constructive and critical advances*. London: Harvester Wheatsheaf.

Abrams, D., & Hogg, M. A. 1998. Prospects for research in group processes and intergroup relations. *Group Processes and Intergroup Relations*, 1: 7–20.

Abrams, D., & Hogg, M. A. (Eds.). 1999. *Social identity and social cognition*. Oxford: Blackwell.

Abrams, D., & Hogg, M. A. In press. Self, group and identity: A dynamic model. In M. A. Hogg & R. S. Tindale (Eds.), *Blackwell handbook of social psychology: Group processes*. Oxford: Blackwell.

Alderfer, C. P., & Thomas, D. A. 1988. The significance of race and ethnicity for understanding organizational behavior. In C. L. Cooper & I. Robertson (Eds.), *International review of industrial and organizational psychology:* 1–41. New York: Wiley.

Anastasio, P. A., Bachman, B. A., Gaertner, S. L., & Dovidio, J. F. 1997. Categorization, recategorization, and common ingroup identity. In R. Spears, P. J. Oakes, N. Ellemers, & S. A. Haslam (Eds.), *The social psychology of stereotyping and group life:* 236–256. Oxford: Blackwell.

Ashforth, B. E., & Humphrey, R. H. 1993. Emotional labor in service roles: The influence of identity. *Academy of Management Review*, 18: 88–115.

Ashforth, B. E., & Mael, F. A. 1989. Social identity theory and the organization. *Academy of Management Review*, 14: 20–39.

Blake, R. R., & Mouton, J. S. 1985. How to achieve integration on the human side of the merger. *Organizational Dynamics*, 13: 41–56.

Brewer, M. B. 1991. The social self: On being the same and different at the same time. *Personality and Social Psychology Bulletin*, 17: 475–482.

Brewer, M. B. 1993. The role of distinctiveness in social identity and group behaviour. In M. A. Hogg & D. Abrams (Eds.), *Group motivation: Social psychological perspectives:* 1–16. London: Harvester Wheatsheaf.

Brewer, M. B. 1996. Managing diversity: The role of social identities. In S. Jackson & M. Ruderman (Eds.), *Diversity in work teams:* 47–68. Washington, DC: American Psychological Association.

Brewer, M. B., & Harasty, A. S. 1996. Seeing groups as entities: The role of perceiver motivation. In E. T. Higgins & R. M. Sorrentino (Eds.), *Handbook of motivation and cognition. Volume 3: The interpersonal context:* 347–370. New York: Guilford.

Brewer, M. B., & Miller, N. 1996. *Intergroup relations*. Milton Keynes, UK: Open University Press.

Brewer, M. B., von Hippel, W., & Gooden, M. P. 1999. Diversity and organizational identity: The problem of entree after entry. In D. A. Prentice & D. T. Miller (Eds.), *Cultural divides: Understanding and overcoming group conflict:* 337–363. New York: Russell Sage Foundation.

Brown, R. J. 1996. Tajfel's contribution to the reduction of intergroup conflict. In W. P. Robinson (Ed.), *Social groups and identities: Developing the legacy of Henri Tajfel:* 169–189. Oxford: Butterworth-Heinemann.

Buono, A. F., & Bowditch, J. L. 1989. *The human side of mergers and acquisitions; Managing collisions between people, cultures, and organizations*. San Francisco: Jossey-Bass.

Burger, J. M. 1985. Temporal effects on attributions for academic performances and reflected-glory basking. *Social Psychology Quarterly*, 48: 330–336.

Campbell, D. T. 1958. Common fate, similarity, and other indices of the status of aggregates of persons as social entities. *Behavioral Science*, 3: 14–25.

Chung, W. V. L. 1997. *Ethnicity and organizational diversity*. New York: University Press of America.

Cialdini, R. B., Borden, R. J., Thorne, A., Walker, M. R., Freeman, S., & Sloan, L. R. 1976. Basking in reflected glory: Three (football) field studies. *Journal of Personality and Social Psychology*, 34: 366–375.

Cialdini, R. B., & de Nicholas, M. E. 1989. Self-presentation by association. *Journal of Personality and Social Psychology*, 57: 626–631.

Cox, T. 1991. The multicultural organization. *Academy of Management Executive*, 5: 34–47.

de Gilder, D., & Wilke, H. A. M. 1994. Expectation states theory and the motivational determinants of social influence. *European Review of Social Psychology*, 5: 243–269.

Deschamps, J.-C., & Brown, R. J. 1983. Superordinate goals and intergroup conflict. *British Journal of Social Psychology*, 22: 189–195.

Dutton, J. E., Dukerich, J. M., & Harquail, C. V. 1994. Organizational images and member identification. *Administrative Science Quarterly*, 39: 239–263.

Eagly, A. H., Karau, S. J., & Makhijani, M. G. 1995. Gender and the effectiveness of leaders: A meta-analysis. *Psychological Bulletin*, 117: 125–145.

Ellemers, N. 1993. The influence of socio-structural variables on identity management strategies. *European Review of Social Psychology*, 4: 27–57.

Ellemers, N., Doosje, B. J., van Knippenberg, A., & Wilke, H. 1992. Status protection in high status minority groups. *European Journal of Social Psychology*, 22: 123–140.

Ellemers, N., van Knippenberg, A., de Vries, N., & Wilke, H. 1988. Social identification and permeability of group boundaries. *European Journal of Social Psychology*, 18: 497–513.

Feather, N. T. 1994. Attitudes towards high achievers and reactions to their fall: Theory and research concerning tall poppies. *Advances in Experimental Social Psychology*, 26: 1–73.

Fielding, K. S., & Hogg, M. A. 1997. Social identity, self-categorization, and leadership: A field study of small interactive groups. *Group Dynamics: Theory, Research, and Practice*, 1: 39–51.

Fielding, K. S., & Hogg, M. A. 1998. *Positive and negative deviance in groups: A social identity analysis*. Unpublished manuscript, University of Queensland.

Fiske, S. T. 1993. Controlling other people: The impact of power on stereotyping. *American Psychologist*, 48: 621–628.

Fiske, S. T., & Dépret, E. 1996. Control, interdependence and power: Understanding social cognition in its social context. *European Review of Social Psychology*, 7: 31–61.

Fiske, S. T., & Taylor, S. E. 1991. *Social cognition* (2nd ed.). New York: McGraw-Hill.

Gaertner, S. L., Dovidio, J. F., Anastasio, P. A., Bachman, B. A., & Rust, M. C. 1993. Reducing intergroup bias: The common ingroup identity model. *European Review of Social Psychology*, 4: 1–26.

Gaertner, S. L., Dovidio, J. F., & Bachman, B. A. 1996. Revisiting the contact hypothesis: The induction of a common ingroup identity. *International Journal of Intercultural Relations*, 20: 271–290.

Gaertner, S. L., Rust, M. C., Dovidio, J. F., Bachman, B. A., & Anastasio, P. A. 1995. The contact hypothesis: The role of a common ingroup identity in reducing intergroup bias among majority and minority group members. In J. L. Nye & A. Brower (Eds.), *What's social about social cognition*: 230–260. Newbury Park, CA: Sage.

Gilbert, D. T., & Jones, E. E. 1986. Perceiver-induced constraint: Interpretations of self-generated reality. *Journal of Personality and Social Psychology*, 50: 269–280.

Gilbert, D. T., & Malone, P. S. 1995. The correspondence bias. *Psychological Bulletin*, 117: 21–38.

Goodwin, S. A., & Fiske, S. T. 1996. Judge not, lest ...: The ethics of power holders' decision making and standards for social judgment. In D. M. Messick & A. E. Tenbrunsel (Eds.),

Codes of conduct: Behavioral research into business ethics: 117–142. New York: Russell Sage Foundation.

Goodwin, S. A., Gubin, A., Fiske, S. T., & Yzerbyt, V. Y. In press. Power can bias impression formation: Stereotyping subordinates by default and by design. *Group Processes and Intergroup Relations.*

Hains, S. C., Hogg, M. A., & Duck, J. M. 1997. Self-categorization and leadership: Effects of group prototypicality and leader stereotypicality. *Personality and Social Psychology Bulletin,* 23: 1087–1100.

Hakansson, H., & Sharma, D. D. 1996. Strategic alliances in a network perspective. In D. Iacobucci (Ed.). *Networks in marketing:* 108–124. Thousand Oaks, CA: Sage.

Hamilton, D. L., & Sherman, S. J. 1996. Perceiving persons and groups. *Psychological Review,* 103: 336–355.

Hamilton, D. L., Sherman, S. J., & Lickel, B. 1998. Perceiving social groups: The importance of the entitativity continuum. In C. Sedikides, J. Schopler, & C. A. Insko (Eds.), *Intergroup cognition and intergroup behavior:* 47–74. Mahwah, NJ: Lawrence Erlbaum Associates.

Haunschild, P. R., Moreland, R. L., & Murrell, A. J. 1994. Sources of resistance to mergers between groups. *Journal of Applied Social Psychology,* 24: 1150–1178.

Hewstone, M. R. C. 1994. Revision and change of stereotypic beliefs: In search of the illusive subtyping model. *European Review of Social Psychology,* 5: 69–109.

Hewstone, M. R. C. 1996. Contact and categorization: Social psychological interventions to change intergroup relations. In C. N. Macrae, C. Stangor, & M. R. C. Hewstone (Eds.), *Stereotypes and stereotyping:* 323–368. London: Guilford.

Hewstone, M. R. C., & Brown, R. J. 1986. Contact is not enough: An intergroup perspective on the "contact hypothesis." In M. R. C. Hewstone & R. J. Brown (Eds.), *Contact and conflict in intergroup encounters*: 1–44. Oxford: Blackwell.

Hogan, E. A., & Overmyer-Day, L. 1994. The psychology of mergers and acquisitions. *International Review of Industrial and Organizational Psychology,* 9: 247–282.

Hogg, M. A. 1987. Social identity and group cohesiveness. In J. C. Turner, M. A. Hogg, P. J. Oakes, S. D. Reicher, & M. S. Wetherell, *Rediscovering the social group: A self-categorization theory:* 89–116. Oxford: Blackwell.

Hogg, M. A. 1992. *The social psychology of group cohesiveness: From attraction to social identity.* London: Harvester Wheatsheaf.

Hogg, M. A. 1993. Group cohesiveness: A critical review and some new directions. *European Review of Social Psychology,* 4: 85–111.

Hogg, M. A. 1996a. Social identity, self-categorization, and the small group. In E. H. Witte & J. H. Davis (Eds.), *Understanding group behavior. Volume 2: Small group processes and interpersonal relations:* 227–253. Mahwah, NJ: Lawrence Erlbaum Associates.

Hogg, M. A. 1996b. Intragroup processes, group structure and social identity. In W. P. Robinson (Ed.), *Social groups and identities*: *Developing the legacy of Henri Tajfel*: 65–93. Oxford: Butterworth-Heinemann.

Hogg, M. A. 1998. *Group identification, leadership, and the exercise of power.* Paper presented at the 1998 convention of the Society for the Psychological Study of Social Issues, Ann Arbor, MI.

Hogg, M. A. 1999. *A social identity theory of leadership.* Unpublished manuscript (submitted for publication), University of Queensland.

Hogg, M. A. In press a. Subjective uncertainty reduction through self-categorization: A motivational theory of social identity processes. *European Review of Social Psychology.*

Hogg, M. A. In press b. Self-categorization and subjective uncertainty resolution: Cognitive and motivational facets of social identity and group membership. In J. P. Forgas, K. D. Williams, & L. Wheeler (Eds.), *The social mind: Cognitive and motivational aspects of interpersonal behavior.* New York: Cambridge University Press.

Hogg, M. A. In press c. Social identity and social comparison. In J. Suls & L. Wheeler (Eds.), *Handbook of social comparison: Theory and research.* New York: Plenum.

Hogg, M. A., & Abrams, D. 1988. *Social identifications: A social psychology of intergroup relations and group processes.* London: Routledge.

Hogg, M. A., & Abrams, D. 1990. Social motivation, self-esteem and social identity. In D. Abrams & M. A. Hogg (Eds.), *Social identity theory: Constructive and critical advances:* 28–47. London: Harvester Wheatsheaf.

Hogg, M. A., & Abrams, D. (Eds.). 1993a. Group motivation: *Social psychological perspectives.* London: Harvester Wheatsheaf.

Hogg, M. A., & Abrams, D. 1993b. Towards a single-process uncertainty-reduction model of social motivation in groups. In M. A. Hogg & D. Abrams (Eds.), *Group motivation: Social psychological perspectives:* 173–190. London: Harvester-Wheatsheaf.

Hogg, M. A., & Abrams, D. 1999. Social identity and social cognition: Historical background and current trends. In D. Abrams & M. A. Hogg (Eds.), *Social identity and social cognition:* 1–25. Oxford: Blackwell.

Hogg, M. A., & Abrams, D. In press. Social categorization, depersonalization and group behavior. In M. A. Hogg & R. S. Tindale (Eds.), *Blackwell handbook of social psychology: Group processes.* Oxford: Blackwell.

Hogg, M. A., Cooper-Shaw, L, & Holzworth, D. W. 1993. Group prototypicality and depersonalized attraction in small interactive groups. *Personality and Social Psychology Bulletin,* 19: 452–465.

Hogg, M. A., & Hains, S. C. 1996. Intergroup relations and group solidarity: Effects of group identification and social beliefs on depersonalized attraction. *Journal of Personality and Social Psychology,* 70: 295–309.

Hogg, M. A., & Hains, S. C. 1998. Friendship and group identification: A new look at the role of cohesiveness in groupthink. *European Journal of Social Psychology,* 28: 323–341.

Hogg, M. A., Hains, S. C., & Mason, I. 1998. Identification and leadership in small groups: Salience, frame of reference, and leader stereotypicality effects on leader evaluations. *Journal of Personality and Social Psychology,* 75: 1248–1263.

Hogg, M. A., & Hardie, E. A. 1991. Social attraction, personal attraction and self-categorization: A field study. *Personality and Social Psychology Bulletin,* 17: 175–180.

Hogg, M. A., & Hardie, E. A. 1992. Prototypicality, conformity and depersonalized attraction: A self-categorization analysis of group cohesiveness. *British Journal of Social Psychology,* 31: 41–56.

Hogg, M. A., & Hardie, E. A. 1997. Self-prototypicality, group identification and depersonalized attraction: A polarization study. In K. Leung, U. Kim, S. Yamaguchi, & Y. Kashima (Eds.), *Progress in Asian social psychology,* vol. 1: 119–137. Singapore: Wiley.

Hogg, M. A., Hardie, E. A., & Reynolds, K. 1995. Prototypical similarity, self-categorisation, and depersonalized attraction: A perspective on group cohesiveness. *European Journal of Social Psychology*, 25: 159–177.

Hogg, M. A., & McGarty, C. 1990. Self-categorization and social identity. In D. Abrams & M. A. Hogg (Eds.), *Social identity theory: Constructive and critical advances:* 10–27. London: Harvester Wheatsheaf.

Hogg, M. A., & Moreland, R. L. 1995. *European and American influences on small group research*. Paper presented at the small groups preconference of the Joint Meeting of the European Association of Experimental Social Psychology and the Society for Experimental Social Psychology, Washington, DC.

Hogg, M. A., & Mullin, B.-A. 1999. Joining groups to reduce uncertainty: Subjective uncertainty reduction and group identification. In D. Abrams & M. A. Hogg (Eds.), *Social identity and social cognition:* 249–279. Oxford: Blackwell.

Hogg, M. A., & Reid, S. In press. Social identity, leadership, and power. In J. Bargh & A. Lee-Chai (Eds.), *The use and abuse of power: Multiple perspectives on the causes of corruption*. Philadelphia: Psychology Press.

Hogg, M. A., & Terry, D. J. (Eds.), In press. *Social identity processes in organizational contexts*. Philadelphia: Psychology Press.

Hogg, M. A., Terry, D. J., & White, K. M. 1995. A tale of two theories: A critical comparison of identity theory with social identity theory. *Social Psychology Quarterly*, 58: 255–269.

Hornsey, M. J., & Hogg, M. A. 1999. Subgroup differentiation as a response to an overly-inclusive group: A test of optimal distinctiveness theory. *European Journal of Social Psychology*, 29: 543–550.

Hornsey, M. J., & Hogg, M. A. In press a. Subgroup relations: A comparison of mutual intergroup differentiation and common ingroup identify models of prejudice reduction. *Personality and Social Psychology Bulletin*.

Hornsey, M. J., & Hogg, M. A. In press b. Intergroup similarity and subgroup relations: Some implications for assimilation. *Personality and Social Psychology Bulletin*.

Ibarra, H. 1995. Race, opportunity, and diversity of social circles in managerial networks. *Academy of Management Journal*, 38: 673–703.

Janis, I. L. 1982. *Groupthink Psychological studies of policy decisions and fiascoes* (2nd ed.). Boston: Houghton Mifflin.

Kandola, R. 1995. Managing diversity: New broom or old hat. *International Review of Industrial and Organizational Psychology*, 10: 131–168.

Kramer, R. M. 1991. Intergroup relations and organizational dilemmas: The role of categorization processes. In L. L. Cummings & B. M. Staw (Eds.), *Research in organizational behavior*, vol. 13: 191–228. Greenwich, CT: JAI Press.

Lalonde, R. N. 1992. The dynamics of group differentiation in the face of defeat. *Personality and Social Psychology Bulletin*, 18: 336–342.

Lester, R. E. 1987. Organizational culture, uncertainty reduction, and the socialization of new organizational members. In S. Thomas (Ed.), *Culture and communication: Methodology, behavior, artifacts, and institutions:* 105–113. Norwood, NJ: Ablex.

Levine, J. M., & Moreland, R. L. 1990. Progress in small group research. *Annual Review of Psychology*, 41: 585–634.

Levine, J. M., & Moreland, R. L. 1994. Group socialization: Theory and research. *European Review of Social Psychology*, 5: 305–336.

Long, K., & Spears, R. 1997. The self-esteem hypothesis revisited: Differentiation and the disaffected. In R. Spears, P. J. Oakes, N. Ellemers, & S. A. Haslam (Eds.), *The social psychology of stereotyping and group life:* 296–317. Oxford: Blackwell.

Lord, R. G., Foti, R. J., & DeVader, C. L. 1984. A test of leadership categorization theory: Internal structure, information processing, and leadership perceptions. *Organizational Behavior and Human Performance*, 34: 343–378.

Mael, F. A., & Ashforth, B. E. 1992. Alumni and their alma mater: A partial test of the reformulated model of organizational identification. *Journal of Organizational Behavior*, 13: 103–123.

Mael, F. A., & Ashforth, B. E. 1995. Loyal from day one: Bio-data, organizational identification, and turnover among newcomers. *Personnel Psychology*, 48: 309–333.

Marcus-Newhall, A., Miller, N., Holtz, R., & Brewer, M. B. 1993. Crosscutting category membership with role assignment: A means of reducing intergroup bias. *British Journal of Social Psychology*, 32: 124–146.

Marques, J. M. 1990. The black-sheep effect: Out-group homogeneity in social comparison settings. In D. Abrams & M. A. Hogg (Eds.), *Social identity theory: Constructive and critical advances:* 131–151. London: Harvester Wheatsheaf.

Marques, J. M., & Paez, D. 1994. The "black sheep effect": Social categorization, rejection of ingroup deviates and perception of group variability. *European Review of Social Psychology*, 5: 37–68.

Marques, J. M., & Yzerbyt, V. Y. 1988. The black sheep effect: Judgmental extremity towards ingroup members in inter- and intra-group situations. *European Journal of Social Psychology*, 18: 287–292.

Marques, J. M., Yzerbyt, V. Y., & Leyens, J.-P. 1988. The black sheep effect: Extremity of judgements towards in-group members as a function of group identification. *European Journal of Social Psychology*, 18: 1–16.

Marris, P. 1996. *The politics of uncertainty: Attachment in private and public life.* London: Routledge.

Moreland, R. L., & Levine, J. M. 1997. *Work group socialization: A social identity approach.* Paper presented at the Second Australian Industrial and Organizational Psychology Conference, Melbourne.

Moreland, R. L., & Levine, J. M. In press. Socialization in organizations and work groups. In M. Turner (Ed.), *Groups at work: Advances in theory and research.* Mahwah, NJ: Lawrence Erlbaum Associates.

Moreland, R. L., Hogg, M. A., & Hains, S. C. 1994. Back to the future: Social psychological research on groups. *Journal of Experimental Social Psychology*, 30: 527–555.

Morris, M. W., & Peng, K. 1994. Culture and cause: American and Chinese attributions for social and physical events. *Journal of Personality and Social Psychology*, 67: 949–971.

Mowday, R. T., & Sutton, R. I. 1993. Organizational behavior: Linking individuals and groups to organizational contexts. *Annual Review of Psychology*, 44: 195–229.

Mullen, B., & Copper, C. 1994. The relation between group cohesiveness and performance: An integration. *Psychological Bulletin*, 115: 210–227.

Nkomo, S. M., & Cox, T., Jr. 1996. Diverse identities in organizations. In S. R. Clegg, C. Hardy, & W. R. Nord (Eds.), *Handbook of organization studies:* 338–356. London: Sage.

Nye, J. L., & Forsyth, D. R. 1991. The effects of prototype-based biases on leadership appraisals: A test of leadership categorization theory. *Small Group Research*, 22: 360–379.

Nye, J. L., & Simonetta, L. G. 1996. Followers' perceptions of group leaders: The impact of recognition-based and inference-based processes. In J. L. Nye, & A. M. Bower (Eds.), *What's social about social cognition: Research on socially shared cognition in small groups:* 124–153. Thousand Oaks, CA: Sage.

Oakes, P. J., Haslam, S. A., & Turner, J. C. 1994. *Stereotyping and social reality*. Oxford: Blackwell.

Oakes, P. J., & Turner, J. C. 1990. Is limited information processing the cause of social stereotyping. *European Review of Social Psychology*, 1: 111–135.

Pettigrew, T. F. 1998. Intergroup contact theory. *Annual Review of Psychology*, 49: 65–85.

Pratt, M. G. In press. To be or not to be? Central questions in organizational identification. In D. Whetten & P. Godfrey (Eds.), *Identity in organizations: Developing theory through conversations*. Thousand Oaks. CA: Sage.

Pratto, F., Sidanius, J., Stallworth, L. M., & Malle, B. F. 1994. Social dominance orientation: A personality variable predicting social and political attitudes. *Journal of Personality and Social Psychology*, 67: 741–763.

Prentice, D. A., & Miller, D. T. (Eds.), 1999. *Cultural divides: Understanding and overcoming group conflict*. New York: Russell Sage Foundation.

Raven, B. H. 1965. Social influence and power. In I. D. Steiner & M. Fishbein (Eds.), *Current studies in social psychology*: 371–382. New York: Holt, Rinehart & Winston.

Reicher, S. D., Spears, R., & Postmes, T. 1995. A social identity model of deindividuation phenomena. *European Review of Social Psychology*, 6: 161–198.

Riordan, C. M., & Shore, L. M. 1997. Demographic diversity and employee attitudes: An empirical examination of relational demography within work units. *Journal of Applied Psychology*, 82: 342–358.

Robinson, W. P. (Ed.). 1996. *Social groups and identities: Developing the legacy of Henri Tajfel*. Oxford: Butterworth-Heinemann.

Ross, L. 1977. The intuitive psychologist and his shortcomings. *Advances in Experimental Social Psychology*, 10: 174–220.

Rubin, M., & Hewstone, M. 1998. Social identity theory's self-esteem hypothesis: A review and some suggestions for clarification. *Personality and Social Psychology Review*, 2: 40–62.

Rush, M. C., & Russell, J. E. A. 1988. Leader prototypes and prototype-contingent consensus in leader behavior descriptions. *Journal of Experimental Social Psychology*, 24: 88–104.

Saks, A. M., & Ashforth, B. E. 1997. Organizational socialization: Making sense of the past and present as a prologue for the future. *Journal of Vocational Behavior*, 51: 234–279.

Sherman, S. J., Hamilton, D. L., & Lewis, A. C. 1999. Perceived entitativity and the social identity value of group memberships. In D. Abrams & M. A. Hogg (Eds.), *Social identity and social cognition*: 80–110. Oxford: Blackwell.

Sigelman, L. 1986. Basking in reflected glory revisited: An attempt at replication. *Social Psychology Quarterly*, 49: 90–92.

Snyder, C. R., Lassegard, M.-A., & Ford, C. E. 1986. Distancing after group success and failure: Basking in reflected glory and cutting off reflected failure. *Journal of Personality and Social Psychology*, 51: 382–388.

Spears, R., Oakes, P. J., Ellemers, N., & Haslam, S. A. (Eds.). 1997. *The social psychology of stereotyping and group life*. Oxford: Blackwell.

Steiner, I. D. 1974. Whatever happened to the group in social psychology? *Journal of Experimental Social Psychology*, 10: 94–108.

Tajfel, H. 1972. Social categorization (English translation of "La catégorisation sociale"). In S. Moscovici (Ed.), *Introduction à la psychologie sociale*, vol. 1: 272–302. Paris: Larousse.

Tajfel, H. 1974a. *Intergroup behavior, social comparison and social change*. Unpublished Katz-Newcomb lectures, University of Michigan, Ann Arbor.

Tajfel, H. 1974b. Social identity and intergroup behaviour. *Social Science information*, 13: 65–93.

Tajfel, H. 1975. The exit of social mobility and the voice of social change. *Social Science Information*, 14: 101–118.

Tajfel, H., & Turner, J. C. 1979. An integrative theory of intergroup conflict. In W. G. Austin & S. Worchel (Eds.), *The social psychology of intergroup relations*: 33–47. Monterey, CA: Brooks-Cole.

Tajfel, H., & Turner, J. C. 1986. The social identity theory of intergroup behavior. In S. Worchel & W. G. Austin (Eds.), *The psychology of intergroup relations:* 7–24. Chicago: Nelson-Hall.

Taylor, D. M., & McKirnan, D. J. 1984. A live-stage model of intergroup relations. *British Journal of Social Psychology*, 23: 291–300.

Taylor, S. E., & Fiske, S. T. 1978. Salience, attention, and attribution: Top of the head phenomena. *Advances in Experimental Social Psychology*, 11: 249–288.

Terry, D. J., & Callan, V. J. 1998. Intergroup differentiation in response to an organizational merger. *Group Dynamics: Theory, Research, and Practice*, 2: 67–87.

Terry, D. J., Carey, C. J., & Callan, V. J. In press. Employee adjustment to an organizational merger: An intergroup perspective. *Personality and Social Psychology Bulletin*.

Terry, D. J., & Hogg, M. A. 1996. Group norms and the attitude-behavior relationship: A role for group identification. *Personality and Social Psychology Bulletin*, 22: 776–793.

Terry, D. J., & Hogg, M. A. (Eds.). 1999. *Attitudes, behavior, and social context: The role of norms and group membership*. Mahwah, NJ: Lawrence Erlbaum Associates.

Trope, Y., & Liberman, A. 1993. The use of trait conceptions to identify other people's behavior and to draw inferences about their personalities. *Personality and Social Psychology Bulletin*, 19: 553–562.

Tsui, A., Egan, T., & O'Reilly, C., III. 1992. Being different: Relational demography and organizational attachment. *Administrative Science Quarterly*, 37: 549–579.

Turner, J. C. 1975. Social comparison and social identity: Some prospects for intergroup behaviour. *European Journal of Social Psychology*, 5: 5–34.

Turner, J. C. 1982. Towards a cognitive redefinition of the social group. In H. Tajfel (Ed.), *Social identity and intergroup relations:* 15–40. Cambridge: Cambridge University Press.

Turner, J. C. 1985. Social categorization and the self-concept: A social cognitive theory of group behavior. In E. J. Lawler (Ed.), *Advances in group processes: Theory and research*, vol. 2: 77–122. Greenwich, CT: JAI Press.

Turner, J. C. 1991. *Social influence*. Milton Keynes, UK: Open University Press.

Turner, J. C. 1996. Henri Tajfel: An introduction. In W. P. Robinson (Ed.), *Social groups and identities: Developing the legacy of Henri Tajfel:* 1–23. Oxford: Butterworth-Heinemann.

Turner, J. C., Hogg, M. A., Oakes, P. J., Reicher, S. D., & Wetherell, M. S. 1987. *Rediscovering the social group: A self-categorization theory.* Oxford: Blackwell.

Turner, M. E., Pratkanis, A. R., Probasco, P., & Leve, C. 1992. Threat, cohesion, and group effectiveness: Testing a social identity maintenance perspective on groupthink. *Journal of Personality and Social Psychology*, 63: 781–796.

Tyler, T. R. 1990. *Why people obey the law.* New Haven, CT: Yale University Press.

van Knippenberg, A., & Ellemers, N. 1993. Strategies in intergroup relations. In M. A. Hogg & D. Abrams (Eds.), *Group motivation: Social psychological perspectives:* 17–32. London: Harvester Wheatsheaf.

van Knippenberg, D. 1997. *A social identity perspective on mergers and acquisitions.* Paper presented at the Second Australian Industrial and Organizational Psychology Conference, Melbourne.

Vaughan, G. M. 1978. Social change and intergroup preferences in New Zealand. *European Journal of Social Psychology*, 8: 297–314.

Wann, D. L., Hamlet, M. A., Wilson, T. M., & Hodges, J. A. 1995. Basking in reflected glory, cutting off reflected failure, and cutting off future failure: The importance of group identification. *Social Behavior and Personality*, 23: 377–388.

Wesolowski, M. A., & Mossholder, K. W. 1997. Relational demography in supervisor-subordinate dyads: Impact on subordinate job satisfaction, burnout, and perceived procedural justice. *Journal of Organizational Behavior*, 18: 351–362.

Williams, K. D., & Sommer, K. L. 1997. Social ostracism by coworkers: Does rejection lead to loafing or compensation? *Personality and Social Psychology Bulletin*, 23: 693–706.

Worchel, S., Morales, J. F., Páez, D., & Deschamps, J.-C. (Eds.). 1998. *Social identity: International perspectives.* London: Sage.

Yukl, G. A., & Falbe, C. M. 1991. Importance of different power sources in downward and lateral relations. *Journal of Applied Psychology*, 76: 416–423.

Zuckerman, M. 1979. Attribution of success and failure revisited, or: The motivational bias is alive and well in attributional theory. *Journal of Personality*, 47: 245–287.

Part 6

ORGANIZATIONAL PERFORMANCE

44

PRINCIPLES OF SOCIOTECHNICAL DESIGN REVISITED

Albert Cherns

Source: *Human Relations* 40(3) (1987): 153–161.

Abstract

This paper is a review of the author's 1976 "Principles of Sociotechnical Design." While most of the principles set out there have stood the test of time and experience, modifications are needed. In particular, the principles that govern the process of design and the activities of the design team are even more closely bound up with the principles governing the design itself. Some new principles are proposed. More attention is given to the needs of the organization as a society.

Introduction

After 10 years, it is not unreasonable to review the paper entitled "Sociotechnical Design" first published in *Human Relations* in 1976 (Cherns, 1976). At that time, there was sufficient experience with new organizations and the redesign of old ones to provide some confidence in the principles that had emerged. The paper itself have been reprinted in a number of compilations and has received wide circulation. Time, however, does not stand still; experience has accumulated. Too few full accounts of the designing of organizations have been published. Lectures, workshops, meetings, and case study presentations abound. Clear divergences have appeared and hardened between Scandinavian and North American approaches and applications. And while the techniques of sociotechnical analysis have been refined and improved they have also tended to become rigid; their demand for considerable effort and understanding have led many to abridge them or to seek tempting short cuts.

Furthermore, the techniques were originally evolved by social scientists for their own use in analyzing and designing organizations. The last decade has seen the realization that the basic data that are needed belong to people, and that they themselves should be involved in the collection and the analysis for two reasons. First, much of the data will otherwise be unreliable and wrongly interpreted; secondly, conclusions from those data in the form of design or redesign will otherwise be only weakly accepted. In targeting engineers as designers of organizations, we sought to provide them with a new perspective, better understanding, and some guidelines so that they could better design organizations as social systems. But, although the "Principle of Compatibility" was placed at the head of the list emphasizing that only participative design could lead to a participative organization, I failed to follow the implications through in the remaining principles. Davis (1982) brought together process and principles and his statement is required reading for anyone who needs to understand just what organization design is and involves. My aim here is different; no one reading this will have all he or she needs to know to understand the whole process or to initiate it. But he or she will be able to assess how appropriate is a given design to the objectives stated for it. And for those involved in design, it is both an aim and a checklist. As for its predecessor, I make no claim for completeness; if anything, I am uneasy that I have not felt the need to amend more, and I hope the next 10 years will teach me more. In this spirit, I offer this revised list.

Principle 1: Compatibility

Everyone can assent readily to the notion that means should fit ends, that the way in which design is done should be compatible with the design's objective. The statement that a design should be "participative" is either too readily accepted which suggests that its meaning has not been fully taken, or dismissed as impractical. How can you involve everyone in design? Surely design is a job for designers. We have to spell out more clearly just what this principle involves. One notorious example of gross misunderstanding is the inevitable failure of a manufacturing company's attempt by way of setting up a "Participation Department"; it is an illustration of the bureaucratic approach, a bureaucratic instrument to de-bureaucratize. From the outset we must recognize that design is an arena for conflict. It has to satisfy an array of objectives, each represented by some organizational element; the way in which this conflict is managed and used to yield positive results sets the pattern for the handling of subsequent conflicts in the newly designed organization. Thus, the design team has to work on its own process and principles of operation, principles no different from those which guide its design. Majority rule, horse trading, or power plays are unacceptable. Members must reveal their assumptions and reach decisions by consensus. Joint "optimization" of technical and social systems is often wrongly interpreted as modification of a technical design for social considerations. It is joint design in which each decision is reached for both technical and social reasons. Experts are needed, whether members of the team or invited for specific issues. But they, too, are required to reveal their assumptions for challenge; for some experts, this is a shock. How they deal with it is at least partly a function of how well the team has prepared them. Again, since the outcome desired is one in which all organizations work together to the same objectives, none can be omitted from the team. And whoever represents a function should truly represent it, which means that he or she is obliged to consult and inform his or her colleagues.

The principle of compatibility is truly the first principle; how well it is adhered to determines how well the remainder can be followed.

Principle 2: Minimal critical specification

As stated, this principle has in my view stood the test of time and I can do no better than repeat it. This principle has two aspects, negative and positive. The negative simply states that no more should be specified than is absolutely essential; the positive requires that we identify what is essential. It is of wide application and implies the minimal critical specification of tasks, the minimal critical allocation of tasks to jobs or of jobs to roles, and the specification of objectives with minimal critical specification of methods of obtaining them. While it may be necessary to be quite precise about what has to be done, it is rarely necessary to be precise about how it is done. In most organizations, there is far too much specificity about how and indeed about what. And a careful observer of people in their work situation will learn how people contrive to get the job done in spite of the rules. As the railwaymen in Britain have demonstrated, the whole system can be brought to a grinding halt by "working to rule." Many of the rules are there to provide protection when things go wrong for the man who imposed them; strictly applied, they totally inhibit adaptation or even effective action.

In any case, it is a mistake to specify more than is needed because by doing so, one closes options that could be kept open. This premature closing of options is a pervasive fault in design; it arises, not only because of the desire to reduce uncertainty, but also because it helps the designer to get his own way. We measure our success and effectiveness less by the quality of the ultimate design than by the quantity of our ideas and preferences that have been incorporated into it.

One way of dealing with the cavalier treatment of options is to challenge each design and demand that alternatives always be offered. This may result in claims that the design process is being expensively delayed. Design proposals may also be defended on the ground that any other choice will run up against some obstacle, such as a company practice, or a trade union agreement, or a manning problem. These obstacles can then be recorded and logged as constraints upon a better sociotechnical solution. When they have all been logged, each can be examined to estimate the cost of removing it. The cost may sometimes be prohibitive, but frequently turns out to be less formidable than supposed or than the engineer has presented it to be.

Again, it is vital that experts and team members reveal their assumptions for challenge. These often turn out to be assumptions about people, that there is one class of person capable of a category of tasks: a maintenance task requires a maintenance mechanic, a cleaning task requires a cleaner, and so on. If we end by assigning a team to a set of tasks which make a coherent whole, we can leave, until the team is recruited, the way in which the tasks should be carried out and who is to do what and when. The extent to which teams can assume responsibility given the right conditions surprises even those who wished it.

Principle 3: Variance control

In my original formulation, I gave this the somewhat pretentious name of "the sociotechnical criterion." The principle has survived the test of time, but the old title indicates that I held too narrow a view of "sociotechnical." True, the principle that variances should not be exported across unit, departmental, or other organizational boundaries is crucial to successful organizational design. True, also, it is the most closely related to the process of sociotechnical analysis; the variance control table brings into immediate prominence inefficiencies in the orgnaization's mode of controlling key variances and prompts suggestions for its improvement. But sociotechnical analysis does not end with the variance control table, important though it is. The social system is more than an effective system for control of technical and raw material variances. And this principle of variance control is very closely associated with Principles 4 and 5.

Principle 4: Boundary location

This was formerly Principle 5, but because of its relationship to principle 3 should come immediately after it. Its essential feature is that boundaries should *not* be drawn so as to impede the sharing of information, knowledge, and learning. The example I gave was of drivers whose departmental organization effectively prohibited their passing on their knowledge and learning about customers and routes to the routing clerks. Many others come to mind including one in a recent design where the location for good practical reasons of two process controllers on the other side of a wall from the process they controlled, placed them, for bad theoretical reasons, under the control of the supervisor of a totally different function. This created a control and information loop which delayed corrective action and promoted endless, if minor, conflicts.

This kind of misplacement arises sometimes from the overvaluing of the merits of tidy geographical commands, sometimes for fear of the advantage that "unsupervised" workers may take. That is less surprising than the willingness to live with what everyone recognizes as indefensible anomalies; there is a perverse pride in organizational "nonsenses." Sociotechnical analysis quickly reveals the confusions of "ownership" which plague existing departmental boundaries.

Principle 5: Information flow

The principle of boundary location counsels against, if it cannot absolutely prohibit, the interruption of information or the insertion of information loops by misplaced organizational boundaries. That by itself will not, however, ensure that information is provided to those who require it when they require it. Obstacles are vertical as well as horizontal. In my observation, information in organizations has three uses: for control, for record, and for action. Its use for *control* of behavior is pernicious, with its associated power games. Its use for *record* is essential but abused. Information systems that provide management with comprehensive and detailed information of the operations constitute a virtually irresistible temptation to intervene, to harass, and to usurp subordinate control and authority. Information required for record should be readily available for call only when and as needed. Information for *action* should be directed *first* to those whose task it is to act. This holds for action to control variances; it holds equally for action to discharge all the actor's responsibilities: for safety, waste control, planning cost control, etc. It is no use holding an individual or a team responsible for any function and doling out information about its performance in arrear and through a higher authority. Under those conditions, the individual or team cannot have ownership of the performance.

This principle is consistent with the need, now increasingly accepted, for information systems to be designed in cooperation with their primary users so long as the designer recognizes that the primary users are those who need to act on the information as well as those who are required to provide such information as is not automatically registered.

Principle 6: Power and authority

Louis E. Davis has coined the term "work authority" to describe two linked concepts. Those who need equipment, materials, or other resources to carry out their responsibilities should have access to them and authority to command them. In return, they accept responsibility for them and for their prudent and economical use. They exercise the power and authority needed to accept responsibility for their performance. But there is also the power and authority that accompanies knowledge and expertise. Confronted by forest fires, authority and power are granted in the U.S. Forest Service to whoever has the knowledge and experience regardless of rank and post; the Admirable Crichton principle.

Principle 6 is closely associated with Principle 5. The diversion of information seduces top management into assuming command of fire fighting, often by remote control. If top management possesses the relevant knowledge and skill, learning and the acquisition of self-confidence are denied to those where the action is. If top management does not possess those attributes, the result is failure, buck passing, and resentment on all sides.

Principle 7: The multifunctional principle

In my original formulation, I trapped myself with too philosophical an account. Consequently, it has been poorly understood and weakly interpreted. The distinction between mechanism and organism *is* relevant, but too metaphorical; an organization is neither one nor the other and concepts like "equifinality" and "directive correlation" are, for all their power as intellectual tools, too remote from organizational concerns as understood by design teams. A more earthy conceptualization is more help.

Organizations need to adapt to their environments; elements of organizations need to adapt to their environments of which the most important are usually other organizational elements. There are two ways of doing so, either by adding new roles or by modifying old ones. (The mechanism adds another specifically designed gadget, the organism learns a new trick). Hiring specialists, experts, is the mechanical response; training to enlarge the repertoire is the organic. Experts add to the problems of organizational integration in many ways; they add to the line-staff confusions of authority; they acquire regulatory as well as advisory functions which add paper work and recording and establish standards which can become disfunctional. The expert as trainer serves the organization quite differently; his role is to enlarge the roles and, hence, the response repertoires of individuals and teams without complicating the lines of command or the allocation of responsibilities.

Principle 8: Support congruence

The implications of sociotechnical analysis and design are comparatively readily accepted for production, maintenance, and quality control. But the support of production teams implies significant and far-reaching changes in reward and information systems, in financial control, and in marketing, sales, purchasing, and planning. At best, each production unit can operate as a profit center; that conflicts with many finance departments' views of financial control. How much control can be exercised by production teams over purchasing, and how much influence they should exert on marketing and sales policy are questions which raise major design issues. You can either start with existing policies and see to what extent they can be modified, or you can adopt a more radical approach; you can design the ideal system to enable production units to operate as "mini-factories" and then modify that to meet practical and policy considerations. The latter conforms better to Principle 2, start with as little baggage as possible, adopt a constraint-free design mode, and build in the unavoidable constraints later. Those may be imposed by government regulation, by corporate policy, or by practical and geographical limitations.

Reward systems offer less problems; common to virtually all sociotechnical designs is the principle of pay for what you know rather than for what you do. Particularly with high technology, the operators' knowledge and understanding of the process is vital; they are there to monitor and initiate corrective action to safeguard production, process, and equipment. Their errors or omissions, their failures of comprehension and anticipation are costly and can be calamitous. Their value is what is in their heads.

Principle 9: Transitional organization

Experience since 1976 is responsible for the addition of this principle. Greenfield sites pose the issue of managing start-up. Redesign on existing sites pose far greater problems; how to maintain production on the old plant while training people to operate the new, and during start-up. In either case, there is a period of transition which requires planning and design; the transitional organization is both different and more complex than either old or new.

As we are engaged in change from a traditional to a new organization, from a traditional to a new philosophy of management, from an old to a new system of values, we need to see the design team and its process as a vehicle of transition. Its design process embodies the new values, its membership constitutes a cadre for diffusing those new values through the organization. Its role in selecting and socializing the new leadership is vital.

The treatment given to those who will not have a part in the new organization, the model of selection of those who will, and the training they receive, all demonstrate the reality of the espoused philosophy. The principle of compatibility is nowhere more in evidence than here.

Facing the task of selection, management too easily resorts to tests and to the use of categories, especially where fewer will be needed to man the new. It is surprising how much realistic self-selection takes place, especially where opportunities are given for people to acquaint themselves with the kind of tasks that will be needed and where they are invited to undertake preliminary training by signing up for courses at local educational establishments. Tests where used should be employed for counseling rather than as hurdles. Those who will no longer be required should be offered help in the labor market. All this is part of the design for transition. Start-up and its debugging should be planned and designed to enhance training; too often the operatives are brushed aside while "experts" manage start-up. A vital learning opportunity is missed in the anxiety to get rolling. Managing the stresses of start-up and shut-down can be prepared for, and that is a task for the design team.

Principle 10: Incompletion or the Forth Bridge principle

Back to the drawing board. Although the myth of stability is essential to enable us to cope with the demands of change, we all know that the present period of transition is not between past and a future stable state but really between one period of transition and another. The stability myth is reassuring but dangerous if it leaves us unprepared to review and revise.

Implementation must begin with the start of design; the principle of compatibility foreshadows this. And with implementation comes evaluation. Sociotechnical analysis reveals the key variances which must be controlled, and training fosters the capacities to manage those which cannot be eliminated; together, they provide the criteria for evaluation, how well the variances are controlled.

Redesign is not the task of a special design team; it is the function of self-regulating operating teams provided with the techniques of analysis, the appropriate criteria and the principles of design. We place a great deal of emphasis on the training of operating teams; not only have they to learn the appropriate operating skills, they have to learn to operate *as a team*, they have to learn how to handle the information of all kinds that their self regulatory function requires, and they have to learn to review and evaluate their performance and to negotiate redesign.

Values

In my 1976 paper I included as my principle 8 'Design and Human Values'. But human (and social) values underpin all of these ten principles. At an early stage of sociotechnical design, a steering committee representing all top management functions, the body which mandates the design team, develops and promulgates its statement of Philosophy enunciating the values with which it charges the design team. These values spell out what the 'socio' in 'sociotechnical' means.

Typically some version of the Emery-Thorsrud 'characteristics of a Good Job' are included, providing people as individuals with challenge, variety, scope for decision making, social support and recognition, social relevance (of the job to life outside), future and an element of choice. They incorporate an understanding of what most people want from work. People do not all share the same wants or needs or expectations. Nor can all be satisfied. What can be done is to apply principles and values with understanding of, and respect for, individual differences.

An organization's responsibilities go beyond those to its members as individuals. As a society, it must have mechanisms for resolving conflict, for ensuring fairness of treatment, which will be accepted as fair, and for generating and maintaining commitment to its goals as an organization. And an organization has responsibilities to all its stakeholders, its members, its customers or clients, its suppliers, its shareholders, the unions which represent its members, and its community. These will all be included in the statement of philosophy, but none is so difficult to define as the last. Some obligations are defined and sanctioned by regulation, ranging from control of pollution to the employment of handicapped people, others call for a conscious social policy. Such a fundamental design question as location raises an issue of social policy; do we seek a greenfield site free of any commitment or do we re-develop in our own community. Familiar in discussion of the "Southern Strategy" of many firms in the USA, similar questions arise in Britain where loyalty to the declining "old" industrial communities is sorely strained.

Questions of value and social responsibility can appear to take us far from the central topic of this paper, the principles of sociotechnical design, but that reflects our tendency to be preoccupied with the design, the organization as an operating system rather than as an open social system with economic goals.

Acknowledgments

I am indebted to my colleagues in Sociotechnics International and to generations of students of our workshops, formerly under the aegis of UCLA, for the stimulus to review the earlier article, and especially to Lou Davis for his suggestions and ideas.

References

Davis, L. E. Organizational design. In G. Salvendy (Ed.), *Handbook of industrial engineering*. New York: Wiley, 1982, pp. 2.1.1–2.1.29.

Cherns, A. B. The principles of sociotechnical design. *Human Relations*, 1976, 9(8), 783–792.

45

MOTIVATION THROUGH THE DESIGN OF WORK

Test of a theory

J. Richard Hackman and Greg R. Oldham

Source: *Organizational Behavior and Human Performance* 16 (1976): 250–279.

Abstract

A model is proposed that specifies the conditions under which individuals will become internally motivated to perform effectively on their jobs. The model focuses on the interaction among three classes of variables: (a) the psychological states of employees that must be present for internally motivated work behavior to develop: (b) the characteristics of jobs that can create these psychological states: and (c) the attributes of individuals that determine how positively a person will respond to a complex and challenging job. The model was tested for 658 employees who work on 62 different jobs in seven organizations, and results support its validity. A number of special features of the model are discussed (including its use as a basis for the diagnosis of jobs and the evaluation of job redesign projects), and the model is compared to other theories of job design.

Introduction

Work redesign is becoming increasingly prominent as a strategy for attempting to improve simultaneously the productivity and the quality of the work experience of employees in contemporary organizations. Although the benefits of work redesign (or "job enrichment" or "job enlargement") are widely touted in the management literature, in fact little is known about the reasons why "enriched" work sometimes leads to positive outcomes for workers and for their employing organizations. Even less is known about the relative effectiveness of various strategies for carrying out the redesign of work (Hackman, 1975).

One reason for this state of affairs is that existing theories of work redesign are not fully adequate to meet the problems encountered in their application. Especially troublesome is the paucity of conceptual tools that are directly useful in guiding the *implementation and evaluation* of work redesign projects. In the paragraphs to follow, we examine several existing theoretical approaches to work redesign, with a special eye toward the measurability of the concepts employed and the action implications of the theorizing (cf. Porter, Lawler, & Hackman, 1975, Chap. 10). We then propose and report a test of a theory of work redesign that focuses specifically on how the characteristics of jobs and the characteristics of people interact to determine when an "enriched" job will lead to beneficial outcomes, and when it will not.

Theoretical approaches to work redesign

Motivation–hygiene theory

By far the most influential theory relevant to work redesign has been the Herzberg two-factor theory of satisfaction and motivation (Herzberg, Mausner, & Snyderman, 1959; Herzberg, 1966). In essence, the theory proposes that the primary determinants of employee satisfaction are factors intrinsic to the work that is done (i.e., recognition, achievement, responsibility, advancement, personal growth in competence). These factors are called "motivators" because they are believed to be effective in motivating employees to superior effort and performance. Dissatisfaction, on the other hand, is seen as being caused by "hygiene factors" that are extrinsic to the work itself. Examples include company policies, supervisory practices, pay plans, working conditions, and so on. The Herzberg theory specifies that a job will enhance work motivation and satisfaction only to the degree that "motivators" are designed into the work itself. Changes that deal solely with "hygiene" factors should not lead to increases in employee motivation.

It is to the credit of the Herzberg theory that it has prompted a great deal of research, and inspired several successful change projects involving the redesign of work (e.g., Ford, 1969; Paul, Robertson, & Herzberg, 1969). Yet there are difficulties with the theory that to some extent compromise its usefulness.

For one, a number of researchers have been unable to provide empirical support for the major tenets of the two-factor theory itself (see for example, Dunnette, Campbell, & Hakel, 1967; Hinton, 1968; King, 1970. For analyses favorable to the theory, see Herzberg, 1966: Whitsett & Winslow, 1967). It appears that the original dichotomization of aspects of the work-place into "motivators" and "hygiene factors" may have been largely a function of methodological artifact, and the present conceptual status of the theory must be considered highly uncertain.

Moreover, the theory does not provide for differences among people in how responsive they are likely to be to "enriched" jobs. In the AT&T studies based on the theory (Ford, 1969), for example, it was assumed that the motivating factors potentially could increase the work motivation of *all* employees. Yet it now appears that some individuals are much more likely to respond positively to an enriched, complex job than are others (Hulin, 1971). The theory provides no help in determining how such individual differences phenomena should be dealt with, either at the conceptual level or in the actual applications.

Finally, the theory in its present form does not specify how the presence or absence of motivating factors can be *measured* for existing jobs. At the least, this increases the difficulty of testing the theory in on-going organizations. It also limits the degree to which the theory can be used to diagnose jobs prior to planned change, or to evaluate the effects of work redesign activities after changes have been carried out.

Activation theory

While psychologists have for many years studied the antecedents and consequences of heightened and depressed levels of psychological and physiological activation in organisms (Berlyne, 1967), only recently have attempts been made to use activation theory to understand the work behavior of individuals in organizations. Scott (1966) has reviewed a number of studies that show how people react to chronic states of underactivation at work by engaging in arousal-enhancing behaviors, some of which have clearly dysfunctional consequences for work effectiveness. The findings Scott summarizes suggest that activation theory may be of considerable use in understanding jobs that are highly repetitive—and in planning for task designs that minimize the dysfunctional consequences of underactivating work. Activation theorists have given relatively little attention to jobs that may be overstimulating, perhaps because few such jobs exist for rank-and-file workers in contemporary organizations.

While activation theory clearly has considerable relevance to both the theory and practice of job design, two thorny problems must be dealt with before the theory can be fully applied to real-world job design problems. First, means must be developed for measuring current levels of activation of individuals is actual work settings (cf. Thayer, 1967), and for assessing the "optimal level" of activation for different individuals. Until such methodologies are developed, it will remain impractical to use activation theory in predicting or changing employee reactions to their jobs except in a very gross fashion; e.g., in situations where it is clear that most employees are enormously over- or understimulated by their jobs.

A second problem has to do with ambiguities regarding the processes by which individuals adapt to *changing* levels in stimulation. Individuals' levels of activation decrease markedly as a function of familiarity with a given stimulus situation. However, after a period of rest, re-presentation of the same stimulus situation will once again raise the level of activation (Scott, 1966). More complete understanding of the waxing and waning of activation in various circumstances could have many implications for job design practices; for example, the practice of "job rotation." Those who advocate job rotation claim that work motivation can be kept reasonably high by rotating individuals through several different jobs, even though each of the jobs would become monotonous and boring if one were to remain on it for a long period of time. If future research can identify ways to maintain activation at near-optimal levels through planned stimulus change, then the theory can contribute substantially to increasing the usefulness of job rotation as a motivational technique. If, however, it turns out that there are general and inevitable decreases in activation over time regardless of how different tasks and rest periods are cycled, then the long-term usefulness of the technique would seem to be limited.

In either case, the potential for applying activation theory to the design of jobs may be limited mainly to those cases in which there are actively dysfunctional affective and behavioral outcomes associated with routine, repetitive jobs. The theory offers less guidance for the design of work that will elicit and maintain positive and self-reinforcing work motivation.

Socio-technical systems theory

The socio-technical systems approach to work redesign provides significant insight into the interdependencies between technical aspects of the work itself and the broader social milieu in which the work is done (Emery & Trist, 1969; Trist, Higgin, Murray, & Pollock, 1963). The theory has evolved from (and has been used as an explanatory device for) numerous planned changes of work systems. Many of these experiments have provided vivid illustration of the interactions between the social and technical aspects of the workplace, and at the same time have proven successful as action projects—in that beneficial outcomes were obtained both for employees and for the organizations in which they worked (cf. Davis & Trist, Note 1; Rice, 1958). Of special interest is the contribution of socio-technical systems theory in developing the notion of the "autonomous work group," in which members of a work team share among themselves much of the decision-making having to do with the planning and execution of the work (Gulowsen, 1972; Herbst, 1962). Creation of autonomous work groups promises to become increasingly prominent and useful as a strategy for redesigning and improving work systems.

Yet for all its merit, the socio-technical systems approach provides few explicit specifications of how (and under what circumstances) the work itself and the social surroundings affect one another. It is, therefore, difficult to test the adequacy of the theory *qua* theory. Moreover, the approach provides little specific guidance about how (and how not to) proceed in carrying out work redesign activities, other than the general dictum to attend to both the technical and social aspects of the work setting and the device of the autonomous work group. Absent from the approach, for example, are explicit means for diagnosing a work system prior to change (to ascertain what "should" be changed, and how), or for evaluating in systematic terms the outcomes of changes that have been completed.

For these reasons, the major value of socio-technical systems theory appears to be its considerable usefulness as a way of thinking about work systems and their redesign. In its present form, it has only limited use in generating new understanding through quantitative tests of theory-specified propositions, or in providing explicit and concrete guidance about what organizational changes to make under what circumstances.

Jobs and individual differences: an interactive approach

Research on work design that focuses on the objective characteristics of jobs is rooted in the work of Turner and Lawrence (1965). These researchers developed measures of six "Requisite Task Attributes" that were predicted to relate positively to employee satisfaction and attendance. A summary measure, the Requisite Task Attributes Index (RTA index) was derived from the six measures and used to test relationships between the nature of jobs and employee reactions to them.

Expected positive relationships between the RTA Index and employee satisfaction and attendance were found only for workers from factories located in small towns. For employees in urban work settings, satisfaction was inversely related to the scores of jobs on the RTA Index, and absenteeism was unrelated to the Index. The investigators concluded that reactions to jobs high on the RTA Index were moderated by differences in the cultural backgrounds of employees. Subsequent research by Blood and Hulin (Blood & Hulin, 1967; Hulin & Blood, 1968) provides support for the notion that subcultural factors moderate worker responses to the design of their jobs.

A study by Hackman and Lawler (1971) provides further evidence that job characteristics can directly affect employee attitudes and behavior at work. These authors suggested that employees should react positively to four "core" dimensions adapted from those used previously by Turner and Lawrence (i.e., variety, task identity, autonomy, feedback). In addition, Hackman and Lawler proposed that individuals who were desirous of growth satisfactions at work should respond especially positively to jobs high on the core dimensions, since these individuals are most likely to value the kinds of opportunities and internal rewards that complex jobs offer.

Results of the study generally supported the hypothesis that employees who work on jobs high on the core dimensions show high work motivation, satisfaction, performance, and attendance. Also, Hackman and Lawler found that a number of dependent measures were moderated as predicted by growth need strength: That is, employees with high measured needs for growth responded more positively to complex jobs than did employees low in growth need strength.

The appropriate conceptualization and measurement of the differences among people that moderate how they respond to complex jobs has been the subject of a number of recent studies. Findings similar to those reported by Hackman and Lawler have been reported by Brief and Aldag (1975), by Oldham (in press), and by Sims and Szilagyi (Note 4), using a measure of growth need strength (although the Brief and Aldag study provided only partial replication). Supportive findings also have been obtained by Robey (1974), using as an individual difference measure "extrinsic" vs "intrinsic" work values. Failures to obtain a moderating effect have been reported by Shepard (1970) (using a measure of alienation from work) and by Stone (1976) (using a measure of employee endorsement of the Protestant work ethic). Wanous (1974) directly compared the usefulness of (a) higher order need strength, (b) endorsement of the Protestant work ethic, and (c) urban vs rural subcultural background as moderators of job effects. All three variables were found to be of some value as moderators, with the need strength measure strongest and the urban–rural measure weakest.

In sum, there is now substantial evidence that differences among people do moderate how they react to the complexity and challenge of their work, and studies using direct measures of individual needs seem to provide more consistent and strong support for this finding than do measures of subcultural background or of generalized work values.

The job characteristics model

The model presented and tested in this paper is an attempt to extend, refine, and systematize the relationships described above between job characteristics and individual responses to the work. The basic job characteristics model is presented in Fig. 1. At the most general level, five "core" job dimensions are seen as prompting three psychological states which, in turn, lead to a number of beneficial personal and work outcomes. The links between the job dimensions and the psychological states, and between the psychological states and the outcomes, are shown as moderated by individual growth need strength. Each of the major classes of variables in the model is discussed in more detail below.

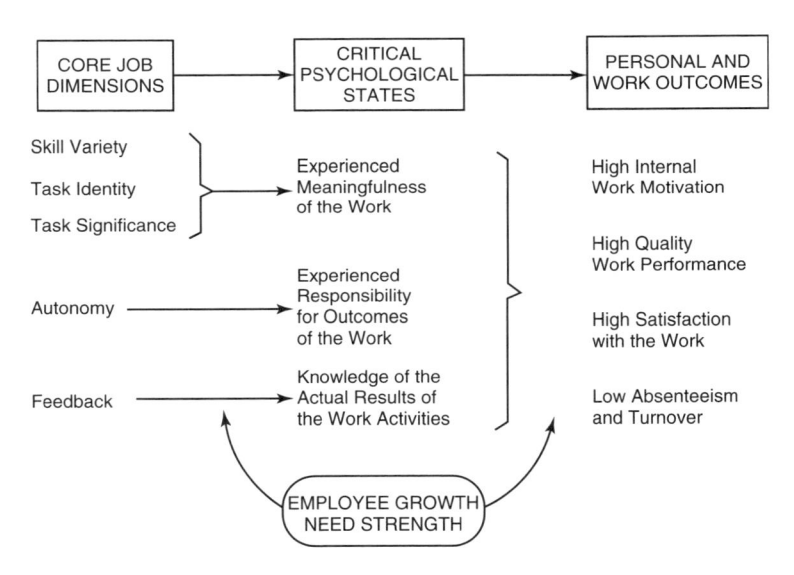

Figure 1 The job characteristics model of work motivation.

Psychological states

The three psychological states (experienced meaningfulness of the work, experienced responsibility for the outcomes of the work and knowledge of the results of the work activities) are the causal core of the model. Following Hackman and Lawler (1971), the model postulates that an individual experiences positive affect to the extent that he *learns* (knowledge of results) that he *personally* (experienced responsibility) has performed well on a task that he *cares about* (experienced meaningfulness).

This positive affect is reinforcing to the individual, and serves as an incentive for him to continue to try to perform well in the future. When he does not perform well, he does not experience an internally reinforcing state of affairs, and he may elect to try harder in the future so as to regain the internal rewards that good performance brings. The net result is a self-perpetuating cycle of positive work motivation powered by self-generated rewards, that is predicted to continue until one or more of the three psychological states is no longer present, or until the individual no longer values the internal rewards that derive from good performance.

It should be noted that self-generated motivation should be highest when all three of the psychological states are present. If the performer feels fully responsible for work outcomes on a meaningful task, but never finds out how well he is performing, it is doubtful that he will experience the internal rewards that can prompt self-generated motivation. Similarly if he has full knowledge of the results of the work, but experiences the task as trivial (or feels no personal responsibility for the results of the work), internal motivation will not be high.

The three psychological states are defined as follows:

> Experienced Meaningfulness of the Work. The degree to which the individual experiences the job as one which is generally meaningful, valuable, and worthwhile;
> Experienced Responsibility for Work Outcomes. The degree to which the individual feels personally accountable and responsible for the results of the work he or she does;
> Knowledge of Results. The degree to which the individual knows and understands, on a continuous basis, how effectively he or she is performing the job.

Job dimensions

Of the five characteristics of jobs shown in Fig. 1 as fostering the emergence of the psychological states, three contributes to the experienced meaningfulness of the work, and one each contributes to experienced responsibility and to knowledge of results.

Toward experienced meaningfulness

Three job characteristics combine additively to determine the psychological meaningfulness of a job. They are:

(1) Skill Variety. The degree to which a job requires a variety of different activities in carrying out the work, which involve the use of a number of different skills and talents of the person.

When a task requires a person to engage in activities that challenge or stretch his skills and abilities, that task almost invariably is experienced as meaningful by the individual. Many parlor games, puzzles, and recreational activities, for example, achieve much of their fascination because they tap and test the intellective or motor skills of the people who do them. When a job draws upon several skills of an employee, that individual may find the job to be of enormous personal meaning—even if, in any absolute sense, it is not of great significance or importance.

(2) Task Identity. The degree to which the job requires completion of a "whole" and identifiable piece of work; that is, doing a job from beginning to end with a visible outcome.

If, for example, an employee assembles a complete product (or provides a complete unit of service) he should find the work more meaningful than would be the case if he were responsible for only a small part of the whole job, other things (such as skill variety) assumed equal.

(3) Task Significance. The degree to which the job has a substantial impact on the lives or work of other people, whether in the immediate organization or in the external environment.

When an individual understands that the results of his work may have a significant effect on the well-being of other people, the meaningfulness of that work usually is enhanced. Employees who tighten nuts on aircraft brake assemblies, for example, are much more likely to perceive their work as meaningful than are workers who fill small boxes with paper clips—again, even though the skill levels involved may be comparable.

Toward experienced responsibility

The job characteristic predicted to prompt employee feelings of personal responsibility for the work outcomes is autonomy. To the extent that a job has high autonomy, the outcomes depend increasingly on the individual's *own* efforts, initiatives, and decisions rather than on the adequacy of instructions from the boss or on a manual of job procedures. In such circumstances, the individual should feel strong personal responsibility for the success and failures that occur on the job. Autonomy is defined as follows:

> Autonomy. The degree to which the job provides substantial freedom, independence, and discretion to the individual in scheduling the work and in determining the procedures to be used in carrying it out.

Toward knowledge of results

The job characteristic that fosters knowledge of results is feedback, which is defined as follows:

> Feedback. The degree to which carrying out the work activities required by the job results in the individual obtaining direct and clear information about the effectiveness of his or her performance.

Summary: the overall "motivating potential" of a job

According to the job characteristics model, the overall potential of a job to prompt internal work motivation on the part of job incumbents should be highest when all of the following are true: (a) the job is high on at least one (and hopefully more) of the three job dimensions that lead to experienced meaningfulness, (b) the job is high on autonomy, and (c) the job is high on feedback.

The Motivating Potential Score (MPS) is a measure of the degree to which the above conditions are met. MPS is computed by combining the scores of jobs on the five dimensions as follows:

$$\text{Motivating Potential Score (MPS)} = \left[\frac{\text{Skill Variety} + \text{Task Identity} + \text{Task Significance}}{3} \right] \times \text{Autonomy} \times \text{Feedback}$$

As can be seen from the formula, a near-zero score of a job on either autonomy or feedback will reduce the overall MPS to near-zero; whereas a near-zero score on one of the three job dimensions that contribute to experienced meaningfulness cannot, by itself, do so.

Individual growth need strength

As noted earlier, there is now substantial evidence that differences among people moderate how they react to their work, and individual need strength appears to be a useful way to conceptualize and measure such differences. The basic prediction is that people who have high need for personal growth and development will respond more positively to a job high in motivating potential than people with low growth need strength.

There are two possible "sites" for this moderating effect in the motivational sequence shown in Fig. 1: (a) at the link between the objective job dimensions and the psychological states, and (b) at the link between the psychological states and the outcome variables. The former would imply that high growth need people are more likely (or better able) to *experience* the psychological states when the objective job is good than are their low growth need counterparts. The latter allows the possibility that nearly everybody may experience the psychological states when job conditions are right, but that individuals with high growth needs respond more positively to that experience. It may be, of course, that growth need strength moderates at *both* points in the sequence, as tentatively shown in Fig. 1. Empirical tests of these alternative "locations" for the moderating effect of growth-need strength are reported later in this paper.

Outcome variables

Also shown in Fig. 1 are several outcome variables that are predicted to be affected by the level of job-based motivation experienced by people at work. Especially critical to the theory is the measure of internal work motivation (Lawler & Hall, 1970; Hackman & Lawler, 1971) because it taps directly the contingency between effective performance and self-administered affective rewards. Typical questionnaire items measuring internal work motivation include: (a) I feel a great sense of personal satisfaction when I do this job well; (b) I feel bad and unhappy when I discover that I have performed poorly on this job; and (c) My own feelings are *not* affected much one way or the other by how well I do on this job (reversed scoring).

Other outcomes listed in Fig.1 are the quality of work performance, job satisfaction (especially satisfaction with opportunities for personal growth and development on the job), absenteeism, and turnover. All of these outcomes are expected to be more positive for jobs with high motivating potential than for jobs low in MPS. Causal priorities *among* the several outcome variables are not explicitly addressed by the model (cf. Oldham, in press).

Method

The job characteristics model was tested using data obtained from 658 employees working on 62 different jobs in seven organizations. The jobs are highly heterogeneous, including blue collar, white collar, and professional work. Both industrial and service organizations are included in the sample, but all are business organizations. The organizations are located in the East, Southeast, and Midwest, in both urban and rural settings.

The primary data collection instrument was the Job Diagnostic Survey (JDS), an instrument specifically designed to measure each of the variables in the job characteristics model. Properties of the JDS (including descriptions of item content and format, and reliabilities of each measure) are described elsewhere (Hackman & Oldham, Note 3; 1975). Included there are the means, standard deviations, and intercorrelations of JDS measures for the respondents whose data are used in this report.

All data were collected on site by one of the authors or their associates. One to four days were spent by the researchers at each organization collecting data. Proceedural steps typically were as follows:

(1) The nature of the research was explained to second- or third-level management, and permission to administer the instrument was secured. Managers were informed that the project had to do with the refinement of an instrument to diagnose jobs, and that it would involve collection of data from employees, from their supervisors, and from company records.
(2) The JDS was administered to groups of employees (ranging from 3 to 25 at a time). Before taking the questionnaire, employees were told about the nature and purposes of the research and were given the option of not participating. Few employees declined to complete the questionnaire. It also was emphasized that all information obtained would be held in confidence, and that no one in the organization would have access to individual responses. Employees were told that it was desirable to have names on questionnaires for research purposes, but that this also was voluntary. About 10% of the respondents declined to provide their names.
(3) Supervisors and the researchers completed the Job Rating Form (Hackman & Oldham, Note 3), which measures the characteristics of the focal job as viewed by individuals who do not work on that job. Prior to completing the Job Rating Form, the researchers observed each job for between 1 and 2 hr.
(4) Members of management were asked to rate the work performance of each respondent on (a) effort expended on the job, (b) work quality, and (c) work quantity. The ratings were made on seven-point scales developed specifically for research purposes. Because the intercorrelations among the three rating scales were high (median = .53), a summary measure of work effectiveness was obtained by averaging ratings across the three scales and across the supervisors who rated each employee. Only the summary measure is used in the analyses reported in this paper.
(5) Absence data were obtained from company records. These data were recorded in terms of the number of days each employee in the sample had been absent during the immediately preceding year.

Employee descriptions of the objective characteristics of their jobs (using the JDS) were compared to similar descriptions made by researcher-observers using the Job Rating Form. Median correlation between the job incumbents and the observers for the five core dimensions is .65 (Hackman & Oldham, 1975). Evidently employees were able to provide rather accurate descriptions of the characteristics of their jobs; hence, employee-generated measures are used for tests of the job characteristics model.[1]

For some jobs in some organizations it was not possible to obtain complete data for all variables. Therefore, some of the results reported in this paper are based on that subset of the total sample for which complete data were available for the variable (or variables) of interest. Also, absence reporting procedures and internal performance standards varied among the seven organizations. Therefore, analyses were performed separately for each of the organizations whenever feasible, and median results are reported. In such cases, statistical significance was determined by combining the p values obtained in the seven separate analyses, following procedures developed by Stouffer *et al.* (1949) and described in Mosteller and Bush (1954, p. 329).

Results

The job characteristics model is sufficiently complex that it cannot be tested in a single analytic step. Therefore, three separate groups of analyses are reported below, each of which bears on a different aspect of the model.

(1) Simple analysis (by zero-order correlation) of the relationships of the job dimensions and the psychological states with the outcome variables.
(2) Analysis (by partial correlation and multiple regression) of the degree to which the psychological states mediate between job characteristics and outcome variables as predicted.
(3) Test of the degree to which employees' reactions to their work are moderated by individual growth-need strength as specified by the model.

Relationships of the job dimensions and psychological states with the outcomes

The median correlations of the job dimensions and the psychological states with each outcome measure are shown in Table 1. In general, results are consistent with expectations from the model: Correlations are in the predicted direction, and most achieve acceptable levels of statistical significance. The psychological states (which in the model are immediately causal of the outcomes) generally correlate higher with the outcome measures than do the job dimensions. The summary Motivating Potential Score (MPS) relates more strongly to the outcomes than do any of its component job dimensions, also as expected. Relationships involving absenteeism and performance, however, are not as strong as expected and are generally smaller than relationships involving the measures of satisfaction and motivation (perhaps simply because absenteeism and performance do not share common method variance with the job characteristics and the psychological states).

Table 1 Median correlations of job dimensions and psychological states with the work outcomes[a]

	Outcome measures				
	Internal motivation	General satisfaction	Growth satisfaction	Absenteeism	Rated work effectiveness
Psychological states					
Experienced meaningfulness	.64**	.64**	.64**	−.03	.13*
Experienced responsibility	.65**	.41**	.51**	−.16	.16**
Knowledge of results	.23**	.33**	.33**	−.11	.10
Job characteristics					
Skill variety	.34**	.32**	.48**	−.15**	.07
Task identity	.25**	.22**	.29**	−.18	.15**
Task significance	.31**	.21**	.35**	.16	.12**
Autonomy	.31**	.38**	.51**	−.24**	.19**
Feedback	.35**	.38**	.45**	−.12	.21**
Motivating potential score	.48**	.43**	.58**	−.25*	.24**

[a]Correlations were computed separately for each of the seven organizations where data were collected, and medians are reported here. See text for explanation of how levels of statistical significance were computed. Total $n = 658$.
*$p < .05$.
**$p < .01$.

Test of the mediating function of the psychological states

The job characteristics model specifies that the three psychological states mediate between the job characteristics and the outcome variables (Fig. 1). The validity of this general proposition is tested by asking three research questions. First, are predictions of the outcome measures from the psychological states maximized when all three of the psychological states are used, or are equally strong relationships obtained using the psychological states singly or in pairs? Second, are the relationships between the job dimensions and the outcome measures empirically dependent on the psychological states, or do the job dimensions predict the outcome measures just as well if the psychological states are ignored? And third, do specific job dimensions relate to specific psychological states as specified in the model, or are the two sets of variables related more complexly (or less so) than predicted?

These three questions are addressed separately below. To maximize the stability of the results (many of which are based on partial and multiple correlations), all 658 subjects were used in the analyses for the three outcome variables that were measured identically in all organizations in the sample: internal motivation, general satisfaction, and growth satisfaction.

Are all three psychological states necessary to maximize prediction of the outcome measures?

To test this question, regressions were computed predicting the outcome measures (a) from each of the three psychological states taken alone (i.e., the zero-order correlations), (b) from the three possible pairs of the psychological states, and (c) from all three psychological states taken together. Results are summarized in Table 2.

Results show that as additional psychological states are added to the regression equations, the amount of outcome measure variance controlled does indeed increase, consistent with the model. It should be noted, however, that the increase in R^2 is substantially greater between one and two predictors than it is between

Table 2 Average variance controlled in regressions predicting outcome measures from one, two and three psychological states

Number of predictors used in regressions	Mean R^2 for outcome measures		
	Internal motivation	General satisfaction	Growth satisfaction
One (EM; ER; KR)[a]	.29	.23	.26
Two (EM + ER; EM + KR; ER + KR)	.45	.39	.43
Three (EM + ER + KR)	.51	.46	.50

[a] $n = 658$, EM = experienced meaningfulness; ER = experienced responsibility; KR = knowledge of results.

two and three. Since measures of the three psychological states are themselves moderately intercorrelated (median = .33), and since some increment in prediction is to be expected on purely statistical grounds when predictors are added to a regression, the conclusion that prediction is maximized when all three psychological states are present must be interpreted with considerable caution.

Are job dimension-outcome variable relationships dependent on the psychological states?

Two complementary methods were used to test this question. First, relationships between each job dimension and the several outcome measures were examined before and after the model-specified mediating psychological state was statistically controlled (by partial correlation). Thus, the effect of experienced meaningfulness was controlled for relationships of skill variety, task identity, and task significance with the outcome measures; experienced responsibility was controlled for the relationships between autonomy and the outcome measures; and knowledge of results was controlled for the relationships between feedback and the outcome measures. If the model is correct, the partial correlations should approach zero and be substantially lower in magnitude than the direct or zero-order correlations between the job dimensions and the outcome measures.

Results are shown in Table 3. In general, substantial support is found for the proposition that the psychological states mediate between the job dimensions and the outcome measures. For each relationship between a job dimension and an outcome measure, statistically controlling the corresponding psychological state substantially lowers the magnitude of the association. In addition, most of the partial correlations are quite low, and many approach zero as predicted.

Results are somewhat less strong for feedback and for autonomy than for the other job dimensions. Although relationships between these variables and the outcome measures do decrease moderately when the corresponding psychological states are controlled for, partial correlations involving feedback do not approach zero for any of the dependent measures, and partials involving autonomy approach zero only for the measure of internal motivation.

An additional and complementary analysis was conducted using multiple regression. For each of the outcome measures, the three psychological states were introduced into a multiple regression equation to serve as primary predictors. Next, the five job dimensions were added to the regression as secondary predictors. If the psychological states do mediate the job dimension-outcome measure relationships as predicted, (a) the psychological states alone should account for a sizable portion of the dependent variable variance, and (b) introduction of the five job dimensions into the equation (as additional predictors) should not substantially increase the amount of dependent variable variance controlled.

Results are shown in Table 4. As predicted, the psychological states account for substantial variance for each of the dependent measures. Moreover, the introduction of the five job dimensions into the regression equations resulted in

Table 3 Relationships between job dimensions and the outcome measures controlling for the effects of the psychological states

Job dimension	Zero-order correlation	Partial correlation[a]	Difference
Internal motivation			
Skill variety	.42	.15	.27
Task identity	.22	.08	.14
Task significance	.32	.07	.25
Autonomy	.33	.08	.25
Feedback	.36	.28	.08
General satisfaction			
Skill variety	.42	.13	.29
Task identity	.22	.07	.15
Task significance	.24	−.06	.30
Autonomy	.43	.29	.14
Feedback	.37	.23	.14
Growth satisfaction			
Skill variety	.52	.28	.24
Task identity	.31	.19	.12
Task significance	.33	.06	.27
Autonomy	.58	.46	.12
Feedback	.44	.31	.13

[a] For each job dimension, the partial correlation reported controls only for the specific psychological state specified by the model to mediate the effects of that dimension. Thus, for relationships involving skill variety, task identity, and task significance, experienced meaningfulness was controlled; for relationships involving autonomy, experienced responsibility was controlled; and for relationships involving feedback, knowledge of results was controlled. ($n = 658$.)

a near-zero increase in the variance controlled for two of the dependent measures and only a small increase for the third.

Examination of the regression coefficients for the individual variables in the equations reveals a few anomalies. Ideally, the standardized coefficients for the psychological states would all be moderate to high, and would all exceed the coefficients for the five job dimensions. It was found, however, that experienced responsibility adds little to prediction for two of the outcome measures (general and growth satisfaction). For both of these outcome measures autonomy (the job dimension theoretically mediated by experienced responsibility) has a relatively larger regression coefficient than does experienced responsibility. In addition, the coefficients for knowledge of results are relatively small (and, for one of the outcome measures, is trivially negative).

In sum, the results in Tables 3 and 4 provide generally strong support for the predictions of the job characteristics model, although some difficulties having to do with certain specific job dimension–psychological state relationships were identified. Additional data relevant to these concerns are reported in the following section.

Table 4 Multiple regressions predicting the outcome measures from all prior variables compared to predictions from the psychological states only[a]

Summary statistics

	Multiple correlation (R) for the full eight-variable equation	R^2 for the three-variable equation (Psychological states only)	R^2 for the full eight-variable equation	Increase in R^2 by adding the five job dimensions to the regression
Internal motivation	.72	.51	.52	.01
General satisfaction	.69	.46	.48	.02
Growth satisfaction	.77	.50	.59	.09

Standardized regression weights (for the full equation)

	Experienced meaningfulness	Experienced responsibility	Knowledge of results	Skill variety	Task identity	Task significance	Autonomy	Feedback
Internal motivation	.31	.43	−.03	.09	−.01	.02	−.05	.08
General satisfaction	.52	.05	.12	.07	−.00	−.07	.10	.03
Growth satisfaction	.38	.07	.09	.13	.03	.02	.24	.07

[a] $n = 658$.

Do specific job dimensions relate to the psychological states as specified by the model?

To test this question, regressions were computed for each of the psychological states, in which the predictors were the job dimensions specified in the model as directly causal of that psychological state. Thus, experienced meaningfulness was predicted from skill variety, task identity, and task significance; experienced responsibility was predicted from autonomy; and knowledge of results was predicted from feedback. Next, the remaining job dimensions (that is, those *not* expected to directly influence the psychological state) were introduced into each regression equation as additional predictors. If the model is correct, the theory-specified job dimensions should account for substantial variance in the psychological states, and the introduction of the remaining job dimensions should not substantially increase the amount of variance controlled.

Results are presented in Table 5, and show that a moderate amount of variance in the psychological states is controlled by the model-specified job dimensions. For the equations predicting experienced meaningfulness and knowledge of results, the addition of job dimensions *not* predicted by the theory to affect these psychological states resulted in very small increases in the level of prediction attained, consistent with the model. The standardized regression weights for the equations predicting these two variables also are as would be expected, with the exception of a very low weight for task identity in predicting experienced meaningfulness.

For the equation predicting experienced responsibility, results are less supportive of the model. The variance controlled in this regression increased .16 (compared to .05 and .02 for the other psychological states) when job dimensions expected *not* to affect experienced responsibility were added. Moreover, examination of the regression weights shows that all five of the job dimensions contribute at a moderate level to the prediction of experienced responsibility. The zero-order correlations between experienced responsibility and each of the job dimensions also were examined, and are consistent with the regression findings: the five correlations are very homogeneous, ranging from .34 to .37 (all statistically reliable at less than the .01 level).

In sum, the results reported above show that the job dimensions predict experienced meaningfulness and knowledge of results generally as would be expected from the job characteristics model. Experienced responsibility, however, turns out to be almost equally affected by all of the job dimensions—not just by autonomy, as specified by the model.

Test of the moderating effect of growth need strength

The job characteristics model specifies that individual growth need strength (GNS) can moderate employees' reactions to their work at two points in the

Table 5 Multiple regressions predicting the psychological states from all job dimensions compared to predictions from the model-specified job dimensions only

Summary statistics

	Multiple correlation (R) for the full equation (All five job dimensions)	R^2 for model-specified job dimensions only[a]	R^2 for the full equation (All five job dimensions)	Increase in R^2 by adding to the regression those job dimensions not specified by the model
Experienced meaningfulness	.66	.38	.43	.05
Experienced responsibility	.57	.17	.33	.16
Knowledge of results	.56	.29	.31	.02

Standardized regression weights

	Skill Variety	Task identity	Task significance	Autonomy	Feedback
Experienced meaningfulness	[.30]	[.05]	[.27]	.17	.17
Experienced responsibility	.21	.17	.19	[.14]	.16
Knowledge of results	−.13	.04	.07	.11	[.51]

[a]The model-specified job dimensions used in computing these regressions are: skill variety, task identity, and task significance to predict experienced meaningfulness; autonomy to predict experienced responsibility; and feedback to predict knowledge of results. Regression coefficients for the model-specified job dimensions are bracketted in the lower half of the table. (n = 658.)

motivational sequence presented in Fig. 1. In particular, it is predicted (a) that the relationship between the three psychological states and the outcome variables will be stronger for individuals with high growth need strength than for individuals with low need for growth; and (b) that the relationship between the core job characteristics and their corresponding psychological states will be stronger for high than for low GNS individuals. In effect, the predictions are that high GNS individuals will be both better able to experience the psychological effects of an objectively enriched job, and more disposed to respond favorably to that experience.

The measure of growth need strength used to test these predictions was obtained from the "job choice" section of the JDS (Hackman & Oldham, 1975). Briefly, respondents indicate their relative preference for 12 pairs of hypothetical jobs (e.g., "A job where you are often required to make important decisions" vs "A job with many pleasant people to work with"). For each item, a job with characteristics relevant to growth need satisfaction is paired with a job having the potential for satisfying one of a variety of other needs. Based on their scores on this measure, the top and bottom quartiles of employees in each organization were identified, and appropriate correlations were computed separately for these two groups. For each relationship tested, it was predicted that the correlation would be higher for employees in the top quartile of the distribution of GNS scores than for those in the bottom quartile.

To test the moderating effects of GNS on the psychological state–outcome measure relationship, it was desirable to use a single measure that would summarize the degree to which all three psychological states simultaneously are present. The product of the three psychological states has this property, and therefore was correlated with each outcome measure, separately for subjects high and low in measured GNS. The top group of correlations in Table 6 show the results. Except for the measure of absenteeism, differences in the magnitude of the correlations for high vs low GNS employees are all in the predicted direction and statistically significant.

The relationships between the core job characteristics and the psychological states for high vs low GNS employees are shown in the middle group of correlations in Table 6. Included is a summary relationship between the overall MPS of the job and the product of the psychological states. All differences between correlations are in the predicted direction and (except for task identity) are statistically significant.

The bottom group of correlations in Table 6 shows results for correlations computed directly between the overall motivating potential of the job and the outcome measures, in effect, bridging the mediating function of the psychological states. Again, all differences between correlations for high vs low GNS employees are in the predicted direction, but the differences are less substantial than the others reported in the table, and statistical significance is achieved only for the measure of internal motivation.

Table 6 Relationships among job dimensions, psychological states, and outcome measures for employees high and low in growth need strength (GNS)[a]

	Median correlations		z (for difference between rs)
	Low GNS	High GNS	
Product of the three psychological states with:			
Internal motivation	.48	.66	1.75*
General satisfaction	.36	.69	3.66**
Growth satisfaction	.42	.69	2.68**
Absenteeism	−.16	−.13	−0.21
Rated work effectiveness	.12	.44	2.06*
Job dimensions with corresponding psychological states			
MPS with product of the psychological states	.59	.70	2.02*
Skill variety with experienced meaningfulness	.23	.57	3.37**
Task identity with experienced meaningfulness	.17	.30	1.08
Task significance with experienced meaningfulness	.15	.52	2.18*
Autonomy with experienced responsibility	.11	.59	2.99**
Feedback with knowledge of results	.42	.63	2.54**
Motivating potential score with:			
Internal motivation	.27	.52	1.64*
General satisfaction	.32	.49	0.93
Growth satisfaction	.55	.65	0.52
Absenteeism	−.23	−.25	0.00
Rated work effectiveness	.20	.44	0.53

[a] Correlations were computed separately for each of the seven organizations, and medians are reported here. Statistical significance of the differences between correlations for high and low GNS subjects was determined by combining the p values obtained in the separate analyses (Mosteller & Bush, 1954, p. 329). Total $n = 356$ (170 and 186, respectively, in the high and low GNS groups; ns are unequal because of tied scores).
*$p < .05$.
**$p < .01$.

Discussion

Empirical validity of the job characteristics model

The results reported above provide generally strong support for the validity of the job characteristics model. A number of specific problems and uncertainties were identified, however, and are explored below.

The basic relationships between the job dimensions and the outcome measures (Table 1) were as predicted and generally of substantial magnitude, although correlations involving absenteeism and work performance were lower than those for the other outcome measures. Similarly, substantial support was found for the proposition that individual growth need strength moderates other model-specified relationships, and that the moderating effect occurs both at the link between the job dimensions and the psychological states, and at the link between the psychological states and the outcome variables (Table 6). This moderating effect was not, however, obtained for the measure of absenteeism.

Both substantive and methodological explanations are possible for the relative weakness of the results involving absenteeism (and, to some extent, work performance). At the substantive level, it may be that these behavioral outcomes are in fact more causally remote from job characteristics than are employees' affective reactions to their work, and therefore are less powerfully affected by the job dimensions. Or the explanation may lie in the fact that the motivation and satisfaction items were in the same questionnaire as the items tapping the job dimensions and the psychological states. For this reason, relationships involving the affective measures may have been inflated because of common method variance, causing the results for absenteeism and performance to appear weaker by comparison. Moreover, relationships involving performance and absenteeism may have been attenuated because of the difficulty in obtaining measures of these criteria that were at the same time psychometrically adequate and comparable across the diversity of jobs and organizations studied. Finally, the results for absenteeism may have been compromised to some extent by a rather prosaic data collection difficulty. Because of idiosyncratic procedures for collecting and recording absenteeism data in some organizations, it was necessary to code all absences terms of the number of *days* individuals were absent in a year (rather than the number of *occasions* they were absent, as originally intended). As a result, when an individual was away from work for a large number of contiguous days (perhaps because of a single serious illness or other personal emergency), that person would receive a very high absenteeism score, when in fact the person may otherwise have had perfect attendance. This data collection problem may have compromised the overall validity of the absenteeism measure used in the research. Unfortunately, the present data do not permit test of the degree to which the various explanations offered above are responsible for the apparent attenuation of the relationships involving absenteeism and work performance effectiveness.

Results presented in Tables 2 through 5 provide general (and sometimes quite strong) support for the proposition that the effects of the core job dimensions on the outcome variables are mediated by the three psychological states. The only noteworthy anomalies identified are that (a) results involving the feedback dimension are in some cases less strong than those obtained for the other job dimensions; and (b) the autonomy-experienced responsibility linkage does not operate as specified by the model in predicting the outcome variables.

The problem with feedback is not a serious one, and may have resulted because the present study dealt *only* with feedback that derived from the job itself. Obviously, feedback is received by employees from many additional sources: supervisors, peers, and so on. Moreover, there is reason to believe that feedback from various sources may interact with one another in affecting individuals' knowledge of the results of their work and their affective reactions to the job as a whole (Greller, Note 2). Therefore, it may be that the present results showing how feedback affects the outcome measures via the psychological states are, in themselves, accurate—but that the results are not as strong as they might be because feedback from other (nonjob) sources was not accounted for in the analyses.

The difficulty with the autonomy-experienced responsibility linkage is more serious, because it raises questions about the validity of part of the model itself. Results showed two findings that were contrary to expectation: (a) experienced responsibility is determined not only by autonomy but by other job dimensions as well (Table 5), and (b) autonomy has *direct* effects on certain of the outcome variables that equal or exceed its predicted indirect impact via experienced responsibility (Table 3 and 4). These results do not cast doubt on the desirability of high autonomy and high experienced responsibility for achieving beneficial work outcomes; the impact of both variables on the outcome measures is, as predicted, positive. But the findings do raise questions about the causal dynamics by which such effects are realized.

The explanation for these anomalies may derive partly from the relationships among the job dimensions themselves. The five dimensions are not empirically independent (Hackman and Oldham, 1975, report a median intercorrelation of .26), nor would they be expected to be: Jobs that are "good" often are good in several ways, and jobs that are "bad" often are generally bad. It also is the case, however, that autonomy is the *least* independent of the five job dimensions (the median correlation of autonomy with the other dimensions is .36). Thus, it may be that autonomy serves, at least in part, to summarize the overall complexity of a job, and that it therefore is both more multiply determined and has a greater diversity of effects than do the other job dimensions. If this is the case, of course, the functions of both autonomy and experienced responsibility in the model-specified causal sequence would be empirically muddied. Additional research will be required to obtain increased specificity and clarity regarding the functions of autonomy and experienced responsibility in the job characteristics model.

MPS as a summary measure of the job characteristics

The Motivating Potential Score (MPS) has been used throughout this paper as a device for summarizing the overall degree to which a job is objectively designed in a way that maximizes the possibility for internal motivation on the part of the people who perform it. The MPS formulation derives directly from the propositions of the job characteristics model, and therefore should be valid to the extent that the model itself has validity. Yet it is important to compare the empirical performance of MPS with that of simpler alternative models because there is increasing evidence that in a wide variety of prediction situations simple, unweighted linear models outperform more complex and subtle formulations (cf. Dawes & Corrigan, 1974). Moreover, special concern about MPS may be warranted, because the MPS formula includes two multiplicative terms. Given that multiplicative operations can compound the effects of measure unreliability (and are rarely warranted in any case by the scale properties of the data), there is cause for concern about how MPS predictions compare to those based on nonmultiplicative models.

Five different models for combining the job dimensions were developed and correlated with the three questionnaire-based dependent measures. The five models and the correlations obtained are shown in Table 7. The results do not meaningfully differentiate among the models. While the full multiplicative model proves to be slightly the worst, and the regression models are slightly the best, the obtained differences are so small as to be of negligible practical significance. Thus, while the model-specified MPS formulation is not disconfirmed by the data, neither has it been shown to represent a more adequate means of combining the job dimensions than other, simpler alternatives.

The nature and effects of growth need strength

Some researchers (e.g., Hackman, Oldham, Janson, & Purdy, 1975; Hulin & Blood, 1968) have suggested that individuals who are low in growth need strength (or who are alienated from middle-class work norms) may react *negatively* to complex or enriched jobs because they will be psychologically "stretched" too far by such jobs, or because they will not value the kinds of outcomes that such jobs provide.

The present findings provide no evidence to support such contentions. While individuals with strong growth needs do react more positively to complex jobs than do individuals with weak needs for growth, the *signs* of the relationships between the job characteristics and the outcome measures are positive even for people in the bottom quartile of the growth need measure. This is of special significance in the present study, because the sample included several groups of employees who scored especially low on the measure of growth need strength.

Table 7 Comparison of several models for combining the job dimensions[a]

Alternative models	Outcome measures		
	Internal motivation	General satisfaction	Growth satisfaction
MPS $\left[\left(\frac{SV+TI+TS}{3}\right) \times A \times F\right]$	.46	.49	.63
Full multiplicative [SV × TI × TS × A × F]	.44	.45	.58
Simple additive [SV + TI + TS + A + F]	.51	.52	.67
Multiple regression	.52	.53	.69
Cross-validated regression	.52	.53	.68

[a] n (except for cross-validated regression) = 658; n for cross-validated regression = 329.

Such individuals may not be primed and ready to respond enthusiastically to a job that is more complex and challenging than the one they now hold. For this reason, those responsible for the implementation of job enrichment programs might be well-advised to proceed slowly and carefully when the target employees have only weak needs for personal growth. And the magnitude of the gains realized in such circumstances may well turn out to be less than would be the case for employees high in growth need strength. But the present findings provide *no* reason to expect that the ultimate impact of working on enriched jobs will be more negative than positive for any group of employees, regardless of their level of growth need strength (see also Stone, 1976).

The present results confirm that the moderators of individuals' reactions to their work can be usefully conceptualized and measured directly in terms of human needs. Questions remain, however, regarding the relationships between such measures and the demographic and subcultural variables that also have been proposed as moderators.

To examine this issue, a summary measure of growth need strength was correlated with a number of demographic and background characteristics of employees in the present sample. Results are shown in Table 8, and suggest that the "typical" high growth need employee is a young and well-educated male who works or lives in a suburban or rural setting. It is noteworthy that the individual's *present* place of work and residence relate most substantially to measured need for growth, whereas the location of socialization is rather weakly associated (cf. Hulin & Blood, 1968; Turner & Lawrence, 1965; Wanous, 1974). Evidently current experiences are more responsible for determining an individual's desire for growth satisfaction than are items of personal history, and therefore are more likely to moderate the relationships between job characteristics and outcome variables.

Table 8 Relationships between growth need strength and demographic characteristics[a]

	Growth need strength	Sex	Age	Education	Rural place of work	Rural current residence	Rural childhood residence
Growth need strength	—						
Sex	−.26	—					
Age	−.15	.02	—				
Education	.46	−.33	−.05	—			
Rural place of work	.16	−.39	−.05	.19	—		
Rural current residence	.14	−.22	.01	.09	.35	—	
Rural childhood residence	.02	−.16	−.03	−.02	.33	.45	—

[a] See Hackman & Oldham (Note 3) for details regarding the measurement of each variable. For psychometric reasons, tests of significance are not appropriate for these correlations. If such tests were appropriate, all correlations ≥ .09 would be significant at the .05 level. $n = 658$.

If this conclusion is accepted, then research examining the effects of job and organizational structures on employee growth needs may prove informative. It may be that individuals' needs *change* or adjust to meet the demands of the situation in which they find themselves. Thus, the needs of an individual may actually become more "growth oriented" when he is confronted with a complex job which seems to demand that the individual develop himself and exercise independent thought and action in his work.

Uses and distinguishing features of the job characteristics model

The job characteristics model was designed so that each of the three focal classes of variables (i.e., objective job characteristics, mediating psychological states, and individual growth need strength) can be directly measured in actual work situations using the Job Diagnostic Survey (Hackman & Oldham, 1975). Therefore, the model can be used as a conceptual basis for the diagnosis of jobs being considered for redesign (e.g., to determine the existing potential of a job for engendering internal work motivation, to identify those specific job characteristics that are most in need of improvement, and to assess the "readiness" of employees to respond positively to enriched work). In addition, the model can serve as a framework for assessing and interpreting measurements collected to evaluate the effects of changes that have been carried out (e.g., to determine which job dimensions did and did not change, to assess the impact of the changes on the affective and motivational responses of employees, and to test for any possible postchange alterations in the growth need strength of the employees whose jobs were redesigned).

The job dimensions specified by the model are directly tied to a set of action principles for redesigning jobs (Hackman, Oldham, Janson & Purdy, 1975; Walters & Associates, 1975). These principles specify what types of changes are most likely to lead to improvements in each of the five core dimensions, and thereby to an overall increase in the motivating potential of a job. The usefulness of the action principles for increasing the MPS of a job has not yet been empirically tested, however; neither has the validity of the job characteristics model itself been assessed in an actual change project. Therefore, further research is required before more than tentative statements can be made regarding the usefulness of the model as a practical guide for work redesign.

It should be noted that the job characteristics model deals only with aspects of jobs that can be altered to create *positive* motivational incentives for the job incumbent. It does not directly address the dysfunctional aspects of repetitive work (as does activation theory), although presumably a job designed in accord with the dictates of the model would not turn out to be routine or highly repetitive.

In addition, the model focuses exclusively on the relationship between individuals and their work. It does not address directly interpersonal, technical, or situational moderators of how people react to their work (as does socio-technical systems theory), even though attention to such factors may be critical in successful installations of actual work changes (Davis & Taylor, 1972; Hackman, 1975). A recent study by Oldham (in press), for example, has shown that inclusion of one such moderator (the quality of interpersonal relationships on the job) significantly improves prediction of employees' responses to their jobs. Specifically, it was found that people who work on complex jobs experience greater internal motivation when they are satisfied with on-the-job relationships than when they are dissatisfied with these relationships.

Finally, the job characteristics model is designed to apply only to jobs that are carried out more-or-less independently by individuals. It offers no explicit guidance for the effective design of work for interacting teams, i.e., when the work is best conceived of as a group task, as is sometimes the case when "autonomous work groups" are formed (Gulowsen, 1972). The model should, nevertheless, be of some use in designing tasks that are motivating to group members: Presumably, a "good" job for a group would have many of the same objective characteristics as a well-designed job intended for an individual.

Yet it also appears that it would be necessary to go well beyond the present limits of the job characteristics model in designing group tasks, for at least two reasons. First, it seems doubtful that translating the core job dimensions from the individual to the group level would be an entirely straightforward process. How, for example, should a group task be designed so that all members would see it as providing high autonomy, and therefore experience substantial *personal* responsibility for the outcome of the *group?* A second problem derives from the fact that how group tasks are designed affects not only the motivation of group members, but the patterns of social interaction that emerge among them as well (Hackman & Morris, 1975). How can group tasks be structured so that they prompt task-effective rather than dysfunctional patterns of interaction among members? Although such questions are crucial to the effective design of tasks for teams, they appear to have no simple answers, nor are they questions for which the job characteristics model in its present form provides explicit guidance.

Acknowledgments

The authors express great appreciation to members of the consulting firm that helped us gain access to the organizations where this research was conducted; to Kenneth Brousseau, Daniel Feldman, and Linda Frank for assistance in data collection and analysis; and to Gerrit Wolf for help in analytic planning.

This report was prepared in connection with research supported by the Office of Naval Research (Organizational Effectiveness Research Program, Contract No. N00014-67A-0097-0026, NR 170-744), and by the Manpower Administration. U.S. Department of Labor (Research and Development Grant No. 21-09-74-14). Since grantees conducting research under government sponsorship are encouraged to express their own judgment freely, this report does not necessarily represent the official opinion or policy of the government.

Note

1 It can reasonably be argued that when the intent is to predict or understand employee attitudes or behavior at work (as is presently the case), employee ratings of the job dimensions are *preferable* to use, since it is an employee's own perceptions of the objective job that is causal of his reactions to it (cf. Hackman & Lawler, 1971).

References

Berlyne, D. E. Arousal and reinforcement. *Nebraska Symposium on Motivation*, 1967, 15, 1–110.

Blood, M. R., & Hulin, C. L. Alienation, environmental characteristics, and worker responses. *Journal of Applied Psychology,* 1967, 51, 284–290.

Brief, A. P., & Aldag, R. J. Employee reactions to job characteristics: A constructive replication. *Journal of Applied Psychology,* 1975, 60, 182–186.

Davis, L. E., & Taylor, J. C. *Design of jobs*. Middlesex, England: Penguin, 1972.

Dawes, R. M., & Corrigan, B. Linear models in decision making. *Psychological Bulletin*, 1974, 81, 95–106.

Dunaette, M. D., Campbell, J. P., Hakel, M. D. Factors contributing to job satisfaction and dissatisfaction in six occupational groups. *Organizational Behavior and Human Performance*, 1967, 2, 143–174.

Emery, F. E., & Trist, E. L. Socio-technical systems. In F. E. Emery (Ed.), *Systems thinking*. London: Penguin, 1969.

Ford, R. N. *Motivation through the work itself*. New York: American Management Association, 1969.

Gulowsen, J. A measure of work group autonomy. In L. E. Davis & J. C. Taylor (Eds.), *Design of jobs*. Middlesex, England: Penguin, 1972.

Hackman, J. R. On the coming demise of job enrichment. In E. L. Cass and F. G. Zimmer (Eds.), *Man and work in society*. New York: Van Nostrand-Reinhold, 1975.

Hackman, J. R., & Lawler, E. E. Employee reactions to job characteristics. *Journal of Applied Psychology Monograph*, 1971, 55, 259–286.

Hackman, J. R., & Morris, C. G. Group tasks, group interaction process, and group performance effectiveness: A review and proposed integration. In L. Berkowitz (Ed.), *Advances in experimental social psychology*. New York: Academic Press, 1975, Vol. 8.

Hackman, J. R., & Oldham, G. R. Development of the Job Diagnostic Survey. *Journal of Applied Psychology,* 1975, 60, 159–170.

Hackman, J. R., & Oldham, G., Janson, R., & Purdy, K. A new strategy for job enrichment. *California Management Review*, Summer, 1975, 57–71.

Herbst, P. G. *Autonomous group functioning*. London: Tavistock, 1962.

Herzberg, F. *Work and the nature of man*. Cleveland: World, 1966.

Herzberg, F., Mausner, B., & Snyderman, B. *The motivation to work*. New York: Wiley, 1959.

Hinton, B. L. An empirical Investigation of the Herzberg methodology and two-factor theory. *Organizational Behavior and Human Performance*, 1968, 3, 286–309.

Hulin, C. L. Individual differences and job enrichment. In J. R. Maher (Ed.), *New perspectives in job enrichment*. New York: Van Nostrand-Reinhold: 1971.

Hulin, C. L., & Blood, M. R. Job enlargement, individual differences, and worker responses. *Psychological Bulletin*, 1968, 69, 41–55.

King, N. A clarification and evaluation of the two-factor theory of job satisfaction. *Psychological Bulletin*, 1970, 74, 18–31.

Lawler, E. E., & Hall, D. T. The relationship of job characteristics to job involvement, satisfaction and intrinsic motivation. *Journal of Applied Psychology*, 1970, 54, 305–312.

Mosteller, F., & Bush, R. L. Selected quantitative techniques. In G. Lindzey (Ed.), *Handbook of social psychology*. Reading, Mass: Addison–Wesley, 1954, Vol. 1.

Oldham, G. R. Job characteristics and internal motivation: The moderating effect of interpersonal and individual variables. *Human Relations*. In press.

Paul, W. J. Jr., Robertson, K. B., & Herzberg, F. Job enrichment pays off. *Harvard Business Review*, 1969, 47, 61–78.

Porter, L. W., Lawler, E. E., & Hackman, J. R. *Behavior in organizations*. New York: McGraw–Hill, 1975.

Rice, A. K. *Productivity and social organization: The Ahmedabad experiment*. London: Tavistock, 1958.

Robey, D. Task design, work values, and worker response: An experimental test. *Organizational Behavior and Human Performance*, 1974, 12, 264–273.

Scott, W. E. Activation theory and task design. *Organizational Behavior and Human Performance*, 1966, 1, 3–30.

Shepard, J. M. Functional specialization, alienation, and job satisfaction. *Industrial and Labor Relations Review*, 1970, 23, 207–219.

Stone, E. F. The moderating effect of work-related values on the job scope–job satisfaction relationship. *Organizational Behavior and Human Performance*, 1976, 15, 147–179.

Stouffer, S. A. et al. *The American soldier, Vol. 1. Adjustment during army life*. Princeton: Princeton Univ. Press, 1949.

Thayer, R. E. Measurement of activation through self-report. *Psychological Reports*, 1967, 20, 663–678.

Trist, E. L., Higgin, G. W., Murray, H., & Pollock, A. B. *Organizational choice*. London: Tavistock, 1963.

Turner, A. N., & Lawrence, P. R. *Industrial jobs and the worker*. Boston: Harvard Graduate School of Business Administration, 1965.

Walters, K. W. & Associates. *Job enrichment for results*. Reading, Mass.: Addison–Wesley, 1975.

Wanous, J. P. Individual differences and reactions to job characteristics. *Journal of Applied Psychology*, 1974, 59, 616–622.

Whitsett, D. A., & Winslow, E. K. An analysis of studies critical of the motivator–hygiene theory. *Personnel Psychology*, 1967, 20, 391–415.

Reference Notes

1. Davis, L. E., & Trist, E. L. *Improving the quality of work life: Experience of the sociotechnical approach*. Background paper commissioned by the U. S. Department of Health, Education, and Welfare for the Work in America Project, June, 1972.
2. Greller, M. *The consequences of feedback*. Unpublished doctoral dissertation, Yale University, 1975.

3. Hackman, J. R., & Oldham, G. R. *The Job Diagnostic Survey: An instrument for the diagnosis of jobs and the evaluation of job redesign projects*. Technical Report No. 4, Department of Administrative Sciences, Yale University, 1974. (Also available from Journal Supplement Abstract Service of the American Psychological Association, Ms. No. 810, 1974.)
4. Sims, H. P., & Szilagyi, A. D. Individual moderators of job characteric relationships. Unpublished manuscript, Graduate School of Business, Indiana University, 1974.

46

WORK CONTROL AND EMPLOYEE WELL-BEING

A decade review

Deborah J. Terry and Nerina L. Jimmieson

Source: C.L. Cooper and I.T. Robertson (eds), *International Review of Indsutrial and Organisation Psychology,* Vol. 14, Chichester: John Wiley, 1999, pp. 95–148.

It is widely recognized that control is a construct that has central importance to our understanding of psychological functioning and adjustment (Skinner, 1996). Indeed, White (1959) saw humans as being intrinsically motivated to control their environment. Moreover, several decades of research—employing both correlational and experimental methodologies—have revealed that a sense of control relates positively to a range of different indicators of well-being (see Miller, 1979; Skinner, 1996; Thompson, 1981). One of the difficulties with the construct of control is that it can be conceptualized at different levels of abstraction (i.e., both personal and societal; C.S. Smith, Tisak, Hahn & Schmieder, 1997) and, despite the fact that there is general agreement that psychologists are most concerned with psychological or personal control (Skinner, 1996; C.S. Smith et al., 1997), a myriad of different constructs has been used to refer to aspects of personal control (see Skinner, 1996). However, as Skinner noted, prototypical definitions of control focus on the link between agents and outcomes; in other words, on the extent to which people are able to influence the outcomes that they experience in their environment.

In common with many areas of psychology, the construct of control has played a central role in industrial and organizational psychology. As Ganster and Fusilier (1989) pointed out in their review of the literature on control in the workplace for the *International Review of Industrial and Organizational Psychology*, much theorizing in this context has been predicated on the basis that jobs that impose limitations on personal control are associated with unfavorable work outcomes. In their review, Ganster and Fusilier (1989; see also Ganster, 1989) presented a comprehensive coverage of the theoretical perspectives in industrial and organizational psychology that have at least, in part, been based on the construct of work control. In addition to research that has focused directly on this construct, Ganster reviewed literature on employee participation in decision-making (e.g., Locke & Schweiger, 1979), job design (e.g., Hackman & Oldham, 1976), and machine-pacing (e.g., Johansson, Aronsson, & Lindstrom, 1978), which are all aspects of the work environment that are assumed to have their impact on work outcomes through their influence on the extent to which employees have control over their work environment. The review was extremely timely, to the extent that it located the construct of work control in the broader literature on industrial and organizational psychology, at the same time as providing a valuable review of the extant literature on the effects of direct measures of employee control.

The present review contrasts with the review conducted by Ganster and Fusilier (1989) in that it is focused entirely on research that, either subjectively or objectively, assessed the construct of work control. As noted above, at the time that Ganster and Fusilier conducted their review, it was timely to conduct a review that reflected the breadth of literature that could be identified as, at least indirectly, revolving around the control construct. A decade later, the challenge is different—the breadth of the domain has been identified, now it is necessary to examine, in depth, the extent of support for the assumption that jobs that impose limitations on personal control are associated with unfavorable work outcomes. To do this in an effective manner, it seemed appropriate to base the discussion on research that has employed direct measures of employee control. Although recent factor analytic work by B.K. Evans and Fischer (1992) suggests that such notions as employee participation and job autonomy are related to a higher-order work control dimension, the unique effects of job characteristics that should impact on outcomes through control (such as job autonomy) are often difficult to ascertain because several task dimensions are manipulated simultaneously (Ganster & Fusilier, 1989). Moreover, there have been several recent reviews of the published literature on the effects of participation (e.g., Cotton, 1995; Sagie, 1995; Wagner, 1994) and job autonomy (Wall & Martin, 1994).

The present review begins with a discussion of the conceptual model that has formed the basis for the majority of the research on the construct of work control—that is, Karasek's (1979; see also Karasek & Theorell, 1990; Theorell & Karasek, 1996) demands–control model. This is followed with: (1) a summary of the results of the early tests of the theory (reviewed in depth by Ganster & Fusilier, 1989; see also Ganster, 1988, 1989; Parkes, 1989); (2) a detailed review of the empirical research pertaining to the demands-control model published since 1989 (papers published in 1988 or 1989 that were not reviewed by Ganster & Fusilier, 1989, are also included in this review); (3) a discussion of the two main responses to the lack of convincing support for the demands–control model—these responses have focused, respectively, on methodological and theoretical issues; and (4) a summary of the other types of effects that direct measures of work control have been found to have on employee adjustment. The chapter concludes with a discussion of possible future directions for research on work control. The central tenet of this final discussion is that the concept of work control should remain an important focus for concern in research on employee well-being, but researchers need to focus more on the mechanisms that underpin the effects of work control, at the same time as addressing the methodological problems that have characterized previous research in the area.

Conceptual background

The job demands–job decision latitude model (Karasek, 1979; Karasek & Theorell, 1990; Theorell & Karasek, 1996)—also referred to as the job demands–job control or demands–control model (as it is in the present review)—has provided the underlying theoretical basis for the majority of studies examining the effects of work control. This model specifies two constructs that can vary independently in the work environment, namely, job demands and job decision latitude. Job demands refer to the psychological stressors existing in the work environment, whereas job decision latitude is defined as the extent to which employees have the potential to control their tasks and conduct throughout the working day. The central tenet of the demands–control model is that job decision latitude mitigates the negative effects of job demands on employee adjustment.

More specifically, Karasek (1979; Karasek & Theorell, 1990; Theorell & Karasek, 1996) refers to jobs characterized by a combination of high job demands and low job decision latitude as 'high strain jobs', whereas low job demands and high job decision latitude result in 'low strain jobs'. A key feature of Karasek's demands–control model is that it proposes that there is a synergistic relationship between job demands and job decision latitude (or control), such that the combined effects of high job demands and low job decision latitude engender a level of strain that exceeds the additive effect of either aspect of the work environment. Thus, the negative effects of high job demands should be most marked for employees whose jobs have little potential for control or, in Karasek's terms, job decision latitude. To the extent that a demanding job is likely to be stressful, the demands–control model is analogous to the stress-buffering hypothesis which proposes that a range of different resources protects individuals from the negative effects of life stressors (see S. Cohen & Edwards, 1989; S. Cohen & Wills, 1985, for reviews). The demands–control model is also in accord with Miller's (1979) minimax hypothesis, which proposes that a belief in situational control reduces negative responses to stressful situations because it provides the individual with the knowledge that they can minimize the maximum aversiveness of a stressful event—in other words, the potential for situational control can be used to avoid the experiences of unbearable adversity.

The demands–control model, however, goes beyond the general stress-buffering hypothesis in that it is proposed that a demanding job may actually engender high levels of employee adjustment when the job is also characterized by high levels of control. Karasek (1979) refers to this combination of work characteristics as an 'active job' which enables the employee to develop new behavior patterns both on and off the job. In other words, job demands, when accompanied by high levels of work control, act as a source of job challenge, rather than as a source of employee strain. 'Passive jobs' are those characterized by low levels of both job demands and job decision latitude—such positions are considered to result in a decline in overall work activities performance and, ultimately, may engender a sense of learned helplessness. Although Karasek envisaged some positive implications of an active job, it should be noted that neither passive or active jobs were seen as having marked effects on well-being.

In the context of understanding work stress, Karasek's job demands–control model is potentially important because it directs attention towards the organizational-level factors that may need to be addressed in order to help mitigate the effects of work stress. There are many individual-level interventions (e.g., employee assistance programs) available for employees who are exhibiting the negative consequences associated with work stress (see Bunce, 1997). Although often successful, individual-level interventions are limited to the extent that they implicitly, at least, attribute primary responsibility for the management of work stress to employees rather than focusing on organizational-level strategies to reduce job demands in the workplace. As noted by Ganster (1989), the identification of organizational-level variables that moderate the effects of stress could have useful practical implications. If such characteristics can be identified, more positive work environments could be created without necessarily reducing workplace demands and expectations (see also Ganster 1988, 1989; Karasek, 1979; Parkes, 1991; Payne, 1979).

Early tests of the demands–control model

Utilizing a range of different occupations in the United States of America (USA) and Sweden, Karasek (1979) was the first to report empirical tests of the demands–control model. In the USA sample, job demands were operationalized with a seven-item measure of quantitative workload, whereas job decision latitude was assessed with eight items that targeted perceptions of both decision authority and skill discretion. In the Swedish data, job both hectic and psychologically demanding), and job decision latitude was a combined measure of intellectual stimulation and expert ratings of skill level required to perform the job. Results revealed some preliminary evidence for the proposed interactive effect of job demands and job decision latitude on employee adjustment. The negative effects of job demands were reduced under conditions of high job decision latitude when predicting exhaustion, job dissatisfaction, and life dissatisfaction among male employees in the USA, and depression among the Swedish sample of male employees.

However, Ganster and Fusilier (1989) cautioned against reaching strong conclusions concerning the extent to which job demands and job decision latitude interact to predict levels of employee adjustment from Karasek's (1979) early research findings. Ganster and Fusilier highlighted several factors that complicate the interpretation of these findings. Specifically, they noted that standard procedures for detecting interaction effects among continuously measured independent variables (i.e., moderated multiple regression analyses in which a multiplicative term is used to test the significance of the proposed demand–control interaction, once the component main effects are controlled) were not utilized (as recommended by Aiken & West, 1991; J. Cohen & P. Cohen, 1983). Instead, Karasek tested the interactive hypothesis by examining mean differences, via analysis of variance (ANOVA) procedures, among the four job quadrants formed by identifying employees experiencing low and high levels of job demands and job decision latitude, respectively. In addition, Ganster and Fusilier questioned the adequacy of the job decision latitude construct as an index of work control by pointing out that the items used by Karasek (1979) to measure job decision latitude in the US sample (this measure has most often been used in subsequent tests of the demands–control model) reflected both decision authority (e.g., freedom over work methods) and skill discretion (e.g., required to learn new things). Moreover, close inspection of the skill discretion items revealed that Karasek confounded the measurement of work control with conceptually different constructs; that is, skill utilization and job complexity. Thus, Ganster and Fusilier concluded that, although the findings reported by Karasek may be interpreted as support for the stress-buffering role of job decision latitude, the same inferences cannot be made for work control.

Ganster and Fusilier (1989) went on to review another methodological approach adopted by Karasek and his colleagues (e.g., Alfredsson, Karasek & Theorell, 1982; Alfredsson, Spetz & Theorell, 1985; Karasek, Russell & Theorell, 1982; LaCroix & Haynes, 1987; Theorell, Alfredsson, Knox et al., 1984; Theorell, Hjemdahl, Ericsson et al., 1985). Utilizing data obtained from a series of national health surveys from the USA and Sweden, levels of job demands and job decision latitude were assigned in these studies on the basis of an individual's occupational classification (i.e., participants' job the relevant variable obtained from employee occupying the same job classification). In the early occupational-level studies, cardiovascular disease and associated risk factors served as the primary outcomes of interest. Ganster and Fusilier concluded that the studies employing aggregated measures of demands and control (i.e., the imputation method) provided modest support for the proposal that the combination of high job demands and low job decision latitude is associated with elevated risks of myocardial morbidity and mortality. However, Ganster and Fusilier (1989; see also Ganster, 1989) argued that research conducted at the occupational-level of analysis is difficult to interpret. They pointed out that occupational classifications based on a broad range of different occupational groups are likely to be confounded with a host of other variables (e.g., socio-economic status, variability in job characteristics within occupations, and individual health behaviors). In addition, it was noted that occupation-level studies of work control overlook the importance of individual perceptions of job demands and job decision latitude within homogeneous occupational groups.

In response to these methodological considerations, a second research approach emerged in which employees' perceptions of work stress and work control were obtained from homogeneous occupational groups. These studies also departed from Karasek's (1979) original methodology by discarding the job decision latitude construct in preference for more focused measures of work control. In this respect, researchers utilized measurement scales that placed a stronger emphasis on Karasek's dimension of decision authority (rather than skill discretion) by asking general questions relating to how much influence employees had over various aspects of their work tasks. In addition, hierarchical multiple regression analyses were used to test the significance of Work Stress × Work Control interactions. Despite these methodological improvements, the individual-level studies reviewed by Ganster and Fusilier (1989) did not find convincing support for the hypothesis that work stress and work control interact to predict employee adjustment. Such research was conducted across a variety of different occupational groups, such as secondary school teachers (e.g., Payne & Fletcher, 1983), clerical workers (Spector, 1987), and healthcare professionals (e.g., McLaney & Hurrell, 1988; Tetrick & LaRocco, 1987).

In summarizing the extant research findings, Ganster and Fusilier (1989) noted that the 'exploration of control as a potential "antidote" to stressful work demands is rich with possibility' (p. 272) and encouraged organizational scholars to continue this line of research. In particular, they highlighted a number of goals for future research, including the need for field experimentation, the importance of distinguishing between various facets of work control, the examination of the indirect effects of work control (i.e., do employees use control to alter their perception of work demands), and the use of objective indicators of the work environment as measures of demands.

Recent tests of the demands–control model

During the past decade, many tests of the demands–control model have continued the trend of discarding the job decision latitude construct in preference for more focused measures of work control, although a number of studies have continued to rely on Karasek's (1979) original methodology. As in the past, it has been common for research of this type to be based on data obtained from participants at one point in time using measures obtained from a single source (i.e., the participant). In other words, the cross-sectional, mono-method design is still frequently employed. The results of the recent cross-sectional tests of the demands–control model are reviewed first, followed by studies that have used more conservative designs—these include: (1) longitudinal studies; (2) studies that have obtained objective measures of demands and/or control; (3) studies that have focused on cardiovascular outcomes; and (4) experimental studies.

Cross-sectional research

Across a wide variety of different occupational settings, recent cross-sectional, self-report tests of the demands–control model have failed to find convincing support for the hypothesis that work stress and work control interact to predict employee adjustment. Based on a sample of 274 prison officers, Morrison, Dunne, Fitzgerald, and Cloghan (1992) found only weak support for the demands–control model on one of seven dependent variables (job satisfaction), there was evidence that the relationship between perceived job demands and job satisfaction was buffered if employees perceived low constraints in the work environment (a construct similar to work control adopted by Payne, 1979). In a cross-sectional study of a relatively small sample of manufacturing employees. Perrewe and Anthony (1990) found no evidence that perceptions of work control (assessed using a 16-item scale that formed the basis for a subsequent 22-item scale of this variable, see Dwyer & Ganster, 1991) interacted with a range of different measures of demands, including work overload, variance in workload, or underutilization of skills. Similarly, in a sample of female social workers, Melamed, Kushnir, and Meir (1991) found no evidence that the effects of a broadly-based measure of work demands were moderated by perceived work control (assessed using a 6-item measure designed as a direct operationalization of the control construct). Using Karasek's (1979) original measures of demands and control, Landsbergis (1988) also found no evidence—when the appropriate moderated regression analyses were conducted—for the demands–control model in a sample of health workers. Using a variety of self-report measures of demands and control, comparable results have been reported in samples of (e.g., Parkes, 1991, Study 1), and retail employees (e.g., Jimmieson & Terry, 1993). In the past decade, a number of other cross-sectional studies have been conducted on heterogeneous samples of workers (see below)—these studies have also failed to find consistent support for the demands–control model.

Longitudinal research

Cross-sectional research that relies on self-report measures (i.e., where all the measures are obtained contemporaneously from the single source) is likely to inflate the observed correlations between predictors and outcomes because of common method variance, which is contributed to by response consistency effects that emanate from the influence of both stable dispositional factors (such as negative affectivity) and unstable occasion factors (such as mood; see Spector, 1992; Spector & Brannick, 1995; Zapf, Dormann, & Frese, 1996). Such confounding effects are likely to make the evidence of main effects of demands and control (see below) difficult to interpret; moreover, as noted by Wall, Jackson, Mullarkey, and Parker (1996), common method variance may obscure the presence of demand by control interactions—this is due to correlated errors that serve to reduce the magnitude of true interaction effects (see M.G. Evans, 1985).

Contrary to the possibility that cross-sectional studies may obscure demands–control effects, recent longitudinal studies have provided only minimal support for the interactive hypothesis of Karasek's (1979) demands-control model. In one of the first longitudinal studies in the area, Bromet, Dew, Parkinson, and

Schulberg (1988) found support for the interactive hypothesis in the prediction of the occurrence of alcohol-related problems, but not for two affective measures of psychological well-being. Using measures of demands and discretion similar in focus to the measures developed by Karasek (1979), Bromet et al. found that self-reported alcohol problems were the highest under conditions of high work demands and low discretion. In contrast, Carayon (1993a) found no evidence of interactive effects involving quantitative workload and work control (essentially a measure of job decision latitude) on a variety of different employee adjustment measures (e.g., anxiety, depression, daily life stress, and physical health). However, Carayon's results should be interpreted with caution. Essentially, the research was cross-sectional in design, given that the focal analyses (i.e., those testing the interactive effects of demands and control) were conducted only on data obtained contemporaneously (either at Time 1 or Time 2).

Using measures derived from Karasek (1979), longitudinal studies conducted by Parkes and her colleagues have also found no support for the critical two-way interaction (Demands × Control) in the prediction of either anxiety and social dysfunction (e.g., Parkes, 1991, Study 2), or scores on a self–report measure of psychosomatic health complaints (Parkes, Mendham, & Von Rabenau, 1994, Study 2). Daniels and Guppy (1994) reported similar results in a sample of accountants— there were no significant interactions involving measures of work stress and either job autonomy or participation in decision-making. The latter studies are important (Daniels & Guppy, 1994; Parkes, 1991; Parkes et al., 1994, Study 2), to the extent that each of the studies controlled for baseline levels of adjustment (as did Bromet et al., 1988). Because of their instability, the effects of occasion factors can be reduced by assessing the predictors and the outcomes at different points in time; however, to fully control for the potential biasing effects of both occasion factors and dispositional factors, the effects of prior adjustment should be controlled in the prediction of subsequent adjustment (Zapf et al., 1996).

Use of objective measures of work characteristics

Another way of controlling common method variance is to avoid same-source measurement; that is, to obtain measures of either the independent or dependent variables from an external source. Interestingly, perhaps the most convincing support for Karasek's demands–control model comes from research that has utilized objective indicators of the work environment (Dwyer & Ganster, 1991; Fox, Dwyer, & Ganster, 1993; Parkes, 1991, Study 1). This research has also made use of objective outcome measures, as has an extensive body of research that is characterized by its focus on cardiovascular outcomes—the latter research is discussed below.

In a study of a sample of 115 manufacturing employees, Dwyer and Ganster (1991) examined the extent to which objective work stress indicators and a measure of perceived work stress interacted with perceptions of work control to predict self-reported job and work satisfaction and a variety of employee withdrawal behaviors.

On the basis of job analysis, Dwyer and Ganster coded each job for a variety of physical (e.g., exposure to chemical hazards) and psychological (e.g., production responsibility) job demands. Perceptions of work control were assessed with a generic 22-item scale that tapped a range of different job control dimensions, whereas the withdrawal data (voluntary absenteeism, tardiness, and days off due to illness) were compiled from computerized records.

Results revealed that the combination of high psychological demands (objectively assessed) and low employee perceptions of work control was associated with high incidences of tardiness and sick leave; thus, work control appeared to buffer the negative effects of high levels of demand on withdrawal behaviors. In addition, the subjective measure of work stress interacted with the work control measure to predict levels of voluntary absenteeism and task satisfaction. Closer inspection of the latter two interactions revealed that, as predicted by the demands–control model, perceived work demands were associated with poor adjustment under conditions of low subjective control. Interestingly, under conditions of high subjective work control, subjective work stress was, in fact, negatively related to voluntary absenteeism and positively related to task satisfaction. This pattern of results provides support for the 'active job' component of Karasek's (1979) demands–control model, namely, that under conditions of high control, high levels of demand are associated positively with employee adjustment.

Parkes (1991, Study 1) also found some support for the demands–control model in relation to withdrawal behaviors. In a study of driving instructors, she analyzed the effects of self-reported demands and discretion (assessed using Karasek's, 1979, measures) on subsequent absenteeism. The absenteeism measure reflected the number of absences (mostly due to minor illness) of less than one week that occurred during the 2-year period following the assessment of demands and control—this information was obtained from personnel records. In support of the demands–control model, Parkes found a weak Demands × Discretion interaction on absenteeism ($p < 0.06$) that reflected the fact that participants low in demands and high in discretion had lower levels of subsequent absenteeism than the other participants.

Fox et al. (1993) also found some support for the demands–control model in a sample of 136 nursing staff from whom a number of objective indicators of work stress (e.g., number of patients under care, percentage of patient contact time, and number of patient deaths witnessed) and employee well-being and performance (e.g., systolic blood pressure, diastolic blood pressure, salivary cortisol levels, and ratings of job performance) were obtained, in addition to a subjective assessment of work control (using Dwyer & Ganster's, 1991, 22-item measure of this variable). Salivary Cortisol levels (at home) were higher for those nurses who had higher patient contact times and low perceptions of work control. There was, however, more consistent support for Karasek's demands–control model when employee perceptions of work stress were taken into account. In this respect, subjective quantitative workload and subjective work control interacted to predict systolic blood pressure (at both work and home), diastolic blood pressure (at home), salivary cortisol levels (at work), and job satisfaction. A subjective measure of the frequency of stressful work events was also found to interact with subjective work control to predict levels of job satisfaction. In each case, the data suggested a buffering role for work control—work stress was related to poor adjustment for those who perceived low levels of work control, but not for those who considered that they had some control over their work environment.

Research on cardiovascular outcomes

In the past decade, a specific focus of research testing the demands–control model has continued to be its predictive utility in relation to physical health outcomes—in particular, indicators of cardiovascular disease. This body of research has been reviewed recently by Schnall, Landsbergis, and Baker (1994), Kristensen (1995), and Theorell and Karasek (1996); thus, it is not reviewed in depth here.

In the recent cardiovascular studies, there has been a continuing reliance on operationalizations of the construct of control as aggregated occupation scores (e.g., Alterman, Shekelle, Vernon, & Burau, 1994; Georges, Wear, & Mueller, 1992; Hammar, Alfredsson, & Theorell, 1994; Moller, Kristensen, & Hollnagel, 1991; Piper, LaCroix, & Karasek, 1989; Reed, LaCroix, Karasek, Miller, & MacLean, 1989; Theorell, deFaire, Johnson, Hall, Perski, & Stewart, 1991); however, the individual-level assessment of control based on Karasek's (1979) measure of this variable has also been common (e.g., Albright, Winkleby, Ragland, Fisher, & Syme, 1992; Georges, Wear, & Mueller, 1992; Green & Johnson, 1990; Light, Turner, & Hinderli, 1992; Schnall, Schwartz, Landsbergis, Warren, & Pickering, 1992; Van Egeren, 1992). A variety of cardiovascular criteria have been considered—these have included diagnosis of coronary heart disease, cardiovascular mortality, myocardial infarction, recurrence of myocardial infarction, and the incidence of risk factors for coronary heart disease (e.g., elevated blood pressure, elevated serum cholesterol, as well as smoking behavior and distribution of body fat).

Taken together, research using cardiovascular disease outcomes as criteria has found only very limited support for the demands–control model. Although the research has linked the two components of the model to a variety of CHD-relevant outcomes (for reviews, see Kristensen, 1995; Schnall, Landsbergis, & Baker, 1994; Theorell & Karasek, 1996; see also the discussion below on the main effects of work control), most of it has been limited by its failure to test for the critical demands–control interaction using moderated regression analyses (see Aiken & West, 1991; J. Cohen & P. Cohen, 1983). Typically, support for the demands–control model has been detected by comparing high strain participants (scoring below the median on discretion and above the mean on demands) with those falling in the other cells formed by dichotomizing scores on the two independent variables. Other methods have included the correlation of quotient scores (demands divided by latitude) with the cardiovascular criteria (e.g., Green & Johnson, 1990; Theorell, deFaire, Johnson et al., 1991; Theorell, Perski,

Orth-Gomer, Hamsten, & deFaire 1991), and the comparison of cardiovascular cases with matched controls on demands and control (or derived quotient scores). However, as Schnall, Landsbergis, and Baker (1994) noted, these methods do not allow detection of true interactive effects between demands and control. If such effects have been directly tested, they have been generally found to be nonsignificant (Chapman, Mandryk, Frommer, Edye, & Ferguson, 1990; Reed et al., 1989; Schaubroeck & Merrit, 1997; cf. Johnson & Hall, 1988).

Experimental research

There have only been a small number of experimental studies that have tested the interactive relationship between work stress and work control in the prediction of employee adjustment. In their review, Ganster and Fusilier (1989) outlined the findings of a laboratory-based study conducted by Perrewe and Ganster (1989), in which levels of work stress and work control were manipulated among a sample of undergraduate students performing a letter-sorting activity. This study provided no evidence to support the hypothesis that objective levels of work control would moderate the effects of objective work stress on levels of anxiety, satisfaction, and several physiological indicators of arousal. However, partial support for Karasek's (1979) demands–control model was found, in that perceptions of behavioral control over the experimental activity (as measured by a post-task manipulation check) weakened the relationship between subjective ratings of work stress and a self-report measure of anxiety.

Subsequent laboratory research has attempted to replicate the pattern of findings reported by Perrewe and Ganster (1989). Given that time pressure is commonly used as an indicator of demand in stress research (e.g., Bandura, Cioffi, C.B. Taylor, & Brouillard, 1988; see also French & Caplan, 1972, for a discussion of this issue), Jimmieson and Terry (in press) followed Perrewe and Ganster's lead and manipulated work stress by varying high and moderate levels of quantitative workload. They, however, attempted to strengthen the experimental design utilized by Perrewe and Ganster by increasing the dimensions of work control manipulated in the experiment.

Consistent with Perrewe and Ganster (1989), Jimmieson and Terry (1998) found no evidence to suggest that objective levels of work stress and work control interacted to predict task satisfaction, post-task mood (after control of initial mood), and subjective task performance. Similarly, at the subjective level of analysis, this study found no support for Karasek's (1979) demands–control model. Since Perrewe and Ganster's (1989) finding that subjective work control buffered the negative effects of subjective work stress on levels of self-reported anxiety was not replicated, Jimmieson and Terry conducted further analyses on the six subscales of the mood questionnaire. These analyses revealed a Subjective Work Stress × Subjective Work Control interaction on the measures of (low) confusion and (low) fatigue. As proposed in Karasek's demands–control model, the negative effects of subjective work stress were most evident for participants who perceived that they possessed low levels of work control over the experimental activity.

Jimmieson and Terry (1997) provided a further test of the demands–control model using a more complex experimental task. As noted by Ganster and Fusilier (1989), sorting letters under time pressure for a period of 20 minutes is unlikely to be of sufficient duration to elicit detrimental effects on levels of adjustment. Furthermore, the simplistic nature of a letter-sorting activity is likely to limit the usefulness of work control in this context. In this respect, Campbell and Gingrich (1986) argued that employee participation during the goal-setting process for complex tasks provides individuals with a better understanding of the task requirements, thus facilitating higher levels of task performance. In contrast, the basic cognitive processing required for the performance of simple tasks may mean that any efforts to increase cognitive processing through employee participation will be ineffective.

In accord with theoretical definitions of task complexity that highlight the need for individuals to make multiple decisions that must take into account poorly defined or possibly antagonistic contingencies (see Campbell, 1988, 1991; Frese, 1989; Kohn & Schooler, 1978, 1979; Wood, 1986), an in-basket activity should include sufficient task components for task-specific information to play an interactive role in determining levels of adjustment. However, Jimmieson and Terry (1997) found only minimal support for an interactive relationship between the objective manipulations of work stress and work control on a variety of measures of adjustment (similar to those used by Jimmieson and Terry, 1998, as well as qualitative and quantitative measures of performance). At the subjective level of analysis, however, there were significant Work Stress × Work Control interactions on the measures of positive mood, subjective task performance, and task satisfaction. The negative effects of subjective work stress were most evident for participants who perceived that they possessed low levels of behavioral control over the experimental activity.

Summary

Although large national health surveys have found some evidence linking demands and control to a range of different indicators of cardiovascular disease, several methodological limitations (including occupational confounds, and failure to employ the appropriate analytic techniques for detecting interactions) have restricted the interpretability of these findings. Other research testing the demands–control model has addressed many of these criticisms; however, it has generally been unsuccessful in establishing empirical support for the proposition that work control buffers the negative effects of work stress on employee adjustment. Failure to support the demands–control model has also been evident in recent research that has employed more sophisticated longitudinal research designs. Utilizing objective indicators of stress and/or strain, research conducted by Dwyer and his colleagues (Dwyer & Ganster, 1991; Fox et al., 1993;

see also Parkes, 1991, Study 1) has, however, revealed some support for the model, as has recent experimental research (at least at the subjective level of analysis).

One conclusion that can be drawn from recent tests of the demands–control model is that, with the exception of the cardiovascular research, studies that have not relied entirely on self-report measures have found stronger support for the demands–control model than have other types of research (i.e., cross-sectional and longitudinal, self-report studies). It is possible that the support for the demands–control model found by Dwyer and her colleagues (Dwyer & Ganster, 1991; Fox et al., 1993; see also Parkes, 1991, Study 1) may be attributable to the fact that the interactive effects were not attenuated due to the presence of common method variance (see Evans, 1985). However, recent longitudinal studies have not found consistent support for the demands–control model; thus, it is difficult to sustain this argument, given that the effects of common method variance are also controlled in this type of design (as long as initial adjustment is controlled in the analyses predicting subsequent adjustment).

An alternative explanation for the supportive results obtained by Dwyer and her colleagues (Dwyer & Ganster, 1991; Fox et al., 1993, see also Parkes, 1991, Study 1) is that the demands–control effect is specific to particular outcomes, a possibility that is discussed in more depth below. Dwyer and Ganster (1991) and Parkes (1991, Study 1) focused on withdrawal behaviors, which are outcomes that have not received much attention on the literature, whereas Fox et al., focused on cortisol level, which is also a relatively unusual outcome variable. However, it should be noted that, in addition to cortisol level, Fox et al., used a number of measures of blood pressure as outcome variables. Such measures have commonly been employed in the cardiovascular research—the discrepancy between the results obtained by Fox et al., and the typical results emerging from the cardiovascular research (i.e., only weak support for the demands-control model) may be related to differences in the assessment of work control (cf. Schaubroeck & Merritt, 1997), an issue that is also discussed below.

The second conclusion that can be reached on the basis of the review of the previous decade of tests of the demands–control model is that, in the context of specific work-related tasks, the perception that high levels of task control are available does appear to mitigate the negative effects of high levels of demands— at least at the subjective level, and particularly in relation to more complex tasks (Jimmieson & Terry, 1997; cf. Jimmieson & Terry, 1998; Perrewe & Ganster, 1987). The results of recent experimental tests of the demands–control model need to be interpreted with caution, given that they were obtained in a laboratory setting using simulated work activities. Nevertheless, they suggest that future research on work control might benefit from a more focused approach. This point is discussed below as part of a broader discussion of the methodological issues that researchers have recently addressed in an effort to account for the lack of more convincing support for the demands–control model.

Methodological developments

In response to the lack of stronger support for the demands–control model, a number of researchers have focused on methodological problems that may account for the weak findings. The potential role of common method variance has been discussed in relation to the results of recent research employing longitudinal designs and designs that have incorporated objective measures. Other methodological issues that have been addressed include: (1) the nature of the sample; (2) the assessment of demands and control and, to a lesser extent; (3) the possibility that interactive effects between demands and control are specific to certain outcomes.

Nature of the sample

The lack of stronger support for the demands–control model in research conducted at the individual level of analysis has been attributed to restricted variance in the work demands and work control variables (see Carayon, 1993a; Karasek, 1979; Payne, 1979; Payne & Fletcher, 1983). Specifically, single occupational groups may not have sufficient variation in job characteristics to detect interactive effects between the two variables. More recently, several large-scale studies have surveyed employees across multiple organizations using perceptual measures of demands and control.

Warr (1990) sampled 1686 managerial, supervisory, and manual workers in his test of Karasek's (1979) demands–control model, and found no significant interactions between perceptions of quantitative workload and job decision latitude in the prediction of anxiety, depression, and satisfaction. Similarly, Kushnir and Melamed (1991) found no evidence of an interactive relationship between work overload (frequency of overtime and perceptions of overload) and work control (assessed with a 6-item scale that focused on the perceived freedom to make work-related decisions) and a variety of different indicators of employee adjustment (e.g., anxiety, irritability, satisfaction, and psychosomatic health) in a sample of 798 managerial and non-managerial employees working in 21 different manufacturing plants. Although Landsbergis, Schnall, Deitz, Friedman, and Pickering (1992) found some support for the model in relation to job satisfaction, job demands and job decision latitude (assessed using Karasek's measures) failed to interact to predict levels of anxiety in 297 employees recruited from eight New York City worksites. More recently, Fletcher and Jones (1993) found no evidence that high levels of self-reported work demands and work control (assessed using Karasek's measures of these variables) interacted to predict job satisfaction, life satisfaction, anxiety, depression, or blood pressure in a sample of over 2000 men and women working in a variety of different occupations; neither did Stansfeld, North, White, and Marmot (1995) in a study of the effects of psychological work demands and perceptions of work control (assessed using measures similar to Karasek's original measures) on psychiatric ill-health and life dissatisfaction among some 10 000 English civil servants (see also Chapman et al., 1990; Kauppinen-Toropainen, Kandolin, & Mutanen, 1983; Marshall, Barnett, Baruch, & Pleck, 1991, for similar results). In a heterogeneous study of 1200 Chinese workers, Xie (1996) did, however, find that the effects of high levels of job demands on anxiety, depression, job satisfaction, and life satisfaction were most evident for those workers who perceived low levels of decision latitude (demands and decision latitude were assessed using Karasek's measures).

Taken together, the results of recent tests of the demands–control model in heterogeneous samples do not suggest that the lack of previous support for the model is a function of a restriction in the range of scores on the measures of demands and control in homogeneous samples. Instead, the results point to the possibility that the stronger support for the demands–control model that was obtained in the early occupation–level research (see Johnson & Hall, 1988) may be due to the confounding effects of sociodemographic and work variables that covary with occupational level (Fletcher, 1991; Ganster, 1989; Ganster & Fusilier, 1989; Payne & Fletcher, 1983).

In light of the fact that the extent of support for the demands–control model does not appear to be a function of the nature of the sample, it may be preferable for researchers to employ relatively homogeneous samples in which pilot work suggests that there is a sufficient range in levels of both demands and control (see Ganster & Fusilier, 1989, for a demonstration that single and multiple occupation samples have similar coefficients of variation on the majority of measures of demands; see also Spector, 1987, for evidence of the full range of demand and control scores in a sample of clerical workers). As noted by Xie (1996), large multi-occupational studies have their drawbacks. Foremost, it is difficult to control for the range of sociodemographic variables that may distinguish employees of different occupations. Furthermore, a large-scale, multi-occupational study, by necessity, requires the use of measures of demands and control that are relevant across the range of occupations under consideration. By relying on such measures, researchers are not able to focus on the particular demands and facets of control that might be most relevant to a particular employee group, which may lessen the likelihood of detecting demand by control interactions. This point is relevant to the next section, which focuses on the possibility that measurement issues may explain the lack of stronger support for the demands–control model in previous research.

Assessment of work control

In their review, Ganster and Fusilier (1989) criticized the use of the job decision latitude construct as a measure of work control (see also Ganster, 1988, 1989; Kasl, 1989). The items used by Karasek (1979) to measure job decision latitude reflect both decision authority (i.e., freedom to make work-related decisions) and skill discretion (i.e., the breadth of skills used in the work context and the opportunity to learn new things). Closer inspection of the skill discretion items, in particular, reveals that Karasek confounded the measurement of work control with conceptually different constructs, including skill utilization, job complexity, and job variety (see also Carayon, 1993a; Kasl, 1989; Kushnir & Melamed, 1991). As noted by Wall et al. (1996), it is not necessarily the case that skill discretion reflects job control—a highly skilled job may, in fact, have little potential for control, a pattern of results that was evident in their distinction between the work characteristics of skilled and unskilled jobs (Wall, Jackson, & Mullarkey, 1995).

In support of the view that Karasek's (1979) measure of job decision latitude comprises two distinct components that may not be tapping the same underlying dimension, C.S. Smith et al. (1997) found that, across multiple, independent samples, the job decision latitude scale loaded on two separate factors reflecting, respectively, decision authority and skill discretion (see also Barnett & Brennan, 1995; Carayon, 1993a). In a subsequent set of analyses that considered Karasek's decision latitude items in addition to items developed by Ganster to assess perceived work control (see Dwyer & Ganster, 1991; C.S. Smith et al., 1997), Ganster's general control items (he also developed some items to assess predictability at work) and the decision authority items did not yield separate factors but the skill discretion items did. Moreover, the correlation between the general control items and the decision authority subscale was higher than the correlation between the two decision latitude subscales (decision authority and skill discretion). Thus, as noted previously, it is unclear whether any of the results reported in support of the demands–control model in studies that have utilized Karasek's measure of work control (i.e., job decision latitude) can be attributed specifically to the control construct, although the findings reported by C.S. Smith et al. do provide some evidence for the concurrent validity of the decision authority subscale as a measure of work control.

Further evidence attesting to the problematic nature of the job decision latitude construct comes from a recent study conducted by Wall et al. (1996; see also Wall, Jackson, & Mullarkey 1995). Wall et al. (1996) proposed that a specific control measure would moderate the relationship between work demands and employee adjustment, but that such an effect would not be evident in relation to the traditional measure of job decision latitude. The specific control measure was a 10-item measure that required employees to indicate the extent to which they could exert control over the timing and methods of their daily work tasks. Results revealed that this operationalization of the work control construct interacted with a measure of cognitive job demands to predict levels of anxiety, depression, and job satisfaction in a large sample of manufacturing employees, such that demands were associated negatively with well-being when control was low but not when it was high. Indeed, when control was perceived to be high, there was some evidence that demands related positively to well-being which is consistent with Karasek's (1979) view that, under the right work conditions, high levels of demands may be a source of challenge, and hence relate positively to employee adjustment. As expected, the job decision latitude measure failed to interact with demands in the prediction of any of the outcome measures.

On the basis of Wall et al.'s (1996) results, it is tempting to conclude that problems with the assessment of control can explain the lack of convincing findings for the demands–control model. However, it should be noted that other researchers have developed and used focused measures of work control. Kushnir and Melamed (1991) used a six-item measure of perceived freedom to make decisions over a range of different work domains, whereas Carayon (1993a) employed five items that assessed perceptions of control over a range of aspects of work. As noted previously, neither of these studies found any support for the demands–control model. Moreover, Kushnir and Melamed conducted their study on a large, heterogeneous sample of employees; thus, Wall et al.'s findings cannot easily be attributed to their use of a focused control measure combined with a heterogeneous sample.

It is possible that Wall et al.'s (1996) findings in support of the demands–control model relate not only to the use of a focused measure of control but also to the manner in which demands were assessed. Wall et al. noted that Karasek's (1979) items assessing work demands reflect affective responses in that the employee is required to indicate perceptions of work stress; for instance, by indicating the extent to which they have experienced 'excessive work'. They argued that the fact that both the independent (demands) and dependent variables (measure of adjustment) assess affective responses means that common method variance is likely to inflate the correlations between the variables (see also Brief, Burke, George, Robinson, & Webster, 1988; Parkes, 1990), and make it difficult to detect true interactive effects. However, as noted previously, this argument cannot easily be sustained because, although there is some support for the demands–control model in studies that have utilized objective measures of work demands (i.e., Dwyer & Ganster, 1991; Fox et al., 1993), longitudinal designs (that also control for common method variance) have not found convincing support for the model. Moreover, most of the support for the demands–control model reported by Fox et al. (1993) and Dwyer and Ganster (1991) was actually found in relation to their subjective, not objective, measures of demands.

Although Wall et al. (1996) found support for the demands–control model using a focused measure of work control and a descriptive measure of work demands, the results need to be replicated, given that the weight of the comparable research evidence is contrary to the model (e.g., Carayon, 1993a; Kushnir & Melamed, 1991). Indeed, as Wall et al. (1996) noted, there is a possibility that their support for the model could be in accord with a general pattern of results that is not supportive of the model, with the occasional report of a supportive finding. Nevertheless, Wall et al. raised some interesting and relevant methodological points that need to be addressed in future research. However, it may also be necessary to take into account recent theoretical developments in the conceptualization of the demands–control model (see below). Such developments are important, in that they may help to clarify the conditions that are most likely to yield evidence for the stress-buffering role of work control.

Specificity in demands–control effects

Parkes (1991) suggested that the effects of high strain jobs (high demands, low control) may be specific to a particular type of affective response. In relation to this point, she pointed out that previous research has not been able to test adequately for specificity of demands–control effects because of the fact that measures of affective state (e.g. burnout, anxiety, depression, satisfaction) are typically moderately intercorrelated. To test for such effects, it is necessary to analyze residualized (rather than raw) outcome scores, in which the effects of the other affective outcomes are controlled (Parkes, 1991). Using such a technique, Broadbent (1985) and Hesketh and Shouksmith (1986) found significant (negative) main effects of work discretion on residualized anxiety but not residualized depression scores. In a similar vein, Parkes (1991) found that the effects of demands and control (moderated by locus of control) predicted residualized anxiety but not social dysfunction scores (also residualized). Future researchers need to follow Parkes's (1991) recommendations in order to determine if demands–control effects are specific to anxiety-related affective responses. In tests of the demands–control model, there is a tendency for researchers to use a number of correlated affective outcomes, which means that the specificity of possible demands–control effects can be examined only if residualized outcome scores are used in the analyses.

The above review of recent tests of the demands–control model suggests that the effects of a high strain (high demands/low control) position may be specific to nonaffective outcomes, in particular absenteeism (Dwyer & Ganster, 1991; Parkes, Study 1, 1991) and health-related outcomes (Fox et al., 1993). This suggestion clearly needs to be verified; nevertheless, it does point to the possibility that Karasek's (1979) focus on illness outcomes should be maintained in future research. Although previous cardiovascular research has failed to yield consistent support for the demands–control model, the methodological problems relating to sampling and to the assessment of the critical predictor variables mean that results of this research are very difficult to interpret.

Summary

In sum, researchers over the past decade have addressed a number of methodological problems that may account for the lack of stronger support for the demands–control model. Taken together, the research indicates little support for the view that evidence for the model would be stronger if heterogeneous samples were studied. There is, however, some support for the view that Karasek's (1979) original measures should be discarded in favor of more focused measures of work control (Wall et al., 1996). Nevertheless, the lack of consistent support for the demands–control model in studies that have employed focused measures of control points to the possibility that other factors need to be taken into account. The possibility that demands–control effects are outcome-specific is one potentially fruitful direction for future research. Other directions for future research relate to theoretical rather than methodological concerns with previous research. The theoretical issues that have been addressed in recent research are discussed below.

Theoretical developments

A number of researchers testing the utility of the demands–decision latitude model have focused their attention on theoretical issues that may account for the lack of stronger support for the model. In this respect, researchers have focused on: (1) the multidimensional nature of the work control construct; and (2) the possibility that there are additional organizational and dispositional characteristics that may interact with high job strain (i.e., high work stress and low work control) to predict employee adjustment.

A multidimensional approach to work control

As previously noted, recent tests of the demands–control model have increasingly employed more focused measures of work control in order to avoid a confounding of work control with other job characteristics (i.e., skill utilization and job complexity). It is important to note, however, that most researchers have typically relied on unidimensional work control measures. In his comprehensive review of the work control literature, Ganster (1988; see also Steptoe, 1989) similarly noted that researchers have tended to view work control as a unidimensional construct, and have, as a consequence, relied on global measures of work control. Work control is, however, a multidimensional construct, to the extent that employees can perceive a sense of personal control over multiple facets of their occupational environment, and that the perception of high levels of control over one facet does not necessarily mean that control will be perceived in relation to other facets.

In an early discussion of the notion of control in the work context, Gardell (1977) made a distinction between instrumental and conceptual forms of personal control. According to Gardell, instrumental control reflects employees' control over their job tasks, whereas conceptual control reflects employees' opportunities to engage in conceptual thought processes that contribute to organizational policies and procedures (see Carayon, 1993b, who found empirical support for this conceptual distinction). Ganster (1988, 1989) developed a more complex work control taxonomy that illustrates the potential multidimensional nature of the work control construct (see also Breaugh's, 1985, discussion of different aspects of work autonomy). Specifically, Ganster proposed that employees may have the opportunity to choose among a variety of different work tasks to complete (i.e., task control), and have the option to choose among available methods for the completion of those work tasks (i.e., method control). Employees may also be able to determine the pace at which they complete work tasks (i.e., pacing control), have varying levels of control over the scheduling of their working hours (i.e., scheduling control), and they may have different opportunities to be involved in wider organizational decision-making processes (i.e., decision control). In addition, Ganster made a distinction between control over the work activities of other employees (e.g., supervision), control over the timing and quantity of interpersonal interaction (e.g., customer contact), and control over the physical aspects of one's working environment (e.g., privacy, noise, lighting, and temperature).

Literature examining the job content implications of advanced manufacturing technology (AMT) has also acknowledged that the notion of personal control may be multidimensional in the work setting. In this respect, Wall, Corbett, Clegg, P.R. Jackson, and Martin (1990) made a distinction between two types of work control: timing and method control. Timing control refers to the ability of employees to determine the scheduling of their job-related activities—the potential for scheduling control contrasts with the situation in which the employee is required to respond to the pace of automated technology systems. Method control reflects the extent to which employees are free from technological prescriptions when deciding how to complete a given work task. Wall and his colleagues employed confirmatory factor analytic procedures to show that measures of method and task control can be empirically distinguished (e.g., P.R. Jackson, Wall, Martin, & Davids, 1993; Wall, Jackson, & Mullarkey 1995). Additional support for the distinction between the measures was provided by the fact that, although the measures had some correlates in common, they each had a number of unique correlates.

Tannenbaum and his colleagues (Tannenbaum, 1962, 1968; & Cooke, 1979; Tannenbaum, Kavcic, Rosner, Vianello, & Weiser, 1974) reported strong empirical evidence that perceptions of work control increase as a function of hierarchical level. Drawing on this early work, Staw noted that the salience of different types of work control may change across different hierarchical levels in the organization (see also Moch, Cammann, & Cooke, 1983). From a related viewpoint, Frese (1989) observed that the salience of work control domains may vary as a function of their proximity to an employee's daily work activities, which relates to the distinction that Hammer and Stern (1980) drew between work control that impinges on a person's own work roles and work control that is gained through more general participation in wider organizational decision-making processes (see also Gardell, 1977; Hammer & Stern, 1980).

It has also been suggested that the traditional job decision latitude construct can be decomposed into more specific work control dimensions. Indeed, Karasek (1979) encouraged future researchers to distinguish among several different aspects of his job decision latitude construct. Söderfeldt, Söderfeldt, Muntaner et al. (1996) argued that, in relation to health care workers, both decision authority and skill discretion should be considered in more depth in order to provide a more focused definition of work control. They contrasted at least four aspects of decision authority, such as closeness of supervision, decisional power within a situation (e.g., control over resources), non-decisional power over a situation (e.g., the setting of informal rules), and ideological control (e.g., control over the operative goals of the organization). Skill discretion concerns not only a choice of skills, but control over the fulfilment of work goals. Söderfeldt et al. also included the notion of administrative control in their taxonomy, and highlighted the need for future research to establish whether these forms of work control have differential effects in determining reactions to stressful working conditions.

Ganster (1988, 1989) argued that the failure of researchers to adopt a multidimensional view of work control might have accounted for the weak and inconsistent findings of the extant tests of Karasek's demands–control model. A multidimensional model of work control is likely to be important not only for statistical purposes (i.e., the presence of relatively independent subscales will impact adversely on the internal consistency of the composite scale and, hence, weaken its predictive utility), but also because global control measures may not reflect the extent to which the employee has control over the aspects of the work environment that are most relevant to the types of work stress being experienced (Ganster, 1989; Sargent & Terry, in press).

To date, only a small number of researchers have attempted to distinguish among different domains of work control when testing Karasek's (1979) demands–control model. In an early study, McLaney and Hurrell (1988) utilized four distinct measures of work control that assessed the extent to which a sample of nurses perceived that they could influence the variety of their work tasks (task control), contribute to organizational decision-making processes (decision control), alter the physical environment in which they worked (environmental control), and access the resources needed to complete their job duties (resource control, cf. Söderfeldt et al., 1996). Although these measures of work control were found to exert positive main effects on levels of job satisfaction (the effects of decision control were substantially weaker), none of the 32 Work Stress × Work Control interactions were significant.

Using the same work control typology, Hurrell and Lindström (1992) found that having control over work tasks was negatively related to the frequency of symptom reporting (e.g., headache, heart symptoms, sleep problems, and stomach trouble) among 231 early-career male managerial staff in Finland and 396 mid-career male managers in the USA. Perceptions of job control over work resources were also related to psychosomatic health complaints in the USA sample of mid-career managers. This study, however, did not report any tests of the demands–control model (Karasek, 1979), but it did provide further empirical support for a multidimensional conceptualization of the notion of work control.

Jimmieson and Terry (1993) examined the extent to which specific domains of work control differentially interacted with levels of task stress (work overload and skill underutilization) and role stress (role conflict and role ambiguity) to predict employee adjustment in a sample of 116 retail employees. Jimmieson and Terry made a distinction between task control (i.e., the extent to which employees could influence the variety, scheduling, and pacing of their work tasks) and decision control (i.e., the extent to which employees had the opportunity to contribute to decision-making processes in the wider organizational environment). There was some evidence to suggest that employees who experienced a combination of high role ambiguity and low task control reported higher levels of depersonalization in their interactions with customers. There was, however, no support for the demands–control model (Karasek, 1979) when levels of decision control were taken into account.

In a recent study that distinguished among different facets of work control, Sargent and Terry (in press) proposed that task-relevant sources of control (such as work pacing, task organization, and scheduling control) would be more likely than peripheral sources of work control (such as mobility, resource allocation, and organizational decision control) to moderate the effects of work demands. This proposal was predicted on the basis of S. Cohen and Wills's (1985; see also S. Cohen & Edwards, 1989) stress-matching hypothesis. According to S. Cohen and Wills, there should be an adequate match between the demands of the situation and the type of buffer under consideration if stress-buffering effects are to be detected. Cohen and Wills's stress-matching hypothesis has received some support in relation to the effects of social support (Terry, Nielsen, & Perchard, 1993), although the hypothesis has yet to be systematically tested. The notion that task-relevant sources of work control are more likely to buffer the negative effects of work stress is also consistent with Jimmieson and Terry's (1993) findings and with Frese's (1989; see also Hammer & Stern, 1980) action sequence proposal, which hypothesizes that the control domains most central to an employees' work activities are likely to have immediate and strong effects on employee adjustment, whereas those control dimensions that are less proximal to daily work activities are likely to have less impact on adjustment.

In a sample of administrative staff employed in a tertiary institution, Sargent and Terry (in press) found some support for the expectation that the stress-buffering effects of work control would be specific to task-related aspects of control. Three facets of work control (i.e., task, scheduling, and decision control) were considered, as were a number of sources of work stress (work overload, underutilization of skills, role conflict, and role ambiguity). As predicted, each of the significant buffering effects involved task control-task control buffered the negative relationship between role ambiguity and job satisfaction (in both cross-sectional and longitudinal analyses) and between work overload and (low) depressive symptomatology (again, in both cross-sectional and longitudinal analyses). Moreover, when a composite measure of work control was used (responses to each item summed, irrespective of focus of control) only very weak support for the demands–control model was obtained, even though the reliability of the combined scale was adequate. Task control is likely to be particularly relevant to a person with ambiguous role demands—such stress should be responsive to the extent to which an employee has the capacity to control how, and in what sequence, task requests are handled. The fact that task control buffered the negative relationship between work overload and low depressive symptoms at both Times 1 and 2 is also interpretable in light of the stress-matching hypothesis, given that a person who has too much to do is likely to be able to handle this stress if the job has some flexibility in terms of its allocation of time and energy to tasks.

Focusing specifically on the distinction between timing and method control, Mullarkey, Jackson, Wall, Wilson, and Grey-Taylor (1997; see also Wall et al., 1990) hypothesized that these two forms of work control would buffer the negative effects of two work stressors specific to AMT work environments (i.e., technological uncertainty and technological abstractness). Using the measures described by P.R. Jackson et al. (1993) and Wall, Jackson, and Mullarkey (1995), it was found that technological demands were related negatively to employee anxiety for those employees who characterized their job as high in timing control, whereas there was a positive relationship between demands and anxiety for those who perceived low levels of timing control—similar but weaker results were evident for technological abstractness. There was, however, no evidence to suggest that method control interacted with either of the indicators of work stress to predict employee adjustment.

Although the positive relationship that Mullarkey et al. (1997) observed between demands and strain under low timing control is consistent with the demands–control model, the strong negative relationship between demands and strain under high control is not entirely consistent with the model. In particular, the high strain observed for low demands, high control positions is inconsistent with Karasek's view of these positions as not having any adverse effects on well-being; however, Karasek did note that 'passive' positions (low demands, low control) may result in a decline in work performance and a sense of helplessness. Mullarkey et al. interpreted their findings in light of the machine-pacing literature that suggests that high timing control may lead to tedious periods of worker inactivity. The operation of slow moving machinery (i.e., high timing control) that makes few technological demands (i.e., low uncertainty and abstractness) is likely to result in a relatively low-challenge job, and a variety of associated negative reactions (e.g., frustration, boredom, and dissatisfaction). In relation to the lack of interactive effects involving method control, it was suggested that the items designed to tap this type of work control were relatively general in nature and, therefore, did not assess an appropriate moderator of the very specific technological demands assessed in the study.

At a broader level, Sutton and Kahn's (1986) stress antidote model distinguished among the extent to which employees can predict the occurrence, duration, and timing of work-related events (predictability) how much they understand how and why things occur in the organization (understanding), and the extent to which employees have the potential to influence events or processes at work (control). Sutton and Kahn proposed that each of these three variables would weaken the negative effects of work stress on employee adjustment. Ganster and Fusilier (1989) located one study that had attempted to test this model (e.g., Tetrick & LaRocco, 1987). Tetrick and LaRocco found that both understanding and control of work-related events moderated the negative effects of role stress on levels of job satisfaction in a sample of healthcare professionals.

Jimmieson and Terry (1993) have since provided a further test of the stress antidote model in a sample of retail employees. They developed scales to measure prediction, understanding, and control, but failed to find empirical support for the distinction among the three variables. Factor analytic procedures revealed that the measures of control (i.e., task control and decision control) could be empirically distinguished from the measures of prediction and understanding. However, the items developed to measure prediction and understanding could not be empirically distinguished. It was suggested that understanding organizational events may be reflected, in part, by the extent to which employees can predict the occurrence, duration, and timing of work-related events. There was support for the stress-buffering effects of the combined measure of prediction and understanding, in that the negative effects of role conflict on feelings of depersonalization and job satisfaction were more marked for employees who rated their job as being low in prediction and understanding. Although offering some support for the stress-antidote model, there is a need for the development of psychometrically sound measures of prediction and understanding. In this respect, the predictability subscale of Dwyer and Ganster's 22-item work control scale (see C.S. Smith et al., 1997) may provide a useful starting point for more systematic research in this area; however, the empirical distinctiveness of the predictability subscale is open to question (Dwyer & Ganster, 1991; Fox et al., 1993; cf. C.S. Smith et al., 1997).

In sum, recent research suggests that the lack of stronger evidence for the demands–control model may be due to a focus on global measures of control. By assessing a single construct of work control, researchers may have masked the fact that some types of control have the potential to buffer the negative effects of job demands, whereas others do not. Sargent and Terry's (in press) research supports the view that focused measures of work control are more likely to show buffering effects if they assess task control rather than more peripheral aspects of work control (also see Jimmieson & Terry, 1993). However, Mullarkey et al.'s (1997) finding that the highest levels of strain among manufacturing workers were experienced under conditions of high timing control and low demands points to the possibility that high levels of control are not always desired (see Bazerman, 1982), a point that is discussed in more detail below. Recent research on dimensions of control also points to the importance of incorporating a range of different control-related variables into stress-buffering models, rather than focusing specifically on the notion of control.

Conjunctive moderator effects

In light of the weak and inconsistent support for Karasek's (1979) demands–control model, other theoretical developments in relation to this model have focused on the possibility that there are additional organizational and dispositional characteristics that may moderate the effects of high strain (i.e., high work stress and low work control) on employee adjustment. As noted by R.E. Smith, Smoll, and Ptacek (1990; see also S. Cohen & Edwards, 1989; Parkes, Mendham, & von Rabenau, 1994), conjunctive moderator effects occur when the effect of a variable is observed only under a particular combination of scores on the two moderator variables. Thus, in the context of the demands–control model, a conjunctive moderator effect would be evident when job demands impacted adversely on adjustment only under conditions of low control and high or low levels of a third variable. In the context of the demands–control model, another way to conceptualize the role of third variables is as secondary conditioning or moderating variables—that is, as variables that further moderate the impact of the primary moderating influence (i.e., work control).

Social support

The variable that has received the most research attention as a possible secondary moderating variable in relation to the job demands–control model is the notion of social support. In 1979, Payne (see also Fletcher, 1991; Payne & Fletcher, 1983) proposed that job strain is a function of three major job characteristics; that is, demands (including the overload component of demands, in addition to other sources of work stress), constraints (e.g., work control and autonomy), and supports (e.g., natural, physical, intellectual, technical, and social resources). He suggested that by adding various supports to the organizational system, such as interpersonal support, less adaptive energy is needed to cope with high job demands under conditions of low control. More recently, Karasek and Theorell (1990) have reconceptualized the demands–control model to include work-related social support. The demands–control–support model predicts that job strain (i.e., high job demands and low job decision latitude) will be most marked when employees have low levels of social support at work. In other words, employee strain should be highest under high work stress combined with low levels of both work control and social support (see Johnson, 1986). This proposal is in line with the stress-buffering model of social support, which proposes that social support protects the individual against the adverse effects of stress (e.g., by helping the person redefine the problem, providing a solution to it; Finney, Mitchell, Cronkite, & Moos, 1984; see also Parkes, Mendham, & von Rabenau, 1994).

Although Payne and Fletcher (1983; see also Melamed, Kushnir, & Meir, 1991) found only weak support for their demands–supports–constraints model, a growing body of research has found stronger support for the joint moderating roles of work control and social support in the stress–strain relationship. In a secondary analysis of national survey data in Sweden, Johnson and Hall (1988) found that low levels of social support accentuated the negative impact of high job demands and low job decision latitude on cardiovascular health indicators; however, unexpectedly, the highest cardiac risk was evident when active work conditions (high demands and high control) were associated with low support (see also Kristensen, 1995; Theorell & Karasek, 1996, for reviews). Landsbergis et al. (1992) similarly found that a lack of social support lessened job satisfaction for those jobs characterized by high job demands and high job decision latitude (i.e., an active job), a pattern of results that they suggested was indicative of the beneficial impact of a cooperative rather than a competitive work environment.

There is also evidence for the demands–control–support model in the prediction of affective work outcomes. Karasek and Theorell (1990) presented some suggestive evidence in this respect. In a more detailed analysis of the joint effects of support, demands, and discretion (demands and discretion were assessed along the lines suggested by Karasek, 1979), Parkes et al. (1994) found that, in both cross-sectional and longitudinal studies, elevated psychosomatic health scores were associated with high strain jobs (i.e., high job demands and low job decision latitude) under conditions of low, but not high, levels of social support at work. In a more recent longitudinal study, Sargent and Terry (in press) similarly found that high levels of supervisor support mitigated the negative effects of high strain jobs on job satisfaction and depersonalization. High levels of non-work support and co-worker support also mitigated the negative effects of high strain jobs on supervisor ratings of work performance.

In sum, there is consistent evidence—across a small number of studies—that the negative effects of a high strain position (high demands and low control) are most marked when levels of social support are low. Future research needs to examine, in more depth, the secondary moderating roles of different types and sources of support. Such research should also examine the mechanisms that underpin the effects of social support—for instance, in relation to colleague support, group norms rather than interpersonal mechanisms may account for the differing effects of high and low work strain as a function of level of support.

Organizational level

In the search for conjunctive moderator variables, other researchers have sought to identify the presence of objective organizational characteristics that may influence the presence of demand by control interactions in the prediction of employee adjustment. In this respect, research attention has focused on a variety of occupational status variables. For instance, Hurrell and Lindström (1992) found that the main effects of job demands and job decision latitude on health status changed as a function of an employee's career stage. Fletcher and Jones (1993) found evidence to suggest that levels of job demands and job decision latitude were higher for white-collar employees than for workers involved in manual labour. Research of this nature points to the possibility that the moderating role of work control in the stress–strain relationship may not occur at all levels of the organization.

Preliminary evidence to suggest that the stress-buffering properties of work control on employee adjustment may vary as a function of hierarchical level was provided by Westman (1992), who found that work control buffered the negative effects of role conflict on psychological health for clerical employees, but not for the managerial employees of a large financial organization. In a consideration of possible explanations for the finding that work control is less important at higher levels of the organization, Westman suggested that organizations may provide employees at the managerial level with other resources such as power, prestige, and higher levels of income that may help to buffer the negative effects of work stress. Because low-status employees tend to lack access to these external coping resources, work control opportunities may be a particularly salient method for dealing with the demands of the job.

In contrast, Xie (1996) proposed that the demands–control model would be less useful in explaining employee adjustment among blue-collar workers than among white-collar employees (see also Fletcher & Jones, 1993). Based on an analysis of the social environment in contemporary China, Xie pointed to the possibility that blue-collar workers are not socialized to seek high levels of personal control at work. In this respect, there is often little opportunity for blue-collar workers to exert personal control over issues directly related to their jobs, whereas more substantive control over operational issues tends to be confined to the managerial employees of an organization (Von Glinow & Teagarden, 1988). Thus, Xie expected that the stress-buffering effects of work control on employee adjustment would be stronger in a sample of managers, professionals, and public servants ($n = 647$) than in a sample of blue-collar employees ($n = 440$) obtained from a variety of Chinese organizations.

In support of his proposal, Xie (1996) found that anxiety, depression, and psychosomatic health complaints were highest among white-collar employees under conditions of job strain (i.e., high job demands and low job decision latitude—assessed using Karasek's 1979, measures). In addition, highest rates of job and life satisfaction occurred for white-collar employees when their jobs were active (i.e., high job demands and high job decision latitude). For blue-collar workers, however, job decision latitude did not buffer the negative effects of job demands (or the two-way interaction was substantially weaker), and in the case of psychosomatic health problems, job decision latitude exacerbated rather than buffered the negative effects of high job demands. Although Chinese cultural norms that discourage complaints about personal sufferings may account for this stress–exacerbating role (see Xie, 1995). More generally, the stress-exacerbating role of job latitude points to the possibility that not all employees desire jobs that are characterized by high work control.

Taken together, the evidence suggesting that the stress-buffering role of work control may vary as a function of organizational level should be interpreted with caution, given that Westman (1992) and Xie (1996) obtained conflicting results; moreover, other researchers have found no evidence for the moderating role of organizational level in relation to the demands–control model (Fletcher & Jones, 1993; Warr, 1990—in both the latter studies, gender also failed to emerge as a secondary moderator variable). The lack of evidence for the secondary moderating role of organizational level is consistent with the general lack of support for the moderating effect of organizational level on the relationship between role stress and employee adjustment (e.g., Fisher & Gitelson, 1983; Pearce, 1981). Thus, it would appear that organizational level does not act as a reliable secondary moderator in relation to the demands–control model and, even if such effects are detected, they can only be explained in very speculative terms. As Xie (1996) noted, a number of factors are likely to distinguish blue-and white-collar workers, or non-managerial and managerial workers. In his work, Xie controlled for a number of the demographic variables that may vary as a function of organizational level. However, there are other contextual work factors that are also likely to be relevant in this regard. Given the equivocal results obtained in relation to organizational level and the difficulty of explaining such effects, researchers should focus on specific contextual work variables rather than pursuing research on the possible moderating effects of organizational level. Recently, research has considered the secondary moderating role that access to work-related information—a contextual work factor—may play. This research is discussed in the next section.

Informational control

Focusing on characteristics of the work environment other than organizational level (and related variables), Jimmieson and Terry (1997, 1998, in press) have, in a series of studies, examined the moderating role of informational control. Drawing on the broader psychological literature, a distinction can be made between behavioral and informational forms of personal control. The majority of early experimental studies conducted in the personal control literature was concerned with manipulations of behavioral control over aversive stimuli. Averill (1973) denned behavioral control as the 'availability of a response which may directly influence or modify the objective characteristics of a threatening event' (pp. 286–287). Miller (1979) and Thompson (1981) provided similar definitions of behavioral control, in that they focused on the extent to which an individual perceives that he or she has the ability to modify an aversive event. Consistent with these definitions, experimental studies have manipulated behavioral control by providing individuals with the option to avoid exposure to a noxious stimulus, reduce some instances of a noxious stimulus, terminate a noxious stimulus prematurely, schedule rest periods from a series of noxious stimuli, limit the intensity of a noxious stimulus, or self-administer a noxious stimulus. Similarly, work control research has focused on the notion of behavioral control as the major construct of interest—typically work control is operationalized as the extent to which employees perceive that they have the ability to directly manipulate various aspects of the occupational environment.

A number of theorists have pointed out that there exists a type of personal control that does not rely for its beneficial effects on the ability of the individual to make an external response (Averill, 1973; R. Katz & Wykes, 1985; Thompson, 1981). As defined by Thompson (1981), cognitive control is the belief that one has a cognitive strategy available to influence the outcome of an aversive event. The types of cognitive strategies that can be used in an effort to satisfy an individual's need for personal control vary considerably (see Rothbaum, Weisz, & Snyder, 1982). Jimmieson and Terry (1997, 1998) focused on the role that informational control may play in the stress–strain relationship. Informational control, unlike other forms of cognitive control, can be objectively manipulated and, therefore, potentially provides organizations with a strategy for improving employee well-being. Thompson (1981) defined informational control as a communication—that is, information gain—that is delivered to an individual prior to an aversive situation. Similarly, Fiske and S.E. Taylor (1991) referred to informational control as a sense of personal control that is achieved when an individual obtains information about a noxious event. Informational control can be conceptualized as a form of cognitive control, because it typically decreases levels of appraised threat associated with an aversive event (Averill, 1973). Furthermore, informational control is a type of personal control that is not reliant for its beneficial effects on the ability of the individual to make an external response (R. Katz & Wykes, 1985).

For several decades, informational control has played an important role in a range of different theoretical models that has been developed to understand human behavior under conditions of stress (see R. Katz & Wykes, 1985, for a review). For instance, the safety signal hypothesis argues that information reduces the amount of time individuals spend in fearful anticipation of the stressful event (Seligman, 1968, 1975). Similarly, the information-seeking perspective argues that information lowers the conflict and, therefore, the arousal associated with unpredictability (Berlyne, 1960). Janis (1958) proposed that informational control stimulates the individual to mentally rehearse the impending stressful event, develop accurate expectations about the characteristics of the impending stressful event, and ultimately, cope better than those individuals who do not have high levels of informational control (see also Lykken, 1962; Perkins, 1968).

It is possible that the effects of behavioral control are contingent on the extent to which individuals perceive that they have access to high levels of informational control. In the goal-setting literature, Earley (1985) found that participants who were provided with choice when performing a class scheduling activity indicated higher levels of assigned and personal goal acceptance when choice was accompanied by high levels of information concerning the experimental activity. Participants also demonstrated better task performance when provided with high levels of both choice and information. These results were replicated in a subsequent field study in which levels of choice and information were manipulated in a sample of 40 animal caregivers whose major responsibility was the cleaning of animal cages.

Given that there is some empirical support for the view that the positive effects of behavioral control are more evident when accompanied by high levels of informational control (e.g., Earley, 1985), Jimmieson and Terry (1998) proposed that the stress-buffering effects of behavioral control may also be more marked at high, rather than low, levels of informational control. In relation to a letter-sorting activity, Jimmieson and Terry manipulated task information, in addition to the manipulations of work stress and behavioral control. A high level of task information was operationalized by providing participants with a communication concerning the step-by-step procedures involved in performing a letter-sorting activity, and temporal information concerning the arrival of additional letters (e.g., introduction by the experimenter on three occasions at regular 5-minute intervals). Contrary to predictions, there was no evidence to suggest that the stress-buffering effects of behavioral control were most marked for participants allocated to the high task information condition. These results may have been due to the relatively simplistic nature of a letter-sorting activity. It is likely that participants possessed the fundamental knowledge, skills, and abilities necessary to perform the letter-sorting activity, thus making the task-specific information provided to participants ineffectual (Daft & Macintosh, 1981; Wood, 1986; see also Chesney & Locke, 1991; Kernan, Bruning, & Miller-Guhde, 1994).

In response, Jimmieson and Terry (in press, Experiment 1) conducted further experimental research to examine the main and interactive effects of stress, behavioral control, and informational control in the context of a complex task—that is, an in-basket activity. High informational control was operationalized by providing participants with procedural information: (1) information concerning the features of a typical in-basket activity; (2) an example in-basket item and a possible response to the in-basket item; (3) information about how much time was available for the activity; and (4) the number of in-basket items to be addressed during the specified time period. There was a consistent pattern of results in support of the stress-buffering role of task information. Specifically, the negative effects of work stress on quantitative performance were stronger for participants who were not provided with procedural information than for participants allocated to the high procedural information condition. When levels of subjective task performance and task satisfaction were considered, procedural information buffered the negative effects of work stress on these outcome variables only under conditions of low behavioral control. In other words, the positive effects of task information (i.e., as a stress buffer) on levels of adjustment were more evident for participants allocated to the low behavioral control condition. Jimmieson and Terry (in press, Experiment 2) partially replicated this pattern of findings in a subsequent laboratory study that extended the experimental design by also manipulating low and high levels of task complexity. In this study, procedural information buffered the negative effects of work stress only under conditions of low behavioral control for participants performing the complex version of the in-basket activity.

In an attempt to interpret this pattern of findings, reference can be made to at least two sequential models of personal control. Based on the early work of Wortman and Brehm (1975), Greenberger and Strasser (1986) argued that employees, rather than entering a state of learned helplessness, respond to a reduction in work control by engaging in a variety of indirect strategies aimed at restoring a sense of personal control at work. In a comprehensive overview of potential response patterns to less than desired levels of control at work, Greenberger and Strasser (1986) suggested that employees may engage in a variety of information-seeking behaviors that serve to restore a sense of prediction and understanding concerning the work environment (see also Greenberger, Porter, Miceli, & Strasser, 1991). Thus, the provision of informational control may play an important role in determining adjustment among employees whose jobs do not provide opportunities for more direct forms of work control (see also Ganster, 1988, 1989). The salience of informational control under conditions of low behavioral control is a process similar to Bell and Staw's (1989) sequential work control model. They argued that outcome control over promotion, remuneration, and other benefits is the most desirable form of personal control in the work context, but when this control strategy is not possible, employees will direct their work control efforts towards job-related behaviors (e.g., determining work schedules). When neither of these work control strategies is possible, employees will strive to gain a sense of prediction and understanding concerning the work environment (see also Staw, 1977, 1986). Given that there are likely to be limited opportunities for behavioral control in many organizations (see Greenberger & Strasser, 1986), the search for other job characteristics that may compensate for low behavioral control, particularly those characterized by high job demands, is an interesting proposal that has received limited research attention in the area of occupational stress and health.

In addition to task-related information, D. Katz and Kahn (1978) highlighted the importance of more contextual forms of information concerning how one's role relates to other organizational functions, and contributes to the overall performance and long-term goals of the organization. Spreitzer's (1995a,b, 1996) definition of job-related information is also consistent with the notion of contextual information. Spreitzer focused on the extent to which employees perceive that they have an understanding of senior management's strategic outlook for the organization (i.e., the vision, mission, and subsequent objectives and goals for the organization). As noted by Sutton and Kahn (1986; see also Jimmieson & Terry, 1993), this type of job-related information provides employees with a sense of prediction and understanding concerning the wider organizational environment.

Jimmieson and Terry (1997) manipulated low and high levels of work stress, behavioral control, and contextual information in a study of 192 psychology students performing an in-basket activity. High levels of contextual information were manipulated by providing participants with information that typically accompanies an in-basket activity (e.g., company profile, mission statement, organizational structure, and quarterly newsletter). This information was intended to provide participants with an understanding of broader organizational issues, such as the importance of their job to the overall performance of the organization and its strategic goals. The manipulation of contextual information had only minimal effects on the outcome measures, a pattern of results that was consistent with Earley's (1986) finding that information about broad organizational outcomes was less important than task-specific information in providing employees with the resources needed for effective job performance. In non-experimental situations, however, contextual information may play a significant role in determining employees' affective responses to the work environment. For instance, D. Katz and Kahn (1978) hypothesized that contextual information is likely to be an important variable in the development of long-term indicators of employee adjustment, such as organizational commitment.

Taken together, the research conducted by Jimmieson and Terry (1997, 1998, in press) points towards a more complex pattern than the proposed conjunctive moderating role of informational control, in that the results suggest that informational control may compensate for the negative impact of low behavioral control. Clearly, the results need to be replicated in the field; nevertheless, they accord with sequential models of work control (Greenberger & Strasser, 1986; Bell & Staw, 1989) and, thus, suggest a possible direction for future research in the area.

Dispositional variables

In addition to examining the effects of secondary moderator variables that relate to the work environment, attention has been directed towards the role that dispositional variables may play in their respect. One obvious variable to take into account in relation to the demands–control model is locus of control, or people's generalized beliefs about the extent to which they have control over their lives. There is evidence that generalized control beliefs are a dispositional predictor of perceptions of work control (Spector, 1992; see also Parkes, 1989). Moreover, it can be argued, on the basis of person–environment theory (French, Caplan, & Van Harrison, 1982; see also Parkes, 1991), that the positive effects of high levels of work control should be most marked for employees with an internal locus of control, whereas externals should respond most favorably to low levels of environmental control. In other words, as Parkes (1991) noted, the effects of control in the work environment should be dependent on the extent to which the degree of available control is dispositionally congruent.

In a review of the early work linking work control and dispositional control beliefs, Jackson (1989) concluded that firm conclusions could not be drawn on the basis of the small number of extant studies. However, there was some support for the congruency hypothesis obtained in a field study conducted by Marino and White (1985): Higher levels of job specificity (assumed to reflect low job autonomy) were positively associated with lower job stress for internals, whereas the opposite was true for the externals. More recently, Parkes (1991) reasoned that, on the basis of the demands–control model, locus of control should emerge as a secondary moderating variable (i.e., that there should be evidence of a demand by control by locus of control interaction). Assuming a congruency model, the impact of high control should be positive for internals but negative for externals.

In a cross-sectional study of civil servants and a longitudinal study of student nurses, Parkes (1991) found that demands and discretion interacted—in the form predicted by Karasek (1979)—for externals but not internals. Inspection of the cell means formed by the crossing of the demands and control scores (assessed using scales derived from Karasek's, 1979, measures) revealed that, under conditions of low demands, externals responded more negatively to high discretion than internals. This pattern of results was consistent with the congruency prediction, but the fact that the impact of high demands and high control was similar for internals and externals was contrary to the congruency prediction, suggesting instead that when demands are high, situational factors override the impact of dispositional variables. Parkes's results provide some support for the view that the effects of different levels of environmental control are dependent on the match between the control and the person's control beliefs. The results, however, need to be replicated, given that Daniels and Guppy (1994), in a longitudinal study of 244 accountants, found that perceptions of high levels of job autonomy buffered the negative effects of stress only for internals (not externals, as found by Parkes, 1991).

In addition to dispositional control beliefs, the Type A behavior pattern (associated with a hard-driving, competitive, and time-pressured disposition; see Friedman & Rosenman, 1974) has been proposed as a possible secondary moderator variable in relation to the demands–control model. In line with the view that Type A individuals have a need to control their environment, Kushnir and Melamed (1991) proposed that Type As would be more distressed by conditions of low work control that Type Bs (individuals who do not display the Type A behavior pattern), and that they would find passive jobs (low demand and low control) particularly distressing. Data collected from a large heterogeneous sample of Israeli workers failed to reveal any perceived control (assessed using a focused 6-item measure) by Type A interactions; however, there were relatively weak workload by control by Type A interactions on job satisfaction and irritability. Inspection of these interactions revealed only weak support (on irritability) for the prediction that Type As would find low demand, low control positions more distressing than Type Bs.

A final dispositional variable that has been looked at in relation to the demands–control model is negative affectivity. According to the stress reactivity hypothesis, individuals with a tendency to experience negative distress will react more negatively to environmental stress than individuals low in negative affect. On the basis of this prediction, O'Brien, Terry, and Jimmieson (1998) proposed that the effects of a high strain work environment (high strain, low control) would impact most negatively on individuals high in negative affectivity. Using the in–basket task developed by Jimmieson and Terry (1997, 1998; in press), O'Brien, Terry, and Jimmieson found, as expected, that demands and control (experimentally manipulated) interacted—in accord with Karasek's (1979) predictions—for participants high in negative affectivity but not for those low in negative affect. This result was evident on a post-experiment measure of task satisfaction, but not on measures of performance (both subjective and objective) or post-task mood (after the effects of pre-task mood were controlled).

In summary, only a few studies have examined the secondary moderating effects of dispositional variables in the context of the demands–control model. In relation to generalized control beliefs, Parkes (1991) found, in two different studies, some support for the view that externals prefer low control situations (but only when demands were low), whereas Daniels and Guppy (1994) found that high levels of autonomy helped buffer the negative effects of job demands only for internals. Taken together, these results provide some support for a congruency model of control; however, the inconsistent pattern of results indicates the need for future research of this type. In relation to Type A behavior and negative affectivity, recent studies have reported some results suggestive of secondary moderating effects; however, these results will need to be replicated before they can be interpreted with any confidence.

Summary

Increasingly, researchers have considered the role of conjunctive or secondary moderating variables in tests of the demands–control model. Such variables are intuitively appealing because their presence could easily explain the lack of stronger evidence for the model. In this respect, there is evidence—across a small number of studies—that the negative effects of a high strain position (high demands and low control) are most marked when levels of social support are low. However, tests of the secondary moderating role of organizational level have failed to yield convincing results—indeed, even if stress-buffering effects of work control were found to be dependent on organizational level it would be very difficult to account, with any confidence, for such effects. In contrast, recent laboratory research has revealed that high levels of informational control may help to compensate for low levels of behavioral control. Such results need to be replicated in the field; however, they are important in that they suggest that the provision of information may serve to buffer high levels of demands in occupations that are inherently low in control. The secondary moderating roles of dispositional variables are unclear—more research needs to consider whether the stress-buffering effects of work control depend on the match between the potential for situational control and the person's generalized control beliefs, and whether they depend on broader dispositional tendencies.

Other effects of work control

Main effects

Although previous research has provided only equivocal evidence for interactive effects of work control, this body of research has demonstrated consistent evidence of significant main effects of work control. Such effects are in line with the view that people have a fundamental motivation to achieve a sense of control over their environment (White, 1959; see also Frese, 1989; Ganster, 1989; Ganster & Fusilier, 1989), which may, at least in part, emanate from the negative consequences of low control for a person's self-image (e.g., reactance theory, Brehm, 1996, & learned helplessness theory, Seligman, 1975; see Thompson, 1981).

Using both Karasek's (1979) measure of decision latitude and more focused measures of work control, research conducted over the past decade has linked high levels of work control to low levels of anxiety (e.g., Carayon, 1993a; Kushnir & Melamed, 1991; Landsbergis et al., 1992; Mullarkey et al., 1997; Payne & Fletcher, 1983; Spector, 1987; Stansfeld et al., 1995; Wall et al., 1996), depression (e.g., Carayon, 1993a; Fletcher & F. Jones, 1993; Mullarkey et al., 1997; Stansfeld et al., 1995; Wall et al., 1996), psychological distress (e.g., Barnett & Brennan, 1995; Marshall et al., 1991), frustration (e.g., Spector, 1987), irritability (e.g., Kushnir & Melamed, 1991), burnout (e.g., Melamed et al., 1991), psychosomatic health complaints (e.g., Carayon, 1993a; Fox et al., 1993; Hurrell & Lindström, 1992; Kushnir & Melamed, 1991), and lifestyle factors, such as alcohol consumption (e.g., Bromet et al., 1988). Positive main effects of work control have also been reported on measures of task satisfaction (e.g., Dwyer & Ganster, 1991), job satisfaction (e.g., Fletcher & F. Jones, 1993; Fox et al., 1993; Greenberger et al., 1989; Kushnir & Melamed, 1991 ; McLaney & Hurrell, 1988; Melamed et al., 1991; Mullarkey et al., 1997; Parkes et al., 1994; Sargent & Terry, in press; Sauter, 1989; Tetrick & LaRocco, 1987; Wall et al., 1996; Warr, 1990), life satisfaction (e.g., Fletcher & F. Jones, 1993; Stansfeld et al., 1995), and job performance (e.g., Greenberger et al., 1989).

Because of the general reliance on cross-sectional designs, the main effects of work control are difficult to interpret. Although negative affectivity is most often considered to be a nuisance variable in relation to the effects of perceived stress, negative affectivity—as well as more transient mood effects—could also inflate that strength of the relationship between perceptions of work control and well-being. Because of a tendency to focus on the negative aspects of themselves and their environment, individuals high in negative affectivity are likely not only to report high levels of subjective distress, but may also perceive low levels of work control.

In general, longitudinal studies have found weaker support for main effects of work control than cross-sectional studies. For example, in two longitudinal studies, Parkes (1991) and Parkes et al. (1994) (cf. Bromet et al., 1988) found non-significant main effects of discretion on subsequent adjustment (after control of initial adjustment), whereas the main effects of discretion were significant in the accompanying cross-sectional studies. Similarly, Sargent and Terry (in press) found a significant main effect of task control on a contemporaneous measure of affective well-being, but the comparable effect was non-significant in the analysis of the subsequent adjustment scores (after control of initial well-being). In studies that have employed objective outcome measures and focused measures of work control, the main effects of work control have also been nonsignificant (Dwyer & Ganster, 1991; Fox et al., 1993; Schaubroeck & Merritt, 1997; cf. Greenberger et al., 1989). Interestingly, both Dwyer and Ganster and Fox et al. found that the main effect of control was significant in the prediction of self-report measures of job satisfaction (assessed at the same time as control). Thus, there is evidence suggesting that the main effects of work control may be due to the confounding influence of common method endemic in mono-method, cross-sectional research.

Nevertheless, it should be noted that significant main effects of job decision latitude have consistently been reported on a range of cardiovascular outcomes (Chapman et al., 1990; Georges, Wear, & Mueller, 1992; Karasek & Theorell,

1990; Pieper, LaCroix, & Karasek, 1989). The discrepancy between the results of these latter studies and others that have focused on objective outcome measures (see above) may be due to the assessment of control—the supportive data have been obtained using Karasek's (1979) measure of job decision latitude, whereas the non-supportive data have been obtained using focused measures of control. Thus, the significant main effects of control on cardiovascular outcomes may be due not to the control component of measures of job decision latitude, but to the component that assesses skill discretion. Indeed, skill underutilization has emerged as a reliable predictor of poor employee adjustment in work stress research (e.g., Jimmieson & Terry, 1993; Sargent & Terry, in press).

In sum, although there have been a large number of reports of significant main effects of work control on a range of different outcome measures, much of the research has been cross-sectional in design. Thus, not only is the direction of causality difficult to determine, significant relationships between perceptions of control and contemporaneous self-report outcome measures may reflect the confounding influence of common method variance. The results of longitudinal studies suggest that this may be the case, as do a number of recent studies employing objective outcome measures. Future research needs to examine the extent to which the significant main effects of control on cardiovascular outcomes may reflect the impact of perceptions of skill utilization, rather than work control. More attention also needs to be paid to the possible indirect effects of work control, given that the lack of evidence of direct effects in longitudinal research may reflect the fact that work control impacts on subsequent adjustment through mediating mechanisms. Such mechanisms are discussed below.

Indirect effects

In their review, Ganster and Fusilier (1989) noted that work control may not only exert direct or interactive effects on levels of employee adjustment. They suggested that one direction for future research was to explore the extent to which employees utilize work control to alter their job demands, thereby reducing levels of strain. Frese (1989) also suggested that work control may act as a stress-reduction mechanism that allows employees to adjust job demands and other job characteristics to their desired level. Similarly, Sutton and Kahn (1986) highlighted the possibility that perceptions of prediction, understanding, and control at work provide employees with the opportunity to reduce both the objective and subjective experience of job demands (see also Parkes, 1989).

To provide evidence of a mediating model, it is necessary to demonstrate that the observed effects of work control are no longer significant when the effects of work stress are statistically controlled (Baron & Kenny, 1986). In support of the indirect effects of work control, Jimmieson and Terry (1993) found that the positive effects of decision control (and two theoretically related control variables; that is, prediction and understanding) were mediated, through their relationships with perceptions of work stress, on subsequent psychological well-being, depersonalization, and job satisfaction (although initial levels of adjustment were not controlled).

Carayon (1993b) posited a different causal sequence to the extent that he hypothesized that work stressors would influence levels of employee adjustment through their effect on work control. Drawing on the job design model proposed by Rosenfield (1989)—which defines control as the central element through which other variables influence mental health—Carayon (1993b) argued that the negative effects of work stress (i.e., workload, speed of work, and cognitive load) on stress outcomes (i.e., psychological complaints and mood disturbances) would occur through their effects on two operationalizations of the work control construct; namely, instrumental control (i.e., control that impacts on daily work activities, such as work pacing) and conceptual control (i.e., control that provides opportunities to participate in wider organizational decision-making). Path analysis revealed partial support for the model in that job demands were related to instrumental control for a sample of office workers. However, job demands exerted a main effect on employee adjustment, irrespective of levels of work control, and work control was not a significant predictor of any of the stress outcomes.

Although relatively few studies have examined indirect effects of work control (or alternative causal pathways; see Carayon, 1993b), the evidence provides some evidence that the effects of work control are mediated through perceptions of work stress (Jimmieson & Terry, 1993). This type of model not only accords with theoretical models of work control (Frese, 1989; Parkes, 1989; Sutton & Kahn, 1986), it also accords with the broader theoretical models of stress and coping, in which subjective evaluations of the potentially stressful context are regarded as critical mediating processes in the relationship between more stable situational (for instance, work control) and person variables and stress outcomes (e.g., Lazarus & Folkman, 1984; Lazarus, 1991; see also Terry, 1994; Terry, Callan, & Sartori, 1996; Terry, Tonge, & Callan, 1995). Despite the theoretical support for indirect effects of work control, future research needs to replicate Jimmieson and Terry's (1993) results. Such research should employ longitudinal research, in an endeavour to establish the temporal relations among work control, demands, and adjustment. Researchers also need to explore the possible mediating role of both subjective evaluations of work demands and more objective assessments of the demands of the work environment.

Curvilinear effects

Warr (1987) has raised another potential relationship between work control and employee adjustment. He argues that a number of job characteristics, including work control, may exhibit a curvilinear association with measures of employee adjustment. His vitamin model of stress and health predicts that a moderate level of work control will have the most beneficial impact on psychological well-being, whereas decrements in psychological well-being will be found at either extremely low or high levels of work control (see also Bazerman, 1982; Rodin,

Reenert, & Solomon, 1980). In this respect, it is argued that extremely high levels of work control will lead to a range of undesirable physiological, psychological, and behavioral consequences due, for instance, to a concern for self-presentation that may be particularly marked when people perceive that they will not be able to perform a task or set of tasks over which they have complete control (see Burger, 1989, for a review; see also Steptoe, 1989).

On methodological rather than substantive grounds, Fletcher and Jones (1993) pointed out that a significant interaction may be a spurious consequence of a curvilinear relationship between the outcome variables and either of the predictor variables (see Lubinski & Humphreys, 1990). It is necessary, therefore, to statistically control for the squared value of the work stress and work control variables (over and above their linear effect) before introducing the two-way interaction term between these variables into the hierarchical regression equation (see also J. Cohen & P. Cohen, 1983).

Warr (1991) provided a test of the vitamin model in a sample of 1686 English workers, and found evidence of a non-linear relationship between job decision latitude and levels of job satisfaction—the increase in satisfaction as a function of decision latitude levelled off at high levels of decision latitude; thus, there was not strong support for the curvilinear hypothesis. Warr found no evidence of demands–control interactions, even when the possible non-linearity in the relations between either of the variables and the outcome under consideration was taken into account. Fletcher and Jones (1993) also provided tests of the demands–control model and the vitamin model. In separate analyses of data obtained from male ($n = 1289$) and female ($n = 985$) employees recruited from a medical facility, there was evidence of a two-way interaction between job demands and job decision latitude for males in the prediction of job and life satisfaction (but not for two measures of psychological well-being). However, additional analyses revealed that, after controlling for the main effects of job demands and job decision latitude and their associated quadratic terms (squared values of the two variables), the two interactions were no longer significant. This pattern of findings can be taken as some evidence of non-linearity in the prediction of job and life satisfaction in the male sample but, overall, Fletcher and Jones concluded that there was only weak support for Warr's (1987) proposition that the effects of work stress and work control on employee adjustment are curvilinear in nature. However, Fletcher and Jones's study does highlight the need for future tests of the demands–control model to adopt this statistical approach in order to identify the presence of spurious interactions due to the non-linear effects of either work demands or work control.

Summary

In summary, recent research has considered some further roles, in addition to the stress buffering role, that work control may have on employee adjustment. With the exception of efforts to test for curvilinear effects of work control, this research focus has been incidental rather than intentional. For this reason, when reviewing previous research on work control, only scant attention has been paid to the possible direct and indirect effects of work control. The present review indicates that there have been numerous reports of significant main effects of work control; however, for the most part, these have been reported in cross-sectional, self-report studies, which suggest that they may be a reflection of the confounding effects of common method variance. Despite Ganster and Fusilier's (1989) call for more research attention on indirect effects of work control, little research of this type has been conducted, although there is some suggestive evidence that perceptions of work stress may play a mediating role in the control–adjustment relationship. In relation to possible curvilinear effects of work control, there is little evidence that moderate levels of control are most beneficial for employee well-being. It should, however, be noted that the studies that have tested for curvilinear effects of work control have been based on relatively heterogeneous samples of employees—it is likely that the adverse effects of high levels of work control will be dependent on both personal dispositions (i.e., desire for control; see Greenberger et al., 1989) and the extent to which the job demands make salient the self–presentational concerns associated with high control.

Conclusions and future directions

The present paper has reviewed the past decade of research testing Karasek's (1979) demands–control model. Building on Ganster and Fusilier's (1989) timely discussion of the construct of work control and how it relates to a range of different areas of interest in industrial and organizational psychology, the aim of the present review was to focus on direct operationalizations of the work control construct. As shown in the review, this construct continues to be a popular area for research, much of which has been designed explicitly to test Karasek's assumption that, when accompanied by high levels of work control, work demands do not impact negatively on employee adjustment.

Taken together, the past decade of research has continued to yield only sporadic support for the demands–control model. It could be concluded that this pattern of results should be interpreted as a general lack of support for the model, and that efforts to identify possible buffers of the negative effects of work demands should be based on alternative theoretical models. However, such a recommendation may be premature. As revealed in this review, recent methodological and theoretical developments have yielded more promising support for the demands–control model. In particular, a number of specific conclusions can be drawn:

1. The evidence suggests that some aspects of work control may be more important than others—in this respect, task-relevant aspects of control appear to act as stress buffers, particularly when the source of stress is task-related.

2. Although research employing multidimensional measures of control has found significant demand–control interactions on affective outcomes, recent studies using composite control measures suggest that stress-buffering effects may be most evident on absenteeism and health-related outcomes. Such results suggest that the lack of more convincing support for the demands–control model in relation to cardiovascular outcomes may be due to the methodological problems with this latter body of research.
3. Recent research supports, in particular, the conjunctive moderating role of social support. Across a relatively small number of studies there is consistent evidence that stress-buffering effects of control are most evident when accompanied by high levels of social support.
4. Under conditions of low control, recent experimental research points to the possible compensatory role of informational control.
5. Although commonly reported in the literature, the main effects of work control may be a spurious outcome of common method variance; however, there is some preliminary evidence to suggest that indirect effects of work control should be examined in future research.

A more general conclusion that is clearly supported by the present review is that Karasek's (1979) concept of decision latitude needs to be refined, both conceptually and methodologically, to focus on the specific construct of work control. Future progress in the understanding of the interplay among work stress, work demands, and employee adjustment will be hampered if researchers continue to rely on a construct that is, operationally, confounded with other salient features of the work environment.

If the second decade of research on work control has sharpened researchers' theoretical and operational treatment of the construct of work control, then the challenge for the next decade of research is to identify the mechanisms that underpin the effects of work control. More specifically, the next decade of research should seek not only to verify the importance of task-relevant dimensions of control, the health and absenteeism-related effects of high demands and low control, and the secondary moderating role of social support, but to identify the mechanisms that underpin these effects. In particular, future research needs to examine the mediating role of: (1) both subjective and objective indicators of work stress; (2) coping responses adopted in the work context; and (3) specific health-related processes (e.g., lifestyle factors, as well as autonomic immunological, and endocrine responses; see Steptoe, 1989). In relation to the possible secondary moderating role of social support, research needs to examine the basis for the effects of a supportive work environment—for instance, the availability of work support may have its beneficial effects at an interpersonal level (e.g., by assisting workers to adopt effective coping responses, e.g., Terry, Rawle, & Callan, 1995), or through group-related mechanisms that render the work unit a cooperative rather than a competitive environment. In addition to examining the mechanisms underlying the effects of work control, researchers need to distinguish among different types of control, and to examine possible compensatory roles of cognitive forms of control. In a related vein, more focused research needs to address the possibility that in some work contexts, or for some people, work control is not desirable—the possible negative effect of high levels of work control remains a relatively unexplored area of research.

The third decade of research on work control will make a significant contribution to the work control literature only if the methodological limitations of previous research continue to be addressed. It is imperative that researchers use focused measures of work control, rather than relying on Karasek's (1979) multifactorial measure of job decision latitude. The reliance on cross-sectional, self-report research also needs to be replaced with the use of longitudinal, multimethod designs. In the context of the demands–control model, the effects of common method variance not only make any main effects of the predictor variables difficult to interpret, they may also obscure the presence of true interactive effects. Longitudinal research (with the appropriate control of initial adjustment) ensures that both transient and more stable sources of common method variance are controlled. Decontaminating the data for the confounding effects of same-source measurement also controls for these sources of common method variance, at the same time as allowing researchers to assess both the non-affective consequences of low work control and the relative importance of subjective and objective characteristics of the work environment. Future research should also avoid the use of large heterogeneous samples—the difficulties involved in interpreting any effects of work control in such samples, combined with the necessity of relying on general measures of work control, make the use of relatively homogeneous work groups more desirable.

In closing, our general conclusion is not much different from Ganster and Fusilier's (1989) conclusion a decade ago: The research conducted during the past decade points to the potential insights that the notion of work control can offer to an understanding of employee responses to work demands. Nevertheless, both conceptually and operationally, researchers need to take a more sophisticated look at this construct. The question as to whether control serves as an effective stress buffer in the work context does not have a simple answer, particularly if the tool that is used to answer the question does not directly reflect the construct that it is designed to assess, or if it is based on an ill-defined conceptualization of the construct. Moreover, any model that is based on the view that work control can help to buffer the negative effects of work stress needs to take into account the other characteristics of the work environment, the characteristics of the employee, and the extent to which there is a match between the type of available control and the source of the stress. Such a model also needs to be able to specify the processes that account for any stress-buffering effects of work control. Thus, the question as to whether work control can act as an antidote to the negative effects of work stress remains viable, but future attempts to answer it need to be more focused and based on a more complex view of the construct of work control than they have been in the past.

References

Aiken, L.S. & West, S.G. (1991). *Multiple Regression: Testing and Interpreting Interactions*. Newbury Park, CA: Sage.

Albright, C.L., Winkleby, M.A., Ragland, D.R., Fisher, J. & Syme, S.L. (1992). Job strain and prevalence of hypertension in a biracial population of urban bus drivers. *American Journal of Public Health*, **82**, 984–989.

Alfredsson, L., Karasek, R.A. & Theorell, T.G. (1982). Myocardial infarction risk and psychosocial work environment: An analysis of the male Swedish working force. *Social Science and Medicine*, **16**, 463–467.

Alfredsson, L., Spetz, C.L. & Theorell, T.G. (1985). Type of occupation and near-future hospitalization for myocardial infarction and some other diagnoses. *International Journal of Epidemiology*, **14**, 378–388.

Alterman, T., Shekelle, R.B., Vernon, S.W. & Burau, K.D. (1994). Decision latitude, psychological demand, job strain, and coronary heart disease in the Western Electric study. *American Journal of Epidemiology*, **139**, 620–627.

Averill, J.R. (1973). Personal control over aversive stimuli and its relationship to stress. *Psychological Bulletin*, **18**, 286–303.

Bandura, A., Cioffi, D., Taylor, C.B. & Brouillard, M.E. (1988). Perceived self-efficacy in coping with cognitive stressors and opioid activation. *Journal of Personality and Social Psychology*, **55**, 479–488.

Barnett, R.C. & Brennan, R.T. (1995). The relationship between job experiences and psychological distress: A structural equation approach. *Journal of Organizational Behavior*, **16**, 259–276.

Baron, R.M. & Kenny, D.A. (1986). The moderator–mediator variable distinction in social psychological research: Conceptual, strategic, and statistical considerations. *Journal of Personality and Social Psychology*, **51**, 1173–1182.

Bazerman, M.H. (1982). Impact of personal control on performance: Is added control always beneficial? *Journal of Applied Psychology*, **67**, 472–479.

Bell, N.E. & Staw, B.M. (1989). People as sculptors versus sculpture: The roles of personality and personal control in organizations. In M.B. Arthur, D.T. Hall, & B.S. Lawrence (Eds), *Handbook of Career Theory* (pp. 232–251). Cambridge: Cambridge University Press.

Berlyne, D.E. (1960). *Conflict, Arousal, and Curiosity*. New York: McGraw-Hill.

Breaugh, J.A. (1985). The measurement of work autonomy. *Human Relations*, **38**, 551–570.

Brehm, J.W. (1996). *A Theory of Psychological Reactance*. New York: Academic Press.

Brief, A.P., Burke, M.J., George, J.M., Robinson, B.S. & Webster, J. (1988). Should negative affectivity remain an unmeasured variable in the study of job stress? *Journal of Applied Psychology*, **73**, 193–199.

Broadbent, D.E. (1985). The clinical impact of job design. *British Journal of Clinical Psychology*, **24**, 33–44.

Bromet, E.J., Dew, M.A., Parkinson, D.K. & Schulberg, H.C. (1988). Predictive effects of occupational and marital stress on the mental health of a male workforce. *Journal of Organizational Behavior*, **9**, 1–13.

Bunce, D. (1997). What factors are associated with the outcome of individual-focused worksite stress management interventions? *Journal of Occupational and Organizational Psychology*, **70**, 1–17.

Burger, J.M. (1989). Negative reactions to increases in perceived personal control. *Journal of Personality and Social Psychology*, **56**, 246–256.

Campbell, D.J. (1988). Task complexity: A review and analysis. *Academy of Management Review*, **13**, 40–52.

Campbell, D.J. (1991). Goal levels, complex tasks, and strategy development: A review and analysis. *Human Performance*, **4**, 1–31.

Campbell, D.J. & Gingrich, K.F. (1986). The interactive effects of task complexity and participation on task performance: A field experiment. *Organizational Behavior and Human Decision Processes*, **38**, 162–180.

Carayon, P. (1993a). A longitudinal test of Karasek's Job Strain model among office workers. *Work and Stress*, **7**, 299–314.

Carayon, P. (1993b). Job design and job stress in office workers. *Ergonomics*, **36**, 463–477.

Chapman, A., Mandryk, J.A., Frommer, M.S., Edye, B.V. & Ferguson, D.A. (1990). Chronic perceived work stress and blood pressure among Australian government employees. *Scandinavian Journal of Work, Environment, and Health*, **16**, 258–269.

Chesney, A.A. & Locke, E.A. (1991). Relationships among goal difficulty, business strategies, and performance on a complex management simulation task. *Academy of Management Journal*, **34**, 400–424.

Cohen, J. & Cohen, P. (1983). *Applied Multiple Regression for the Behavioral Sciences*, New York: Erlbaum.

Cohen, S. & Edwards, J.R. (1989). Personality characteristics as moderators of the relationship between stress and disorder. In R.W.J. Neufeld (Ed.), *Advances in the Investigation of Psychological Stress* (pp. 235–283). New York: Wiley.

Cohen, S. & Wills, T.A. (1985). Stress, social support, and the buffering hypothesis. *Psychological Bulletin*, **98**, 310–357.

Cotton, J.L. (1995). Participation's effect on performance and satisfaction: A reconsideration of Wagner. *Academy of Management Review*, **20**, 276–278.

Daft, R.L. & Macintosh, N.B. (1981). A tentative exploration into the amount and equivocality of information processing in organizational work units. *Administrative Science Quarterly*, **26**, 207–224.

Daniels, K. & Guppy, A. (1994). Occupational stress, social support, job control, and psychological well-being. *Human Relations*, **47**, 1523–1544.

Dwyer, D.J. & Ganster, D.C. (1991). The effects of job demands and control on employee attendance and satisfaction. *Journal of Organizational Behavior*, **12**, 595–608.

Earley, P.C. (1985). Influence of information, choice, and task complexity upon goal acceptance, performance, and personal goals. *Journal of Applied Psychology*, **70**, 481–491.

Earley, P.C. (1986). Supervisors and shop stewards as sources of contextual information in goal setting: A comparison of the United States with England. *Journal of Applied Psychology*, **71**, 111–117.

Edwards, J.R. & Cooper, C.L. (1990). The person–environment fit approach to stress: Recurring problems and some suggested solutions. *Journal of Organizational Behavior*, **11**, 293–307.

Evans, B.K. & Fischer, D.G. (1992). A hierarchical model of participatory decision-making, job autonomy, and perceived control. *Human Relations*, **45**, 1169–1189.

Evans, M.G. (1985). A Monte Carlo study of the effects of correlated method variance in moderated multiple regression analysis. *Organizational Behavior and Human Decision Processes*, **36**, 305–323.

Finney, J.W., Mitchell, R.C., Cronkite, R.C. & Moos, R.H. (1984). Methodological issues in estimating main and interactive effects: Examples for the coping/social support and stress field. *Journal of Health and Social Behavior*, **19**, 23–24.
Fisher, C.D. & Gitelson, R. (1983). A meta-analysis of the correlates of role conflict and ambiguity. *Journal of Applied Psychology*, **68**, 320–333.
Fiske, S.T. & Taylor, S.E. (1991). *Social Cognition*. New York: McGraw-Hill.
Fletcher, B.C. (1991). *Work, Stress, Disease, and Life Expectancy*. Chichester, UK: Wiley.
Fletcher, B.C. & Jones, F. (1993). A refutation of Karasek's demand–discretion model of occupational stress with a range of dependent measures. *Journal of Organizational Behavior*, **14**, 319–330.
Fox, M.L., Dwyer, D.J. & Ganster, D.C. (1993). Effects of stressful job demands and control on physiological and attitudinal outcomes in a hospital setting. *Academy of Management Journal*, **36**, 289–318.
French, J.R.P. & Caplan, R.D. (1972). Organizational stress and individual strain. In A.J. Marrow (Ed.), *The Failure of Success* (pp. 30–68). New York: Amacon.
French, Jr J.R.P., Caplan, R.D. & Van Harrison, R. (1982). *The Mechanisms of Job Stress and Strain*. New York: Wiley.
Frese, M. (1989). Theoretical models of control and health. In S.L. Sauter, J.J. Hurrell & C.L. Cooper (Eds), *Job Control and Worker Health* (pp. 107–128). Chichester, UK: Wiley.
Friedman, M. & Rosenman, R. (1974). *Type A Behaviour and Your Heart*. New York: Knopf.
Ganster, D.C. (1988). Improving measures of work control in occupational stress research. In J.J. Hurrell, L.R. Murphy, S.L. Sauter, & C.L. Cooper (Eds), *Occupational Stress: Issues and Developments in Research* (pp. 88–99). New York: Taylor & Francis.
Ganster, D.C. (1989). Worker control and well-being: A review of research in the workplace. In S.L. Sauter, J.J. Hurrell & C.L. Cooper (Eds), *Job Control and Worker Health* (pp. 3–24). Chichester, UK: Wiley.
Ganster, D.C. & Fusilier, M.R. (1989). Control in the workplace. In C.L. Cooper & I.T. Robertson (Eds), *International Review of Industrial and Organizational Psychology* (Vol. 4, pp. 235–280). Chichester, UK: Wiley.
Gardell, B. (1977). Autonomy and participation at work. *Human Relations*, **30**, 515–533.
Georges, E., Wear, M.L. & Mueller, W.H. (1992). Body fat distribution and job stress in Mexican-American men of Hispanic Health and Nutrition Examination Survey. *American Journal of Human Biology*, **80**, 1368–1371.
Green, K.L. & Johnson, J.V. (1990). The effects of psychosocial work organization on patterns of cigarette smoking among male chemical plant employees. *American Journal of Public Health*, **80**, 1368–1371.
Greenberger, D.B., Porter, G., Miceli, M.P. & Strasser, S. (1991). Responses to inadequate personal control in organizations. *Journal of Social Issues*, **47**, 111–128.
Greenberger, D.B. & Strasser, S. (1986). Development and application of a model of personal control in organizations. *Academy of Management Review*, **11**, 164–177.
Greenberger, D.B. & Strasser, S. (1991). The role of situational and dispositional factors in the enhancement of personal control in organizations. In L.L. Cummings & B.M. Staw (Eds), *Research in Organizational Behavior* (pp. 111–145). Greenwich, CT: JAI Press.
Greenberger, D.B., Strasser, S., Cummings, L.L. & Dunham, R.B. (1989). The impact of personal control on performance and satisfaction. *Organizational Behavior and Human Decision Processes*, **43**, 29–51.

Hackman, J.R. & Oldham, G.R. (1976). Motivation through the design of work: Test of a theory. *Organizational Behavior and Human Performance*, **16**, 250–279.
Hammar, N., Alfredsson, L. & Theorell, T.G. (1994). Job characteristics and incidence of myocardial infarction. *International Journal of Epidemiology*, **23**, 277–284.
Hammer, T.H. & Stern, R.N. (1980). Employee ownership: Implications for the organizational distribution of power. *Academy of Management Journal*, **23**, 78–100.
Hesketh, B. & Shouksmith, G. (1986). Job and non-job activities, job satisfaction, and mental health among veterinarians. *Journal of Occupational Behavior*, **7**, 325–339.
Hurrell, J.J. & Lindström, K. (1992). Comparison of job demands, control, and psychosomatic complaints at different career stages of managers in Finland and the United States. *Scandinavian Journal of Work, Environment, and Health*, **18**, 11–13.
Hurrell, J.J. & McLaney, M.A. (1989). Control, job demands, and job satisfaction. In S.L. Sauter, J.J. Hurrell, & C.L. Cooper (Eds), *Job Control and Worker Health* (pp. 97–103). Chichester, UK: Wiley.
Jackson, S.E. (1989). Does job control control job stress? In S.L. Sauter, J.J. Hurrell, & C.L. Cooper (Eds), *Job Control and Worker Health* (pp. 25–53). Chichester, UK: Wiley.
Jackson, P.R., Wall, T.D., Martin, R. & Davids, K. (1993). New measures of job control, cognitive demand, and production responsibility. *Journal of Applied Psychology*, **78**, 753–762.
Janis, I.L. (1958). *Psychological Stress*. New York: Wiley.
Jimmieson, N.L. & Terry, D.J. (1993). The effects of prediction, understanding, and control: A test of the stress antidote model. *Anxiety, Stress, and Coping*, **6**, 179–199.
Jimmieson, N.L. & Terry, D.J. (1997). Responses to an in-basket activity: The role of work stress, behavioral control, and informational control. *Journal of Occupational Health Psychology*, **2**, 72–83.
Jimmieson, N.L. & Terry, D.J. (1998). An experimental study of the effects of work stress, work control, and task information on adjustment. *Applied Psychology: An International Review*, **47**, 343–369.
Jimmieson, N.L. & Terry, D.J. (in press). The moderating role of task characteristics in determining responses to a stressful work simulation. *Journal of Organizational Behavior*.
Johansson, G., Aronsson, G. & Lindstrom, B.O. (1978). Social psychological and neuroendocrine reactions in highly mechanized work. *Ergonomics*, **21**, 583–589.
Johnson, J.V. (1986). The impact of workplace social support, job demands, and work control upon cardiovascular disease in Sweden. In *Division of Environmental and Organisational Psychology Research Report* (Vol. 1). Stockholm: University of Stockholm.
Johnson, J.V. & Hall, E.M. (1988). Job strain, work place social support, and cardiovascular disease: A cross-sectional study of a random sample of the Swedish working population. *American Journal of Public Health*, **78**, 1336–1342.
Karasek, R.A. (1979). Job demands, job decision latitude, and mental strain: Implications for job redesign. *Administrative Science Quarterly*, **24**, 285–308.
Karasek, R.A., Russell, R. & Theorell, T.G. (1982). Physiology of stress and regeneration in job related cardiovascular illness. *Journal of Human Stress*, **3**, 29–42.
Karasek, R.A. & Theorell, T.G. (1990). *Healthy Work: Stress, Productivity, and the Reconstruction of Working Life*. New York: Basic Books.
Kasl, S.V. (1989). An epidemiological perspective on the role of control in health. In S.L. Sauter, J.J. Hurrell & C.L. Cooper (Eds), *Job Control and Worker Health* (pp. 161–190). Chichester, UK: Wiley.

Katz, D. & Kahn, R.L. (1978). *The Social Psychology of Organizations*. New York: Wiley.
Katz, R. & Wykes, T. (1985). The psychological difference between temporally predictable and unpredictable stressful events: Evidence for information control theories. *Journal of Personality and Social Psychology*, **48**, 781–790.
Kauppinen-Toropainen, K., Kandolin, I. & Mutanen, P. (1983). Job dissatisfaction and work-related exhaustion in male and female work. *Journal of Occupational Behavior*, **4**, 193–207.
Kernan, M.C., Bruning, N.S. & Miller-Guhde, L. (1994). Individual and group performance: Effects of task complexity and information. *Human Performance*, **7**, 273–289.
Kohn, M.L. & Schooler, C. (1978). The reciprocal effects of the substantive complexity of work and intellectual flexibility: A longitudinal assessment. *American Journal of Sociology*, **84**, 24–52.
Kohn, M.L. & Schooler, C. (1979). The reciprocal effects of the substantive complexity of work and intellectual flexibility: A longitudinal assessment. In M.W. Riley (Ed.), *Aging from Birth to Death: Interdisciplinary Perspectives* (pp. 47–75). Boulder, CO: Westview Press.
Kristensen, T.S. (1995). The demand–control–support model: Methodological challenges for future research. *Stress Medicine*, **11**, 17–26.
Kushnir, T. & Melamed, S. (1991). Work-load, perceived control, and psychological distress in Type A/B industrial workers. *Journal of Organizational Behavior*, **12**, 155–168.
LaCroix, A.Z. & Haynes, S.G. (1987). Gender differences in the stressfulness of workplace roles: A focus on work and health. In R.C. Barnett, G.K. Baruch, & L. Biener (Eds), *Gender and Stress* (pp. 96–121). New York: Free Press.
Landsbergis, P.A. (1988). Occupational stress among health care workers: A test of the job demands–control model. *Journal of Organizational Behavior*, **9**, 217–239.
Landsbergis, P.A., Schnall, P.L., Deitz, D., Friedman, R. & Pickering, T. (1992). The patterning of psychological attributes and distress by 'job strain' and social support in a sample of working men. *Journal of Behavioral Medicine*, **15**, 379–405.
Lazarus, R.S. (1991). Psychological stress in the workplaces. *Journal of Social Behavior and Personality*, **6**(7), 1–13.
Lazarus, R.S. & Folkman, S. (1984). *Stress Appraisal, and Coping*, New York: Springer-Verlag.
Light, K.C., Turner, J.R. & Hinderli, A.L. (1992). Job strain and ambulatory work blood pressure in healthy young men and women. *Hypertension*, **20**, 214–218.
Locke, E.A. & Schweiger, D.M. (1979). Participation in decision-making: One more look. In B. Staw (Ed.), *Research in Organizational Behavior* (pp. 265–339). Greenwich, CT: JAI Press.
Lubinski, D. & Humphreys, L.G. (1990). Assessing spurious 'moderator effects': Illustrated substantively with the hypothesized ('synergistic') relation between spatial and mathematical ability. *Psychological Bulletin*, **107**, 385–393.
Lykken, D.T. (1962). Perception in the rat: Autonomic response to shock as a function of length of warning interval. *Science*, **137**, 665–666.
Marino, K.E. & White, S.E. (1985). Departmental structure, locus of control, and job stress: The effect of a moderator. *Journal of Applied Psychology*, **45**, 168–175.
Marshall, N.L., Barnett, R.C, Baruch, G.K. & Pleck, J.H. (1991). More than a job: Women and stress in caregiving occupations. In H. Lapata & J. Levy (Eds), *Current Research on Occupations and Professions* (pp. 61–81). Greenwich, CT: JAI Press.

McLaney, M.A. & Hurrell, J.J. (1988). Control, stress, and job satisfaction in Canadian nurses. *Work and Stress*, **2**, 217–224.

Melamed, S., Kushnir, T. & Meir, E.I. (1991). Attenuating the impact of job demands: Additive and interactive effects of perceived control and social support. *Journal of Vocational Behavior*, **39**, 40–53.

Miller, S.M. (1979). Controllability and human stress: Method, evidence, and theory. *Behavior Research and Therapy*, **17**, 287–304.

Moch, M., Cammann, C. & Cooke, R.A. (1983). Organizational structure: Measuring the distribution of influence. In S.E. Seashore, E.E. Lawler, P.H. Mirvis, & C. Cammann (Eds), *Assessing Organisational Change: A Guide to Methods, Measures, and Practices* (pp. 177–201). New York: Wiley.

Moller, L., Kristensen, T.S. & Hollnagel, H. (1991). Social class and cardiovascular risk factors in Danish men. *Scandinavian Journal of Social Medicine*, **19**, 116–126.

Morrison, D.L., Dunne, M.P., Fitzgerald, R. & Cloghan, D. (1992). Job design and levels of physical and mental strain among Australian prison officers. *Work and Stress*, **6**, 13–31.

Mullarkey, S., Jackson, P.R., Wall, T.D., Wilson, J.R. & Grey-Taylor, S.M. (1997). The impact of technology characteristics and job control on worker mental health. *Journal of Organizational Behavior*, **18**, 471–489.

O'Brien, A., Terry, D.J. & Jimmieson, N.L. (1998). Negative affectivity and responses to work stress: An experimental study. Manuscript submitted for publication.

Parkes, K.R. (1989). Personal control in an occupational context. In A. Steptoe & A. Appels (Eds), *Stress, Personal Control, and Health* (pp. 21–47). Chichester, UK: Wiley.

Parkes, K.R. (1990). Coping, negative affect and the work environment: Additive and interactive predictors of mental health. *Journal of Applied Psychology*, **75**, 399–409.

Parkes, K.R. (1991). Locus of control as moderator: An explanation for additive versus interactive findings in the demand–discretion model of work stress? *British Journal of Psychology*, **82**, 291–312.

Parkes, K.R., Mendham, C.A. & von Rabenau, C. (1994). Social support and the demand–discretion model of job stress: Tests of additive and interactive effects in two samples. *Journal of Vocational Behavior*, **44**, 91–113.

Payne, R.L. (1979). Demands, supports, constraints, and psychological health. In C.J. Mackay & T. Cox (Eds), *Response to Stress: Occupational Aspects* (pp. 85–105). London: International Publishing Corporation.

Payne, R.L. & Fletcher, B.C. (1983). Job demands, supports, and constraints as predictors of psychological strain among schoolteachers. *Journal of Vocational Behavior*, **22**, 136–147.

Pearce, J.L. (1981). Bringing some clarity to role ambiguity research. *Academy of Management Review*, **6**, 665–674.

Perkins, C.C. Jr (1968). An analysis of the concept of reinforcement. *Psychological Review*, **75**, 155–172.

Perrewe, P.L. & Anthony, W.P. (1990). Stress in a steel pipe mill: The impact of job demands, personal control, and employee age on somatic complaints. *Journal of Social Behavior and Personality*, **5**, 77–90.

Perrewe, P.L. & Ganster, D.C. (1989). The impact of job demands and behavioral control on experienced job stress. *Journal of Organizational Behavior*, **10**, 213–229.

Pieper, C.F., LaCroix, A.Z. & Karasek, R.A. (1989). The relation of psychosocial dimensions of work with coronary heart disease risk factors: A meta analysis of five United States data bases. *American Journal of Epidemiology*, **129**, 483–494.

Reed, D.M., LaCroix, A.Z., Karasek, R.A., Miller, D.W. & MacLean, C.A. (1989). Occupational strain and the incidence of coronary heart disease. *American Journal of Epidemiology*, **129**, 495–502.

Rodin, J., Reenert, K. & Solomon, S.K. (1980). Intrinsic motivation for control: Fact or fiction? In A. Baum, J.E. Singer & S. Valins (Eds), *Advances in Environmental Psychology*, 2, Hillsdale, NJ: Erlbaum.

Rosenfield, S. (1989). The effects of women's employment: Personal control and sex differences in mental health. *Journal of Health and Social Behavior*, **30**, 77–91.

Rothbaum, F., Weisz, J.R. & Snyder, S.S. (1982). Changing the world and changing the self: A two-process model of perceived control. *Journal of Personality and Social Psychology*, **42**, 5–37.

Sagie, A. (1995). Employee participation and work outcomes: An end to the dispute? *Academy of Management Review*, **20**, 278–280.

Sargent, L.D. & Terry, D.J. (in press). The effects of work control and job demands on employee adjustment and work performance. *Journal of Occupational and Organizational Psychology*.

Sargent, L.D. & Terry, D.J. (1998). The moderating role of social support in Karasek's job strain model. Manuscript submitted for publication.

Sauter, S.L. (1989). Moderating effects of job control on health complaints in office work. In S.L. Sauter, J.J. Hurrell & C.L. Cooper (Eds), *Job Control and Worker Health* (pp. 91–103). Chichester, UK: Wiley.

Schaubroeck, J. & Merritt, D.E. (1997). Divergent effects of job control on coping with work stressors: The key role of self-efficacy. *Academy of Management Journal*, **40**, 738–754.

Schnall, P.L., Landsbergis, P.A. & Baker, D.B. (1994). Job strain and cardiovascular disease. *Annual Review of Public Health*, **15**, 381–411.

Schnall, P.L., Schwartz, J.E., Landsbergis, P.A., Warren, K. & Pickering, T. (1992). The relationship between job strain, alcohol, and ambulatory blood pressure. *Hypertension*, **19**, 488–494.

Schwartz, J.E., Pieper, C.F. & Karasek, R.A. (1988). A procedure for linking psychosocial job characteristics data to health surveys. *American Journal of Public Health*, **78**, 904–909.

Seligman, M.E.P. (1968). Chronic fear produced by unpredictable electric shock. *Journal of Comparative Physiological Psychology*, **66**, 402–411.

Seligman, M.E.P. (1975). *Helplessness: On Depression, Development, and Death*. New York: Freeman.

Skinner, E.A. (1996). A guide to constructs of control. *Journal of Personality and Social Psychology*, **71**, 549–570.

Smith, C.S., Tisak, J., Hahn, S.E. & Schmieder, R.A. (1997). The measurement of job control. *Journal of Organisational Behavior*, **18**, 225–237.

Smith, R.E., Smoll, F.L. & Ptacek, J.T. (1990). Conjunctive moderator variables in vulnerability and resiliency research: Life stress, social support and coping skills, and adolescent sports injuries. *Journal of Personality and Social Psychology*, **58**, 360–369.

Söderfeldt, B., Söderfeldt, M., Muntaner, C., O'Campo, P., Warg, L. & Ohlson, C. (1996). Psychosocial work environment in human service organizations: A conceptual analysis and development of the demand–control model. *Social Science Medicine*, **42**, 1217–1226.

Spector, P.E. (1987). Interactive effects of perceived control and job stressors on affective reactions and health outcomes for clerical workers. *Work and Stress*, **1**, 155–162.

Spector, P.E. (1992). A consideration of the validity and means of self-report measures of job conditions. In C.L. Cooper & I.T. Robertson (Eds), *International Review of Industrial and Organizational Psychology* (Vol. 7, pp. 123–151). Chichester, UK: Wiley.

Spector, P.E. & Brannick, M.T. (1995). The nature and effects of method variance in organizational research. In C.L. Cooper & I.T. Robertson (Eds), *International Review of Industrial and Organizational Psychology* (Vol. 10, pp. 249–274). Chichester, UK: Wiley.

Spreitzer, G.M. (1995a). Psychological empowerment in the workplace: Dimensions, measurement, and validation. *Academy of Management Journal*, **38**, 1442–1465.

Spreitzer, G.M. (1995b). An empirical test of a comprehensive model of interpersonal empowerment in the workplace. *American Journal of Community Psychology*, **23**, 601–629.

Spreitzer, G.M. (1996). Social structural characteristics of psychological empowerment. *Academy of Management Journal*, **39**, 483–504.

Stansfeld, S.A., North, F.M., White, I. & Marmot, M.G. (1995). Work characteristics and psychiatric disorder in civil servants in London. *Journal of Epidemiology and Community Health*, **49**, 48–53.

Staw, B.M. (1977). Motivation in organizations: Toward synthesis and redirection. In B.M. Staw & G.R. Salancik (Eds), *New Directions in Organizational Behavior* (pp. 55–95). Chicago, IL: St Clair Press.

Staw, B.M. (1986). Beyond the control graph: Steps toward a model of perceived control in organizations. In R.N. Stern & S. McCarthy (Eds), *The Organizational Practice of Democracy* (pp. 305–321). Chichester, UK: Wiley.

Steptoe, A. (1989). Psychophysiological mechanisms relating control, coping and health. In S.L. Sauter, J.J. Hurrell, & C.L. Cooper (Eds), *Job Control and Worker Health* (pp. 191–203). Chichester, UK: Wiley.

Sutton, R.I. & Kahn, R.L. (1986). Prediction, understanding, and control as antidotes to organizational stress. In J. Lorsch (Ed.), *Handbook of Organizational Behavior* (pp. 272–285). Englewood Cliffs, NJ: Prentice-Hall.

Tannenbaum, A.S. (1962). Control in organizations: Individual adjustment and organizational performances. *Administrative Science Quarterly*, **1**, 236–257.

Tannenbaum, A.S. (1968). *Control in Organizations*. New York: McGraw-Hill.

Tannenbaum, A.S. & Cooke, R.A. (1979). Organizational control: A review of studies employing the control graph method. In C.J. Lammers & D.C. Hickson (Eds), *Organizations Alike and Unlike* (pp. 183–210). London: Routledge & Kegan Paul.

Tannenbaum, A.S., Kavcic, B., Rosner, M., Vianello, M. & Weiser, G. (1974). *Hierarchy in Organizations*. San Francisco, CA: Jossey-Bass.

Terry, D.J. (1994). The determinants of coping: The role of stable and situational factors. *Journal of Personality and Social Psychology*, **66**, 895–910.

Terry, D.J., Callan, V.J. & Sartori, G. (1996). A test of a stress-coping model of adjustment to a large-scale organizational change. *Stress Medicine*, **2**, 105–120.

Terry, D.J., Nielsen, J. & Perchard, L. (1993). Effects of work stress on psychological well-being and job satisfaction: The stress buffering role of social support. *Australian Journal of Psychology*, **45**, 168–175.

Terry, D.J., Rawle, & Callan, V.J. (1995). The effects of social support on adjustment: The mediating role of coping. *Personal Relationships*, **3**, 97–124.

Terry, D.J., Tonge, L. & Callan, V.J. (1995). Employee adjustment to stress: The role of coping resources, situational factors, and coping responses. *Anxiety, Stress, and Coping*, **8**, 1–24.

Tetrick, L.E. & LaRocco, J.M. (1987). Understanding, prediction, and control as moderators of the relationships between perceived stress, satisfaction, and psychological well-being. *Journal of Applied Psychology*, **72**, 538–543.

Theorell, T.G., Alfredsson, L., Knox, S., Perski, A., Svensson, J. & Wallers, D. (1984). On the interplay between socio-economic factors, personality, and work environment in the pathogenesis of cardiovascular disease. *Scandinavian Journal of Work, Environment, and Health*, **10**, 373–380.

Theorell, T.G., deFaire, U., Johnson, J., Hall, E.M., Perski, A. & Stewart (1991). Job strain and ambulatory blood pressure profiles. *Scandinavian Journal of Work Environmental Health*, **17**, 380–385.

Theorell, T.G., Hjemdahl, F., Ericsson, F., Kallner, A., Knox, S., Perski, A., Svensson, J., Tidgren, B. & Wallers, D. (1985). Psychosocial and physiological factors in relation to blood pressure at rest: A study of Swedish men in their upper twenties. *Journal of Hypertension*, **3**, 591–600.

Theorell, T.G. & Karasek, R.A. (1996). Current issues relating psychosocial job strain and cardiovascular disease research. *Journal of Occupational Health Psychology*, **1**, 9–26.

Theorell, T.G., Perski, A., Orth-Gomer, K., Hamsten, A. & deFaire, U. (1991). The effects of the strain of returning to work on the risk of cardiac death after a first myocardial infarction before age 45. *International Journal of Cardiology*, **30**, 61–67.

Thompson, S.C. (1981). Will it hurt less if I can control it? A complex answer to a simple question. *Psychological Bulletin*, **90**, 89–101.

Van Egeren, L.F. (1992). The relationship between job strain and blood pressure at work, at home, and during sleep. *Psychosomatic Medicine*, **54**, 337–343.

Von Glinow, M.A. & Teagarden, M.B. (1988). The transfer of human resource management technology in Sino-US cooperative ventures: Problems and solutions. *Human Resource Management*, **27**, 201–229.

Wagner, J.A. (1994). Participation's effects on performance and satisfaction: A reconsideration of research evidence. *Academy of Management Review*, **19**, 312–330.

Wall, T.D., Corbett, J.M., Clegg, C.W., Jackson, P.R. & Martin, R. (1990). Advanced manufacturing technology and work design: Towards a theoretical framework. *Journal of Organizational Behavior*, **11**, 201–219.

Wall, T.D., Jackson, P.R. & Mullarkey, S. (1995). Further evidence on some new measures of job control, cognitive demand, and production responsibility. *Journal of Organizational Behavior*, **16**, 431–455.

Wall, T.D., Jackson, P.R., Mullarkey, S. & Parker, S.K. (1996). The demands–control model of job strain: A more specific test. *Journal of Occupational and Organizational Psychology*, **69**, 153–166.

Wall, T.D. & Martin, R. (1994). Job and work design. In C.L. Cooper & I.T. Robertson (Eds), *Key Reviews in Managerial Psychology* (pp. 158–188). Chichester, UK: Wiley.

Warr, P.B. (1987). *Work, Unemployment, and Mental Health*. Oxford: Oxford University Press.

Warr, P.B. (1990). Decision latitude, job demands, and employee well-being. *Work and Stress*, **4**, 285–294.

Warr, P.B. (1990). Decision latitude, job demands, and employee well-being. *Work and Stress*, **4**, 285–294.
Westman, M. (1992). Moderating effect of decision latitude on stress–strain relationship: Does organizational level matter? *Journal of Organizational Behavior*, **13**, 713–722.
White, R.W. (1959). Motivation reconsidered: The concept of competence. *Psychological Review*, **66**, 297–333.
Wood, R.E. (1986). Task complexity: Definition of the construct. *Organizational Behavior and Human Decision Processes*, **37**, 60–82.
Wortman, C. & Brehm, J.C. (1975). Responses to uncontrollable outcomes: An integration of reactance theory and the learned helplessness model. In L. Berkowitz (Ed.), *Advances in Experimental Social Psychology* (pp. 278–336). New York: Academic Press.
Xie, J.L. (1995). Research on Chinese organizational behavior and human resource management: Conceptual and methodological considerations. In S.B. Prasad (Ed.), *Advances in International Comparative Management* (pp. 15–42). Greenwich, CT: JAI Press.
Xie, J.L. (1996). Karasek's model in the people's Republic of China: Effects of job demands, control, and individual differences. *Academy of Management Journal*, **39**, 1594–1618.
Zapf, D., Dormann, C. & Frese, M. (1996). Longitudinal studies in organizational stress research: A review of the literature with reference to methodological issues. *Journal of Occupational Health Psychology*, **1**, 145–169.

47

ORGANIZATIONAL CHANGE AND DEVELOPMENT

Karl E. Weick and Robert E. Quinn

Source: *Annual Review of Psychology* 50 (1999): 361–386.

Abstract

Recent analyses of organizational change suggest a growing concern with the tempo of change, understood as the characteristic rate, rhythm, or pattern of work or activity. Episodic change is contrasted with continuous change on the basis of implied metaphors of organizing, analytic frameworks, ideal organizations, intervention theories, and roles for change agents. Episodic change follows the sequence unfreeze-transition-refreeze, whereas continuous change follows the sequence freeze-rebalance-unfreeze. Conceptualizations of inertia are seen to underlie the choice to view change as episodic or continuous.

Introduction

Analyses of organizational change written since the review by Porras & Silvers (1991) suggest that an important emerging contrast in change research is the distinction between change that is episodic, discontinuous, and intermittent and change that is continuous, evolving, and incremental. This contrast is sufficiently pervasive in recent work and sufficiently central in the conceptualization of change that we use it as the framework that organizes this review.

The contrast between episodic and continuous change reflects differences in the perspective of the observer. From a distance (the macro level of analysis), when observers examine the flow of events that constitute organizing, they see what looks like repetitive action, routine, and inertia dotted with occasional episodes of revolutionary change. But a view from closer in (the micro level of analysis) suggests ongoing adaptation and adjustment. Although these adjustments may be small, they also tend to be frequent and continuous across units, which means they are capable of altering structure and strategy. Some observers (e.g. Orlikowski 1996) treat these ongoing adjustments as the essence of organizational change. Others (e.g. Nadler et al 1995) describe these ongoing adjustments as mere incremental variations on the same theme and lump them together into an epoch of convergence during which interdependencies deepen. Convergence is interrupted sporadically by epochs of divergence described by words like revolution, deep change, and transformation.

We pursue this contrast, first by a brief overview of change as a genre of analysis and then by a more detailed comparison of episodic and continuous change using a framework proposed by Dunphy (1996).

Change as a genre of organizational analysis

The basic tension that underlies many discussions of organizational change is that it would not be necessary if people had done their jobs right in the first place. Planned change is usually triggered by the failure of people to create continuously adaptive organizations (Dunphy 1996). Thus, organizational change routinely occurs in the context of failure of some sort. A typical storyline is "First there were losses, then there was a plan of change, and then there was an implementation, which led to unexpected results" (Czarniawska & Joerges 1996:20).

Representative descriptions of change vary with the level of analysis. At the most general level, "change is a phenomenon of time. It is the way people talk about the event in which something appears to become, or turn into, something else, where the 'something else' is seen as a result or outcome" (Ford & Ford 1994:759). In reference to organizations, change involves difference "in how an organization functions, who its members and leaders are, what form it takes, or how it allocates its resources" (Huber et al 1993:216). From the perspective of organizational development, change is "a set of behavioral science-based theories, values, strategies, and techniques aimed at the planned change of the organizational work setting for the purpose of enhancing individual development and improving organizational performance, through the alteration of organizational members' on-the-job behaviors" (Porras & Robertson 1992:723).

The concepts used to flesh out these definitions have been surprisingly durable over the years. Lewin's (1951) three stages of change—unfreeze, change, and refreeze—continue to be a generic recipe for organizational development. As Hendry (1996) notes, "Scratch any account of creating and managing change and the idea that change is a three-stage process which necessarily begins with a process of unfreezing will not be far below the surface. Indeed it has been said that the whole theory of change is reducible to this one idea of Kurt Lewin's" (p. 624). Lewin's assertion that "you cannot understand a system until you try to change it" (Schein 1996:34) survives in Colville et al's (1993) irony of change: "one rarely fully appreciates or understands a situation until after it has changed" (p. 550). Lewin's concept of resistance to change survives in O'Toole's (1995:159–66) list of 30 causes of resistance to change and in renewed efforts to answer the question, "Just whose view is it that is resisting change?" (Nord & Jermier 1994). The distinction between incremental and radical change first articulated by Watzlawick et al (1974) and Bateson (1972) as the distinction between first-and second-order change continues to guide theory construction and data collection (Roach & Bednar 1997; Bartunek 1993). The rhythms of change (Greiner 1972) continue to be described as periods of convergence marked off from periods of divergence by external jolts (e.g. Bacharach et al 1996). The continuing centrality of these established ideas may suggest a certain torpor in the intellectual life of scholars of change. We think, instead, that this centrality attests to the difficulty of finding patterns when difference is the object of study.

While work within the past 10 years has become theoretically richer and more descriptive, there is a continuing debate about whether change research is developing as a cumulative and falsifiable body of knowledge. Kahn's (1974:487) assessment of organizational change research in the 1970s is cited by Macy & Izumi (1993:237) as a statement that remains relevant: "A few theoretical propositions are repeated without additional data or development; a few bits of homey advice are reiterated without proof or disproof; and a few sturdy empirical observations are quoted with reverence but without refinement or explication." Similar sentiments are found in Woodman (1989), in Golembiewski & Boss (1992), and in the withering popular books on "the change business" titled *The Witch Doctors* (Micklethwait & Wooldridge 1996) and *Dangerous Company* (O'Shea & Madigan 1997). The tone of these critiques is illustrated by the obvious pleasure the authors of *The Witch Doctors* take in their observation that "the reason American businessmen talk about gurus is because they can't spell the word charlatan" (Micklethwait & Wooldridge 1996:11).

Remedies to the above problems are seen to lie in the direction of the following, all coupled with greater efforts to articulate the situated nature of organizational action (e.g. Laurila 1997): (*a*) cross-organizational meta-analysis (e.g. Macy & Izumi 1993), (*b*) cross-organizational interview-surveys (e.g. Huber & Glick 1993), (*c*) simulations that are cross-organizational by virtue of their generality (e.g. Sastry 1997), (*d*) ethnographies (e.g. Katz 1997) and case studies (e.g. Starbuck 1993) that are treated as prototypes, (*e*) reconceptualization of organizational change as institutional change (e.g. Greenwood & Hinings 1996), and (*f*) cross-disciplinary borrowing (e.g. Cheng & Van de Ven 1996). Coupled with efforts to improve the quality of evidence in change research have been parallel efforts to better understand the limitations of inquiry (e.g. Kilduff & Mehra 1997, McKelvey 1997). When these are combined, there appears to be simultaneous improvement of tools and scaling down of the tasks those tools must accomplish.

The sheer sprawl of the change literature is a continuing challenge to investigators who thrive on frameworks (e.g. Mintzberg & Westley 1992). An important recent attempt to impose order on the topic of organizational change is the typology crafted by Van de Ven & Poole (1995). They induced four basic process theories of change, each characterized by a different event sequence and generative mechanism:

1. Life cycle theories have an event sequence of start-up, grow, harvest, terminate, and start-up. They have a generative mechanism of an immanent program or regulation.
2. Teleological theories have an event sequence of envision/set goals, implement goals, dissatisfaction, search/interact, and envision/set goals. They have a generative mechanism of purposeful enactment and social construction.
3. Dialectical theory has an event sequence of thesis/antithesis, conflict, synthesis, and thesis/antithesis. It has a generative mechanism of pluralism, confrontation, and conflict.
4. Evolutionary theory has an event sequence of variation, selection, retention, and variation. It has a generative mechanism of competitive selection and resource scarcity.

These four motors are classified along two dimensions: (*a*) the unit of change, which depicts whether the process focuses on the development of a single organizational entity (life cycle, teleological) or on interactions between two or more entities (evolution, dialectic) and (*b*) the mode of change, which depicts whether the sequence of change events is prescribed by deterministic laws and produces first-order change (life cycle, evolution) or whether the sequence is constructed, emerges as the process unfolds, and generates novel second-order change (dialectic, teleology).

The language of motors is useful because it alerts investigators to missing motors in change theories that aspire to comprehensiveness, it draws attention to mechanisms of interplay among motors and the necessity for balance (Van de Ven & Poole 1995:534), it tempts people to look for a "fifth motor" and other hybrids, and (because the language of motors is a language of process rather than of outcome) it enables investigators to identify what is happening before it has concluded (p. 524). Because the authors propose a detailed list of conditions that must be met if a motor is to operate (Van de Ven & Poole 1995:525, Figure 2), they imply that when change interventions fail, there is a mismatch between the prevailing conditions and the kind of motor activated by the change intervention.

Van de Ven & Poole's review (1995) suggested that mode of change and unit of change were important partitions of the change literature. Our review suggests that tempo of change, defined as "characteristic rate, rhythm, or pattern of work or activity" (Random House 1987:1954), is also a meaningful partition. We explore the contrast between episodic and continuous change by comparing the two forms on five properties that Dunphy (1996:543) suggests are found in any comprehensive theory of change (Table 1). These properties are (*a*) a basic metaphor of the nature of organization; (*b*) an analytical framework to understand the organizational change process; (*c*) an ideal model of an effectively functioning organization that specifies both a direction for change and values to be used in assessing the

Table 1 Comparison of episodic and continuous change

	Episodic change	*Continuous change*
Metaphor of organization	Organizations are inertial and change is infrequent, discontinuous, intentional.	Organizations are emergent and self-organizing, and change is constant, evolving, cumulative.
Analytic framework	Change is an occasional interruption or divergence from equilibrium. It tends to be dramatic and it is driven externally. It is seen as a failure of the organization to adapt its deep structure to a changing environment. Perspective: macro, distant, global. Emphasis: short-run adaptation. Key concepts: inertia, deep structure of interrelated parts, triggering, replacement and substitution, discontinuity, revolution.	Change is a pattern of endless modifications in work processes and social practice. It is driven by organizational instability and alert reactions to daily contingencies. Numerous small accommodations cumulate and amplify. Perspective: micro, close, local. Emphasis: long-run adaptability. Key concepts: recurrent interactions, shifting task authority, response repertoires, emergent patterns, improvisation, translation, learning.
Ideal organization	The ideal organization is capable of continuous adaptation.	The ideal organization is capable of continuous adaptation.
Intervention theory	The necessary change is created by intention. Change is Lewinian: inertial, linear, progressive, goal seeking, motivated by disequilibrium, and requires outsider intervention. 1. Unfreeze: disconfirmation of expectations, learning anxiety, provision of psychological safety. 2. Transition: cognitive restructuring, semantic redefinition, conceptual enlargement, new standards of judgment. 3. Refreeze: create supportive social norms, make change congruent with personality.	The change is a redirection of what is already under way. Change is Confucian: cyclical, processional, without an end state, equilibrium seeking, eternal. 1. Freeze: make sequences visible and show patterns through maps, schemas, and stories. 2. Rebalance: reinterpret, relabel, resequence the patterns to reduce blocks. Use logic of attraction. 3. Unfreeze: resume improvisation, translation, and learning in ways that are more mindful.
Role of change agent	Role: prime mover who creates change. Process: focuses on inertia and seeks points of central leverage. Changes meaning systems: speaks differently, communicates alternative schema, reinterprets revolutionary triggers, influences punctuation, builds coordination and commitment.	Role: Sense maker who redirects change. Process: recognizes, makes salient, and reframes current patterns, Shows how intentional change can be made at the margins. Alters meaning by new language, enriched dialogue, and new identity. Unblocks improvisation, translation, and learning.

success of the change intervention (e.g. survival, growth, integrity); (*d*) an intervention theory that specifies when, where, and how to move the organization closer to the ideal; and (*e*) a definition of the role of change agent. Because we are building a composite picture using portions of work that may have been designed to answer other questions, readers should treat our placement of specific studies as evocative rather than definitive.

Episodic change

The phrase "episodic change" is used to group together organizational changes that tend to be infrequent, discontinuous, and intentional. The presumption is that episodic change occurs during periods of divergence when organizations are moving away from their equilibrium conditions. Divergence is the result of a growing misalignment between an inertial deep structure and perceived environmental demands. This form of change is labeled "episodic" because it tends to occur in distinct periods during which shifts are precipitated by external events such as technology change or internal events such as change in key personnel.

Basic metaphors: organizing for episodic change

The metaphor of organization implied by conceptualizations of episodic change is of a social entity that combines the following characteristics: dense, tightly coupled interdependencies among subunits; efficiency as a core value; a preoccupation with short-run adaptation rather than long-run adaptability; constraints on action in the form of the invisible hand of institutionalization; powerful norms embedded in strong subcultures; and imitation as a major motivation for change. The importance of interdependencies as a precondition for episodic change is found in discussions of alignment (e.g. Pfeffer 1998:Ch. 4), configurations (e.g. Miller 1990), and cultural inertia (e.g. Tushman & O'Reilly 1996). The importance of imitation is reflected in Sevon's (1996) statement that "every theory of organizational change must take into account the fact that leaders of organizations watch one another and adopt what they perceive as successful strategies for growth and organizational structure" (pp. 60–61).

Images of organization that are compatible with episodic change include those built around the ideas of punctuated equilibria, the edge of chaos, and second-order change. The image of an organization built around the idea of a punctuated equilibrium (Tushman & Romanelli 1985) depicts organizations as sets of interdependencies that converge and tighten during a period of relative equilibrium, often at the expense of continued adaptation to environmental changes. As adaptation lags, effectiveness decreases, pressures for change increase, and a revolutionary period is entered. As these pressures continue to increase, they may result in an episode of fundamental change in activity patterns and personnel, which then becomes the basis for a new equilibrium period. Apple Computer illustrated a series of discontinuous changes in strategy, structure, and culture as it moved from the leadership of Steve Jobs through that of John Sculley, Michael Sprindler, Gil Amelio, and back to Jobs (Tushman & O'Reilly 1996). Romanelli & Tushman (1994) found this pattern of discontinuous episodic change when they examined changes in the activity domains of strategy, structure, and power distribution for 25 minicomputer producers founded between 1967 and 1969. Changes in these three domains were clustered, as would be predicted from a punctuated change model, rather than dispersed, as would be predicted from a model of incremental changes that accumulate.

The image of an organization built around the idea of operating at "the edge of chaos" (McDaniel 1997, Stacey 1995) depicts the organization as a set of simple elements tied together by complex relationships involving nonlinear feedback (Arthur 1995). An important property of nonlinear systems is bounded instability or what is referred to as the edge of chaos. Here a system has developed both negative and positive feedback loops and is hence simultaneously capable of stability and instability. Behavior at the edge of chaos is paradoxical because the system moves autonomously back and forth between stability and instability. Applied to organizations, Cheng & Van de Ven (1996), for example, show that biomedical innovation processes are nonlinear systems that move episodically from stages of chaos to greater order within a larger context containing random processes. Browning et al (1995) show how the unprecedented successful alliance called Sematech emerged from a set of small, discrete events that occurred at a point of irreversible disequilibrium when the entire US semiconductor industry was about to collapse.

The image of an organization built around the idea of second-order change in frames of reference depicts the organization as a site where shared beliefs operate in the service of coordinated action (Langfield-Smith 1992, Bougon 1992). These shared frames of reference may be "bent" when first-order changes produce minor alterations in current beliefs or "broken" when second-order changes replace one belief system with another (Dunbar et al 1996). First-order change is illustrated by a shift of culture at British Rail from a production-led bureaucracy to a market-led bureaucracy (the firm remained a top-down bureaucracy). Second-order change is illustrated by the later culture shift at British Rail from a market-led bureaucracy to a network-partnership culture in which power was distributed rather than concentrated (Bate 1990). Second-order change is episodic change and "refers to changes in cognitive frameworks underlying the organization's activities, changes in the deep structure or shared schemata that generate and give meaning to these activities" (Bartunek & Moch 1994:24). Recently, it has been proposed that there exists a third order of change that basically questions the adequacy of schemas themselves and argues for direct exposure to the "ground for conceptual understanding" in the form of music, painting, dance, poetry, or mystical experience. Organizational change thus gains intellectual power through alignment with aesthetics (e.g. Sandelands 1998). Examples of third-order change are found in the work of Torbert (1994), Nielsen & Bartunek (1996), Mirvis (1997), Olson (1990), and Austin (1997).

In each of these three images, organizational action builds toward an episode of change when preexisting interdependencies, patterns of feedback, or mindsets produce inertia.

Analytic framework: the episodic change process

Episodic change tends to be infrequent, slower because of its wide scope, less complete because it is seldom fully implemented, more strategic in its content, more deliberate and formal than emergent change, more disruptive because programs are replaced rather than altered, and initiated at higher levels in the organization (Mintzberg & Westley 1992). The time interval between episodes of discontinuous change is determined by the amount of time organizations expend in other stages of organizational development. If, for example, the stages of organizational change are labeled development, stability, adaptation, struggle, and revolution (Mintzberg & Westley 1992), then episodic change is contemplated when adaptation begins to lag. It takes provisional form as organizations struggle to confront problems and experiment with solutions, and it produces actual shifts in systems during the stage of revolution. The frequency of revolutions and episodic change depends on the time spent in the four prior stages, which varies enormously. This temporal variation in processes building up to revolution is the reason why this form of change is best described as episodic, aperiodic, infrequent.

Three important processes in this depiction of episodes are inertia, the triggering of change, and replacement. Inertia, defined as an "inability for organizations to change as rapidly as the environment" (Pfeffer 1997:163), takes a variety of forms. Whether the inability is attributed to deep structure (Gersick 1991), first-order change (Bartunek 1993), routines (Gioia 1992), success-induced blind spots (Miller 1993), top management tenure (Virany et al 1992), identity maintenance (Sevon 1996), culture (Harrison & Carroll 1991), complacency (Kotter 1996), or technology (Tushman & Rosenkopf 1992), inertia is a central feature of the analytic framework associated with episodic change. Romanelli & Tushman (1994) are representative when they argue that it takes a revolution to alter "a system of interrelated organizational parts that is maintained by mutual dependencies among the parts and with competitive, regulatory, and technological systems outside the organization that reinforce the legitimacy of managerial choices that produced the parts" (p. 1144). Because interrelations are dense and tight, it takes larger interventions to realign them. An example of processes of inertia is Miller's research (1993, 1994) demonstrating that inertia is often the unintended consequence of successful performance. Successful organizations discard practices, people, and structures regarded as peripheral to success and grow more inattentive to signals that suggest the need for change, more insular and sluggish in adaptation, and more immoderate in their processes, tending toward extremes of risk-taking or conservatism. These changes simplify the organization, sacrifice adaptability, and increase inertia.

Although inertia creates the tension that precedes episodic change, the actual triggers of change come from at least five sources: the environment, performance, characteristics of top managers, structure, and strategy (Huber et al 1993). Huber et al found that all five were associated with internal and external changes, but in ways specific to the kind of change being examined (ten specific changes were measured; see Huber et al 1993:223). For example, consistent with Romanelli & Tushman's data, Huber et al found that downturns in growth (a potential revolutionary period) were positively related to externally focused changes and to changes in organizational form. Interestingly, upturns in growth were also positively related to externally focused changes, a finding interpreted to suggest that "desirable but risky changes might be held in abeyance until performance improves" (Huber et al 1993:230).

A final property of the analytic framework associated with episodic change is that it often assumes that change occurs through replacement (Ford & Backoff 1988, Ford & Ford 1994). The idea of replacement is that "one entity sequentially takes the place of or substitutes for a second. The first identity does not *become* the second but is substituted for it. ... [T]he change process becomes a sequence of events in which a person (a) determines or defines what currently exists (what is A), (b) determines or defines its replacement (Not-A), (c) engages in action to remove what is currently there, and (d) implants its replacement" (Ford & Ford 1994:773, 775). Beer et al (1990) demonstrate that replacement of one program with another seldom works. The problem with such a logic is that it restricts change to either-or thinking. The only way to prevent A is to apply its reciprocal or a counterbalance or its opposite, which precludes the possible diagnosis that both A and not-A may be the problem. For example, authoritarian decision making may be counterbalanced by mandating that decisions be made at lower levels (Roach & Bednar 1997). However, this change is simply authoritarian decision-abdication, which means that authoritarian control from the top persists. As lower-level managers try harder to guess what the right decisions are (i.e. those decisions top management would have made) and err in doing so, the mandate is reaffirmed more forcefully, which worsens performance even more and creates a vicious circle. What was really intended was the creation of expectations of individual autonomy that allowed decisions to be made at the level where the expertise and information are lodged.

In conclusion, the basic analytical framework involving episodic change assumes in part that inertia is a force to contend with. When inertia builds, some trigger usually precipitates an episode of replacement. To understand episodic change is to think carefully about inertia, triggers, and replacements.

Ideal episodic organizations

There is no one "ideal model of an effectively functioning organization" that suggests directions for episodic change and values to be used in judging the success of an episodic change intervention (e.g. survival, growth). This is so for the simple reason that episodic change is a generic description applicable across diverse organizational forms and values. There is no direct parallel in the case of episodic change for Dunphy's (1996) assertion that the ideal model of an effectively functioning sociotechnical system is "a representative democratic community composed of semi-autonomous work groups with the ability to learn continuously through participative action research" (p. 543). If organizational change generally occurs in the context of failures to adapt, then the ideal organization is one that continuously adapts. And this holds true whether the focus is episodic or continuous change. The ideal in both cases would resemble the successful self-organizing firms that Brown & Eisenhardt (1997) found in the computer industry. Successful firms did not rely on either a purely mechanistic or purely organic process and structure. Instead, successful firms had well-defined managerial responsibilities and clear project priorities while also allowing the design processes to be highly flexible, improvisational, and continuously changing. Successful firms also had richly connected communication systems, including informal and electronic grapevines, and a very high value on cross-project communication. Two important features that encouraged both episodic and continuous change were (*a*) semi structures poised between order and disorder with only some features being prescribed and (*b*) intentional links in time between present projects and future probes to reduce discontinuity and preserve direction. The authors interpret this pattern as an instance of bounded instability and argue that it may be more motivating, more attuned to sense-making in a fast-changing environment, and more flexible (as a result of capabilities for improvisation) than patterns that are pure instances of either mechanistic or organic systems.

A more generic ideal, suited for both episodic and continuous-change interventions, is found in Burgelman's (1991) attempt to show how organizations adapt by a mixture of continuous strategic initiatives that are within the scope of the current strategy (induced processes) and additional episodic initiatives that are outside the current strategy (autonomous processes). An ideal model framed more in terms of management practices is Pfeffer's (1998) description of seven "high performance management practices" that produce innovation and productivity, are difficult to copy, and lead to sustained profitability. These practices are employment security, selective hiring, self-managed teams and decentralization, extensive training, reduction of status differences, sharing of information, and high and contingent compensation.

Intervention theory in episodic change

Episodic change tends to be dramatic change, as Lewin made clear: "To break open the shell of complacency and self-righteousness it is sometimes necessary to bring about deliberately an emotional stir-up" (Lewin 1951, quoted in Marshak 1993:400). While strong emotions may provide "major sources of energy for revolutionary change" (Gersick 1991), they may also constrain cognition and performance in ways analogous to those of stress (Barr & Huff 1997, Driskell & Salas 1996).

Because episodic change requires both equilibrium breaking and transitioning to a newly created equilibrium, it is most closely associated with planned, intentional change. Intentional change occurs when "a change agent deliberately and consciously sets out to establish conditions and circumstances that are different from what they are now and then accomplishes that through some set or series of actions and interventions either singularly or in collaboration with other people" (Ford & Ford 1995:543). And this is where Lewin comes into his own.

Lewin's ideas remain central to episodic change because they assume that inertia in the form of a quasi-stationary equilibrium is the main impediment to change (Schein 1996). Lewin's insight was that an equilibrium would change more easily if restraining forces such as personal defenses, group norms, or organizational culture were unfrozen. Schein's (1996) work suggests that unfreezing basically involves three processes: (*a*) disconfirmation of expectations, (*b*) induction of learning anxiety if the disconfirming data are accepted as valid and relevant (we fear that "if we admit to ourselves and others that something is wrong or imperfect, we will lose our effectiveness, our self-esteem, and maybe even our identity," p. 29), and (*c*) provision of psychological safety that converts anxiety into motivation to change.

Schein's (1996) work also suggests an updated understanding of what happens after unfreezing. Change occurs through cognitive restructuring in which words are redefined to mean something other than had been assumed, concepts are interpreted more broadly, or new standards of judgment and evaluation are learned. Thus, when Lewin persuaded housewives during World War II to serve kidneys and liver, he cognitively redefined their standards of what was acceptable meat by means of a process that mixed together identification with positive role models, insight, and trial-and-error learning. When unfreezing occurs and people are motivated to learn something, they tend to be especially attentive to ideas that are in circulation, a mechanism discussed later as "translation." Refreezing that embeds the new behavior and forestalls relapse is most likely to occur when the behavior fits both the personality of the target and the relational expectations of the target's social network.

Lewin also remains relevant to episodic change because his other five assumptions about change are compatible with its analytical framework. These five assumptions (Marshak 1993) are (*a*) linear assumption (movement is from one state to another in a forward direction through time); (*b*) progressive assumption (movement is from a lesser state to a better state); (*c*) goal assumption (movement is toward a specific end state); (*d*) disequilibrium assumption (movement requires disequilibrium); and (*e*) separateness assumption (movement is planned and managed by people apart from the system). Summarized in this form, Lewin's change model resembles "Newtonian physics where movement results from the application of a set of forces on an object" (Marshak 1993:412). Complexity theory is the least "Newtonian" of the several formulations associated with episodic change, and its continued development may broaden our understanding of episodic interventions. For example, complexity theory implies that improved performance may at times be linked to the surrender of control, which is a very different image from one of attacking inertia through coercive means (e.g. Dunphy & Stace 1988).

Newer analyses relevant to episodic change suggest how difficult it is to unfreeze patterns but also that attempts at unfreezing start earlier than was previously thought. Both conclusions are the result of microlevel research on smoking cessation and weight loss by Prochaska and his colleagues (Grimley et al 1994, Prochaska et al 1992). They propose that when people are exposed to change interventions, they are at one of four stages: precontemplation, contemplation, action, and maintenance. Precontemplators are unaware of any need to change, whereas contemplators are aware that there is a problem and they are thinking about change but have not yet made a commitment. People can remain in the contemplation stage for long periods, up to two years in the case of smokers. Action, the stage most change agents equate with change, is the stage in which people actually alter their behaviors, in any change intervention, few people are in the action stage. In smoking cessation programs, for example, empirical findings suggest that only 15% of the smokers in any given worksite are ready for action.

The important result, in the context of episodic change, is the finding that most people who reach the action stage relapse and change back to previous habits three or four times before they maintain the newer sequence. Beer et al (1990:50) found several false starts in renewal efforts at General Products. This suggests that change is not a linear movement through the four stages but a spiral pattern of contemplation, action, and relapse and then successive returns to contemplation, action, and relapse before entering the maintenance and then termination stages. Relapse should be more common in discrete episodic change than in cumulative continuous change because larger changes are involved. What is interesting is that 85% of the relapsers return to the stage of contemplation, not to the stage of precontemplation. This means that they are closer to taking action again following relapse than change agents suspected. The fact that change passes through a contemplation stage also means that people are changing before we can observe any alterations in their behavior. This suggests that interventions may have value even when no action is observed.

Role of change agent in episodic change

The role of the change agent in episodic change is that of prime mover who creates change. Macy & Izumi (1993:245–50) list 60 work design changes made by prime movers in North American interventions. The steps by which people enact the role of prime mover (e.g. Kotter 1996, Nadler 1998) look pretty much the same. What is different in newer work is the demonstration that one can be a prime mover on a larger scale than in the past (Weisbord 1987). Many practitioners are focusing on larger gatherings (Axelrod 1992, Dannemiller & Jacobs 1992) with more issues on the table for immediate action (e.g. Ashkenas & Jick 1992), concentrated in shorter periods of time (Torbert 1994). Large-scale change in very large groups is counterintuitive, since size and participation tend to be negatively related (e.g. Pasmore & Fagans 1992, Gilmore & Barnett 1992). Normally, large group settings induce stereotyping, decreased ownership of ideas, increased abstraction, and less willingness to express unique thoughts. The challenge for prime movers is to neutralize these tendencies. To do so requires that they abandon several traditional organizational development (OD) assumptions. Large-scale interventions rely less on action theory and discrepancy theory and more on systems theory; less on closely held, internal data generation and more on gathering data from the environment and sharing it widely; less on slow downward cascades and more on real-time analysis and decision making; less on individual unit learning and more on learning about the whole organization; less on being senior management driven and more on a mixed model of being driven by both senior management and the organization; less consultant centered and more participant centered; less incremental and more fundamental in terms of the depth of change (Bunker & Alban 1992).

There has also been an increasingly refined understanding of specific ways in which change agents can be effective prime movers. As Rorty (1989) observed, "a talent for speaking differently rather than for arguing well, is the chief instrument of cultural change" (p. 7). Language interventions are becoming a crucial means for agents to create change (e.g. Bate 1990, O'Connor 1995). Bartunek (1993) argues that to produce second-order change in a preexisting shared schema requires a strong alternative schema, presented clearly and persistently. Barrett et al (1995) demonstrate that changes symbolizing a successful revolution are basically interpretations that point to a new alignment of the triggers that initiated the revolutionary period.

Wilkof et al (1995) report on their attempt to intervene in the relationships between two companies in a difficult partnership. Their initial attempts to improve cooperation focused on feeding back problems from a traditional data collection. This failed and led to the discovery that although there were technical or structural solutions available, the actors could not agree because of a vast difference in cultural lenses and diametrically opposed interpretations of meaning. The consultant, therefore, changed her strategy. She began meeting independently with the actors from each organization. In the meetings she would meet each condemnation not with data or argument but with an alternative interpretation from the cultural lens of the other company. She calls the process "cultural consciousness raising." The authors underscore the importance of working with actors to interpret the actions of others not as technical incompetence but as behaviors that are consistent with a particular cultural purpose, meaning, and history.

Continuous change

The phrase "continuous change" is used to group together organizational changes that tend to be ongoing, evolving, and cumulative. A common presumption is that change is emergent, meaning that it is "the realization of a new pattern of organizing in the absence of explicit a priori intentions" (Orlikowski 1996:65). Change is described as situated and grounded in continuing updates of work processes (Brown & Duguid 1991) and social practices (Tsoukas 1996). Researchers focus on "accommodations to and experiments with the everyday contingencies, breakdowns, exceptions, opportunities, and unintended consequences" (Orlikowski 1996:65). As these accommodations "are repeated, shared, amplified, and sustained, they can, over time, produce perceptible and striking organizational changes" (p. 89). The distinctive quality of continuous change is the idea that small continuous adjustments, created simultaneously across units, can cumulate and create substantial change. That scenario presumes tightly coupled interdependencies. When interdependencies loosen, these same continuous adjustments, now confined to smaller units, remain important as pockets of innovation that may prove appropriate in future environments.

Basic metaphors: organizing for continuous change

The metaphor of organization that is implicit in conceptualizations of continuous change is not the reciprocal of metaphors associated with episodic change. The dynamics are different, as would be expected from a shift to a more micro perspective and to the assumption that everything changes all the time (Ford & Ford 1994). From closer in, the view of organization associated with continuous change is built around recurrent interactions as the feedstock of organizing, authority tied to tasks rather than positions, shifts in authority as tasks shift, continuing development of response repertoires, systems that are self-organizing rather than fixed, ongoing redefinition of job descriptions, mindful construction of responses in the moment rather than mindless application of past responses embedded in routines (Wheatley 1992:90), and acceptance of change as a constant. Although these properties may seem prescriptive rather than descriptive and better suited to describe the "ideal organization" than the "basic metaphor," they are straightforward outcomes when people act as if change is continuous, organizing constitutes organization, and stability is an accomplishment.

Images of organization that are compatible with continuous change include those built around the ideas of improvisation, translation, and learning. The image of organization built around improvisation is one in which variable inputs to self-organizing groups of actors induce continuing modification of work practices and ways of relating. This image is represented by the statement that change "is often realized through the ongoing variations which emerge frequently, even imperceptibly, in the slippages and improvisations of everyday activity" (Orlikowski 1996:88–89). Improvisation is said to occur when "the time gap between these events [of planning and implementation] narrows so that in the limit, composition converges with execution. The more improvisational an act, the narrower the time gap between composing and performing, designing and producing, or planning and implementing" (Moorman & Miner 1998a). Empirically, Moorman & Miner (1998b) found that improvisation often replaced the use of standard procedures in new product development and, in the presence of developed organizational memory, had positive effects on design effectiveness and on cost savings. Orlikowski (1996), in her study of changes in an incident tracking system, found repeated improvisation in work practices that then led to restructuring. Similar descriptions are found in Crossan et al (1996), Brown & Eisenhardt (1997), and Weick (1993).

The image of organization built around the idea of translation is one of a setting where there is continuous adoption and editing (Sahlin-Andersson 1996) of ideas that bypass the apparatus of planned change and have their impact through a combination of fit with purposes at hand, institutional salience, and chance. The idea that change is a continuous process of translation derives from an extended gloss (Czarniawska & Sevon 1996) of Latour's observation that "the spread in time and place of anything—claims, orders, artefacts, goods—is in the hands of people; each of these people may act in many different ways, letting the token drop, or modifying it, or deflecting it, or betraying it or adding to it, or appropriating it" (Latour 1986:267). The controlling image is the travel of ideas and what happens when ideas are turned into new actions in new localities (Czarniawska & Joerges 1996). Translation is not a synonym for diffusion. The differences are crucial. The impetus for the spread of ideas does not lie with the persuasiveness of the originator of the idea. Instead, the impetus comes from imitators and from their conception of the situation, their self-identity and others' identity, and their analogical reasoning (Sevon 1996). The first actor in the chain is no more important than the last; ideas do not move from more saturated to less saturated environments; it is impossible to know when the process concludes, since all ideas are in the air all the time and are implemented depending on the purpose at hand (Czarniawska & Joerges 1996). A match between a purpose and an idea does not depend on inherent properties of the idea. Instead, it is assumed that "most ideas can be proven to fit most problems, assuming good will, creativity, and a tendency to consensus" (p. 25). Thus, the act of translation creates the match.

The image of organization built around the idea of learning is one of a setting where work and activity are defined by repertoires of actions and knowledge and where learning itself is defined as "a change in an organization's response repertoire" (Sitkin et al 1998). What this adds to the understanding of continuous change is the idea that it is a range of skills and knowledge that is altered rather than a specific action, as well as the idea that a change is not just substitution but could also include strengthening existing skills. A change in repertoire is also a change in the potential for action, which means action may not be manifest at the time of learning (Pye 1994). To specify learning in terms of a response repertoire is also to specify a mechanism by which change is retained (Moorman & Miner 1997). Other retention-learning mechanisms discussed in the literature include organizational routines (March 1994), know-how embedded in communities of practice (Brown & Duguid 1991), distributed memory (Wegner 1987), distributed information processing systems (Tsoukas 1996), structures of collective mind (Weick & Roberts 1993), and organizational memory (Walsh & Ungson 1991). Summaries of recent work on organizational learning can be found in Huber (1991), Miller (1996), Easterby-Smith (1997), Mirvis (1996), and Lundberg (1989).

In each of these three images, organizations produce continuous change by means of repeated acts of improvisation involving simultaneous composition and execution, repeated acts of translation that convert ideas into useful artifacts that fit purposes at hand, or repeated acts of learning that enlarge, strengthen, or shrink the repertoire of responses.

Analytic framework: the continuous change process

The following description summarizes the analytic framework of continuous change:

> Each variation of a given form is not an abrupt or discrete event, neither is it, by itself discontinuous. Rather, through a series of ongoing and situated accommodations, adaptations, and alterations (that draw on previous variations and mediate future ones), sufficient modifications may be enacted over time that fundamental changes are achieved. There is no deliberate orchestration of change here, no technological inevitability, no dramatic discontinuity, just recurrent and reciprocal variations in practice over time. Each shift in practice creates the conditions for further breakdowns, unanticipated outcomes, and innovations, which in turn are met with more variations. Such variations are ongoing; there is no beginning or end point in this change process.
>
> (Orlikowski 1996:66)

Implicit in that description are several important processes, including change through ongoing variations in practice, cumulation of variations, continuity in place of dramatic discontinuity, continuous disequilibrium as variations beget variations, and no beginning or end point. What is less prominent in this description are key properties of episodic change, such as inertia, triggers, and replacement. Continuous change could be viewed as a series of fast mini-episodes of change, in which case inertia might take the form of tendencies to normalization (Vaughan 1996) or competency traps (Levinthal & March 1993). Triggers to change might take the form of temporal milestones (Gersick 1989, 1994) or dissonance between beliefs and actions (Inkpen & Crossan 1995). Replacements might take the form of substituting expert practices for practices of novices (Klein 1998). But the more central issues in the case of continuous change are those of continuity and scale.

Issues of continuity are associated with the concept of organizational culture (Trice & Beyer 1993). Culture is important in continuous change because it holds the multiple changes together, gives legitimacy to nonconforming actions that improve adaptation and adaptability (Kotter & Heskett 1992), and embeds the know-how of adaptation into norms and values (O'Reilly & Chatman 1996). Culture as the vehicle that preserves the know-how of adaptation is implied in this description: "If we understand culture to be a stock of knowledge that has been codified into a pattern of recipes for handling situations, then very often with time and routine they become tacit and taken for granted and form the schemas which drive action" (Colville et al 1993:559). Culture, viewed as a stock of knowledge, serves as a scheme of expression that constrains what people do and a scheme of interpretation that constrains how the doing is evaluated. To change culture is to change climate (e.g. Schneider et al 1996), uncover the tacit stock of knowledge by means of experiments that surface the particulars (Colville et al 1993), or deconstruct organizational language paradigms (Bate 1990). Although culture has been a useful vocabulary to understand stability and change, there are growing suggestions that as one moves away from treating it as a social control system, the concept may become less meaningful (Jordan 1995).

The separate issue of scale arises because continuous changes in the form of "situated micro-level changes that actors enact over time as they make sense of and act in the world" (Orlikowski 1996:91) are often judged to be too small, too much a follower strategy (Huber & Glick 1993:385), and even too "unAmerican" (Hammond & Morrison 1996:Ch. 3) to be of much importance when hyperturbulence and quantum change confront organizations (Meyer et al 1993).

The analytical framework associated with continuous change interprets scale in a different way. The fact that the changes are micro does not mean that they are trivial (Staw & Sutton 1993, Staw 1991). Representative of this view is Ford & Ford's (1995) observation, "The macrocomplexity of organizations is generated, and changes emerge through the diversity and interconnectedness of many microconversations, each of which follows relatively simple rules" (p. 560). Small changes do not stay small, as complexity theory and the second cybernetics (Maruyama 1963) make clear. Small changes can be decisive if they occur at the edge of chaos. Furthermore, in interconnected systems, there is no such thing as a marginal change, as Colville et al (1993) demonstrated in their study of small experiments with culture change at British Customs. Microlevel changes also provide the platform for transformational change and the means to institutionalize it. Depictions of successful revolutions, however, tend to downplay the degree to which earlier sequences of incremental changes made them possible. This oversight is serious because people tend to attribute the success of revolution to its break with the past and its vision of the future, whereas that success may actually lie in its connection with the past and its retrospective rewriting of what earlier micro-changes meant.

In conclusion, the basic analytical framework for continuous change assumes that revolutions are not necessary to shatter what basically does not exist. Episodic change is driven by inertia and the inability of organizations to keep up, while continuous change is driven by alertness and the inability of organizations to remain stable. The analytic framework for continuous change specifies that contingencies, breakdowns, opportunities, and contexts make a difference. Change is an ongoing mixture of reactive and proactive modifications, guided by purposes at hand, rather than an intermittent interruption of periods of convergence.

Ideal continuous organizations

The "ideal organizations" described above in the context of episodic change serve just as well as ideals for continuous change, since those ideals incorporate capabilities for both forms of change. Thus, that discussion is compatible with the metaphors and analytical framework for continuous change.

Intervention theory in continuous change

Lewin's change model, with its assumptions of inertia, linearity, progressive development, goal seeking, disequilibrium as motivator, and outsider intervention, is relevant when it is necessary to create change. However, when change is continuous, the problem is not one of unfreezing. The problem is one of redirecting what is already under way. A different mindset is necessary, and Marshak (1993) has suggested that one possibility derives from Confucian thought. The relevant assumptions are (*a*) cyclical assumption (patterns of ebb and flow repeat themselves), (*b*) processional assumption (movement involves an orderly sequence through a cycle and departures cause disequilibrium), (*c*) journey assumption (there is no end state), (*d*) equilibrium assumption (interventions are to restore equilibrium and balance), (*e*) appropriateness assumption (correct action maintains harmony), and (*f*) change assumption (nothing remains the same forever).

In the face of inertia, it makes sense to view a change intervention as a sequence of unfreeze, transition, refreeze. But in the face of continuous change, a more plausible change sequence would be freeze, rebalance, unfreeze. To freeze continuous change is to make a sequence visible and to show patterns in what is happening (e.g. Argyris 1990). To freeze is to capture sequences by means of cognitive maps (Fiol & Huff 1992, Eden et al 1992, Cossette & Audet 1992), schemas (Bartunek 1993, Tenkasi & Boland 1993), or war stories (Boje 1991, O'Connor 1996). To rebalance is to reinterpret, relabel, and resequence the patterns so that they unfold with fewer blockages. To rebalance is to reframe issues as opportunities (Dutton 1993), reinterpret history using appreciative inquiry (e.g. Cooperrider & Srivasta 1987, Hammond 1996), to differentiate more boldly among "the external world, the social world, and the world of inner subjectivity" (Thachankary 1992:198), or to be responsive to concerns about justice (Novelli et al 1995). Thus, a story of intense but unproductive meetings is rewritten as a story affirming the value of "corporateness" in an international nonprofit organization (Thachankary 1992:221). Finally, to unfreeze after rebalancing is to resume improvisation, translation, and learning in ways that are now more mindful of sequences, more resilient to anomalies, and more flexible in their execution.

An important new means of rebalancing continuous change is the use of a logic of attraction, which is the counterpart of the logic of replacement in episodic change. As the name implies, people change to a new position because they are attracted to it, drawn to it, inspired by it. There is a focus on moral power, the attractiveness or being state of the change agent, the freedom of the change target, and the role of choice in the transformational process. Kotter (1996) asks the question, is change something one manages or something one leads? To manage change is to tell people what to do (a logic of replacement), but to lead change is to show people how to be (a logic of attraction). RE Quinn (1996) argues that most top managers assume that change is something that someone with authority does to someone who does not have authority (e.g. Boss & Golembiewski 1995). They overlook the logic of attraction and its power to pull change.

To engage this logic of attraction, leaders must first make deep changes in themselves, including self-empowerment (Spreitzer & Quinn 1996). When deep personal change occurs, leaders then behave differently toward their direct reports, and the new behaviors in the leader attract new behaviors from followers. When leaders model personal change, organizational change is more likely to take place. A similar logic is implicit in Cohen & Tichy's (1997) recent emphasis on top managers developing a teachable point of view. Leaders who first consolidate their stories and ideas about what matters undergo personal change before organizational change is attempted. Subsequent organizational change is often more effective because it is led by more attractive leaders. Beer et al (1990:194–95) raise the interesting subtlety, based on their data, that inconsistency between word and action at the corporate level does not affect change effectiveness, but it does have a negative effect for leaders at the unit level. Their explanation is that inconsistency at the top is seen as necessary to cope with diverse pressures from stockholders and the board but is seen as insincerity and hypocrisy at other levels.

Role of change agent in continuous change

If continuous change is altered by freezing and rebalancing, then the role of the change agent becomes one of managing language, dialogue, and identity, as we saw above. Change agents become important for their ability to make sense (Weick 1995) of change dynamics already under way. They recognize adaptive emergent changes, make them more salient, and reframe them (Bate 1990). They explain current upheavals, where they are heading, what they will have produced by way of a redesign, and how further intentional changes can be made at the margins.

To redirect continuous change is to be sensitive to discourse. Schein (1993) argues that dialogue, which he defines as interaction focused on thinking processes and how they are preformed by past experience, enables groups to create a shared set of meanings and a common thinking process. "The most basic mechanism of acquiring new information that leads to cognitive restructuring is to discover in a conversational process that the interpretation that someone else puts on a concept is different from one's own" (Schein 1996:31). Barrett et al (1995) and Dixon (1997) also argue that the most powerful change interventions occur at the level of everyday conversation. J Quinn (1996) demonstrates in the context of strategic change that good conversation is vocal, reciprocating, issues-oriented, rational, imaginative, and honest. And Ford & Ford (1995) argue that change agents produce change through various combinations of five kinds of speech acts: assertives or claims, directives or requests, commissives or promises, expressives that convey affective state, and declarations that announce a new operational reality. These speech acts occur in different combinations to constitute four different conversations: conversations of change, understanding, performance, and closure.

Conclusion

Our review suggests both that change starts with failures to adapt and that change never starts because it never stops. Reconciliation of these disparate themes is a source of ongoing tension and energy in recent change research. Classic machine bureaucracies, with their reporting structures too rigid to adapt to faster-paced change, have to be unfrozen to be improved. Yet with differentiation of bureaucratic tasks comes more internal variation, more diverse views of distinctive competence, and more diverse initiatives. Thus, while some things may appear not to change, other things do. Most organizations have pockets of people somewhere who are already adjusting to the new environment. The challenge is to gain acceptance of continuous change throughout the organization so that these isolated innovations will travel and be seen as relevant to a wider range of purposes at hand.

Recent work suggests, ironically, that to understand organizational change one must first understand organizational inertia, its content, its tenacity, its interdependencies. Recent work also suggests that change is not an on-off phenomenon nor is its effectiveness contingent on the degree to which it is planned. Furthermore, the trajectory of change is more often spiral or open-ended than linear. All of these insights are more likely to be kept in play if researchers focus on "changing" rather than "change." A shift in vocabulary from "change" to "changing" directs attention to actions of substituting one thing for another, of making one thing into another thing, or of attracting one thing to become other than it was, A concern with "changing" means greater appreciation that change is never off, that its chains of causality are longer and less determinate than we anticipated, and that whether one's viewpoint is global or local makes a difference in the rate of change that will be observed, the inertias that will be discovered, and the size of accomplishments that will have been celebrated.

Acknowledgments

We acknowledge with appreciation fruitful discussions of key points with Dave Schwandt, Lance Sandelands, Jane Dutton, Wayne Baker, Anjali Sastry, and Matt Brown, with special thanks to Kathleen Sutcliffe for thoughtful commentary on various drafts of the complete argument.

Literature cited

Argyris C. 1990. *Overcoming Organizational Defenses*: Facilitating Organizational Learning. Boston: Allyn & Bacon

Arthur WB. 1995. Positive feedbacks in the economy. In *Increasing Returns and Path Dependence in the Economy*, ed. T Kuran, pp. 1–32. Ann Arbor: Univ. Mich. Press

Ashkenas RN, Jick TD. 1992. From dialogue to action in GE work-out: developmental learning in a change process. *Res. Organ. Change Dev.* 6:267–87

Austin JR. 1997. A method for facilitating controversial social change in organizations: Branch Rickey and the Brooklyn Dodgers. *J. Appl. Behav. Sci.* 33:101–18

Axelrod D. 1992. Getting everyone involved: how one organization involved its employees, supervisors, and managers in redesigning the organization. *J. Appl. Behav. Sci.* 28:499–509

Bacharach SB, Bamberger P, Sonnenstuhl WJ. 1996. The organizational transformation process: the micropolitics of dissonance reduction and the alignment of logics of action. *Admin. Sci. Q.* 41:477–506

Barr PS, Huff AS. 1997. Seeing isn't believing: understanding diversity in the timing of strategic response. *J. Manage. Stud.* 34:337–70

Barrett FJ, Thomas GF, Hocevar SP. 1995. The central role of discourse in large-scale change: a social construction perspective. *J. Appl. Behav. Sci.* 33:352–72

Bartunek JM. 1993. The multiple cognitions and conflicts associated with second order organizational change. In *Social Psychology in Organizations*: Advances in Theory and Research, ed. JK Murnighan, pp. 322–49. Englewood Cliffs. NJ: Prentice Hall

Bartunek JM, Moch MK. 1994. Third-order organizational change and the western mystical tradition. *J. Organ. Change Manage.* 7:24–41

Bate P. 1990. Using the culture concept in an organization development setting. *J. Appl. Behav. Sci.* 26:83–106

Bateson G. 1972. *Steps to An Ecology of Mind*. New York: Ballantine

Beer M, Eisenstat RA, Spector B. 1990. *The Critical Path to Corporate Renewal*. Boston, MA: Harv. Bus. Sch.

Boje D. 1991. The storytelling organization: a study of story performances in an office-supply firm. *Admin. Sci. Q.* 36:106–26

Boss RW, Golembiewski RT. 1995. Do you have to start at the top? The chief executive officer's role in successful organization development efforts. *J. Appl. Behav. Sci.* 31:259–77

Bougon MG. 1992. Congregate cognitive maps: a unified dynamic theory of organization and strategy. *J. Manage. Stud.* 29:369–89

Brown JS, Duguid P. 1991. Organizational learning and communities-of-practice: toward a unified view of working, learning, and innovation. *Organ. Sci.* 2:40–57

Brown SL, Eisenhardt KM. 1997. The art of continuous change: linking complexity theory and time-paced evolution in relent-lessly shifting organizations. *Admin. Sci. Q.* 42:1–34

Browning LD, Beyer JM, Shetler JC. 1995. Building cooperation in a competitive industry: Sematech and the semiconductor industry. *Acad. Manage. J.* 38:113–51

Bunker BB, Alban BT. 1992. Conclusion: what makes large group interventions effective? *Appl. Behav. Sci.* 28:579–91

Burgelman RA. 1991. Intraorganizational ecology of strategy making and organizational adaptation: theory and field research. *Organ. Sci.* 2:239–62

Cheng YT, Van de Ven AH. 1996. Learning the innovation journey: order out of chaos? *Organ. Sci.* 7:593–614

Cohen E, Tichy N. 1997. How leaders develop leaders. *Train Dev.* 51:58–74

Colville I, Dalton K, Tomkins C. 1993. Developing and understanding cultural change in HM customs and excise: there is more to dancing than knowing the next steps. *Public Admin.* 71:549–66

Cooperrider DL, Srivasta S. 1987. Appreciative inquiry in organizational life. In *Research in Organizational Change and Development*, ed. RW Woodman, WA Pas-more. 1:129–69. Greenwich, CT: JAI

Cossette P, Audet M. 1992. Mapping of an idiosyncratic schema. *J. Manage. Stud.* 29:325–47

Crossan MM, Lane HW, White RE, Klus L. 1996. The improvising organization; where planning meets opportunity. *Organ. Dyn.* 24:20–35

Czarniawska B, Joerges B. 1996. Travels of ideas. See Czarniawska & Sevon 1996, pp. 13–48

Czarniawska B, Sevon G, eds. 1996. *Translating Organizational Change.* New York: Walter de Gruyter

Dannemiller KD, Jacobs RW. 1992. Changing the way organizations change: a revolution of common sense. *J. Appl. Behav. Sci.* 28:480–98

Dixon NM. 1997. The hallways of learning. *Organ. Dyn.* 25:23–34

Driskell JE, Salas E, eds. 1996. *Stress and Human Performance.* Mahwah, NJ: Erlbaum

Dunbar RLM, Garud R, Raghuram S. 1996. A frame for deframing in strategic analysis. *J. Manage. Inq.* 5:23–34

Dunphy D. 1996. Organizational change in corporate setting. *Hum. Relat.* 49(5):541–52

Dunphy DC, Stace DA. 1988. Transformational and coercive strategies for planned organizational change: beyond the OD model. *Organ. Stud.* 9(3):317–34

Dutton JE. 1993. The making of organizational opportunities: an interpretive pathway to organizational change. *Res. Organ. Behav.* 15:195–226

Easterby-Smith M. 1997. Disciplines of organizational learning: contributions and critiques. *Hum. Relat.* 50:1085–113

Eden C, Ackerman F, Cropper S. 1992. The analysis of cause maps. *J. Manage. Stud.* 29:309–23

Fiol CM, Huff AS. 1992, Maps for managers: where are we? Where do we go from here? *J. Manage. Stud.* 29:267–85

Ford J, Backoff R. 1988. Organizational change in and out of dualities and paradox. In *Paradox and Transformation*, ed. R Quinn, K Cameron, pp. 81–121. Cambridge, MA: Ballinger

Ford JD, Ford LW. 1994. Logics of identity, contradiction, and attraction in change. *Acad. Manage. Rev.* 19:756–85

Ford JD, Ford LW. 1995. The role of conversations in producing intentional change in organizations. *Acad. Manage. Rev.* 20(3):541–70

Gersick CJG. 1989. Marking time: predictable transitions in task groups. *Acad. Manage. J.* 32:274–309

Gersick CJG. 1991. Revolutionary change theories: a multilevel exploration of the punctuated equilibrium paradigm. *Acad. Manage. Rev.* 16:10–36

Gersick CJG. 1994. Pacing strategic change: the case of a new venture. *Acad. Manage. J.* 37:9–45

Gilmore TN, Barnett C. 1992. Designing the social architecture of participation in large groups to effect organizational change. *J. Appl. Behav. Sci.* 28:534–48

Gioia DA. 1992. Pinto fires and personal ethics: a script analysis of missed opportunities. *J. Bus. Ethics* 11:379–89

Golembiewski RT, Boss RW. 1992. Phases of burnout in diagnosis and intervention: individual level of analysis in organization development and change. *Res. Organ. Change Dev.* 6:115–52

Greenwood R, Hinings CR. 1996. Understanding radical organizational change: bringing together the old and the new institutionalism. *Acad. Manage. Rev.* 21:1022–54

Greiner L. 1972. Evolution and revolution as organizations grow, *Harv. Bus. Rev.* 50(4): 37–46

Grimley D, Prochaska JO, Velicer WF, Blais LM. DiClemente CC. 1994. The transtheoretical model of change. In *Changing the Self: Philosophies, Techniques, and Experiences*, ed. M Brinthaupt, pp. 201–27. New York: State Univ. NY Press

Hammond J, Morrison J. 1996. *The Stuff Americans Are Made Of.* New York: Macmillan

Hammond SA. 1996. *The Thin Book of Appreciative Inquiry*. Plano, TX: Kodiak Consult.

Harrison JR, Carroll G. 1991. Keeping the faith: a model of cultural transmission in formal organization. *Admin. Sci. Q.* 36:552–82

Hendry C, 1996. Understanding and creating whole organizational change through learning theory. *Hum. Relat.* 49:621–41

Huber GP. 1991. Organizational learning: an examination of the contributing processes and a review of the literatures. *Organ. Sci.* 2:88–115

Huber GP, Glick WH, eds. 1993. *Organizational Change and Redesign*. New York: Oxford Univ. Press

Huber GP, Sutcliffe KM, Miller CC, Glick WH. 1993. Understanding and predicting organizational change. See Huber & Glick 1993, pp. 215–65

Inkpen AC, Crossan MM. 1995. Believing is seeing: joint ventures and organization learning. *J. Manage. Stud.* 32:595–618

Jordan AT. 1995. Managing diversity: translating anthropological insight for organization studies. *J. Appl. Behav. Sci.* 31:124–40

Kahn RL. 1974. Organizational development: some problems and proposals. *J. Appl. Behav. Sci.* 10:485–502

Katz J. 1997. Ethnography's warrants. *Sociol. Methods Res.* 25:391–423

Kilduff M, Mehra A. 1997. Postmodernism and organizational research. *Acad. Manage. J.* 22:453–81

Klein G. 1998, *Sources of Power*. Cambridge. MA: MIT Press

Kotter JP. 1996. *Leading Change*. Boston, MA: Harv. Bus. Sch.

Kotter JP, Heskett JL. 1992. *Corporate Culture and Performance*. New York: Free Press

Langfield-Smith K. 1992. Exploring the need for a shared cognitive map. *J. Manage. Stud.* 29:349–68

Latour B. 1986. The powers of association. In *Power, Action, and Belief*, ed. J Law, pp. 264–80. London: Routledge & Kegan

Laurila J. 1997. The thin line between advanced and conventional new technology: a case study on paper industry management. *J. Manage. Stud.* 34:219–39

Levinthal DA, March JG. 1993, The myopia of learning. *Strateg. Manage. J.* 14:95–112

Lewin K. 1951. *Field Theory in Social Science*. New York: Harper & Row

Lundberg CC. 1989. On organizational learning: implications and opportunities for expanding organizational development. *Res. Organ. Change Dev.* 3:61–82

Macy BA, Izumi H. 1993. Organizational change, design, and work innovation: a meta-analysis of 131 North American field studies—1961–1991. *Res. Organ. Change Dev.* 7:235–313

March JG. 1994. *A Primer on Decision Making.* New York: Free Press

Marshak RJ. 1993. Lewin meets Confucius: a review of the OD model of change. *J. Appl. Behav. Sci.* 29:393–415

Maruyama M. 1963. The second cybernetics: deviation-amplifying mutual causal processes. *Am. Sci.* 51:164–79

McDaniel RR Jr. 1997. Strategic leadership: a view from quantum and chaos theories. *Health Care Manage. Rev.* Winter: 21–37

McKelvey B. 1997. Quasi-natural organization science. *Organ. Sci.* 8:352–80

Meyer AD, Goes JB, Brooks GR. 1993. Organizations reacting to hyperturbulence. See Huber & Glick 1993, pp. 66–111

Micklethwait J, Wooldridge A. 1996. *The Witch Doctors.* New York: Times Books

Miller D. 1990. Organizational configurations: cohesion, changes, and prediction. *Hum. Relat.* 43:771–89

Miller D. 1993. The architecture of simplicity. *Acad. Manage. Rev.* 18:116–38

Miller D. 1994. What happens after success: the perils of excellence. *J. Manage. Stud.* 31:325–58

Miller D. 1996. A preliminary typology of organizational learning: synthesizing the literature. *J. Manage.* 22:485–505

Mintzberg H, Westley F. 1992. Cycles of organizational change. *Sirateg. Manage. J.* 13:39–59

Mirvis PH. 1996. Historical foundations of organization learning. *J. Organ. Change Manage.* 9:13–31

Mirvis PH. 1997. Crossroads: "social work" in organizations. *Organ. Sci.* 8:192–206

Moorman C, Miner AS. 1997. The impact of organizational memory on new product performance and creativity. *J. Mark. Res.* 34:91–106

Moorman C, Miner AS. 1998a. Organizational improvisation and organizational memory. *Acad. Manage. Rev.* In press

Moorman C, Miner AS. 1998b. The convergence of planning and execution: improvisation in new product development. *J. Mark.* In press

Nadler DA. 1998. *Champions of Change.* San Francisco: Jossey-Bass

Nadler DA, Shaw RB, Walton AE. 1995. *Discontinuous Change.* San Francisco: Jossey-Bass

Nielsen RP, Bartunek JM. 1996. Opening narrow routinized schemata to ethical stakeholder consciousness and action. *Bus. Soc.* 35:483–519

Nord WR, Jermier JM. 1994. Overcoming resistance to resistance: insights from a study of the shadows. *Public Admin. Q.* 17:396–409

Novelli L, Bradley LK, Shapiro DL, 1995. Effective implementation of organizational change: an organizational justice perspective. In *Trends in Organizational Behavior*, ed. CL Cooper, 2:15–37. London: Wiley & Sons

O'Connor ES. 1995. Paradoxes of participation: textural analysis and organizational changes. *Organ. Stud.* 16(5):769–803

O'Connor ES. 1996. Telling decisions: the role of narrative in decision making. In *Organizational Decision Making*, ed. Z Shapiro, pp. 304–23. New York: Cambridge Univ. Press

Olson EE. 1990. The transcendent function in organizational change. *J. Appl. Behav. Sci.* 26:69–81

O'Reilly CA, Chatman JA. 1996. Culture as social control: corporations, cults and commitment. *Res. Organ. Behav.* 18:157–200

Orlikowski WJ. 1996. Improvising organizational transformation overtime: a situated change perspective. *Inf. Syst. Res.* 7(1):63–92

O'Shea J, Madigan C. 1997. *Dangerous Company*. New York: Times Books

O'Toole J. 1995. *Leading Change*. San Francisco: Jossey-Bass

Pasmore WA, Fagans MR. 1992. Participation. individual development, and organizational change: a preview and synthesis. *J. Manage.* 18:375–97

Pfeffer J. 1997. *New Directions For Organization Theory*. New York: Oxford Univ. Press

Pfeffer J. 1998. *The Human Equation*. Boston: Harv. Bus. Sch.

Porras JI, Robertson PJ. 1992. Organizational development: theory, practice, research. *Handbook of Organizational Psychology*, ed. MD Dunnette, LM Hough, 3:719–822. Palo Alto, CA: Consult. Psychol. Press. 2nd ed.

Porras JI, Silvers RC. 1991, Organization development and transformation. *Annu. Rev. Psychol.* 42:51–78

Prochaska JO, DiClemente CC, Norcross JC. 1992. In search of how people change: applications to addictive behaviors. *Am. Psychol*, 47:1102–14

Prochaska JO, DiClemente CC, Norcross JC. 1997. In search of how people change: applications to addictive behaviors. In *Addictive Behaviors*: *Readings on Etiology, Prevention, and Treatment*, ed. G Marlatt, pp. 671–96, Washington, DC: Am. Psychol. Assoc.

Pye A. 1994. Past, present and possibility: an integrative appreciation of learning from experience. *Manage. Learn.* 25:155–73

Quinn JJ. 1996. The role of 'good conversation' in strategic control. *J. Manage. Stud.* 33:381–94

Quinn RE. 1996. *Deep Change*: *Discovering the Leader Within*. San Francisco: Jossey-Bass

Random House Dictionary of The English Language. 1987. New York: Random House. 2nd ed, unabridged

Roach DW, Bednar DA. 1997. The theory of logical types: a tool for understanding levels and types of change in organizations. *Hum. Relat.* 50:671–99

Romanelli E, Tushman ML. 1994. Organizational transformation as punctuated equilibrium: an empirical test. *Acad. Manage. J.* 37:1141–66

Rorty R. 1989. *Contingency, Irony, and Solidarity*. New York: Cambridge Univ. Press

Sahlin-Andersson K. 1996. Imitating by editing success: the construction of organizational fields. See Czarniawska & Sevon 1996, pp. 69–92

Sandelands L. 1998. *Feeling and Form In Social Life*. Lanham, MD: Rowman & Little-field

Sastry MA. 1997. Problems and paradoxes in a *model* of punctuated organizational change. *Admin. Sci. Q.* 42:237–75

Schein EH. 1993. On dialogue, culture, and organizational learning. *Organ. Dyn.* 21: 40–51

Schein EH. 1996. Kurt Lewin's change theory in the field and in the classroom: notes toward a model of managed learning. *Syst. Pract.* 9:27–47

Schneider B, Brief AP, Guzzo RA. 1996. Creating a climate and culture for sustainable organizational change. *Organ. Dyn.* 24:7–19

Sevon G. 1996. Organizational imitation in identity transformation. See Czarniawska & Sevon I996, pp. 49–68

Sitkin SB, Sutcliffe KM, Weick KE. 1998. Organizational learning. In *The Technology Management Handbook*, ed. R Dorf. Boca Raton, FL: CRC Press. In press

Spreitzer GM, Quinn RE. 1996. Empowering middle managers to be transformational leaders. *J. Appl. Behav. Sci.* 32(3):237–61

Stacey RD. 1995. The science of complexity: an alternative perspective for strategic change processes. *Strateg. Manage. J.* 16:477–95

Starbuck WH. 1993. Keeping a butterfly and an elephant in a house of cards: the elements of exceptional success. *J. Manage. Stud.* 30:885–921

Staw BM. 1991. Dressing up like an organization: when psychological theories can explain organizational action. *J. Manage.* 17:805–19

Staw BM, Sutton RI. 1993. Macro organizational psychology. In *Social Psychology in Organizations: Advances in Theory and Research*, ed. JK Murnighan, pp. 350–84. Englewood Cliffs, NJ: Prentice Hall

Tenkasi RV, Boland RJ. 1993. Locating meaning making in organizational learning: the narrative basis of cognition. *Res. Organ. Change Dev.* 7:77–103

Thachankary T. 1992. Organizations as "texts": hermeneutics as a model for understanding organizational change. *Res. Organ. Change Dev.* 6:197–233

Torbert WR. 1994. Managerial learning, organizational learning: a potentially powerful redundancy. *Manage. Learn.* 25:57–70

Trice HM, Beyer JM. 1993. *The Culture of Work Organizations*. Englewood Cliffs, NJ: Prentice Hall

Tsoukas H. 1996. The firm as a distributed knowledge system: a constructionist approach. *Strateg. Manage. J.* 17:11–26

Tushman ML, O'Reilly CA III. 1996. The ambidextrous organization: managing evolutionary and revolutionary change. *Calif. Manage. Rev.* 38:1–23

Tushman ML, Romanelli E. 1985. Organizational revolution: a metamorphosis model of convergence and reorientation. *Res. Organ. Behav.* 7:171–222

Tushman ML, Rosenkopf L. 1992. Organizational determinants of technological change: toward a sociology of technological evolution. *Res. Organ. Behav.* 14:311–47

Van de Ven AH, Poole MS. 1995. Explaining development and change in organizations. *Acad. Manage. Rev.* 20(3):510–40

Vaughan D. 1996. *The Challenger Launch Decision*. Chicago: Univ. Chicago Press

Virany B, Tushman ML. Romanelli E. 1992. Executive succession and organization outcomes in turbulent environments: an organization learning approach. *Organ. Sci.* 3:72–91

Walsh JP, Ungson GR, 1991. Organizational memory. *Acad. Manage. Rev.* 16:57–91

Watzlawick P, Weakland J, Fisch R. 1974. *Change*. New York: Norton

Wegner DM. 1987. Transactive memory: a contemporary analysis of the group mind. In *Theories of Group Behavior*, ed. B Mullen, GR Goethals, pp. 185–208. New York: Springer-Verlag

Weick KE. 1993. Organizational redesign as improvisation. In *Organizational Change and Redesign*, ed. GP Huber, WH Glick, pp. 346–79. New York: Oxford Univ. Press

Weick KE. 1995. *Sensemaking in Organizations*. Thousand Oaks. CA: Sage

Weick KE, Roberts KH. 1993. Collective mind in organizations: heedful interrelating on flight decks. *Admin. Sci. Q.* 38:357–81

Weisbord MR. 1987. *Productive Workplaces*. San Francisco: Jossey-Bass

Whealtey MJ. 1992. *Leadership and the New Science*. San Francisco: Berrett-Koehler

Wilkof MV, Brown DW, Selsky JW. 1995. When the stories are different: the influence of corporate culture mismatches on interorganizational relations. *J. Appl. Behav. Sci.* 31:373–88

Woodman RW. 1989. Organizational change and development: new arenas for inquiry and action. *J. Manage.* 15:205–28

48

OVERCOMING RESISTANCE TO CHANGE

Lester Coch and John R. P. French, Jr.

Source: *Human Relations* 1(4) (1948): 512–532.

Introduction

It has always been characteristic of American industry to change products and methods of doing jobs as often as competitive conditions or engineering progress dictates. This makes frequent changes in an individual's work necessary. In addition, the markedly greater turnover and absenteeism of recent years result in unbalanced production lines which again makes for frequent shifting of individuals from one job to another. One of the most serious production problems faced at the Harwood Manufacturing Corporation has been the resistance of production workers to the necessary changes in methods and jobs. This resistance expressed itself in several ways, such as grievances about the piece rates that went with the new methods, high turnover, very low efficiency, restriction of output, and marked aggression against management. Despite these undesirable effects, it was necessary that changes in methods and jobs continue.

Efforts were made to solve this serious problem by the use of a special monetary allowance for transfers, by trying to enlist the cooperation and aid of the union, by making necessary layoffs on the basis of efficiency, etc. In all cases, these actions did little or nothing to overcome the resistance to change. On the basis of these data, it was felt that the pressing problem of resistance to change demanded further research for its solution. From the point of view of factory management, there were two purposes to the research: (1) Why do people resist change so strongly? and (2) What can be done to overcome this resistance?

Starting with a series of observations about the behavior of changed groups, the first step in the overall program was to devise a preliminary theory to account for the resistance to change. Then on the basis of the theory, a real life action experiment was devised and conducted within the context of the factory situation. Finally, the results of the experiment were interpreted in the light of the preliminary theory and the new data.

Background

The main plant of the Harwood Manufacturing Corporation, where the present research was done, is located in the small town of Marion, Virginia. The plant produces pajamas and, like most sewing plants, employs mostly women. The plant's population is about 500 women and 100 men. The workers are recruited from the rural, mountainous areas surrounding the town, and are usually employed without previous industrial experience. The average age of the workers is 23; the average education is eight years of grammar school.

The policies of the company in regard to labor relations are liberal and progressive. A high value has been placed on fair and open dealing with the employees and they are encouraged to take up any problems or grievances with the management at any time. Every effort is made to help foremen find effective solutions to their problems in human relations, using conferences and role-playing methods. Carefully planned orientation, designed to help overcome the discouragement and frustrations attending entrance upon the new and unfamiliar situation, is used. Plant-wide votes are conducted where possible to resolve problems affecting the whole working population. The company has invested both time and money in employee services such as industrial music, health services, lunch-room, and recreation programs. In the same spirit, the management has been conscious of the importance of public relations in the local community; they have supported both financially and otherwise any activity which would build up good will for the company. As a result of these policies, the company has enjoyed good labor relations since the day it commenced operations.

Harwood employees work on an individual incentive system. Piece rates are set by time study and are expressed in terms of units. One unit is equal to one minute of standard work: 60 units per hour equal the standard efficiency rating. Thus, if on a particular operation the piece rate for one dozen is 10 units, the operator would have to produce 6 dozen per hour to achieve the standard efficiency rating of 60 units per hour. The skill required to reach 60 units per hour is great. On some jobs, an average trainee may take 34 weeks to reach the skill level necessary to perform at 60 units per hour. Her first few weeks of work may be on an efficiency level of 5 to 20 units per hour.

The amount of pay received is directly proportional to the weekly average efficiency rating achieved. Thus, an operator with an average efficiency rating of 75 units per hour (25 per cent. more than standard) would receive 25 per cent. more than base pay. However, there are two minimum wages below which no operator may fall. The first is the plantwide minimum, the hiring-in wage; the second is a minimum wage based on six months' employment and is 22 per cent. higher than the plant-wide minimum wage. Both minima are smaller than the base pay for 60 units per hour efficiency rating.

The rating of every piece worker is computed every day and the results are published in a daily record of production which is shown to every operator. This daily record of production for each production line carries the names of all the operators on that line arranged in rank order of efficiency rating, with the highest rating girl at the top of the list. The supervisors speak to each operator each day about her unit ratings. Because of the above procedures, many operators do not claim credit for all the work done in a given day. Instead, they save a few of the piece rate tickets as a "cushion" against a rainy day when they may not feel well or may have a great amount of machine trouble.

When it is necessary to change an operator from one type of work to another, a transfer bonus is given. This bonus is so designed that the changed operator who relearns at an average rate will suffer no loss in earnings after change. Despite this allowance, the general attitudes toward job changes in the factory are markedly negative. Such expressions as, "When you make your units (standard production), they change your job," are all too frequent. Many operators refuse to change, preferring to quit.

The transfer learning curve

An analysis of the after-change relearning curves of several hundred experienced operators rating standard or better prior to change showed that 38 per cent. of the changed operators recovered to the standard unit rating of 60 units per hour. The other 62 per cent. either became chronically sub-standard operators or quit during the relearning period.

The average relearning curve for those who recover to standard production on the simplest type job in the plant (Figure I) is eight weeks long, and, when smoothed, provides the basis for the transfer bonus. The bonus is the percent. difference between this expected efficiency rating and the standard of 60 units per hour. Progress is slow for the first two or three weeks, as the relearning curve shows, and then accelerates markedly to about 50 units per hour with an increase of 15 units in two weeks. Another slow progress area is encountered at 50 units per hour, the operator improving only 3 units in two weeks. The curve ends in a spurt of 10 units progress in one week, a marked goal gradient behavior. The individual curves, of course, vary widely in length according to the simplicity or difficulty of the job to be relearned; but in general, the successful curves are consistent with the average curve in form.

It is interesting to note in Figure I that the relearning period for an experienced operator is longer than the learning period for a new operator. This is true despite the fact that the majority of transfers—the failures who never recover to standard—are omitted from the curve. However, changed operators rarely complain of "wanting to do it the old way," etc., after the first week or two of change; and time and motion studies show few false moves after the first week of change. From this evidence it is deduced that proactive inhibition or the interference of previous habits in learning the new skill is either non-existent or very slight after the first two weeks of change.

Figure II, which presents the relearning curves for 41 experienced operators who were changed to very difficult jobs, gives a comparison between the recovery rates

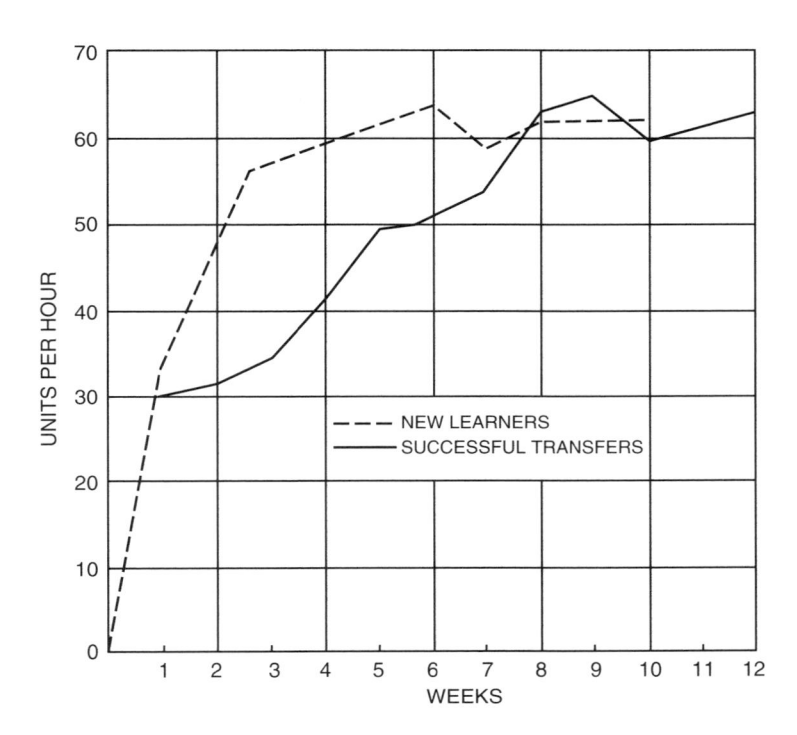

Figure I A comparison of the learning curve for new, inexperienced employees with the relearning curve for only those transfers (38 per cent.) who eventually recover to standard production.

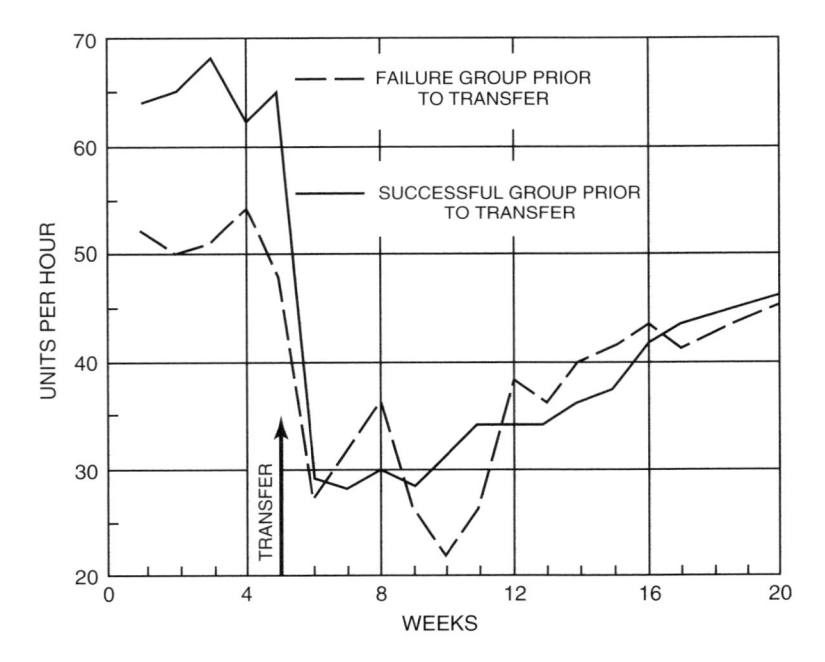

Figure II The drop in production and the rate of recovery after transfer for skillful and for sub-standard operators.

for operators making standard or better prior to change, and those below standard prior to change. Both classes of operators dropped to a little below 30 units per hour and recovered at a very slow but similar rate. These curves show a general (though by no means universal) phenomenon: that the efficiency rating prior to change does not indicate a faster or slower recovery rate after change.

A preliminary theory of resistance to change

The fact that relearning after transfer to a new job is so often slower than initial learning on first entering the factory would indicate, on the face of it, that the resistance to change and the slow relearning is primarily a motivational problem. The similar recovery rates of the skilled and unskilled operators shown in Figure II tend to confirm the hypothesis that skill is a minor factor and motivation is the major determinant of the rate of recovery. Earlier experiments at Harwood by Alex Bavelas demonstrated this point conclusively. He found that the use of group decision techniques on operators who had just been transferred resulted in very marked increases in the rate of relearning, even though no skill training was given and there were no other changes in working conditions.(2)

Interviews with operators who have been transferred to a new job reveal a common pattern of feelings and attitudes which are distinctly different from those of successful non-transfers. In addition to resentment against the management for transferring them, the employees typically show feelings of frustration, loss of hope of ever regaining their former level of production and status in the factory, feelings of failure, and a very low level of aspiration. In this respect these transferred operators are similar to the chronically slow workers studied previously.

Earlier unpublished research at Harwood has shown that the non-transferred employees generally have an explicit goal of reaching and maintaining an efficiency rating of 60 units per hour. A questionnaire administered to several groups of operators indicated that a large majority of them accept as their goal the management's quota of 60 units per hour. This standard of production is the level of aspiration according to which the operators measure their own success or failure; and those who fall below standard lose status in the eyes of their fellow employees. Relatively few operators set a goal appreciably above 60 units per hour.

The actual production records confirm the effectiveness of this goal of standard production. The distribution of the total population of operators in accordance with their production levels is by no means a normal curve. Instead there is a very large number of operators who rate 60 to 63 units per hour and relatively few operators who rate just above or just below this range. Thus we may conclude that:

(1) There is a force acting on the operator in the direction of achieving a production level of 60 units per hour or more. It is assumed that the strength of this driving force (acting on an operator below standard) increases as she gets nearer the goal—a typical goal gradient (see Figure I).

On the other hand restraining forces operate to hinder or prevent her from reaching this goal. These restraining forces consist among other things of the difficulty of the job in relation to the operator's level of skill. Other things being equal, the faster an operator is sewing the more difficult it is to increase her speed by a given amount. Thus we may conclude that:

(2) The strength of the restraining force hindering higher production increases with increasing level of production.

In line with previous studies, it is assumed that the conflict of these two opposing forces—the driving force corresponding to the goal of reaching 60 and the restraining force of the difficulty of the job—produces frustration. In such a conflict situation, the strength of frustration will depend on the strength of these forces. If the restraining force against increasing production is weak, then the frustration will be weak. But if the driving force toward higher production (i.e., the motivation) is weak, then the frustration will also be weak. Probably both of the conflicting forces must be above a certain minimum strength before any frustration is produced; for all goal-directed activity involves some degree of conflict of this type, yet a person is not usually frustrated so long as he is making satisfactory progress toward his goal. Consequently we assume that:

(3) The strength of frustration is a function of the weaker of these two opposing forces, provided that the weaker force is stronger than a certain minimum necessary to produce frustration.(1)

An analysis of the effects of such frustration in the factory showed that it resulted, among other things, in high turnover and absenteeism. The rate of turnover for successful operators with efficiency ratings above standard was much lower than for unsuccessful operators. Likewise, operators on the more difficult jobs quit more frequently than those on the easier jobs. Presumably the effect of being transferred is a severe frustration which should result in similar attempts to escape from the field.

In line with this theory of frustration, and the finding that job turnover is one resultant of frustration, an analysis was made of the turnover rate of transferred operators as compared with the rate among operators who had not been transferred recently. For the year September, 1946, to September, 1947, there were one hundred and ninety-eight operators who had not been transferred recently, that is, within the thirty-four week period allowed for relearning after transfer. There was a second group of eighty-five operators who had been transferred recently, that is, within the time allowed for relearning the new job. Each of these two groups was divided into seven classifications according to their unit rating at the time of quitting. For each classification the percent. turnover per month, based on the total number of employees in that classification, was computed.

The results are given in Figure III. Both the levels of turnover and the form of the curves are strikingly different for the two groups. Among operators who have not been transferred recently the average turnover per month is about $4\frac{1}{2}$ per cent.; among recent transfers the monthly turnover is nearly 12 per cent. Consistent with the previous studies, both groups show a very marked drop in the turnover curve

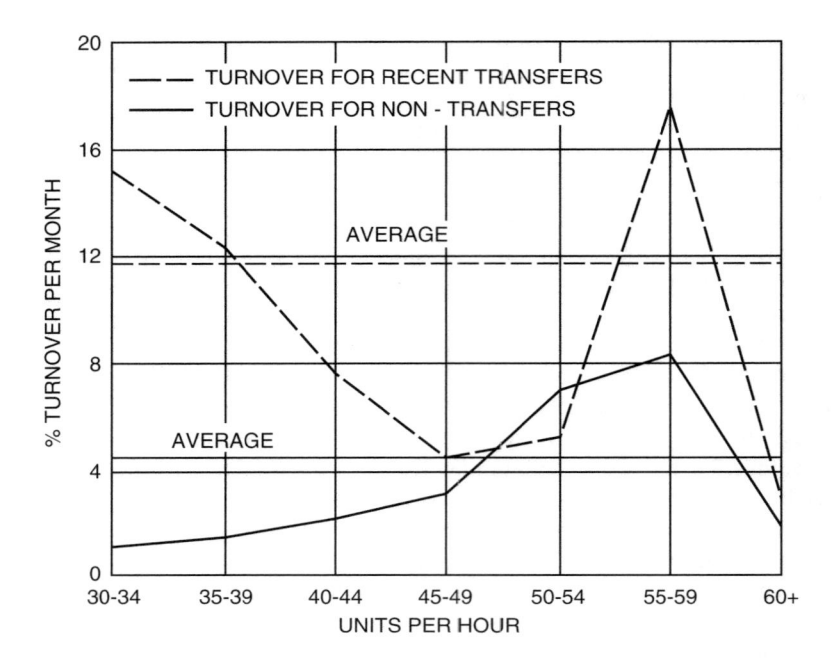

Figure III The rate of turnover at various levels of production for transfers as compared with non-transfers.

after an operator becomes a success by reaching 60 units per hour or standard production. However, the form of the curves at lower unit ratings is markedly different for the two groups. The non-transferred operators show a gradually increasing rate of turnover up to a rating of 55 to 59 units per hour. The transferred operators, on the other hand, show a high peak at the lowest unit rating of 30 to 34 units per hour, decreasing sharply to a low point at 45 to 49 units per hour. Since most changed operators drop to a unit rating of around 30 units per hour when changed and then drop no further, it is obvious that the rate of turnover was highest for these operators just after they were changed and again much later just before they reached standard. Why?

It is assumed that the strength of frustration for an operator who has *not* been transferred gradually increases because both the driving force towards the goal of reaching 60 and the restraining force of the difficulty of the job increase with increasing unit rating. This is in line with hypotheses (1), (2) and (3) above. For the transferred operator on the other hand the frustration is greatest immediately after transfer when the contrast of her present status with her former status is most evident. At this point the strength of the restraining forces is at a maximum because the difficulty is unusually great due to proactive inhibition. Then as she overcomes the interference effects between the two jobs and learns the new job, the difficulty and the frustration gradually decrease and the rate of turnover declines until the operator reaches 45—49 units per hour. Then at higher levels of production the difficulty starts to increase again and the transferred operator shows the same peak in frustration and turnover at 55—59 units per hour.

Though our theory of frustration explains the forms of the two turnover curves in Figure IV, it hardly seems adequate to account for the markedly higher level of turnover for transfers as compared to non-transfers. On the basis of the difficulty of the job, it is especially difficult to explain the higher rate of turnover at 55—59 units per hour for transfers. Evidently additional forces are operating.

Another factor which seems to affect recovery rates of changed operators is the amount of we-feeling. Observations seem to indicate that a strong psychological sub-group with negative attitudes toward management will display the strongest resistance to change. On the other hand, changed groups with high we-feeling and positive cooperative attitudes are the best relearners. Collections of individuals with little or no we-feeling display some resistance to change but not so strongly as the groups with high we-feeling and negative attitudes toward management. However, turnover for the individual transfers is much higher than in the latter groups. This phenomenon of the relationship between we-feeling and resistance to change is so overt that for years the general policy of the management of the plant was never to change a group as a group but rather to scatter the individuals in different areas throughout the factory.

An analysis of turnover records for changed operators with high we-feeling showed a 4 per cent. turnover rate per month at 30 to 34 units per hour, not

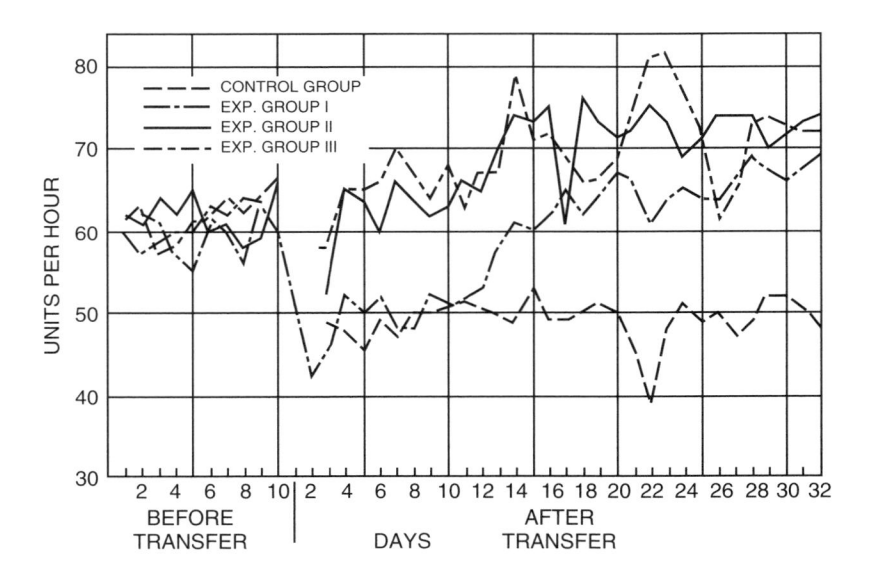

Figure IV The effects of participation through representation (group 1) and of total participation (groups 2 and 3) on recovery after an easy transfer.

significantly higher than in unchanged operators but significantly lower than in changed operators with little or no we-feeling. However, the acts of aggression are far more numerous among operators with high we-feeling than among operators with little we-feeling. Since both types of operators experience the same frustration as individuals but react to it so differently, it is assumed that the effect of the in-group feeling is to set up a restraining force against leaving the group and perhaps even to set up driving forces toward staying in the group. In these circumstances, one would expect some alternative reaction to frustration rather than escape from the field. This alternative is aggression. Strong we-feeling provides strength so that members dare to express aggression which would otherwise be suppressed.

One common result in a sub-group with strong we-feeling is the setting of a group standard concerning production. Where the attitudes toward management are antagonistic, this group standard may take the form of a definite restriction of production to a given level. This phenomenon of restriction is particularly likely to happen in a group that has been transferred to a job where a new piece rate has been set; for they have some hope that if production never approaches the standard, the management may change the piece rate in their favor.

A group standard can exert extremely strong forces on an individual member of a small sub-group. That these forces can have a powerful effect on production is indicated in the production record of one presser during a period of forty days.

In the group

Days	Production per day
1—3	46
4—6	52
7—9	53
10—12	56
Scapegoating begins	
13—16	55
17—20	48
Becomes a single worker	
21—24	83
25—28	92
29—32	92
33—36	91
37—40	92

For the first twenty days she was working in a group of other pressers who were producing at the rate of about 50 units per hour. Starting on the thirteenth day, when she reached standard production and exceeded the production of the other members, she became a scapegoat of the group. During this time her production decreased toward the level of the remaining members of the group. After twenty days the group had to be broken up and all the other members were transferred to other jobs leaving only the scapegoat operator. With the removal of the group, the group standard was no longer operative; and the production of the one remaining operator shot up from the level of about 45 to 96 units per hour in a period of four days. Her production stabilized at a level of about 92 and stayed there for the remainder of the twenty days. Thus it is clear that the motivational forces induced in the individual by a strong sub-group may be more powerful than those induced by management.

The experiment

On the basis of the preliminary theory that resistance to change is a combination of an individual reaction to frustration with strong group-induced forces it seemed that the most appropriate methods for overcoming the resistance to change would be group methods. Consequently an experiment was designed employing two variations of democratic procedure in handling groups to be transferred. The first variation involved participation through representation of the workers in designing the changes to be made in the jobs. The second variation consisted of total participation by all members of the group in designing the changes. A third control group was also used. Two experimental groups received the total participation treatment. The three experimental groups and the control group were roughly matched with respect to: (1) the efficiency ratings of the groups before transfer; (2) the degree of change involved in the transfer; (3) the amount of we-feeling observed in the groups.

In no case was more than a minor change in the work routines and time allowances made. The control group, the eighteen hand pressers, had formerly stacked their work in one-half dozen lots on a flat piece of cardboard the size of the finished product. The new job called for stacking their work in one half dozen lots in a box the size of the finished product. The box was located in the same place the cardboard had been. An additional two minutes per dozen was allowed (by the time study) for this new part of the job. This represented a total job change of 8.8 per cent.

Experimental group 1, the thirteen pajama folders, had formerly folded coats with pre-folded pants. The new job called for the folding of coats with unfolded pants. An additional 1.8 minutes per dozen was allowed (by time study) for this new part of the job. This represented a total job change of 9.4 per cent.

Experimental groups 2 and 3, consisting of eight and seven pajama examiners respectively, had formerly clipped threads from the entire garment and examined every seam. The new job called for pulling only certain threads off and examining every seam. An average of 1.2 minutes per dozen was subtracted (by time study) from the total time on these two jobs. This represented a total job change of 8 per cent.

The control group of hand pressers went through the usual factory routine when they were changed. The production department modified the job, and a new piece rate was set. A group meeting was then held in which the control group was told that the change was necessary because of competitive conditions, and that a new piece rate had been set. The new piece rate was thoroughly explained by the time study man, questions were answered, and the meeting dismissed.

Experimental group 1 was changed in a different manner. Before any changes took place, a group meeting was held with all the operators to be changed. The need for the change was presented as dramatically as possible, showing two identical garments produced in the factory; one was produced in 1946 and had sold for 100 per cent. more than its fellow in 1947. The group was asked to identify the cheaper one and could not do it. This demonstration effectively shared with the group the entire problem of the necessity of cost reduction. A general agreement was reached that a savings could be effected by removing the "frills" and "fancy" work from the garment without affecting the folders' opportunity to achieve a high efficiency rating. Management then presented a plan to set the new job and piece rate:

(1) Make a check study of the job as it was being done.
(2) Eliminate all unnecessary work.
(3) Train several operators in the correct methods.
(4) Set the piece rate by time studies on these specially trained operators.
(5) Explain the new job and rate to all the operators.
(6) Train all operators in the new method so they can reach a high rate of production within a short time.

The group approved this plan (though no formal group decision was reached), and chose the operators to be specially trained. A sub-meeting with the "special" operators was held immediately following the meeting with the entire group. They displayed a cooperative and interested attitude and immediately presented many good suggestions. This attitude carried over into the working out of the details of the new job; and when the new job and piece rates were set, the "special" operators referred to the resultants as "our job," "our rate," etc. The new job and piece rates were presented at a second group meeting to all the operators involved. The "special" operators served to train the other operators on the new job.

Experimental groups 2 and 3 went through much the same kind of change meetings. The groups were smaller than experimental group 1, and a more intimate atmosphere was established. The need for a change was once again made dramatically clear; the same general plan was presented by management. However, since the groups were small, all operators were chosen as "special" operators; that is, all operators were to participate directly in the designing of the new jobs, and all operators would be studied by the time study man. It is interesting to note that in the meetings with these two groups, suggestions were immediately made in such quantity that the stenographer had great difficulty in recording them. The group approved of the plans, but again no formal group decision was reached.

Results

The results of the experiment are summarized in graphic form in Figure IV. The gaps in the production curves occur because these groups were paid on a time-work basis for a day or two. The control group improved little beyond their early efficiency ratings. Resistance developed almost immediately after the change occurred. Marked expressions of aggression against management occurred, such as conflict with the methods engineer, expression of hostility against the supervisor, deliberate restriction of production, and lack of cooperation with the supervisor. There were 17 per cent. quits in the first forty days. Grievances were filed about the piece rate, but when the rate was checked, it was found to be a little "loose."

Experimental group 1 showed an unusually good relearning curve. At the end of fourteen days, the group averaged 61 units per hour. During the fourteen days, the attitude was cooperative and permissive. They worked well with the methods engineer, the training staff, and the supervisor. (The supervisor was the same person in the cases of the control group and experimental group 1). There were no quits in this group in the first forty days. This group might have presented a better learning record if work had not been scarce during the first seven days. There was one act of aggression against the supervisor recorded in the first forty days. It is interesting to note that the three special representative operators in experimental group 1 recovered at about the same rate as the rest of their group.

Experimental groups 2 and 3 recovered faster than experimental group 1. After a slight drop on the first day of change, the efficiency ratings returned to a pre-change level and showed sustained progress thereafter to a level about 14 per cent. higher than the pre-change level. No additional training was provided them after the second day. They worked well with their supervisors and no indications of aggression were observed from these groups. There were no quits in either of these groups in the first forty days.

A fourth experimental group, composed of only two sewing operators, was transferred by the total participation technique. Their new job was one of the most difficult jobs in the factory, in contrast to the easy jobs for the control group and the other three experimental groups. As expected, the total participation technique again resulted in an unusually fast recovery rate and a final level of production well above the level before transfer. Because of the difficulty of the new job, however, the rate of recovery was slower than for experimental groups 2 and 3, but faster than for experimental group 1.

In the first experiment, the control group made no progress after transfer for a period of 32 days. At the end of this period the group was broken up and the individuals were reassigned to new jobs scattered throughout the factory. Two and a half months after their dispersal, the thirteen remaining members of the original control group were again brought together as a group for a second experiment.

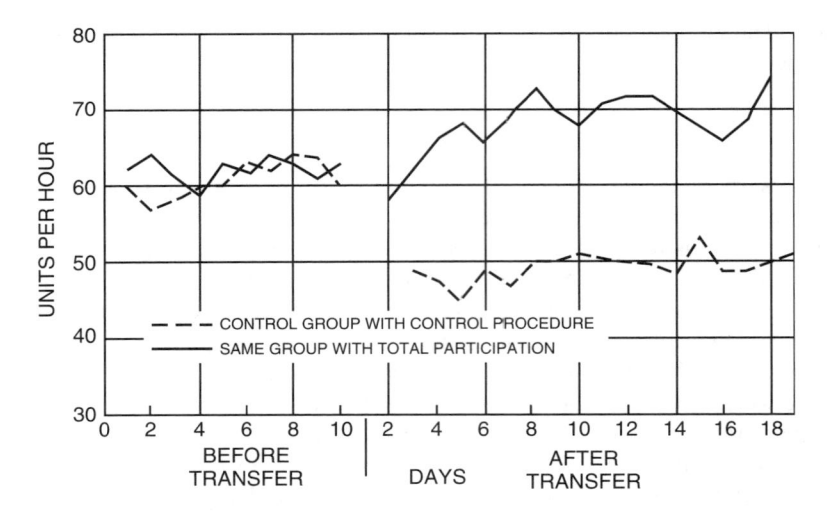

Figure V A comparison of the effect of the control procedure with the total participation procedure on the same group.

This second experiment consisted of transferring the control group to a new job, using the total participation technique in meetings which were similar to those held with experimental groups 2 and 3. The new job was a pressing job of comparable difficulty to the new job in the first experiment. On the average it involved about the same degree of change. In the meetings no reference was made to the previous behavior of the group on being transferred.

The results of the second experiment were in sharp contrast to the first (see Figure V). With the total participation technique, the same control group now recovered rapidly to their previous efficiency rating, and, like the other groups under this treatment, continued on beyond it to a new high level of production. There was no aggression or turnover in the group for 19 days after change, a marked modification of their previous behavior after transfer.

Some anxiety concerning their seniority status was expressed, but this was resolved in a meeting of their elected delegate, the union business agent, and a management representative. It should be noted in Figure V that the prechange level on the second experiment is just above 60 units per hour; thus the individual transfers had progressed to just above standard during the two and a half months between the two experiments.

Interpretation

The purpose of this section is to explain the drop in production resulting from transfer, the differential recovery rates of the control and the experimental groups, the increases beyond their former levels of production by the experimental groups, and the differential rates of turnover and aggression.

The first experiment showed that the rate of recovery is directly proportional to the amount of participation, and that the rates of turnover and aggression are inversely proportional to the amount of participation. The second experiment demonstrated more conclusively that the results obtained depended on the experimental treatment rather than on personality factors like skill or aggressiveness, for identical individuals yielded markedly different results in the control treatment as contrasted with the total participation treatment.

Apparently total participation has the same type of effect as participation through representation, but the former has a stronger influence. In regard to recovery rates, this difference is not unequivocal because the experiment was unfortunately confounded. Right after transfer, experimental group number 1 had insufficient material to work on for a period of seven days. Hence their slower recovery during this period is at least in part due to insufficient work. In succeeding days, however, there was an adequate supply of work and the differential recovery rate still persisted. Therefore we are inclined to believe that participation through representation results in slower recovery than does total participation.

Before discussing the details of why participation produces high morale, we will consider the nature of production levels. In examining the production records of hundreds of individuals and groups in this factory, one is struck by the constancy of the level of production. Though differences among individuals in efficiency rating are very large, nearly every experienced operator maintains a fairly steady level of production given constant physical conditions. Frequently the given level will be maintained despite rather large changes in technical working conditions.

As Lewin has pointed out, this type of production can be viewed as a quasi-stationary process—in the on-going work the operator is forever sewing new garments, yet the level of the process remains relatively stationary. Thus there are constant characteristics of the production process permitting the establishment of general laws.

In studying production as a quasi-stationary equilibrium, we are concerned with two types of forces: (1) forces on production in a downward direction, (2) forces on production in an upward direction. In this situation we are dealing with a variety of both upward forces tending to increase the level of production and downward forces tending to decrease the level of production. However, in the present experiment we have no method of measuring independently all of the component forces either downward or upward. These various component forces upward are combined into one resultant force upward. Likewise the several downward component forces combine into one resultant force downward. We can infer a good deal about the relative strengths of these resultant forces.

Where we are dealing with a quasi-stationary equilibrium, the resultant forces upward and the forces downward are opposite in direction and equal in strength at the equilibrium level. Of course either resultant forces may fluctuate over a short period of time, so that the forces may not be equally balanced at a given moment.

However, over a longer period of time and on the average the forces balance out. Fluctuations from the average occur but there is a tendency to return to the average level.

Just before being transferred, all of the groups in both experiments had reached a stable equilibrium level at just above the standard production of 60 units per hour. This level was equal to the average efficiency rating for the entire factory during the period of the experiments. Since this production level remained constant, neither increasing nor decreasing, we may be sure that the strength of the resultant force upward was equal to the strength of the resultant force downward. This equilibrium of forces was maintained over the period of time when production was stationary at this level. But the forces changed markedly after transfer, and these new constellations of forces were distinctly different for the control and the experimental groups.

For the control group the period after transfer is a quasi-stationary equilibrium at a lower level, and the forces do not change during the period of thirty days. The resultant force upward remains equal to the resultant force downward and the level of production remains constant. The force field for this group is represented schematically in Figure VI. Only the resultant forces are shown. The length of the vector represents the strength of the force; and the point of the arrow represents the point of application of the force, that is, the production level and the time at which the force applies. Thus the forces are equal and opposite only at the level of 50 units per hour. At higher levels of production the forces downward are greater than the forces upward; and at lower levels of production the forces upward are

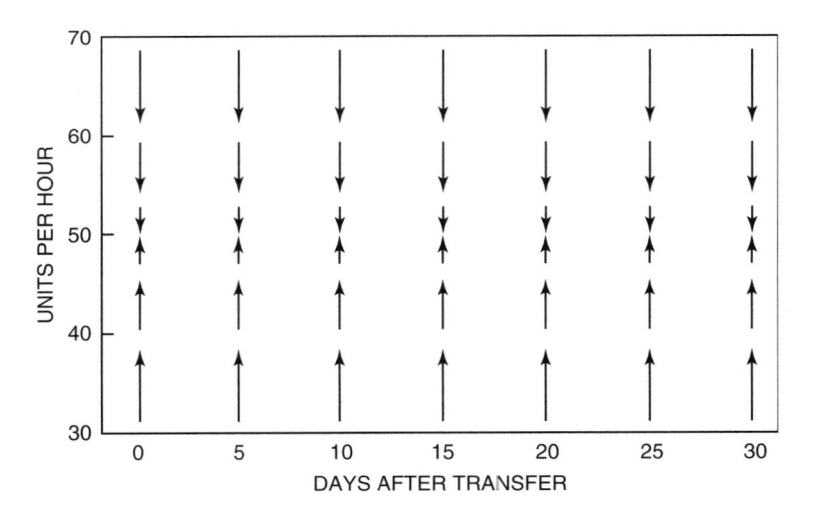

Figure VI A schematic diagram of the quasi-stationary equilibrium for the control group after transfer.

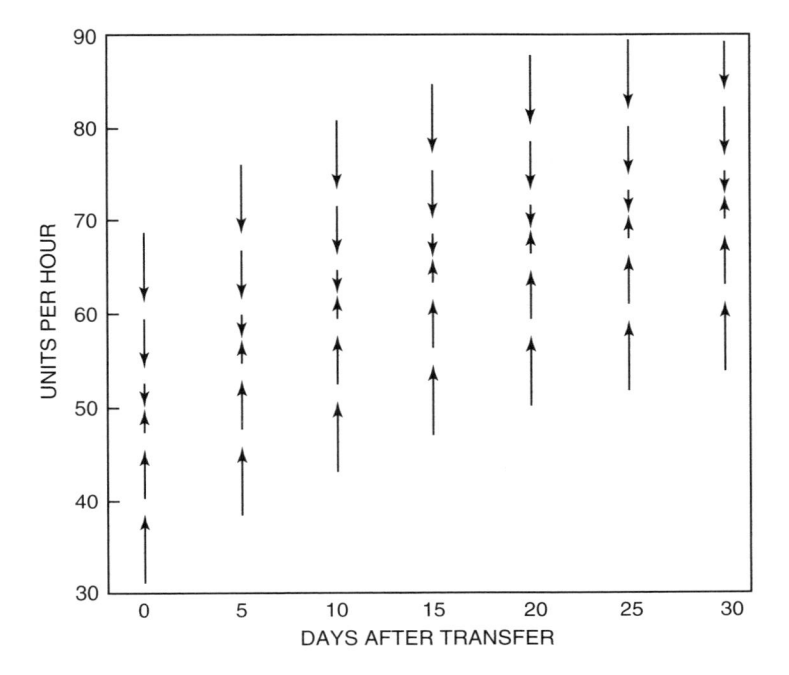

Figure VII A schematic diagram of the quasi-stationary equilibrium for the experimental groups after transfer.

stronger than the forces downward. Thus there is a tendency for the equilibrium to be maintained at an efficiency rating of 50.

The situation for the experimental groups after transfer can be viewed as a quasi-stationary equilibrium of a different type. Figure VII gives a schematic diagram of the resultant forces for the experimental groups. At any given level of production, such as 50 units per hour or 60 units per hour, both the resultant forces upward and the resultant forces downward change over the period of thirty days. During this time the point of equilibrium, which starts at 50 units per hour, gradually rises until it reaches a level of over 70 units per hour after thirty days. Yet here again the equilibrium level has the character of a "central force field" where at any point in the total field the resultant of the upward and the downward forces is in the direction of the equilibrium level.

To understand how the difference between the experimental and the control treatments produced the differences in force fields represented in Figures VI and VII, it is not sufficient to consider only the resultant forces. We must also look at the component forces for each resultant force.

There are three main component forces influencing production in a downward direction: (1) the difficulty of the job (see p. 517); (2) a force corresponding to avoidance of strain; (3) a force corresponding to a group standard to restrict production to a given level. The resultant force upward in the direction of greater production is composed of three additional component forces; (1) the force corresponding to the goal of standard production (see p. 516); (2) a force corresponding to pressures induced by the management through supervision; (3) a force corresponding to a group standard of competition. Let us examine each of these six component forces.

1. Job difficulty

For all operators the difficulty of the job is one of the forces downward on production. The difficulty of the job, of course, is relative to the skill of the operator. The given job may be very difficult for an unskilled operator but relatively easy for a highly skilled one. In the case of a transfer a new element of difficulty enters. For some time the new job is much more difficult, for the operator is unskilled at that particular job. In addition to the difficulty experienced by any learner, the transfer often encounters the added difficulty of proactive inhibition. Where the new job is similar to the old job there will be a period of interference between the two similar but different skills required. For this reason a very efficient operator whose skills have become almost unconscious may suffer just as great a drop as a much less efficient operator (see Figure II). Except for group 4, the difficulty of these easy jobs does not explain the differential recovery rates because both the initial difficulty and the amount of change were equated for these groups. The two operators in group 4 probably dropped further and recovered more slowly than any of the other three groups under total participation because of the greater difficulty of the job.

2. Strain avoidance

The force toward lower production corresponding to the difficulty of the job (or the lack of skill of the person) has the character of a restraining force—that is, it acts to prevent locomotion rather than as a driving force causing locomotion. However, in all production there is a closely related driving force towards lower production, namely "strain avoidance." We assume that working too hard and working too fast is an unpleasant strain; and corresponding to this negative valence there is a driving force in the opposite direction, namely towards taking it easy or working slower. The higher the level of production the greater will be the strain and, other things being equal, the stronger will be the downward force of strain avoidance. Likewise, the greater the difficulty of the job the stronger will be the force corresponding to strain avoidance. But the greater the operator's skill the smaller will be the strain and the strength of the force of strain avoidance. Therefore:

(4) The strength of the force of strain avoidance

$$= \frac{\text{job difficulty} \times \text{production level}}{\text{skill of operator}}$$

The differential recovery rates of the control group in both experiments and the three experimental groups in Experiment I cannot be explained by strain avoidance because job difficulty, production level, and operator skill were matched at the time immediately following transfer. Later, however, when the experimental treatments had produced a much higher level of production, these groups were subjected to an increased downward force of strain avoidance which was stronger than in the control group in Experiment I. Evidently other forces were strong enough to overcome this force of strain avoidance.

3. The goal of standard production

In considering the negative attitudes toward transfer and the resistance to being transferred, there are several important aspects of the complex goal of reaching and maintaining a level of 60 units per hour. For an operator producing below standard, this goal is attractive because it means success, high status in the eyes of her fellow employees, better pay, and job security (see p. 516). On the other hand, there is a strong force against remaining below standard because this lower level means failure, low status, low pay, and the danger of being fired. Thus it is clear that the upward force corresponding to the goal of standard production will indeed be strong for the transfer who has dropped below standard.

It is equally clear why any operator, who accepts the stereotype about transfer, shows such strong resistance to being changed. She sees herself as becoming a failure and losing status, pay, and perhaps the job itself. The result is a lowered level of aspiration and a weakened force toward the goal of standard production.

Just such a weakening of the force toward 60 units per hour seems to have occurred in the control group in Experiment I. The participation treatments, on the other hand, seem to have involved the operators in designing the new job and setting the new piece rates in such a way that they did not lose hope of regaining the goal of standard production. Thus the participation resulted in a stronger force toward higher production. However, this force alone can hardly account for the large differences in recovery rate between the control group and the experimental groups; certainly it does not explain why the latter increased to a level so high above standard.

4. Management pressure

On all operators below standard the management exerts a pressure for higher production. This pressure is no harsh and autocratic treatment involving threats. Rather it takes the form of persuasion and encouragement by the supervisors. They attempt to induce the low rating operator to improve her performance and to attain standard production.

Such an attempt to induce a psychological force on another person may have several results. In the first place the person may ignore the attempt of the inducing agent, in which case there is no induced force acting on the person. On the other hand, the attempt may succeed so that an induced force on the person exists. Other things being equal, whenever there is an induced force acting on a person, the person will locomote in the direction of the force. An induced force, which depends on the power field of an inducing agent—some other individual or group—will cease to exist when the inducing power field is withdrawn. In this report it is different from an "own" force which stems from a person's own needs and goals.

The reaction of a person to an effective induced force will vary depending, among other things, on the person's relation to the inducing agent. A force induced by a friend may be accepted in such a way that it acts more like an own force. An effective force induced by an enemy may be resisted and rejected so that the person complies unwillingly and shows signs of conflict and tension. Thus in addition to what might be called a "neutral" induced force, we also distinguish an *accepted* induced force and a *rejected* induced force. Naturally the acceptance and the rejection of an induced force can vary in degree from zero (i.e., a neutral induced force) to very strong acceptance or rejection. To account for the difference in character between the acceptance and the rejection of an induced force, we make the following assumptions:

(5) The acceptance of an induced force sets up additional own forces in the same direction.
(6) The rejection of an induced force sets up additional own forces in the opposite direction.

The grievances, aggression, and tension in the control group in Experiment I indicate that they rejected the force toward higher production induced by the management. The group accepted the stereotype that transfer is a calamity, but the control procedure did not convince them that the change was necessary and they viewed the new job and the new piece rates set by management as arbitrary and unreasonable.

The experimental groups, on the contrary, participated in designing the changes and setting the piece rates so that they spoke of the new job as "our job" and the new piece rates as "our rates". Thus they accepted the new situation and accepted the management induced force toward higher production.

From the acceptance by the experimental groups and the rejection by the control group of the management induced forces, we may derive (by (5) and (6) above) that the former had additional own forces toward higher production whereas the latter had additional own forces toward lower production. This difference helps to explain the better recovery rate of the experimental groups.

5. Group standards

Probably the most important force affecting the recovery under the control procedure was a group standard, set by the group, restricting the level of production to 50 units per hour. Evidently this explicit agreement to restrict production is related to the group's rejection of the change and of the new job as arbitrary and unreasonable. Perhaps they had faint hopes of demonstrating that standard production could not be attained and thereby obtain a more favorable piece rate. In any case there was a definite group phenomenon which affected all the members of the group. We have already noted the striking example of the presser whose production was restricted in the group situation to about half the level she attained as an individual (see p. 519). In the control group, too, we would expect the group to induce strong forces on the members. The more a member deviates above the standard the stronger would be the group-induced force to conform to the standard, for such deviations both negate any possibility of management's increasing the piece rate and at the same time expose the other members to increased pressure from management. Thus individual differences in levels of production should be sharply curtailed in the control group after transfer.

An analysis was made for all groups of the individual differences within the group in levels of production. In Experiment I the 40 days before change were compared with the 30 days after change; in Experiment II the 10 days before change were compared to the 17 days after change. As a measure of variability, the standard deviation was calculated each day for each group. The average daily standard deviations *before* and *after* change were as follows:

Group	Variability		
Experiment I	Before Change		After Change
Control group	9.8	...	1.9
Experimental 1	9.7	...	3.8
Experimental 2	10.3	...	2.7
Experimental 3	9.9	...	2.4
Experiment II			
Control group	12.7	...	2.9

There is indeed a marked decrease in individual differences within the control group after their first transfer. In fact the restriction of production resulted in a lower variability than in any other group. Thus we may conclude that the group standard at 50 units per hour set up strong group-induced forces which were important components in the central force field shown in Figure VI. It is now evident that for the control group the quasi-stationary equilibrium after transfer has a steep gradient around the equilibrium level of 50 units per hour—the strength of the forces increase rapidly above and below this level. It is also clear that the group standard to restrict production is a major reason for the lack of recovery in the control group.

The table of variability also shows that the experimental treatments markedly reduced variability in the other four groups after transfer. In experimental group 1 (participation by representation) this smallest reduction of variability was produced by a group standard of individual competition. Competition among members of the group was reported by the supervisor soon after transfer. This competition was a force toward higher production which resulted in good recovery to standard and continued progress beyond standard.

Experimental groups 2 and 3 showed a greater reduction in variability following transfer. These two groups under total participation were transferred on the same day. Group competition developed between the two groups. This group competition, which evidently resulted in stronger forces on the members than did the individual competition, was an effective group standard. The standard gradually moved to higher and higher levels of production with the result that the groups not only reached but far exceeded their previous levels of production.

Turnover and aggression

Returning now to our preliminary theory of frustration, we can see several revisions. The difficulty of the job and its relation to skill and strain avoidance has been clarified in proposition (4). It is now clear that the driving force toward 60 is a complex affair; it is partly a negative driving force corresponding to the negative valence of low pay, low status, failure, and job insecurity. Turnover results not only from the frustration produced by the conflict of these two forces, but also as a direct attempt to escape from the region of these negative valences. For the members of the control group, the group standard to restrict production prevented escape by increasing production, so that quitting their jobs was the only remaining escape. In the participation groups, on the contrary, both the group standards and the additional own forces resulting from the acceptance of management-induced forces combined to make increasing production the distinguished path of escape from this region of negative valence.

In considering turnover as a form of escape from the field, it is not enough to look only at the psychological present; one must also consider the psychological future. The employee's decision to quit the job is rarely made exclusively on the basis of a momentary frustration or an undesirable present situation; she usually quits when she also sees the future as equally hopeless. The operator transferred by the usual factory procedure (including the control group) has in fact a realistic view of the probability of continued failure because, as we have already noted, 62 per cent. of transfers do in fact fail to recover to standard production. Thus the higher rate of quitting for transfers as compared to non-transfers results from a more pessimistic view of the future.

The control procedure had the effect for the members of setting up management as a hostile power field. They rejected the forces induced by this hostile power field, and group standards to restrict production developed within the group in opposition to management. In this conflict between the power field of management and the power field of the group, the control group attempted to reduce the strength of the hostile power field relative to the strength of their own power field. This change was accomplished in three ways: (1) the group increased its own power by developing a more cohesive and well-disciplined group, (2) they secured "allies" by getting the backing of the union in filing a formal grievance about the new piece rate, (3) they attacked the hostile power field directly in the form of aggression against the supervisor, the time study engineer, and the higher management. Thus the aggression was derived not only from individual frustration but also from the conflict between two groups. Furthermore, this situation of group conflict both helped to define management as the frustrating agent and gave the members strength to express any aggressive impulses produced by frustration.

Conclusions

It is possible for management to modify greatly or to remove completely group resistance to changes in methods of work and the ensuing piece rates. This change can be accomplished by the use of group meetings in which management effectively communicates the need for change and stimulates group participation in planning the changes.

For Harwood's management, and presumably for managements of other industries using an incentive system, this experiment has important implications in the field of labor relations. A majority of all grievances presented at Harwood have always stemmed from a change situation. By preventing or greatly modifying group resistance to change, this concomitant to change may well be greatly reduced. The reduction of such costly phenomena as turnover and slow relearning rates presents another distinct advantage.

Harwood's management has long felt that action research such as the present experiment is the only key to better labor-management relations. It is only by discovering the basic principles and applying them to the true causes of conflict that an intelligent, effective effort can be made to correct the undesirable effects of the conflict.

Acknowledgments

Grateful acknowledgements are made by the authors to Dr. Alfred J. Marrow, president of the Harwood Manufacturing Corporation, and to the entire Harwood staff for their valuable aid and suggestions in this study.

The authors have drawn repeatedly from the works and concepts of Kurt Lewin for both the action and theoretical phases of this study.

Many of the leadership techniques used in the experimental group meetings were techniques developed at the first National Training Laboratory for Group Development held at Bethel, Maine, in the summer of 1947. Both authors attended this laboratory.

References

French, John R. P., Jnr.: The Behaviour of Organized and Unorganized Groups under Conditions of Frustration and Fear, Studies in Topological and Vector Psychology, III, *University of Iowa Studies in Child Welfare*, 1944, Vol. XX, pp. 229–308.

Lewin, Kurt: Frontiers in Group Dynamics, *Human Relations*, Vol. I, No. 1, 1947, pp. 5–41.

49

COUNTERPRODUCTIVE BEHAVIOURS AT WORK

Adrian Furnham and John Taylor

Source: *A. Furnham and J. Taylor, The Dark Side of Behaviour at Work: Understanding and Avoiding Employees Leaving, Thieving and Deceiving,* Basingstoke: Palgrave Macmillan, 2004 pp. 83–129.

Introduction

The list of antisocial, deviant and destructive behaviours at work is long: absenteeism, accidents, bullying, corruption, disciplinary problems, drug and alcohol abuse, sabotage, sexual harassment, tardiness, theft, whistle-blowing, white collar crime and violence are typical examples of what one could list as counterproductive behaviours or CWBs.

The term CWB is often used synonymously with antisocial, deviant, dysfunctional, retaliative and unethical behaviour at work (Marcus 2000). It costs organizations billions every year and many of them invest in ways to prevent, reduce or catch those most likely to offend. There are many different words to describe CWBs, such as: organizational delinquency, production and property deviance, workplace deviance. All agree it is a multifaceted behavioural syndrome that is characterized by hostility to authority, impulsivity, social insensitivity, alienation and lack of moral integrity. People feel frustrated or powerless or unfairly dealt with and act accordingly.

CWB is intentional and contrary to the interests of the organization. CWB may not in the shortfall be reflected in counterproductivity which is the cost of CWBs. The essence of a CWB is wrongdoing: not counternormativeness or hurting the organization. Thus taking sick leave when not sick may be a common occurrence, indeed the norm, yet still a CWB.

So what are we talking about? Sackett (2002) listed 11 groups of CWB:

1 Theft and related behaviour (theft of cash or property; giving away of goods or services, misuse of employee discount).

2   Destruction of property (deface, damage, or destroy property; sabotage production).
3   Misuse of information (reveal confidential information; falsify records).
4   Misuse of time and resources (waste time, alter time card, conduct personal business during work time).
5   Unsafe behaviour (failure to follow safety procedures; failure to learn safety procedures).
6   Poor attendance (unexcused absence or tardiness; misuse sick leave).
7   Poor quality work (intentionally slow or sloppy work).
8   Alcohol use (alcohol use on the job; coming to work under the influence of alcohol).
9   Drug use (possess, use, or sell drugs at work).
10 Inappropriate verbal actions (argue with customers; verbally harass co-workers).
11 Inappropriate physical actions (physically attack co-workers; physical sexual advances toward co-worker). (pp 5–6)

A central question for both the scientist and the manager is whether these eleven types of CWB are discrete or related. In other words, does each CWB have its own unique characteristics or are they are all related and the product of a mix of different personality types and organization situations?

At the heart of the matter is whether people who engage in one type of CWB (for example sabotage) are also likely to engage in others (for example theft). It should of course be recognized that work contexts limit and provide opportunities for specific types of CWB. However, various studies using different groups have revealed a fairly strong correlation between self-reported CWBs (Sackett 2002). In other words, people seem likely to (or not) take part in any/all or no counterproductive behaviours. Thus it seems that people could be put on a continuum in terms of how likely they are to engage in CWBs from very unlikely to very likely.

No doubt the choice of CWB to the individual is limited. Some thieve, others destroy, some go absent a lot, others do shoddy work. Perhaps their personality, opportunity, level of courage or anger determines how they act but the essential point is that people seek their vengeance where they can. Put another way, the essential causes of theft, sabotage, whistle-blowing or lying and cheating are probably the same.

Classification of bad behaviours

There are few more distressing experiences in the workplace for managers than having to cope with an employee who has deliberately done wrong. The implications of not taking action are often even greater and if situations are handled badly managers compound the errors.

The sooner problems can be identified the easier they are to handle and, if managed well, the potential costs of counterproductive behaviour are reduced.

Staff are often described as a company's most valuable resource. It is often said and quoted by CEOs. The published material on managing employees prefers to emphasize the positive: how to maximize potential, retaining great employees, motivating for success, win-win. The list is long and extensive.

In an earlier study that tried to classify deviant behaviours, Robinson and Bennett (1995) came up with the impressive list on the page opposite.

- Employee stealing customer's possessions.
- Boss verbally abusing employee.
- Employee sabotaging equipment.
- Employee coming to work late or leaving early.
- Employee lying about hours worked.
- Employee gossiping about manager.
- Employee starting negative rumours about company.
- Boss sexually harassing employee.
- Employee physically abusing customer.
- Employee taking excessive breaks.
- Employee sabotaging merchandise.
- Employee overcharging on services to profit him or herself.
- Employee intentionally making errors.
- Employee covering up mistakes.
- Employee leaving job in progress with no directions so the job is done wrong.
- Boss following rules to the letter of the law.
- Employee gossiping about co-worker.
- Employee intentionally working slowly.
- Boss unjustifiably firing employee.
- Employee sexually harassing co-worker.
- Employee accepting kickbacks.
- Employee endangering him or herself by not following safety procedures.
- Boss leaving early and leaving his/her work for employees to do.
- Employee hiding in back room to read the newspaper.
- Employee stealing company equipment/merchandise.
- Employee acting foolishly in front of customers.
- Employee verbally abusing customers.
- Employee working unnecessary overtime.
- Employee calling in sick when not.
- Boss showing favouritism to certain employees.
- Boss gossiping about employees.
- Employee talking with co-worker instead of working.
- Employee stealing money from cash drawer.
- Employee misusing discount privilege.
- Employee wasting company resources by turning up the heat and opening the windows.
- Employee blaming co-worker for mistakes.
- Employee misusing expense account.

COUNTERPRODUCTIVE BEHAVIOURS AT WORK

- Employee going against boss's decision.
- Employees competing with co-workers in a non-beneficial way.
- Boss blaming employees for his/her mistakes.
- Boss refusing to give employee his/her earned benefits or pay.
- Employee making personal long-distance calls or mailing personal packages from work.
- Employee endangering co-workers by reckless behaviour.
- Employee stealing co-worker's possessions.
- Boss asking employee to work beyond job description.

Robinson and Bennett (1997a) describe CWBs as 'voluntary behaviour of organizational members that violates significant organizational norms and, in so doing, threatens the well-being of the organization and/or its members' (p 7). They also offer two-by-two categorization of CWBs (see Figure 4.1).

They offer both a simple model of the path to deviance (see Figure 4.2) and also a more detailed model that tries to predict which type of deviance will occur (Robinson and Bennett 1997b p 15).

They have five propositions based on this model:

P1: If the provocation produces an expressive motivation, an employee will be more likely to direct his or her actions at the perceived source of the provocation (individual or organization), with one of the most legitimate/least deviant action that is available, satisfying and unconstrained.

P2: If the provocation produces an expressive motivation, an employee will be more likely to engage in a more serious deviant act to the extent that more minor deviant acts are unavailable, unsatisfying, and/or constrained.

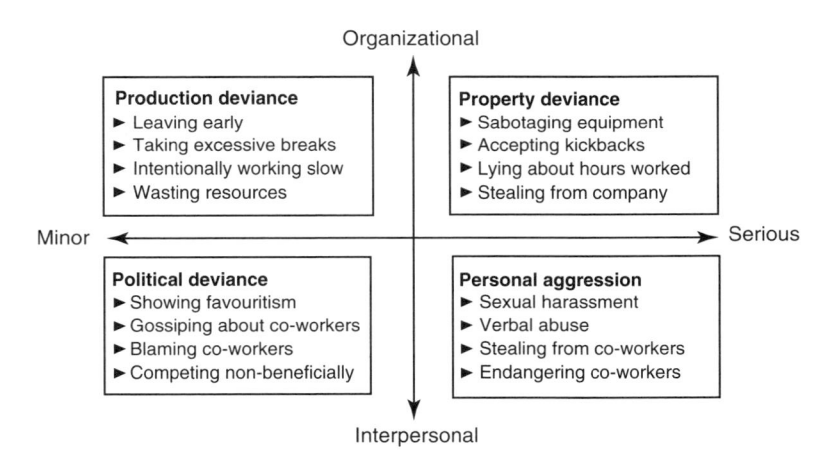

```
                          Organizational
                               ▲
         ┌──────────────────────┬──────────────────────┐
         │ Production deviance  │ Property deviance    │
         │ ► Leaving early      │ ► Sabotaging equipment│
         │ ► Taking excessive   │ ► Accepting kickbacks │
         │   breaks             │ ► Lying about hours   │
         │ ► Intentionally      │   worked              │
         │   working slow       │ ► Stealing from       │
         │ ► Wasting resources  │   company             │
Minor ◄──┼──────────────────────┼──────────────────────┼──► Serious
         │ Political deviance   │ Personal aggression  │
         │ ► Showing favouritism│ ► Sexual harassment   │
         │ ► Gossiping about    │ ► Verbal abuse        │
         │   co-workers         │ ► Stealing from       │
         │ ► Blaming co-workers │   co-workers          │
         │ ► Competing non-     │ ► Endangering         │
         │   beneficially       │   co-workers          │
         └──────────────────────┴──────────────────────┘
                               ▼
                          Interpersonal
```

Figure 4.1 Typology of deviant workplace behaviour. (*Source:* Robinson and Bennett 1997a.)

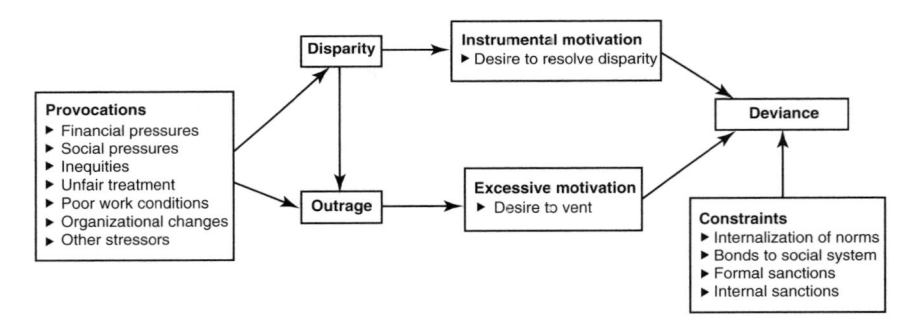

Figure 4.2 A model of workplace deviance. (*Source:* Robinson and Bennett 1997b p 15.)

P3: If the provocation produces an expressive motivation, an employee will be more likely to direct his or her actions at a target other than the perceived source of the provocation to the extent that minor and serious forms of deviance directed at the perceived source are unavailable, unsatisfying, and/or contained. (p 22)

P4: If the provocation produces an instrumental motivation, an employee will be more likely to direct his or her actions at the target (individual or organization) that is most pertinent to resolving the disparity, with the most legitimate/least deviant action mat is available, effective, and unconstrained.

P5: If the provocation produces an instrumental motivation, an employee will be more likely to engage in more serious deviant acts to the extent that more minor deviant acts are unavailable, ineffective, and/or constrained. (p 23)

Various researchers have placed emphasis on slightly different features. Thus Grover (1993) believes role conflict at work is a major cause of CWB. Triggers (felt injustice, stressors) provoke a deviant reaction; because of lack of constraints there are opportunities to perform CWBs in individuals with poor self-control.

There are not many theories specifically of CWBs but one exception is that of Martinko et al. (2002) who developed what they called a Causal Reasoning Perspective. Their aim was to demonstrate the relationships and similarities between and among various forms of CWBs. They define CWBs as those 'characterized by a disregard for societal and organizational rules and values; actions that threaten the well being of an organization and its members and break implicit and explicit rules about appropriate, civil and respectful behaviour'.

Martinko et al. (2002) reviewed over 20 relevant studies that looked at individual difference variables and situational variables that seemed related to CWB; individual differences included personality (for example neuroticism, Machiavellianism), demography (age, sex), morality (integrity), organizational experience (tenure, commitment) and self-perceptions (self-esteem, self-concept). The situational or organizational variables included organizational policies, practices, norms, rules, resource scarcity, job autonomy and appraisals.

Note that the attribution must be about stable causes, meaning stable over time. Unstable causes by definition come and go and lead to quite different attributions. Thus lack of ability is a stable attribution, but being in a bad mood or having a cold is an unstable attribution.

The theory shown diagrammatically (Figure 4.3) goes like this. An individual in a particular work situation, say a person with low self-esteem and low integrity in a difficult competitive work environment with adverse work conditions feels that things are not fair. The model talks of perceived disequilibria, or feelings of injustice or inequity. Associated with this feeling of unfairness is the cause or attribution that the person makes for this state of affairs. If they believe *they personally* are the cause (internal stable attribution) they are likely to take part in self-destructive behaviours, but if they feel the cause is *external* (that is, their boss, unfair company rules) they are likely to take part in retaliation behaviour.

What is attractive about this model is essentially three things. First, it attempts to differentiate between different types of CWB, here called self destructive and retaliatory behaviour. Second, it offers a process whereby CWBs are likely to occur. Third, it describes some of the more important individual difference factors that are associated with CWBs.

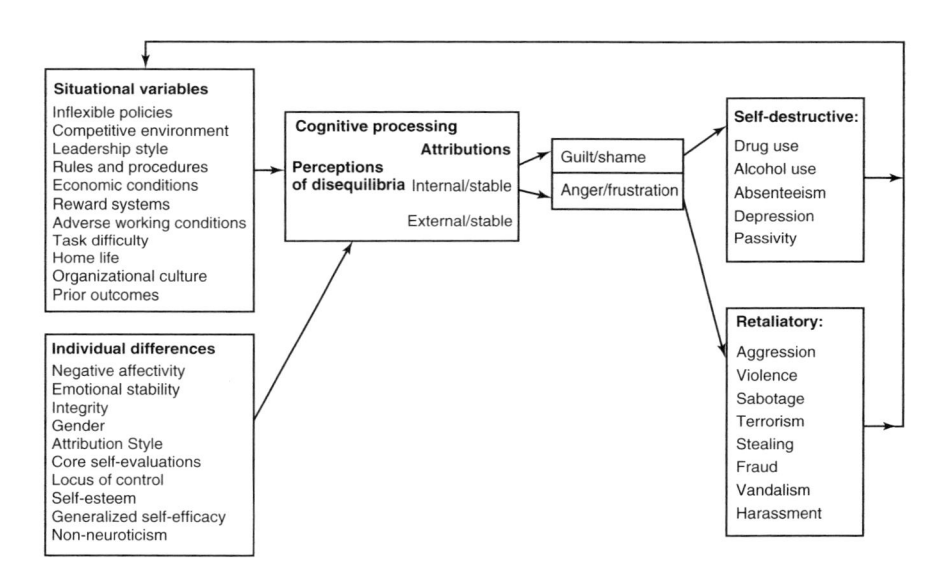

Figure 4.3 A causal reasoning model of counterproductive behaviour. (*Source:* Adapted from Martinko et al. 2002.)

Martinko et al. (2002) describe in detail six individual difference factor they believe to be heavily implicated in CWBs:

1. *Gender:* Overwhelmingly CWBs are more likely to be the province of males because they make more aggressive attributions and tend to be more self-serving by blaming others for their failure.
2. *Locus of control:* Those who are fatalistic, believing their lives are determined by chance or powerful others, compared with instrumentalists who believe they control their own life outcomes, are more likely to commit CWBs.
3. *Attribution/explanation style:* Those with hostile and pessimistic attribution styles, in other words, those who attribute person failure either to external, stable and intentional causes (that is, a nasty boss) or internal, stable and global causes (that is, I have no ability) tend to cause more CWBs. In other words, how people characteristically describe their own success and failure is a good predictor of their likelihood to become involved in CWBs.
4. *Core self-evaluations:* These are fundamental beliefs about self and are similar to self-esteem. Hardy, stable, 'can do' people are less likely to feel victims or experience organizational paranoia and less likely to be involved in CWBs.
5. *Integrity*: People with integrity tend to be agreeable, conscientious, emotionally stable and reliable. They are clearly less likely to get involved in CWBs.
6. *Neuroticism* (negative affectivity): This refers to the extent to which individuals experience anger, anxiety, fear and hostility. Stable individuals tend to be more satisfied with their lives and focus on the positive. Neurotics often feel people in their environment are demanding, distant and threatening. Neurotics are more prone to CWBs.

Certainly this model is a promising start. The authors are wary of limitations but make a good cause for specifying a reasonable process which explains how, why and when individuals in certain work situations do, and do not, get involved in CWBs.

Theft

> *Companies around the world will spend an estimated US$75 billion this year on security-related products and services. That sum will include mountains of high-tech equipment, investigators' fees, and salaries for thousands of security officers. With losses from corporate fraud put at between US$250 billion and US$400 billion annually, the obvious question is: Is this money well spent?*
> *The Enemy Within*—report by Stephen Payne February 2000 http://www.cfoasia.com/archives/200002-20.htm

Organizations often label theft as 'inventory shrinkage' and it may be 2–3% of retail sales. Up to half of this can be employee theft. These figures differ from country to country, sector to sector and year to year but are serious enough for many organizations to call for expensive countermeasures. Electronic security tags, cameras and observation mirrors, locks and chains and armed security guards are commonplace in many shops. They may or may not act as deterrents. They can make matters worse (see Chapters 9 and 10).

It is impossible to get accurate and reliable statistics on employee theft. Estimates vary as a function of the research and the business domains. It is also difficult to define theft or to suggest that 'taking home' a few envelopes is equivalent to stealing large sums of money or valuable goods. 'Ball-park' figures vary considerably that from a quarter to two-thirds of all employees are involved in some sort of theft at work.

There are all sorts of definitional issues. Employers and employees have different definitions particularly when the words thief and victim are used. Also there is trivial theft (a few paper clips), semi-trivial (pens and paper) and non-trivial theft (computers). It is possible to distinguish between *production theft* (poor output) and *material theft* (property/money). Production theft includes work slow-downs while material theft is quite clearly property theft. There is also theft of time (absenteeism) and theft of goods produced by the company.

Some have distinguished between *altruistic theft* (giving stolen goods to others) and *selfish theft*. This is often a post-rationalization of the thief who claims that he/she is more like Robin Hood than a common criminal. There is also *preventable* vs. *non-preventable theft*. This may be a more fuzzy distinction than can be made here. There is scarcely any crime that is totally non-preventable, although the risks can be significantly reduced.

Essentially theft is the unlawful taking, transfer or control of another's (the employer) property with the aim of benefiting the thief (and others) who are not entitled to that property.

In every company or organization there are staff who thieve. It may be mostly petty theft, but the extent is often surprising. The evidence is growing that employees regularly steal from their employers. Estimates vary considerably from researcher to researcher, from business sector to business sector and from country to country. But the overall picture is compelling: employee theft is hurting companies and organizations.

There is no single database that details the extent of the problem. The retail industry has always recognized that 'shrinkage' of its stocks is a problem. Until recently the blame was put on the customer and described as shoplifting. Now employers recognize that employees are also responsible. The 2002 National Retail Security Survey produced by the University of Florida reported that 'retailers attributed 48% of their inventory shrinkage to employee theft'. Shoplifting, often thought to be retailer's biggest problem, is only 32% (see Figure 4.4).

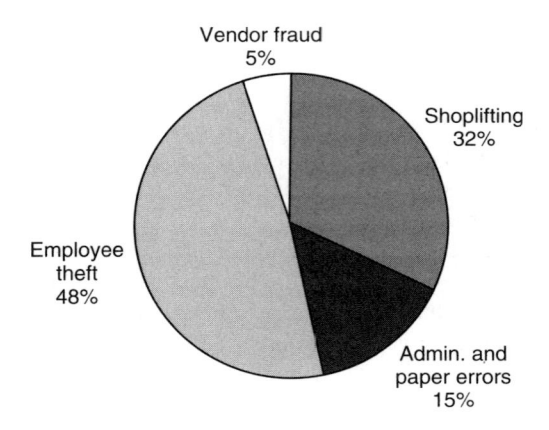

Figure 4.4 Sources of shrinkage in US 2002. (*Source:* University of Florida, National Retail Security Survey 2002.)

The report goes on:

> Assuming a total shrinkage dollar total of approximately $31.3 billion, this translates into an annual employee theft price tag of slightly over $15 billion ... There is no other form of larceny that annually costs American citizens more money than employee theft.

According to this report convenience stores and supermarkets suffer the greatest losses (Hollinger 2002).

In Europe the situation is a little different. The third report of the European Retail Theft Barometer collected data from 16 European countries. The report estimates the costs of shrinkage in Europe to be €27,258 million in the year 2002/03 or 1.37% of turnover. Customers who shoplift represent 48% and internal error is 17%. Another 7% is the responsibility of the suppliers (Figure 4.5).

Taking each country separately the shrinkage problem is most acute in the UK, where staff theft accounts for 36% of shrinkage, with Denmark, Norway and The Netherlands 32%. Portugal and Germany have less staff theft at 22% and 23%, but, by the same analysis, a higher shoplifting rate (Table 4.1).

Retailers have responded by increasing the amount invested in security. They now spend €6364 million on security, an increase of 22% over the previous year (2001/02), but this figure includes measures to combat theft by customers and suppliers.

The opportunity for thieving is perhaps greater in a shop than, say, an employment agency, but opportunities exist in all businesses.

COUNTERPRODUCTIVE BEHAVIOURS AT WORK

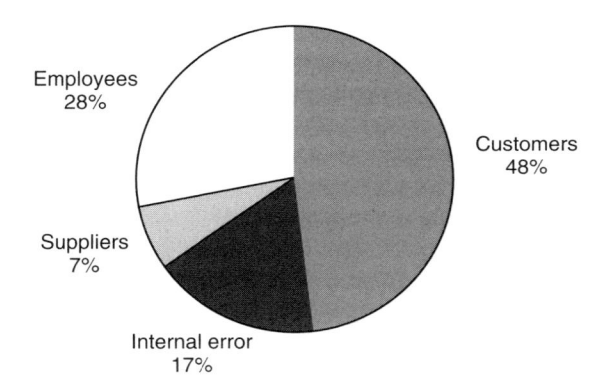

Figure 4.5 Sources of shrinkage in Europe 2002/03. (*Source: The European Retail Theft Barometer*, Centre for Retail Research February–May 2003.)

Table 4.1 2002/03 sources of shrinkage by country

	Customers %	Staff %	Suppliers %	Internal error %
Austria	53.0	23.5	6.0	17.5
Belgium/Luxemburg	46.5	29.5	6.0	18.0
Denmark	45.5	32.5	7.0	15.0
Finland	47.0	31.0	9.0	13.0
France	48.0	28.3	6.5	17.2
Germany	50.7	23.0	8.3	18.0
Greece	55.0	20.0	7.0	18.0
Ireland	46.2	29.2	7.2	17.4
Italy	52.3	22.9	10.8	14.0
The Netherlands	45.9	32.0	7.1	15.0
Norway	46.0	32.0	6.0	16.0
Portugal	53.0	22.3	9.7	15.0
Spain	52.0	26.5	5.5	16.0
Sweden	45.0	27.0	9.2	18.8
Switzerland	52.5	23.5	8.5	15.5
United Kingdom	42.4	36.1	4.0	17.5
Averages	47.8	28.5	6.8	16.9

Source: The European Retail Theft Barometer, Centre for Retail Research, February–May 2003.

In 2002 a dental practice in London discovered that their much loved receptionist had stolen over £5000 from the till over the previous three years. The receptionist had simply creamed off £20 or £30 every time she was on duty. Any one who has access to company cash has the potential to steal.

The hotel and catering industries suffer as much as any:

> *I started to get bored, so I began stealing small things like food and beer from the kitchen. But when I start stealing from a job it's like a snowball effect, an addiction, I can't stop it ... I stole TV sets, lamps, chairs and furniture. (Martin Sprouse 1992 p 45, quoting a security guard in a hotel in the US)*
>
> *Members of all the housekeeping groups band together when it comes time for stealing ... For more major thefts it's back to the rooftop. Workers with pick-up trucks drive to the back of the hotel. Others throw boxes of linen, shower curtains, towels just anything, into the waiting trucks. (Martin Spouse 1992 p 43, quoting a chambermaid)*

In 1999 Michael G. Kessler & Associates, Ltd, the leading international investigative and forensic accounting firm specializing in corporate issues affecting today's workplace, completed an exhaustive study surveying over 500 employees in the US on the issue of employee theft in the workplace. Their report showed that employee theft is the cause for one out of every three business failures in the US today. Their study 'disclosed that employees readily admitted to stealing office supplies, falsifying expense reports and taking inventory, and almost 87% of those surveyed admitted to falsifying time sheets because they regularly stole time from their employers and were paid for hours they did not work. Those surveyed also indicated that these practices were increasing at an alarming rate. Previous studies revealed that the price tag on employee theft in the US was over $120 billion a year' (www.investigation.com/articles/library/1999articles/articles22). Their research also discovered that: 21% will never steal from an employer; 13% will steal from an employer and 66% will steal if they see others do so without consequence.

A UK-wide survey, for Bank of Scotland Business Banking by the Opinion Research Business, revealed that 24% of small and medium-sized businesses—almost 900,000 across the UK—reported having suffered staff fraud. Whilst losses of more than £5000 are very rare, the figures show small firms are more susceptible to cases of petty fraud and theft. Some 11% have lost up to £1000 through theft or fraud and 4% have lost between £1000 and £5000.

Whilst 19% of firms with fewer than 15 employees have experienced staff fraud, this figure more than doubles to 48% for businesses with over 36 staff. For some reason, firms headed by men are more likely to experience staff fraud than those headed by women (25% compared with 18%). Nearly one in ten respondents said that they have sacked or disciplined a member of staff as a result of fraud or theft over the last three years (www.smallbusiness-centre.net—24 July 2003).

Singer (1996) noted 12 danger signs that possible indicate employees are embezzling a company:

1. Rewriting records for the sake of 'neatness'.
2. Refusing to take vacations; never taking personal or sick days.
3. Working overtime voluntarily and excessively and refusing to release custody of records during the day.
4. Unusually high standard of living, considering salary.
5. Gambling in any form beyond ability to withstand losses.
6. Refusal of promotion.
7. Replying to questions with unreasonable explanations.
8. Getting annoyed at reasonable questions.
9. Inclination toward covering up inefficiencies and mistakes.
10. Pronounced criticisms of others (to divert suspicion).
11. Frequent association with, and entertainment by, a member of supplier's staff.
12. Excessive drinking or associating with questionable characters.

People in human resources are becoming interested in theft prevention. Niehoff and Paul (2000 p 61) offer ten guidelines:

Procedural guidelines

1. Install security systems and implement internal accounting controls for any process involving money or company assets.
2. Use integrity tests in selection process, but only if you can assure that such tests are valid.
3. Conduct background checks as thoroughly as the laws allow.
4. Review and revise, if necessary, any job or organizational information presented to prospective employees, assuring that all information is accurate and consistent.
5. Conduct orientation programs that discuss the company's code of ethics and formal procedures to be followed in case of problems.

Interactive guidelines

1. Initiate and model a culture of honesty in the organization, with clear reinforcement for honesty and punishment for dishonesty (including for all levels of management).
2. Provide support or encouragement for employee personal and skill development.
3. Contract with an employee-assistance program for counselling troubled employees.
4. Review compensation and benefit packages for internal and external equity.

5. Get to know employees through effective communication and implement programs that create bonds between employees and the company.

Theories of theft

Inevitably the perceived cause of the problems leads to an appropriate strategy for prevention. Most researchers in the area, like Greenberg and Barling (1996), recognize that different forces together impact on when, how and why theft takes place. Their simple model is shown in Figure 4.6.

There appear to be three types of theories of theft based on different levels:

1. *Personal:* This focuses on the personality, demographic and criminological profits of the individual whose background and morality lead to their thieving. Impulsive, excitement-seeking, people with poor moral development and education are the most common types.
2. *Social:* This focuses on theft as both/either a response to unfair treatment/ violation of psychological contract *and/or* a compliance with organizational norms that support, endorse and even require thieving. The focus is not on the individual's personality but his/her feelings of betrayal, distress, injustice, revenge and retaliation after being badly treated.
3. *Systemic:* This focuses on two features with theft as compensation for perceived poor (inequitable) pay and poor control systems that allow individuals to get away with it.

Personal factors
- Need
- Deviant background
- Greed, opportunity
- Moral laxity
- Marginality

Workplace factors
- Organizational climate
- Deterrence doctrine
- Perceived fairness

Person x workplace interactions
- Marginality x fairness
- Greed x deterrence
- Opportunity x climate

→ Employee theft

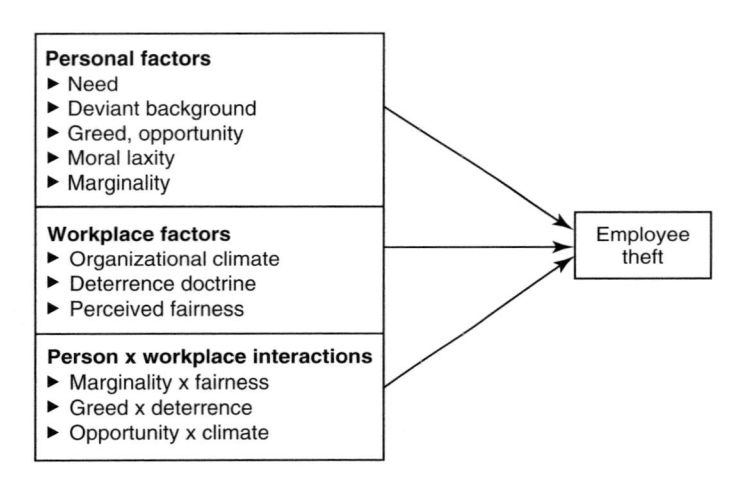

Figure 4.6 Different forces on theft. (*Source:* Adapted from Greenberg and Barling 1996.)

There are many factors involved in employee theft. Greenberg and Barling (1996) suggest that they can be grouped into three types:

1   *Person theories:* these are concerned with the essentially psychological problem of explaining why some individuals (and not others) are involved with pilfering and theft:

   A   *Financial needs.* The idea is that stealing occurs as a function of financial need. But others' needs are implicated, such as social or belongingness needs, because people may steal in order to obtain goals/money that allows them to become a 'club member'. It is a weak theory as it does not distinguish the origin or type of need (for example drug addiction, gambling, sick relatives).
   B   *Deviant personality/background.* The concept is that there is a person type who is more vulnerable to opportunities to steal as well as personally more likely to rationalize stealing behaviour. The theory is weak and tautological—people who steal are the stealing type—stealing types steal!
   C   *Greed/tempted opportunities.* The idea is that people are inherently greedy and steal when they can: they are inherently untrustworthy. However, it fails to explain why there are systematic differences in greed.
   D   *Moral laxity.* Here the theme is that some groups (especially young people) do not possess the same ethical standards or trustworthy qualities as other groups. Again the argument is poor: it is tautological and does not explain individual differences.
   E   *Marginality.* People who are marginal have less static jobs with no tenure or social standing and steal as a way of expressing grievances. Because they have had no opportunities to develop commitment—they steal.

   Each of these theories is profoundly problematic for the same specific reasons.

2   *Workplace theories* emphasize rather different factors:

   A   *Organizational climate:* In effect this refers to a moral atmosphere than can even endorse dishonesty or at least turn a blind eye towards it. The idea is that the prevailing climate sends clear messages to employers about whether, what, which and when dishonest behaviours are acceptable or not.
   B   *Deterrence doctrine:* This refers to the existency, explicitness and retributive nature of company antitheft policies and the perceived certainty and severity of punishment, as well as the visibility of that punishment. The idea is simple: get tough with deterrence and theft will be reduced.
   C   *Perceived organizational fairness:* This 'theory' suggests it is exploitation by the employer that causes pilferage. Note that it is perceived unfairness on the part of the organization that is the crucial factor. Pay cuts in particular lead to this activity.

There is also possibly the interaction between personal and workplace factors. There must be opportunity but it is the combination of person characteristics and workplace characteristics that probably predicts theft most accurately. Thus a morally lax individual in a morally lax workplace that offers opportunity for stealing would be an extreme case. Equally a greedy, opportunistic individual who works in an organization he/she believes to be exploitative is also a situation likely to lead to theft.

In a recent study Greenberg (2002) showed that the moral development of an individual and the actual victim of a theft (individual vs. organization) actually determine when and why people steal money. That is, it is the particular interaction between the person and the job that leads to thieving.

Dissatisfaction, injustice and theft

Many researchers have tried to understand theft at work in terms of theories of injustice and justice (distributive justice, equity justice). The idea is simple. People are in a *social exchange relationship* at work: they give and they get (inputs and outputs). They 'sell' their time, expertise, labour and loyalty and, in return, get a salary, pension, paid holidays and so on. Where the 'equation' is balanced all is well. Where not, people are motivated to reestablish it. Thus people can, if they believe they are inappropriately rewarded, ask for a raise, leave, work less hard, go absent *or steal.*

People who feel frustrated, cheated, humiliated or undervalued often steal as revenge and to right a wrong. This is not to say that all dissatisfied people thieve. But there is evidence that thieving is often a *restitution and retaliative* response to perceived unfairness. People steal partly because of the way they are treated. People *strike back* with reciprocal deviance if they feel poorly or unfairly treated:

> In summary, it appears that employee theft is more than simply an attempt to restore a mathematical balance between outcomes and inputs. Such inequities appear to be necessary for theft to occur, but may not always be sufficient. What needs to be added to the formula for employee theft is improper social treatment—variously called social insensitivity, lack of dignity, rudeness, disrespect, or lack of compassion. Although inequitable outcomes may be necessary to instigate employee theft, they may be insufficient to do so. Showing social insensitivity to those outcomes may also be required to trigger the theft response.
> (Greenberg and Scott 1996 p 14)

Greenberg and Scott (1996) asked the fundamental question as to why theft at work seems so widely acceptable. They believe there is a *cycle of employee theft acceptance* based on three factors: people's willingness to harm (particularly big) organizations; organizations too infrequently prosecute employees caught thieving; many employees feel complete lack of guilt over stealing.

Often large organizations are seen as very rich abusers of power, bullies of their workforce and competitors and hence just 'victims' or targets of 'Robin Hood' thieving. Companies do not prosecute, however, because of the cost, the nature of the evidence they have, the poor publicity and the effect on the other staff. And because companies do not often prosecute employees don't see the activity as necessarily wrong and hence steal happily and without guilt.

Equally supervisory norms may condone and even encourage theft. This may occur because of *parallel deviance* or *passive imitation* which simply means that people follow the lead of their bosses who they notice abusing the system and thieving. If the supervisor calls theft 'a perk' so do the staff. Next there is the *invisible wage structure* or system of *controlled larceny* which effectively means that supervisors allow, help and even organise employee theft. They often say they do this to enrich jobs and more efficiently motivate staff.

However, even more common are work-group norms that support and regulate employee theft. Becoming part of a group may involve being taught how to, when and where to steal. Indeed work-group thieving may ritualistically and symbolically be linked to becoming a successful employee. Thieving norms involve how people divide the spoils/outcomes of theft. Further, the group help 'neutralise' their acts with a raft of excuses/explanations like denials of responsibility, injury, the company being a victim, appeals to higher authority and a condemnation of the condemner. Group norms often spell out the parameters of thieving behaviour—that is, what is and is not stolen, and the worth of what has been stolen.

So how can the manager reduce employee thefts? The first tiling is to *break the social norms* that accept and rationalize theft. Some companies have had success with simply printing theft statistics on the intranet. It is essential to stop employees seeing their theft as appropriate and desirable. Business ethic talks can help this, but they are insufficient and can be seen as preaching.

Profit-sharing also helps align the interests of employer and employees. Activities that lower profitability (pilfering in employee-owned companies) soon become taboo. Where this is not possible, having a clear social contract prohibiting theft may help.

If perceived (note, not actual) fairness is an issue, it is important to emphasize continually the *fairness* of the company's *compensation system*. Company hotlines for just whistle-blowing have been shown to have a significant effect. Some companies have suggested that the issue of theft should be brought into the open and employees should be encouraged to discuss how it is to be defined and treated. This helps to flag that the company is serious about theft and helps ensure employees' commitment.

Companies are now so worried about the issue that they are attempting serious preventive, proactive, rather than reactive, methods. This involves integrity testing and background checks at selection. It also involves employer publications and, more ominously, a tightening up of internal controls and security.

Most employers would prefer to avert the problem in the first place perhaps with some pre-employment screening such as giving people integrity tests. Yet Greenberg and Barling (1996) point to some severe limitations with that idea.

> Although integrity tests have been shown to predict on-the-job theft, they still need to be used with caution for several reasons: it is ironical and unreasonable to expect dishonest people to answer questions truthfully about their own attitudes toward theft and past dishonest behaviour. Attitudes about theft or personality tendencies are only moderately correlated with theft behaviours. Opportunity for theft does not necessarily lead to greater occurrences of theft. In fact, most employees in various occupations have access to money or merchandise but choose not to steal. Labelling someone a 'thief' may become a self-fulfilling prophesy and would certainly make it more difficult for that person to obtain alternative employment. Privacy issues and most importantly, this approach ignores [sic] the potential contribution of workplace factors that might lead to employee theft. (p 59)

Greenberg (1998) has argued that there are forces that both encourage and discourage theft at various levels. They work first at the level of the individual. Thus the personality and the moral development of the individual may be either an encouraging or an inhibiting force while various life pressures (for more money to fund gambling debts, secret love affairs and so on) may encourage the individual to thieve.

Individuals have to make the decision to thieve which then usually results in their justifications (to self and others) of that act. After the theft they then usually try to manage the interpretation of that action and label it according to their own ends. Many try to legitimate a clearly illegitimate act. Their personality, morality and intelligence are powerful determinants in how, when and why this is done.

At the group level there may well be peer pressure to take part in group-organized and accepted thieving. Equally there may well be peer-based pressure not to take part in any or specific types of theft. Paradoxically some organizations encourage theft by tacitly accepting it as an invisible wage structure. Most say that they (or indeed try to) induce inhibiting forces by a mixture of a code of ethics, ethical leadership and having a non-bureaucratic structure.

All organizations attempt to weaken forces that seem to encourage theft and equally strengthen those that try to inhibit it. Greenberg and Barling (1996) have argued that some deterrent actions nearly always seem successful and should be recommended always to reduce theft. These include treating employees with dignity and respect; getting them involved in what is defined as theft; opening and regularly communicating the cost of organizational theft and making sure that no one (particularly leaders) is a role model for unethical behaviour.

Less successful methods include reducing bureaucracy, using preselection screening, rotating group membership constantly and having assistance programmes for people in financial trouble.

Recent research into employee theft

▶ *Employee theft is the cause for one out of every three business failures in this country*

▶ *87% of those surveyed admitted to falsifying time sheets because they regularly stole time from their employers and were paid for hours they did not work*

▶ *19% of firms in the UK with fewer than 15 employees have experienced staff fraud, this figure more than doubles to 48% for businesses with over 36 staff*

▶ *In German retail companies 22.5% of shrinkage is the result of employee theft; in Ireland it is 32%*

▶ *Workers who help themselves to software, hardware and other office equipment are costing Britain's small businesses £1.2 billion a year*

▶ *Fraudulent activities such as submitting false expense claims and making long-distance phone calls from the office cost UK businesses £831 million a year*

▶ *30 US-based retail chains—with sales of $355 billion—caught 73,326 dishonest employees in 2000, a 10% increase over the 1999 figure*

▶ *Employee theft costs US businesses over $53 billion annually and affects every type of organization. The majority of unexplained inventory losses involve employee theft*

▶ *70% of all corporate fraud and theft problems are caused by employees—and not outsiders. When outsiders are actually involved in defrauding a business, you can bet they've got a partner working at the company*

▶ *It is estimated that 95% of all businesses experience employee theft and management is seldom aware of the actual extent of losses or even the existence of theft*

Fraud

The difference between employee theft and fraud is largely about scale. In the previous section 'petty' theft of cash, goods on shelves or in cupboards has been discussed. Here the theft is more determined and larger scale.

Fraud is defined by David Davies (2000 p 2) in one of the standard works on fraud as:

> All those activities involving dishonesty and deception that can drain value from a business, directly or indirectly, whether or not there is a personal benefit to the fraudster.

> Merrill Lynch was plunged into fresh controversy yesterday when allegations emerged that a former energy trader had embezzled $43 million from the firm.
>
> *Guardian* 12 August 2003

There is also an issue about position in the company. Theft and pilfering are done by blue collar less well-paid workers; fraud is something usually done by white collar workers. The only purpose for the distinction between the two is that their motivations may be different.

Fraud comes in various forms. PricewaterhouseCoopers, in its 2003 report on economic crime, identifies seven different forms of fraud:

1 Asset misappropriation
2 Financial misrepresentation
3 Corruption and bribery
4 Money laundering
5 Cyber crime
6 Industrial espionage
7 Product piracy.

Not all are committed by employees, but most of those identified in the list above are perpetrated by those inside the organization.

On 14 September 1999 *People Management* (the magazine for the Chartered Institute of Personnel and Development—CIPD), quoting from a report commissioned by Business Defence Europe, revealed that the £5 billion of serious fraud every year in the UK is the tip of the iceberg and that the majority of fraud is committed by middle management (p 11).

PricewaterhouseCoopers (PWC) has for three years produced an Economic Crime Survey. In 2003, it found that well over a third of respondent companies worldwide (37%) said they had suffered from one or more serious frauds during the previous two years. While there were regional differences, the impact was wide-spread. The percentage of respondents who reported serious fraud in each region is shown in Figure 4.7 The research also showed which sectors were most vulnerable (Figure 4.8).

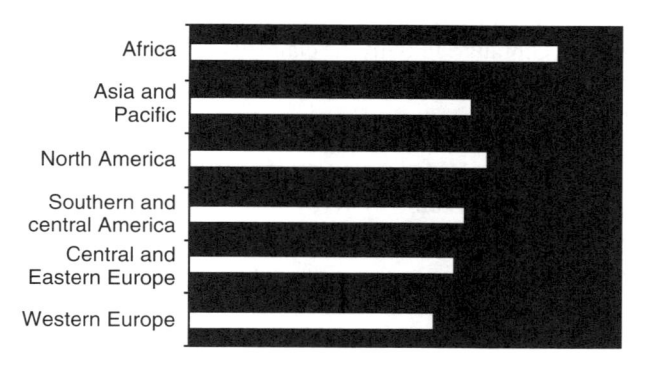

Figure 4.7 Percentage of companies suffering serious fraud. (*Source:* Investigations and Forensic Services Department of PricewaterhouseCoopers 2003.)

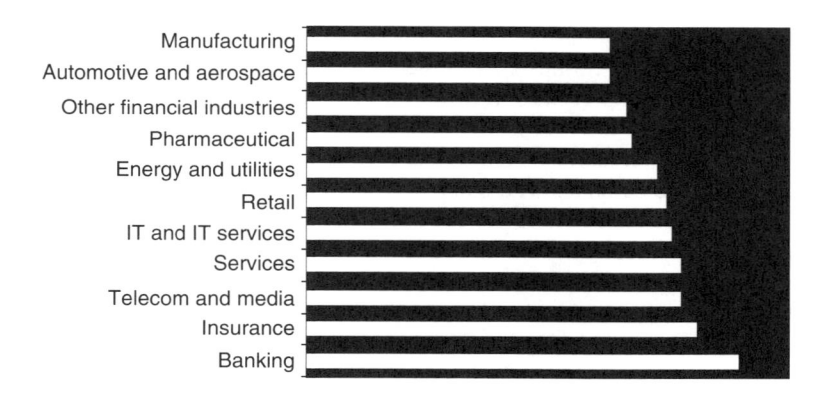

Figure 4.8 Victims of fraud worldwide. (*Source:* Investigations and Forensic Services Department of PricewaterhouseCoopers 2003.)

> *According to a recent joint report by the Australian Institute of Criminology and PricewaterhouseCoopers, the problem costs Australia about $3.5 billion a year. Many see this estimate as conservative.*

Of those companies which PWC surveyed and which had suffered fraud, the average loss was over $2 million. But the report recognizes that this figure is partial. Many companies knew they had been the subject of fraud but could not quantify the cost.

Fraud or embezzlement is not restricted to companies. In 2003 a former UN official in Kosovo went on trial in Germany. Joe Trutschler, 37, admitted to stealing

$4.3 million from the Kosovo Electricity Company and depositing the money in private accounts in Gibraltar. Initially, he claimed that he had been setting the cash aside to secretly raise the salaries of Kosovo's energy workers (*France Presse* 16 June 2003).

Norwich acts on '£1.5m fraud'
Simon Bowers Guardian *Thursday 19 June 2003*

Norwich Union, the insurance firm owned by Aviva, confirmed yesterday that it had filed a high court claim against a former employee and a number of people outside the firm over allegations that £1.5m had been illegally siphoned out of company coffers in a decade-long fraud.

www.guardian.co.uk

In 2000, Paul van Buitenen, an official in the European Union, went public with details of corruption, cronyism and abuse of power in the Commission. The entire team of 20 commissioners, headed by then president Jacques Santer, resigned in a symbolic gesture to demonstrate their commitment to cleaning up the Commission's act.

Buitenen was eventually forced to leave his job and return to his home town, Breda, in The Netherlands. The story however continued as Marta Andreasen, former chief accountant of the European Union, has reported that the Commission's systems failed to meet even the most basic accounting standards. In August this year, a leaked report from the EU Court of Auditors found that the £63 billion a year budget was open to fraud and abuse. The report warned that the EU systems were 'out of control' with 'obvious risks as regards liability'. Ms Andreasen said she believed that a lack of security left the system open to fraud at any time which could not be traced (www.news.bbc.co.uk 3 October 2002).

Increasingly fraud cases have an international dimension. In the UK the Serious Fraud Office (SFO) is responsible for investigating and prosecuting cases:

> This can require our investigators to obtain evidence from abroad, interview witnesses in other countries or sometimes deal with an extradition, all of which requires liaison with the authorities in foreign jurisdictions.

Examples of cases with a foriegn dimension
R v Roger Crow and James Lovat

Crow was a senior manager at the London branch of the Hungarian International Bank. Lovat ran a printing company that provided services to the bank. Both defendants conspired to steal over £½ million from the bank. Crow manipulated the bank's payments system to disguise the purchase of a printing press for the benefit of Lovat's company by debiting the sum from a dormant account not subject to internal scrutiny. The fraud was uncovered when the bank went into voluntary liquidation. Thirty-five days into the trial, on 29 January 2003, the defendants pleaded guilty to the charge of conspiracy to steal. On the following day both men were sentenced to 21 months' imprisonment, suspended for two years.

R v Christopher Freeman and Alan Hodgkinson
The defendants were charged in January 2002 with conspiracy to defraud, fraudulent trading, false accounting and forgery in connection with Universal Bulk Handling Ltd of which they were directors. The business went into receivership in February 1999 with debts of £10 million. Freeman pleaded guilty on 7 November 2002 to fraudulent trading, false accounting and forgery. Sentencing of Freeman was held over, pending the outcome of proceedings against Hodgkinson and a third defendant.

R v Roddam Twiss
In July 2001 Twiss was charged with theft, conspiracy to steal and conspiracy to defraud. He was acting for The Grosvenor Trust. The allegation is that funds held by the Trust on behalf of investors for the purpose of high-yield investment schemes were not applied for investment purposes. Instead the funds were transferred to Twiss and another person (Emile Coury) and disbursed by them. Coury is awaiting extradition from Switzerland to the UK and it is intended to join him on the same indictment as Twiss. The trial is scheduled for March 2004.

SFO 2002/03 report pp 24–30

Davies (2000 pp 23–4) identifies 22 common indicators and risk factors when considering the potential for fraud in an organization:

▷ Autocratic management style
▷ Mismatch of personality and status
▷ Unusual behaviour
▷ Illegal acts
▷ Expensive lifestyles
▷ Untaken holidays
▷ Poor quality staff
▷ Low morale
▷ High staff turnover
▷ Compensation tied to performance
▷ Results at any cost
▷ Poor commitment to control
▷ No code of business ethics
▷ Unquestioning obedience of staff
▷ Complex structures
▷ Remote locations poorly supervised
▷ Several firms of auditors

▷ Poorly defined business strategy
▷ Profits well in excess of industry norms
▷ Mismatch between growth and systems development
▷ Poor reputation
▷ Liquidity problems

According to Davies (2000) people commit fraud for a whole variety of reasons: pressure to perform (for example to reach targets); personal pressures (gambling); the joy of beating the system (alienated hacker); greed, boredom and revenge. Fraudsters, he believes, come in four types: the boaster, the manipulator, the deceiver and the loner.

Davies (2000) clearly paints the picture of organizations that provide a fertile field for fraudsters. The downsized, delayered organization, eager to outsource and in a state of constant flux and change, is typically where fraud occurs. A command-and-control organization with a blame culture and highly aggressive targets and a dysfunctional board is where fraud occurs most.

To illustrate the sheer number and complexity of variables in this issue he provided a wonderful fraud-watch chessboard, shown in Table 4.2.

But how are we to really manage this growing blue collar, highly counterproductive behaviour? Davies (2000) maintains the first task is to persuade the board—usually by showing the cost of fraud—*the cost of not doing anything*. He believes an antifraud strategy has five components. *First*, being very clear about ethics, values, standards and what is and is not acceptable behaviour. The message is clear: there are rules that are logical and fair and those who break them cheat the company and the shareholder.

Second, human resource policies need to be developed for serious screening—the morally desirable in and the undesirable out. They need to monitor work patterns and holidays, attempt fair appraisals and do regular surveys to identify issues and problems early. *Third*, they need a fraud reporting channel that people will not be frightened to use and they need a fraud response plan. *Fourth*, they need to put in place a good fraud awareness programme to make managers more vigilant about the causes and manifestations of fraud. *Fifth*, managers need to be taught how to incisively but successfully interview/interrogate their staff to find out the 'who, when and why' fraud at all levels is occurring.

Fraud is in many ways similar to petty thieving. Whilst successful fraud may involve the loss of many millions by clever trained professionals, the reasons why people steal are much the same. It is only the methods and values that differ, usually as a function of opportunity. Resentment, greed, opportunity are key ingredients in fraud. Indeed, fraud and petty theft are controlled in much the same way, which underlines the fact that they result from similar causes.

Table 4.2 Fraud-watch chessboard

STRATEGY	Nepotism	High staff turnover	Ethical dilemmas not dealt with	Structure conflicts with risk management	Complex structures	Poor learning from other businesses	Overly aggressive targets
Weak strategy	Skills gaps	CULTURE and ETHICS	STRUCTURE	Defensive business units	Multiple audit relationships	Poor communication of fraud and ethics policies	Core business processes not clearly defined
Poor implementation plans	Inappropriate career moves	Cultural confusion	Dysfunctional board	Front and back office skills and status mismatch	REWARD STRUCTURES	FRAUD RISK MANAGEMENT	Gaps in processes and controls not identified
Poor communication of strategy	Low morale	Cultural pressures	Confusion between chairman and chief executive	Structure does not fit strategy	Impact of bonus and other structures not recognized	No antifraud strategy	Low focus on areas most vulnerable to fraud
Strategic drift	Low level of fraud awareness	Sub-cultures	Confused reporting lines	Centre and business units in conflict	Risks relating to earn-outs not managed	Fraud implications of business strategy not assessed	FRAUD RESPONSE
PEOPLE	Untaken holiday	Need-to-know culture. Concentrations of power	Management structure not aligned to reward structures	Poor role definition	Relative disparities in pay-to-market rates	No fraud risk profiling	No fraud policy
Weak recruitment screening	Lifestyles inconsistent with salary	Business units not assimilated into culture	Special reporting arrangements	Responsibilities for managing fraud risk poorly defined	COMMUNICATIONS	Fraud risks not matched with controls	Poor fraud reporting channels and protections
Prior business relationships	Autocratic management style	Weak ethical code and values	Lack of expertise to operate structure	Low status of finance	Poor organizational learning	Performance measures manipulated	No fraud response plan to follow up fraud incidents.

Source: Davies 2000.

Deceit

Estimating the costs of this kind of fraud is difficult, not least because some deceptions are not motivated by personal gain but are designed to enhance or maintain a person's reputation. Some of the great names in science have been guilty of falsehoods. For a thousand years astronomers credited Ptolemy with theories about the positions of planets. Historians now believe that his writings were based on the observations of an earlier astronomer, Hipparchus of Rhodes. Newton is suspected of actively trying to discredit his competitors as well as falsifying or massaging data to fit his existing theories. Mendel was so convinced of the correctness of his theories he made the data fit his hypothesis perfectly.

Fraud in the field of science and medical research in particular, is surprisingly frequent and at least in the last 30 years reasonably well documented. In 1981 the US House of Representatives investigated scientific misconduct. Al Gore, Chairman of the Committee on Science and Technology, opened the hearing with these words: 'We need to discover whether recent incidents are merely episodes that will drift into the history of science as footnotes, or whether we are creating situations and incentives ... that makes such cases as these "the tip of the iceberg" '. The reaction from the scientific community was hostile. Phillip Handler, President of the National Academy of Sciences, called the issue 'grossly exaggerated' (Lock and Wells 1996 pp 5, 6). But the evidence of consistent and prevalent fraud and misconduct is strong.

Lock collated details of 71 case histories broken down between the following countries: Australia 4, Canada 1, UK 14, and US 52. They include some extraordinary examples, including the notorious case of William Summerlin at the Sloan-Kettering Institute, New York, who faked transplantation results by darkening transplanted skin patches in white mice with a black felt tip pen (Lock and Wells 1996 pp 15–28). In 1997 a German investigative committee uncovered evidence that two biomedical scientists had falsified data in as many as 37 publications between 1988 and 1996.

Lock himself conducted a small survey in 1988 of 80 people in the medical research fields and in a response rate of 100% (itself an indicator of the interest people have in the subject) found that over half knew of some instance of fraud or misconduct. His colleague Frank Wells was responsible for reporting 26 cases to the General Medical Council in the UK.

In Australia cases of deceit have taken on a high profile. In 1991 Dr William McBride faced 15 complaints brought against him by the Health department. He admitted publishing false and misleading data, claiming it was 'in the long-term interests of humanity'. He was found guilty and struck off. The Medical Tribunal said his 'acts demonstrated a course of premeditated deception in the field of medical research and indicate a serious flaw or defect in his character, a trait of dishonesty' (Lock and Wells 1996 p 135).

Professor Michael Briggs was dean at Geelong University and worked in the field of oral contraceptives. He was a man with a quick wit, and an ability to attract large sums of money from drug companies. In the early 1980s there was considerable controversy over his research, culminating in his resignation and move to Marbella in Spain. The *Sunday Times* in London drew a partial admission from him of generalizing from a small amount of data (Lock and Wells 1996 p 130).

Husson et al. (1996 p 211) identify three types of fraud in clinical and medical research:

1   Falsification of data
2   Concealment of data
3   Creation of data.

But the detection and prevention are still fraught with problems. There is home movement to bring the approach in the western world to fraud together and to show consistency.

C. Kristina Gunsalus distinguishes two types of deceivers, the straightforward crooks and the 'jerks'. The latter tend to be 'bright but without social skills; are aggressively competitive; are idiosyncratic; drive each other hard and have a variety of unclassified characteristics including corner cutting, self delusion, and incompetence' (Lock, in Lock and Wells 1996 p 30).

The theme of self-delusion or self-deception is taken up by William Broad and Nicholas Wade: 'Self-deception is so potent a human capability that scientists, supposedly trained to be the most objective of observers, are in fact peculiarly vulnerable to deliberate deception by others' (Broad and Wade 1985 p 116).

Deviant, dysfunctional, counterproductive behaviour takes place in many organizations. Universities are one such place. Brockway et al. (2002) showed how student cynicism may well lead to variable behavioural problems among cynical students. Interestingly they distinguished between policy cynicism, academic cynicism, social cynicism and institutional cynicism. Jackson et al. (2002) also found personality factors in fact predicted student cheating behaviour at university.

Cizek (1999) noted how prevalent misconduct is. He also noted typical reasons students give. These include:

▷   The instructor assigns too much material.
▷   The instructor left the room during the test.
▷   A friend asked me to cheat and I couldn't say no.
▷   The instructor doesn't seem to care if I learn the material.
▷   The course information seems useless.
▷   The course material is too hard.
▷   Everyone else seems to be cheating.
▷   In danger of losing scholarship because of low grades.
▷   Don't have time to study because I am working to pay for school.
▷   People sitting around me made no attempt to cover their papers.

Table 4.3 Top five circumstances related to planned and spontaneous cheating

Rank	Circumstances that increase cheating	Circumstances that decrease cheating
	Planned cheating	
1	Student perception that instructor doesn't care about cheating	Punishment for cheating (for example expulsion)
2	Student financial support depends on grades	Essay examination format
3	Student perception that test is unfair	Student perception of high instructor vigilance during examination
4	Student perception of low instructor vigilance during examination	Student perception that test is fair
5	Direct effect of course grade on student's long-term goals	Course material highly valued by student
	Spontaneous cheating	
1	Student financial support depends on grades	Punishment for cheating (for example expulsion)
2	Student perception that instructor doesn't care about cheating	Essay examination format
3	Direct effect of course grade on student's long-term goals	Student perception of high instructor vigilance during examination
4	Student perception of low instructor vigilance	Students seated far apart during examination
5	Student perception that test is unfair	Student perception that test is fair

Source: Adapted from Cizek 1999.

He noted the circumstances where cheating occurs and these are shown in Table 4.3.

Deception is also frequent in business. In the late 1990s Roger Eden and Geoffrey Brailey—former directors of Corporate Services Group plc—dishonestly caused and permitted the company's financial statements for 1997 to be prepared in such a way as to overstate the true extent of its profitability and sought to do the same in 1998. In 1997, the overstatement amounted to just over £3 million. In 1998, the accounting irregularities came to light before the statements could be published. The potential overstatement of profit for 1998 is estimated to exceed at least £25 million (Serious Fraud Office press release 17 September 2003).

Information leakage (citizenship espionage)

Information itself is a commodity which can be sold or used to damage a company or organization, though in some cases the perpetrators can reasonably claim that their action was for the public good. Although the individuals will feel they are giving a fair account of what has happened, or of the data, this is often disputed and sometimes there is no attempt to tell the truth. In most cases of information leakage a third party has to be involved. The questions to be asked are: did the employee know he or she was passing useful information, did the employee deliberately seek out a third person or did the third person seek out the employee?

It is also possible for individuals to take information away from an organization for their personal use later. Whenever anyone moves job, they take with them information and experience which will help them make better judgements as they make decisions in their new job. They might, for example, decide to pursue (or not) a particular client because they know what they need from earlier experience with the former company. For the purposes of this section we are concerned mainly with those employees who pass information to another, as this is what causes the real damage.

> 'Gossip is the cement which holds organizations together,' said Ms Doyle. 'Providing communal space, such as coffee areas or lunch rooms, allows employees to share information, knowledge and build relations that benefits both the company and the employee.'
>
> A study by the Industrial Society reported by www.bbc.co.uk 20 November 2000

Information leakage, which is the responsibility of employees, as opposed to external stealing, can be for the following six reasons:

1. *Accidental.* The loss of papers or electronic data, which might be found by other interested parties. It might also be the result of indiscreet comments made over the phone or overheard in a bar. The person concerned does not intend to cause damage.
2. *Casual gossip.* A conversation motivated by the individual's desire to discuss either other people's private lives or the company's business.
3. *Deliberate gossip* or bad-mouthing. This is the result of an individual feeling hurt or resentful about something which has happened in the office, which they feel is unfair.
4. *Deliberate passing of information* to expose some wrongdoing in the company or organization (whistle-blowing).
5. *Deliberate and clandestine passing of information* (orally or in paper or electronic format), which benefits the business of the third party. In this case the individual benefits, usually financially, but stays in the company.
6. *Taking confidential information* on departure from an organization that will be of direct benefit to that individual in his or her new employment.

Accidental loss can be put down to carelessness and the responsibility of the individual. The employers would have to accept some responsibility if they had not trained the individuals concerned sufficiently or were working them so hard that mistakes begin to happen out of tiredness or out of having top much to do.

Can one man's journey be responsible for kickstarting America's textile manufacturing industry? At least one American president thought so. Heralded as the father of the American Industrial Revolution by President Jackson, Samuel Slater's decision to emigrate to the United States had consequences far beyond his own life. Derbyshire born Slater gained his expertise in the textile industry as an apprentice to Jedediah Strutt in one of his mills at Milford. To reach America, he betrayed his employers, deceived his family and broke the law. However, the rewards were rich; on his death in America, his fortune was worth $1,200,000.

www.bbc.co.uk/legacies

A chief executive who sent his staff an email accusing them of being lazy and threatening them with the sack has seen the share price of his company plummet after his message was posted on the internet.

In the three days after publication of his outburst—which gave managers a two-week ultimatum to shape up—stock on the American healthcare company dropped by 22 per cent over concerns about staff morale. It is now trading at more than a third less than it was before the email was sent. Neal Patterson, head of the Cerner Corporation, based in Kansas City, has spent the past three weeks trying to assuage investors.

His email to managers rad: 'We are getting less than 40 hours of work from a large number of our EMPLOYEES. The parking lot is sparsely used at 8am; likewise at 5pm. As managers, you either do not know what your EMPLOYEES are doing or you do not CARE. In either case, you have a problem and you will fix it or I will replace you.'

His email read: 'NEVER in my career have I allowed a team which worked for me to think they had a 40-hour job. I have allowed YOU to create a culture which is permitting this. NO LONGER.' He added that 'hell will freeze over' before he increased employee benefits. He wanted to see the car park nearly full by 7.30am and half full at weekends. He wrote: 'You have two weeks. Tick, tock.'

A week later, the email appeared on a Yahoo financial message board and Wall Street analyst began receiving calls from worried shareholders.

Daily Telegraph 6 April 2001

People at work spy on their bosses. They may betray their colleagues, their bosses or the company as a whole. They may even become a traitor by committing treason. Countries have laws about treason, espionage, sedition and mutiny to discourage their enemies.

The enemy within can be a thief but is often worse: a betrayer of trust. They are the sorts of industrial or organizational spies that tend to be portrayed in novels: they tend to be in some sense outside conventional society; they are somehow invisible; their attachment to others is superficial; they are fascinated with the power of secrecy and they are individualistic (autonomous, self-reliant). The enemy within, the citizen spy, is often caught only after selling trade secrets.

Eoyang (1994 pp 85–6; emphases in original) believes that classically there is a behaviour chain or typical sequence of events that occur:

> The chain begins with *intention*, which is some level of interest and motivation in violating security. Next is the formulation *of plans* either along or with others to transform the intentions into concrete actions. The third essential step is to gain access to locations, persons, or sources that retain restricted information. Once access has been achieved, the actual *acquisition* of the information must be effected. Since most perpetrators of espionage wish to minimize the risks of their trade, they typically engage in deception to hide their activities and their responsibility for it. As most consumers of espionage products are governments, spies must have *contact* with some foreign agency to whom they can confer the stolen information and from whom they can receive their compensation (*exchange*). The actual transmittal of the information may take many forms, some of which have been celebrated in innumerable spy novels. Although the rewards of espionage are rarely munificent, the consumption of the gains from espionage can sometimes arouse suspicions when it shows as unusual or unexplained affluence. Finally, it may be necessary for spies to flee (escape) to avoid capture and punishment or to enjoy the fruits of their clandestine endeavours without retribution.

He also notes possible countermeasures used to catch spies in the organization, as shown in Table 4.4.

Morris and Moberg (1994) note how work organizations are often excellent contexts for betrayal. People need to be, and are, trusted at work for various specific reasons. Many work tasks are ambiguous and dynamic so organizations can prescribe how they are done. They have to trust the employee to do his/her best. Also, inevitably, many work behaviours are difficult to observe and therefore the employee has to be trusted to do them. Often the work outcomes are difficult to assess, so organizations have to balance the mixture of putting in place (expensive) control systems and of trusting individuals. Certainly in some jobs die trust factor is less important than in others.

Trust is a two-way street: a contract. The person puts trust in the organization and vice versa. A victim who feels that they have intentionally and individually

Table 4.4 Possible countermeasures used to catch spies in the organization

INTENTION	Clearances	Training, education	Leadership/counselling, Situational matching
PLANNING/ CONSPIRACY	Periodic reinvestigation, polygraph	Informants search warrants	Personnel rotation
ACCESS	Clearances	Compartmentalization	Position vulnerability
ACQUISITION	Special access programmes	Classification management, document control	Need to know
DECEPTION	Periodic reinvestigation, polygraph	Inspections	Group cohesion, integrity
FOREIGN CONTACT	Periodic reinvestigation, alien prohibitions	Surveillance	Continuing assessment
EXCHANGE	Periodic reinvestigation, polygraph	Punishment	Sting operations
CONSUMPTION	Periodic reinvestigation,	Tax enforcement	Employee assistance
ESCAPE	Travel checks	Travel restrictions	Plea bargaining, double agents

Source: Eoyang 1994.

been harmed by the organization with little opportunity for adequate redress is ripe for betrayal. Morris and Moberg (1994 p 187) note:

> From the standpoint of managerial practice and policy, the themes that we have developed here yield few revelations, but they do support much of what is already accepted as sound, if well-worn, advice. First, hire people who are believed to be trustworthy. Recognize the three particular features of work that make interdependent people vulnerable to one another's actions and the need for personal trust that such situations require. Respond to these situations by encouraging the emergence of internal control systems to support and sustain personal trust between functionally dependent members—but only after ensuring that what is possible has been done to reduce the need for personal trust in the first place. We hope we have made clear that personal trust between interdependent workers can be crucial to getting the job done; but when alternatives are available, it is wrong for organizations to freeload on personal trust between their members because it is the members themselves, and not necessarily the organization, who may be victimized by

violations of such personal trust. In addition, no matter how irrational such acts may seem we can only wonder how many crimes or other transgressions against organizations were precipitated by unredressed breaches of personal trust between individual members.

Hogan and Hogan (1994) make four important observations about organizational betrayal by citizenship espionage. First, it is rare (a low base-rate phenomenon) and therefore very hard to predict. Second, the greatest danger to organizations comes from those within them (not without). Third, people who are as used to competition as opposed to cooperation at work are experts in deceptive communication. Those who take part in treachery and betrayal are often unusually socially skilled (charismatic, charming, intelligent, socially poised and self-confident).

From their research Hogan and Hogan (1994) suggested that there are four characteristics of the ideal or prototypic betrayer. They are attractive, interesting, charming and past-masters at flattery and ingratiation. However, they also have unusual degrees of egocentrism, self-absorption and selfishness. These people are, however, privately self-doubting, unhappy and unsure about their self-worth. Finally, they are particularly prone to self-deception—in short they lie to themselves. The betrayer—an essentially hollow man or woman—retains only the mask of integrity.

Whistle-blowing

Very few people attempt to defend stealing from, or sabotage in, an organization by an employee. Whilst it is conceivable to do this, say in times of war or in other exceptional circumstances, these behaviours are normally deviant and considered both morally and legally wrong.

Whistle-blowing, however, has begun to have a rather different reputation. Indeed there are now on the web numerous international sites that purport to help (and encourage) whistle-blowing. Whistle-blowing is, or at least should be, about organizational wrongdoing. It is where, often, many senior people conspire to do things which are illegal, immoral, and dangerous but benefit themselves.

What constitutes wrongdoing is very questionable. One study (Keenan 1990) categorized actions into three categories: *minor fraud* (that is, fiddling expenses, stealing office supplies), *harm to others* (discrimination, violating health and safety rules), and *serious fraud* (bribery, overtime abuse). That study also found:

1   the great majority (70%) work in organizations without a formal written policy for suspected dishonest and fraudulent activities that includes a description as to what is to be done if wrongdoing is observed or suspected
2   a sizeable number (37%) are uncertain about the adequacy of their company's protection of employees who report illegal or wasteful activities within company operations

3   a sizeable number (21%) believe that there is an unfair and inconsistent treatment of wrongdoing in their organizations because of the position held by the suspected wrongdoers or length of service; and
4   fear of retaliation is a major factor influencing perceptions about company encouragement of whistle blowing and having enough information on where to blow the whistle. (p 233)

Consider four examples:

1   *An engineer believes the plans for a building are wrong and would lead to an unsafe construction that does not follow industry guidelines. He reports this first to his boss, then the CEO, then his professional body. None acts so he contacts the media.*
2   *An employee from an ethnic minority has noticed that the rejection to acceptance rate of applicants from his particular racial group is higher than that of the dominant group. He reports this to his boss and then the head of human resources who both deny any form of racial discrimination. The individual is unconvinced and turns to the Commission for Racial Equality, the media and activists at the same time.*
3   *A person working in the pharmaceuticals business finds out that, contrary to the organization's public statements, some of its materials are tested on animals. She reports this to a director who denies it and challenges that evidence. She believes she is right and, met with further denials, phones the local antivivisection group.*
4   *A loyal worker gets passed over for promotion a number of times. She feels that this is unfair and age discriminatory. She therefore waits until a voluntary severance programme goes embarrassingly wrong before leaking it to the media as a revenge for her frustration.*

So what is whistle-blowing? The term supposedly arises from sport where referees blow a whistle to indicate foul play. As we shall see, whistle-blowing can take many forms. It appears to have three components. First, that an individual or group working, or recently working, in an organization perceive something 'morally amiss'. That is, they believe organizational policy, practices, acts or intentions to be morally wrong. Second, they communicate that information to people outside the organization: these may be journalists, competitors, the police. Third, the perception by at 'least a number' of people inside the organization is that the communication should not have been made.

There are three 'actors' in every whistle-blowing case: the wrongdoer, the whistle-blower and the recipient of the information. From a legal perspective, whistle-blowing is warranted if the person believes in good faith the wrongdoing has implications for public policy. From a philosophic perspective, the question arises whether the act is ethical. However, from an auditor's perspective the central question is whether the wrongdoing is sufficient to pursue the problem. Whistle-blowers need to decide between internal and external channels for complaint, which are clearly very different in outcome. They also need a reasonable supposition of success in that they believe their action will lead to the wrongdoing being stopped.

Near and Miceli (1996) in an extensive review considered two myths. First, that *whistle-blowers are crackpots*. The results of numerous studies, though not entirely consistent, seem to indicate the precise opposite. Compared to 'silent, inactive' observers, whistle-blowers tend to be older, more senior, better educated, with better job performance and commitment and believe they have a role responsibility to report wrongdoing through appropriate channels:

> To date, empirical evidence has shown that whistle-blowing is more likely in organizations that support whistle-blowing in various ways, but not including incentives for it, and where whistle-blowers report greater value congruence with top managers. Organizations with higher rates of whistle-blowing seem to be high performing, to have slack resources, to be relatively non-bureaucratic, and tend to cluster in particular industries or in the public rather than private or not-for-profit sectors. Finally, group size is positively related to whistle-blowing, while quality of supervisor is not. (pp 512–13)

Researchers have questioned whistle-blowers' morality and loyalty. The latter naturally questions who the loyalty is to. Near and Miceli (1996) conclude that there is no evidence for the crackpot myth and that most whistle-blowers simply have the opportunity to observe the wrongdoing because of the nature of their jobs.

NHS inspector praises whistle-blowers

Patrick Butler
Wednesday 15 November 2000
Staff who blew the whistle on poor standards of hospital care have been praised by the government's health standards regulator for their courage in attempting to alert the authorities to care abuses.

Peter Homa, chief executive of the Commission for Health Improvement (CHI), criticized North Lakeland NHS trust in Cumbria for not acting after abuses were

> reported by staff in 1996, and blamed that failure for further alleged mistreatment of patients in 1998.
> Mr Homa today praised the 'courage' of whistle-blowers who battled to expose mistreatment of elderly mentally ill patients at North Lakeland.
> www.society.guardian.co.uk

Second that *all whistle-blowers suffer retaliation*. Despite looking at all sorts of factors (personal characteristics of whistle-blowers that predict retaliation, situational factors such as organizational structure and culture) the authors found little evidence and:

> can only conclude that: a) retaliation against whistle-blowers is not universal (and perhaps not even widespread); b) retaliation, when it does occur, may take many forms (ranging from less severe to more severe), all of which are highly subject to personal interpretation by the whistle-blower; and c) whistle-blowers claim that it does not deter them, either currently in the future cases, although fear of retaliation may cause them to seek external channels for whistle-blowing, to the obvious dismay of the organization. To date, however, most state and federal legal statutes have been written with the primary goal of preventing retaliation under the assumption that retaliation will deter future whistle-blowing—despite empirical evidence to the contrary, (p 523)

When are whistle-blowers effective? Most, it seems go public once organizations attempt to cover-up wrongdoing and retaliate against the whistle-blower. Where whistle-blowers are powerful, with unique skills, resources and secrets the organization needs (and cannot easily replace), they are more likely to succeed. The more competent, confident, credible and objective they seem, the more they are listened to. Experts with legitimate power are likely to be more effective particularly with internal whistle-blowing.

Near and Miceli (1995) have done an excellent job in looking at the characteristics that predict effective whistle-blowing. They divide these into individual and situational variables and present two explanatory flow charts (Figures 4.9 and 4.10).

This model is based on 12 simple but crucial propositions. Whistle-blowing effectiveness is enhanced when managers, co-workers and the compliant recipient see the whistle-blower as credible and relatively powerful in the organization and when the whistle-blower identifies him/herself at the outset rather than looking for anonymity. Effectiveness increases when the compliant recipients are supportive of the whistle-blower's actions and when the wrongdoer has little power and credibility.

COUNTERPRODUCTIVE BEHAVIOURS AT WORK

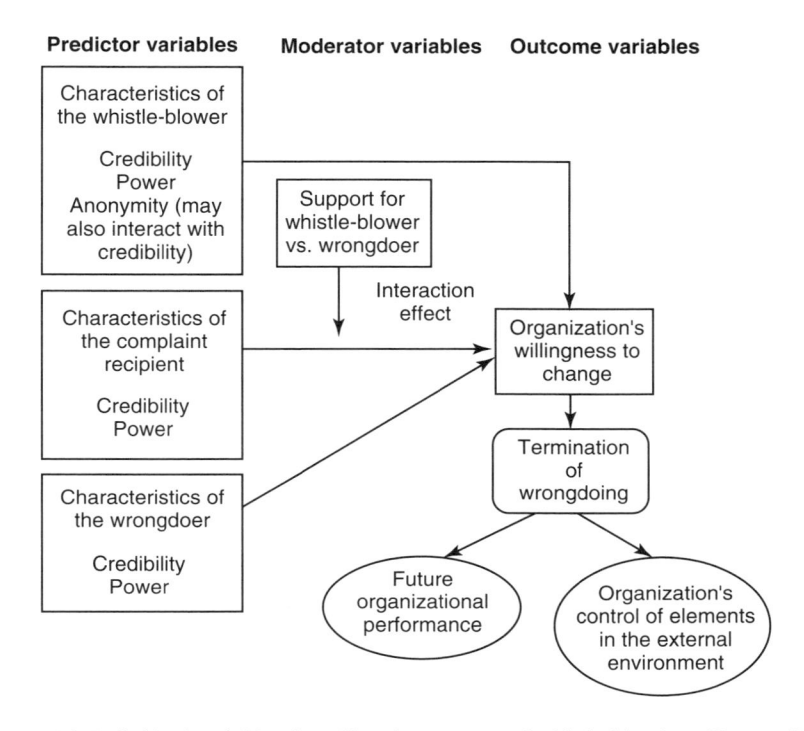

Figure 4.9 Individual variables that affect the outcome of whistle-blowing. (*Source:* Near and Miceli 1995.)

They assert that the greater the dependence of the organization on the wrongdoing the less likely internal and the more likely external whistle-blowing will be. The more evidence provided and the more unambiguously illegal the acts, the more likely the effectiveness. Further, the whistle-blower needs to be seen to use appropriate channels and means. Naturally, effectiveness is enhanced in organizations where the climate discourages wrongdoing and actually encourages whistle-blowing and discourages retaliation. It is most effective in organizations with bureaucratic structures but only where there are formal and operating mechanisms to encourage internal whistle-blowing. Finally, effectiveness will be enhanced in organizations that have low power in their environment particularly if external channels of reporting are used.

The problem for the organization, the researcher and the law is to determine the *real motive* of the whistle-blower (Casal and Zalkind 1995; Miceli et al. 1991; Somers and Casal 1994). The disgruntled, passed-over, vengeful employee may take to whistle-blowing to 'get even'. Hopefully close investigations of whistle-blowing accusations can help determine just from unjust whistle-blowers.

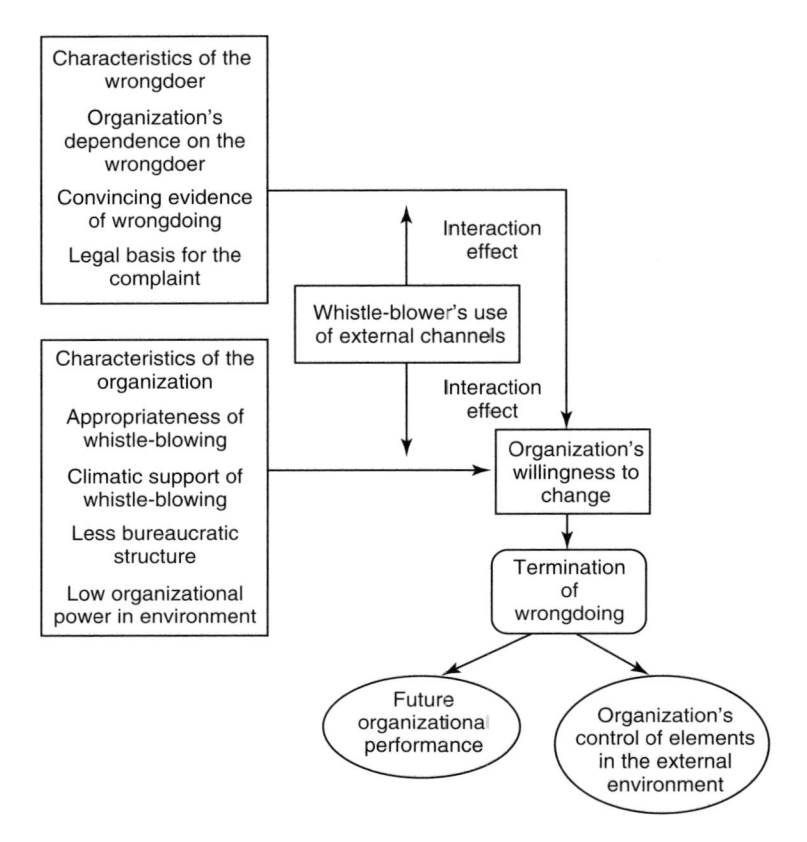

Figure 4.10 Situational variables that affect the outcome of whistle-blowing. (*Source:* Near and Miceli 1995.)

But the reputation and legal cost to an organization falsely accused can be enormous. It can break organizations as well as individuals.

Some whistle-blowers feel guilty and do so because by 'telling the truth' they feel in part able to redeem themselves for their complicity, collusion and participation in the wrongdoing.

From the top-down perspectives in organizations, the whistle-blower is disloyal, a traitor, one who indulges in title-tattle. From the bottom-up perspective, whistle-blowers can be seen as heroes: courageous, fighters for truth. Some of the lionized whistle-blowers talk of personal sacrifice (the retaliation) for a noble cause; acting because they had no choice; being unable not to act knowing what they know. There is a lot of talk about identification with victims, a sense of collective guilt and shame (working for the company), even being a part of history. Seeking revenge or the limelight is never discussed.

It is quite simply too easy to be a whistle-blower: media experts explain how frequently they are called by people with all sorts of impossible stories and little evidence to support them. Their motives are often a curious mix of the personal and the political. Justice, ethics and fairness are concepts that are bandied about with abandon.

Rothschild and Miethe (1999 p 107) did a survey of whistle-blowing in the US and found:

> data the authors collected on whistle-blowers and on silent observers that shows a) whistle-blowing is more frequent in the public sector than in the private: b) there are almost no sociodemographic characteristics that distinguish the whistle-blower from the silent observer; c) whistle-blowers suffer severe retaliation from management, especially when their information proves significant; and d) no special method of disclosure or personal characteristics can insulate the whistle-blower from such retaliation. Furthermore, the authors found that retaliation was most certain and severe when the reported misconduct was systematic and significant—when the practices exposed were part of the regular, profit accumulation process of the organization. The authors conclude from their interviews that the journey to exoneration that follows a whistle-blower's disclosures often alters the whistle-blowers identity, leading them to see themselves as people who resist hurtful or criminal conduct in the workplace.

The question then is, essentially, when is whistle-blowing justified? This may refer to the manner as well as the reasons for it. Those who believe whistle-blowing to be both a good thing and a safety valve talk of the suppression of dissent and give advice on how to be an effective resister. It has been portrayed as an effective anticorruption device. Some organizations, clearly worried by the threat of whistle-blowing, often more euphemistically referred to as 'raising concerns at work', actually have policies and procedures to deal with it. Thus they may have a job entitled 'Whistle-blowing Champion' and set out who to contact, how 'the investigation' is dealt with by internal inquiry, and what occurs if this is not satisfactorily dealt with by the organization according to the whistle-blower.

In surveys, it has been shown that the overwhelming majority of people support the concept of legal protection for people who report corruption. A clear majority say they would probably or definitely not report corruption without legal protection. Clearly job loss and other reprisals are seen to be the major deterrent to reporting corruption. Where people have faith in the management who will respond to reports not by shooting the messenger but investigating and confronting the problem, the need for whistle-blowing is significantly reduced.

It is, however, sensible for the organization to put into practice whistles-blower procedures that state the issue of malpractice is both serious and will be dealt with firmly. It must accept the right to raise issues confidentially and without fear of repercussions. It needs also to have guidelines and time limits for the consequent investigations. Perhaps most wisely of all, its procedures should specify the consequences and penalties for making false and malicious allegations in the first place.

Some countries pass legal statutes. For example, The British Public Interest Disclosure Act gives legitimate whistle-blowers legal protection against reprisal, victimization and, usually, dismissal. This Act applies to those who have 'genuine concerns' about such things as criminal activity, civil offence, and breaches of health and safety regulations, miscarriages of justice, environmental damage, and so on.

The Act states that whistle-blowers must have an honest and *reasonable suspicion* that a malpractice has/is likely to occur and have made a *disclosure/representation* to their employer. The Act protects them if they reasonably believe they would be victimized if they raised concerns with senior people *internally* or with the *prescribed regulator;* that evidence would be concealed or destroyed if raised internally; or that they believed the disclosure was of an exceptionally serious nature.

Whistle-blowing is a serious act. The 'just' whistle-blower needs to be completely sure of his/her facts and have evidence sufficiently reliable and robust to stand up in a court of law. They may be advised to seek legal help first. They need to follow current procedure, be prepared to compromise and take advice.

So when is whistle-blowing justified? This refers to the manner and matter of disclosure as well as to the reasons/motives behind the whistle-blower. Various criteria may be set:

1. *Utilitarianism*
   This is about working out the harm/good, ends/means ratio. There are nearly always positive and negative consequences of whistle-blowing. Whistle-blowing might cause a company to fail and innocent employees to lose their jobs. If the end is not justified by the means it probably means it is not justified at all. There are those who are not utilitarians and absolutists who believe that the *truth must be known* whatever the cost. It is a supposedly virtuous and moral necessity whatever the consequences.
2. *Correcting and preventing wrongdoing*
   If an act of whistle-blowing is disinterested in prevention but only seeks restitution (and revenge), it may be a sign of insincerity. Pessimists who talk of 'the system' claim it cannot be changed, will always be corrupt and no, even altruistic, act can change that. On the other hand, if the whistle-blower seems genuinely interested in seeking that this event could (and should) not re-occur, it may be a sign of justifiability.
3. *'Responsible whistle-blowing'*
   It may seem oxymoronic to some and quite natural to others that a code of conduct should be followed. To be responsible means things like: getting

facts correct without distortion, exaggeration or fabrication; avoiding personalizing or vindictiveness; avoiding hurt, pain or embarrassment to innocent parties; consulting colleagues and relevant others before acting; choosing the appropriate time, manner and target for the whistle-blowing. Of course all these rules must be seen in context and balanced. But the extent and reason for why they are broken gives a good insight into the real motives of the whistle-blower.

4   *Channels exhausted*
All organizations have policies and procedures about 'complaints'. The sincerity and honesty of a whistle-blower may be judged by the extent he/she gave the organization warnings and a chance to rectify wrongs. It is true that within some organizations channels for complaints, disciplinary procedures and grievance may be absent, or biased, or negative, dealing only with complaints and not prevention. Whistle-blowers often say it is dangerous, even suicidal, to try the 'official' route but that is something they must prove themselves in order to justify their actions.

Sabotage

Sabotage is not exclusively the domain of a lunatic with explosives or a weapon. It is the cold calculation of a person intent on revenge and there are many manifestations. Sabotage can have a wide and very specific meaning. It has, most often two distinct connotations: the intention to damage company property and/or subvert company operations. This involves, quite simply the destruction or tampering with (but strictly speaking not theft of) machinery and goods as well as attempting to stop, or slow down production. The reasons for sabotage are manifold: protect one's job; protect family/friends from a boss or simply employ the principle of an eye-for-an-eye.

Faking application forms and shrinkage seem almost trivial compared with industrial sabotage. Chemical products (medicines, foods) can easily be 'tampered' with. A virus can be introduced into a company's vital computer destroying all records and files. Large crucial mechanical equipment can be 'disabled' so preventing a whole series of jobs being done. Perhaps the most widespread and growing forms of sabotage involve the web: sabotaging others' computer files. All sorts of industries seem vulnerable and have been targeted. They include food and drink processors, cosmetic companies, supermarkets and restaurants and other high-tech organizations. Sabotage takes place during strikes. It is often seen by psychologists as the cathartic destruction of property.

Crino (1994) has defined sabotage as work-related behaviour specifically designed to 'damage, disrupt, or subvert the organization's operations for the personal purpose of the saboteur by creating unfavourable publicity, embarrassment, delays in production, damage to property, the destruction of working relationships, or the harming of employees or customers' (p 312).

An examination of the sabotage literature suggests commonly five predominant motives (Ambrose et al. 2002):

1 A reaction to powerlessness where people feel they have no freedom or autonomy at work. It is an attempt to attain control for its own sake.
2 Chronic and acute organizational frustration that originates from such things as inadequate resources to do the job.
3 To make work easier to accomplish like breaking rules, restructuring social relationships. It may involve non-sanctioned means to achieve sanctioned ends.
4 Boredom: entertainment and fun can certainly be had when things go wrong.
5 Evening the score through a sense of injustice typically generated by disrespect, being passed over for promotion, given additional responsibilities without power.

> *Still stinging after the violence of last June's anticapitalist riots in the City, police are taking seriously the threat of sabotage from anarchists who may try to infiltrate big companies to coincide with this year's protests, planned for May 1. Last week, they issued, a warning to companies in the country's financial heart to be on their guard against temporary workers who may come to work with a hidden agenda.*
>
> *Guardian* Monday 17 April 2000

In the world of anarchism and terrorism which exists today there is a sixth reason—that of the terrorist or anarchist infiltrating organizations to sabotage key business or public services.

It is quite impossible to get valid sabotage statistics for two reasons. First, organizations do not always know when it has occurred. Second, where they do, for obvious reasons of poor publicity they do not report it.

Sabotage was the tool of labour movements in the nineteenth century. However, in the twenty-first century increased technological complexity of products and greater customer demand for quality and safety have meant sabotage is both more important and difficult to detect. For some writers saboteurs tend to be characterized as hostile, angry, vengeful, impulsive, narcissistic, paranoid or psychopaths (Klein et al. 1996).

Indeed sabotage has different aims: destroy machinery or goods, stop production or reduce the work being done. It should not be assumed that sabotage is exclusively the lot of *workers*. There is also *management* sabotage: indeed they are often in a better position to be more successful at it. Management sabotage has been shown to be caused by things like the perception of uneven work distribution, arbitrarily made investments, wages being unrelated to productivity and unfair promotions.

Sabotage has different goals but many refer to simple retaliation. There are also different targets—managers, machinery, customers. Usually the target is the same as the perceived cause of the injustice and frustration. The severity of the injustice is also important: the amount, type and source of perceived injustice or unfairness relates logically to the severity of the injustice (Ambrose et al. 2002).

Further, one can distinguish between *instrumental* and *demonstrative* sabotage. The former is aimed at achieving demands or changing the power structure, while the latter is about castigating management, protesting about injustice or simply showing one's rejection of company values and policies. Sabotage may be a 'publicity stunt' aimed primarily at spoiling a company's image.

Saboteurs may be vengeful, defensive, lazy or self-promotional. Some are retaliative and try to 'get even' while others are more involved in self-presentation trying, somewhat bizarrely to meet perceived expectations or requirements or organizational success.

Using interesting examples Crino (1994) listed a number of motivations for sabotage.

1. To make a statement or send a message. They hope to gain maximum publicity and sympathy for their position which may be based on political, moral or religious beliefs.
2. To prevent or encourage corporate change. Some want to stop mergers or stock sales by scaring off bidders. Others sabotage old equipment forcing a company to buy new machines.
3. To establish personal worth or simply be the centre of attention. They may want to increase their status or join particular subcultures. This is rarely politically motivated sabotage but more likely pathologically motivated sabotage.
4. To gain a competitive advantage over co-workers. They may destroy others work or, withholding or lying about important information, losing important documents; compromising others reputation (rumour, blame, altered records) or encouraging them to take part in self-defeating behaviours. The idea is to enhance one's own reputation at the expense of others.
5. To gain revenge against management and co-workers. Workers who have been shown disrespect, passed over for promotion, given added responsibility but no commensurate reward, or not been given support from colleagues become disgruntled. Arson, bomb threats and attempted poisoning is not unusual for these saboteurs.
6. To have an impact in a large, faceless, distant bureaucracy. People are loyal to their local group and resent the interference by anonymous people from head office often many miles away. Curiously sabotage can increase a sense of control: they (personally) can slow down production, make errors, let faulty products leave the factory. It allows them to think, quite negatively, that they can make a difference.

7 To obtain thrills and satisfy a need to destroy. Bored sensation seekers love a fire, a line of cars with slashed tyres, a building with broken windows. Sabotage is a game and an exciting one at that. One can beat the system and out smart pompous authority figures.
8 To avoid responsibility for failure, incompetence or to avoid work. Sabotage can refocus attention away from them. It can also be used to intimidate or implicate others or even encourage them to conspire to avoid work.
9 For personal gain. Sabotage may well create conditions for additional compensation, compromising data, setting up good jobs with competitors. Clever IT sabotage can lead to access to data on managed funds, customer records, and so on.
10 To vent anger created by one's personal life. The disappointed, disillusioned and frustrated may take out their anger at work quite simply because they spend a lot of their time there. The acts are random, unplanned and gratuitous aimed simply to vent anger and feel more control.

One study gathered data from 44 HR managers and 164 supervisors in 10 American companies (Di Battista 1991, 1996). It attempted to discuss the forms, reasons for and best ways of reducing the risk of sabotage. They listed 15 forms of sabotage, later made up to 30.

1 Doing 'personal work' on company time with company supplies and telephone.
2 Writing on company furniture and walls.
3 Flattening tyres and scratching company cars.
4 Stealing to compensate for low pay and poor work conditions.
5 Self-creating 'down time'.
6 Switching paperwork around the office.
7 Snipping cables on word processors.
8 Passing on defective work and parts to the next station.
9 Calling OSHA representative as a scare tactic.
10 Altering the time on the punch clock.
11 Punching someone else's time card.
12 Calling upon the union to intervene.
13 Setting up the foreman to get him/her in trouble.
14 Pulling the fire alarm and bomb threats.
15 Turning on a machine and walking away, knowing it will crash.
16 Instructing others to engage in activities which will be harmful to the company.
17 Altering or deleting data stored in computer databases.
18 Falsifying information on company records.
19 Disclosing secret information to competitors.

20 Allowing defective parts to pass inspection.
21 Lowering the quality of the product by purposely using lower quality parts.
22 Altering company records.
23 Placing a false order.
24 Wrecking the office of an executive you don't like.
25 Damaging someone else's work.
26 Insulting customers.
27 Losing important files and papers.
28 Ruining relations with other companies.
29 Lying to management about important data.
30 Interrupting mail so that it fails to get to people on time.

Some of these seem more trivial than others and some people do consider poisoning products or serious luddite destruction of machines quite acceptable. Over 200 people came up with 10 reasons for sabotage:

1 Self-defence
2 Revenge
3 Pressure of the work environment
4 To protect oneself from boss/company
5 To protect friends or family from boss/company
6 To protect one's job
7 The foreman/company deserved it
8 Just for fun/laughs
9 No one was hurt by the action
10 Frustration with employee situation.

However, being HR professionals, they seemed better at listing attempts to reduce sabotage. They came up with eight interpersonal approaches and ten structural or 'organizational' approaches:

Interpersonal approaches

1 Manage the suggestion system.
2 Monitor the flow of written and oral messages.
3 Improve interviewing skills.
4 Encourage feedback from subordinates.
5 Develop workable communication programmes.
6 Let subordinates know the direction in which they make progress in the organization.
7 Provide a record for assessment of the department or unit as a whole and show where each person fits into the larger picture.
8 Insist, for certain employees, that improvement is necessary.

Structural approaches

1. Setting up a quality circle.
2. Implementing job enlargement programmes.
3. Setting up autonomous production groups.
4. De-emphasizing the corporate role in decision making.
5. Expanding strategic planning to cross-functionally develop key employees.
6. Storing copies of data at another site.
7. Using biometrics devices as ID cards for workers. These machines can scan voice reflections and handprints.
8. Using antiviral programs to detect viruses.
9. Prohibiting employees from loading contested software into the system.
10. Encrypt data and program the computer to accept calls only from authorized phones.

Di Battista (1996) argues that sabotage crises move through various stages: *pre-crises* (where small warning signs can be detected), *acute crises* (when the event has just occurred and demands swift, sure management) and *chronic crises* (when the crises are not resolved) and the *crisis resolution* stage. He believes management can forecast the effect by considering five factors:

1. Intensity of consequences
2. Scrutiny to the normal operations of the business
3. Interference to the normal operations of the business
4. Damage to the public image
5. Cost both in hard (profits, ROI) and soft (morale, stress) currency.

In a study of 121 American HR managers, he found that of the actual sabotage events reported by the respondents:

- 3% escalated in intensity
- 24% were subject to close scrutiny
- 15% were subject to close government scrutiny
- 82% interfered with normal business operations
- 62% damaged the company's bottom line
- 18% damaged the company's public image.

Di Battista (1996 p 51) concluded:

> Research shows that organizations can no longer look to prevent sabotage occurrences, but rather to anticipate and manage the event to a quick resolution. It is in management's best interest to avoid the acute and chronic stages of an event. At these stages, the organization may find the event to escalate in intensity, to fall under close media and governmental

scrutiny, to interfere with the normal operations of business, to jeopardize its public image, and to damage its bottom line. Therefore once management can admit that an act may occur, it can access the impact of it on the organization and its public. With this combination of assessing an impact assuming a probability, management has developed a forecast procedure that it can make as part of a comprehensive plan to manage risk.

Some researchers have become very interested in very specific sabotage. Logan (1993) looked at product tampering which frequently triggers 'an avalanche of false alarms, copycat cases, tampering threats and falsified reports of suspected tampering' (p 918). A favoured method is placing cyanide in food such as cakes and also in toothpaste, fresh produce and drinks. Interestingly, threats of tampering are much more common than actual tampering. Motives have been found to vary from sociopolitical, malicious mischief and revenge to economic terrorism.

Logan (1993 p 925) concluded:

The extent of tampering crime, and the potential for its expansion, highlights the vulnerability of the food, drink, and drug supply to tampering, and the potential economic and social consequences that this crime or even its threat has. It is evident that the public has a morbid fascination with this type of public safety threat, as evidenced by the deluge of reports to the authorities following even a single documented episode of tampering. The potential for hysteria is very high and underscores the need for responsible reporting in the media and tactful handling of information by public health agencies. Manufacturers and food, drug and produce suppliers need to be keenly aware of the threat when planning marketing and packaging strategies for their products. The public needs to be educated in the importance of inspecting the tamper evident packaging at the point of sale, and prior to consuming or storing food, and to accept that part of the responsibility for protection from adulterated products is their own. The penalties for product tampering need to be more widely publicized, possibly through the use of warnings on food and drug packaging material, similar to alcohol warnings. Perversely however, heightened warnings regarding product tampering could lead to new outbreaks.

Recommendations at reducing sabotage are not fundamentally different from those causing other types of problem. Many are obvious (Crino 1994).

1 Assess job applicants carefully, verifying particularly job history, especially frequent changes in jobs and the reason why this occurred. One should look for signs of persecution feelings (multiple claims of maltreatment at work)

and whether they have all the requisite skills. Integrity testing may be used most beneficially.

2. Train employees to minimize disorientation and frustration particularly in times of change. Training should make the employee feel important and valued and worthy of investment. Job enrichment and having self-managed teams can prevent alienation.

3. Create an atmosphere of fairness, justice and trust by equitable award and appraisal. Employees need to be kept informed and consistent, ethical not political, standards need to be set up. Regular, honest, supportive performance appraisals can go a long way to reduce feelings of bitterness and revenge. All disciplinary action needs to match the offence. Managers need to keep their word.

4. Stress the compatibility of employee/employer interests. If employees believe they personally suffer when sabotage takes place they are naturally less likely to do it or condone it. Companies need to ensure workers feel supported and that demands of work and family are nicely counterbalanced.

5. Take security seriously because carelessness and patchy security provide perfect options for the saboteur. Employees need to be made accountable for security issues which need to be seen as part of the job that interferes with real work. Security issues can easily be introduced to job descriptions, orientation and appraisal to attempt to create a real security culture.

6. Limit access to facilities, information and production, particularly through computer networks. Through usual techniques of passes, passwords, identification badges, it is possible to reduce 'easy' sabotage.

7. Improve the ability to trace sabotage. Saboteurs do not want to be caught. Video cameras, authorized (and traceable) computer and building access can ensure that authorities know where people are and what they are doing.

8. Assume sabotage will occur and plan for it. Limiting the impact of behaviour is important. This may mean having backup programs and databases offsite as well as running antiviral programs. Companies need to have a plan for recalling products, informing the public, handling media interest and managing liability when necessary.

Resignations

Few companies or organizations offer young people a career for life. The emphasis from career advisers and in recruitment agencies is to move jobs regularly in order to develop talents fully. Retention of their talented, knowledgeable and hard-working employees is therefore becoming an endemic problem for employers.

Recent Hay studies reveal that about one-third of employees surveyed worldwide plan to resign in three years. In the previous five years, employee attrition surged by more than 25%. The Hay Group report showed that for companies with revenues of $500 million the loss could amount to 4% of revenues amounting to 40% of profits, assuming those companies earned 10% on revenues. The report gives an example from a consumer products group which recruits 100 executives a year, a quarter of whom leave within 12 months. The average direct cost of recruitment and training was $6.25—if they could have held on to 10 of those 25 they would have saved $2.5 million per year (Hay Group 2001).

In the UK, a survey in 2001 showed that 22% of doctors intended to quit direct patient care in the next five years. In 1998 the figure was 14%. The principal reason was a reduction in job satisfaction (Sibbald et al. 2003 p 1). The cost of recruitment throughout the UK was estimated by Simon Howard in 2002 as £7 billion, 'which is a lot of money in anyone's book' (Howard 2002 p 58).

There has been a great deal of research on employee turnover: why, when and how employees choose voluntarily to leave organizations. What have all these studies demonstrated? In their exhaustive meta-analysis Griffeth et al. (2000) came to the following conclusions:

▷ There are *proximal* and *distal* causes that lead to the decision to leave which takes place over time in a fairly well-described dynamic process. The general decision to leave is usually initiated by job dissatisfaction. This leads to a search for an alternative. The distal factors that have been consistently shown to be important are: job content, stress, work-group cohesion, autonomy, leadership, distributive justice and promotional chances. These affect commitment and satisfaction which leads to ideas about leaving.

▷ The turnover rate in companies is not necessarily a powerful factor determining whether any one individual will leave.

▷ The turnover rate for women is quite similar to that of men.

▷ Companies that have merit-based reward systems tend to keep people longer. Where collective reward programmes replace individual incentive, their introduction seems to increase turnover.

▷ Organizations (like the military) that have specific compulsory contracts to discourage resignations in a fixed period certainly experience far less turnover and a more stable workforce.

▷ Personality factors—specifically neuroticism and conscientiousness—do predict turnover over and above other factors.

Resignations form the most frequent and perhaps the most innocent reason for staff turnover, but are often a manifestation of discontent and the one which costs most. And so many could be avoided!

Conclusion

This chapter has looked at some of the very specific types of CWBs. There is a separate research literature on these topics: theft, fraud, deceit, information leakage, whistle-blowing, sabotage and excessive turnover. Yet many similar themes occur. These CWBs occur in a variety circumstances most of which are predictable and preventable. Certainly specific characteristics of individuals seem related to the particular CWB. A rather different sort of individual chooses to become a saboteur as opposed to a whistle-blower, though they may be motivated by very similar circumstances.

Opportunity, work-group norms, and management practices are the factors that most obviously account for specific CWBs. Theft, petty and serious, may be condemned by junior management; deceit may be the norm in some settings, and mass turnover after expensive training and selection a common reaction to particular circumstances.

Integrity researchers in those specific areas offer similar advice. They maintain, with good empirical evidence, that those CWBs can be significantly reduced (though probably never eliminated). They all talk of more careful selection better management practices and the introduction, where appropriate, of surveillance equipment. Organizations have gone (and will go) out of business because of the preventable CWBs of their employees. No matter how good the product or service, or how hungry the market for it, if the employees are disgruntled and vengeful because of the way they are treated the organization may yet fail.

Hence the importance of taking the dark side of work behaviour seriously. CWBs are damaging; they affect profits and productivity. But disloyalty and indifference can be turned round and, with the right policies and management organizations, one can create a workforce that is loyal and committed.

References

Ambrose, M., Seabright, M. and Schminke, M. (2002) Sabotage in the work place: The role of organizational injustice. *Organizational Behaviour and Human Decision Processes*, **89**, 947–65.

Broad, W. and Wade, N. (1985) *Betrayers of the Truth: Fraud and Deceit in Science* Oxford: OUP.

Brockway, J., Carlson, K., Jones, S. and Bryant, F. (2002) Development and validation of a scale for measuring cynical attitudes towards college. *Journal of Educational Psychology*, **94**, 1–15.

Casal, J. and Zalkind, S. (1995) Consequences of whistle-blowing. *Psychological Reports*, **77**, 795–802.

Cizek, G. (1999) *Cheating on Tests* Mahway, NJ: LEA.

Crino, M. (1994) Employee sabotage: a random or preventable phenomenon. *Journal of Managerial Issues*, **6**, 311–30.

Davies, D. (2000) *Fraud Watch* London: ABG.

Di Battista, R. (1991) Creating new approaches to recognise and deter sabotage. *Public Personnel Management*, **20**, 347–53.

Eoyang, C. (1994) Models of Espionage. In T. Sarbin (ed.) *Citizen Sabotage* New York: Praeger, pp 69–92.

Greenberg, J. (1998) The cognitive geometry of employee theft: negotiating 'the line' between taking and theft. In R.W. Griffin, A. O'Leary-Kelly and J. Collins (eds) *Nonviolent behaviors in organizations (Vol. 2). Dysfunctional behaviors in organizations*, pp 147–93. Greenwich, CT: JAI

Greenberg, J. (2002) Who stole the money, and when? Individual and situational determinants of employee theft. *Organizational Behaviour and Human Decision Processes*, **89**, 985–1003.

Greenberg. J. and Scott, K. (1996) Why do workers bite the hands that feed them? *Research in Organizational Behaviour*, **18**, 111–56.

Greenberg, L. and Barling, J. (1996) Employee theft. In C. Cooper and D. Rousseau (eds) *Trends in Organizational Behaviour*, **3**, 49–67. Chichester: Wiley.

Griffeth, R., Hom. and Gaertner, S. (2000) A meta-analysis of antecedents and correlates of employee turnover. *Journal of Management*, **26**, 463–88.

Grover, S. (1993) Lying, deceit and subterfuge: A model of dishonesty in the workplace. *Organizational Science*, **4**, 478–95.

Hay Group (2001) *The Retention Dilemma* www.haygroup.com.

Hogan, R. and Hogan, J. (1994) The mask of integrity. In T. Sarbin (ed.). *Citizen Espionage*. New York: Praeger, pp 93–105.

Hollinger, R. (2002) *National Retail Security Survey Final Report* University of Florida.

Howard, S. (2002) The Missing £7 Billion. *People Management*, 21 March 2001.

Husson, J.M., Bugaievsky, J., Huidberg, E., Schwarz, J. and Chadha, D. (1996) Fraud in clinical research on medicines in the European Union: facts and proposals. In Lock and Wells (eds).

Jackson, C., Levine, S., Furnham, A. and Burr, N. (2002) Predictors of cheating behaviour at university. *Journal of Applied Social Psychology*, **32**, 1–18.

Keenan, J. (1990) Upper-level managers and whistle blowing. *Journal of Business and Psychology*, **5**, 223–35.

Klein, R., Leong, G. and Silva, J. (1996) Employee sabotage in the workplace: A biopsychosocial model. *Journal of Forensic Sciences*, **41**, 52–5.

Lock, S. and Wells, F. (1996) (eds) *Fraud and Misconduct in Medical Research* London: BMJ Publishing Group.

Logan, B. (1993) Product tampering crime: A review. *Journal of Forensic Sciences*, **38**, 918–27.

Martinko, M., Gundlach, M. and Douglas, S. (2002) Towards an integrative theory of counter productive workplace behaviour. *International Journal of Selection and Assessment*, **10**, 36–50.

Miceli, M., Dozier, J. and Near, J. (1991) Blowing the whistle on data fudging. *Journal of Applied Social Psychology*, **21**, 271–95.

Morris, J. and Moberg, D. (1994) Work organization as contexts for trust and betrayal. In T. Sarbin (ed.) *Citizen Espionage* New York: Praegar, pp 189–202.

Near, J. and Miceli, M. (1995) Effective whistle-blowing. *Academy of Management Review*, **20**, 679–706.

Near, J. and Miceli, M. (1996) Whistle-blowing: Myth and reality. *Journal of Management*, **22**, 507–26.

Nicehoff, B. and Paul, R. (2000) Causes of employment theft and strategies that HR managers can use for prevention. *Human Resources Management*, **39**, 51–69.

Robinson, S. and Bennett, R. (1997a) A typology of deviant work-place behaviours. *Academy of Management Journal*, **38**, 555–72.

Robinson, S. and Bennett, R. (1997b) Workplace deviance: its definition, its manifestations and its causes. *Research on Negotiations in Organizations*, **6**, 3–27.

Rothschild, J. and Miethe, T. (1999) Whistle-blower and management retaliation. *Work and Occupations*, **26**, 107–25.

Sibbald, B., Bojke, C. and Gravelle, H. (2003) Primary Care: National survey of job satisfaction and retirement intentions amongst general Practitioners in England. *British Medical Journal*, 1 January 2003.

Singer, T. (1996) Stop thief! Are new employees robbing you blind? *Entrepreneur*, January: 144–53.

Somers, M. and Casal, J. (1994) Organizational commitment and whistle-blowing. *Group and Organizational Management*, **19**, 270–84.

50
WHAT *IS* THE DIFFERENCE BETWEEN ORGANIZATIONAL CULTURE AND ORGANIZATIONAL CLIMATE?
A native's point of view on a decade of paradigm wars

Daniel R. Denison

Source: *Academy of Management Review* 21(3) (1996): 619–654.

Abstract

Recently, organizational culture researchers have applied quantitative survey methods and identified comparative "dimensions" of culture in a way that appears to contradict some of the original foundations of culture research within organizational studies. This new quantitative culture research also bears a strong resemblance to earlier research on organizational climate. This article examines the implications of this development by first considering the differences between the literatures on organizational culture and organizational climate and then examining the many similarities between these two literatures. The literatures are compared by focusing on their definition of the phenomena, their epistemology and methodology, and their theoretical foundations. The implications of the differing theoretical foundations and their underlying assumptions about the phenomenon are discussed at some length, as are some of the consequences of the continued separation of these two literatures. The final discussion focuses on the implications of these developments for future research on organizational cultures and contexts.

Since the early 1980s, when the culture perspective originally burst onto the organizational studies scene, the literature has evolved through many interesting stages. Early on, as Meyerson (1991: 256) noted, "culture was the code word for the subjective side of organizational life... its study represented an ontological rebellion against the dominant functionalist or 'scientific' paradigm." This reaction against the pervasive positivism, quantification, and managerialism of mainstream organizational studies helped initiate a decade-long reexamination of the foundations of organizational studies that still continues (Alvesson, 1989; Burrell & Morgan, 1979; Czarniawska-Joerges, 1992).

By the mid-1980s, however, many researchers were concerned that culture research was falling short of its promise (Alvesson, 1985; Frost, 1985; Frost, Moore, Louis, Lundberg, & Martin, 1991; Smircich & Calás, 1987). The "paradigm wars" that challenged the dominant perspective had sharpened researchers' skills at epistemological repartee, but culture research still seemed to have fallen short of theoretical and practical expectations, even as it became an established area in the field. Since that time, the area has "matured" in a number of ways, including the publication of several books on organizational culture, such as the integrative overviews offered by Schein (1985, 1992), Ott (1989), Trice and Beyer (1992), and Alvesson (1993); new perspectives introduced by Sackmann (1991), Martin (1992), Alvesson and Berg (1992), and Czarniawska-Joerges (1992); and new empirical studies and ethnographies presented by Denison (1990), Kunda (1992), and Kotter and Heskett (1992).

A more curious development in the literature, however, is the appearance of a number of articles that apply quantitative research methods to the study of culture (Calori & Sarnin, 1991; Chatman, 1991; Chatman & Caldwell, 1991; Denison & Mishra, 1995; Gordon & DiTomaso, 1992; Hofstede, Neuijen, Ohayv, & Sanders, 1990; Jermier, Slocum, Fry, & Gaines, 1991). In general, these authors have applied survey methods to study comparative "dimensions" of culture in a way that appears to contradict the epistemological foundations of culture research within organizational studies. Some of these studies have combined qualitative and quantitative methods, but they nonetheless bear a strong resemblance to the type of research that served as the antithesis of culture research a decade ago. With some alarm, Siehl and Martin (1990: 274) argued that this type of research runs the risk of reducing culture to "just another variable in existing models of organizational performance."

Even more perplexing, however, is the fact that many of these recent quantitative culture studies have become virtually indistinguishable from the research in the older and now neglected tradition of organizational climate. Why is it, for example, that when Chatman (1991) asked questions about risk taking as an organizational trait, the field of organizational studies labeled it as "organizational culture," yet when Litwin and Stringer (1968) asked similar questions about risk taking, that the field labeled it as "organizational climate"? Why is it that when Joyce and Slocum (1982) examined person-environment fit, this was perceived as a "climate study," but when O'Reilly, Chatman and Caldwell (1991) examined person-environment fit, it was called a "culture study"? What implications do these similarities and differences have for the recent history and future trajectory of research on organizational culture?

Several authors have attempted to compare these two literatures and explore areas of integration (Pettigrew, 1990; Reichers & Schneider, 1990; Schneider, 1985; 1990), but the similarities and differences between culture and climate research generally have been neglected in discussions of the culture perspective (Alvesson, 1993; Schein, 1990; Smircich & Calás, 1987; Trice & Beyer, 1992). This article attempts to examine these issues more carefully by comparing and contrasting the culture and climate literatures in an effort to understand the differences and similarities between these two perspectives and their implications for future research.

This article begins with a review of the differences between culture and climate as they have typically been presented in the literature. The second section of this article, however, explores a more controversial alternative, arguing that the primary difference between these two literatures is not a substantive difference in the phenomena under investigation, but rather it is a difference in the perspective *taken* on the phenomenon. This thesis is explored through an examination of the definitions, epistemologies, and methods applied in this literature as well as the more fundamental differences in their theoretical foundations. The article also explores the implications of these theoretical foundations as well as some of the unfortunate consequences of the separation between these two literatures. The final discussion section then focuses on some suggestions regarding future research on organizational cultures.

Contrasting the organizational culture and organizational climate literatures

During the early evolution of the culture perspective, the distinction between culture and climate was quite clear. Schwartz and Davis (1981: 32) perhaps put it most simply when they said that whatever culture is, it is *not* climate ("one way to understand culture is to understand what it is not"). Studying culture required qualitative research methods and an appreciation for the unique aspects of individual social settings. Studying organizational climate, in contrast, required quantitative methods and the assumption that generalization across social settings not only was warranted but also was the primary objective of the research. If researchers carried field notes, quotes, or stories, and presented qualitative data to support their ideas, then they were studying culture. If researchers carried computer printouts and questionnaires and presented quantitative analysis to support their ideas, then they were studying climate.

Other factors also helped to distinguish these two topics in the literature. Culture researchers were more concerned with the evolution of social systems over time (Mirvis & Sales, 1990; Mohr, 1982; Pettigrew, 1979; Rohlen, 1974; Schein, 1985, 1990; Van Maanen, 1979), whereas climate researchers were generally less concerned with evolution but more concerned with the impact that organizational systems have on groups and individuals (Ekvall, 1987; Joyce & Slocum, 1984; Koyes & DeCotiis, 1991). Culture researchers argued for the importance of a deep understanding of underlying assumptions (Kunda, 1992; Schein, 1985, 1990), individual meaning (Geertz, 1973; Pondy, Frost, Morgan, & Dandridge, 1983), and the insider's point of view of the organization. Climate researchers, in contrast, typically placed greater emphasis on organizational members' perceptions of "observable" practices and procedures that are closer to the "surface" of organizational life (Guion, 1973; James & Jones, 1974) and the categorization of these practices and perceptions into analytic dimensions defined by the researchers.

The culture perspective has many exemplars, but it is perhaps best represented by book-length ethnographies, by authors such as Jaques (1951), Dalton (1959), Rohlen (1974), Schein (1985), or Kunda (1992). It is worth noting that many of these works appeared before the culture perspective itself emerged within organizational studies and, in contrast, that relatively few have appeared since. In addition, these early studies often are not distinct from more general contributions to organizational studies, such as Crozier's (1964) or Selznick's (1957) works, that were based on comparative case analyses. Rohlen's (1974) ethnography of white-collar workers in a Japanese bank is an exemplary piece of organizational culture research, presenting a thorough analysis of social structure, career pathways, organizational cultures, individual meaning, and organizational adaptation in a wholistic manner that illustrates the insights that can be gained from applying ethnographic methods to a modem organization.

Article-length descriptions of cultural analyses have also made an important contribution to the organizational culture literature. One of the classics is certainly Whyte's (1949) analysis of the social structure of a restaurant, which presents organization as a negotiated set of interaction patterns among different status, gender, and occupational groupings as it examines these factors as the context within which work occurs. More recent examples include Barley's (1983) analysis of the semiotics of the organizational and occupational cultures of funeral parlors and his analysis of the structuration processes that occur when new technology is introduced in medical imaging departments (Barley, 1986). Both of these analyses portray organizational cultures as the confluence of occupational cultures (Van Maanen & Barley, 1984) that define the nature of individual meaning and practice at work. Other worthy contributions include Martin, Sitkin, and Boehm's (1985) analyses of how the different meanings attributed to an organizational story can be used to distinguish the "old guard" from the "new guard" during an organizational transition; Van Maanen's studies of new police recruits (1973,1975); Rosen's (1985,1991) analyses of the symbolism of power, status, prosperity, and greed within an advertising firm; and Trice and Beyer's (1992) analysis of the importance of rituals. More cognitive approaches to the study of cultures were offered by Geertz (1971) through his analysis of the symbolism and meaning in a Balinese cock fight and by Weick and Roberts (1993) in their focus on the cognitive representations of coordination shared by the crew of an aircraft carrier. Other authors such as Geertz (1973), Smircich (1983), Allaire and Firsirotu (1984), Frost, Moore, Louis, Lundberg, and Martin (1985, 1991),

Smircich and Calás (1987), Czarniawska-Jorges (1992), Martin (1992), and Trice and Beyer (1992) also have made important contributions through their analyses of the culture literature.

The evolution of the climate perspective has followed a very different pattern. The concept has its roots in Lewin's studies of experimentally created social climates (Lewin, 1951; Lewin, Lippit, & White, 1939) and qualitative observation of natural organizational settings (Barker, 1965; Likert, 1961). Within the field of organizational studies, attention was first focused on climate as a topic of study in two books published in 1968. The first (Tagiuri & Litwin, 1968) was a widely cited collection of essays that presented a variety of approaches ranging from climate as an "objective" set of organizational conditions to climate as the "subjective interpretation" of individual and organizational characteristics. The second book (Litwin & Stringer, 1968) focused on the consequences of organizational climate for individual motivation, thus supporting the general idea that climate encompasses both organizational conditions and individual reactions. Likert (1961, 1967) and Campbell, Dunnette, Lawler, and Weick (1970) also contributed to this early literature by each defining a set of dimensions thought to represent the most salient aspects of organizational climate. Litwin and Stringer (1968), for example, sought to define organizational environments in terms of nine climate dimensions: structure, responsibility, reward, risk, warmth, support, standards, conflict, and identity.

After this initial burst of activity, a major issue of concern became the integration of climate research with the rest of the growing field of organizational studies. Thus, for example, there is an extensive literature that attempts to distinguish climate from seemingly "adjacent" topics such as individual satisfaction (Guion, 1973; Johanneson, 1976; LaFollette & Sims, 1975; Payne, Fineman, & Wall, 1976; Schneider & Snyder, 1975) and organizational structure (Drexler, 1977; James, 1982; Lawler, Hall, & Oldham, 1974; Payne & Pugh, 1976). A series of review articles in the mid-1970s (Hellriegel & Slocum, 1974; James & Jones, 1974; Payne & Pugh, 1976) helped to clarify this issue by building consensus around three distinct approaches to the study of climate: (a) the perceptual measurement of individual attributes, (b) the perceptual measurement of organizational attributes, and (c) the multiple measurement of organizational attributes combining perceptual and more "objective" measurements. These perspectives were distinguished by characterizing the first as "psychological climate" and characterizing the second and third perspectives as "organizational climate."

The central issue of whether climate is a "shared perception" or a "shared set of conditions" has remained a basic issue of debate in the climate literature. In one of the more memorable statements of this era, Guion (1973), using one meteorological analogy to clarify another, suggested that the concept of organizational climate was actually like the wind chill index, in that it involved the subjective perception of the joint effects of two objective characteristics, temperature and wind speed. This reasoning was used to argue that research on organizational climate would require the measurement of both objective organizational conditions and the individual perceptions of those conditions. More recently, Glick's (1985, 1988) debate with James, Joyce, and Slocum (1988) provided a spirited inquiry into the logic associated with both the psychological and the organizational perspectives on climate research.

Perhaps in part because of the growing influence of the culture perspective in the 1980s, climate researchers became more concerned with the formation of organizational climates and began to ask a more fundamental question, "Where do organizational climates come from?" Schneider and Reichers (1983), Schneider (1987), and Reichers (1987) explored this issue through what they called the "attraction-selection-retention" process. This process, interestingly, portrays the dynamics of climate formation in terms of membership changes coupled with socialization processes. Several other notable authors (Ashforth, 1985; Poole, 1985; Poole & McPhee, 1983) have taken a social construction approach to the formation of organizational climates and have provided a persuasive rationale for viewing "climates" as an outgrowth of the more basic value systems of organizations.

This brief overview of these two literatures helps to sketch out the dominant perspectives that have existed in these areas over the past decade. The two literatures present contrasting perspectives with little overlap in style or substance. This contrast tends to support perhaps the most widely accepted distinction between the two phenomena: *Culture* refers to the deep structure of organizations, which is rooted in the values, beliefs, and assumptions held by organizational members. Meaning is established through socialization to a variety of identity groups that converge in the workplace. Interaction reproduces a symbolic world that gives culture both a great stability and a certain precarious and fragile nature rooted in the dependence of the system on individual cognition and action. *Climate*, in contrast, portrays organizational environments as being rooted in the organization's value system, but tends to present these social environments in relatively static terms, describing them in terms of a fixed (and broadly applicable) set of dimensions. Thus, climate is often considered as relatively temporary, subject to direct control, and largely limited to those aspects of the social environment that are consciously perceived by organizational members.

Table 1 presents a summary of this widely accepted view of these two literatures by pointing out contrasts in epistemology, point of view, methodology, level of analysis, temporal orientation, theoretical foundations, and disciplinary base of the culture and climate perspectives.

After presenting the basic distinction between these two topics, however, I now turn to a more controversial thesis: Although it is clear that culture and climate are, in fact, very different perspectives on organizational environments, it is far less clear that they actually examine distinct organizational phenomena. In this next section, I present a more detailed comparison of some of the central issues in each literature, giving careful attention to areas in which the two perspectives overlap.

Table 1 Contrasting organizational culture and organizational climate research perspectives

Differences	Culture literature	Climate literature
Epistemology	Contextualized and idiographic	Comparative & nomothetic
Point of view	Emic (native point of view)	Etic (researcher's viewpoint)
Methodology	Qualitative field observation	Quantitative survey data
Level of analysis	Underlying values and assumptions	Surface-level manifestations
Temporal orientation	Historical evolution	Ahistorical snapshot
Theoretical foundations	Social construction; critical theory	Lewinian field theory
Discipline	Sociology & anthropology	Psychology

Are culture and climate different phenomena or different points of view?

The differences noted thus far help to describe the dominant perspectives taken in these two literatures. However, at many points, it is unclear whether culture and climate represent two entirely separate phenomena or whether they represent closely related phenomena that are examined from different perspectives. Thus, the second part of this discussion explores the possibility that organizational culture and organizational climate have similarities as well as differences and that the differences may be more closely linked to differences of perspective rather than differences of substance. Both perspectives, for example, could be regarded as examining *the internal social psychological environment of organizations and the relationship of that environment to individual meaning and organizational adaptation*. Both perspectives entertain the possibility of a shared, holistic, collectively defined social context that emerges over time as organizations struggle with the joint problems of adaptation, individual meaning, and social integration.

Several of these areas of similarity are apparent through even a simple comparison between well-known definitions of culture and climate. For example, Schein (1985: 19, 1992: 12) defined culture as "a pattern of shared basic assumptions that the group learned as it solved its problems of external adaptation and internal integration, that has worked well enough to be considered valid and, therefore, to be taught to new members as the correct way to perceive, think, and feel in relation to those problems." Values and behavior, Schein argued, are more superficial representations of this underlying structure. Tagiuri and Litwin (1968: 25), defined climate as "the relatively enduring quality of the total [organizational] environment that (a) is experienced by the occupants, (b) influences their behavior, and (c) can be described in terms of the values of a particular set of characteristics (or attributes) of the environment." To this definition, he added that climate is "phenomenologically external" yet "in the actor's head." Although Tagiuri and Litwin's definition places more emphasis on the way in which the social environment is *experienced* by the actors, and Schein's definition places more emphasis on how the social environment is *created* by the actors, both authors focused on the collective cognitive representation of patterns of social learning over time. These two definitions also show similarities in other areas: Both attempt to describe the holistic nature of social contexts in organizations, the durability of these organizational contexts over time, and the roots of these contexts in the organization's system of beliefs, values, and assumptions. Comparing these two definitions thus suggests that these two literatures may have a far more complex set of similarities and differences than those suggested by the presentation of the literature in the first part of this article.

Further comparison of other definitions of culture and climate help to support the idea that there are both differences and similarities in the phenomena under investigation in these two literatures. This potential overlap thus requires a more careful examination of the research that is actually done when authors use these concepts. Thus, the following sections present a more careful and deliberate comparison of these two literatures in terms of their central theoretical issues, their content and substance, their methodologies and epistemologies, and their theoretical foundations. These similarities between the two literatures are summarized in Table 2.

Central theoretical issues

Several examples help to illustrate how theorists in both areas have struggled with a highly similar set of generic problems. As a first illustration, both perspectives attempt to address the problem of social contexts simultaneously being the *product* of individual interaction and a powerful *influence* on individual interaction. That is, organizations are made up of individual interactions but are also a determining context for those interactions (Ashforth, 1985; Barley, 1986; Giddens, 1979; Golden, 1992; Moran & Volkwein, 1992; Poole, 1985; Poole & McPhee, 1983; Riley, 1983; Schneider & Reichers, 1983). Authors of both literatures have attempted to understand this process of reciprocal evolution, but they often have been more successful at explaining one process or the other, rather than both at the same time. As the Schein (1985, 1992) and Tagiuri and Litwin (1968) definitions showed, the culture literature often focuses on how social contexts develop out of interaction, whereas the climate literature is more likely to focus on the perception of social contexts and their impacts. Nonetheless, both literatures address a similar generic problem.

A second example, closely related to the first, is the "multilayered" nature of both culture and climate (Glick, 1985; James & Jones, 1974; Lundberg, 1982; Schein, 1985, 1990). The alternatives presented in each of the perspectives once again have notable similarities. In culture research, for example, there is a frequent distinction

Table 2 Areas of convergence in the culture and climate literature

Areas of convergence	Examples of convergence
Definition of the phenomenon	Both focus on the internal social psychological environment as a holistic, collectively defined social context
Central theoretical issues	Shared dilemma: context is created by interaction, but context determines interaction
	Definition of domain varies greatly by individual theorist
	Dynamics between the whole and the part
	- Multiple layers of analysis
	- Dimensions vs. holistic analysis
	- Subcultures vs. unitary culture
Content & substance	High overlap between the dimensions studied by quantitative culture researcher and earlier studies by climate researchers
Epistemology & methods	Recent emergence of quantitative culture studies and qualitative climate studies
Theoretical foundations	Roots of culture research are in social constructionism
	Roots of climate research are in Lewinian field theory
	Many recent studies have crossed or combined these traditions

made between the overt, surface manifestations of a culture such as artifacts, structures, symbols, rituals, or practices and the underlying assumptions or values that those manifestations exemplify. In climate research, a similar debate exists surrounding the quasi-objective "set of conditions" that exist in an organizational system and the subjective perception of those conditions by organizational members. Some theorists in fact argue that the set of conditions is the climate, whereas others argue that the climate is in fact the selective perceptions (Glick, 1988; James, Joyce, & Slocum, 1988). A careful comparison of Schein's (1985, 1990) hierarchy of artifacts, values, beliefs, and assumptions in culture research with James and Jones's (1974) or Glick's (1985) discussion of the levels of organizational and psychological climate also shows several parallels.

For example, Schein (1985), Lundberg (1982), and others have distinguished levels of analysis, ranging from core assumptions that represent the deepest level of culture, to beliefs and values as an intermediate level, to norms and artifacts that are visible at the surface level. Climate researchers also have relied on a three-part typology (Glick, 1985; James & Jones, 1974) that distinguishes psychological climate (James, James, & Asch, 1990), or the experienced organizational environment perceived by organizational members, from a social psychological set of conditions called organizational climate, to an objective and structural set of socially constructed conditions also called organizational climate. Although these levels of analysis used in the two literatures do not, of course, match directly, their common attempt to distinguish the manifest from the latent, the cognitive from the social, and the object from the subject share many similarities. Both literatures also might be criticized for giving more attention to the distinction among levels of culture, rather than to the integration across levels (Weick & Roberts, 1993).

A third issue that appears in both literatures stems from the holistic or global nature of the phenomena (Ekvall, 1987; Schneider, 1975; Schneider & Reichers, 1983). In both literatures researchers struggle with the inherent expansiveness of an explicitly broad and inclusive phenomenon. Accordingly, it is often difficult, if not impossible, to define the content of the domain of culture or climate independent of the interests of individual theorists and researchers. Thus, the content of culture as defined by Schein (1985, 1990), Hofstede (1991), Martin (1992), Kunda (1992), Kotter and Heskett (1992), Hofstede (1991), or Peters and Waterman (1982) varies greatly. Climate research, as Denison (1990) noted, shows a very similar pattern: The content varies by theorist, and there seems to be no natural limit to the climate domain other than the ability of theorists, researchers, and practitioners to evoke new adjectives to describe perceived social psychological environments.

The typical focus of the climate literature on the features of organizational contexts has often led to the conclusion that climate refers to the features rather than to the underlying context itself. As Poole (1985: 86) noted, "these types [i.e., contexts] can be *rated* on dimensions—for example, a democratic climate is high in supportiveness, low in structure, and emphasizes rewards rather than punishments—but cannot be *reduced* to dimensions, because they are wholes." Describing holistic contexts in terms of features can be a useful strategy for research—it can aid in the discovery of new contexts and can enable comparisons among types. However, "featurization" can often do violence to the representation of climate as a holistic phenomenon because there is always much more to a context than can be encompassed by any list of dimensions or attributes (Poole, 1985).

The relationship between the unitary whole and its constituent parts is also reflected in several other ways in the two literatures (Drexler, 1977; Ekvall, 1987; Gregory, 1983; Joyce & Slocum, 1984; Martin, 1992; Riley, 1983; Van Maanen & Barley, 1984). For example, many authors have written about the importance of subcultures (Martin, 1992) or distinctive subunit climates (Joyce & Slocum, 1982) and their relationships to the organizational whole. In addition, this issue is also reflected in each literature when specific content areas are defined, such as a climate for creativity (Cummings, 1965), safety (Zohar, 1980), or service (Bowen & Schneider, 1988) or a culture of absence (Nicholson & Johns, 1985).

Also, neither literature is immune from the problems of an intrigue with one aspect of the problem leading to a neglect of the whole. As Czarniawska-Joerges (1992: 108) noted,

> Organization theorists have located new aspects of organizational life and its function to study during the second half of the decade. Among these

we can find jokes, coffee breaks, how people are dressed, how they behave at the corporation's Christmas party, how they sit at meetings, how they get fired (the "rite" of getting fired), what stories about present and former figures of authority are told, and so on. ... It could be argued that these are of marginal importance compared to, for example, the organization's hierarchy and the way in which work is organized, controlled, and carried out.

This section has outlined a common set of problems, including the reciprocal nature of the social construction of organizational environments, the understanding of organizational contexts as a multilevel phenomenon, and the problem of the relationship between the organizational whole and its constituent parts. As such, it reveals a number of instances in which the two literatures may well be compatible, if not complementary, and suggests that organizational theory might in fact benefit from more explicit integration between the culture and climate literatures.

Content and substance

Another area of surprising similarity between these two literatures becomes apparent when the "content" of traditional climate research is compared to the "content" of recent culture studies. Of course, not all (nor perhaps even most) culture researchers would choose to describe culture in terms of comparative traits or dimensions. However, when they do, the content of the culture domain begins to take on a strong resemblance to the topics that climate researchers have been concerned with for decades. For example, Hofstede's concept of power distance—the appropriate social and emotional distance that should be maintained between individuals of different status and power—is highly similar to the concept of "aloofness" introduced in one of the earliest studies of organizational climate (Halpin & Croft, 1962). Interestingly, Haplin and Crofts, working in the context of American public school systems, cast this dimension in a pejorative light, whereas Hofstede's observations across national cultures appear to lead him to cast this in far more neutral terms. Nonetheless, the underlying substance of these two dimensions is highly similar.

A careful comparison of the content of culture and climate studies yields many such similarities. Schwartz and Davis (1981), after carefully pointing out that whatever culture is, it is clearly not climate, go on to list a set of "tasks" that can reveal an organization's culture. Their list includes dimensions such as decision making, communicating, and organizing. Thus, these authors show an interesting overlap with Taylor and Bowers (1973), who list decision-making practices, communication flow, and the organization of work among their key climate dimensions. Other examples abound: O'Reilly, Chatman, and Caldwell's (1991) dimension of risk taking is highly similar to Litwin and Stringer's (1968); Joyce and Slocum's (1982) emphasis on peer relations is similar to Schein's (1985, 1992); Wilkins's (1978) concept of social control bears some similarity to Porter and Lawler's (1973) concept of autonomy; and Campbell, Dunnette, Lawler, and Weick's (1970) dimension of consideration closely resembles Cooke and Rousseau's (1988) concept of humanistic culture.

Table 3 presents a partial summary of some of these similarities by examining a set of five dimensions that have been described by six different authors, three from the culture literature and three from the climate literature. Closer examination of the individual items in these scales also shows a striking set of similarities (Gordon & Christensen, 1993).

The purpose of this comparison, of course, is not to deny the differences between the two literatures, but rather to highlight some of the similarities. These similarities become most apparent when a particular type of culture research—that which has tried to make generalizations about the features or dimensions of organizational cultures—is compared to earlier climate research. Culture researchers who have not made explicit generalizations about the features and dimensions of the social contexts they study may, of course, show fewer similarities to the climate literature. Nonetheless, this similarity and overlap suggest that a more thoughtful dialogue between these two literatures may have value.

Methodology and epistemology

As indicated by the quote from Meyerson (1991) at the beginning of this article, culture research in organizational studies came about, in part, as a reaction to the existing orthodoxy in organizational studies. This reaction also was a part of a broader trend of the growing influence of postmodernism on the social sciences. As Parker noted, postmodernists often have indicted positivist social science for "elevat[ing] a faith in reason to a level at which it becomes equated with progress" (1992: 3). As such, postmodernists often are harshly critical of attempts to systematize, define, and impose rational comparative logics on the social and organizational world. Instead, it is suggested that "all of our attempts to discover truth should be seen for what they are—forms of discourse" (Parker, 1992: 3). Following this logic, knowledge must then be situated in time and place and hence relativized. As Bruno LaTour (1988: 179) wrote in *The Pasteurization of France*, "the very act of comparing, an effort to uncover similarities and differences, is a meaningless activity because postmodern epistemology holds it impossible ever to define adequately the elements to be contrasted and likened."

This perspective, of course, wreaked havoc with the classic positivist approach of climate researchers, who often took as their central mandate the development of a universal set of dimensions that would allow for comparative generalizations regarding perceived social and psychological environments. The primary epistemological issues framed in the climate literature centered on whether climate was a property of the individual, the social environment, or the interaction of the two, and researchers generally did not question the validity of comparing any of these features of social context. The epistemological critique of positivism that

Table 3 A comparison of selected dimensions used by culture and climate researchers

	Culture researchers				Climate researchers		
	Hofstede (1990)	O'Reilly & Chatman (1992)	Cooke & Rousseau (1988)		Litwin & Stringer (1968)	Hellriegel & Slocum (1974)	Koya & DeCotiis (1991)
Structure	Authority	Stability	Conventional culture		Structure	Centralization	????
Support	Power distance	Respect for people	Humanistic culture		Support	Supportiveness	Support
Risk	Security	Innovation	Avoidance culture		Risk	Innovation	Innovation
Cohesiveness	Collectivism	Teamwork	Affiliative culture		Identity	Peer relations	Cohesion
Outcome orientation	Results orientation	Outcome orientation	Achievement culture		Standards	Motivation to achieve	Pressure

was so central to the early evolution of culture research made it easy for scholars to dismiss earlier climate research as a prime example of "what not to do" and to resist discussion of areas of integration and overlap, suggesting instead that research on the phenomenon of organizational culture could only be conducted from a postmodern perspective that pursued a qualitative understanding of the unique aspects of individual social contexts.

From these reformist beginnings, research from the culture perspective made an impact in a number of different topic areas, including socialization (Louis, 1980; Van Maanen & Schein, 1979), symbolism (Alvesson & Berg, 1992; Dandridge, 1983; Pondy, Frost, Morgan, & Dandridge, 1983; Smircich & Calás, 1987), and organizational change (Frost et al., 1985, 1991; Martin et al., 1985; Schein, 1985, 1992). Nonetheless, by the mid-1980s the influence of the culture perspective had begun to wane (Calás & Smircich, 1987), leading culture researchers to talk about "Rekindling the Flame" (Frost, 1985). Even though culture researchers had developed a distinctive point of view, they had done less to define a substantive research agenda and paradigm. The critique of positivism, once made, did not necessarily suggest a future direction. This perhaps echoes one of Terry Eagleton's (1983: 144) more provocative comments about the limits of the postmodernist critique in the field of literature: "It allows you to drive a coach and horses through anyone else's beliefs while not saddling you with the inconvenience of having to adopt any yourself."

Since this period of the middle 1980s, however, the perspectives of culture researchers have expanded in several significant ways. In addition to authors whose work continued to reflect the image of "culture" research established in the early 1980s (Kunda, 1992; Martin, 1992; Smircich, 1983; Smircich & Calás, 1987; Van Maanen, 1988), "culture" research also took a curious turn as authors included studies that pursued a more conventional agenda of comparison and generalization, exemplified by a series of more recent culture articles that have used either quantitative methods exclusively or some combination of quantitative and qualitative methods (Chatman, 1991; Denison & Mishra, 1995; Gordon & DiTomaso, 1992; Hofstede, Neuijen, Ohayv, & Sanders, 1990; Jermier et al., 1991; O'Reilly et al., 1991). These most recent studies, although extending culture research in several important directions, present many overlaps with the methods and epistemology represented by the climate literature and thus invite a more careful analysis of the similarities.

In this context, the work of Geert Hofstede (1980a,b, 1986,1991; Hofstede et al., 1990) represents an interesting example. Hofstede's quantitative and comparative work on *national* culture received wide acclaim during the early and mid-1980s (Sondergaard, 1994), during a period when researchers of *organizational* culture studiously avoided quantitative methods and comparison across settings (Schein, 1985). Thus, it is important to ask, "How is it that quantitative comparisons of national culture across many nations received widespread acceptance, at a time when quantitative comparisons of organizational cultures within a single cultural context (usually Western, English-speaking, and often American at that) were seen as unfounded?" Comparative logic was rejected in the relatively homogeneous settings that concerned researchers of organizational culture at the same time that it was largely accepted in the relatively heterogeneous setting that concerned researchers of national culture. Hofstede and his colleagues further confounded the epistemological sensibilities of traditional culture researchers when they published a study of organizational culture comparing 20 Dutch and Danish firms. They showed that there were substantial differences between firms on several dimensions of organizational culture, which were closely linked to the dimensions of national culture developed in earlier research (Hofstede et al., 1990).

A similar example is provided by the work of O'Reilly and colleagues (1991). Their use of quantitative measures of culture, a comparative framework, and a concern with person-organization fit shows many similarities to earlier research in the climate literature. In fact, this study has virtually the same design as Joyce and Slocum's (1982) study of the discrepancy between psychological climate and organizational climate as a predictor of performance and job satisfaction. In addition, Martin and colleagues (1985), writing in the culture literature and using qualitative methods, also used a similar design to distinguish members of the old guard and the new guard based upon their perceptions of the organizational context.

A very different set of overlaps is suggested by the work of authors who have examined the formation of organizational climates (Ashforth, 1985; Moran & Volkwein, 1992; Poole, 1985; Poole & McPhee, 1983; Schneider, 1987; Schneider & Reichers, 1983). These authors vary in the degree to which they consciously incorporate the tenets of postmodern epistemology, but this stream of climate literature nonetheless shares much in common with the methodological and epistemological sensibilities of culture researchers.

An interesting example of this overlap was provided by Poole (1985) and Poole and McPhee (1983). Poole drew on Giddens's (1979) concept of generative rules and resources as the basis of the social reproduction process to define climate as a "belief and value structure members employ as they act in the organization" (Poole, 1985: 101). Ashforth (1985) also took a similar approach in his examination of the formation of organizational climates. One might even argue that the approach taken by Schneider (1987) and Schneider and Reichers (1983), although far less consciously postmodern than either Poole's or Ashforth's, still describes the creation of organizational climates in a manner that fits well with the implicit assumptions about the situated nature of social contexts and the inherently problematic nature of comparison.

Although the methods and epistemologies of culture and climate research generally are very different, a careful analysis of the culture literature reveals a broad range of epistemological approaches that overlap to a significant degree with earlier research on organizational climate. By the same token, more recent research on the formation of organizational climates reflects the emphasis on postmodern epistemology and qualitative methods that has been advocated by culture researchers.

Like the convergence of substance and content described in the previous section, this trend also makes it more difficult to distinguish culture and climate research solely on the basis of epistemology or method.

Theoretical foundations: the difference that makes a difference

Perhaps the most significant difference between the culture and climate literatures lies not in the nature of the phenomenon or the methods used to study it, but in the theoretical traditions that have been borrowed from other branches of the social sciences. The climate literature has its roots in the field theory of Kurt Lewin (1951), whereas the culture literature is grounded in the symbolic interaction and social construction perspectives developed by Mead (1934) and Berger and Luckmann (1966). This section contrasts the different ontologies (Smircich, 1983; Smircich & Calás, 1987) that underlie these two perspectives and examines the influence that they have had on the literatures.

Many of the differences between climate and culture can be understood by examining Lewin's basic concept of the relationship between individuals and their social environments and then considering the implications of this framework for the study of organizations. Lewin expressed his basic formulation in terms of a simple equation:

$$B = f(P, E)$$

in which B = behavior, E = the environment, and P = the person.

Quite apart from the unending complexities of actually computing the predictions of such an equation, Lewin's framework makes a far more basic assumption that has had a strong influence on the study of organizational climates. According to Lewinian field theory, the social world can be neatly divided into Bs, Ps, and Es. Thus, in order to study a phenomenon such as organizational climate (or culture) from Lewin's perspective, *the person must, by definition, be analytically separate from the social context*. This perspective characterizes the approach taken in the climate literature quite well. The "agents" of an organizational system, such as management, are often assumed, but seldom studied directly. They create the climate that others work in. The "subjects" of that system, most often employees, workers, or subordinates, are the primary objects of study. They work within the climate, but they do not create it. The impacts that the system has on its subjects are primarily examined with a nonrecursive logic (Poole, Ashforth, & Schneider notwithstanding) that conveniently neglects the process by which the social environment is constructed by the individual members it comprises.

In contrast to proponents of the Lewinian logic who analytically separate the person from the environment and tend to assume that individuals are either subjects or agents of a social system, users of the symbolic interaction perspective (Mead, 1934) and the social construction perspective (Berger & Luckman, 1966) underlying the organizational culture literature assume that the individual cannot be analytically separated from the environment and that the members of social systems are best regarded as being agents and subjects simultaneously. Thus, social context is regarded as both the medium and the outcome of social interaction. Furthermore, this literature often defines the primary topic of interest as the recursive dynamics between the individual and the system (Giddens, 1979; Lave & Wenger, 1990; Riley, 1983), rather than the impact of the system on its members.

Some implications of the different theoretical foundations

These seemingly modest theoretical differences in the conceptualization of social contexts have wide-ranging ramifications. Three are examined here. The first is the capacity of each of these perspectives for developing an understanding of the evolution of social process over time. The second is the potential of each of these perspectives for comparing contexts across different organizational settings, and the third is the connection of each of these perspectives to the ideology of managerialism. These three implications are summarized in Table 4.

Social process and evolution

One of the distinct advantages of the symbolic interactionist and social constructionist frameworks is the perspective that they provide on the evolution of social process over time. The simultaneous creation of meaning and social structure, the evolution of interaction patterns into systems of normative control, and the

Table 4 Some implications of the theoretical foundations of culture and climate research

Implications for	Theoretical foundations	
	Social constructionism	Lewinian field theory
Social process & evolution	Highly valuable for understanding the evolution of social context on a case-by-case basis	Difficult to use for understanding evolution; useful for understanding the impact of social context
Comparative research	Difficult to make comparisons, except for studies with a small number of cases	Useful for comparison; less useful for an in-depth understanding of individual cases
Managerial ideology	Control of the organization's value system is contested by varied stakeholders, power groups, and subcultures	Accepts the distinction between the managerial creators of "context" and the nonmanagerial employees that are affected by the context

close connection between the symbolic and material world can be well understood through the culture perspective. This facet of the culture perspective has been elaborated by authors such as Rohlen (1974), Van Maanen (1979), Mohr (1982), Schein (1985, 1990, 1992), Kunda (1992), and Hatch (1993).

The Lewinian perspective, in contrast, provides an awkward framework within which to understand the evolution of social process. By analytically separating the person from the social environment, it becomes quite difficult to devise a theory of how that social environment evolves. Despite several noteworthy attempts at conceptualizing the formation and evolution of social contexts that appear in the climate literature (Ashforth, 1985; Poole, 1985; Poole & McPhee, 1983; Schneider & Reichers, 1983), the Lewinian perspective still appears to be more useful for conceptualizing the influence of context on human behavior than for understanding the process by which social context develops.

The strength of the Lewinian perspective is in conceptualizing a particular type of social process involving the influence of an established context on organizational members who are in subordinate positions of power. Thus, for studies of the impact of the system on its members, particularly when a time lag occurs between the systemic stimulus and the individual response, the Lewinian framework is a highly useful perspective. As this article has shown, researchers from both literatures have adopted a Lewinian perspective to study these types of problems.

Two substantive examples help to illustrate the utility of this contrast. Research on socialization (Chatman, 1991; O'Reilly, Chatman, & Caldwell, 1991; Schneider & Reichers, 1983; Van Maanen, 1973, 1975; Van Maanen & Schein, 1979) illustrates a phenomenon in which the agents of socialization, who are representatives of the system, are quite distinct from the subjects of the system, who are newcomers being socialized. Within this context, Lewinian field theory with its core concept of separate individuals and environments provides a useful conceptual framework. Interestingly, even authors who write about socialization from a clinical perspective (e.g., Van Maanen, 1973, 1975; Van Maanen & Schein, 1979) and view socialization as a process of learning a culture maintain a relatively clear distinction between agents and subjects of socialization. At the beginning of this process, newcomers are highly distinct from other organizational members, whereas at the end of the process, they are much less distinct.

Innovation, in contrast, provides an example in which it may be less useful to separate the individuals from the environment that they are a part of. For example, Kidder's (1981) analysis of a team designing a new computer makes a good case for the coevolution of team culture and individual identity. The innovation process thus becomes difficult to understand when studied within a framework that analytically separates the individual from the environment. Barley (1986) reached a similar conclusion from his study of the adoption of a new form of medical technology. Thus, the evolutionary processes in innovation are difficult to understand, unless there is a core concept of the coevolution of the individual and the environment as suggested by the social constructionist perspective.

The viability of comparative research

The differences between these two theoretical perspectives also have strong implications for a second point, the viability of comparative research. If environments are considered as existing independently of individuals, as in Lewinian field theory, then they are more likely to be conceptualized, dimensionalized, measured, and compared as social entities. In addition, the relationship between organizational contexts and individual perceptions also can be conceptualized and operationalized in a way that allows for generalization across social settings. This logic fits well with the climate metaphor, and it is congruent with the idea that social environments exist separately from the individuals who comprise them. In contrast, the idea of comparing, generalizing, and dimensionalizing cultures clashes quite badly with the concept of cultures as unique social constructions that create unique meaning systems for their members. Thus, if all social action is situated, as suggested by the social construction and symbolic interaction perspectives (Lave & Wenger, 1990), then comparison across settings becomes a much more questionable enterprise (LaTour, 1988).

Some examples from the two literatures help to illustrate the different logics of comparison that derive from the Lewinian and social construction frameworks. For example, Joyce and Slocum (1984) argued that individuals who experience a similar set of social psychological conditions should be regarded as sharing the same "climate," even if they have no interaction, interdependence, collective history, or identity. Poole (1985) referred to this same phenomenon as "co-orientation." In this example, climate is conceptualized as a characteristic of individual-organizational dyads that can be disaggregated or reaggregated with little attention to the original situation in which the climate originated. Not only can climate be generalized and dimensionalized, but the climate itself also can be analytically detached from the social setting in which it was generated and then reaggregated.

In contrast, many culture researchers have argued that meaning and symbolic representation can be understood only with respect to specific settings. All cultures are thus unique, and attempts at generalization are inherently futile. Thus, the goal of research must be to understand and describe individual cultures at a level that allows for an understanding of individual meaning and organizational symbolism, or what Geertz (1973) called *thick description*. In this case, generalizations about the relationship between the individual and the organizational environment cannot, with confidence, be carried beyond the situations in which they arise.

Given this context, the recent turn of organizational culture research to the comparative and quantitative approaches noted previously in this article becomes very interesting. One must ask, "*Which* cultural phenomenon are these studies comparing and generalizing?" Authors of these studies acknowledge the existence of "levels of culture" and the limitations of comparative research to truly understand deeper levels of culture such as assumptions and beliefs. However, each of these studies selects an "intermediate" level of culture, such as values and cultural traits, about which to generalize. This approach does not deny the existence of either deeper level assumptions unique to a culture or the more surface-level practices, artifacts, and symbols that may have highly situational meaning. Instead, each of the studies has been focused on generalizing about cultures at an intermediate level of values or traits.

Several examples help to illustrate how this intermediate level of culture may be more useful for comparison and generalization than either the deeper level of cultural assumptions or the more superficial level of cultural artifacts and symbols. First, consider O'Reilly and colleagues' (1991) concept of innovation. Their analysis does not assume that innovation has the same deep cultural meaning across organizational settings or that organizational members attribute the same meaning to risk taking in each of the organizations they studied. In contrast, they also do not focus on the symbolic representation of risk or the particular practices used to manage innovation in the organizations that they studied. Instead, they focus on the intermediate level of values or traits as a means to generalize about culture.

As a second example, Trompenaars (1993) described differences among individualistic and collectivistic cultures by contrasting the way that individuals from those cultures react to different scenarios. This contrast does not address the underlying meaning of individualism and collectivism in each of the cultures, and it does not deal with the specific meaning of the artifacts and symbols that are used at a more superficial level to represent individualism and collectivism in each culture. Like the previous example, Trompenaars' research was focused on the intermediate level of values and traits. Trompenaars also gave an interesting example of how the same symbol or artifact may, in fact, have *exactly the opposite* meaning in two different contexts. As he explained, Japanese in Tokyo will often wear a face mask when they have a cold to prevent it from spreading to others, whereas Americans in New York or Los Angeles are far more likely to wear the same face mask to protect *themselves* from the effects of smog or airborne disease. These examples from O'Reilly and colleagues (1991) and Trompenaars (1993) help to illustrate how several authors conducting comparative culture research appear to have chosen the level of values and traits as the point of comparison.

The ideology of managerialism

The theoretical foundations underlying culture and climate research also have implications for the positions taken in each literature with respect to managerial ideology. Within the culture literature, a number of authors have been critical of the manipulation inherent in the managerial perspective (Alvesson, 1985, 1989; Frost et al., 1985, 1991; Kunda, 1992; Martin, 1992), whereas others have taken an approach that is openly managerial (Barney, 1986; Kotter & Heskett, 1992; Schein, 1985, 1992; Wilkins, 1989; Wilkins & Ouchi, 1983). Climate researchers, in contrast, appear to be less critical of managerial ideology. They tend to accept the organizational contexts created by management as a given, while concentrating on the perceptions and reactions of the individuals who work within those contexts

(Ekvall, 1987; Glick, 1985; Guion, 1973; James & Jones, 1974; Koys & Decotiis, 1991).

Once again, the key analytical step of separating the person from the environment appears to be central to this distinction. A "separate" environment, as suggested by Lewinian framework, is more consistent with both the illusion and the reality of unidirectional managerial control. This classic Lewinian distinction between the managerial creators of the organizational context and the survey respondents who perceive the context clearly reflects a managerial bias. However, climate researchers often counter this bias by directing their primary interests and concerns to their nonmanagerial respondents James et al., 1990). This approach often leaves climate researchers in the tacit position of playing both sides of the managerial issue. They seldom contest the managerial creation of organizational contexts, but they often represent the interests and perspectives of the nonmanagerial employees who operate within that context.

In contrast to the climate literature, in which issues of managerialism are seldom addressed directly, culture researchers frequently discuss the political and ideological consequences of their work. For example, Alvesson (1985, 1989, 1993), who wrote from the perspective of a critical theorist (Burrell & Morgan, 1979; Habermas, 1971; Mills, 1978), was highly critical of the managerialism of culture research and organizational studies in general and argued that the most important role of organization and management theory should be to further the emancipatory interests of organizational members. As a theorist, Alvesson appears to have achieved an "emancipatory high ground" through his critique, but it comes at the cost of a principled detachment that seems to ensure that the emancipation he sought for organizational members will be difficult to achieve on either practical or conceptual terms. Interestingly, in a more recent applied case study of a computer consultancy company, Alvesson's (1992) interest in emancipation showed many similarities to the focus of those who have studied participation and empowerment in more traditional applied ways (Block, 1991; Lawler, 1986; Semler, 1989).

Because the social construction framework that serves as a foundation for most culture research presumes that social environments are created through emergent social processes, politics and ideology become a much more salient issue. Thus, it is far less clear who is in "control" of the organizational context. Top management? Labor? Bioengineers? New executives from the consumer goods industry? The Dutch? Men? Women? Blacks? Whites? New Yorkers? Californians? In short, with social construction as an organizing framework, competing cultural influences are engaged in a power struggle to define the organizational culture. As Jermier (1991) noted, "organizational culture is a contested reality." Subcultures (Martin, 1992; Van Maanen & Barley, 1984) may thus be of as much interest as organizational cultures, and the value system of the elite is but one influence on the ultimate form of the organization. The political agendas of culture researchers thus range from a focus on the emancipatory interests of organizational members (Alvesson, 1989; Staeblein & Nord, 1985) to a focus on building corporate character (Wilkins, 1989). Culture researchers present a variety of viewpoints on the issue of managerialism and cultural control, but nearly all of these issues are rooted in the inherent diversity of social construction rather than the tidy distinction between person and environment provided by the Lewinian framework.

Some unfortunate consequences of the disjuncture between these two literatures

The lack of integration between the culture and climate literatures and their research traditions has a number of consequences that deserve further consideration. In general, a tendency to view these two research areas as competing perspectives in a paradigm war allows for far less integration than might otherwise occur based on the similarities of the substantive agenda. In this section I focus on three specific consequences of the separation between these two research traditions.

A tendency to overplay the implications of each perspective

The juxtaposition of the logics of culture and climate research has resulted in a tendency to define two contrasting orthodoxies in the study of social contexts. However, as Czarniawska-Joerges (1992: 66) noted,

> The phenomena are complex, so why do we persist in studying them with such simple methods? Or worse yet, contorting the phenomenon through selective definition and proscriptive repartee until it becomes that which can only be legitimately "seen" through a very selective set of lenses.

In short, the conceptualizations of organizational contexts provided by the culture and climate literature often tend to create a contrast between the two literatures that is more apparent than real. The inadequacies of one approach become the justification for the other. The interests of researchers in each "camp" may in fact be served by maintaining the ongoing paradigm wars, even though these dynamics may detract from progress in understanding the underlying phenomenon.

This tendency also may result in more attention being given to extreme, rather than integrative, points of view. To build on an earlier example, the climate literature has presented what might be called a "radically de-situated" view of climate (James, Demaree, Mulaik, & Ladd, 1992; Joyce & Slocum, 1984; Poole, 1985), which argues that individuals do not need to share the same social setting to experience the same perceived climate, thus redefining a contextual construct as a cognitive one. In contrast, the culture literature has presented a "radically situated" view of culture (LaTour, 1988; Parker, 1992), summarized previously in this article, implying that no valid generalization can be made outside of a particular setting. Both of these extremes appear to receive more attention in the respective literatures than does the central question of the relative uniqueness and generality of culture in different organizational settings (Martin, Feldman, Hatch, & Sitkin, 1983; Rentsch, 1990).

Differences of perspective also tend to become confused with differences of phenomenon. For example, Martin (1992) discussed three different perspectives on culture, describing them as though they were three different phenomena. Although these three perspectives provide a useful and insightful overview of the culture literature, issues of integration among the three perspectives were generally neglected. Thus, the reader is left with the impression that the field deals with three distinct phenomena, rather than the single phenomenon of organizational context, viewed from three different perspectives. This divergence is all the more interesting when one notes that the three perspectives elaborated by Martin (1992) were originally presented by Meyerson and Martin (1987) in their analysis of the Peace Corps, a single organizational context that they analyzed from three perspectives.

As another example of the tendency to overplay the implications of the culture and climate perspectives, culture researchers often have criticized positivist organizational research, focusing on its comparative logic, quantitative methods, and managerial bias. This critique has generated some interesting repartee. A noteworthy example was provided by Siehl and Martin (1990) in their commentary on the research linking organizational culture and performance (e.g., Calori & Sarnin, 1991; Denison, 1984, 1990; Denison & Mishra, 1995; Gordon, 1985; Gordon & DiTomaso, 1992; Hansen & Wernerfelt, 1989; Kotter & Heskett, 1992). Each of these studies, to varying degrees, is quantitative and comparative, and they represent examples of the type of culture research that bears some similarity to earlier research on organizational climate.

A brief analysis of their critique shows that Siehl and Martin (1990) questioned the contribution of quantification and comparison and infer that research on the links between culture and performance is intended to legitimate the direct managerial control of organizational cultures. Based on this analysis, they warned of the "pernicious social effects" of linking culture and performance (Siehl & Martin, 1990: 273). Interestingly, however, a very similar set of findings regarding culture and performance can be found in research conducted from a labor perspective linking employee involvement and cooperative labor relations with effectiveness criteria such as quality and productivity (e.g., Cooke, 1992, 1993; Cutcher-Gershenfeld, 1991; Ichniowski, Shaw, & Prennushi, 1994; Kochan, Gobeille, & Katz, 1983). Thus, Siehl and Martin (1990) seemed to group the elements that they viewed as *pernicious* (managerial manipulation, comparative research, survey data, and positivist epistemology) into one convenient target. A more thoughtful and fine-grained analysis might reveal a more complex yet more integrative set of dynamics underlying these issues.

A lack of legitimacy for research combining the two perspectives

With limited dialogue between these two perspectives, integrative studies that combine sufficient depth of analysis to gain a qualitative understanding with a broad enough sample to give some comparative leverage are very unlikely to occur. The experience of authors of qualitative culture research encountering positivist reviewers who demanded comparative analysis and the experience of authors of quantitative culture research encountering reviewers who demanded to know how their research was different from climate research are both common symptoms of a parochial outlook that currently exists regarding research on organizational context. Greater dialogue can legitimate more integrative research combining these perspectives.

My own experience in attempting to publish research that combines qualitative case studies with quantitative analysis bears this out. In an integrative article attempting to develop and test a theory of culture and effectiveness, my coauthor and I selected a set of five case studies based on prior analysis, used those to develop a model, and then collected quantitative survey data from a large sample of firms to test the model (Denison & Mishra, 1995). To our dismay, when we tried to get this work published, we found that Reviewer A said, "I love these case studies, but you should get rid of the survey data." Reviewer B added, "the quantitative study is very solid, but I would omit the case studies—they add very little." Reviewer C (predictably) suggested that we "focus on theory building—the article is too 'data driven.'"[1]

This lack of integration poses an interesting question: Which tradition "owns" those research designs that study more than one case, but fewer cases than would be needed for a "statistically valid" sample? Currently, this type of design is not "owned" or legitimated by either tradition and thus is more difficult to apply. Interestingly, however, this state of affairs clashes rather badly with the major contributions that traditionally have been made in organizational studies using this type of design (Blau, 1995; Burns & Stalker, 1961; Clark, 1970, 1972; Crozier, 1964; Dalton, 1959; Eisenhardt, 1989; Gouldner, 1954; Jackall, 1988; Lawrence & Lorsch, 1967; Schein, 1985, 1992). In each of these cases, researchers took a comparative perspective on a relative small sample of organizations (a sample size of 3–8 covers most of these examples) and have studied each of those organizations with a deep understanding, while still trying to develop generalizations that can explain the differences and similarities among the firms.

Increased distance from the phenomenon

When organizational culture research began in the early 1980s, it was all about being close to the phenomenon. Culture researchers originally gained great energy from the observation that organizational research had lost much of its fidelity—the verisimilitude with respect to organizational life itself—and suggested that the antidote to this problem was in description, ethnography, and an attempt to understand the native's point of view. Unfortunately, many of the original champions of "up close and personal" haven't hit the field in years. The paradigm wars over epistemology and methodology have directed researchers' energy away from the sizable investment of time required to do thick description. Thus, as Kunda (1993) pointed out, "thin description" may now be a more accurate description of most field research on organizational culture.

Interestingly, the call for staying close to the phenomenon also can be heard within the climate literature. Note Payne and Pugh's (1976: 1168) comments in their well-known review of the climate literature:

> Future research can ignore most of these [quantitative climate] studies and utilize a completely different approach. We need deep involvement from the members of a complex system to gather meaningful data which accurately reflect these people's experience...the researcher needs to swap data interpretations with his subjects so that interpretations are more realistic.

Climate researchers often have seemed inextricably (and inexplicably?) wedded to a limited form of contact with the organizations that they study: the collection of questionnaire data, the sine qua non of climate research (Trice & Beyer, 1992). This approach may require some contact with a research site (at least by mail), but it seldom requires direct contact with the social psychological phenomena that are the primary objects of study.

Thus, in both literatures, the discussion of research methods and approaches often outweighs the discussion of the organizational contexts that are ostensibly under investigation. Several authors have openly questioned whether organizational studies should be regarded as the study of *organizations* or the study of *discourse about organizations* (Parker, 1992; Smircich & Calás, 1987). The problems inherent in this position have perhaps been best described by Czarniawska-Joerges (1992: 192):

> Revolutionary attempts to reform organizational theory finish up by theorizing about organizational theory. There is no objection to this, but I would insist on learning something about social reality that is beyond social science. Otherwise, the following sarcastic comment will find its full application: "The language of science became the object of science and what had begun as perception unmediated by concepts became conception unmediated by percepts (Tyler, 1986: 124).

Distance from the phenomenon often helps sustain the powerful generalizations that fuel paradigm wars (Czarniawska-Joerges, 1995), but unfortunately these same powerful generalizations also can deter integration. As a result, the paradigms and the conflicts between them become the phenomenon of study rather than organizational life itself. This poses difficult problems for progress in the study of organizational contexts, because as Czarniawska-Joerges (1992: 192) put it, "When all is said and done, there is one main obstacle to the emergence of an anthropology of complex organizations: access." In contrast, a focus on the phenomenon, drawing in an eclectic manner from a variety of theories, methods, and perspectives, seems far more likely to make a contribution to the substantive understanding of organizational cultures.

Discussion

This article has attempted to address a remarkable paradox in the culture literature: With the recent appearance of culture studies based upon quantitative survey research methods, culture research has begun to emulate a substantive and epistemological research agenda that served as its antithesis less than a decade ago. Culture research is now being published in the leading organizational journals, but (ironically) only by emulating the same positivist research model that culture researchers originally deplored. Furthermore, a comparison of this recent culture research with the organizational "climate" literature of the 1960s and 1970s shows a curious similarity and suggests that it is becoming increasingly difficult to distinguish some of the current culture research from the earlier climate paradigm on the basis of either the substantive phenomenon or the methods and epistemology.

On the surface, the distinction between organizational climate and organizational culture may appear to be quite clear: Climate refers to a *situation* and its link to thoughts, feelings, and behaviors of organizational members. Thus, it is temporal, subjective, and often subject to direct manipulation by people with power and influence. Culture, in contrast, refers to an *evolved context* (within which a situation may be embedded). Thus, it is rooted in history, collectively held, and sufficiently complex to resist many attempts at direct manipulation. The two perspectives have generated distinct theories, methods, and epistemologies as well as a distinct set of findings, failings, and future agendas.

However, at a deeper level, when one begins to compare the individual studies that make up these two literatures, these seemingly clear distinctions begin to disappear. Over time, the underlying similarity of the two research topics has led a number of culture researchers to apply the quantitative, comparative, and Lewinian approaches associated with climate research, whereas several climate researchers have studied the evolution of social contexts from a social constructionist point of view that makes it difficult to distinguish from culture research. Despite these points of convergence, however, considerable effort is still devoted to the maintenance of a narrow orthodoxy within each literature that makes it difficult, if not impossible, to build on some of the obvious points of integration.

I have argued that one of the most enduring differences between culture and climate stems from their respective theoretical foundations. Both are rooted in the dominant theoretical traditions of their time, climate research growing out of Lewinian field theory (Lewin, 1951) and culture research growing out of the social construction framework (Berger & Luckmann, 1966; Mead, 1934). However, even this boundary is not always so clear. The research of Chatman (1991) and O'Reilly and colleagues (1991) reflects many aspects of the Lewinian framework, and the works of Ashforth (1985), Poole and McPhee (1983), Poole (1985), and Schneider and Reichers (1983) can easily be viewed as describing the social construction of organizational contexts.

The analysis in this article has led me to conclude that these two research traditions should be viewed as differences in *interpretation* rather than differences in the *phenomenon*. I also have argued that this approach will provide a stronger foundation for integration than the currently held assumption that culture and climate are fundamentally different and nonoverlapping phenomena. This conclusion has several implications. First, at a minimum, this conclusion provides a strong rationale for the continued integration of quantitative and qualitative methods in the study of organizational culture and the continued borrowing of theoretical foundations, epistemological arguments, and research strategies from either tradition in order to serve future research. Different researchers will, of course, generate different forms of evidence and different ways of interpreting each other's results, sustaining a rich source of diversity. But the endless debate over what constitutes the "right" kind of data can be given a decent burial. The debate over whether rituals or regressions or surveys or semiotics constitute the best data can become subordinate to the debate over what these multiple data sources and strategies can reveal about social contexts and their influence on individuals and organizations. Perhaps this conclusion also will temper the temerity of reviewers or editors whose knee-jerk reaction to uncovering quantitative data in a culture study is to ask, "but then, isn't this really a climate study?" Data, one must conclude, are actually rather benign. It is our interpretations that bring meaning to them, label the phenomenon, and conceptualize the link between research and action. The capacity to tolerate (and encourage) multifaceted interpretations of eclectic forms of evidence may in fact be a requisite level of complexity for understanding the extraordinarily complex topic of organizational culture.

Second, a stronger interpretation of my conclusions is that the culture and climate literatures actually address a common phenomenon: the creation and influence of social contexts in organizations. If one raises the level of abstraction slightly, it then becomes clear that this article is a discussion of two dominant traditions in the study of organizational contexts over a period of several decades. Because the culture literature is the more recent of these two traditions, it seems fair to assume that this tradition is more dominant at the present time. This conclusion implies that the future study of organizational *contexts* can perhaps best be served if researchers more explicitly incorporate the traditions of climate research within the culture literature, so that the lessons of both literatures can be applied to future research.

Nowhere is the need to achieve better integration between these two traditions greater than when one encounters practicing managers. The epistemological debates that have consumed culture researchers for the past decade (including many of the arguments in this article!) typically mean nothing to them. They can't tell the difference. Confronted with this observation, one of my colleagues recently observed, "that's because we are smarter than they are!" Although I would like to believe that there is perhaps some truth in this observation, sounder advice would suggest that culture, climate, or social context researchers who work directly with managers, executives, and other practitioners would do well to understand and adopt the natural language that organizational members use to describe their own context. That natural language may refer to culture, climate, context, the work environment, "this organization," or other ways of describing the phenomenon we are studying. Once they learn the local language, it is far easier for scholars and researchers to apply their insights. Transplanting our own language, with all of its implicit assumptions about the finer points of theory and epistemology, can be confusing and misleading. Many practitioners have now become sophisticated managers of social contexts and cultures and frequently apply our research in an eclectic, problem-driven manner. However, the effective translation of the insights of our research literature usually depends on a clear understanding of the existing concepts and vocabulary that an organization uses to describe its own context.

Finally, it is important to remember that one of the most powerful contributions of the culture literature in the early 1980s was the observation that organizational research had lost much of its fidelity with respect to organizational life itself. The efforts of these early culture researchers served to return organizational life, as it is understood by those who experience it, to center stage in the literature. But much of that basic insight has now been lost amid the paradigm wars. Can this fundamental insight be reinstated as a strength of the culture literature? I hope it can be, and I hope the debate over how research should be conducted and which conceptual and methodological resources should be applied can assume a secondary role, subordinate to the primary goal of understanding the evolution and influence of social contexts in organizations.

Acknowledgments

My thanks to Geert Hofetede and his colleagues and students at Rijksuniversiteit Limburg in Maastricht, The Netherlands, for their insights during my presentation of the first version of this article in November, 1992. I thank Nancy Adler, Mary Yoko Brannen, Paul Carlile, Michael Cohen, Dick Daft, Jane Dutton, Karen Golden-Biddle, George Gordon, Peter Manning, Debra Meyerson, Joan Rentsch, Maijen Schultz, John Slocum, Bob Sutton, John Van Maanen, and Karl Weick for their contributions to this article. I am also indebted to *AMR's* editor and reviewers for their useful comments, critiques, and suggestions. Finally, I thank Ikujiro Nonaka and the Institute of Business Research at Hitotsubashi University for the support that they provided during my final revision of this article.

Note

1 A few years ago there was a great debate raging: statistics versus the case study. The debate is no longer waged publicly, but it still troubles many of us. On the one hand, we see that an individual case study, skillfully analyzed, yields interesting insights—but

not scientific knowledge. On the other hand, we find that nearly all statistical work in sociology has dealt with the characteristics of aggregates: How much of a given phenomenon is to be found in a given population? Such an approach does not tell us anything about the relations among the individuals making up that population. And yet, if we are to believe the textbooks, the relations among individuals, the group life they lead, are the very heart of sociology.

So let us have more individual case studies, but let us also place the individual in the social system in which he participates and note how his attitudes and goals change with changes in the relations he experiences. And let us have more quantitative work, but let us at last bring it to bear upon the heart of sociology, measuring the relations among individuals in their organizations. (Whyte, 1949: 310).

This article is written from the perspective of one member of the community of scholars who study organizational cultures. This "native" was originally drawn to the social sciences by studying George Herbert Mead's symbolic interactionism as an undergraduate student, later indoctrinated in Parsonian structural-functionalism as a master's student in sociology, and then trained in general systems theory and survey research as a doctoral student in organizational psychology. After completing a quantitative dissertation on organizational culture and financial performance, I was driven by a desire to find out what was behind the statistical results (and by a distinct preference for interacting with human beings rather than statistical analysis packages...) and went into the field to do a series of case studies as a complement to the quantitative study. Combining qualitative theory building with quantitative theory testing felt like a constructive and integrative result.

Gaining acceptance for integrative work, however, proved much more difficult than I had anticipated. Narrow and parochial perspectives were very powerful and made it difficult to combine theory and practice. I was attracted to the field and the topic in part because it offered the opportunity to do work that was theoretical and applied, and was quantitative and qualitative, but the "culture of organizational culture research" made it seem far easier to declare allegiance to one single approach than to attempt to combine them. In addition, the experiences of many of my culture colleagues with the review process suggested that an inordinate amount of time was being spent on epistemological posturing. Many felt that their articles were often accepted or rejected primarily because of the perspective they had taken, rather than what they had learned about organizations and their cultures. This brief background helps explain some of the influences that led me to write this essay.

References

Allaire, Y. & Firsirotu, M. 1984. Theories of organizational culture. *Organization Studies*, 5: 193–226.

Alvesson, M. 1985. A critical framework for organizational analysis. *Organization Studies*, 6: 117–138.

Alvesson, M. 1989. The culture perspective on organizations: Instrumental values and basic features of culture. *Scandinavian Journal of Management*, 5(2): 123–136.

Alvesson, M. 1992. Leadership as social integrative action: A study of a computer consultancy company. *Organization Studies*, 13: 185–209.

Alvesson, M. 1993. *Cultural perspectives on organizations*. Cambridge, England: Cambridge University Press.

Alvesson, M., & Berg, D. O.1992. *Corporate culture and organisational symbolism*. New York: de Gruyter.

Ashforth, B. 1985. Climate formation: Issues and extensions. *Academy of Management Review*, 10: 837–847.

Barker, R. 1965. Explorations in ecological psychology. *American Psychologist*, 20: 1–14.

Barley, S. R. 1983. Semiotics and the study of occupational and organizational cultures. *Administrative Science Quarterly*, 28: 393–413.

Barley, S. 1986. Technology as an occasion for structuring: Observations on CT scanners and the social order of radiology departments. *Administrative Science Quarterly*, 31: 78–108.

Barney, J. 1986. Organizational culture: Can it be a source of competitive advantage? *Academy of Management Review*, 11: 656–665.

Berger, P., & Luckmann, T. 1966. *The social construction of reality*. New York: Penguin.

Blau, P. 1955. *The dynamics of bureaucracy*. Chicago: University of Chicago Press.

Block, P. 1991. *The empowered manager: Positive political skills at work*. San Francisco: Jossey-Bass.

Bowen, D., & Schneider, B. 1988. Services marketing and management: Implications for organizational behavior. In B. M. Staw & L. L. Cummings (Eds.), *Research in organizational behavior*, vol. 10: 43–80. Greenwich, CT: JAI Press.

Burns, T., & Stalker, G. 1961. *The management of innovation*. London: Tavistock.

Burrell, G., & Morgan, G. 1979. *Sociological paradigms and organizational analysis*. London: Heinemann.

Calás, M., & Smircich, L. 1987. *Post-culture: Is the organizational culture literature dominant but dead?* Paper presented at the international conference of Organizational Symbolism and Corporate Culture, Milan, Italy.

Calori, R., & Sarnin, P. 1991. Corporate culture and economic performance: A French study. *Organization Studies*, 12: 49–74.

Campbell, J., Dunnette, M. D., Lawler, E. E., & Weick, K. E. 1970. *Managerial behavior, performance, and effectiveness*. New York: McGraw-Hill.

Chatman, J. 1991. Matching people and organizations: Selection and socialization in public accounting firms. *Administrative Science Quarterly*, 36: 459–484.

Clark, B. 1970. *The distinctive college: Antioch, Reed, and Swathmore*. Chicago: Aldine.

Clark, B. 1972. The organizational saga in high education. *Administrative Science Quarterly*, 17: 178–183.

Cooke, W. 1992. Product quality improvement through employee participation: The effects of unionization and joint union-management administration. *Industrial and labor Relations Review*, 46: 119–134.

Cooke, W. 1993. *Employee participation, group-based pay incentives, and company performance: A union-non-union comparison*. Working paper, School of Business, Wayne State University, Detroit, MI.

Cooke, R., & Rousseau, D. 1988. Behavioral norms and expectations. A quantitative approach to the assessment of organizational culture. *Group and Organizational Studies*, 13: 245–273.

Crozier, M. 1964. *The bureaucratic phenomenon*. Chicago: University of Chicago Press.

Cummings, L. L. 1965. Organizational climates far creativity. *Academy of Management Journal*, 8: 837–847.

Cutcher-Gershenfeld, J. 1991. The impact on economic performance of a transformation in workplace relations. *Industrial and Labor Relations Review*, 44: 241–260.

Czarniawska-Joerges, B. 1992. *Exploring complex organizations: A cultural perspective*. Beverly Hills, CA: Sage.

Czarniawska-Joerges, B. 1995. Narration or science? Collapsing the division in organization studies. *Organization*, 2(1): 11–33.
Dalton, M. 1959. *Men who manage*. New York: Wiley.
Dandridge, T. 1983. Symbols' function and use. In L. Pondy, P. Frost, G. Morgan, & T. Dandridge (Eds.), *Organizational symbolism*: 69–73. Greenwich, CT: JAI Press.
Denison, D. 1984. Bringing corporate culture to the bottom line. *Organizational Dynamics*, 13(2): 4–22.
Denison, D. 1990. *Corporate culture and organizational effectiveness*. New York: Wiley.
Denison, D., & Mishra, A. 1995. Toward a theory of organizational culture and effectiveness. *Organisation Science*, 6: 204–223.
Drexler, J. 1977. Organizational climate: Its homogeneity within organizations. *Journal of Applied Psychology*, 62: 38–42.
Eagleton, T. 1983. *Literary theory*. Oxford: Basil Blackwell.
Eisenhardt, K. 1989. Making fast strategic decisions in high-velocity environments. *Academy of Management Journal*, 32: 543–576.
Ekvall, G. 1987. The climate metaphor in organizational theory. In B. Bass & P. Drenth (Eds.), *Advances in organizational psychology*, 177–190. Beverly Hilts, CA: Sage.
Frost, P. 1985. *Rekindling the flame*. Symposium presented at the annual meeting of the Academy of Management, San Diego, CA.
Frost, P., Moore, L., Louis, M., Lundberg. C., & Martin, J. 1985. *Organizational culture*. Beverly Hills, CA: Sage.
Frost, P., Moore, L., Louis, M., Lundberg, C, & Martin, J. 1991. *Reframing organizational culture*. Beverly Hills, CA: Sage.
Geertz, C. 1971. Deep play: Notes on the Balinese cockfight. In C. Geertz (Ed.), *Myth, symbol, and culture:* 1–37. New York: Norton.
Geertz, C. 1973. *The interpretation of cultures*. New York: Basic Books.
Giddens, A. 1979. *Central problems in social theory: Action, structure, and contradiction in social analysis*. Berkeley: University of California Press.
Glick, W. 1985. Conceptualizing and measuring organization and psychological climate. Pitfalls in multilevel research. *Academy of Management Review*, 10: 601–616.
Glick, W. 1988. Response: Organizations are not central tendencies: Shadowboxing in the dark, Round 2. *Academy of Management Review*, 13: 133–137.
Golden, K. A. 1992. The individual and organizational culture: Strategies for action in highly-ordered contexts. *Journal of Management Studies*, 29: 1–21.
Gordon, G. 1985. The relationship of corporate culture to industry sector and corporate performance. In R. H. Kilman, M. J. Saxton, R. Serpa, & Associates (Eds.), *Gaining control of the corporate culture:* 103–125. San Francisco: Jossey-Bass.
Gordon, G., & Christensen, E. 1993. *Industry influences on the relationship between management culture and performance*. Paper presented at the annual meeting of the Academy of Management, Atlanta, GA.
Gordon, G., & DiTomaso, N. 1992. Predicting corporate performance from organizational culture. *Journal of Management Studies*, 29: 783–798.
Gouldner, A. 1954. *Patterns of industrial bureaucracy*. New York: Free Press.
Gregory, K. 1983. Native view paradigms: Multiple cultures and culture conflict in organizations. *Administrative Science Quarterly*, 28: 359–376.
Guion, R. 1973. A note on organizational climate. *Organizational Behavior and Human Performance*, 9: 120–125.

Habermas, J. 1971. *Toward a rational society.* London: Heinemann.
Halpin, A., & Croft, D. 1962. *The organizational climate of schools.* St. Louis: Washington University Press.
Hansen, G., & Wernerfelt, B. 1989. Determinants of firm performance: The relative importance of economic and organizational factors. *Strategic Management Journal,* 10: 399–411.
Hatch, M. J. 1993. The dynamics of culture. *Academy of Management Review,* 18: 657–693.
Hellriegel, D., & Slocum, I. W., Jr. 1974. Organizational climate: Measures, research and contingencies. *Academy of Management Journal,* 17: 255–280.
Hofstede, G. 1980a. *Culture's consequences: International differences in work-related values.* Beverly Hills, CA: Sage.
Hofstede, G. 1980b. Motivation, leadership and organization: Do American leadership theories apply abroad? *Organizational Dynamics,* 9(1): 42–63.
Hofstede, G. 1986. The usefulness of the "organizational culture" concept. *Journal of Management Studies,* 23: 253–257.
Hofstede, G. 1991. *Culture and organizations: Software of the mind.* New York: McGraw-Hill.
Hofstede, G., Neuijen, B., Ohayv, D., & Sanders, G. 1990. Measuring organizational cultures: A qualitative and quantitative study across twenty cases. *Administrative Science Quarterly,* 35: 286–316.
Ichniowski, C., Shaw, K., & Prennushi, G. 1994. *The effects of human resource management practices on productivity.* Working paper, Columbia University, Graduate School of Business, New York.
Jackall, R. 1988. *Moral mazes: The world of corporate managers.* New York: Oxford University Press.
Jaques, E. 1951. *The changing culture of a factory.* New York: Dryden Press.
James, L. 1982. Aggregation bias in estimates of perceptual agreement. *Journal of Applied Psychology,* 76: 214–224.
James, L., Demaree, R., Mulaik, S., & Ladd, R. 1992. Validity generalization in the context of situational models. *Journal of Applied Psychology,* 77: 3–14.
James, L., James, L., & Asch, D. 1990. The measuring of organizations: The role of cognition and values. In B. Schneider (Ed.), *Organizational climate and culture:* 40–89. San Francisco: Jossey-Bass.
James, L., & Jones, A. 1974. Organizational climate: A review of theory and research. *Psychological Bulletin,* 18: 1096–1112.
James, L., Joyce, W., & Slocum, J. 1988. Comment: Organizations do not cognize. *Academy of Management Review,* 13: 129–132.
Jermier, J. 1991. Reflections on *street corner society.* In P. Frost, L. Moore, M. Louis, C. Lundberg, & J. Martin (Eds.), *Reframing organizational culture:* 223–233. Newbury Park, CA: Sage.
Jermier, J., Slocum, J., Fry, L., & Gaines, J. 1991. Organizational subcultures in a soft bureaucracy: Resistance behind the myth and facade of an official culture. *Organization Science,* 2: 170–194.
Johanneson, R. F. 1976. Some problems in the measurement of organizational climate. *Organizational Behavior and Human Performance,* 10: 95–103.
Joyce, W. F., & Slocum, J. 1982. Climate discrepancy: Refining the concepts of psychological and organizational climate. *Human Relations,* 35: 951–972.

Joyce, W. F., & Slocum, J. 1984. Collective climate: Agreement as a basis for defining aggregate climate in organizations. *Academy of Management Journal*, 27: 721–742.

Kidder, T. 1981. *The soul of a new machine*. Boston: Little Brown.

Kochan, T., Gobeille, K., & Katz, H. 1983. Industrial relations performance, economic performance, and QWL programs: An interplant analysis. *Industrial and Labor Relations Review*, 37: 3–17.

Kotter, J., & Heskett, J. 1992. *Corporate culture and performance*. New York: Free Press.

Koys, D., & Decotiis, T. 1991. Inductive measures of psychological climate. *Human Relations*, 44: 265–285.

Kunda, G. 1992. *Engineering culture*. Philadelphia: Temple University Press.

Kunda, G. 1993. *Engineering culture*. Paper presented at the annual meeting of the Academy of Management, Atlanta, GA.

Lafollette, W. R., & Sims, H. P. 1975. Is satisfaction redundant with organizational climate? *Organizational Behavior and Human Performance*, 13: 257–278.

LaTour, B. 1988. *The pasteurization of France*. Cambridge, MA: Harvard University Press.

Lave, J., & Wenger, S. 1990. *Situated learning*. Cambridge, England: Cambridge University Press.

Lawler, E. 1986. *High involvement management: Participative strategies for improving organizational performance*. San Francisco: Jossey-Bass.

Lawler, E. E., Hall, D. T., & Oldham, G. R. 1974. Organizational climate: Relationship to organizational structure, process, and performance. *Organizational Behavior and Human Performance*. 11:139–155.

Lawrence, P. R., & Lorsch, J. W. 1967. *Organization and environment: Managing differentiation and integration*. Boston: Harvard University.

Lewin, K. 1951. *Field theory in social science*. New York: Harper & Row.

Lewin, K., Lippit, R., & White, R. 1939. Patterns of aggressive behavior in experimentally created social climates. *Journal of Social Psychology*, 10: 271–299.

Likert, R. L. 1961. *New patterns of management*. New York: McGraw-Hill.

Likert, R. L. 1967. *The human organization*. New York: McGraw-Hill.

Litwin, G., & Stringer, 1968. *Motivation and organizational climate*. Cambridge, MA: Harvard University Press.

Louis, M. R. 1980. Surprise and sense making: What newcomers experience in entering unfamiliar organizational settings. *Administrative Science Quarterly*, 25: 226–250.

Lundeberg, C. 1982. *Organizational culture change: An organizational development critique*. Paper presented at the annual meeting of the Academy of Management, Dallas, TX.

Martin, J. 1992. *Cultures in organizations: Three perspectives*. New York: Oxford University Press.

Martin, J., Feldman, M., Hatch, M., & Sitkin, S. 1983. The uniqueness paradox in organizational stories. *Administrative Science Quarterly*, 28: 438–453.

Martin, J., Sitkin, S., & Boehm, M. 1985. Founders and the elusiveness of a cultural legacy. In P. Frost, L. Moore, M. Louis, C. Lundberg, & J. Martin (Eds.), *Organizational culture*: 99–124. Beverly Hills, CA: Sage.

Mead, G. 1934. *Mind, self, and society*. Chicago: University of Chicago Press.

Meyerson, D. 1991. Acknowledging and uncovering ambiguities. In P. Frost, L. Moore, M. Louis, C. Lundberg, & J. Martin (Eds.), *Reframing organizational culture*. Beverly Hills, CA: Sage.

Meyerson, D., & Martin, J. 1987. Cultural change: An integration of three different views. *Journal of Management Studies*, 18: 1–26.
Mills, C. W. 1978. *The sociological imagination*. Harmondsworth, England: Penguin.
Mohr, L. 1982. *Explaining organizational behavior*. San Francisco: Jossey-Bass.
Moran, E. T., & Volkwein, J. F. 1992. The cultural approach to the formation of organizational climate. *Human Relations*, 45: 19–47.
Nicholson, N., & Johns, G. 1985. The absence culture and the psychological contract—Who's in control of absence? *Academy of Management Review*, 10: 397–407.
O'Reilly, C., Chatman, J., & Caldwell, D. 1991. People and organizational culture: A profile comparison approach to assessing person-environment fit. *Academy of Management Journal*, 34: 487–516.
Ott, J. S. 1989. *The organizational culture perspective*. Chicago: Dorsey Press.
Parker, M. 1992. Post-modern organizations or postmodern organization theory? *Organizational Studies*, 12: 1–17.
Payne, R. L., Fineman, S., & Wall, T. D. 1976. Organizational climate and job satisfaction: A conceptual synthesis. *Organizational Behavior and Human Performance*, 16: 45–62.
Payne, R., & Pugh, D. 1976. Organizational structure and climate. In M. Dunnette (Ed.), *Handbook of industrial and organizational psychology*. Chicago: Rand McNally.
Peters, T., & Waterman, R. 1982. *In search of excellence: Lessons from America's best run companies*. New York: Harper & Row.
Pettigrew, A. 1979. On studying organizational cultures. *Administrative Science Quarterly*, 24: 570–581.
Pettigrew, A. 1990. Organizational climate and culture: Two constructs in search of a role. In B. Schneider (Ed.), *Organizational climate and culture:* 413–433. San Francisco: Jossey-Bass.
Pondy, L., Frost, P., Morgan, G., & Dandridge, T. 1983. *Organizational symbolism*. Greenwich, CT: JAI Press.
Poole, M. S. 1985. Communication and organization climates. In R. D. McPhee & P. K. Thompkins (Eds.), *Organizational communication: Traditional themes and new directions*, 79–108. Beverly Hills, CA: Sage.
Poole, M. S., & McPhee, R. D. 1983. A struturational analysis of organizational climates. In L. Putnam & M. Pacanowsky (Eds.), *Communication and organizations: An interpretive approach:* 195–220. Beverly Hills, CA: Sage.
Porter, L., & Lawler, E. 1973. *Managerial attitudes and performance*. Homewood, IL: Irwin.
Reichers, A. 1987. An interactionist perspective on newcomer socialization rates. *Academy of Management Review*, 12: 278–287.
Reichers, A., & Schneider, B. 1990. Climate and culture: An evolution of constructs. In B. Schneider (Ed.), *Organizational climate and culture:* 5–39. San Francisco: Jossey-Bass.
Rentsch, J. 1990. Climate and culture: Interaction and qualitative differences in organizational meanings. *Journal of Applied Psychology*, 75: 668-681.
Riley, P. 1983. A structurationist account of political cultures. *Administrative Science Quarterly*, 28: 414–437.
Rohlen, T. 1974. *For harmony and strength: Japanese white-collar organization in anthropological perspective*. Berkeley: University of California Press.
Rosen, M. 1985. Breakfast at Spiro's: Dramaturgy and dominance. *Journal of Management*, 11(2):31–48.

Rosen, M. 1991. Scholars, travelers, and thieves: On concept, method, and cunning in organizational ethnography. In P. Frost, L. Moore, M. Louis, C. Lundberg, & J. Martin (Eds.), *Reframing organizational culture:* 271–284. Beverly Hills, CA: Sage.

Sackmann, S. 1991. *Cultural knowledge in organizations: Exploring the collective mind.* Newbury Park, CA: Sage.

Schein, E. 1985. *Organizational culture and leadership.* San Francisco: Jossey-Bass.

Schein, E. 1990. Organizational culture. *American Psychologist,* 45: 109–119.

Schein, E. 1992. *Organizational culture and leadership* (2nd ed.). San Francisco: Jossey-Bass.

Schneider, B. 1975. Organizational climate: *An essay. Personnel Psychology,* 28: 447–479.

Schneider, B. 1985. Organizational behavior. *Annual Review of Psychology,* 36: 573–611.

Schneider, B. 1987. The people make the place. *Personnel Psychology,* 40: 437–453.

Schneider, B. 1990. *Organizational climate and culture.* San Francisco: Jossey-Bass.

Schneider, B., & Reichers, A. 1983. On the etiology of climates. *Personnel Psychology,* 36:19–39.

Schneider, B., & Snyder, R. A. 1975. Some relationships between job satisfaction and organizational climate. *Journal of Applied Psychology,* 60: 318–328.

Schwartz, H., & Davis, S. 1981. Matching corporate culture and business strategy. *Organizational Dynamics,* 10(1): 30–38.

Selznick, P. 1957. *Leadership in administration.* New York: Harper & Row.

Semler, R. 1989. Managing without managers: Participative management at Brazil's Semco. *Harvard Business Review,* 67(5): 76–84.

Siehl. C. & Martin, J. 1990. Organizational culture: A key to financial performance? In B. Schneider (Ed.), *Organizational climate and culture.* San Francisco: Jossey-Bass.

Smircich, L. 1983. Concepts of culture and organizational analysis. *Administrative Science Quarterly,* 28: 339–358.

Smircich, L., & Calás, M. F. 1987. Organizational culture: A critical assessment. In F. Jablin, L. Putnam, K. Roberts, & L. Porter (Eds.), *Handbook of organizational communication:* 228–263. Beverly Hills, CA: Sage.

Sondergaard, M. 1994. Research note: Hofstede's consequences: A study of reviews, citations, and replications. *Organization Studies,* 15: 447–456.

Staeblein, R., & Nord, W. 1985. Practical and emancipatory interests in organizational symbolism: A review and evaluation. *Journal of Management,* 11: 13–28.

Tagiuri, R., & Litwin, G. (Eds.). 1968. *Organizational climate: Explorations of a concept.* Boston: Harvard Business School.

Taylor, J., & Bowers, D. 1973. *The survey of organizations.* Ann Arbor, MI: Institute for Social Research.

Trice, H., & Beyer, J. 1992. *The cultures of work organizations.* Englewood Cliffs, NJ: Simon & Schuster.

Trompenaars, F. 1993. *Riding the waves of culture: Understanding diversity in global business.* Homewood, IL: Irwin.

Tyler, S. A. 1986. Post-modem ethnography. In J. Clifford & G. E. Marcus (Eds.), *Writing culture: The poetics and politics of ethnography:* 122–140. Berkeley: University of California Press.

Van Maanen, J. 1973. Observations on the making of policemen. *Human Organization,* 32: 407–417.

Van Maanen, J. 1975. Police socialization: A longitudinal examination of job attitudes in an urban police department. *Administrative Science Quarterly,* 20: 207–228.

Van Maanen, J. 1979. Qualitative research. *Administrative Science Quarterly*, 24: 570–581.

Van Maanen, J. 1988. *Tales of the field.* Chicago: University of Chicago Press.

Van Maanen, J., & Barley, S. 1984. Occupational communities: Cultural control in organizations. *Research in Organizational Behavior*, 6: 287–365.

Van Maanen, J., & Schein, E. 1979. Toward a theory of organizational socialization. *Research in Organizational Behavior*, 11: 209–259.

Weick, K., & Roberts, K. 1993. Collective mind in organizations: Heedful interrelating on flight decks. *Administrative Science Quarterly*, 38: 357–381.

Whyte, W. F. 1949. The social structure of the restaurant. *American Journal of Sociology*, 54: 302–310.

Wilkins, A. 1978. *Organizational stories as an expression of management philosophy.* Unpublished doctoral dissertation, Stanford University.

Wilkins, A. 1989. *Developing corporate character: How to successfully change an organization without destroying it.* San Francisco: Jossey-Bass.

Wilkins, A., & Ouchi, W. 1983. Efficient cultures: Exploring the relationship between culture and organizational performance. *Administrative Science Quarterly*, 28: 468–481.

Zohar, D. 1980. Safety climate in industrial organizations: Theoretical and applied implications. *Journal of Applied Psychology*, 65: 96–117.